OCP
Oracle® Database 12c
Administrator Certified
Professional

Study Guide

Robert G. Freeman

Charles A. Pack

Senior Acquisitions Editor: Jeff Kellum
Development Editor: Tom Cirtin
Technical Editors: Pete Sharman; Syed Jaffar Hussain
Production Editor: Dassi Zeidel
Copy Editor: Linda Recktenwald
Editorial Manager: Pete Gaughan
Vice President and Executive Group Publisher: Richard Swadley
Associate Publisher: Chris Webb
Media Project Manager 1: Laura Moss-Hollister
Media Associate Producer: Doug Kuhn
Media Quality Assurance: Josh Frank
Book Designer: Judy Fung
Compositor: Craig Woods, Happenstance Type-O-Rama
Proofreader: Sara Wilson
Indexer: Ted Laux
Project Coordinator, Cover: Patrick Redmond
Cover Designer: Wiley
Cover Image: ©Getty Images Inc./Jeremy Woodhouse

Dear Reader,

Thank you for choosing *OCP: Oracle Database 12c Administrator Certified Professional Study Guide*. This book is part of a family of premium-quality Sybex books, all of which are written by outstanding authors who combine practical experience with a gift for teaching.

Sybex was founded in 1976. More than 30 years later, we're still committed to producing consistently exceptional books. With each of our titles, we're working hard to set a new standard for the industry. From the paper we print on, to the authors we work with, our goal is to bring you the best books available.

I hope you see all that reflected in these pages. I'd be very interested to hear your comments and get your feedback on how we're doing. Feel free to let me know what you think about this or any other Sybex book by sending me an email at contactus@sybex.com. If you think you've found a technical error in this book, please visit http://sybex.custhelp.com. Customer feedback is critical to our efforts at Sybex.

Best regards,

Chris Webb
Associate Publisher
Sybex, an Imprint of Wiley

For my Carrie, my kids, and my parents.
—*Robert G. Freeman*

For my wife, Donna, and our daughter, Jenny.
—*Charles A. Pack*

Acknowledgments

Writing a book is such a vast undertaking that it's hard to know where to start with the acknowledgments. I also hate writing this part because, frankly, someone always gets forgotten. That being said, here we go.

Thanks to my patient wife, Carrie, who sits across from me in the bedroom as I write away. I'm sure she is tired of being a book/work widow. Thanks to my little bundle of joy, Amy, who is now 8 months old. She and Carrie both remind me daily of what is truly important in the world. Thanks to my awesome older kids. It's so odd to have an 8-month-old and then five kids from ages 28 to 21. Thanks to all the folks at Oracle with whom I work, they are way too many to name.

Writing books is a long, complex, and often frustrating task. Thanks to all the folks at Sybex who participated in the making of this book. Thanks especially to Jeff Kellum, who was my acquisitions editor, for getting me involved in this project. I'd worked with Jeff before on my very first book, and apparently he didn't remember the pain I caused him well enough, since he asked me to write this book anyway. Jeff put up with a lot on this book; we really made the schedule something of a joke, I'm afraid. Thanks to Tom Cirtin, who tried so hard to get us back on track schedule-wise.

Finally, a very important thanks goes out to *you*. Thanks for buying this book. Thanks for wanting to become an Oracle Certified Professional. Thanks for any nice comments you might leave on websites here and there. Thanks for trusting us to help you succeed at the test!

—Robert G. Freeman

Thanks to Robert Freeman and Jeff Kellum for the opportunity to write this book. Thanks to my colleagues at CSX, some of the brightest and hardest working people I've ever known, for continuously challenging me to stay technically sharp.

This book would not have been written without my wife's permission, of course. Thank you, Donna, for your support through these fun projects of mine. Thank you to my daughter Jenny, who is now 13 and is sitting next to me on the sofa sketching MLP characters on her iPad while I write about "the Oracle."

—Charles A. Pack

About the Authors

Robert G. Freeman   lives in Las Vegas, Nevada, and loves it. He is a Master Principal Database Expert at Oracle Corporation. He works in the Engineered Systems Group (Public Sector) and deals with things like Exadata and Oracle databases all the time.

Besides working with Oracle databases (that's his story and he's sticking to it), Robert writes an occasional book (at last count over a dozen), flies airplanes, enjoys karate, and has a family that is awesome. He met Charles Pack, who is a fellow Okie (even if he sometimes roots for the wrong school), years ago and to this day wonders if Charles will ever walk around without wearing sunglasses to hide his eyes and the deep meaning contained in them. Robert is the husband of the patient Carrie and father of six (and counting!) wonderful, if not occasionally misguided, children.

Charles A. Pack   is an Oracle Certified Professional DBA with over 25 years of IT experience. His career has included PC repairman, network administrator, systems operator, COBOL programmer, backup and storage engineer, DBA, architect, project manager, and people manager. He earned a bachelor of science degree from Oklahoma State University, an MBA from The University of Oklahoma, and a master of science in computer science from Texas A&M University—Corpus Christi. He has taught Oracle DBA classes at Florida State College—Jacksonville and has presented on the subject at universities and to professional organizations. He authored the Oracle Press *OCP Oracle9i Database: Performance Tuning Exam Guide* and collaborated with co-author Robert Freeman on *Oracle 8 to 8i Upgrade Exam Cram*.

At CSX Technology in Jacksonville, Florida, he has been responsible for storage, backups, and capacity planning, as well as enterprise content management and collaboration. In his current role as Technical Director of Infrastructure Architecture, he and his teams are responsible for strategic infrastructure design, capacity planning, and system performance. He is a true cowboy at heart, and he loves to barbecue.

About the Technical Reviewers

Pete Sharman is a principal product manager with the Enterprise Manager product suite group in the Server Technologies Division at Oracle Corporation. He has worked with Oracle for the past 18 years in a variety of roles from education to consulting to development and has used Enterprise Manager since its 0.76 beta release. Pete is a member of the Oak Table Network and has presented at conferences around the world from Oracle Open World (both in Australia and the United States), RMOUG Training Days, the Hotsos. He coauthored two books, one on Enterprise Manager 12c and another on Oracle Database Appliance, and authored a book on how to pass the Oracle8*i* Database Administration exam for the Oracle Certified Professional program. He lives in Canberra, Australia, with his wife and three children.

Syed Jaffar Hussain has more than 21 years of IT experience that includes more than 14 years of production Oracle database administration. Oracle has honored him with the prestigious Oracle ACE Director role and named him DBA of the Year for 2011, both for his vast knowledge and for contributions to the Oracle community. He is an Oracle Certified Master (OCM) for Oracle Database 10*g*, a status granted only after passing extensive challenges in a hands-on environment. He is also an Oracle Database 10*g* RAC Certified Expert. Syed Jaffar is a well-known Oracle speaker and he coauthored *Expert Oracle RAC12* and *Oracle 11g R1/R2 Real Application Clusters Essentials*. He blogs regularly at http://jaffardba.blogspot.com.

Contents at a Glance

Contents

Table of Exercises

Introduction

There is high demand for professionals in the information technology (IT) industry, and Oracle certifications are the hottest credentials in the database world. You have made the right decision to pursue your Oracle certification because it will give you a distinct advantage in this highly competitive market.

Many readers may already be familiar with Oracle and do not need an introduction to Oracle databases. For those who aren't familiar with the company, Oracle, founded in 1977, sold the first commercial relational database and is now the world's leading database company and second-largest independent software company, with revenues of more than $37 billion, and is headquartered in Redwood City, California.

Oracle databases are the de facto standard for large Internet sites, mission-critical enterprise applications, and cloud solutions. With the acquisition of Sun Microsystems, Oracle offers complete enterprise business solutions with engineered systems capable of running world-class databases and applications. Enterprise Resource Planning (ERP) application suites, data warehouses, and business applications at many large and medium-size companies rely on Oracle. The demand for DBA resources remains higher than for other professions during weak economic times.

This book is intended to help you pass the Oracle Database 12c: Advanced Administration exam, which will establish your credentials as an Oracle Certified Professional (OCP). The OCP certification is a prerequisite for obtaining an Oracle Certified Master (OCM) certification. Using this book and a practice database, you can learn the necessary skills to pass the 1Z0-063 Oracle Database 12c: Advanced Administration exam.

Why Become Oracle Certified?

The number-one reason to become an OCP is to gain more visibility and greater access to the industry's most challenging opportunities. Oracle certification is the best way to demonstrate your knowledge and skills in Oracle database systems.

Certification is proof of your knowledge and shows that you have the skills required to support Oracle core products. The Oracle certification program can help a company to identify proven performers who have demonstrated their skills and who can support the company's investment in Oracle technology. It demonstrates that you have a solid understanding of your job role and the Oracle products used in that role.

OCPs are among the best paid in the IT industry. Salary surveys consistently show the OCP certification to yield higher salaries than other certifications, including Microsoft, Novell, and Cisco.

So whether you are beginning your career, changing your career, or looking to secure your position as a DBA, this book is for you!

Oracle Certifications

Oracle certifications follow a track that is oriented toward a job role. The primary certification tracks are Database, Applications, Java, Enterprise Management, Virtualization, and Operating Systems. Within each track, Oracle has a tiered certification program of OCA and OCP. Only the Database track has OCM. The Database track is clearly for the database administrator job role.

> For the latest certification information on all of Oracle certification paths, please visit the Oracle website at http://education.oracle.com/pls/web_prod-plq-dad/db_pages.getpage?page_id=39&p_org_id=1001&lang=US.

The role of database administrator (DBA) has become a key to success in today's highly complex database systems. The best DBAs work behind the scenes but are in the spotlight when critical issues arise. They plan, create, maintain, and ensure that the database is available for the business. They have tools to proactively monitor the database for performance issues and to prevent unscheduled downtime. The DBA's job requires broad understanding of the architecture of Oracle database and expertise in solving problems.

Sybex has Oracle certification study guides for the Database track. In the following sections, I will introduce you to the different tiers in the Oracle Database 12*c* certification track.

Oracle Database 12*c* Administrator Certified Associate

The Oracle Certified Associate (OCA) credential is the first step toward achieving the Oracle Certified Professional (OCP) certification. OCA shows that you have the fundamental knowledge and skills to support an Oracle Database 12*c* database. This certification requires you to pass two exams that demonstrate your Oracle basics:

- 1Z0-061: Oracle Database 12*c*: SQL Fundamentals
- 1Z0-062: Oracle Database 12*c*: Installation and Administration

If you have already passed any one of the following tests, you need not take the 1Z0-061 exam; you need to pass only 1Z0-062.

- 1Z0-051: Oracle Database 11*g*: SQL Fundamentals I
- 1Z0-047: Oracle Database SQL Expert

The 1Z0-061 exam can be taken at a testing location or from your home using the Internet. The 1Z0-062 test is offered at a Pearson VUE facility.

> To register for the test, visit Pearson VUE at http://www.pearsonvue.com.

Oracle Database 12*c* Administrator Certified Professional

The Oracle Certified Professional credential shows that you have the skill and technical expertise to manage and implement enterprise databases. The OCP tier challenges you to demonstrate your continuing experience and knowledge of Oracle technologies. The OCP test will measure your knowledge in setting up and managing multitenant architecture databases and in backup and recovery. The Oracle Database 12*c* Administrator Certified Professional certification requires you to have the OCA certification as well as to pass the following exam:

- 1Z0-063: Oracle Database 12*c*: Advanced Administration

In addition, the OCP candidate must take one instructor-led Oracle University hands-on requirement class.

 You should verify the list of approved hands-on courses at the Oracle education website at http://education.oracle.com/pls/web_prod-plq-dad/db_pages.getpage?page_id=244#5.

Oracle Database 12*c* Administrator Certified Master

The highest level of certification available in any track is the Oracle Certified Master. The OCM certification credential shows that you have the highest level of expertise in an Oracle product. To become a certified master, you must first achieve OCP status and then complete two advanced instructor-led classes at an Oracle education facility. You must also pass a hands-on examination at an Oracle education facility. At the time of writing this book, the Oracle Database 12*c*: Certified Master exam has not been released.

More Information and Resources

You can find most current information about Oracle certification at http://education .oracle.com/certification. You may be asked to choose your country of residence before being directed to the site. Follow the links under Certifications to choose the track and learn more.

Choose the Database track to view the different certification versions available. Choose Oracle Database 12*c* Administrator Certified Associate, and then click on the test to know more about the test contents, the objectives covered in the test, and the passing score and to register for the test.

The Oracle documentation is available online at http://tahiti.oracle.com. Oracle documentation contains a wealth of information, which can be used to supplement what you learn from this book.

Oracle provides training series with step-by-step instructions to perform a variety of Oracle Database 12c tasks. The Oracle by example (OBE) tutorial can be found at `http://apex.oracle.com/pls/apex/f?p=44785:1`.

Oracle Technology Network (`http://www.oracle.com/technology/index.html`) is a great resource for database administrators and developers. You can read articles, view sample code, access documentation, participate in forums, and most importantly, download Oracle Database 12c, Oracle Enterprise Manager Cloud Control 12c, and other Oracle products.

OCA/OCP Study Guides

The Oracle Database 12c administration track certification consists of three tests: two for OCA and one for OCP. Sybex offers study guides to help you achieve OCA and OCP certification.

- *OCA: Oracle Database 12c Administrator Certified Associate Study Guide* (9781118643952)—Covers exams 1Z0-061: Oracle Database 12c: SQL Fundamentals and 1Z0-062: Oracle Database 12c: Installation and Administration.

- *OCP: Oracle Database 12c Administrator Certified Professional Study Guide* (9781118644072)—Covers exam 1Z0-063: Oracle Database 12c: Advanced Administration.

These two books are offered in a boxed set as *OCP: Oracle Certified Professional on Oracle Database 12c Certification Kit* (9781118957684).

Oracle Exam Requirements

The Oracle Database 12c: Advanced Administration exam covers several core subject areas. As with many typical multiple-choice exams, there are several tips that you can follow to maximize your score on the exam.

Oracle Database 12c: Advanced Administration (1Z0-063) Requirements

To pass the Oracle 12c: Advance Administration exam, you need to master the following subject areas in Oracle 12c:

- Oracle Database 12c: Backup and Recovery
- Oracle Data Protection Solutions
- Performing Basic Backup and Recovery
- Configuring for Recoverability
- Using the RMAN Recovery Catalog
- Implementing Backup Strategies

- Performing Backups
- Configuring RMAN Backup Options and Creating Backup of Non-Database Files
- Using RMAN-Encrypted Backups
- Diagnosing Failures
- Recovering Files Using RMAN
- Using Oracle Secure Backup
- Using Flashback Technologies
- Using Flashback Database
- Transporting Data
- Duplicating a Database
- Monitoring and Tuning of RMAN Operations
- Oracle Database 12*c*: Managing Multitenant Architecture
- Multitenant Container and Pluggable Database Architecture
- Creating Multitenant Container and Pluggable Databases
- Managing a CDB and PDBs
- Managing Storage in a CDB and PDBs
- Managing Security in a CDB and PDBs
- Managing Availability
- Managing Performance
- Moving Data, Performing Security Operations, and Interacting with Other Oracle Products

Tips for Taking the Oracle Database 12*c*: Advanced Administration Exam

The following tips are presented to help you prepare for and pass the exam.

- The exam consists of between 70 and 95 questions to be completed in 120 to 150 minutes. Answer the questions you are sure of first, before you run out of time.

The exam details were not released at the time of this writing. These above details are based on the Oracle 11*g* exam. Check Oracle's website at education.oracle.com for specifics.

- Many questions on the exam have answer choices that at first glance look identical. Read the questions carefully. Do not jump to conclusions. Make sure you clearly understand what each question asks.

- Most questions are based on scenarios. Some of the scenarios contain nonessential information and exhibits. You need to be able to identify what's important and what's not.

- Do not leave any questions unanswered. There is no negative scoring. After selecting an answer, you can mark difficult questions or the ones you are unsure of and come back to them later.

- When answering questions you are not sure about, use a process of elimination to get rid of the obviously incorrect answers first. Doing this greatly improves your odds if you need to make an educated guess.

- If you are not sure of your answer, mark it for review and then look for other questions that may help you eliminate any incorrect answers. At the end of the test, you can review the questions you marked earlier.

You should be familiar with exam objectives, which are included at the beginning of each chapter. Please check the objectives list on the Oracle Education website for any changes or updates. The detail page for each exam shows the passing score, number of questions, and minutes allocated along with exam fees and any other requirements.

What Does This Book Cover?

This book covers everything you need to pass the Oracle Database 12*c*: Advanced Administration exam. Each chapter begins with a list of exam objectives.

Chapter 1: Performing Oracle User-Managed Backups   This chapter introduces Oracle user-managed backup and recovery. A review of Oracle's architecture with respect to backup and recovery is presented. Management of the Oracle database with respect to backup and recovery is included. The chapter covers putting the database in ARCHIVELOG mode as well as Oracle offline and online backups.

Chapter 2: Performing Oracle User-Managed Database Recoveries   This chapter introduces the reader to Oracle user-managed recoveries. Both complete and incomplete recoveries are examined. Backup and recovery of the database control file are included along with the recreation of the temporary tablespace data files. Finally, we discuss recovery from the loss of online redo logs and the password files.

Chapter 3: Configuring and Backing Up Oracle Databases Using RMAN   This chapter introduces the reader to RMAN and discusses configuration of RMAN for backup and recovery operations. Both offline and online backups are discussed. The chapter then proceeds to cover backups of an Oracle database by RMAN.

Chapter 4: Using the RMAN Recovery Catalog   This chapter provides an introduction to the RMAN recovery catalog. It also provides information on when you might want to use a recovery catalog, how to set up a recovery catalog, and how to register a database with the recovery catalog. We also discuss the use of RMAN's new virtual private catalog.

Chapter 5: Recovering Databases with RMAN   This chapter dives into RMAN recoveries. It examines RMAN recoveries in both NOARCHIVELOG and ARCHIVELOG mode and discusses recoveries using both full backups and incremental backups. We explore faster recoveries using image copies as well as recoveries using a backup control file.

Chapter 6: Tuning and Monitoring RMAN and the Automatic Diagnostic Workflow   This chapter covers RMAN reporting, monitoring, and tuning. It discusses the use of various views to monitor and report on RMAN operations. The RMAN REPORT and LIST commands are also covered in this chapter. We discuss various RMAN administration commands as well.

Chapter 7: Performing Oracle Advanced Recovery   This chapter explores advanced RMAN recovery topics, including incomplete recoveries using RMAN. The chapter also discusses using RMAN for database duplication and tablespace point-in-time recoveries. It includes a discussion on using RMAN in disaster recovery situations. We close out Chapter 7 with a discussion on backup and recovery for Oracle multitenant databases.

Chapter 8: Understanding Flashback Technology   In this chapter, we provide a brief overview of Flashback functionality and examine Automatic Undo Management, the cornerstone upon which key Flashback technologies rely. We discuss Flashback Drop and the Recycle Bin, Flashback Query, Flashback Versions Query, Flashback Transaction, Flashback Temporal Validity Query, Flashback Table, Flashback Data Archive, and Flashback Database.

Chapter 9: Diagnosing the Database and Managing Performance   In this chapter, you'll learn about the tools that help the DBA diagnose problems in the database and about the tools that assist with detecting and resolving performance issues.

Chapter 10: Managing Database Resources   This chapter discusses resumable space allocation, transportable tablespaces and databases, shrinking segments, and storage resource management in the Oracle 12*c* multitenant architecture, specifically how permanent and temporary tablespaces are managed in container databases (CDBs) and pluggable databases (PDBs).

Chapter 11: Creating Oracle Multitenant Databases   This chapter is an introduction to the concepts of the Oracle multitenant architecture, new to Oracle 12*c*, and an introduction to creating multitenant CDBs and PDBs.

Chapter 12: Managing Oracle Multitenant Databases   In this chapter, we explore how to manage the multitenant database environment that is based on the Oracle Database 12*c* multitenant architecture. We differentiate between CDBs and PDBs. You will learn how to connect to, start up, and shut down CDBs and PDBs.

Chapter 13: Oracle Utilities   This chapter describes the use of Oracle-supplied database utilities in the Oracle Database 12*c* multitenant architecture. We discuss moving data, performing security operations, and interacting with other Oracle products in the multitenant environment.

Chapter 14: Oracle Security in CDBs and PDBs   This chapter focuses on security considerations in the Oracle Database 12*c* multitenant architecture. We discuss managing common and local users, common and local privileges, and common and local roles. We also discuss enabling common users to access data in specific PDBs.

What's Available Online?

The book includes a number of companion study tools, which can be downloaded from www.sybex.com/go/ocp12csg. See Appendix B for information on how to access and install these tools:

Test Preparation Software   The test preparation software prepares you for the 1Z0-063 exam. You'll find all the review and assessment questions from the book *plus* two additional practice exams that appear exclusively from the downloadable study tools.

Electronic Flashcards   The companion study tools include hundreds of flashcards specifically written to hit you hard, so don't get discouraged if you don't ace your way through them at first! They're there to ensure that you're really ready for the exam. And no worries—armed with the review questions, practice exams, and flashcards, you'll be more than prepared when exam day comes!

Bonus Lab Appendix   We have included a number of bonus labs designed to give you additional hands-on practice.

Glossary   A complete glossary of common terms is available at www.sybex.com/go/ocp12csg.

How to Use This Book

This book provides a solid foundation for the serious effort of preparing for the Oracle Database 12*c*: Advanced Administration exam. To best benefit from the book, use the following study method:

1. Take the assessment test immediately following this introduction. (The answers are at the end of the test.) Carefully read the explanations for any questions you get wrong, and note in which chapters the material is covered. This information should help you plan your study strategy.

2. Study each chapter carefully, making sure you fully understand the information and the test objectives listed at the beginning of each chapter. Pay close attention to any chapter related to questions you missed in the assessment test.

3. Complete all hands-on activities in the chapter, referring to the chapter so that you understand the reason for each step you take. It is best to have an Oracle Database 12*c* database available to try out the examples and code provided in the book.

4. Answer the review questions related to that chapter. Note the review questions that confuse or trick you, and study those sections of the book again.

5. Take the two bonus exams included in the downloadable study tools. They will give you a complete overview of what you can expect to see in the real test.

6. Answer all the flashcard questions included with the study tools.

7. Remember to use the study tools included with this book. The electronic flash cards and Sybex test engine exam-preparation software have been specifically designed to help you study and pass your exams.

> The additional study tools can be downloaded from www.sybex.com/go/ ocp12csg.

To learn all the material covered in this book, you will need to apply yourself regularly and with discipline. Try to set aside the same time period every day to study, and select a comfortable and quite place to do so. If you work hard, you will be surprised at how quickly you learn this material. You can also find supplemental reading material and Oracle documentation references on my blog that will deepen your knowledge of what you read in this book. All the best!

> Prebuilt Oracle Database 12*c* can be downloaded and set up on VirtualBox. This is convenient especially if you are new to Oracle. Prebuilt Oracle VMs can be downloaded from http://www.oracle.com/technetwork/ community/developer-vm. You will have to install and set up Oracle VM VirtualBox to use the prebuilt VMs.

How to Contact Sybex

Sybex strives to keep you supplied with the latest tools and information you need for your work. Please check our website at www.sybex.com, where we'll post additional content, errata, and updates that supplement this book if the need arises. Enter search terms? in the Search box (or type the book's ISBN—97811186444072), and click Go to get to the book's update page.

Exam Objectives

Exam 1Z0-063 Oracle Database 12*c*: Backup and Recovery: Objectives Map

- 1.1 Oracle Data Protection Solutions, Chapter 1
  - Explain Oracle backup and recovery solutions
- Performing Basic Backup and Recovery, Chapters 1 and 2
  - Back up and recover a NOARCHIVELOG database, Chapters 1 and 2
- Configuring for Recoverability, Chapters 1 and 3
  - Configure and manage RMAN settings, Chapter 3
  - Configure the Fast Recovery Area, Chapter 3
  - Configure control files and redo log files for recoverability, Chapter 1
- Using the RMAN Recovery Catalog, Chapter 4
  - Create and use an RMAN recovery catalog, Chapter 4
  - Protect the RMAN recovery catalog, Chapter 4
- Implementing Backup Strategies, Chapter 3
  - Use various RMAN backup types and strategies, Chapter 3
- Performing Backups, Chapter 3
  - Perform full and incremental backups, Chapter 3
  - Manage backups, Chapter 3
- Configuring RMAN Backup Options and Creating Backup of Non-Database Files, Chapter 3
  - Use techniques to improve backups, Chapter 3
  - Perform backup of non-database files, Chapter 3
- Using RMAN-Encrypted Backups, Chapter 3
  - Create RMAN-encrypted backups, Chapter 3
- Diagnosing Failures, Chapter 9
  - Describe the Automatic Diagnostic Workflow, Chapter 9 and Chapter 6
  - Handle block corruption, Chapter 9

- Performing Restore and Recovery Operations, Chapters 1 and 5
  - Describe and tune instance recovery, Chapter 1
  - Perform complete and incomplete recovery, Chapter 5
- Recovering Files Using RMAN, Chapters 5 and 7
  - Perform recovery for spfile, password file, control file, redo log files, Chapter 5
  - Perform table recovery from backups, Chapter 7
  - Perform recovery of index and read-only tablespaces, temp file, Chapter 5
  - Restore a database to a new host, Chapter 7
- Using Oracle Secure Backup, Chapter 7
  - Configure and use Oracle Secure Backup, Chapter 7
- Using Flashback Technologies, Chapter 8
  - Describe the Flashback technologies, Chapter 8
  - Use Flashback to query data, Chapter 8
  - Perform Flashback Table operations, Chapter 8
  - Describe and use Flashback Data Archive, Chapter 8
- Using Flashback Database, Chapter 8
  - Perform Flashback Database operations, Chapter 8
- Transporting Data, Chapter 10
  - Describe and use transportable tablespaces and databases, Chapter 10
- Duplicating a Database, Chapter 7
  - Choose a technique for duplicating a database, Chapter 7
  - Create a backup based duplicate database, Chapter 7
  - Duplicate a database based on a running instance, Chapter 7
- Monitoring and Tuning of RMAN Operations, Chapter 6
  - Tune RMAN performance, Chapter 6

Exam 1Z0-063 Oracle Database 12*c*: Managing Multitenant Architecture: Objectives Map

- Multitenant Container and Pluggable Database Architecture, Chapter 11
  - Describe the multitenant architecture, Chapter 11
  - Explain pluggable database provisioning, Chapter 11

- Creating Multitenant Container and Pluggable Databases, Chapter 11
  - Configure and create a CDB, Chapter 11
  - Create a PDB using different methods, Chapter 11
  - Unplug and drop a PDB, Chapter 11
  - Migrate a non-CDB database to PDB, Chapter 11
- Managing a CDB and PDBs, Chapter 12
  - Establish connections to CDB/PDB, Chapter 12
  - Start up and shut down a CDB and open and close PDBs, Chapter 12
  - Evaluate the impact of parameter value changes, Chapter 12
- Managing Storage in a CDB and PDBs, Chapter 10
  - Manage permanent and temporary tablespaces in CDB and PDBs, Chapter 10
- Managing Security in a CDB and PDBs, Chapter 14
  - Manage common and local users, Chapter 14
  - Manage common and local privileges, Chapter 14
  - Manage common and local roles, Chapter 14
  - Enable common users to access data in specific PDBs, Chapter 14
- Managing Availability, Chapter 7
  - Perform backups of a CDB and PDBs, Chapter 7
  - Recover PDB from PDB datafiles loss, Chapter 7
  - Use Data Recovery Advisor, Chapter 7
  - Duplicate PDBs using RMAN, Chapter 7
- Managing Performance, Chapter 9
  - Monitor operations and performance in a CDB and PDBs, Chapter 9
  - Manage allocation of resources between PDBs and within a PDB, Chapter 9
  - Perform Database Replay, Chapter 9
- Moving Data, Performing Security Operations, and Interacting with Other Oracle Products, Chapters 7 and 13
  - Use Data Pump, Chapter 7
  - Use SQL*Loader, Chapter 13
  - Audit operations, Chapter 13
  - Use Other Products with CDB and PDBs—Database Vault, Data Guard, LogMiner, Chapter 13

Assessment Test

1. What Oracle process runs when the database is in ARCHIVELOG mode but not when it is in NOARCHIVELOG mode?

   A. MMON

   B. LGWR

   C. ARCH

   D. ARWR

   E. COPY

2. You are peer-reviewing a fellow DBA's backup plan for his NOARCHIVELOG mode database, as shown here:

   1. Put the tablespaces in backup mode.

   2. Back up the data files for all tablespaces.

   3. Take the tablespaces out of backup mode.

   4. Back up all archived redo logs.

   Your colleague asks you to comment on his plan. Which response would be correct?

   A. The plan will work as is.

   B. The plan needs to be modified to allow for an archive-log switch after step 3.

   C. The plan needs to be modified so that a backup of the archived redo logs occurs before step 1.

   D. The plan needs to be adjusted to shut down the database after step 1 and to restart the database after step 2.

   E. The plan cannot work as presented.

3. Which of the following statements is true when the database is in ARCHIVELOG mode and tablespaces are in hot backup mode?

   A. Archive log generation is suspended until the tablespaces are taken out of hot backup mode.

   B. Data files are not written to during hot backups.

   C. Changes to the database are cached during the backup and not written to the data files to ensure that the data files are consistent when recovered.

   D. The data file headers are not updated during the backup.

   E. The way data is written to the online redo logs is unchanged during the backup.

4. When you create a backup control file, where is the resulting file written to?

    A. The database user dump destination directory

    B. The database diagnostic destination directory

    C. `$ORACLE_HOME/rdbms`

    D. `$ORACLE_HOME/admin`

    E. The directory and filename you specify in the command

5. If a log file becomes corrupted, it may cause the database to stall. How would you correct such a situation?

    A. Recover the online redo log from backup.

    B. Delete and recreate the log file.

    C. Use the `ALTER DATABASE CLEAR LOGFILE` command to clear the log file.

    D. Shut down the database and restart it.

    E. Shut down the database and then mount it. Clear the log file with the `ALTER DATABASE CLEAR LOGFILE` command and then restart the database with `ALTER DATABASE OPEN RESETLOGS`.

6. You have lost data files 1 and 3 from your database, and the database has crashed. In what order should you perform the following steps to recover your database?

    1. Take the data files that were lost offline.

    2. Issue `STARTUP MOUNT` to start up the database.

    3. Issue the `ALTER DATABASE OPEN` command.

    4. Restore the data files that were lost.

    5. Recover the data files with the `RECOVER DATAFILE` command.

    6. Bring the data files back online.

    7. Recover the database with the `RECOVER DATABASE` command.

    A. 2, 1, 3, 4, 5, 6

    B. 2, 4, 5, 3

    C. 4, 7, 3

    D. 2, 4, 7, 3

    E. 2, 7, 3

7. Which command is used to open the database after an incomplete recovery?

    A. `ALTER DATABASE OPEN`

    B. `ALTER DATABASE OPEN REPAIRLOG`

    C. `ALTER DATABASE OPEN RESETLOGS`

    D. `ALTER DATABASE OPEN RESETLOG`

    E. `ALTER DATABASE RESETLOGS OPEN`

8. Your database has a backup that was taken yesterday (Tuesday) between 13:00 and 15:00 hours. This is the only backup you have. You have lost all the archived redo logs generated since the previous Monday, but you have archived redo logs available from the previous Sunday and earlier. You now need to restore your backup due to database loss. To which point can you restore your database?

   A. 13:00 on Tuesday.

   B. 15:00 on Tuesday.

   C. Up until the last available archived redo log on Sunday.

   D. To any point; all the redo should still be available in the online redo logs.

   E. The database is not recoverable.

9. Which of the following files cannot be backed up by RMAN? (Choose all that apply.)

   A. Database data files

   B. Control files

   C. Online redo logs

   D. Database pfiles

   E. Archived redo logs

10. Which of the following RMAN structures can data from a data file span?

   A. RMAN backup-set pieces spanning backup sets

   B. RMAN backup-set pieces within a given backup set

   C. RMAN backups

   D. RMAN channels

   E. None of the above

11. Which RMAN backup command is used to create the block-change tracking file?

   A. `ALTER DATABASE CREATE BLOCK CHANGE TRACKING FILE`

   B. `ALTER DATABASE ENABLE BLOCK CHANGE FILE`

   C. `ALTER DATABASE ENABLE BLOCK CHANGE TRACKING USING FILE '/ora01/opt/ block_change_tracking.fil'`

   D. `ALTER SYSTEM ENABLE BLOCK CHANGE TRACKING USING FILE '/ora01/opt/block_ change_tracking.fil'`

   E. `ALTER SYSTEM BLOCK CHANGE TRACKING ON`

12. A shoot-out has erupted between your MS development teams using .NET and your Linux development teams using Java. Knowing that your database is in danger, which command would you use to back up your NOARCHIVELOG mode database using RMAN with compression?

   A. BACKUP DATABASE ALL

   B. BACKUP COMPRESSED DATABASE

   C. BACKUP AS COMPRESSED BACKUPSET DATABASE;

   D. BACKUP AS COMPRESSED BACKUP DATABASE PLUS ARCHIVELOG ALL;

   E. BACKUP AS COMPRESSED BACKUPSET DATABASE PLUS COMPRESS ARCHIVELOG ALL;

13. What is the purpose of the RMAN recovery catalog? (Choose all that apply.)

   A. Make backups faster

   B. Store RMAN metadata

   C. Store RMAN scripts

   D. Provide the ability to do centralized backup reporting

   E. Make recovery faster

14. RMAN provides more granular catalog security through which feature?

   A. Virtual private database

   B. Virtual private catalog

   C. RMAN virtual database

   D. RMAN secure catalog

   E. Oracle Database Vault

15. True or false? You can back up the RMAN recovery catalog with RMAN.

   A. True

   B. False

16. What RMAN command must you use before you can back up a database using the recovery catalog?

   A. CREATE CATALOG

   B. INSTALL DATABASE

   C. CATALOG DATABASE

   D. MERGE CATALOG WITH DATABASE

   E. REGISTER DATABASE

17. You have control-file autobackups enabled. When starting your database from SQL*Plus, you receive the following error message. Using RMAN, how would you respond to this error?

```
SQL> startup
ORA-01078: failure in processing system parameters
LRM-00109: could not open parameter file
'C:\ORACLE\PRODUCT\11.1.0\DB_1\DATABASE\INITORCL.ORA'
```

   A. Issue the STARTUP NOMOUNT command and then issue the RESTORE PARAMETER FILE command from the RMAN prompt.

   B. Issue the STARTUP NOMOUNT command and then issue the RESTORE SPFILE command from the RMAN prompt.

   C. Issue the STARTUP NOMOUNT command and then issue the RESTORE SPFILE FROM AUTOBACKUP command from the RMAN prompt.

   D. Issue the STARTUP NOMOUNT command and then issue the RESTORE SPFILE FROM BACKUP command from the RMAN prompt.

   E. Issue the RESTORE SPFILE FROM AUTOBACKUP command from the RMAN prompt.

18. While working on a data problem, Curt, Bill, Ben, Mike, and Matt introduced a vast amount of corrupted data into the database. Pablo has discovered this problem and he needs you to recover the database to the point in time prior to the introduction of the corruption. The logical corruption was introduced at 6:30 P.M. on September 6, 2013. Which of the following would be the correct commands to use to restore the database to a point in time before the corruption?

   A. RESTORE DATABASE UNTIL TIME '06-SEP-2013 06:30:00');RECOVER DATABASE UNTIL TIME '06-SEP-2013 06:30:00'); ALTER DATABASE OPEN;

   B. RESTORE DATABASE UNTIL TIME '06-SEP-2013 06:30:00');RECOVER DATABASE UNTIL TIME '06-SEP-2013 06:30:00'); ALTER DATABASE OPEN RESETLOGS;

   C. RESTORE DATABASE UNTIL TIME '06-SEP-2013 18:29:55');RECOVER DATABASE UNTIL TIME '06-SEP-2013 18:29:55');ALTER DATABASE OPEN RESETLOGS;

   D. RESTORE DATABASE UNTIL TIME '06-SEP-2013 18:29:55');ALTER DATABASE OPEN RESETLOGS;

   E. RESTORE DATABASE UNTIL TIME '06-SEP-2013 18:29:55');RECOVER DATABASE;ALTER DATABASE OPEN RESETLOGS;

19. What is the purpose of the UNTIL CHANGE option of the RESTORE command?

   A. It allows you to select the SCN that you want to restore to.

   B. It allows you to select the log sequence number you want to restore to.

   C. It allows you to select the timestamp you want to restore to.

   D. It allows you to manually stop the restore at any time as online redo logs are applied.

   E. None of the above.

20. What is the purpose of the RECOVER command? (Choose all that apply.)

    A. Recover database data files from physical disk backup sets.

    B. Recover required incremental backups from physical disk backup sets.

    C. Recover required archived redo logs from physical disk backup sets.

    D. Apply incremental backups to recover the database.

    E. Apply archived redo logs to recover the database.

21. What is an obsolete backup set?

    A. A backup set that is missing one or more backup set pieces

    B. A backup that has exceeded the retention criteria and is no longer needed

    C. A backup set that does not include archived redo logs

    D. A backup set that cannot be recovered due to corruption

    E. A backup set superseded by a data file copy

22. What is the purpose of the LIST EXPIRED BACKUP command?

    A. List all backups impacted by a RESETLOGS command.

    B. List all backups that are subject to retention criteria.

    C. List all backups that are missing associated physical backup set pieces.

    D. List the status of data file backup failures due to the use of the DURATION command.

    E. List backups that cannot be used by the RESTORE command because they have been marked as disabled.

23. What is the purpose of the CATALOG command?

    A. To review RMAN control file and recovery catalog metadata and ensure that it's correct

    B. To delete RMAN backup-related metadata from the recovery catalog

    C. To create metadata in the control file and the recovery catalog related to backup set pieces

    D. To create a report that lists database backups

    E. To rebuild the recovery catalog

24. Which of the following commands will fail?

    A. REPORT SCHEMA;

    B. REPORT NEED BACKUP;

    C. REPORT NEED BACKUP DAYS 3;

    D. REPORT USER;

    E. REPORT OBSOLETE;

25. What are the two different types of database duplication? (Choose two.)

   A. Active

   B. Passive

   C. Online

   D. Backup-based

   E. Failure-driven

26. When you're performing a tablespace point-in-time recovery, which tablespaces will always be restored to the auxiliary instance? (Choose all that apply.)

   A. The SYSTEM tablespace.

   B. The UNDO tablespace.

   C. All tablespaces with tables.

   D. All tablespaces with indexes.

   E. No tablespaces are automatically restored.

27. Which operation requires that you create an auxiliary instance manually before executing the operation? (Choose all that apply.)

   A. Backup-based database duplication.

   B. Active database duplication.

   C. Tablespace point-in-time recovery.

   D. No operation requires the creation of an auxiliary instance.

28. What RMAN command is used to execute a tablespace point-in-time recovery?

   A. RECOVER

   B. DUPLICATE

   C. RESTORE

   D. COPY

   E. None of the above

29. RMAN provides the ability to back up a PDB from the root of the CDB. True or false?

   A. True

   B. False

30. Which of the following EXPDP commands will successfully export the mydb PDB?

   A. EXPDP SYS/PASSWORD@mydb DIRECTORY=ROBERT FULL=Y

   B. EXPDP 'SYS/PASSWORD@mydb' DIRECTORY=ROBERT FULL=Y

   C. EXPDP 'SYS/PASSWORD@mydb AS SYSDBA' DIRECTORY=ROBERT FULL=Y

   D. EXPDP 'SYS/PASSWORD@mydb AS EXPDBA' DIRECTORY=ROBERT FULL=Y

   E. EXPDP 'SYS/PASSWORD@mydb AS EXPORT_FILE' DIRECTORY=ROBERT FULL=Y

31. Which of the following lists the correct steps when using the Data Recovery Advisor to correct a problem with the database?

   A. Start SQL*Plus.

   Issue the LIST FAILURE command.

   Issue the ADVISE FAILURE command.

   Issue the REPAIR FAILURE command.

   B. Start RMAN.

   Issue the LIST FAILURE command.

   Issue the ADVISE FAILURE command.

   Issue the REPAIR FAILURE command.

   C. Start RMAN.

   Issue the ADVISE FAILURE command.

   Issue the LIST FAILURE command.

   Issue the REPAIR FAILURE command.

   D. Start SQL*Plus.

   Issue the ADVISE FAILURE command.

   Issue the LIST FAILURE command.

   Issue the REPAIR FAILURE command.

   E. Start the dravsr command-line tool.

   Issue the ADVISE FAILURE command.

   Issue the LIST FAILURE command.

   Issue the REPAIR FAILURE command.

32. Which of the following is not supported by RMAN?

   A. A complete backup of a CDB

   B. A complete backup of a PDB

   C. An incremental backup of more than one PDB

   D. Point-in-time recovery of a PDB

   E. None of the above

33. The Oracle expdp utility does not support which of the following operations? (Choose all that apply.)

   A. Full export of a PDB

   B. Table-level export of a PDB

   C. Schema-level export of a PDB

   D. Point-in-time recovery of a PDB

   E. None of the above

34. A user performs an update on a table. Shortly after committing the transaction, they realize that they had an error in their WHERE clause, causing the wrong rows to be updated. Which Flashback option would allow you to undo this transaction and restore the table to its previous state?

    A. Flashback Drop

    B. Flashback Query

    C. Flashback Versions Query

    D. Flashback Transaction Query

    E. Flashback Table

35. A developer calls and reports that he accidentally dropped an important lookup table from a production database. He needs the table to be recovered. What action would you take?

    A. Initiate an incomplete recovery operation using RMAN.

    B. Copy the table from a development database.

    C. Advise the user to rekey the data.

    D. Perform a Flashback Drop operation.

    E. Perform a Flashback Recovery operation.

36. In a Database Replay workload capture, what client request information is gathered? (Choose all that apply.)

    A. SQL text

    B. Shared server requests (Oracle MTS)

    C. Bind variable values

    D. Information about transactions

    E. Remote DESCRIBE and COMMIT operations

37. Which of the following are true concerning block media recovery? (Choose all that apply.)

    A. Any gap in archive logs ends the recovery.

    B. If a gap in archive logs is encountered, RMAN will search forward for newer versions of the blocks that are not corrupt.

    C. Uncorrupted blocks from the flashback logs may be used to speed recovery.

    D. The database can be in NOARCHIVELOG mode.

    E. None of the above

38. A user performs an update on a table. Shortly after committing the transaction, he realizes that he had an error in the WHERE clause, causing the wrong rows to be updated. Which Flashback option would allow you to undo this transaction and restore the table to its previous state?

    A. Flashback Drop

    B. Flashback Query

    C. Flashback Versions Query

    D. Flashback Transaction Query

    E. Flashback Table

39. A developer calls and reports that he accidentally dropped an important lookup table from a production database. He needs the table to be recovered. What action would you take?

    A. Initiate an incomplete recovery operation using RMAN.

    B. Copy the table from a development database.

    C. Advise the user to rekey the data.

    D. Perform a Flashback Drop operation.

    E. Perform a Flashback Recovery operation.

40. In a Database Replay workload capture, what client request information is gathered? (Choose all that apply.)

    A. SQL text

    B. Shared server requests (Oracle MTS)

    C. Bind variable values

    D. Information about transactions

    E. Remote DESCRIBE and COMMIT operations

41. Which of the following are true concerning block media recovery? (Choose all that apply.)

    A. Any gap in archive logs ends the recovery.

    B. If a gap in archive logs is encountered, RMAN will search forward for newer versions of the blocks that are not corrupt.

    C. Uncorrupted blocks from the flashback logs may be used to speed recovery.

    D. The database can be in NOARCHIVELOG mode.

    E. None of the above.

42. You notice that a long-running transaction is suspended due to a space constraint, and there is no AFTER SUSPEND triggered event addressing the issue. You also note that the critical transaction is just about to reach the RESUMABLE_TIMEOUT value. Which of these actions is appropriate?

A. Abort the session, fix the space problem, and then resubmit the transaction.

B. Use the DBMS_RESUMABLE.SET_SESSION_TIMEOUT procedure to extend the time-out for the session while you fix the problem.

C. Do nothing, let the transaction fail, and then fix the problem.　　　.

D. Use Segment Shrink to clean up the table.

E. Use the DBMS_RESUMABLE.SET_TIMEOUT procedure to extend the time-out for the session while you fix the problem.

43. Which of the following are not components of the multitenant container database? (Choose all that apply.)

A. CDB$SEED

B. PDB$SEED

C. PDB$ROOT

D. Zero or more PDBs

E. CDB$ROOT

44. As a common user with DBA privileges, you can use which of these SQL*Plus commands to create a PDB?

A. CREATE PDB lneND;

B. CREATE PLUGGABLE DATABASE lneND USING pdb1;

C. CREATE PLUGGABLE DATABASE lneND FROM PDB$SEED;

D. CREATE PLUGGABLE DATABASE lneND FROM pdb1;

45. Of the following statements, which are not true regarding a local user? (Choose all that apply.)

A. A local user is created at the CDB$ROOT.

B. A local user has access to the CDB$ROOT and the local PDB.

C. A local user has access to all PDBs but not the CDB$ROOT.

D. A local user has access only to the local PDB.

46. Which of the following are valid shutdown scenarios in the CDB? (Choose all that apply.)

   A. SHUTDOWN NORMAL when you're ready to perform a cold backup within a constrained time window

   B. SHUTDOWN FORCE when SHUTDOWN IMMEDIATE doesn't succeed

   C. SHUTDOWN TRANSACTIONAL to end all pending transactions and then SHUTDOWN NORMAL

   D. SHUTDOWN IMMEDIATE when SHUTDOWN ABORT doesn't work

   E. None of the above

47. Which of the following are use cases for Oracle Data Pump? (Choose all that apply.)

   A. Connect to CDB$ROOT and import root objects into the CDB.

   B. Connect to PDB$SEED and import objects into the PDB.

   C. Connect to a common user and import objects into a PDB.

   D. Connect to a local user and import objects into a PDB.

48. When using Oracle Data Guard, after you create a PDB in a primary CDB, what must you also do in each associated standby CDB? (Choose all that apply.)

   A. Nothing; Data Guard always keeps the physical standby databases synchronized with the primary.

   B. You must clone the primary PDB to the standby CDBs.

   C. You must copy the PDB data files to the standby prior to plugging in the PDB in the primary.

   D. None of the above

49. In the Oracle 12c multitenant architecture, which of the following is a characteristic of a common user?

   A. It has the same identity in a non-CDB or a CDB.

   B. It has the same identity in all PDBs in a CDB.

   C. It can access only the CDB$ROOT.

   D. It is Oracle-supplied only.

50. When plugging a non-CDB into a PDB, what happens to the non-CDB users?

   A. Oracle-supplied administrative user accounts overwrite the target PDB local user accounts.

   B. Oracle-supplied administrative user account passwords overwrite the target common user account passwords.

   C. Non-CDB defined user accounts become common user accounts in the target CDB.

   D. Non-CDB defined user accounts become local user accounts in the target PDB.

Answers to Assessment Test

1. **C.** The ARCH process starts up when the database is in ARCHIVELOG mode. It is responsible for moving the online redo logs to the various archived redo log destination directories. For more information, see Chapter 1, "Performing Oracle User-Managed Backups."

2. **E.** Since the database is in NOARCHIVELOG mode, the entire plan will not work since you cannot perform hot backups in NOARCHIVELOG mode. If the database was in ARCHIVELOG mode, then you would choose option B. For more information, see Chapter 1, "Performing Oracle User-Managed Backups."

3. **D.** When a tablespace is in hot backup mode, the related data file headers are not updated. The headers will be updated after the tablespaces are taken out of hot backup mode. For more information, see Chapter 1, "Performing Oracle User-Managed Backups."

4. **E.** When you issue the `ALTER DATABASE BACKUP CONTROLFILE TO 'DIRECTORY/ FILENAME'` command, Oracle will write the backup control file to the directory and filename that you choose. For more information, see Chapter 1, "Performing Oracle User-Managed Backups."

5. **C.** Use the `ALTER DATABASE CLEAR LOGFILE` command to clear the log file and free up the database. If the log file has not been archived, you may have to use the `ALTER DATABASE CLEAR UNARCHIVED LOGFILE` command instead. For more information, please see Chapter 2, "Performing Oracle User-Managed Database Recoveries."

6. **B.** You will have to issue `STARTUP MOUNT` to start up the database and then restore the database data files that were lost (you could, of course, restore the files first). You will then need to recover the data files with the `RECOVER DATAFILE` command. Once the data files are recovered, you can then open the database. You may wonder why online recovery is not possible in this case. Data file 1 is always the SYSTEM tablespace. The database cannot be opened if the SYSTEM tablespace is not available. Also, the use of the `RECOVER DATABASE` command is not the best choice in this case. Oracle always wants you to answer the question with the best choice. In this case, data file recovery is the best choice. For more information, please see Chapter 2, "Performing Oracle User-Managed Database Recoveries."

7. **C.** The `ALTER DATABASE OPEN RESETLOGS` command is used to open an Oracle database after an incomplete recovery. For more information, please see Chapter 2, "Performing Oracle User-Managed Database Recoveries."

8. **E.** The database is not recoverable. You would need all the archived redo logs generated during the backup on Tuesday, at least, to restore the database after that backup. The online redo logs are very unlikely to have all the redo that would be required. For more information, please see Chapter 2, "Performing Oracle User-Managed Database Recoveries."

9. **C, D.** RMAN will not back up online redo logs or database parameter files. RMAN will back up database server parameter files (spfiles), however. For more information, see Chapter 3, "Configuring and Backing Up Oracle Databases Using RMAN"

10. **B.** RMAN backup set pieces within the same backup set can contain data from a given data file. For more information see Chapter 3, "Configuring and Backing Up Oracle Databases Using RMAN."

11. **C.** Use the `ALTER DATABASE ENABLE BLOCK CHANGE TRACKING USING FILE` command, followed by the path and filename in single quotes, to create the block change tracking file. For more information, see Chapter 3, "Configuring and Backing Up Oracle Databases Using RMAN."

12. **C.** You would use the `BACKUP AS COMPRESSED BACKUPSET DATABASE PLUS ARCHIVELOG ALL` command to back up your database. Of course, the command is so long-winded that the war would be over by the time you finished typing it all in. For more information, see Chapter 3, "Configuring and Backing Up Oracle Databases Using RMAN."

13. **B, C, D.** The RMAN recovery catalog provides a centralized location for all RMAN-related metadata. Thus it makes centralized reporting much easier. Additionally, you can store scripts in the recovery catalog for use across all databases that use RMAN. For more information, see Chapter 4, "Using the RMAN Recovery Catalog."

14. **B.** The RMAN virtual private catalog provides the ability to allow users granular access to RMAN recovery catalog records based on database name. Thus, specific users can see only the records they are allowed to see. For more information, see Chapter 4, "Using the RMAN Recovery Catalog."

15. **A.** You can back up any database without connecting to the recovery catalog, including the recovery catalog database. In fact, you can back up the recovery catalog database while connected to the recovery catalog. For more information, see Chapter 4, "Using the RMAN Recovery Catalog."

16. **E.** The `REGISTER DATABASE` command is used to indicate that the target database should be registered in the recovery catalog. For more information, see Chapter 4, "Using the RMAN Recovery Catalog."

17. **C.** You would first need to start the database with the `STARTUP NOMOUNT` command from the RMAN prompt. Then you would restore the spfile using the `RESTORE SPFILE FROM AUTOBACKUP` command. For more information, see Chapter 5, "Recovering Databases with RMAN."

18. **C.** You would first need to restore the database to the correct point in time with the `RESTORE DATABASE` command. You would include the `UNTIL TIME` parameter to indicate what point in time you want to restore to. You would then recover the database with the `RECOVER DATABASE` command, which will apply the appropriate incremental backups and archived redo logs. Again, you would use the `UNTIL TIME` command to indicate the time to recover to. Finally, you would open the database with the `ALTER DATABASE OPEN RESETLOGS` command. For more information, see Chapter 5, "Recovering Databases with RMAN."

19. A. The UNTIL CHANGE option of the RESTORE command provides the ability to restore the database to a specific SCN. For more information, see Chapter 5, "Recovering Databases with RMAN."

20. B, C, D, E. The RECOVER command will recover the needed incremental backup and archived redo logs from backup sets for recovery purposes. The RECOVER command will then apply the incremental backups and archived redo logs as needed to recover the database. For more information, see Chapter 5, "Recovering Databases with RMAN."

21. B. An obsolete backup set is one that has exceeded the retention criteria. As a result, it is subject to automatic removal in the flash recovery area. For more information, see Chapter 6, "Tuning and Monitoring RMAN and the Automatic Diagnostic Workflow."

22. C. An expired backup is one that is missing one or more physical backup set pieces. The LIST EXPIRED BACKUP command lists these types of backups. For more information, see Chapter 6, "Tuning and Monitoring RMAN and the Automatic Diagnostic Workflow."

23. C. The CATALOG command is used to catalog backup set pieces or image copies in both the control file and the recovery catalog so RMAN can use those backup set pieces or image copies. For more information, see Chapter 6, "Tuning and Monitoring RMAN and the Automatic Diagnostic Workflow."

24. D. There is no REPORT USER command. For more information, see Chapter 6, "Tuning and Monitoring RMAN and the Automatic Diagnostic Workflow."

25. A, D. Active database duplication takes place using network connections between the target database and the auxiliary database instance. Backup-based duplication requires that the RMAN backup set pieces be available on the server where the duplicate database will be created. For more information, see Chapter 7, "Performing Oracle Advanced Recovery."

26. A, B. The SYSTEM and UNDO tablespaces will always be restored during a tablespace point-in-time recovery operation. For more information, see Chapter 7, "Performing Oracle Advanced Recovery."

27. A, B. Database duplication (either backup-based or active) requires that you create the parameter files for the auxiliary database instance and have the auxiliary database instance started in NOMOUNT mode. For more information, see Chapter 7, "Performing Oracle Advanced Recovery."

28. A. You use the RECOVER TABLESPACE command to perform a tablespace point-in-time recovery. For more information, see Chapter 7, "Performing Oracle Advanced Recovery."

29. A. True—you use the BACKUP PLUGGABLE DATABASE command to back up a PDB from the root of a CDB. See Chapter 7, "Performing Oracle Advanced Recovery."

30. C. The command shown in answer C will result in a successful backup. All the other commands will fail. See Chapter 7, "Performing Oracle Advanced Recovery."

31. **B.** You start RMAN and then issue the `ADVISE FAILURE` command. Then you issue the `LIST FAILURE` and `REPAIR FAILURE` commands.

32. **E.** All of the operations listed are supported by RMAN. See Chapter 7, "Performing Oracle Advanced Recovery."

33. **D.** Of course, expdp does not support a point-in-time recovery of a PDB since expdp does not support point-in-time recoveries. See Chapter 7, "Performing Oracle Advanced Recovery."

34. **E.** Only the Flashback Table option recovers a table to a previous point in time. The other options allow viewing of past states of the data (B, C, D) or restoration from the Recycle Bin (A), but they do not recover a table to a previous point in time. For more information, see Chapter 8, "Understanding Flashback Technology."

35. **D.** A Flashback Drop option would allow you to restore the table from the Recycle Bin. Although A, B, and C may all be valid recovery options, they are much less desirable than Flashback Drop. E is an invalid option altogether. For more information, see Chapter 8, "Understanding Flashback Technology."

36. **A, C, D.** Shared server requests and remote `DESCRIBE` and `COMMIT` operations are not captured in a workload. For more information, see Chapter 9, "Diagnosing the Database and Managing Performance."

37. **B, C.** Option A is incorrect because a gap in archive logs does not automatically end the recovery. RMAN will search forward for uncorrupted newer blocks; if RMAN finds one, it will continue with the restore and recovery operation. RMAN will check the flashback logs for uncorrupted copies of the block before it checks the backups. Option D is incorrect because the database must be in ARCHIVELOG mode. For more information, see Chapter 9, "Diagnosing the Database and Managing Performance."

38. **E.** Only the Flashback Table option recovers a table to a previous point in time. The other options allow viewing of past states of the data (B, C, D) or restoration from the Recycle Bin (A), but they do not recover a table to a previous point in time. For more information, see Chapter 8, "Understanding Flashback Technology."

39. **D.** A Flashback Drop option would allow you to restore the table from the Recycle Bin. Although A, B, and C may all be valid recovery options, they are much less desirable than Flashback Drop. E is an invalid option altogether. For more information, see Chapter 8, "Understanding Flashback Technology."

40. **A, C, D.** Shared server requests and remote `DESCRIBE` and `COMMIT` operations are not captured in a workload. For more information, see Chapter 9, "Diagnosing the Database and Managing Performance."

41. **B, C.** Option A is incorrect because a gap in archive logs does not automatically end the recovery. RMAN will search forward for uncorrupted newer blocks; if it finds one, it will continue with the restore and recovery operation. RMAN will check the flashback logs for uncorrupted copies of the block before it checks the backups. Option D is incorrect because the database must be in ARCHIVELOG mode. For more information, see Chapter 9, "Diagnosing the Database and Managing Performance."

42. **B.** Since you're running short on time, extend the time-out for the session that's in jeopardy and fix the space problem. Don't put the transaction at risk while you try to find free space and run the commands, and don't kill the transaction—unless you know that the space condition and extended suspend has caused other issues. For more information, see Chapter 10, "Managing Database Resources."

43. **A, C.** CDB$SEED and PDB$ROOT are not components of the multitenant container database architecture. For more information, see Chapter 11, "Creating Oracle Multitenant Databases."

44. **D.** Option A is incorrect because CREATE PDB is not a valid command. Option B is not correct because the USING clause is not valid. Option C is not correct because you did not specify the target admin user and password. For more information, see Chapter 11, "Creating Oracle Multitenant Databases."

45. **A, B, C.** Answer D is the only true answer: the local user by definition has access only to the one PDB it was created in. For more information, see Chapter 12, "Managing Oracle Multitenant Databases."

46. **E.** Answer A is not correct because you need to shut down the database as soon as possible. Answer B is not correct because SHUTDOWN FORCE is not valid. SHUTDOWN TRANSACTIONAL will wait for all pending transactions to complete, so option C is not valid. Use SHUTDOWN ABORT when no other option will work, so option D is not valid. For more information, see Chapter 12, "Managing Oracle Multitenant Databases."

47. **C, D.** Option A is incorrect because Data Pump does not allow any CDB-wide operations (CDB$ROOT). For the same reason B is incorrect; Oracle Data Pump doesn't allow import operations on PDB$SEED. For more information, see Chapter 13, "Oracle Utilities."

48. **C.** Answer A is not correct because Data Guard does not automatically create the PDB in the standby databases. Answer B is incorrect because you do not have to clone the PDB to the standby CDBs. For more information, see Chapter 13, "Oracle Utilities."

49. **B.** Answer B is correct because a common user has the same identity in all containers in a CDB. Option A is incorrect because only Oracle-supplied common users in a CDB would appear similar to Oracle-supplied users in a non-CDB; however, non-CDBs do not have common or local users. Answer C is not correct because a common user has the capability to access all containers. Common users can create common users, so D is incorrect. For more information, see Chapter 14, "Oracle Security in CDBs and PDBs."

50. **D.** Option A is incorrect because the user accounts are merged, not overwritten. Option B is incorrect because the passwords are not overwritten. Option C is incorrect because the plugged-in user accounts become local user accounts, not common users. For more information, see Chapter 14, "Oracle Security in CDBs and PDBs."

Chapter

1

Performing Oracle User-Managed Backups

ORACLE DATABASE 12*c*: ADVANCED ADMINISTRATION EXAM OBJECTIVES COVERED IN THIS CHAPTER:

✓ Explain Oracle backup and recovery solutions

✓ Describe types of database failures

✓ Describe the tools available for backup and recovery tasks

✓ Describe RMAN and maximum availability architecture

✓ Back up and recover a NOARCHIVELOG database

✓ Perform backup and recovery in NOARCHIVELOG mode

✓ Configure control files and redo log files for recoverability

✓ Multiplex control files

✓ Multiplex redo log files

✓ Describe and tune instance recovery

✓ Enable ARCHIVELOG mode

✓ Backup a control file to trace

This chapter begins your introduction to the information you need to pass your Oracle Database 12c: Certified Professional exam. Perhaps the main job of an Oracle DBA involves using your knowledge to ensure that your database is always backed up and recoverable.

This might sound simple. However, the expertise needed to ensure that your backup and recovery plan is effective is not easy to come by. This is one reason why the job of the DBA is in high demand. With your passing of the Oracle Database 12c Administration II exam, you will be able to present credentials to employers that indicate that you have a particular set of knowledge that will permit you to protect their data.

There is a lot to cover in this chapter. From the basics of how Oracle works and how that relates to backup and recovery, to configuring online redo log files and control file for higher availability. Also in this chapter, we will discuss manually backing up your database when it's in NOARCHIVELOG mode, and many more topics that you will want to know as you prepare for your Oracle OCP exam.

Exam objectives are subject to change at any time without prior notice and at Oracle's sole discretion. Please visit Oracle's Training and Certification website (http://www.oracle.com/education/certification/) for the most current exam-objectives listing.

Oracle Database Data Protection Options

There are a number of things to consider with respect to backup and recovery. There are different kinds of failures, different types of backups, and different tools that can be used to back up and restore an Oracle Database. In this section, we will look at the various Oracle Data protection options that are available to the DBA.

What Kind of Failures Can Happen to a Database

There are literally numberless combinations of things that can go wrong with an Oracle database. Like any technology, there are always opportunities for failure. Throughout this book you will see a number of examples of these types of failures. The most common failures include:

Physical failures – This includes the loss of disk drives, controller cards, memory, or even the server itself.

Logical failures – this includes failures that corrupt data, failures of software (such as bugs) and application failures corrupt data.

Networking failures – These are errors where one component cannot talk to another component. This can lead to a number of problems.

User errors – These are errors where the user accidently or purposely corrupts data.

Disasters – Things like earthquakes, tornadoes, and flooding happen from time to time and you have to be prepared for failures on a more massive scale.

When considering an overall backup and recovery architecture, you need to consider each of these kinds of failures and how to recover from them. Each type of failure requires a different approach when trying to protect from and mitigate the results of that failure. We will discuss these things in a number of places in this book.

Physical and Logical Backups

There are two different kinds of Oracle backup and recovery. The first is a physical backup and the second is a logical backup. A physical backup involves backing up the physical files of the database to some backup medium, such as another disk or a tape drive.

The logical backup extracts the data from the database and stores it in a separate backup file. Thus, the physical component of the database is not backed up, only the data and meta data needed to reconstruct the database if the logical backup should need to be used to restore the database.

In general the logical backup is of less use than a physical backup. This is because the recovery variations available with physical backups are generally greater than with logical backups. Another benefit of physical backups over logical backups is that large logical backups will usually take longer to restore than a physical backup from the same database.

Other benefits of physical backups are that they can be done in a consistent manner and they provide the ability to restore the database to any given point in time that is required. Logical backups do not provide this point-in-time recovery functionality.

Tools for Backup and Recovery

There are different ways of performing backup and recovery of an Oracle database. The most common tools that you will find in use are:

RMAN – Perhaps the most commonly used tool, RMAN is a free tool provided by Oracle that performs physical backups of the Oracle database. RMAN is easy to implement and use.

Oracle Data Pump – Oracle Data Pump is a method of performing logical backups of the Oracle Database.

Oracle Flashback features – Oracle Database provides a number of features that revolve around its Flashback Database functionality. These flashback features include the following:

- Flashback Database
- Flashback Query
- Flashback Version Query
- Flashback Transaction Query

* Flashback Transaction
* Flashback table
* Flashback table drop

As you can see there are a number of different variations on the Flashback features, specific to different kinds of needs.

Manual backups – You can write scripts that perform manual backups of your database. You can then take those manual backups and manually restore them.

Oracle MAA Recommendations

The Oracle database provides a number of ways to protect the enterprise from data loss. The different kinds of protection range from basic offline backup and recovery procedures to more complex functionality to provide disaster recovery and multisite solutions.

Oracle provides guidance with respect to data protection in a series of recommended best practices collectively called the Maximum Availability Architecture (MAA) best practices. These best practices describe the architectures, processes, standards, and procedures that should be followed to ensure that your database is protected to the maximum extent possible. The MAA practices actually extend to the various layers in the Enterprise computing landscape, including application and infrastructure.

Various Oracle database features and products are part of the MAA best practices including the following and many other topics:

* Backup and recovery
* High availability
* Disaster recovery
* Data replication and distribution
* Database rolling upgrades

As you will see in the next several chapters, the Oracle Database has a rich set of features to protect your database from data loss. This book concentrates a great deal on Oracle Database backup and recovery. Likewise, the OCP exam contains a large number of questions related to database backup and recovery, specifically those associated with RMAN. Backup and recovery is one of the most fundamental architectural features of the Oracle Database with respect to data protection.

However, there are other things that need to be considered when planning your enterprise data-protection strategy. These include topics such as high availability, disaster recovery, how to correct user or application data corruptions, and data replication. Solutions to these problems involve the following Oracle Database features and products:

Oracle Real-Application Clusters   High availability is provided through the use of Oracle Real-Application Clusters (RAC). With RAC you can have more than one computer connected to your database. Thus, if one of the computers fails, the remaining computers can continue to run.

Oracle Data Guard   Disaster recovery is provided through the Oracle Data Guard product. Oracle Data Guard makes it possible to duplicate your database to one or more sites and keep those duplicate databases synchronized with your primary database. When the primary database site fails, you can switch over operations to one of the Oracle Data Guard databases with minimum or zero data loss. The Oracle OCP exam does not contain any questions specific to Oracle Data Guard.

Oracle Flashback Database   Accidental data corruption and data loss can be rectified through the use of Oracle Flashback Database. Oracle Flashback Database is a subject of the OCP exam and is covered in Chapter 8, "Understanding Flashback Technology," of this book.

Oracle GoldenGate   Data replication is provided through the Oracle GoldenGate product. This product provides the ability to replicate data between both Oracle databases and non-Oracle databases. The OCP exam does not have any questions on Oracle GoldenGate.

Understanding the Oracle Database as It Relates to Backup and Recovery

As a DBA, recovering your database should be important to you. Correspondingly, recovery is also important to Oracle, so the database product has been built to be robust with respect to backup and recovery. We'll start this chapter with a quick primer on how Oracle supports backup and recovery. In this section, we'll give you the background you need to understand backup and recovery and to be successful with your OCP exam. In the following sections, we will discuss these topics:

- Oracle processes related to backup and recovery
- Oracle memory structures related to backup and recovery
- The data dictionary
- Oracle data files and tablespaces
- Online redo logs
- Control files
- Parameter files
- NOARCHIVELOG and ARCHIVELOG modes
- The Oracle instance and the Oracle Database

Note this is not the "kitchen sink" when it comes to an Oracle architecture discussion. We assume you are already somewhat familiar with the Oracle Database architecture (since to take the OCP exam you must first have completed the OCA certification track, which consists of two exams), so this is just a review of the pieces of it that are involved in backup and recovery in some way.

There are two different kinds of Oracle recoveries: instance/crash recovery and media recovery. *Instance recovery* is automatically managed by Oracle when you restart the database. *Media recovery* is a manual process done by the DBA and involves the use of Oracle Database backups.

Oracle Processes Related to Backup and Recovery

The front-line support for Oracle backup and recovery is the Oracle architecture. One part of this architecture is the processes related to the Oracle Database. Although the Oracle Database has a number of processes, only a few really matter with respect to backup and recovery and will be mentioned in this text. These processes are as follows:

- LGWR
- DBW
- ARCH
- Multithreaded Oracle
- User processes

Let's discuss each of these processes next so you can better understand how they impact database recovery.

LGWR Process

The *log writer process (LGWR)* is responsible for keeping the online redo logs up to date. The job of the LGWR process is to move redo from the volatile (nonpersistent) redo log buffer in the System (sometimes called Shared) Global Area (SGA) to the persistence of the online redo logs. A number of different things cause LGWR to wake up and write the redo data, among them are database session commit operations and when the redo log buffer fills to a certain point.

DBW Processes

The *database writer processes (DBWn)* (the *n* indicates that there might be more than one of these processes) are responsible for writing to the database data files. This writing occurs during events called *checkpoints.* A database checkpoint may, in reality, happen at just about any time while the database is running. DBW has very little to do with recovery of the database (other than to support it by writing to the data files) because database data file writes are often delayed and the blocks within the data files themselves are not consistent with the current state of the data inside of the SGA. By default, Oracle starts only one DBW process, but if needed, additional DBW processes can be utilized, though this is rare.

ARCH Processes

The *archiver processes (ARCn)* are responsible for the creation of archived redo logs. In a later section in this chapter, we will discuss how redo logs are filled with redo. Once the redo log file fills, a log switch occurs and Oracle will begin to write to the next online redo log. If the database is in ARCHIVELOG mode (see the section "NOARCHIVELOG and ARCHIVELOG Modes"), the ARCH process will be responsible for taking that filled archived redo log and copying it to one or more backup locations.

If the database is in ARCHIVELOG mode, then the ARCH process will start automatically. Oracle can also start more than one ARCH process if multiple redo logs need to be archived. For ARCH to work properly, you will need to configure the appropriate archiving locations (see "Configuring the Database for Backup and Recovery" later in this chapter for more information). The ARCH process is so vital to backup and recovery of the database that if it cannot copy the archived redo logs to the mandatory archived log destinations, the database will eventually stall until the problem is corrected.

Database Architecture

You might wonder why we spend time talking about the architecture of the database. We don't want you to just understand *how* to do something; we want you to understand *why* you do it. Understanding backup and recovery requires knowing the architecture of the Oracle Database. This knowledge may well make the difference when you face a question and you are not sure of the answer. If you understand how something works, then figuring out an answer to a question becomes easier because you also know how it does not work.

If you are unsure of an answer to an OCP exam question, try to work out which answers are not correct and eliminate them. By knowing how the architecture works, you will be able to eliminate questions more easily and find the correct answer more often.

Multithreaded Oracle

Oracle Database 12*c* introduced an optional multithreaded process/threaded model for operating systems such as Unix and Linux. In this model, most of the database background processes are spawned as threads of a few primary processes. The Oracle multithreaded model should not be confused with Oracle Shared Servers. Shared Servers is a user connection pooling mechanism, whereas multithreaded Oracle is a different way of spawning the processes that make Oracle run.

You can enable multithreaded Oracle through the use of the THREADED_EXECUTION parameter. When this parameter is set to TRUE, there will no longer be a one-to-one relationship between an Oracle background process and an operating system process.

User Processes

User processes are the processes that are started by client programs to connect to the database. In the case of local user processes (also called foreground processes to distinguish them from background database instance processes) on the database server, they will connect directly to the database without the need of a listener. User processes coming from the network will use the Oracle listener to establish a connection to the database. The listener is a program that "listens" for clients to make database connections on a specific port. The listener then spawns a foreground process and connects the network connection to that spawned process.

At first glance, it might seem that the user processes are not all that important to backup and recovery. As you will see, user processes are actually an integral part of backup and recovery since you have to be able to connect to the database instance with these processes. You will also find as you proceed through this book that you will need the listener up and running in order to perform certain functions.

Oracle Memory Structures Related to Backup and Recovery

The principle SGA memory structure to be aware of when it comes to backup and recovery is the *redo log buffer*. This is typically a small area of memory that is configured for Oracle to store redo records in. This is a very transient area of memory and its size can impact the performance of your database. Although the redo log buffer will not have a direct impact on backup and recovery, it's still important to be aware of it in the light of any discussion on backup and recovery.

The Oracle Data Dictionary

The *Oracle data dictionary* is a critical piece of the backup and recovery landscape. In the following sections, we will introduce you to the data dictionary. We will then give you some information on the basic format of the data dictionary so it will be more familiar to you when you actually use it. Finally, we will provide a list of views that you will find useful during your backup and recovery efforts.

Overview of the Data Dictionary

The data dictionary is a set of views and tables that expose metadata about your Oracle Database. For example, if you want to know the name of your database, you can look at the NAME column in a view called V$DATABASE.

The data dictionary is important because it will give you information on the following critical components of the database:

- Tablespaces
- Data files
- Redo logs
- RMAN backup–related information
- Database configuration

This information will be essential when configuring for backups and also when you need to recover your database from failure. Throughout this book you will be using the data dictionary, and it behooves you to become comfortable with it.

Forms of the Data Dictionary

The data dictionary views are named using a common naming convention. This convention can be used to identify the source of the data and when a view can be queried. The main types of data dictionary views are as follows:

> We are introducing the CDB_* views here. We will not be covering the Multitenant Database option of the Oracle Database in detail in this chapter. Please see Chapter 12, "Managing Oracle Multitenant Databases," for more details on this option.

Static Data Dictionary Views   The *static data dictionary views* are sourced from tables and views created when the database was first created. These tables and views are owned by the SYS schema and are located in the SYSTEM tablespace. The views typically contain structural metadata about the database, including such things as tables, indexes, and other database objects.

If you are running Oracle Multitenant, you will find versions of these views in each pluggable database (PDB) contained within the container database (CDB). Also you will find versions of these views in the root container. The scope of what is contained in these views varies depending on the PDB you are in, the user you are connected as, and the state of the database. Please see the chapters on Oracle multitenant databases for more information on what is contained in these views when using Oracle Multitenant.

The names of these views are all prefixed to indicate the scope of the data contained within that view. There are four main prefixes:

DBA_*   The DBA_* views allow those with DBA privileges to see all data contained in the view. For example, if you were a DBA and you wanted to see all tables in the database named MY_DATA, you could query the DBA_TABLES view, as shown here:

```
Select owner, table_name from dba_tables
Where owner='MY_DATA';
```

ALL_*   The scope of the ALL_* views is more reduced than that of the DBA_* views. When you query the ALL_* views, you see only those objects for which you have been granted some form of access. For example, if you wanted to see all instances of a table called MY_DATA that you had access to, you could query the ALL_TABLES view, as shown here:

```
Select owner, table_name from all_tables;
```

USER_*   The USER_* views are the most restrictive of the data dictionary views. When you query the USER_* views, you see only those objects that are in the schema you are currently logged into. For example, if you wanted to see if there was a table called MY_DATA in your schema, you could query the USER_TABLES view, as shown here:

```
Select table_name from user_tables;
```

CDB_* With the advent of Oracle Database 12c, Oracle has added a completely new set of data dictionary views. These views help you to deal with Oracle multitenant databases. The views are prefixed with CDB, and they allow you to look at the various pluggable databases within the Oracle container database. We will cover these views in a lot more detail in chapter 12.

> Notice in the example query against USER_TABLES that we removed the owner column. It is quite common that the DBA_* and ALL_* views will have an owner column but that the USER_* views will not. This is because the user in the USER_* views is assumed to be the user you are logged in as.

Dynamic Performance Data Dictionary Views The *dynamic performance data dictionary views* typically start with a V$ prefix, such as V$DATABASE or V$SESSION. The views are often used for database monitoring and tuning, but there are times when they will be the only database views available to you for recovery purposes.

The data in these views source from either the database control file or C structures that are part of the Oracle Database kernel. Typically these views are available when the database instance is mounted (see "Oracle Database Startup and Shutdown" later in this chapter), but some views are available only after the instance has started.

⊕ Real World Scenario

Using Data Dictionary Views

In the real world, DBAs use the data dictionary a great deal. Although Oracle offers a nice graphical database administration tool called Oracle Enterprise Manager Cloud Control 12c that helps reduce the DBAs' need to use the data dictionary, the typical DBA will often need to access the data dictionary.

For example, recently we needed to know which users were on the system and what their OS process IDs were so we could kill a process. We were already in SQL*Plus, and it was easier to just query the data dictionary than to open a browser, log into the OEM, and surf to the page that would give us the information we wanted.

Our boss thought we were crazy for not using OEM, so we had a race to see who could get the information faster. Want to guess who won? Often DBAs will create their own set of scripts to access the data dictionary views. This makes it even faster to get the information you want without having to switch back and forth to OEM. OEM is a great tool, but sometimes it just pays to know the data dictionary. Plus, there are some places that don't use it at all.

Common Data Dictionary and Dynamic Performance Views You Will Use

During your backup and recovery experiences as an Oracle DBA, you will have occasion to use the data dictionary. Table 1.1 provides a list of some data dictionary views that you will want to be aware of and that will be helpful to you on your OCP exam.

TABLE 1.1   Examples of Data Dictionary/Dynamic Performance Views Useful for Recovery

View Name	Description
V$DATABASE	Provides basic database-related information, including the logging mode
V$INSTANCE	Provides basic instance information
V$DATAFILE	Provides database data file information stored in the control file
V$LOGFILE	Provides information on the individual redo log file members from the control file
V$LOG	Provides information on the redo log groups from the control file
V$ARCHIVED_LOG	Provides archive log information from the control file
V$LOG_HISTORY	Provides information on redo log switches in the database
DBA_DATA_FILES	Provides data file information
DBA_TABLESPACES	Provides information on tablespaces in the database

You can find all the data dictionary views available in Oracle by looking at the Oracle reference guide in the Oracle documentation available at http://tahiti.oracle.com.

Oracle Data Files and Tablespaces

Oracle data is stored in tablespaces, which comprise one or more data files. It is very important to understand data files and tablespaces and their relationships when it comes to backup and recovery. In the following sections, we will briefly reintroduce you to the important components of the Oracle Database.

Oracle Data Files

The Oracle Database *data files* are critical database physical files that are used to store all your Oracle data (well, almost all!). The physical data files are the structures most likely to be lost and subsequently recovered during a database-recovery operation. You are probably aware that database data files are preallocated in size and that they can be configured to grow automatically.

When you perform a physical backup of your database, the database data files will be the principle structures you back up. When you restore your database due to a media failure, you will be restoring one or more data files. You may also have to restore other database files such as the control file, the online redo logs, and the archived redo logs, which we will discuss later in this section.

 Another type of database backup is called a logical backup. We will discuss logical backups in future chapters.

Data files can be in two different states. They can be online (the default) or offline. Some Oracle database restore operations will require that you take one or more data files offline.

Oracle Tablespaces

A *tablespace* is a logical, named entity in the database that is used to store database objects. For example, your database might have a table called STORES that contains data about stores in your organization. The table STORES will be assigned to a tablespace, perhaps called STORE_DATA.

A tablespace is assigned to one or more database data files, and the size of the tablespace is related to the size of the underlying database data files. Several recovery options exist with respect to tablespaces, including tablespace point-in-time recovery, which we will discuss in later chapters of this book.

Tablespaces can be in four different states. They can be online (the default), offline, read-write (the default), or read-only. If you put your tablespace in read-only mode, then you will need to back up the data files associated with that tablespace only once as long as the tablespace is in read-only mode. Some recovery operations require the database be offline to perform restore and recovery operations.

Redo Logs

The redo logs of the database are the principle vehicle for backup and recovery. In the following sections, we will cover two different types of redo logs. First, we will discuss the online redo log, and then we will discuss the archived redo log.

Online Redo Logs

Online redo logs are used by Oracle to store all the changes that occur in the database. Think of them as something akin to a videotape recording of everything that is going on.

Later on, you can rewind that videotape and replay it to see what happened. During recovery, Oracle does just that, using the online redo logs.

In this section we will discuss online redo log file basics, redo log file groups, redo log file members, and redo log file sequence numbers.

Redo Log File Basics

Online redo logs are created when the database is created. You must have a minimum of two redo logs in any Oracle database. When the database starts running, it will write to the first redo log group. Once that log fills up, it will switch over and begin to write to the next log. Once the second log fills up, the database will clear the first log and begin to write redo into that log. Thus, redo log files are used in a round-robin style.

Redo Log File Groups

Each online redo log file is a member of a specific *redo log file group*. In the case where there are just two online redo logs (the minimum allowed), there will be two groups, likely named group 1 and group 2. You can create new online redo log groups and drop existing groups (until you are down to just two groups) anytime online.

Redo Log File Members

As you might gather, the online redo log files are an important component of the database. If you lose the online log files, you could permanently lose data. To protect against this, Oracle provides for multiplexing of online redo logs within each group. Each copy of the online redo log is considered a *redo log file member*, often called just a member.

Multiplexing allows you to indicate to Oracle that it should create and maintain duplicate copies of the online redo log files. When multiplexing online redo logs, it's a good idea to put each member on a different disk for many reasons, even on a SAN.

Redo Log Sequence Numbers

Each time an online redo log group is used, that group is assigned a unique *redo log sequence number* (typically 1 for a new database). As you can see in Figure 1.1, you have two online redo log groups. You start writing to the first online redo log group, which is log sequence 1. Once that log group fills up, you start writing to online group 2, which was assigned sequence number 2. Once that group fills up, you switch back to redo log group 1, reusing that redo log group. The sequence number is incremented, though, and the redo associated with that online redo log group will be part of sequence 3. Once that group fills up, Oracle will switch to online log group 3. Once that group fills up, Oracle switches back to redo log group 1, reusing that redo log group.

Sequence numbers can be very important when it comes to recovering your database, as you will see in later chapters.

Archived Redo Logs

You may have noticed from the previous discussion on online redo logs that the redo log files get reused over and over. As a result, the records in those log files will be lost forever when the log file is reused. This overwriting of the online redo logs limits the recovery options available for you to use with Oracle.

FIGURE 1.1   Redo log file round-robin writing

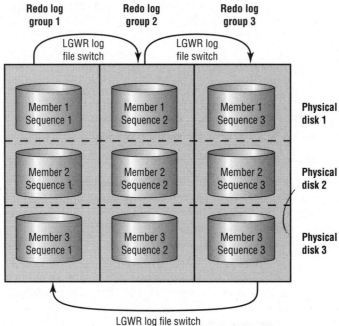

When the database is put in ARCHIVELOG mode (see the section "NOARCHIVELOG and ARCHIVELOG Modes"), Oracle will make copies of the online redo logs after they have been filled and after Oracle starts to write to the next online redo log group. The copies of the online redo logs are called *archived redo logs*. Archived redo logs are critical to advanced recoveries such as point-in-time recoveries and point-of-failure recoveries.

To protect the database transactions, online redo logs will not be reused until the archived redo logs have been successfully written. This can cause database operations to be suspended if the archived redo logs cannot be written successfully.

Control File

The *control file* of the database is kind of a central repository of important database related metadata. It's a binary file that contains information about physical database structures, redo logs, and archived redo logs; RMAN information is stored here too. The control file is critical to a good backup and recovery strategy, as you will see in this chapter and other chapters of this book.

Parameter Files

In this section, we will address what parameter files and parameters are. We will then discuss the two types of parameter files available in Oracle: the parameter file (pfile) and server parameter file (spfile).

Parameter Files and Parameters

Every Oracle Database has a *parameter file*. Inside the parameter file you'll find a variety of parameters that define global settings for that database. Parameter files are stored, by default, in ORACLE_HOME/dbs or ORACLE_HOME/database, depending on the operating system in use.

Each parameter file will contain many different parameters. Parameters are used to configure memory settings, auditing settings, destination directories for log files, and archived redo log files. When configuring a database for backup and recovery, you will configure several parameters, as you will see in the section "Configuring the Database for Backup and Recovery."

Parameters come in two flavors, static and dynamic. You must change static parameters and restart the database in order for the parameters to take effect. Dynamic parameters can be changed on the fly, without the need to restart the database.

> **NOTE** You can find all the database parameters available in Oracle by looking at the Oracle reference guide in the Oracle documentation available at http://tahiti.oracle.com.

Parameter Files

The pfile is a text-based parameter file. To modify settings in this file, you simply open the file with your editor and change it. Once your changes are complete, save the file. You will then need to bounce the database to have those settings take effect.

Pfiles are kept, by default, in the $ORACLE_HOME/dbs (Unix) or %ORACLE_HOME%\database (Windows) directory. The default name for a pfile is init<oracle_sid>.ora. So if your Unix database is called ORCL, your pfile will be called initORCL.ora by default. Note that case sensitivity applies here based on the operating system.

Server Parameter Files

The spfile is an Oracle database managed parameter file managed by the Oracle server. We will first look closer at the spfile itself, and then we will discuss how to set parameters when using an spfile.

What Is an Spfile?

An Oracle spfile differs from a text-based parameter file in that the Oracle server manages it, and you as the DBA should never edit the file directly. The spfile is partly nontext (it has a header and a footer), but the actual parameter settings are in plain text (so you can view the file if you like and see what parameters are set to in the spfile).

Spfiles are kept, by default, in the $ORACLE_HOME/dbs (Unix) or %ORACLE_HOME%\
database (Windows) directory. The spfile naming convention is sp<oracle_sid>.ora
by default. When the DBA starts the Oracle database/instance, Oracle will first look
for an spfile using the default filename. If one is not found, it will look for a file called
spfile<oracle_sid>.ora in the same default directory. Finally, if no spfile is found,
Oracle will look for a regular pfile as described previously. If no parameter file is found,
then the database will signal an error and the startup will abort. Oracle generally recommends using an SPFILE over a text parameter file.

Note that if you try to start the database from RMAN without an spfile or
pfile available, Oracle will use the default parameter settings and actually
start the database. This does not happen if you try to start the database
from SQL*Plus or OEM. We will discuss RMAN more in Chapter 3, "Configuring and Backing Up Using RMAN."

How Do You Set Parameter Values When Using an Spfile?

To modify a parameter when using an spfile, you use the alter system command. For
example, if you want to change the parameter DB_RECOVERY_FILE_DEST_SIZE, which is a
dynamic parameter (so it can be changed on the fly), you would issue the following alter
system command:

```
Alter system set db_recovery_file_dest_size=100m;
```

The previous command only changes the parameter as long as the database instance is
running. The parameter would be reset in this case unless you used the scope=both parameter. In this case, the parameter would be changed for the running instance, dynamically,
and also the parameter would be changed in the database spfile so that the change would
persist through an instance restart. Here is an example:

```
Alter system set db_recovery_file_dest_size=100m scope=both;
```

As we said earlier, some parameters are not dynamic. In this case, you have to indicate
that you want to change only the parameter file. To do this, use the alter system command
and include the scope=spfile keyword, as shown here:

```
Alter system set memory_max_target=200m scope=spfile;
```

In some cases, you may want to change the parameter in just the current instance of
the database, but you will not want that change to persist after the next shutdown. In
this case, use the scope=memory keyword when issuing the alter system command, as
shown here:

```
Alter system set db_recovery_file_dest_size=100m scope=memory;
```

NOARCHIVELOG and ARCHIVELOG Modes

Oracle Database runs in two principal modes, NOARCHIVELOG (the default) and ARCHIVELOG. The logging bit has to do with archived redo logs and if they are saved or not, which makes a difference in the kinds of recoveries that you can do. Let's look at each mode in a bit more detail.

> For manual backup and recovery questions in the OCP exam you will only have to be concerned with databases in NOARCHIVELOG mode. When you are asked RMAN questions you may be asked about either ARCHIVELOG mode or NOARCHIVELOG mode. So we cover both modes here.

NOARCHIVELOG MODE

NOARCHIVELOG mode is the default logging mode. In NOARCHIVELOG mode, the online redo logs are overwritten over time and no backups are created. Because of this, you are limited in the way you can back up your database and how you can recover it.

Backups are limited to cold or offline backups. This means that you must shut down your database before you can back it up. As you will see in later sections of this chapter, you will back up all the data files of the database plus the online redo logs and the control file(s).

Recovery in NOARCHIVELOG is equally limited. In NOARCHIVELOG mode, you can restore the database only to the point in time that the backup was taken. Thus you will lose any changes to the database that took place after the backup was complete and the database was opened for business. This is typically not an acceptable solution for production databases.

We will discuss how to back up your database in NOARCHIVELOG mode later in this chapter. In Chapter 2, "Performing Oracle User-Managed Database Recoveries," we will discuss recovering your database with backups taken in NOARCHIVELOG mode. In Chapter 3 we will discuss using RMAN to perform offline backups, and in Chapter 5, "Recovering Databases with RMAN," we will discuss using RMAN to restore these backups.

ARCHIVELOG MODE

ARCHIVELOG mode is a much more flexible method of operating your database and is strongly recommended for all production databases. In this mode, you can back up your database while it's up and running, allowing users to work at the same time that the backups are running.

When the database is in ARCHIVELOG mode, changes are recorded in the online redo logs as usual. What is different is that the archived redo logs are copied to a backup directory once they have filled up. These copies of the redo log files are called *archived redo logs* and the Oracle Database process that copies them is called the *ARCH process*. In Oracle Database 12*c*, the ARC*n* process starts automatically when the database is in ARCHIVELOG mode.

The archived redo logs may be copied to one or a number of different destinations. We will discuss configuring where Oracle should copy these archived redo logs to in the section "Configuring the Database for Backup and Recovery."

We will discuss how to back up your database in ARCHIVELOG mode later in this chapter. In Chapter 2 we will discuss recovering your database with backups taken in ARCHIVELOG mode. In Chapter 3 we will discuss using RMAN to perform online backups, and in Chapter 5 we will discuss using RMAN to restore these backups. Finally, in Chapter 7, "Performing Oracle Advanced Recovery," we will discuss more-advanced recoveries with backups taken in ARCHIVELOG mode.

The Oracle Instance and the Oracle Database

In the following sections, we will first review knowledge you should already have on the basics of the Oracle instances and the Oracle Database. Then we will discuss the startup and shutdown of the Oracle instance and the Oracle Database.

Oracle Instances and Oracle Databases: a Review

With respect to backup and recovery of Oracle databases, it is important to understand that there is a difference between an Oracle instance and an Oracle database. This is because certain backup and recovery operations must occur while the Oracle instance is running and the database is not. Other operations will require that the database be open (which presumes the instance is already running).

No doubt you are already somewhat familiar with the notion of the instance from your OCA experience as well as your actual database experience. To review, an Oracle *instance* is the collection of shared memory (SGA) and processes (LGWR, DBWR, and so on). When these are all up and running, the instance is said to be started (see the next section for more details on starting and stopping a database).

The Oracle *database* is essentially the collection of database data files, the control file, and online redo log files. When the instance is running, Oracle will attach to the database and open it for business. Once the database is open, users can begin to do their work, assuming there are no problems during the database open process that prevents it from opening.

 Sybex's *OCA: Oracle Database 12c Administrator Certified Associate Study Guide* provides complete coverage of the Oracle Database memory and processes. In this text, we assume you have already taken and passed the OCA exam and that you understand the body of knowledge consanguineous to that exam.

Oracle Database Startup and Shutdown

It is important to understand the startup and shutdown process of an Oracle database. In this section, we will first discuss the different stages of the Oracle database startup and shutdown processes. We will then discuss the mechanics of actually starting and stopping the database in its different phases. We will quickly discuss restricted-mode database operations, and finally we will discuss the different stages the database must be in for specific types of backup and recovery operations to occur.

Exploring the Stages of Database Startup and Shutdown

When an Oracle database is started, it goes through four different and distinct stages:

Shutdown   When the database and instance are shut down, they are at rest. There are no processes present, no memory is allocated, and nothing is going on. It is important to note that even though the database/instance may be shut down and closed, other Oracle processes (like the listener or OEM agents) may be still running.

Nomount   When the database is in nomount mode, the instance has been started. Thus, processes have been started and memory allocated.

Mount   When the database is in mount mode (or mounted), the instance is started and the database has opened the control file. The control file is read, but its contents are not validated. Note that the database is not open at this time.

Open   When the database is opened, the control file contents have been validated against the physical database. The data files are all confirmed to be present, and they are opened. Oracle will then analyze the data files to determine if the database is in a consistent state. If the database is not in a consistent state, some form of recovery will be required.

Typically, the form of recovery required, *crash or instance recovery*, does not require any DBA involvement. If instance recovery is not possible, then *media recovery* is required. Media recovery requires the application of backups and recovery operations to bring the database current to the point of failure (if this is possible). The principal determining factors for media recovery are the presence of the needed data files and the availability in the online redo logs of the redo needed to bring those files current. If either of these conditions does not exist, then media recovery is required.

Database shutdowns occur in much the same way as startups, except in reverse. There are two different kinds of shutdowns, however: consistent and inconsistent.

Consistent Shutdowns   If your database shutdown is a *consistent shutdown*, then the database data files and the database control file will be synchronized upon shutdown. The dirty buffers in the database buffer cache will be flushed out to the database data files, making them consistent. A consistent shutdown is a nice, tidy shutdown.

Inconsistent Shutdowns   An *inconsistent shutdown* is another term for a mess. When your database is shut down in an inconsistent manner, it is in an indeterminate state and will require some form of recovery (typically instance recovery, which requires no DBA intervention) when it is restarted. Inconsistent shutdowns, however bad they might sound, often are the only way to shut down a database in a timely manner.

About Instance Recovery

We mentioned instance recovery earlier, and there may be a question or two about instance recovery on your OCP exam, so let's talk about that for a second. In this section, we will discuss:

- Checkpoints
- The system change number
- Instance recovery
- Fast-start fault recovery
- Tuning database instance recovery times
- Monitoring cache recovery
- The mean time to recover advisor

Checkpoints   The reason there is a variance between the current state of the database and the state of the database as represented in the database data files is that Oracle reduces the writes to disk in order to improve database performance. The DBW process typically writes to the database data files in a lazy fashion. This is so that the IO associated with the writes by the DBW processes will be minimized. Each time a write occurs, this is called a checkpoint.

Checkpoints occur irregularly most of the time, triggered by various events. It is quite possible that a changed block in memory will not be written to disk for a period of seconds or even minutes after a commit occurs. Thus, a commit does not cause a checkpoint. A commit only causes the redo change records (called change vectors) that have been generated in the redo log buffer to be flushed to the online redo log of the database. Since the online redo logs reside on disk, they provide the persistent image that, when added to the database data files, represent the most current image of the database to the most recent commit.

The System Change Number   Oracle keeps track of all of the activity in the database through the use of the system change number (SCN). The SCN is a counter, and its job is to keep track of everything going on inside the database and assign it a temporal identity. This serves to keep transactions that occurred in a particular order in the same order later down the road (such as during recovery). You need to preserve the order of transactions because of dependencies that occur between transactions. For example, if you have a parent table and a child table, you want to make sure that during recovery all inserts into the parent table occur before inserts into the child table. This is because of the foreign key constraint that exists between the two tables to ensure the integrity of that parent/child relationship. The SCN helps Oracle to track the temporal flow of those changes, and thus the parent table insert will have a lower SCN than the child table insert. As a result, in the end, all is right with the world.

SCNs are loosely coupled with time. Thus, 12:30 p.m. local time would be associated with a specific SCN in a given individual database. The thing to remember is that 12:30 p.m. local time will most likely be associated with a different SCN in each database, so the coupling is very loose. The concept of the SCN is very important because there may be times when you will want to restore your database to a specific SCN. This is supported during recovery operations. Also, Oracle's Flashback features support the use of the SCN when flashing back the database. See Chapter 8 for more information on the vast number of features available with Oracle Flashback Database.

Instance Recovery   There are two different flavors of instance recovery: instance recovery and crash recovery. *Instance recovery* is associated with the crash of the entire database, including all of its instances, and the recovery of the database after that crash. *Crash recovery* occurs when a RAC database node fails, and the other nodes recover the transactions of the failed node. In the context of the Oracle OCP exam, you will need to understand instance recovery and how to tune the database to reduce the time it takes to do instance recovery. You will not need to be concerned with crash recovery.

Understanding and controlling the time it takes to perform instance recovery is important because your customers may require that you adhere to specific requirements with respect to how long it takes your database to open after it has crashed (say, for example, because of power loss). The maximum time allowed for your database to come back up is typically called the recovery time objective (RTO).

When starting the database, Oracle will check the SCN in each individual data file against what is called the checkpoint SCN in the database control file. The checkpoint SCN is a number that represents the SCN recorded after the completion of the last successful checkpoint.

If the SCNs are all the same when the database is started, then no instance recovery is required and the database is opened. This is the quickest way to get an Oracle database open.

If the SCNs in the data files differ from the checkpoint SCN in the control file, then instance recovery will be required. Instance recovery occurs in two stages. The first is cache recovery, where Oracle will apply the changes from the online redo logs, including any that might be recorded in the online redo logs that are not committed. Cache recovery is the portion of instance recovery that you need to tune because this is the process that is keeping the database from opening.

Once cache recovery is complete, Oracle will open the database and start the second stage of instance recovery, called transaction recovery. During transaction recovery, Oracle will roll back any uncommitted transactions that were applied during cache recovery. However, the database is open and fully functional.

As you might expect, as the version of the data on disk diverges from the version of the data at the current point in time, the time to perform instance recovery increases. While this improves performance at run time, it can also negatively impact performance during instance recovery. This balancing act between instance recovery and database performance is managed by Oracle's Fast-Start Fault Recovery feature, which we will discuss next.

Fast-Start Fault Recovery   Fast-Start Fault Recovery provides ways to adjust DBW so that it will maintain write IO at a rate sufficient to maintain a specific target RTO while also enabling maximum database performance. Thus, you balance the frequency of DBW writing against the time it takes to do instance recovery.

Fast-Start Fault Recovery manages the recovery time by managing the data latency between the persistent storage (disk) and the database cache in memory. You control Fast-Start Fault Recovery through the use of the FAST_START_MTTR_RECOVERY parameter.

The FAST_START_MTTR_RECOVERY parameter indicates the maximum number of seconds that any instance recovery should take. The DBW process will then manage database writes in such a way as to attempt to meet the number of seconds that FAST_START_MTTR_RECOVERY is set to.

Some parameters can disable Fast-Start Fault Recovery. These include the parameters FAST_START_IO_TARGET, LOG_CHECKPOINT_INTERVAL, and LOG_CHECKPOINT_TIMEOUT. If your database is using these parameters, then you are not taking advantage of Fast-Start Fault Recovery.

Monitoring Instance Recovery   Because instance recovery is the instance-recovery process that is the most time sensitive, you will want to monitor your critical databases to make sure that they can meet your instance recovery time SLAs. The view V$INSTANCE_RECOVERY provides information on both the target mean time to recover the database and the currently estimated mean time to recover the database. The ESTIMATED_MTTR column represents the mean time to recover (MTTR) for the current system based on its current activity.

The Mean Time To Recover Advisor   Trying to correctly set the FAST_START_MTTR_RECOVERY parameter can be difficult. If you are sensitive to performance but also are sensitive to instance recovery time, the Mean Time to Recover Advisor (MTTR Advisor) can be of assistance. If you look at the V$INSTANCE_RECOVERY view, you will see the column TARGET_MTTR. This column represents the maximum attainable MTTR for that database and is calculated by the MTTR Advisor. Both the ESTIMATED_MTTR and TARGET_MTTR columns will vary based on database activity.

You can view the results of the MTTR Advisor through the V$MTTR_TARGET_ADVICE view. This view provides an analysis of the current setting of the FAST_START_MTTR_RECOVERY parameter and how adjustments of that parameter will impact instance recovery time.

> **NOTE** Sybex's OCA preparation guide for Oracle Database 12c, *OCA: Oracle Database 12c Administrator Certified Associate Study Guide: Exams 1Z0-061 and 1Z0-062* (Sybex, 2014) by Biju Thomas, provides complete coverage on starting the Oracle Database and the different stages of opening the Oracle Database, so this is just a quick review.

Starting and Stopping the Database

During backup and recovery operations, you will need to know how to start up and shut down your database correctly. To start up the database in any of the modes described in the previous section, you will use the STARTUP command or the ALTER DATABASE command, as required. To stop the database, you will use the SHUTDOWN command. Typically, database startup operations are performed from SQL*Plus or Oracle Enterprise Manager.

The STARTUP Command   This command is used to start the instance and/or database only when the database is in a shutdown state. The STARTUP command can be used to completely open the database, as shown in this code snippet:

```
SQL> startup
```

The STARTUP command also has options that you can use to indicate that you want Oracle to start the startup operation at a certain point. For example, you can indicate that you want the instance to be started only by using the STARTUP NOMOUNT command:

```
SQL> startup nomount
```

Or perhaps you want to start the instance and mount the database. In this case, the command would be as follows:

```
SQL> startup mount
```

Sometimes you want to shut down the database and start it up in one command. You can use the STARTUP FORCE command to perform this action. Note that the STARTUP FORCE command will shut down your database in an inconsistent manner (which we discussed earlier in this chapter), and some operations (such as putting the database in ARCHIVELOG mode) will not complete successfully if the database was shut down in an inconsistent manner. Here is an example of the STARTUP FORCE command:

```
SQL> startup force
```

The SHUTDOWN Command   The SHUTDOWN command does what it says; it shuts down the database. As with the SHUTDOWN command, it comes with a few options. First there is the plain-Jane SHUTDOWN command, which will shut down the database if absolutely nothing is going on and if absolutely no one is logged in. You can guess how often those conditions happen in reality! Until its conditions are met, the SHUTDOWN command will just sit there, waiting for its opportunity to shut down the database.

Here is an example of the SHUTDOWN command:

```
SQL> shutdown
```

If waiting is not your forte, then you may want to try the shutdown immediate command. The shutdown immediate command will prevent new logons, roll back any uncommitted transactions, and then bring the database down. It's a consistent-shutdown, no-waiting approach to stopping the database, and lots of DBAs like it. Here is an example:

```
SQL> shutdown immediate
```

The cousin of SHUTDOWN IMMEDIATE is SHUTDOWN TRANSACTIONAL (we are not sure if it's a first cousin or second cousin; Oracle has not defined this within the body of the Oracle documentation yet). The main difference here is that the SHUTDOWN TRANSACTIONAL command will wait for active transactions to complete (commit) before shutting down those sessions. As a result, the SHUTDOWN TRANSACTIONAL command can take a while longer to complete its task, but on the positive side, users might be a little bit happier (if they are actually able to be happy anytime the database comes down). Here is an example of the SHUTDOWN TRANSACTIONAL command:

```
SQL> shutdown transactional
```

The bad boy of database shutdowns is the SHUTDOWN ABORT command. If you want your database to come down without debate, this is the way to do it. This is like pulling the power cord on your database; it is a crash of the database, shutting it down in an inconsistent manner. Here is an example of the SHUTDOWN ABORT command:

```
SQL> shutdown abort
```

The SHUTDOWN ABORT Command: The Truth Is Out There

As long as the SHUTDOWN ABORT command has been around it has been surrounded in controversy. It is believed by some that the Seven-Day War was actually started as the result of a disagreement between DBAs over the SHUTDOWN ABORT command (they conveniently ignore the fact that Oracle didn't even exist then). The truth is that the SHUTDOWN ABORT command is the fastest way to shut down your database. Because the database will be shut down in an inconsistent manner, it may result in a delayed database startup because of the recovery process that Oracle must go through internally. Often, though, SHUTDOWN ABORT may well be the way to get your database shut down and started back up in the shortest amount of time possible.

The ALTER DATABASE Command   The ALTER DATABASE command is used to move the database from one state to another. For example, if the instance was started with the STARTUP NOMOUNT command, you may want to mount the database. To do so, you would use the ALTER DATABASE MOUNT command, as shown here:

```
SQL> alter database mount;
```

If the database is already mounted and you want to open it, then the ALTER DATABASE OPEN command would be appropriate, as shown in this example:

```
SQL> alter database open;
```

Performing Database Restricted-Mode Operations

Sometimes it's nice to have the house to yourself, isn't it? Oracle allows you the equivalent of having the house to yourself when you put the database in restricted mode. When the database is in restricted mode, only those with the restricted session privilege can access it. Since DBA accounts have restricted session privileges, this means you can log into the database and do your work, feeling secure that other users won't get in and cause problems. You may find that during certain recovery operations a restricted session will help when you need to get into the database to perform some DBA-related activities but you don't want other users to log in yet.

To open the database in restricted mode, you issue the STARTUP RESTRICT command. If your database is already open, you can put it in restricted mode with the ALTER DATABASE ENABLE RESTRICTED SESSION command. This will not impact existing users, but new users will not be able to connect unless they have the restricted session privilege. To disable the restricted session and allow users to connect to the database, use the ALTER DATABASE DISABLE RESTRICTED SESSION command.

Performing Backup and Recovery Operations and Getting Database Status

So, what kind of operations would you perform given the different open or closed combinations of the database? Here are some examples:

Operations while the instance is down and the database is not open:

- Copy the spfile to a pfile
- Copy the pfile to an spfile
- Perform manual cold backups

Operations while the instance is open and the database is not open:

- Create a database
- Create a database control file
- Restore the database control file or spfile from RMAN

Operations while the instance is mounted and the database is not open:

- Cold backup with RMAN
- Recovery of critical data files (SYSTEM, UNDO tablespaces)
- Offline recovery of entire database

Operations while the instance is mounted and the database is open:

- Online data file or tablespace recovery of noncritical tablespaces
- Online backups of the database

Configuring the Database for Backup and Recovery

The ARCHIVELOG and NOARCHIVELOG modes of the database really boil down to what your backup and recovery needs and requirements are. If your recovery needs are simple, and you just want to restore to the point of your last backup, then you can leave your database in NOARCHIVELOG mode and do offline backups. If your database uptime requirements provide time to shut down the database for your backup, then NOARCHIVELOG mode will work fine for you.

If you are going to do offline backups of your database in NOARCHIVELOG mode, then you can pretty much ignore this section. All you will need to do there (as we will cover in the next section) is determine the location of the files you need to back up and the location to which you want to back them up, shut down the database, and back it up.

When you want to perform online backups, or if you want to be able to recover offline backups beyond the time of the backup, then the database needs to be in ARCHIVELOG mode. Putting the database in ARCHIVELOG mode requires some configuration, which we will discuss first. Once you have configured the database, you will then actually put it in ARCHIVELOG mode, which we will cover next.

You will need to understand both NOARCHIVELOG and ARCHIVELOG mode for the OCP exam. While manual database backup and recovery–related questions will only ask you about NOARCHIVELOG mode situations, RMAN questions may well ask you about backup and recovery in both modes.

In the following sections, we will discuss configuring the database for ARCHIVELOG mode operations (no additional configuration for NOARCHIVELOG mode operations is required unless you want to configure the Fast Recovery Area for RMAN, which is covered in Chapter 3), and then we will discuss actually putting the database in ARCHIVELOG mode. Finally, we will discuss some database views that will be useful when managing a database in ARCHIVELOG mode.

Configuring for ARCHIVELOG Mode

The first step to putting the database in ARCHIVELOG mode is to set the database parameters. You need to set the database parameters so that the ARCH process will work correctly when it needs to archive the online redo logs, creating archived redo logs.

You will want to consider setting several parameters when you are going to put the database in ARCHIVELOG mode. A number of parameters are directly associated with user-managed backup and recovery in ARCHIVELOG mode. Table 1.2 describes these parameters.

Real World Scenario

Mixing NOARCHIVELOG and ARCHIVELOG Modes

In the real world, you might find that some of your databases are running in NOARCHIVELOG mode and some of your databases are running in ARCHIVELOG mode. For example, your development and test databases may be able to be shut down at night for backups. Additionally, they might not have a need for point-in-time or point-of-failure recovery. Thus, NOARCHIVELOG mode is just fine for them.

You may find that your production databases have different requirements. First, it may be that shutting down your production systems for backups at any time is not acceptable to your customer. Further, you probably will also find that people prefer not to lose data in production and that they would prefer to be able to restore the database and then recover all work that occurred after the last backup. You will have to put your database in ARCHIVELOG mode to satisfy those requirements.

Perhaps you are asking yourself, "What about this Fast Recovery Area thing I've been hearing about?" Since the Fast Recovery Area (FRA, previously called the Flash Recovery Area) typically is not used for manual backups, we will defer discussion of the FRA until we discuss RMAN in later chapters. Thus, the parameters related to the RMAN and the FRA are not included in Table 1.2.

TABLE 1.2   Oracle Parameters Associated with User-Managed Backup and Recovery

Parameter Name	Description
LOG_ARCHIVE_DEST	Indicates the destination to copy archived redo logs to. Typically this parameter is not set and the LOG_ARCHIVE_DEST_n parameter is set instead.
LOG_ARCHIVE_DEST_n	Indicates one of up to 10 destinations to copy archived redo logs to. The first destination starts with 1 (LOG_ARCHIVE_DEST_01).
LOG_ARCHIVE_DEST_STATE_n	Indicates the state of LOG_ARCHIVE_DEST_n (ENABLED, DEFERRED, or ALTERNATE).
LOG_ARCHIVE_FORMAT	Indicates the format of the archived redo log filenames.

Assume that you have a database called orcl and you have decided that you want Oracle to back up your archived redo logs to a directory called c:\oracle\archivelog\orcl (in Unix, perhaps it's called /oracle/archivelog/orcl). You would first have to create the file system directory structures, and then you would need to set the appropriate parameters. In this case, you would use the ALTER SYSTEM command to set the LOG_ARCHIVE_DEST_1 parameter to point to c:\oracle\archivelog\orcl, as shown in this code example:

```
Alter system set log_archive_dest_1='location=c:\oracle\archivelog\orcl';
```

You can also clear this parameter setting by just using blank quotes, as shown in this example:

```
Alter system set log_archive_dest_1='';
```

With the LOG_ARCHIVE_DEST_n parameter, you can configure up to 31 different archive-log destination directories. This feature can be used to provide redundant backup locations for your archive logs to protect them in the event of a failure of one or more of those locations. For example, you could archive to a local disk, and you could archive to an NFS-mounted disk. In that case, you would have two LOG_ARCHIVE_DEST_n parameters set like this:

```
-- Local mount on C: drive
Alter system set log_archive_dest_1='location=c:\oracle\archivelog\orcl';
-- NFS Mount on Z: drive
Alter system set log_archive_dest_2='location=Z:\oracle\archivelog\orcl';
```

Oracle will archive to both destinations, in parallel. This type of configuration is also used in more advanced database setups such as standby databases.

> Archive-log destination directories can take on different states, such as ENABLED, DEFERRED, or ALTERNATE (I tried to get the folks at Oracle to add a state of EXAUSTION or FRUSTRATION; they said no, but they did seem to like the suggestion of a state of CONFUSION). They can also be defined as MANDATORY or OPTIONAL. You will not need to be aware of these advanced settings for your OCP exam, but you might need to use these options as a part of your normal duties. You can find more information on these different attributes in the Oracle documentation.

You may also want to control how Oracle names the archived redo logs. This is done with the LOG_ARCHIVE_FORMAT parameter. For example, you may want to put the database name in the name of the archive logs being created, but you also want them to be numbered in such a way that the name will always be unique. You can set the LOG_ARCHIVE_FORMAT string to a value of orcl_%s_%t_%r_%d.arc, as shown in this example:

```
Alter system set log_archive_format='orcl_%s_%t_%r_%d.arc' scope=spfile;
```

You may wonder what the %s, %t, %r, and %d represent. These are variables that represent values for particular components of the archived redo log. The %s represents the sequence number, which is always unique for a given database (until a RESETLOGS command occurs, which we will discuss in Chapter 2). The %t is the thread number that represents an individual node on a cluster when your database is running on Oracle's Real Application Clusters (RAC). The %r represents the reset logs number (see Chapter 2). Finally, the %d represents the DBID that should be unique for each database. Together, this string of variables will make the archive log filenames unique for every database on your system.

Every database in Oracle has a DBID, which is a unique identifier for the database (see the DBID column in V$DATABASE to see your DBID). Be careful, though! It is possible to have databases on two different boxes with the same name and even with the same DBID. If you will be sharing an ARCHIVELOG mount point between boxes (say, via NFS), you will need to make sure you do not accidentally overwrite archived redo logs originating from databases with the same name and/or DBID! You won't need to know about the DBID for your OCP exam, but we thought we'd tell you anyway!

Putting the Database in ARCHIVELOG Mode

Putting the database in ARCHIVELOG mode is as easy as following these steps:

1. Configure archiving-related parameters as shown in the previous section.

2. Shut down the database in a consistent state using the SHUTDOWN, SHUTDOWN IMMEDIATE, or SHUTDOWN TRANSACTIONAL command.

3. Mount the database with the STARTUP MOUNT command.

4. Put the database in ARCHIVELOG mode with the ALTER DATABASE ARCHIVELOG command.

5. Open the database with the ALTER DATABASE OPEN command.

One thing to be aware of when the database is in ARCHIVELOG mode is that if you have not configured archiving correctly, you could find yourself with a database that just stops running. If Oracle cannot archive the online redo logs, it will suspend all database operations once it cycles through all the online redo log groups. So, for example, if your database does log switches every 10 minutes and has three redo log groups, your database will mysteriously freeze after 30 minutes. Lack of configuration is not as big of a problem in Oracle Database 12*c* as it was in earlier versions since Oracle defaults to using the Fast Recovery Area (discussed in Chapter 3).

Similar problems can occur if the archive-log destination directory runs out of space or if the permissions are not set correctly. If Oracle starts to have problems of this sort, it will log an error in the alert log of the database. Here is an example of an error you might see in the alert log (we discuss finding the alert log of the database later in this chapter):

```
All online logs needed archiving
ARCH: Archival stopped, error occurred. Will continue retrying
ORA-16014: log 2 sequence# 29 not archived, no available destinations
ORA-00312: online log 2 thread 1: 'C:\ORACLE\ORADATA\ORCL\REDO02.LOG'
```

Also, users logging into the database will find their logins just hanging until the archive-log problems are solved.

We've covered the parameters needed to put the database in ARCHIVELOG mode and the basic steps involved in the process. Let's look at an example of actually putting the database in ARCHIVELOG mode. Exercise 1.1 provides an example of doing just that.

 Real World Scenario

Online Redo Logs Stop Being Archived

We can't tell you how many times this has happened to us as DBAs. You are busy designing some cool model and the operations guys call. "Hey," they say, "we are getting calls. The database isn't working anymore."

"What?" you respond. "What do you mean it's not working?"

"The user sessions are just stalled, sitting there not doing anything. It's like the database has gone out to lunch or something," the operations guy says.

Immediately you are pretty sure you know what's wrong. So you ask the operations guy, "So, the mount point for the archived redo logs. Are you possibly getting an alert that it's full?"

The operations guy fumbles around to look at the alerts. Sure enough, the archived redo log destination is filled up. "Oh, yeah ... I was going to call you about that but I forgot."

So, you proceed to back up the archived redo logs and then remove them from the system to free up space. You also follow up to make sure some additional disk space is added to the file system.

This kind of situation happens a lot if you do not have enough space available for your archived redo logs or if your backups stop working. I've seen this happen frequently in shops where the database was originally designed for a certain amount of use and that usage has increased significantly.

EXERCISE 1.1

Putting a Database in ARCHIVELOG Mode

In this exercise you will take a database that is in NOARCHIVELOG mode and put it in ARCHIVELOG mode.

1. First, validate that the database is in NOARCHIVELOG mode using the V$DATABASE column LOG_MODE:

```
SQL> Select log_mode from v$database;
LOG_MODE
------------
NOARCHIVELOG
```

2. Next, look at the settings for the parameters (note that we have removed some of the LOG_ARCHIVE_DEST_*n* parameter to save trees) LOG_ARCHIVE_DEST_1 and LOG_ARCHIVE_FORMAT:

```
SQL> show parameter log_archive_dest_1
NAME                                 TYPE        VALUE
------------------------------------ ----------- -----------
log_archive_dest_1                   string
log_archive_dest_10                  string
SQL> show parameter log_archive_format
NAME                                 TYPE        VALUE
------------------------------------ ----------- -----------
log_archive_format                   string      ARC%S_%R.%T
```

3. Create the archive log directory c:\oracle\arch\orcl:

```
SQL> host mkdir c:\oracle\arch\orcl
```

4. You want to modify LOG_ARCHIVE_DEST_1 and LOG_ARCHIVE_FORMAT so that they are set correctly. LOG_ARCHIVE_DEST_1 should be set to c:\oracle\arch\orcl and LOG_ARCHIVE_FORMAT should be orcl_%r_%t_%s.arc. You will use the ALTER SYSTEM command to set these parameters. You will then check to make sure they are set correctly.

```
Alter system set log_archive_dest_1='location=c:\oracle\arch\orcl';
-- Note that we have to use the scope=spfile on this next parameter.
-- This is because it's not dynamic!
Alter system set log_archive_format='orcl_%r_%t_%s.arc' scope=spfile;
```

5. Next, shut down the database in a consistent manner with the SHUTDOWN IMMEDIATE command:

```
SQL> shutdown immediate
Database closed.
Database dismounted.
ORACLE instance shut down.
```

6. Now mount the database with the STARTUP MOUND command:

```
SQL> startup mount;
ORACLE instance started.
Total System Global Area  418484224 bytes
Fixed Size                  1333592 bytes
Variable Size             348128936 bytes
Database Buffers           62914560 bytes
Redo Buffers                6107136 bytes
Database Mounted.
```

7. Put the database in ARCHIVELOG mode with the ALTER DATABASE ARCHIVELOG command:

```
SQL> alter database archivelog;
Database altered.
```

8. Open the database for operations:

```
SQL> alter database open;
Database altered.
```

9. Make sure the database is in ARCHIVELOG mode:

```
SQL> Select log_mode from v$database;
LOG_MODE
------------
ARCHIVELOG
```

10. It is a good idea to make sure that everything is configured correctly and that the archived redo logs are getting generated in the place where you expect them to be generated. So, first you will force an archive-log switch with the ALTER SYSTEM

SWITCH LOGFILE command. This will cause a log switch to the next redo log group, and ARCH will need to copy the redo log to an archived redo log:

```
SQL> alter system switch logfile;
System altered.
```

11. Look in the c:\oracle\arch\orcl directory. You should see a file in that directory:

```
SQL> host dir c:\oracle\arch\orcl
 Volume in drive C has no label.
 Volume Serial Number is 08DE-E1AB
 Directory of c:\oracle\arch\orcl
08/02/2013  12:44 PM    <DIR>          .
08/02/2013  12:44 PM    <DIR>          ..
08/02/2013  12:44 PM        41,032,192 ORCL_658485967_1_2.ARC
               1 File(s)     41,032,192 bytes
               2 Dir(s)  17,065,476,096 bytes free
```

The ORCL_659495967_1_2.ARC file is your archive log file, so ARCH is copying the log file to the correct location. Excellent job!

What If the Archived Redo Logs Are Not Getting Created?

So, what if you don't see an archived redo log in the directory where you think it's supposed to be? Double-check the LOG_ARCHIVE_DEST_1 parameter and make sure it's set correctly. This is usually the problem. You can issue the command SHOW PARAMETER LOG_ARCHIVE_DEST_1 from SQL*Plus to do this. Make sure the directory exists, check the security permissions on the directory, and make sure you have enough space available on the file system.

If the archive logs are not getting created correctly, you will need to quickly figure out why. If Oracle switches through all of the available online redo logs and tries to switch into one that has previously been used and is waiting to be archived, all database activity will be suspended until the archived redo log can be completely written out.

Using ARCHIVELOG Mode Data Dictionary Views

Oracle provides several data dictionary views that can be used to monitor and manage the online and archived redo logs. Table 1.3 describes those views.

TABLE 1.3   Oracle Dynamic Performance Views Associated with User-Managed Backup and Recovery

View Name	Description
V$ARCHIVE	The V$ARCHIVE view provides information on redo logs that are in need of being archived.
V$ARCHIVE_DEST	The V$ARCHIVE_DEST view provides information on each individual archive-log destination. Typically this view is used for Oracle Data Guard.
V$ARCHIVE_DEST_STATUS	The V$ARCHIVE_DEST_STATUS view provides status information on each of the individual archive-log destination directories.
V$ARCHIVE_PROCESSES	The V$ARCHIVE_PROCESSES view provides information on the different ARCH processes running on your system.
V$ARCHIVED_LOG	The V$ARCHIVED_LOG view provides information on individual archived redo logs.
V$LOG	The V$LOG view provides information on the online redo log groups.
V$LOGFILE	The V$LOGFILE view provides information on specific online redo logs.
V$LOG_HISTORY	The V$LOG_HISTORY view provides historical information on all online/archived redo logs.

Using the V$ views is easy to do, and they can tell you a lot about the status of both online and archived redo logs, as shown in Exercise 1.2.

EXERCISE 1.2

Putting the V$ Views to Work

The V$ views are very useful when you want to find out something about your database related to backup or recovery. In this exercise, we will look at some V$ views related to the database online redo logs.

1. Let's look at the current redo logs that have been archived:

```
SQL> select name, thread#, sequence# from v$archived_log;
NAME                                            THREAD#   SEQUENCE#
-------------------------------------------- ---------- ----------
C:\ORACLE\ARCH\ORCL\ORCL_658485967_1_2.ARC           1           2
```

```
C:\ORACLE\ARCH\ORCL\ORCL_658485967_1_3.ARC          1          3
C:\ORACLE\ARCH\ORCL\ORCL_658485967_1_4.ARC          1          4
C:\ORACLE\ARCH\ORCL\ORCL_658485967_1_5.ARC          1          5
```

In the output, you will find the name of the archived redo log. You also see the thread number (in case you are running RAC) and the log sequence number. Note that since you have put the database in ARCHIVELOG mode, you have generated four archived redo logs.

2. You can see where your online redo logs are by using the V$LOGFILE view, as shown in this example:

```
SQL> select group#, status, member from v$logfile;
   GROUP# STATUS  MEMBER
---------- ------- ---------------------------------
        3          C:\ORACLE\ORADATA\ORCL\REDO03A.LOG
        2          C:\ORACLE\ORADATA\ORCL\REDO02.LOG
        1          C:\ORACLE\ORADATA\ORCL\REDO01.LOG
        3          C:\ORACLE\ORADATA\ORCL\REDO03B.LOG
```

In this output, you can see you have three online redo log groups. It is interesting to note that group 3 actually has two members, whereas groups 1 and 2 have one member each.

3. You can see which is the current online redo log group by querying the V$LOG view, as shown here:

```
SQL> select group#, sequence#,  status from v$log;
   GROUP#  SEQUENCE# STATUS
   ---------- ---------- ----------------
        1     13 CURRENT
        2     11 ACTIVE
        3     12 ACTIVE
```

In this example, log group 1 (marked with a CURRENT status) is the group that Oracle is currently writing to. Note that sequences 11 and 12 are marked active. This implies that they have not been archived yet or that they are being archived. They will be marked inactive once ARCH has finished archiving them.

Performing Oracle Offline Backups

We have been talking a lot about ARCHIVELOG mode and preparing for online backups, but we first need to talk about how to do offline backups in Oracle. Offline backups are actually quite easy to do, as you will see in Exercise 1.3, where you will be backing up a database with an offline backup.

     This is the kind of manual backup you may be asked about in the OCP exam.

EXERCISE 1.3

Executing an Offline Backup

In this exercise, you will be executing an offline backup of your database. Follow these steps to back up a database with an offline backup:

1. First, you need to determine which files to back up. You will need to know the location of the data files, the control file, and the online redo logs. You use the FILE_NAME column of the DBA_DATA_FILES view to find the data files:

    ```
    SQL> Select file_name from dba_data_files;
    FILE_NAME
    -------------------------------------------
    C:\ORACLE\ORADATA\ORCL\USERS01.DBF
    C:\ORACLE\ORADATA\ORCL\UNDOTBS01.DBF
    C:\ORACLE\ORADATA\ORCL\SYSAUX01.DBF
    C:\ORACLE\ORADATA\ORCL\SYSTEM01.DBF
    C:\ORACLE\ORADATA\ORCL\REVEAL_DATA_01.DBF
    C:\ORACLE\ORADATA\ORCL\REVEAL_INDEX_01.DBF
    C:\ORACLE\ORADATA\ORCL\USERS02.DBF
    7 rows selected.
    ```

2. You use the MEMBER column in the V$LOGFILE view to find the location of all the online redo logs:

    ```
    SQL> select member from v$logfile;
    MEMBER
    -----------------------------------
    C:\ORACLE\ORADATA\ORCL\REDO03A.LOG
    ```

```
C:\ORACLE\ORADATA\ORCL\REDO02.LOG
C:\ORACLE\ORADATA\ORCL\REDO01.LOG
C:\ORACLE\ORADATA\ORCL\REDO03B.LOG
```

3. You use the `NAME` column in `V$CONTROLFILE` to find the control files:

```
SQL> select name from v$controlfile;
NAME
-------------------------------------
C:\ORACLE\ORADATA\ORCL\CONTROL01.CTL
C:\ORACLE\ORADATA\ORCL\CONTROL02.CTL
C:\ORACLE\ORADATA\ORCL\CONTROL03.CTL
C:\ORACLE\ORADATA\ORCL\CONTROL04.CTL
```

4. Having found all the files you will need for your backup, create a directory to back up all your files to. Of course, you might back up your files to tape or a thumb drive or some such thing. In this case, you will just copy the files to a directory that you will create called `c:\backup\orcl\backup1`:

```
SQL> host mkdir c:\backup\orcl\backup1
```

5. Having created your backup directory, you need to shut down the database with the `SHUTDOWN IMMEDIATE` command before you start your backup:

```
SQL> shutdown immediate
Database closed.
Database dismounted.
ORACLE instance shut down.
SQL> exit
```

6. Now copy the files that you found in steps 1, 2, and 3 to the backup directory created in step 4. Notice that all the files in this example reside in one directory, `c:\oracle\ora-data\orcl`, so the `COPY` command is quite easy. Backups can take a while, so be patient. It's probably a good time to go grab a cool refreshment from the vending machine!

```
C:\>copy c:\oracle\oradata\orcl\*.* c:\backup\orcl\backup1
c:\oracle\oradata\orcl\CONTROL01.CTL
c:\oracle\oradata\orcl\CONTROL02.CTL
c:\oracle\oradata\orcl\CONTROL03.CTL
c:\oracle\oradata\orcl\CONTROL04.CTL
c:\oracle\oradata\orcl\REDO01.LOG
```

```
c:\oracle\oradata\orcl\REDO02.LOG
c:\oracle\oradata\orcl\REDO03A.LOG
c:\oracle\oradata\orcl\REDO03B.LOG
c:\oracle\oradata\orcl\REVEAL_DATA_01.DBF
c:\oracle\oradata\orcl\REVEAL_INDEX_01.DBF
c:\oracle\oradata\orcl\SYSAUX01.DBF
c:\oracle\oradata\orcl\SYSTEM01.DBF
c:\oracle\oradata\orcl\TEMP01.DBF
c:\oracle\oradata\orcl\UNDOTBS01.DBF
c:\oracle\oradata\orcl\USERS01.DBF
c:\oracle\oradata\orcl\USERS02.DBF
        16 file(s) copied.
```

7. Once the copy is complete, verify that the backup is where you expect it to be:

```
C:\>dir c:\backup\orcl\backup1
 Volume in drive C has no label.
 Volume Serial Number is 08DE-E1AB
 Directory of c:\backup\orcl\backup1
08/02/2013  02:16 PM    <DIR>          .
08/02/2013  02:16 PM    <DIR>          ..
08/02/2013  02:02 PM        10,174,464 CONTROL01.CTL
08/02/2013  02:02 PM        10,174,464 CONTROL02.CTL
08/02/2013  02:02 PM        10,174,464 CONTROL03.CTL
08/02/2013  02:02 PM        10,174,464 CONTROL04.CTL
08/02/2013  02:02 PM        52,429,312 REDO01.LOG
08/02/2013  02:02 PM        52,429,312 REDO02.LOG
08/02/2013  02:02 PM       104,858,112 REDO03A.LOG
08/02/2013  02:02 PM       104,858,112 REDO03B.LOG
08/02/2013  02:02 PM        15,736,832 REVEAL_DATA_01.DBF
08/02/2013  02:02 PM        15,736,832 REVEAL_INDEX_01.DBF
08/02/2013  02:02 PM       851,386,368 SYSAUX01.DBF
08/02/2013  02:02 PM       754,982,912 SYSTEM01.DBF
08/02/2013  02:02 PM        50,339,840 TEMP01.DBF
08/02/2013  02:02 PM       519,053,312 UNDOTBS01.DBF
08/02/2013  02:02 PM       581,246,976 USERS01.DBF
08/02/2013  02:02 PM        10,493,952 USERS02.DBF
              16 File(s)  3,154,249,728 bytes
               2 Dir(s)  13,330,685,952 bytes free
```

EXERCISE 1.3 *(continued)*

8. Start the database. Your backup is complete!

```
SQL> startup
ORACLE instance started.
Total System Global Area  418484224 bytes
Fixed Size                  1333592 bytes
Variable Size             348128936 bytes
Database Buffers           62914560 bytes
Redo Buffers                6107136 bytes
Database mounted.
Database opened.
```

NOTE   You could always decide to compress the backup files with a utility like PKZIP to save space if you wanted. By the way, RMAN can do this for you!

That's all there is to an offline database backup. In the next chapter, you will see that recovering the database using this backup is just as easy!

Temporary Tablespaces and Backups

Temporary tablespaces created with the CREATE TEMPORARY TABLESPACE command do not need to be backed up. The tempfiles associated with temporary tablespaces can be recreated on the fly as needed. This is true with both online backups and offline backups. If you are using the old-style temporary tablespaces that are not using tempfiles, you will still need to back up those data files.

To recreate tempfiles, simply use the ALTER TABLESPACE command with the ADD TEMPFILE keyword, as shown here:

```
Alter tablespace my_temp
Add tempfile '/u01/db01/mytempfile01.dbf' size 100m;
```

Performing Oracle Online Backups

Oracle online backups are not difficult to do; they just require a few additional steps. In this section, we will introduce you to Oracle online backups. First, we will discuss online backups and generally how to do them. We will then present an example of performing an online backup.

The Mechanics of Online Backups

To do Oracle online backups, your database must be in ARCHIVELOG mode. You can back up the entire database or you can choose to back up a specific tablespace or set of tablespaces. If you choose to back up only specific tablespaces, you will not be able to recover your database until you have at least a base backup of all of its tablespaces. That said, you can back up the tablespaces at different times if you prefer (though this is not common practice). For example, you could back up the SYSTEM tablespace on Monday, the USERS tablespace on Tuesday, and so on. As long as you have a complete cumulative backup of the database (taken at different times), you can recover it.

To start an online backup, you will need to put each tablespace in hot backup mode. This can be done by using the ALTER DATABASE BEGIN BACKUP command, or you can individually put tablespaces in hot backup mode with the ALTER DATABASE BEGIN BACKUP command. After you have put the tablespaces in hot backup mode, you back up the underlying data files of that tablespace. If you need to know where the data files related to that tablespace reside, you can use the DBA_DATA_FILES view.

> ### When a Tablespace Is in Hot Backup Mode
>
> When you put a tablespace in hot backup mode, Oracle will start writing block-sized records to the redo logs. These records are much bigger than the normal-sized records, so this can cause performance problems.
>
> One odd misconception we hear from time to time is that Oracle will stop writing to the database data files during a hot backup. In fact Oracle will continue to write changes to the data files; however, it will not update the data file headers until the backup is complete.

When you put a tablespace in hot backup mode, you are really putting the underlying data files of that tablespace in hot backup mode. You can determine if a data file is in hot backup mode by querying the V$BACKUP view. The STATUS column will indicate ACTIVE if the given data file is in hot backup mode. Here is an example of such a query where our USERS tablespace is in hot backup mode, as indicated by the ACTIVE status:

```
SQL> select a.tablespace_name, b.status
  2   from dba_data_files a, v$backup b
  3   where a.file_id=b.file#
  4   order by tablespace_name;


TABLESPACE_NAME                 STATUS
------------------------------  -----------
REVEAL_DATA                     NOT ACTIVE
REVEAL_INDEX                    NOT ACTIVE
SYSAUX                          NOT ACTIVE
SYSTEM                          NOT ACTIVE
UNDOTBS1                        NOT ACTIVE
USERS                           ACTIVE
USERS                           ACTIVE
```

Another thing to be aware of is what happens if the database is shut down while data files are in hot backup mode. First, Oracle will not allow you to shut down a database with most shutdown commands (SHUTDOWN, SHUTDOWN IMMEDIATE, or SHUTDOWN TRANSACTIONAL) while a tablespace is in hot backup mode. Instead it will generate an error, as shown here:

```
ORA-01149: cannot shutdown - file 4 has online backup set
ORA-01110: data file 4: 'C:\ORACLE\ORADATA\ORCL\USERS01.DBF'
```

This error identifies the data file that is in hot backup mode. You would need to determine which tablespace the data file is assigned to by looking at the DBA_DATA_FILES view. You would then issue the ALTER TABLESPACE END BACKUP command to take it out of hot backup mode.

If you issue a SHUTDOWN ABORT, STARTUP FORCE, or if the database crashes for some reason or the server shuts down without shutting down the database in a natural fashion, Oracle will not restart with a data file in hot backup mode. You will see the following error when you try to restart the database:

```
ORA-10873: file 4 needs end backup before opening a database
ORA-01110: data file 4: 'C:\ORACLE\ORADATA\ORCL\USERS01.DBF'
```

You simply issue the command ALTER DATABASE END BACKUP to take the data files out of hot backup mode and then ALTER DATABASE OPEN to open the database.

You can take the tablespaces out of hot backup mode with the ALTER DATABASE END BACKUP command, or you can individually take each tablespace out of hot backup mode by issuing the ALTER TABLESPACE END BACKUP command.

Once you complete the online backup, one more very important step is to back up the archived redo logs that were generated during the backup. You will need each log that was generated from the time you issued the ALTER DATABASE BEGIN BACKUP command until you issued the ALTER DATABASE END BACKUP command. After the backup, use the ALTER SYSTEM SWITCH LOGFILE command to force a log switch to cause the current online redo log (which contains redo generated during the backup) to be archived after you have completed the backup. You will need the redo in this log file, and any other archived redo logs that might have been generated during the backup, in order to recover the database from the backup you just completed.

In addition to regular online backups, you will want to schedule regular backups of your archived redo logs to protect them as much as possible. For example, if the online backup in the exercise ended at 4 p.m., you would be able to restore the database up to 4 p.m. with the archived redo logs you backed up. Archived redo logs will continue to be generated, though, and if you want to be able to recover your database to a point beyond 5 p.m., you will need to have those later-generated archived redo logs available (more on recovery in the next chapter). Thus it is a good idea to have regular backups of your archived redo logs!

In Exercise 1.4, we walk you through the process of doing an online backup.

EXERCISE 1.4

Executing an Online Backup

In this exercise you will be performing an online database backup. As mentioned in the text, your database will need to be in ARCHIVELOG mode to successfully execute this backup.

1. We assume your database is already running in ARCHIVELOG mode. If it's not, return to Exercise 1.1 and put your database in ARCHIVELOG mode.

2. As with the previous offline/cold backup, you need to know what data files need to be backed up:

```
SQL> Select file_name from dba_data_files;
FILE_NAME
-------------------------------------------
C:\ORACLE\ORADATA\ORCL\USERS01.DBF
C:\ORACLE\ORADATA\ORCL\UNDOTBS01.DBF
C:\ORACLE\ORADATA\ORCL\SYSAUX01.DBF
C:\ORACLE\ORADATA\ORCL\SYSTEM01.DBF
C:\ORACLE\ORADATA\ORCL\REVEAL_DATA_01.DBF
C:\ORACLE\ORADATA\ORCL\REVEAL_INDEX_01.DBF
C:\ORACLE\ORADATA\ORCL\USERS02.DBF
7 rows selected.
```

EXERCISE 1.4 *(continued)*

3. Having determined which data files need to be backed up, you need to know where the archived redo logs are being copied to.

```
SQL> show parameter log_archive_dest_1
NAME                         TYPE         VALUE
-------------------------    -----------  ------------------------------
log_archive_dest_1           string       location=c:\oracle\arch\orcl
```

4. You should note the current online redo log sequence number at this point. You will need this, plus all log sequences generated during the backup, to be able to perform your recovery. You can get this number from the V$LOG view:

```
SQL> select group#, sequence#, status from v$log;
    GROUP#  SEQUENCE# STATUS
---------- ---------- ----------------
        1         13 INACTIVE
        2         14 CURRENT
        3         12 INACTIVE
```

In this case, you see that you will need all log files from sequence number 14 on in order to restore the backup you are preparing to use.

5. You now need to put the database in hot backup mode. Oracle Database 12*c* provides the command ALTER DATABASE BEGIN BACKUP for this purpose. You can also back up specific tablespaces with the ALTER TABLESPACE BEGIN BACKUP command:

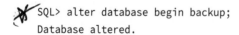

```
SQL> alter database begin backup;
Database altered.
-- ALTERNATE - Run this for each tablespace to be backed up.
-- alter tablespace users begin backup;
```

6. The database data files are now ready to be backed up. You will copy the files to a directory that you will create called c:\backup\orcl\backup2:

```
SQL> host mkdir c:\backup\orcl\backup2
```

7. Now copy all the database data files to this directory. In this case, all the files are in the directory c:\oracle\oradata\orcl, and the filenames all end with an extension of .DBF, so the command to copy them is pretty easy. Once you have started the data file copy, go get something to eat. It might take a while.

```
SQL> host copy c:\oracle\oradata\orcl\*.dbf c:\backup\orcl\backup2
c:\oracle\oradata\orcl\REVEAL_DATA_01.DBF
```

```
c:\oracle\oradata\orcl\REVEAL_INDEX_01.DBF
c:\oracle\oradata\orcl\SYSAUX01.DBF
c:\oracle\oradata\orcl\SYSTEM01.DBF
c:\oracle\oradata\orcl\TEMP01.DBF
c:\oracle\oradata\orcl\UNDOTBS01.DBF
c:\oracle\oradata\orcl\USERS01.DBF
c:\oracle\oradata\orcl\USERS02.DBF
        8 file(s) copied.
```

8. Having patiently waited for the backup to complete, you now need to take the database out of hot backup mode. Oracle Database 12*c* provides the command ALTER DATABASE END BACKUP for this purpose. You can also back up specific tablespaces with the ALTER TABLESPACE END BACKUP command:

```
SQL> alter database end backup;
Database altered.
-- ALTERNATE - Run this for each tablespace to be backed up.
-- alter tablespace users end backup;
```

9. Next, you need to determine the current log file sequence number. You will need the earlier log file that you identified and all log files generated during the backup up to the current log file to be able to restore this backup. The query is the same as the query against the V$LOG view that we showed you earlier in this chapter:

```
SQL> select group#, sequence#, status from v$log;
    GROUP#  SEQUENCE# STATUS
---------- ---------- ----------------
         1         13 INACTIVE
         2         14 ACTIVE
         3         15 CURRENT
```

In this example, you can see that during the backup you had a log file switch, from sequence number 14 to sequence number 15. You see that 15 is the current sequence number. You know now that you will need to back up the logs with sequence numbers 14 and 15 in order to be able to restore this backup.

10. You now need to force a log switch so the log with sequence number 15 (the current online redo log sequence number) will be archived. To do this, you issue the ALTER SYSTEM SWITCH LOGFILE command. This will cause Oracle to switch to the next log file (sequence 16), and the current archive log (sequence 15) will be copied to the archive-log directory by the ARC*n* processes.

```
SQL> Alter system switch logfile;
System altered.
```

EXERCISE 1.4 *(continued)*

11. Having switched log files, you need to wait for ARCH to complete copying the last log file to the archive-log directory. You can check for this completion by looking at the V$ARCHIVED_LOG view:

```
SQL> Select sequence#, archived, status from v$archived_log
  2  Where sequence# between 14 and 15;
 SEQUENCE# ARC S
---------- --- -
        14 YES A
        15 YES A
```

    Here you see that the logs with sequence numbers 14 and 15 (already identified as critical to restoring this backup) have been archived successfully. The ARCHIVED column indicates this with the use of the YES value.

12. Now back up all archived redo logs, ensuring that all logs with numbers between sequence *x* and sequence *y* are backed up. You will simply copy all archived redo logs from the directory identified in step 3 (c:\oracle\arch\orcl) to your backup directory:

```
SQL> Host copy c:\oracle\arch\orcl\*.* c:\backup\orcl\backup2
c:\oracle\arch\orcl\ORCL_658485967_1_10.ARC
c:\oracle\arch\orcl\ORCL_658485967_1_11.ARC
c:\oracle\arch\orcl\ORCL_658485967_1_12.ARC
c:\oracle\arch\orcl\ORCL_658485967_1_13.ARC
c:\oracle\arch\orcl\ORCL_658485967_1_14.ARC ⊠ Log sequence 14
c:\oracle\arch\orcl\ORCL_658485967_1_15.ARC ⊠ Log sequence 15
c:\oracle\arch\orcl\ORCL_658485967_1_2.ARC
c:\oracle\arch\orcl\ORCL_658485967_1_3.ARC
c:\oracle\arch\orcl\ORCL_658485967_1_4.ARC
c:\oracle\arch\orcl\ORCL_658485967_1_5.ARC
c:\oracle\arch\orcl\ORCL_658485967_1_6.ARC
c:\oracle\arch\orcl\ORCL_658485967_1_7.ARC
c:\oracle\arch\orcl\ORCL_658485967_1_8.ARC
c:\oracle\arch\orcl\ORCL_658485967_1_9.ARC
        14 file(s) copied.
```

    You can tell that the logs with sequence numbers 14 and 15 were backed up since you know that the log sequence number is part of the filename (it's the number right before the extension). We also marked them for you in the output just because we are nice guys. After copying the archived redo logs to the backup location, you can delete the source location if you want to save space. Once the backup of the archived redo logs is complete, your database backup is done.

NOTE   We hope you also realize that you will need to back up files like the database parameter file, any other Oracle-related configuration files (such as for networking), and the Oracle Database software itself. Backing up these structures (except for the spfile, which is a special RMAN case we will cover in Chapter 3) is beyond the scope of the OCP exam.

Backing Up the Control File

Finally, we need to talk about control-file backups. In Oracle there are three ways to manually back up a control file (again, RMAN methods will be covered in Chapter 3):

- Backing up the original control file during a cold backup
- Creating a backup control file
- Creating a trace file with the CREATE CONTROL FILE command in it

We have already covered the first method in this chapter. Let's look at the remaining two methods in some more detail. We will address recovering from a lost control file in Chapter 2.

Creating a Backup Control File

The backup control file is almost the same as a regular control file. It has some areas in it that are marked such that Oracle recognizes that it's a backup control file. When a backup control file is used, some form of recovery will be required (typically just involving the use of the archived and online redo logs if the database is otherwise intact).

To create the backup control file, simply issue the ALTER DATABASE BACKUP CONTROLFILE TO command, indicating at the end of the command where you want the control file to be created.

For example, if you wanted to create a backup control file after the online backup you performed in Exercise 1.4, you would simply need to issue the following command:

```
SQL> alter database backup controlfile to
'c:\backup\orcl\backup2\backup_control.ctl';
Database altered.
```

The result is the creation of a backup control file called backup_control.ctl found in the c:\backup\orcl\backup2 directory, as you can see here:

```
SQL> host dir c:\backup\orcl\backup2\backup_control.ctl
 Volume in drive C has no label.
 Volume Serial Number is 08DE-E1AB
 Directory of c:\backup\orcl\backup2
```

```
08/02/2013  03:24 PM        10,174,464 BACKUP_CONTROL.CTL
                1 File(s)    10,174,464 bytes
                0 Dir(s)   9,930,571,776 bytes free
```

We will cover recovering from control-file loss using a backup control file in Chapter 2.

Creating a Trace File with the *Create CONTROLFILE* Command in It

If all else fails and you do not have a backup control file, don't worry; you have another option, the CREATE CONTROLFILE command. Normally, manually executing the command can be challenging because you need to know a lot of information about your database (like the names and locations of all the database data files). However, you can prepare for the possibility of having to use the CREATE CONTROLFILE command by creating one in advance. The ALTER DATABASE BACKUP CONTROLFILE TO TRACE command will create a trace file with the CREATE CONTROLFILE command in it for you. The trace file is stored in the new diagnostic directory structure in Oracle Database 12*c*.

The diagnostic directory structure is a new standard introduced in Oracle Database 12*c* that defines where Oracle stores files related to database troubleshooting and diagnostics. The base directory of this structure is defined by the parameter DIAGNOSTIC_DEST. Here is an example of the setting of DIAGNOSTIC_DEST on an Oracle Database:

```
SQL> show parameter diag
NAME                                  TYPE         VALUE
------------------------------------- ------------ ---------
diagnostic_dest                       string       C:\ORACLE
```

A whole book could be written on the new 12*c* diagnostic capabilities, but what we are interested in is where user-generated trace files get created because when we issue the ALTER DATABASE BACKUP CONTROLFILE TO TRACE command, the resulting file will be a user-generated trace file.

> **NOTE** We would be remiss if we didn't mention that the database alert log is contained in the diagnostic destination directory structure. It is contained in the same directory as the trace files we are discussing in this section. Each database (or database instance if you are running RAC) will have its own alert log. The filename format for the alert log is alert_{instance name}.log. The alert log is an important diagnostic and monitoring tool, so you should become familiar with it.

In this case, the trace file will be created in a directory structure under DIAGNOSTIC_DEST\diag\rdbms\orcl\orcl\trace, as shown in this code example:

```
SQL> alter database backup controlfile to trace;
Database altered.
```

```
C:\oracle\diag\rdbms\orcl\orcl\trace>dir
 Volume in drive C has no label.
 Volume Serial Number is 08DE-E1AB
 Directory of C:\oracle\diag\rdbms\orcl\orcl\trace
08/02/2013  03:38 PM    <DIR>          .
08/02/2013  03:38 PM    <DIR>          ..
08/02/2013  03:38 PM         1,027,520 alert_orcl.log
08/02/2013  03:38 PM             9,572 orcl_ora_12120.trc
08/02/2013  03:38 PM                91 orcl_ora_12120.trm
               4 File(s)      1,037,183 bytes
               4 Dir(s)   9,964,507,136 bytes free
```

The trace file is called orcl_ora_12120.trc (it's easy to tell since there are no other trace files in the directory). If you have a number of trace files in the directory, you can sort the contents ascending by date and time and generally the correct trace file will be at the top (i.e., the LS -ALT command). Also, the V$PROCESS view has a TRACEFILE column in it that will display the name of the trace file for that process.

Another option with the ALTER DATABASE BACKUP CONTROLFILE TO TRACE command is to define an alternate location for the trace file. The syntax for this command is as follows:

```
alter database backup controlfile to trace as '/tmp/my_control_trace.trc';
```

If you look in the file, you will find a trace-file header in it first. Later down the trace file, you will find two different versions of the CREATE CONTROLFILE command. Here is an example of the CREATE CONTROLFILE command that you might find in this file:

```
CREATE CONTROLFILE REUSE DATABASE "ORCL" NORESETLOGS  ARCHIVELOG
    MAXLOGFILES 16
    MAXLOGMEMBERS 3
    MAXDATAFILES 100
    MAXINSTANCES 8
    MAXLOGHISTORY 292
LOGFILE
  GROUP 1 'C:\ORACLE\ORADATA\ORCL\REDO01.LOG'  SIZE 50M,
  GROUP 2 'C:\ORACLE\ORADATA\ORCL\REDO02.LOG'  SIZE 50M,
  GROUP 3 (
    'C:\ORACLE\ORADATA\ORCL\REDO03A.LOG',
    'C:\ORACLE\ORADATA\ORCL\REDO03B.LOG'
  ) SIZE 100M
-- STANDBY LOGFILE
DATAFILE
  'C:\ORACLE\ORADATA\ORCL\SYSTEM01.DBF',
  'C:\ORACLE\ORADATA\ORCL\SYSAUX01.DBF',
```

```
  'C:\ORACLE\ORADATA\ORCL\UNDOTBS01.DBF',
  'C:\ORACLE\ORADATA\ORCL\USERS01.DBF',
  'C:\ORACLE\ORADATA\ORCL\REVEAL_DATA_01.DBF',
  'C:\ORACLE\ORADATA\ORCL\REVEAL_INDEX_01.DBF',
  'C:\ORACLE\ORADATA\ORCL\USERS02.DBF'
CHARACTER SET WE8MSWIN1252;
```

You will notice that this output includes the data file names, the location and names of the online redo logs, and other information needed by the CREATE CONTROLFILE command. The trace file contains other output that will be required to complete the recovery process, so you should back up the trace file as it is. In Chapter 2, we will address the process of recovering from a control-file loss using the output contained in the trace files.

 Exam objectives are subject to change at any time without prior notice and at Oracle's sole discretion. Please visit Oracle's Training and Certification website (http://www.oracle.com/education/certification/) for the most current exam-objectives listing.

Summary

Backups in Oracle can be a big deal. There are a number of different situations you will find yourself in, and finding a strategy to use depends on your knowledge of how to do backup and recovery. That's why the OCP exam has a great deal of backup and recovery focus.

We started this chapter introducing you to the Oracle architecture. This knowledge is critical to understanding what is required for any kind of Oracle database backup and recovery.

At the time we wrote this book, the Oracle 12*c* OCP exam contents with respect to manual backups and recovery specifically say "Backup and recover a NOARCHIVELOG database."

In this chapter we covered that particular topic in depth.

Then, we moved a little deeper to give you a firm understanding of more complex backup procedures, such as online backups and point-in-time recovery. We did this because later chapters will be discussing these kinds of backups and restores in the context of Oracle's backup tool called Recovery Manager (RMAN). You will understand RMAN operations much better if you understand the basic things that Oracle does under the covers to facilitate database recovery.

It is probably clear to you that recovery in Oracle can be quite complex. It becomes even harder when you are actually doing it under the gun, when people are breathing down your neck to get that database up. So, build your skills in this area now. They will serve you well in the future.

Exam Essentials

The following topics are specifically listed as essential test items and part of the content of the Oracle Database 12c OCP Exam.

Describe types of database failures.   Understand the kinds of database failures that can occur. Also understand what causes those failures and what kind of recovery is required in the event those failures occur.

Describe tools available for backup and recovery tasks.   Understand the various tools/ methods (ie: shell scripts) that are available to backup and recover and Oracle database. Describe generally how each tool works.

Describe RMAN and maximum availability architecture.   Understand and be able to describe the benefits of Oracle's Maximum Availability Architecture (MAA). Also be able to describe what RMAN is and what it's used for.

Configure your control file and online redo logs for recoverability.   Understand the benefit of multiplexing the control files and the online redo logs. Understand why it is important to back up your control file. Understand the different methods of backing up your control file. Understand what a backup control file is.

Describe and tune instance recovery.   Understand what instance recovery is and why it's critical to database availability. Describe how to monitor and configure the database for optimal instance recovery performance.

Perform backup and recovery in NOARCHIVELOG mode.   Understand the steps that need to be performed to do an offline backup. Understand the difference between an offline backup and an online backup and how these differences can be used to decide the optimal backup strategy.

Enable ARCHIVELOG mode.   Understand what ARCHIVELOG mode is, and how to configure the database so that it's running in ARCHIVELOG mode. Understand what archived redo logs are and why they are important, how they are created and where they are created.

Back up a control file to trace.   Understand how to create a backup of the control file to a trace file, and where that trace file is located.

Review Questions

1. What are the different archiving modes available in the Oracle Database? (Choose all that apply.)

   A. LOGGING mode

   B. NOLOGGING mode

   C. ARCHIVELOG mode

   D. ARCHIVING mode

   E. NOLOGFILE mode

   F. NOARCHIVELOG mode

   G. RECOVERY mode

2. Your database is in NOARCHIVELOG mode. You start to do a backup, but your users complain that they don't want you to shut down the database to perform the backup. What options are available to you?

   A. Put the database in hot backup mode and perform an online backup, including backing up the archived redo logs.

   B. Just back up the database data files without shutting down the database.

   C. You will have to wait until you can shut down the database to perform the backup.

   D. Mark each data file as backup in progress, back them up individually, and then mark them as backup not in progress. No archived redo logs will need to be backed up.

   E. Back up only the data files that the user will not be touching. Once the user has finished what they were doing, you can shut down the database and back up the data files the user changed during the course of the remaining backup.

3. Your database backup scripts keep failing on the ALTER TABLESPACE BEGIN BACKUP command. Your junior DBA informs you that the failure is because the database is in ARCHIVELOG mode. Is he correct?

   A. Yes

   B. No

   C. There is insufficient information to decide the answer to this question.

4. What parameter is used to tune instance recovery in Oracle Database 12c?

   A. INSTANCE_RECOVERY_TIME

   B. FAST_START_RECOVERY_TIME

   C. FAST_MTTR_RECOVERY

   D. FAST_START_MTTR_RECOVERY

   E. None of the above

5. Which files do you need to back up for a database that is in ARCHIVELOG mode to ensure recovery? (Choose all that apply.)

   A. Database data files

   B. Online redo logs

   C. Archived redo logs

   D. Backup control file

   E. Control file from a backup

6. What does the SCN represent?

   A. The system change number, which is a marker indicating a point in time relative to transactions within a given database.

   B. A number that represents time. Thus, at 1300 hours, the SCN is the same on all databases.

   C. The security change number, which represents the security code that is needed to access any database structure.

   D. A conversion factor that converts internal database time to external clock time.

   E. UTC time in the database, providing a standardized way of tracking time in Oracle.

7. Which command(s) are used to back up the control file? (Choose all that apply.)

   A. ALTER SYSTEM BACKUP CONTROLFILE

   B. ALTER DATABASE BACKUP CONTROLFILE TO TRACE

   C. ALTER DATABASE BACKUP CONTROL FILE

   D. ALTER DATABASE BACKUP CONTROLFILE TO 'FILENAME'

   E. ALTER CONTROLFILE BACKUP

8. What is the purpose of MAA?

   A. MAA is a set of practices that Oracle has created to help you better administer your databases.

   B. MAA is a set of practices that standardizes Oracle database creation, file naming conventions and operating system directory names.

   C. MAA is a set of practices that align around providing maximum availability for Oracle databases.

   D. MAA is a new form of Oracle martial arts.

   E. MAA is an online document available from oracle.com that provides a list of current critical issues related to database backup and recovery.

9. Which of the following will cause instance recovery to occur? (Choose all that apply.)

   A. Power failure causes the database server to crash.

   B. You issue a `SHUTDOWN IMMEDIATE` command from the SQL prompt.

   C. You issue the `ALTER DATABASE CHECKPOINT` command.

   D. You issue the `SHUTDOWN ABORT` command from the SQL prompt.

   E. You issue the `SHUTDOWN TRANSACTIONAL` command from the SQL prompt.

10. What parameter controls how often the database checkpoints and also tries to reduce the time that instance recovery will take?

    A. `FAST_START_RECOVERY`

    B. `MTTR_TARGET`

    C. `RESTART_FAST`

    D. `CHECKPOINT_TIME`

    E. `FAST_START_MTTR_RECOVERY`

11. Which of the following database processes have some purpose in Oracle database operations that apply to database backup and recovery? (Choose all that apply.)

    A. DBW

    B. LGWR

    C. DNNR

    D. THREADn

    E. PQOn

12. What is most impacted by the delay between committing a transaction and the time that the data associated with that change is written to disk?

    A. Media recovery

    B. Archiving

    C. Instance recovery

    D. Transaction completion time

    E. Database creation time

13. Which of the following files are likely to be found in the diagnostic destination directory of an Oracle database?

    A. Database trace files

    B. Database data files

    C. Listener files

    D. Database parameter files

    E. Database alert log

14. Your database is ARCHIVELOG mode. Given the following steps, which option provides the steps to do this backup in the right order and the most efficiently?

  1. ALTER DATABASE BEGIN BACKUP.

  2. ALTER TABLESPACE {TABLESPACE NAME} BEGIN BACKUP.

  3. Back up the database data files.

  4. ALTER DATABASE END BACKUP.

  5. ALTER TABLESPACE {TABLESPACE NAME} END BACKUP

  6. Back up the online redo logs.

  7. Perform a redo log switch.

  8. Back up the archived redo logs.

  A. 2,3,4,6,8

  B. 1,2,3,5,4,7,8

  C. 1,3,4,7,8

  D. 8,7,4,3,1

  E. 1,7,8,9

15. From the answers available below, choose the two types of backups that can be taken of an Oracle database.

  A. Metadata backup

  B. Logical backup

  C. Physical backup

  D. Consistent backup

  E. Inconsistent backup

16. What database files would you need to back up if you are doing a NOARCHIVELOG recovery?

  A. Database data files

  B. Online redo logs

  C. Archived redo logs

  D. Database control file

  E. Database command file

17. What database view would you query to determine if the database is in ARCHIVELOG mode?

    A. DBA_ARCHIVELOG_MODE

    B. V$LOG_MODE

    C. V$LOGGING_MODE

    D. V$ARCHIVELOG_MODE

    E. V$DATABASE

18. What database view would you query to determine what the current archiving status of an online redo log is?

    A. V$LOGFILE

    B. DBA_ARCHIVED_LOG

    C. DBA_ARCHIVLOG_HISTORY

    D. V$ARCHIVELOG_HISTORY

    E. V$ARCHIVED_LOG

19. Which of the following are the names of an Oracle database process architecture? (Choose all that apply.)

    A. Multithreaded

    B. Multigenerational

    C. Multiprocess

    D. Multiplied

    E. Multitasked

20. Which of the following is not the name of an Oracle Database process?

    A. DBWn

    B. LGWR

    C. ARCH

    D. ORCL

    E. All are database processes

Chapter

2

Performing Oracle User-Managed Database Recoveries

ORACLE DATABASE 12c: ADVANCED ADMINISTRATION EXAM OBJECTIVES COVERED IN THIS CHAPTER:

✓ Perform Basic Backup and Recovery

✓ Back up and recover a NOARCHIVELOG database

✓ Perform backup and recovery in NOARCHIVELOG mode

In Chapter 1, "Performing Oracle User-Managed Backups," we showed you how to perform user-based database backups in both NOARCHIVELOG and ARCHIVELOG mode. Of course, those backups are of little good if you don't know how to use them to restore your database. In this chapter, we will show you how to restore your database with user-based backups.

First, we will show you how to use the offline backup you took in NOARCHIVELOG mode and use it to restore your database. Recovering a database in NOARCHIVELOG mode is the main activity that we cover in this chapter that is covered in the OCP exam. However, the other things contained in this chapter are related to concepts you will need to understand throughout the exam. Trust us on that one.

After talking about recovery in NOARCHIVELOG mode, we will address restoring online backups taken in ARCHIVELOG mode. We will then talk about different kinds of user-based incomplete recoveries, also called *point-in-time* recoveries. While the exam will not cover these advanced types of manual, user-based recoveries, it will cover these types of recoveries from an RMAN prospective. Thus, you need to be familiar with all the concepts that will be presented in this chapter, including those associated with point-in-time recovery.

Finally, we will cover other recovery processes, such as recovering from a lost control file and a lost temporary tablespace tempfile, recovering from the loss of an online redo log group, and recovering from the loss of a password file. So, buckle in, keep your hands and arms inside the vehicle at all times, and enjoy the ride!

Exam objectives are subject to change at any time without prior notice and at Oracle's sole discretion. Please visit Oracle's Training and Certification website (http://www.oracle.com/education/certification/) for the most current exam-objectives listing.

Performing a Recovery in NOARCHIVELOG Mode

Recovering a database that was backed up in NOARCHIVELOG mode is perhaps the easiest recovery task to do. The thing to keep in mind is that there are no archived redo logs to apply. You simply will be restoring your database to the point in time of the backup you took. It does not matter if you lost one data file or the entire enchilada; you have to restore all the files you backed up to recover the database.

The process is simple. You copy all the files you backed up during your offline backup (data files, control files, redo logs) and then start the database. You simply must copy all of these files; you can't pick and choose what to recover. Exercise 2.1 provides an example of such a recovery operation.

EXERCISE 2.1

Restoring a Database Using a Cold Backup

In this exercise, you will be restoring the database with a cold backup. It is assumed the database is in NOARCHIVELOG mode.

1. Make sure the database is shut down.

2. Copy the files on the backup media to the original location. You would copy the following files:

- Database data files

- Database control files

- Database online redo logs

If the original location of the database files is not available, copy them to an alternate location. Having copied the files to an alternate location, you will likely need to execute an optional step 3 for the control files and optional step 4 for all database files and/or online redo logs. Here is an example of the COPY command:

```
C:\Documents and Settings\Robert>copy c:\oracle\oradata\orcl\cold\*.*
c:\backup\orcl\backup1
```

3. (Optional) If you copied the database control files to a location other than their original location, you will need to modify the database parameter CONTROL_FILES to point to the control files in their new location.

If you are using a text-based parameter file (pfile), simply edit the file and change the CONTROL_FILES parameter value contained within that file.

If you are using a server-based parameter file (spfile), then you will need to start the database in NOMOUNT mode and change the SPFILE entry for the CONTROL_FILES parameter using the ALTER SYSTEM command. You will have to use the SCOPE=SPFILE keyword when issuing the ALTER SYSTEM command since changing the CONTROL_FILES parameter is not supported as a dynamic change.

After you have changed the parameter file (manually or using the ALTER SYSTEM command), use the SHUTDOWN command to shut down the database (the parameter file will be reread when you open it again in the next steps). Here is an example:

```
SQL> startup nomount
ORACLE instance started.
Total System Global Area  397557760 bytes
```

```
Fixed Size                  1333452 bytes
Variable Size             289408820 bytes
Database Buffers          100663296 bytes
Redo Buffers                6152192 bytes
SQL> alter system set control_files='C:\ORACLE\ORADATA\ORCL\CONTROL01.CTL',
'C:\ORACLE\ORADATA\ORCL\CONTROL02.CTL',
'C:\ORACLE\ORADATA\ORCL\CONTROL03.CTL' scope=spfile;
System altered.
SQL> shutdown immediate
ORA-01507: database not mounted
ORACLE instance shut down.
```

4. (Optional) If you copied the database online redo logs or the database data files to a different location, you will need to indicate to Oracle that you have done so. This is so Oracle will know where the files are now so it can open them. This is known as a rename operation. (Don't be fooled, though. It renames only the files inside of Oracle; it does not rename them on the operating system).

To rename the database files (redo log and data files) you must have the database mounted first. Once the database is mounted, you will issue the ALTER DATABASE RENAME FILE command for each database file that needs to be changed.

Here is an example where we have moved the online redo logs and database data files from c:\oracle\oradata\orcl to c:\oracle\oradata\orclnew. You need to indicate to Oracle that you have made this change by using the ALTER DATABASE RENAME FILE command. This will change the pointers to the database files inside the control file so Oracle will be looking for the files in the correct location.

Note that for the rest of this exercise we will assume that the files were moved to their original locations. In this example, you rename the online redo logs and then you rename the database data files:

```
SQL> startup mount
ORACLE instance started.
Total System Global Area  397557760 bytes
Fixed Size                  1333452 bytes
Variable Size             272631604 bytes
Database Buffers          117440512 bytes
Redo Buffers                6152192 bytes
Database mounted.
SQL>alter database rename file 'c:\oracle\oradata\orcl\REDO01.LOG' to
```

EXERCISE 2.1 *(continued)*

```
  'c:\oracle\oradata\orclnew\REDO01.LOG';
SQL>alter database rename file 'c:\oracle\oradata\orcl\REDO02.LOG' to
  'c:\oracle\oradata\orclnew\REDO02.LOG';
SQL>alter database rename file 'c:\oracle\oradata\orcl\REDO03.LOG' to
  'c:\oracle\oradata\orclnew\REDO03.LOG';
SQL>alter database rename file 'c:\oracle\oradata\orcl\SYSAUX01.DBF' to
  'c:\oracle\oradata\orclnew\SYSAUX01.DBF';
SQL>alter database rename file 'c:\oracle\oradata\orcl\SYSTEM01.DBF' to
  'c:\oracle\oradata\orclnew\SYSTEM01.DBF';
SQL>alter database rename file 'c:\oracle\oradata\orcl\TEMP01.DBF' to
  'c:\oracle\oradata\orclnew\TEMP01.DBF';
SQL>alter database rename file 'c:\oracle\oradata\orcl\UNDOTBS01.DBF' to
  'c:\oracle\oradata\orclnew\UNDOTBS01.DBF';
SQL>alter database rename file 'c:\oracle\oradata\orcl\USERS01.DBF' to
  'c:\oracle\oradata\orclnew\USERS01.DBF';
```

5. Now that the files are copied into place, you can start up the database:

```
SQL> alter database open
Database opened.
```

That's it. You have recovered your database! Query to your heart's delight!

 **Real World Scenario**

Recovering in NOARCHIVELOG Mode

Because of its limitations, you might ask yourself whether anyone really uses a database in NOARCHIVELOG mode. The answer is yes.

The main benefit to running in NOARCHIVELOG mode is that you are not generating archived redo logs. Archived redo logs require more space (sometimes a lot more space). Often development or test databases do not require online backups or point-in-time recovery, so running them in NOARCHIVELOG mode might make sense. Most large shops will run all databases in ARCHIVELOG mode because of the added flexibility it provides.

Performing a Full Database Recovery in ARCHIVELOG Mode

You might think there's something slightly mystical about database recoveries in ARCHIVELOG mode the first few times you do them. You take a backup that may be days or even weeks old, apply some magic in the form of application of the archived redo logs, and *voilà* (Robert's wife, the French expert, will appreciate that word), your database is up to date and ready to roll.

It's true that some DBAs (and managers) actually don't believe that you can back up a database while it's up and running and be able to restore it fully without losing any data. Well, we're here to tell you that you can, that it works, and that it's not magic but just some good programming. It's reliable too. We've been working with Oracle for a very long time. We've yet to see an online backup that's not recoverable unless someone did something wrong, and it's pretty hard to do something wrong unless you are just not paying attention.

In the following sections, we will talk about user-based recovery of your database when it's in ARCHIVELOG mode. We will talk about preparing for the recovery and then we will talk about the actual recovery process. Note that we are discussing a full database recovery to the point of failure of the database and not a point-in-time recovery. We assume that the online redo logs are intact since full point-of-failure recovery requires this.

The OCP exam may ask you about conditions where the online redo logs have been lost, you have to use a backup control file, or all the files associated with the database are lost. See the sections "Performing User-Based Incomplete Recoveries" and "Performing Other Types of Recoveries" for more details on these special types of database recoveries.

Loss of Online Redo Logs or Control Files

Remember, if you have lost your online redo logs, then recovery becomes more complex (the OCP exam is likely to ask you questions about these kinds of losses). We will discuss these kinds of losses later in this chapter.

Preparing for the Recovery

When preparing for recovery, you have to consider what kind of data file loss you have experienced. There are three types you might experience:

- Loss of all data files
- Loss of one or more non-SYSTEM or -UNDO tablespace data files
- Loss of the SYSTEM or UNDO tablespace data file

The recovery for each of these types of data file losses is similar. Some recoveries can be done online (with the database up and running) and other recoveries will require that the database be shut down (though in these cases it's likely going to have crashed anyway). We will cover each of these types of loss in the following sections.

Restoring Data Files after the Loss of All Data Files

If you have lost all of your database data files, then you will need to perform a database recovery with the database down. It is most likely in these cases that the database will have already crashed anyway (or refused to restart); Oracle does not do well if all of the database data files go missing.

The procedure in this case is simple:

1. Restore the data file backups from your backup media.

   You can restore these data files to their original locations or to new locations depending on your needs.

2. Once you have restored the data files, you are ready to recover the entire database.

   We discuss full database recovery in the section "Recovering the Database" (an original title, we know).

Restoring Data Files after the Loss of the SYSTEM or UNDO Tablespace Data File

If you have lost only data files related to the SYSTEM or UNDO tablespace, then you should restore only those data files. You will still need to do an offline recovery, but the recovery will be much quicker since all you will need to do is recover those database data files. Once you have recovered the data files from your backup media, perform a tablespace- or data file–level recovery, which is covered in the section "Recovering the Database."

Specific Recovery Actions

The OCP exam expects you to answer a question with the best answer. For example, in the case of the loss of a single, non-SYSTEM or -UNDO tablespace data file, the best answer is to restore just that data file and not all database data files. Sure you can restore all the data files, but that would not be the best course of action.

Restoring Data Files after the Loss of One or More Non-SYSTEM or -UNDO Tablespace Data Files

If you lose a data file related to a tablespace other than the SYSTEM or UNDO tablespace, then you can actually perform online recovery of the database. In these cases, it is unlikely that the database will crash, and if the database is started up, it will seem to start up normally, although if anyone should try to use data that is in the missing data file they will get an error. To perform this kind of recovery, you will need to first indicate to the database that the file is in an offline state. You do this by using the ALTER DATABASE command, as shown here:

```
alter database datafile 4 offline;
alter database datafile 'C:\ORACLE\ORADATA\ORCL\USERS01.DBF' offline;
```

Now you will find that the STATUS column for this data file in V$DATAFILE will show that the file has a RECOVER status, as shown here:

```
SQL> select file#, status from v$datafile;
    FILE# STATUS
---------- -------
        1 SYSTEM
        2 ONLINE
        3 ONLINE
        4 RECOVER
```

You should also note that the status of the data file in the DBA_DATA_FILES view does not change when you offline a file. It will still show as AVAILABLE. A row will also appear for the data file you have taken offline in the V$RECOVER_FILE view.

Data File IDs

Did you notice in the ALTER DATABASE command where we used a number instead of the location of the data file? This is the data file ID, and you can use the data file ID in lieu of the entire path many times. You can find the data file ID in the V$DATAFILE and DBA_DATA_FILES views, as shown here:

```
SQL> select file_id, file_name from dba_data_files;
   FILE_ID FILE_NAME
---------- ---------------------------------------
        4 C:\ORACLE\ORADATA\ORCL\USERS01.DBF
        3 C:\ORACLE\ORADATA\ORCL\UNDOTBS01.DBF
        2 C:\ORACLE\ORADATA\ORCL\SYSAUX01.DBF
        1 C:\ORACLE\ORADATA\ORCL\SYSTEM01.DBF
```

Recovering the Database

If you restore the database files to different locations, you will need to modify the database parameter file and/or the database control file with the new file locations using the ALTER SYSTEM command as demonstrated in optional steps 3 and 4 of Exercise 2.1.

Recovering the database depends, again, on the type of data file outage you have experienced. In the next sections, we will cover the RECOVER DATABASE command first. Then we'll cover restoring the database after loss of all data files, loss of SYSTEM or UNDO tablespace data files, and loss of non-SYSTEM or -UNDO tablespace data files.

Renaming Database Files

Sometimes during a recovery you will need to restore database files to different locations. If this is the case, you will need to indicate to Oracle where the new location is. The types of files you are likely to move are control files, online redo logs, and database data files.

If you are restoring control files to a different location, then simply change the CONTROL_ FILES parameter.

If the relocation involves the online redo logs or the database data files, then you will need to use the ALTER DATABASE RENAME FILE command. This command works only when the database is mounted and in some cases when it's open (like when data files to be renamed are offline).

To rename a file, restore the files to the new location and issue the ALTER DATABASE RENAME FILE command, as shown here:

```
alter database rename file '/ora01/oracle/oradata/orcl/system01.dbf'
To '/ora02/oracle/oradata/orcl/system01.dbf';
```

This will rename the file in the control file. Note that it has no impact on the actual physical file.

Using the *RECOVER DATABASE* Command

The RECOVER DATABASE command is used in Oracle to recover the database from the SQL prompt. When you issue the RECOVER DATABASE command without any parameters, Oracle will assume a *point-of-failure recovery* or *complete recovery*. That is, it will try to recover the database up to the last redo-log entry. This results in a complete recovery of your database down to the last transaction. During recovery operations, Oracle will inspect the data file headers and the control file and determine where data file recovery needs to begin for each data file. To do this, Oracle will inspect the SCN contained in each database data file. It will use the SCN to determine where it needs to start recovering the data file.

What is the SCN? The system change number (SCN) is a counter, and its job is to keep track of everything going on inside the database and assign it a temporal identity. This serves to keep transactions that occurred in a particular order in the same order later down the road (such as during recovery). You need to preserve the order of transactions because of dependencies that occur between transactions. For example, if you have a parent and child table, you want to make sure that during recovery all INSERTs into the parent table occur before INSERTs into the child table. This is because of the foreign key constraint that exists between the two tables to ensure the integrity of that parent/child relationship. The SCN helps Oracle to track the temporal flow of those changes, and thus the parent table INSERT will have a lower SCN than the child table INSERT. As a result, in the end, all is right with the world.

SCNs are loosely coupled with time. Thus, 12:30 P.M. local time would be associated with a specific SCN in a given individual database. The thing to remember is that 12:30 P.M. local time will most likely be associated with a different SCN in each database, so the coupling is very loose. The concept of the SCN is very important because there may be times when you will want to restore your database to a specific SCN. This is supported during recovery operations. Also, Oracle's Flashback features support the use of the SCN when flashing back the database. See Chapter 8 "Understanding Flashback Technology," for more information on the vast number of features available with Oracle Flashback Database.

When you issue the RECOVER DATABASE command from the SQL prompt, you have a number of options. You can recover the entire database with RECOVER DATABASE, you can recover a specific tablespace with RECOVER TABLESPACE, and you can recover a data file with RECOVER DATAFILE. As you progress through this chapter, you will see several examples of the use of the RECOVER DATABASE command, including the use of the database SCN to recover your database.

After you have issued the RECOVER DATABASE command, you will be prompted for the archived redo log it thinks it needs to apply. You can simply press the Enter key and Oracle will apply the redo in that archived redo log. Once the redo has been applied, the RECOVER DATABASE command will prompt you for the next redo log in the sequence, and you press Enter again.

As you can imagine, this can get a little long-winded if you have to apply a number of archived redo logs. Another thing you can do at the prompt is type in **AUTO**. This will cause the RECOVER DATABASE command to automatically start applying archived redo-log files without prompting you for the name or location of those files. This is much easier!

Recovering the Database after the Loss of All Data Files

You can use the RECOVER DATABASE command to recover the entire database all at once. Having restored all the database data files from the backup media, you would follow these steps:

1. Log into the database as SYS using the SYSDBA privilege.
2. Mount the database with the STARTUP MOUNT command.
3. Issue the RECOVER DATABASE command from the SQL prompt.

   The RECOVER DATABASE command will recommend to you the correct archived redo log to apply.

4. At the prompt, type **AUTO**; the RECOVER DATABASE command automatically starts applying all redo until the database is recovered.

   Once database recovery is complete, the RECOVER DATABASE command will return you to the SQL prompt.

5. Issue the ALTER DATABASE OPEN command to open the database for business.

Note that in this case you have performed a full recovery. Your database should have been completely restored without any data loss. There is no need to perform a special backup after this recovery (other than your regularly scheduled backups). In Exercise 2.2, you'll be doing a full recovery of your database after it has lost all data files.

EXERCISE 2.2

Recovering the Database from the Loss of All Data Files

In this exercise, you will perform a full (complete) database recovery, restoring all data files. It is important to note that this recovery presupposes that the online redo logs and control files of the database are intact.

1. Back up the database. Details on how to do a full online database backup are found in Chapter 1.

2. In summary, follow these steps:

   ▪ First, put the database in hot backup mode.

   ▪ Copy all database data files to a backup location.

   ▪ Take the database out of hot backup mode.

   ▪ Force a log switch. Back up the archived redo logs.

   Here is an example of a backup:

```
[oracle@localhost orcl]$ sqlplus "/ as sysdba"
SQL*Plus: Release 12.1.0.1.0 Production on Tue Feb 18 12:24:53 2014
Copyright (c) 1982, 2013, Oracle.  All rights reserved.
Connected to:
Oracle Database 12c Enterprise Edition Release 12.1.0.1.0 - 64bit Production
With the Partitioning, OLAP, Advanced Analytics and Real Application Testing
options
Enter password:


SQL> alter database begin backup;
Database altered.
SQL> host cp /oracle01/oradata/orcl/*.dbf /oracle01/backup/orcl
SQL> alter database end backup;
```

```
Database altered.
SQL> alter system switch logfile;
System altered.
SQL> host cp /oracle01/backup/arch/* /oracle01/backup/orcl/*
SQL> alter database backup controlfile to trace;
Database altered.
SQL> alter database backup controlfile to '/oracle01/oradata/orcl/control1.bak';
Database altered.
```

3. Now remove all data files from the database. On some operating-system platforms (Linux, for example), you can do this with the database up and running, and on others (Windows) you will have to shut down the database.

```
SQL> quit
Disconnected from Oracle Database 12c Enterprise Edition
Release 12.1.0.1.0 - 64bit Production
With the Partitioning, OLAP, Advanced Analytics and Real Application Testing
options [oracle@localhost orcl]$ pwd
/oracle01/oradata/orcl
[oracle@localhost orcl]$ ls -al *.dbf
-rw-r-----  1 oracle oinstall  104865792 Aug 17 15:49 example01.dbf
-rw-r-----  1 oracle oinstall  104865792 Aug 17 15:49
my_second_secure_tbs_01.dbf
-rw-r-----  1 oracle oinstall  104865792 Aug 17 15:49 my_secure_tbs_01.dbf
-rw-r-----  1 oracle oinstall  104865792 Aug 17 15:49 retention_archives_01.
dbf
-rw-r-----  1 oracle oinstall  778051584 Aug 17 15:49 sysaux01.dbf
-rw-r-----  1 oracle oinstall  744497152 Aug 17 15:49 system01.dbf
-rw-r-----  1 oracle oinstall  182525952 Aug 17 14:03 temp01.dbf
-rw-r-----  1 oracle oinstall 1121984512 Aug 17 15:49 undotbs01.dbf
-rw-r-----  1 oracle oinstall  159326208 Aug 17 15:49 users01.dbf
[oracle@localhost orcl]$ rm *.dbf
```

4. Connect to the database and shut it down. It may be possible that you will not be able to connect to the database, and yet the database will still be running. In this case you will have to manually kill the Oracle processes if you are running in Unix or shut down the database service in Windows. In our case, we are not able to log into the database, so we kill the LGWR process.

```
[oracle@localhost trace]$ sqlplus "/ as sysdba"
SQL*Plus: Release 12.1.0.1.0 Production on Fri Dec 27 10:20:57 2013
```

```
Copyright (c) 1982, 2013, Oracle.  All rights reserved.
Enter password:
ERROR:
ORA-01075: you are currently logged on
Enter user-name:
ERROR:
ORA-01017: invalid username/password; logon denied
Enter user-name:
ERROR:
ORA-01017: invalid username/password; logon denied
SP2-0157: unable to CONNECT to ORACLE after 3 attempts, exiting SQL*Plus
[oracle@localhost trace]$ ps -ef|grep orcl|grep lgwr
oracle   23118    1  0 15:48 ?        00:00:01 ora_lgwr_orcl
[oracle@localhost trace]$ kill -9 23118
```

5. Once you are sure the database is down, restore the database data files from their backup location to the location where the database files belong.

```
[oracle@localhost orcl]$ pwd
/oracle01/backup/orcl
[oracle@localhost orcl]$ cp *.dbf /oracle01/oradata/orcl/*
```

6. Now connect to the database and issue the STARTUP MOUNT command.

```
[oracle@localhost orcl]$ sqlplus / as sysdba
SQL*Plus: Release 12.1.0.1.0 Production on Tue Feb 18 12:24:53 2014
Copyright (c) 1982, 2013, Oracle.  All rights reserved.
Connected to:
Oracle Database 12c Enterprise Edition Release 12.1.0.1.0 - 64bit Production
With the Partitioning, OLAP, Advanced Analytics and Real Application Testing
options
SQL> startup mount
ORACLE instance started.
Total System Global Area  167395328 bytes
Fixed Size                  1298612 bytes
Variable Size             142610252 bytes
Database Buffers           20971520 bytes
Redo Buffers                2514944 bytes
Database mounted.
SQL>
```

7. To recover the database, issue the RECOVER DATABASE command. The command may return a response that says "media recovery complete," as shown here:

```
SQL> recover database
Media recovery complete.
```

You may also be prompted to apply archived redo logs. Simply enter **AUTO** at the prompt:

```
SQL> recover database
ORA-00279: change 5071334 generated at 08/17/2013 15:35:51 needed for thread 1
ORA-00289: suggestion :
/oracle01/fast_recovery_area/ORCL/archivelog
/2013_08_17/o1_mf_1_5_4bk6onh8_.arcORA-00280:
change 5071334 for thread 1 is in sequence #5
Specify log: {<RET>=suggested | filename | AUTO | CANCEL}
auto
ORA-00279: change 5071583 generated at 08/17/2013
15:40:04 needed for thread 1
ORA-00289: suggestion :
/oracle01/fast_recovery_area/ORCL/archivelog
/2013_08_17/o1_mf_1_6_4bk76kwk_.arcORA-00280:
change 5071583 for thread 1 is in sequence #6
ORA-00279: change 5091960 generated at 08/17/2013
15:49:05 needed for thread 1
ORA-00289: suggestion :
/oracle01/fast_recovery_area/ORCL/archivelog
/2013_08_17/o1_mf_1_7_4bk9ksb4_.arcORA-00280:
change 5091960 for thread 1 is in sequence #7
ORA-00279: change 5112317 generated at 08/17/2013
16:29:13 needed for thread 1
ORA-00289: suggestion :
/oracle01/fast_recovery_area/ORCL/archivelog
/2013_08_17/o1_mf_1_8_4bk9p236_.arcORA-00280:
change 5112317 for thread 1 is in sequence #8
ORA-00279: change 5112647 generated at 08/17/2013
16:31:29 needed for thread 1
```

```
ORA-00289: suggestion :
/oracle01/fast_recovery_area/ORCL/archivelog
/2013_08_17/o1_mf_1_9_4bk9p2mz_.arcORA-00280:
change 5112647 for thread 1 is in sequence #9
Log applied.
Media recovery complete.
```

8. Oracle will apply the needed redo and then return you to the SQL prompt. Assuming no errors occur, you can now open the database with the ALTER DATABASE OPEN command, as shown here:

```
SQL> alter database open;
Database altered.
```

Recovering the Database after the Loss of the SYSTEM or UNDO Tablespace Data File

In this case, we will just restore the tablespaces or data files that were lost. Of course, because these are critical tablespace objects, the database itself is down. After restoring the data files that were lost (do not restore any data files that are intact), recover the database following these steps:

1. Log into the database as SYS using SYSDBA authentication.

2. Mount the database with the STARTUP MOUNT command.

   For recovery, you have two options. You can use the RECOVER TABLESPACE or the RECOVER DATAFILE command to recover the data files that were lost. It's kind of up to you which one you want to use (we like the RECOVER TABLESPACE command in this situation more because it's easier to do since it covers all the data files). The various recover commands (RECOVER DATABASE, RECOVER TABLESPACE, and RECOVER DATAFILE) will recommend the correct archived redo log to apply.

3. At the prompt, type **AUTO**.

   The RECOVER DATABASE command (as well as RECOVER TABLESPACE or RECOVER DATAFILE) automatically starts applying all redo until the database is recovered.

4. Once database recovery is complete, the RECOVER DATABASE command will return you to the SQL prompt. You can then issue the ALTER DATABASE OPEN command to open the database for business.

Recovery of the UNDO Tablespace

There are cases where the UNDO tablespace can be recovered online. If the database was shut down in a consistent manner before the UNDO tablespace was lost, it may be that all you will need to do is take the UNDO tablespace data files offline (you won't be able to take the tablespace itself offline) and then open the database.

Oracle has a default SYSTEM tablespace that would be used in this case, when the database initially comes up. You could then just create a new UNDO tablespace and drop the old one. This might be a quicker recovery method in some cases.

Recovering the Database after the Loss of One or More Non-SYSTEM or -UNDO Tablespace Data Files

If the tablespace/data file you lost is not associated with the SYSTEM or UNDO tablespaces, then you are in luck. You don't even need to shut down the database to recover! All you need to do is take the data files offline, restore the impacted data files, recover the data files (or the tablespace), and bring them back online.

The nice thing about this is if your users are not using the tablespace, they will never know there was a problem. If the users are using the tablespace, they will be impacted only if they try to use the data files that are offline (which is one good reason in some cases to take just the data files offline rather than the whole tablespace).

The first question is, how do you know which data files are missing? There are a couple of things that will give you a clue. First of all, your users will start getting these messages:

```
SQL> select * from scott.emp;
select * from scott.emp
                    *
ERROR at line 1:
ORA-00376: file 4 cannot be read at this time
ORA-01110: data file 4: 'C:\ORACLE\ORADATA\ORCL\USERS01.DBF'
```

You can also look at the V$RECOVER_FILE view for more information on data files that need recovery. Here is an example of such a query:

```
SQL> select file#, 'online', online_status, error from v$recover_file;
     FILE# ONLINE  ONLINE_ ERROR
---------- ------- ------- -------------------- ---------- ---------
         4 ONLINE   ONLINE FILE NOT FOUND
```

> **Missing Data Files**
>
> Don't expect that these errors indicating data files are missing will always show up in the alert log. Sometimes they will (for example, on database startup), but often they won't (for example, when a query fails because a data file is offline). If you want to monitor for this problem reliably, then the V$RECOVER_FILE view is the way to go.

So, here is the general recovery process from such an error. In this case, we assume the database is up and running:

1. Take the data file offline using the ALTER DATABASE DATAFILE OFFLINE command as shown here:

   ```
   alter database datafile 'C:\ORACLE\ORADATA\ORCL\USERS01.DBF' offline;
   ```

   As an alternative, you can use FILE_ID as shown in this example:

   ```
   alter database datafile 4 offline;
   ```

   FILE_ID will appear in the error message, or you can use the FILE_ID column of DBA_DATA_FILES or the FILE# column in the V$DATAFILE view.

2. Restore the missing data files.

3. Restore all archived redo logs that will be needed for recovery. This would be all archived redo logs generated from the beginning of the backup image you restored in step 2.

> **WARNING**   When you are restoring backup files, never restore backed-up online redo logs over the existing online redo logs. This is so important, in fact, that when we talked about hot backups in Chapter 1, we did not even back up the online redo logs. Restoring old online redo logs over your existing ones will lead to data loss. Fair warning!

4. Recover the missing data files with the RECOVER DATAFILE or RECOVER TABLESPACE command.

5. Bring the data files or the tablespace online with the ALTER DATABASE or ALTER TABLESPACE command.

So, what do you do if your database was down and you discover the files are lost when you start it up? That's simple too:

1. Log in as SYS and start up the database.

   If a data file is missing, you will get an error message that looks something like this:

   ```
   SQL> startup
   ORACLE instance started.
   ```

```
Total System Global Area  397557760 bytes
Fixed Size                  1333452 bytes
Variable Size             289408820 bytes
Database Buffers          100663296 bytes
Redo Buffers                6152192 bytes
Database mounted.
ORA-01157: cannot identify/lock data file 4 - see DBWR trace file
ORA-01110: data file 4: 'C:\ORACLE\ORADATA\ORCL\USERS01.DBF'
```

It may be that you are missing more than data file 4, since Oracle will alert you to only the first data file that it finds missing.

2. Use the V$RECOVER_FILE, V$DATAFILE, and V$TABLESPACE views to determine exactly which data files are missing and which tablespaces they are associated with, as shown in this example:

```
SQL> l
  1  select b.name ts_name, a.error, c.name datafile
  2  from v$recover_file a, v$tablespace b, v$datafile c
  3  where a.file#=c.file#
  4* and b.ts#=c.ts#
SQL> /

TS_NAME    ERROR                 DATAFILE
---------  --------------------  ------------------------------------
USERS      FILE NOT FOUND        C:\ORACLE\ORADATA\ORCL\USERS01.DBF
```

3. Review the results of the query.

As long as the missing data files are not part of the SYSTEM or UNDO tablespace, you can simply take those data files offline and open the database. The intent will be to recover those tablespaces/data files with the database open.

4. First use the ALTER DATABASE DATAFILE OFFLINE command to take the tablespaces offline:

```
SQL> alter database
datafile 'C:\ORACLE\ORADATA\ORCL\USERS01.DBF' offline;
Database altered.
```

5. Next, open the database with the ALTER DATABASE OPEN command:

```
alter database open
```

6. Now restore the database backup data files from your hot backup media.

7. Restore all archived redo logs that will be needed for recovery. You will need to restore all archived redo logs generated from the beginning of the backup image you restored in step 2.

Figuring Out Which Archived Redo Logs You Need

If you need to figure out exactly which archived redo logs you need to restore your backup (so, perhaps, you can restore those files off of backup media), you can use the V$RECOVER_FILE and the V$LOG_HISTORY views. The V$RECOVER_FILE view provides the last change number (in the CHANGE# column) present in the file(s) needing recovery. The V$LOG_HISTORY view will tell you which archived redo logs the changes are in. Here is an example:

```
ORA-01157: cannot identify/lock data file 4- see DBWR trace file
ORA-01110: data file 4: 'C:\ORACLE\ORADATA\ORCL\USERS01.DBF'
SQL> host copy users01.dbf.backup users01.dbf
        1 file(s) copied.
SQL> Select a.file#, a.change#, b.first_change#, b.next_change#, b.sequence#
  2  From v$recover_file a, v$log_history b
  3  Where a.change#<=b.next_change#;
     FILE#    CHANGE# FIRST_CHANGE# NEXT_CHANGE#  SEQUENCE#
---------- ---------- ------------- ------------ ----------
         4    1418889       1417349      1438925         20
```

You could also find the name of the actual archived redo logs needed for recovery by querying the V$ARCHIVED_LOG view. In some cases, the log sequence number will not show up here if the associated online redo log file has not yet been archived.

```
SQL> Select a.file#, a.change#, b.first_change#, b.next_change#,
  2  b.sequence#, b.name
  3  From v$recover_file a, v$archived_log b
  4  Where a.change#<=b.next_change#;
     FILE#    CHANGE# FIRST_CHANGE# NEXT_CHANGE#  SEQUENCE#
---------- ---------- ------------- ------------ ----------
NAME
-------------------------------------------------
         4    1418889       1417349      1438925         20
C:\ORACLE\ARCH\ORCL\ARC00020_0662757171.001
```

8. Recover the data files or tablespaces using the RECOVER DATAFILE or RECOVER TABLESPACE command.

   ```
   SQL> recover datafile 4;
   ```

9. Bring the data files or tablespaces online using the ALTER DATABASE DATAFILE ONLINE or ALTER TABLESPACE ONLINE command. Once you have done this, you have recovered the missing tablespace data files and your database is back to normal.

   ```
   SQL>Alter database datafile 4 online;
   ```

Backing Up after the Recovery

There really is no requirement to do a special backup after a data file or tablespace recovery. All your backup files are still usable, and Oracle will keep generating archived redo logs just like before.

 Real World Scenario

Performing Database Recoveries in the Real World

In this book, we are providing you with some of the most common recovery situations that you might face and that appear on the OCP exam. The reality is that in the real world, recovery can quickly become very complex and overwhelming. You have people looking over your shoulder, 200 opinions on how to fix the problem (all of them different, of course), and you face an issue that does not quite neatly fit into the backup and recovery case studies that you have experienced in your training.

The key to figuring out what to do is to sit back and think about what the problem is and why it is happening. Another key is if you feel that you might be getting in over your head, get Oracle Support on the line. Sometimes it takes a while to get them geared up to really help you, and the sooner you get them engaged, the better off you will be in the end.

Finally, when you are troubleshooting, don't shotgun solutions. If you are not sure about your solution, think it out very carefully. Talk to other DBAs around you and get their opinions. Nothing makes a bad day worse than having a database failure and then realizing that you just made it a bigger problem by screwing up the recovery process.

Performing User-Based Incomplete Recoveries

Incomplete recovery (also called *point-in-time recovery*) is the process of recovering the database to a different point in time than the most current point in time. Why would one do such a thing, you ask? There may be a number of reasons:

* Loss of one of the online redo log groups, making full recovery impossible
* User error requiring a recovery of the database to a different point in time
* Creation of a duplicate database to a point in time other than that of the source database

In the following sections, we will cover the basics of incomplete recovery. First, we will discuss the requirements for and mechanics of incomplete recovery, and then we will cover preparation for incomplete recovery. Finally, we will walk through the process of an actual incomplete recovery.

Requirements for and Mechanics of an Incomplete Recovery

The requirements for incomplete recovery are much like those of a complete recovery from an online backup. First, the database must be in ARCHIVELOG mode. Second, you have to have a backup of the database (online or offline) and all of the archived redo logs required to get your database to the point in time that you are interested in.

Preparing for an Incomplete Recovery

The first step in performing an incomplete recovery is to restore the database from a backup that was taken before the point in time to which you want to restore the database.

Notice that you have to restore the entire database. This can sometimes confuse less-experienced DBAs. With incomplete recovery, you must restore the entire database, and it must be restored to a point in time before the point in time that you wish to recover to.

For example, suppose it's 2:00 P.M. and you wish to recover just the USERS tablespace objects to 1:00 P.M. because someone messed something up. To do so, it's not just as simple as restoring the USERS tablespace data files to 1:00 P.M. You have to restore the entire database to 1:00 P.M.

Oracle is persnickety about data file consistency. Recall the concept of the SCN, which is Oracle's internal counter for all operations. When you do an insert, it is assigned an SCN. When you then commit that insert, it is assigned a different, higher SCN. This way, Oracle knows the insert came first and the commit came second.

When you start the Oracle Database, it's a demanding bit of software. It requires that the SCN in each data file be the same before it will open the database (there is an exception to this with read-only tablespaces). Also, there are SCNs stored in the control file that have to jibe with the SCNs in the data files. If the SCNs don't jibe, then some form of recovery is required.

Tablespace Point-in-Time Recovery

There is a concept of tablespace point-in-time recovery that allows you to restore just a tablespace to a point in time different from that of the database. We will discuss tablespace point-in-time recovery using RMAN in Chapter 7, "Performing Oracle Advanced Recovery." The OCP exam does not require that you know how to do tablespace point-in-time recovery manually, so we are not covering that topic in this book.

So, if the entire database is at SCN 12345 (see Figure 2.1) and you restore the USERS tablespace to SCN 1234, that will be a problem. Oracle will detect the different SCNs and require a complete recovery. Not quite what you hoped for.

FIGURE 2.1   Database with data files restored incorrectly for incomplete recovery

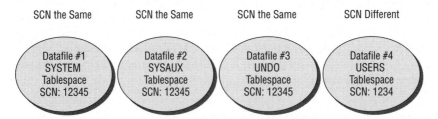

You want to recover to SCN 1234. Datafiles 1, 2, and 3 are at SCN 12345, which is after SCN 1234. Incomplete recovery to SCN 1234 is not possible because recovery rolls forward SCNs, not backward.

So, when you want to perform an incomplete database recovery, you have to restore all the data files to a point in time at or before the point in time that you actually want to recover to. In Figure 2.2, you can see that all the data files are recovered to SCN 1230 or lower, so you can now begin an incomplete recovery to SCN 1234 as you wish.

Note that you do not need to restore the control file to a previous version for incomplete recovery to work. Once you have finished the incomplete-recovery process, Oracle will reset the control file so that it will correctly reflect the current state of the database.

You will also need to restore all archived redo logs that were generated from the time of the backup image until the point that you want to restore to. You can determine which archived redo log sequence numbers you want to restore by looking at the V$ARCHIVED_LOG view (we provided a query using the V$ARCHIVED_LOG view in a note earlier in this chapter). Keep in mind that you may also need redo contained in an online redo log that has not been archived yet. Since you will not be restoring any online redo logs, this won't be a problem.

FIGURE 2.2   Database with data files restored correctly for incomplete recovery

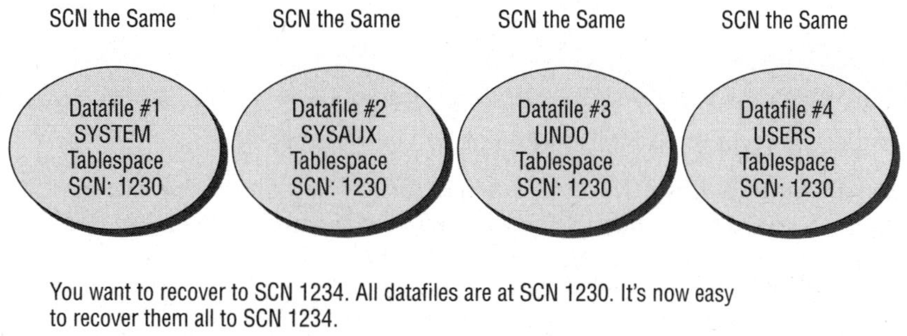

You want to recover to SCN 1234. All datafiles are at SCN 1230. It's now easy
to recover them all to SCN 1234.

Now that you have restored all the database data files and the needed archived redo logs,
you are ready to execute your incomplete database recovery.

Performing an Incomplete Recovery

Having restored the database data files, recovery is pretty easy. First, you determine the type of
recovery that you want to do, and then you perform the recovery using the RECOVER DATABASE
command. Finally, you open the database. Let's look at these steps in some more detail next.

Determining the Type of Point-in-Time Recovery

There are three types of point-in-time recovery that you can perform:

Time-Based Recovery   *Time-based recovery* is based on the time that you want to recover
your database to. Time-based recovery is granular to the nearest second.

Log Sequence–Based Recovery   *Log sequence–based recovery* is based on defining the log
sequence number you wish the database to be recovered to. You will need to determine the
correct log sequence number. The V$ARCHIVED_LOG and V$LOG views may be helpful in making
this determination.

Change-Based Recovery   *Change-based recovery* is based on the SCN that you wish
to restore your database to. You can determine what the current SCN of the database is
by querying the CURRENT_SCN column of the V$DATABASE view. You can also associate a
given time to an approximate SCN by using the TIMESTAMP_TO_SCN, SCN_TO_TIMESTAMP,
or SMON_SCN_TIME view.

Perform Your Point-in-Time Recovery

Regardless of which of the three point-in-time recoveries you choose to perform, the overall
process is very similar. You will use the RECOVER DATABASE command for your recovery. Each
recovery type will take a different keyword, as shown here:

Time-Based Recovery   To perform time-based recovery, use the RECOVER DATABASE UNTIL
TIME command. The format of the time in the command is 'yyyy-mm-dd:hh24:mi:ss',
which is consistent in each Oracle database (so it is not dependent on parameters such as

NLS_DATE_FORMAT). Here is an example of the use of the RECOVER DATABASE UNTIL TIME command:

```
Recover database until time '2013-10-23:13:00:00'
```

In this example, the database will be recovered up to October 23, 2013 at 1:00 P.M. Any transactions that are committed after that point will be rolled back.

Log Sequence–Based Recovery   To perform log sequence–based recovery, use the RECOVER DATABASE UNTIL SEQUENCE command. This example recovers to log sequence 34:

```
Recover database until sequence 34;
```

Change-Based Recovery   To perform change-based recovery, use the RECOVER DATABASE UNTIL CHANGE command followed by the SCN you wish to recover to. In this example, we recover to SCN 1234:

```
Recover database until change 1234;
```

Once the recovery begins, you will be prompted for the appropriate archived redo logs to apply just as with a complete database recovery. The main difference is that the application of archived redo logs (and possibly online redo logs) will automatically cease once the point in time, change, or SCN has been reached. Once the redo has been applied, the database is ready to be opened.

Opening the Database

Having recovered the database, you will want to open it. A point-in-time recovery will result in a new incarnation of the database. A new incarnation is a new logical version of the database. The data remains the same, of course, but the redo stream essentially starts over. The log sequence number is reset to 1 (the SCN is not reset) and a new life begins for the database.

To indicate to Oracle that you are doing an incomplete recovery, you will open the database in a slightly different way. You will still use the ALTER DATABASE OPEN command, but you will also include the keyword RESETLOGS. The RESETLOGS command indicates to Oracle that it should reset the control file and the redo log sequence number and open the database as a brand-new incarnation. The entire command looks like this:

```
alter database open resetlogs;
```

Through Oracle Database 10g, Oracle recommended that you back up the database anytime you issue a RESETLOGS operation. This was because Oracle did not support recovering a database through a RESETLOGS operation. Since Oracle Database 11g, Oracle allows you to perform a recovery through RESETLOGS. This is supported through the new %r format string available in the LOG_ARCHIVE_FORMAT parameter (see Chapter 1 for more on this parameter). This format string will include a RESETLOGS number in the naming of each archived redo log. This will help Oracle keep the redo-log stream straight.

If you should need to do a recovery after a RESETLOGS operation, simply restore the same backup that you used to do the point-in-time recovery and recover using that backup. You can do full recovery or point-in-time recovery using the redo associated with the new incarnation. In Exercise 2.3, you'll perform a point-in-time recovery.

EXERCISE 2.3

Performing a Point-in-Time Recovery

In this exercise, you will do a point-in-time recovery by restoring the database to a previous SCN.

1. Back up the database. Details on how to do a full online database backup are found in Chapter 1. In summary, follow these steps:

   - First, put the database in hot backup mode.

   - Copy all database data files to a backup location.

   - Take the database out of hot backup mode.

   - Force a log switch. Back up the archived redo logs.

   Here is an example of a backup:

   ```
   [oracle@localhost orcl]$ sqlplus "/ as sysdba"
   SQL*Plus: Release 12.1.0.1.0 Production on Tue Feb 18 14:22:34 2014
   Copyright (c) 1982, 2013, Oracle.  All rights reserved.
   Connected to:
   Oracle Database 12c Enterprise Edition Release 12.1.0.1.0 - 64bit Production
   With the Partitioning, OLAP, Advanced Analytics and Real Application Testing
   options
   SQL> alter database begin backup;
   Database altered.
   SQL> host cp /oracle01/oradata/orcl/*.dbf /oracle01/backup/orcl
   SQL> alter database end backup;
   Database altered.
   SQL> alter system switch logfile;
   System altered.
   SQL> host cp /oracle01/backup/arch/* /oracle01/backup/orcl/*
   SQL> alter database backup controlfile to trace;
   Database altered.
   SQL> alter database backup controlfile to '/oracle01/oradata/orcl/control1.bak';
   Database altered.
   ```

2. Next, log into the database as SCOTT/TIGER and create a new table. Insert two records into the new table and commit the insert:

```
SQL> connect scott/tiger
Connected.
SQL> create table test_table (id number);
Table created.
SQL> insert into test_table values (1);
1 row created.
SQL> insert into test_table values (2);
1 row created.
SQL> commit;
Commit complete.
```

3. Now, log in as SYS and determine the current SCN by using the CURRENT_SCN column of the V$DATABASE table. Your SCN will be different from that in the example:

```
SQL> connect sys as sysdba
Enter password:
Connected.
SQL> select current_scn from v$database;
CURRENT_SCN
-----------
    5135413
```

4. Log back in as SCOTT/TIGER and add two more records. Commit the inserts:

```
SQL> connect scott/tiger
Connected.
SQL> insert into test_table values (3);
1 row created.
SQL> insert into test_table values (4);
1 row created.
SQL> commit;
Commit complete.
```

5. Log in as SYS again and query the current SCN by using the CURRENT_SCN column of the V$DATABASE table. Notice that the SCN has changed:

```
SQL> connect sys as sysdba
Enter password:
Connected.
SQL> select current_scn from v$database;
CURRENT_SCN
```

```
-----------
    5135522
```

6. Shut down the database.

```
SQL> shutdown abort
ORACLE instance shut down.
```

7. Once you are sure the database is down, restore the database data files from their backup location to the location where the database files belong:

```
[oracle@localhost orcl]$ pwd
/oracle01/backup/orcl
[oracle@localhost orcl]$ cp *.dbf /oracle01/oradata/orcl/*
```

8. Mount the database:

```
[oracle@localhost orcl]$ sqlplus "/ as sysdba"
SQL*Plus: Release 12.1.0.1.0 Production on Tue Feb 18 14:22:34 2014
Copyright (c) 1982, 2013, Oracle.  All rights reserved.
Connected to an idle instance.
SQL> startup mount
ORACLE instance started.
Total System Global Area  167395328 bytes
Fixed Size                  1298612 bytes
Variable Size             142610252 bytes
Database Buffers           20971520 bytes
Redo Buffers                2514944 bytes
Database mounted.
```

9. Recover the database using the RECOVER DATABASE UNTIL CHANGE command. You will use the SCN you queried in step 3 as the SCN to recover to. Enter **AUTO** when prompted for an archived redo log to apply:

```
SQL> Recover database until change 5135413;
ORA-00279: change 5071334 generated at 08/17/2013 15:35:51 needed for thread 1
ORA-00289: suggestion :
/oracle01/fast_recovery_area/ORCL/archivelog/2013_08_17
/o1_mf_1_5_4bk6onh8_.arc
ORA-00280: change 5071334 for thread 1 is in sequence #5
Specify log: {<RET>=suggested | filename | AUTO | CANCEL}
auto
```

```
ORA-00279: change 5071583 generated at 08/17/2013 15:40:04 needed for thread 1
ORA-00289: suggestion :
/oracle01/fast_recovery_area/ORCL/archivelog/2013_08_17
/o1_mf_1_6_4bk76kwk_.arc
ORA-00280: change 5071583 for thread 1 is in sequence #6
ORA-00279: change 5091960 generated at 08/17/2013 15:49:05 needed for thread 1
ORA-00289: suggestion :
/oracle01/fast_recovery_area/ORCL/archivelog/2013_08_17
/o1_mf_1_7_4bk9ksb4_.arc
ORA-00280: change 5091960 for thread 1 is in sequence #7
ORA-00279: change 5112317 generated at 08/17/2013 16:29:13 needed for thread 1
ORA-00289: suggestion :
/oracle01/fast_recovery_area/ORCL/archivelog/2013_08_17
/o1_mf_1_8_4bk9p236_.arc
ORA-00280: change 5112317 for thread 1 is in sequence #8
ORA-00279: change 5112647 generated at 08/17/2013 16:31:29 needed for thread 1
ORA-00289: suggestion :
/oracle01/fast_recovery_area/ORCL/archivelog/2013_08_17
/o1_mf_1_9_4bk9p2mz_.arc
ORA-00280: change 5112647 for thread 1 is in sequence #9
ORA-00279: change 5112649 generated at 08/17/2013 16:31:30 needed for thread 1
ORA-00289: suggestion :
/oracle01/fast_recovery_area/ORCL/archivelog/2013_08_17
/o1_mf_1_10_4bk9p3gz_.arc
ORA-00280: change 5112649 for thread 1 is in sequence #10
Log applied.
Media recovery complete.
```

10. Open the database with the ALTER DATABASE OPEN RESETLOGS command. The data-base will open:

```
SQL> alter database open resetlogs;
Database altered.
```

11. Log into the SCOTT schema. Do a SELECT * FROM TEST_TABLE. You should have only two records in the table:

```
SQL> Connect scott/tiger
Connected.
SQL> Select * from test_table;
        ID
```

EXERCISE 2.3 *(continued)*

```
    ----------
             1
             2
```

Performing Other Types of Recoveries

You will need to be prepared for other types of user-managed recoveries when taking your OCP exam or just in the course of managing your Oracle Database. In the following sections, we will talk about the following types of user-managed recoveries:

- Loss of a tempfile
- Loss of an online redo log group
- Loss of the control file
- Loss of the password file
- Loss of everything

Recovering from the Loss of a Tempfile

Tempfiles are used with temporary tablespaces. As discussed in Chapter 1, you do not need to back up a tempfile. Because of its temporary nature, the contents of a tempfile are not needed during a recovery. You will need to recreate the tempfile after any recovery that includes the temporary tablespace. This is done by using the ALTER TABLESPACE ADD TEMPFILE command as shown in this example, where we add a tempfile to the TEMP tablespace:

```
ALTER TABLESPACE TEMP ADD TEMPFILE '/oracle01/oradata/orcl/temp01.dbf'
SIZE 200m  REUSE AUTOEXTEND ON;
```

Recovering from the Loss of an Online Redo Log Group

Loss of the online redo logs comes in four different flavors:

- Loss of a redo log file group member
- Loss of an inactive online redo log group
- Loss of an active but not current online redo log group
- Loss of the current online redo log group

Any loss of an entire online redo log group makes for a very bad day. Loss of the last two categories (loss of an active or current online redo log) is often a disaster.

Recall that the redo logs are written to as soon as there is a commit (other events can cause writes too). Remember also that the database data files are written to later, some-times much later. Thus, the database data files are often way out of synchronization with the actual current state of the database. If the database crashes, then often the database data files are not up to date, and this forces Oracle to apply redo to get them current when you start up the database. Normally, Oracle will do this automatically in a process called *instance recovery.*

As a result of the fact that the database data files are often out of synch with the actual state of the database, loss of an active or the current online redo log group can be disastrous. Loss of an active online redo log can result in loss of data. Loss of the current online redo log will likely result in data loss, but this is not always the case. Thus, redo logs are quite important. You may wonder what the difference between the current, active, and inactive redo logs is:

Current   Current online redo log group.

Active   Not currently in use but the dirty blocks associated with the redo in the log file still need to be written to the data files by DBWR. Also, the group may still need to be archived.

Inactive   Not currently in use and dirty blocks associated with the redo in the log file have been written to data files by DBWR.

You can see the status of an online redo log group by querying the STATUS column of the V$LOG view. Let's look at what to do when it comes to recovering from loss of redo log groups.

Dealing with the Loss of an Inactive Online Redo Log Group Member

If you have lost one or more members of an online redo log group (but not the entire group), then the response is pretty easy. You can simply recreate the member using the ALTER DATABASE ADD LOGFILE MEMBER command. For example, you might see this error in the alert log:

```
ORA-00313: open failed for members of log group 2 of thread 1
ORA-00312: online log 2 thread 1: 'C:\ORACLE\ORADATA\ORCL\REDO02.LOG'
```

If the database has not shut down, you should immediately attempt to checkpoint the database using the ALTER SYSTEM CHECKPOINT command. The ALTER SYSTEM CHECKPOINT command forces the database to write any dirty blocks from the database buffer cache to the database data files in an urgent manner. This will be helpful in the event the database crashes because of this missing online redo log.

Once the checkpoint has completed, you would issue the ALTER DATABASE ADD LOGFILE command to recreate the redo log group member redo02.log:

```
SQL>alter database add logfile member
'C:\ORACLE\ORADATA\ORCL\REDO02.LOG' reuse to group 2;
```

If the database happened to crash before you could add the log file, you would mount the database and then issue the `ALTER DATABASE ADD LOGFILE` command. You should then be able to open the database.

Another option is to shut down the database in a consistent manner (`SHUTDOWN`, `SHUTDOWN IMMEDIATE`, `SHUTDOWN TRANSACTIONAL`, `SHUTDOWN NORMAL`) and then copy another member of the redo log group to the location of the missing member. You can then restart the database normally.

Dealing with the Loss of an Inactive Online Redo Log Group

Loss of an inactive online redo log group is not a terribly big deal in and of itself and is quite easy to recover from. There are two different situations you will need to be prepared for. First is loss of an inactive online redo log group during database startup. Second is loss of an inactive online redo log group during database operations. Let's look at these two situations in more detail.

Dealing with the Loss of an Inactive Online Redo Log Group on Startup

First, if you start up the database and the inactive online redo log group cannot be opened, you will get the following error message:

```
ORA-00313: open failed for members of log group 2 of thread 1
ORA-00312: online log 2 thread 1: 'C:\ORACLE\ORADATA\ORCL\REDO02.LOG'
```

The response to this condition is to drop the log-file group using the `ALTER DATABASE` command, as shown here:

```
SQL> alter database drop logfile group 2;
```

You can then recreate the online redo log group using the `ALTER DATABASE ADD LOGFILE` command:

```
SQL> alter database add logfile group 2
 'c:\oracle\oradata\orcl\redo02A.log' size 50m;
SQL> alter database add logfile group 2
 'c:\oracle\oradata\orcl\redo02B.log' size 50m;
```

Dealing with the Loss of an Inactive Online Redo Log Group When the Database Is Running

If you lose an inactive online redo log group (or it becomes corrupted) while the database is running, the database will sometimes keep operating. It will sometimes skip the online redo log group that went missing and continue to operate normally. In this case, you can issue an `ALTER SYSTEM CHECKPOINT` command and then clear the log-file group with the `ALTER DATABASE CLEAR LOGFILE GROUP` command, as shown here:

```
SQL>alter system checkpoint;
SQL>alter database clear logfile group 1;
```

It may be that when you try to clear the log file you will receive an error that indicates that the log file needs to be archived:

```
SQL> alter database clear logfile group 1;
alter database clear logfile group 1
*
ERROR at line 1:
ORA-00350: log 1 of instance orcl (thread 1) needs to be archived
ORA-00312: online log 1 thread 1: '/oracle01/oradata/orcl/redo01.log'
```

Since the log file is not there, it cannot be archived. You can use the ALTER DATABASE CLEAR UNARCHIVED LOGFILE command to clear the unarchived log file and rebuild the log file in its current location, as shown here:

```
SQL> alter database clear
2 unarchived logfile '/oracle01/oradata/orcl/redo01.log';
```

You will need to back up your database in this case, since an archived redo log will have been lost.

Sometimes the database will not crash but will freeze. In this case, you will open another SQL*Plus session as a user with SYSDBA privileges and issue the ALTER SYSTEM CHECKPOINT command followed by either the ALTER DATABASE CLEAR LOGFILE or the ALTER DATABASE CLEAR UNARCHIVED LOGFILE command, depending on the type of recovery required. After issuing these commands, the database should operate as usual.

Back Up the Database after Clearing Unarchived Log Files

Sometimes the database will crash as a result of the loss of the online redo log group. In this case, you will need to follow this procedure:

1. From SQL*Plus, log in as SYS using SYSDBA privileges.

2. Mount the database using the STARTUP MOUNT command.

3. Issue the ALTER DATABASE CLEAR LOGFILE GROUP SQL command.

4. Open the database with the ALTER DATABASE OPEN command.

Dealing with the Loss of an Active but Not Current Online Redo Log Group

Loss of an ACTIVE (as shown in V$LOG column status) online redo log group requires the use of the ALTER DATABASE CLEAR UNARCHIVED LOGFILE command, as shown in the previous section.

This is because the active online redo log will not have been archived and you need to indicate to Oracle that this is okay. This command will rebuild the online redo log and allow Oracle to proceed with normal operations. You should always back up the database after this operation.

Dealing with the Loss of the Current Online Redo Log Group

Losing the current online redo log group is perhaps the worst disaster your Oracle Database could encounter. This is because there is a significant risk of loss of data in such cases. When you lose the current online redo log group, you can expect that the database will crash.

If the database has not yet shut down, you should immediately attempt to checkpoint the database using the ALTER SYSTEM CHECKPOINT command and then shut down the database afterward as soon as it is practical. The ALTER SYSTEM CHECKPOINT command forces the database to write any dirty blocks from the database buffer cache to the database data files in an urgent manner.

It may be that you can open the database without any recovery being required. This is the best-case situation. To try to restart the database do the following:

1. Issue the STARTUP MOUNT command.

2. Issue the ALTER DATABASE CLEAR UNARCHIVED LOGFILE command for the redo log group that was lost.

   Examples of this command can be seen in earlier sections of this chapter.

3. Issue the ALTER DATABASE OPEN command.

If the database opens successfully, you are in luck. If the database fails to open, you are in a bad way. You will need to perform incomplete recovery of the database as discussed in the section "Performing an Incomplete Recovery." You can see an example of recovering the database as a result of the loss of the current online redo log group in Exercise 2.1.

Recovering from the Loss of a Control File

Recovery from loss of a control file depends on the nature of the loss. There are two different situations you might encounter. You might lose one or more but not all control files. You might also lose all control files. Let's look at what to do in these cases.

Dealing with the Loss of One or More Control Files but Not All

If you have at least one control file left, recovery is quite simple. Follow these steps:

1. Shut down the database normally.

2. Copy one of the remaining control files to the location of the lost control files and give it the same name as the lost control file.

3. Restart the database.

Recovering from Loss of All Control Files

If you lose your control files, Oracle is not shy about telling you. If you are trying to start up your database and your control files are missing, you will see an error like this:

```
SQL> startup
ORACLE instance started.
Total System Global Area   171581440 bytes
Fixed Size                    1298640 bytes
Variable Size              146804528 bytes
Database Buffers            20971520 bytes
Redo Buffers                 2506752 bytes
ORA-00205: error in identifying control file, check alert log for more info
```

This error will occur on startup if any of your control files are missing. If your database is running, the loss of some of your control files will not cause it to stop operating. As a result, you can plan to shut down your database and then simply copy a surviving copy of the control file to the location of the lost control file. If the location is no longer available, you can modify the CONTROL_FILES parameter so that it points to the location of the new control file.

If you lose your control files while the database is running, it is quite likely that the database will crash in short order. There are some cases where it might stay up for a little while, but it will eventually come down on you.

Loss of all control files will require that you use a backup control file or issue the CREATE CONTROLFILE command from the SQL prompt. We discussed the creation of a backup control file in Chapter 1. We also discussed how to create a trace file with the CREATE CONTROLFILE command in it in Chapter 1. Let's look at each of these recoveries in a bit more detail.

Recovering Lost Control Files with a Backup Control File

If you have a backup control file, follow these steps to recover from the loss of all your control files:

1. Copy the backup control file to the location of each control file defined by the parameter CONTROL_FILES.
2. Modify the CONTROL_FILES parameter if required.
3. Mount the database with the STARTUP MOUNT command.
4. Recover the database using the RECOVER DATABASE USING BACKUP CONTROLFILE command.
5. At the prompt, type in **AUTO** to apply all archived redo logs.

   Recovery will end, likely with an error. This is because the final redo log sequence number you need to apply is not in an archived redo log but is in one of the online redo logs.
6. Issue the RECOVER DATABASE USING BACKUP CONTROLFILE command again. This time, when prompted for the archived redo log to apply, enter one of your online redo log names (for example, **redo01.log**).

7. Continue to attempt to apply each online redo log group until you find the correct log sequence number.

   Once the final online redo log is applied, recovery will complete automatically and without error.

8. You can now open the database using the ALTER DATABASE OPEN RESETLOGS command.

Recovering Lost Control Files Using the *CREATE CONTROLFILE* Command

In Chapter 1, we introduced the ALTER DATABASE BACKUP CONTROLFILE TO TRACE command. This created a trace file that you can use to recreate your control file. If you lose your control files, a backup control file is the easiest way to manually recover. However, if you do not have a backup control file, you have two options:

* Use the contents of the script created as a result of the ALTER DATABASE BACKUP CONTROLFILE TO TRACE command.

* Manually issue the CREATE CONTROLFILE command.

As already discussed in Chapter 1, the ALTER DATABASE BACKUP CONTROLFILE TO TRACE command creates a script that you can use to recover your control file. The script will need to be modified before it can be used.

The script contains the following sections:

* Trace-file header

* List of parameters related to archiving

* NORESETLOGS case for recreating the control file

* RESETLOGS case for recreating the control file

As you can see, the script has two different versions of the CREATE CONTROLFILE command. One is for recoveries where the online redo logs are intact. You will want to edit the script so that the correct type of recovery is done. Each version of the script also contains code to register archived redo logs, recover the database, and then open the database automatically.

Let's look at the following code, which is an example of using the NORESETLOGS case. The script is designed to do it all without any DBA interference. First, it starts the database instance. It then proceeds to issue the CREATE CONTROLFILE command. The script records some archived redo log records in the control file that will be needed for recovery. The database is then recovered and opened. Finally, the temporary tablespace tempfile is recreated. You may want to use the RMAN Catalog command to catalog all of the backup sets after this recovery, since the RMAN metadata will be missing from the control file.

```
STARTUP NOMOUNT
CREATE CONTROLFILE REUSE DATABASE "ORCL" NORESETLOGS  ARCHIVELOG
    MAXLOGFILES 16
    MAXLOGMEMBERS 3
    MAXDATAFILES 100
    MAXINSTANCES 8
    MAXLOGHISTORY 292
```

```
LOGFILE
  GROUP 1 (
    '/oracle01/oradata/orcl/redo01.log',
    '/oracle01/oradata/orcl/redo01a.log'
  ) SIZE 100M,
  GROUP 2 (
    '/oracle01/oradata/orcl/redo02.log',
    '/oracle01/oradata/orcl/redo02a.log'
  ) SIZE 50M,
  GROUP 3 (
    '/oracle01/oradata/orcl/redo03.log',
    '/oracle01/oradata/orcl/redo03a.log'
  ) SIZE 50M
-- STANDBY LOGFILE
DATAFILE
  '/oracle01/oradata/orcl/system01.dbf',
  '/oracle01/oradata/orcl/sysaux01.dbf',
  '/oracle01/oradata/orcl/undotbs01.dbf',
  '/oracle01/oradata/orcl/users01.dbf',
  '/oracle01/oradata/orcl/example01.dbf',
  '/oracle01/oradata/orcl/retention_archives_01.dbf',
  '/oracle01/oradata/orcl/my_secure_tbs_01.dbf',
  '/oracle01/oradata/orcl/my_second_secure_tbs_01.dbf'
CHARACTER SET WE8MSWIN1252
;
-- Configure RMAN configuration record 1
VARIABLE RECNO NUMBER;
EXECUTE :RECNO :=
SYS.DBMS_BACKUP_RESTORE.SETCONFIG('COMPRESSION ALGORITHM','''BZIP2''');
-- Configure RMAN configuration record 2
VARIABLE RECNO NUMBER;
EXECUTE :RECNO := SYS.DBMS_BACKUP_RESTORE.SETCONFIG('CONTROLFILE
AUTOBACKUP','ON');
-- Commands to re-create incarnation table
-- Below log names MUST be changed to existing filenames on
-- disk. Any one log file from each branch can be used to
-- re-create incarnation records.
-- ALTER DATABASE REGISTER LOGFILE
'/oracle01/fast_recovery_area/ORCL/archivelog/2013_08_16/o1_mf_1_1_%u_.arc';
-- ALTER DATABASE REGISTER LOGFILE
  '/oracle01/fast_recovery_area/ORCL/archivelog/2013_08_16/o1_mf_1_1_%u_.arc';
```

```
-- ALTER DATABASE REGISTER LOGFILE
 '/oracle01/fast_recovery_area/ORCL/archivelog/2013_08_16/o1_mf_1_1_%u_.arc';
-- Recovery is required if any of the datafiles are restored backups,
-- or if the last shutdown was not normal or immediate.
RECOVER DATABASE
-- Set Database Guard and/or Supplemental Logging
ALTER DATABASE ADD SUPPLEMENTAL LOG DATA (PRIMARY KEY) COLUMNS;
-- All logs need archiving and a log switch is needed.
ALTER SYSTEM ARCHIVE LOG ALL;
-- Database can now be opened normally.
ALTER DATABASE OPEN;
-- Commands to add tempfiles to temporary tablespaces.
-- Online tempfiles have complete space information.
-- Other tempfiles may require adjustment.
ALTER TABLESPACE TEMP ADD TEMPFILE '/oracle01/oradata/orcl/temp01.dbf'
    SIZE 182517760  REUSE AUTOEXTEND ON NEXT 655360  MAXSIZE 32767M;
```

Recovering from the Loss of the Password File

If you lose the database password file, it is simple to recover. First, if you have backed up the password file and it has not changed since the backup, you can simply restore it. If you did not have a backup of the password file, all you need to do is rerun the ORAPWD command to recreate the password file. The ORAPWD command is used to create password files. It's executed from the command line, as shown in this example:

```
[oracle@localhost dbs]$ cd $ORACLE_HOME/dbs
[oracle@localhost dbs]$ orapwd file=orapwtest entries=20 password=Robert
```

In this example, we first changed to the $ORACLE_HOME/dbs directory where password files are stored. Next, we ran the ORAPWD command to create the password file. We passed the name of the password file using the FILE= parameter. Password files always start with ORAPW followed by the name of the database (TEST in this case). The ENTRIES parameter indicates the number of SYSADM entries that are allowed for, and PASSWORD indicates the password associated with the SYS account.

Recovering from the Loss of Everything

Loss of everything might rightly be called the "full-meal deal." It's the worst possible case of data loss. If you have lost everything, you will need the following to recover your database when running in ARCHIVELOG mode:

- Oracle software
- Oracle networking–related parameter files

- Oracle Database parameter file
- Oracle Database data files
- Backup control file or `CREATE CONTROLFILE` command ready to run

The procedure to fully restore your database is as follows:

1. Create any new directories required.

2. Restore the Oracle software.

3. Restore or recreate the Oracle networking parameter files.

4. Restore the Oracle parameter file.

5. Rebuild the Oracle password file if required.

6. Restore the Oracle Database data files.

7. Start up the database in mount mode.

8. Recover the database using the procedure outlined in the section titled "Recovering from Loss of All Control Files."

Summary

As you can see, backup and recovery in Oracle can be a big deal. There are a number of different situations you will find yourself in. Sometimes these situations take some deep thinking to get out of them. Often, understanding how Oracle actually works will help guide you through the problem and find a solution.

The Oracle 12c OCP exam contains a number of recovery-related questions, so you will want to know this stuff well. You should also work through the different exercises so that you understand what to do in different situations. In this chapter, we discussed a number of recovery cases:

- NOARCHIVELOG recovery
- ARCHIVELOG recovery
- Point-in-time recoveries
- Special recovery cases

It is probably clear to you that recovery in Oracle can be quite complex. It becomes even harder when you are actually doing it under the gun, when people are breathing down your neck to get that database up.

Exam Essentials

The following topics are specifically listed as essential test items and part of the content of the Oracle Database 12*c* OCP exam.

Explain Oracle backup and recovery solutions.   Understand the different Oracle backup and recovery solutions. Understand concepts such as multiplexing control files and online redo logs. Understand various high availability and disaster recovery options that are available for you to use.

Back up and recover a NOARCHIVELOG database.   Understand how to restore and recover your database in NOARCHIVELOG mode. Understand that you have to shut down the database and that you have to restore all the data files, the control files, and the online redo logs from your backup.

The following topics are not specifically listed as essential test items or part of the content of the Oracle Database 12*c* OCP exam. However, these topics are covered in this chapter because they are key foundational concepts to understanding topics that are covered in the Oracle Database 12*c* OCP exam.

Understand the Oracle Database backup and recovery architecture.   Understand the underlying architecture that the Oracle Database uses to facilitate the backup and recovery of the physical Oracle Database.

Restore and recover your database to the point of failure in ARCHIVELOG mode.   Understand how to restore and recover your database in ARCHIVELOG mode. Understand that you can recover the entire database or just a given tablespace or data file. Understand which recoveries can be done with the database up and which require that the database be shut down.

Restore and recover your database to a different point in time.   Understand how to perform point-in-time recovery with your database. Understand how to restore the data files. Understand the types of recovery that are available (time-based, change-based, and SCN-based). Understand how to use the RECOVER DATABASE command to perform point-in-time recovery and how to open the database after recovery has been completed.

Recover your database in the event of a lost online redo log.   Understand how to recover your database if you lose an inactive or current online redo log file. Understand the benefit of using the ALTER SYSTEM CHECKPOINT command if you have lost an online redo log group and the database is still running. Understand how to use the ALTER DATABASE CLEAR command to clear unarchived redo log files and to recreate lost online redo log files. Understand the impacts of losing the current or an active online redo log file.

Recover your database in the event of a lost control file.   Understand how to recover your database if you lose one or more control files. Learn how to recover a lost control file by using a backup control file. Learn how to recover a lost control file by using the CREATE CONTROLFILE command contained in the trace file resulting from the ALTER DATABASE BACKUP CONTROLFILE TO TRACE command.

Review Questions

1. Your NOARCHIVELOG database has experienced a loss of data file users_01.dbf, which is associated with a tablespace called USERS. The database is still running. Which of the following is the most correct answer?

   A. You can take the data file offline, restore the data file from a backup, and then recover the data file using the archived redo logs. You would then bring the data file back online.

   B. You will have to shut down the database and restore the database, online redo logs, and control files that were contained in the last backup. You can then restart the database. There will be data loss.

   C. You will have to shut down the database and restore the database, online redo logs, and control files that were contained in the last backup. You can then restart the database. There will be no data loss.

   D. This failure is not recoverable. You will need to force open the database and then force a recovery.

   E. None of the above is correct.

2. As soon as you discover that you have lost an online redo log, if the database is still functioning, what should be your first action?

   A. Shut down the database.

   B. Clear the online redo log.

   C. Back up the database.

   D. Checkpoint the database.

   E. Call Oracle support.

   F. Panic.

3. You have lost all your SYSTEM tablespace data files (system_01.dbf and system_02.dbf) and the database has crashed. The database is in ARCHIVELOG mode and you have a current backup. What would be the appropriate order of operations to correct the situation?

   1. Mount the database with the STARTUP MOUNT command.

   2. Take the SYSTEM data file offline with the ALTER DATABASE command.

   3. Restore the SYSTEM_01.dbf data file from backup media with the required archived redo logs.

   4. Restore all SYSTEM tablespace–related data files from backup media.

   5. Issue the RECOVER TABLESPACE SYSTEM command.

   6. Issue the RECOVER DATAFILE SYSTEM_01.DBF command.

7. Open the database with the `ALTER DATABASE OPEN` command.

8. Open the database with the `ALTER DATABASE OPEN RESETLOGS` command.

   A. 1,3,6,7

   B. 2,4,5,8

   C. 1,2,3,6,7

   D. 4,1,5,7

   E. 2,3,6,5,7

4. You have discovered that one of three control files has been lost. What steps would you follow to recover that control file?

   1. Shut down the database.

   2. Restore a control-file copy from backup media.

   3. Use the `CREATE CONTROLFILE` command to create a new control file.

   4. Copy the backup control file into place.

   5. Create a new copy of the control file from one of the surviving control files.

   6. Recover the database using the `RECOVER DATABASE USING BACKUP CONTROLFILE` command.

   7. Start up the database.

   A. 1,2,6,7

   B. 3,6,7

   C. 1,4,6,7

   D. 1,6,7

   E. 1,5,7

5. Which files will you need to perform a full recovery of a database backed up in NOARCHIVELOG mode? (Choose all that apply.)

   A. Database data files

   B. Control files

   C. Archived redo logs

   D. Online redo logs

   E. Flashback logs

6. Which are the correct steps, in order, to deal with the loss of an online redo log if the database has not yet crashed?

   1. Issue a checkpoint.

   2. Shut down the database.

   3. Issue an `ALTER DATABASE OPEN` command to open the database.

4. STARTUP MOUNT the database.

5. Issue an ALTER DATABASE CLEAR LOGFILE command.

6. Recover all database data files.

A. 1,2,3,4

B. 2,4,5,6

C. 1,2,4,5,3

D. 2,6,4,6,3

E. 2,4,1,3

7. What methods of point-in-time recovery are available in ARCHIVELOG mode? (Choose all that apply.)

A. Change-based

B. Cancel-based

C. Time-based

D. Sequence number-based

E. Transaction number-based

8. Which files are required for a full recovery of the database in ARCHIVELOG mode? (Choose three.)

A. Database data files

B. Online redo logs

C. Archived redo logs

D. Backup control file

E. Control file from a backup

9. What methods of point-in-time recovery are available in NOARCHIVELOG mode?

A. Change-based

B. Cancel-based

C. Time-based

D. Sequence number-based

E. None of the above

10. Upon starting your ARCHIVELOG mode database, you receive the following error:

```
SQL> startup
ORACLE instance started.
Total System Global Area  171581440 bytes
Fixed Size                  1298640 bytes
```

```
Variable Size               146804528 bytes
Database Buffers             20971520 bytes
Redo Buffers                  2506752 bytes
Database mounted.
ORA-00313: open failed for members of log group 1 of thread 1
ORA-00312: online log 1 thread 1: '/oracle01/oradata/orcl/redo01.log'
ORA-00312: online log 1 thread 1: '/oracle01/oradata/orcl/redo01a.log'
```

You can choose from the following steps:

1. Restore the database data files.

2. Issue the ALTER DATABASE CLEAR UNARCHIVED LOGFILE GROUP command.

3. Issue the ALTER DATABASE OPEN command.

4. Issue the ALTER DATABASE OPEN RESETLOGS command.

5. Recover the database using point-in-time recovery.

6. Issue the STARTUP MOUNT command to mount the database.

7. Back up the database.

Which is the correct order of these steps in this case?

A. 1,6,5,4,7

B. 6,5,4

C. 6,2,3,7

D. 1,6,3

E. The database cannot be recovered.

11. A user sends you an email with the following error message:

```
create table idtable(id number)
*
ERROR at line 1:
ORA-01116: error in opening database file 4
ORA-01110: data file 4: '/oracle01/oradata/orcl/users01.dbf'
ORA-27041: unable to open file
Linux Error: 2: No such file or directory
Additional information: 3
```

You can choose from the following steps:

1. Restore the missing database data file.

2. Take the missing data file offline.

3. Shut down the database.

4. Issue the RECOVER TABLESPACE USERS command.

5. Issue the STARTUP MOUNT command to mount the database.

6. Bring the USERS tablespace online.

7. Issue the ALTER DATABASE OPEN command.

Which is the correct order of these steps in this case?

A. 2,1,4,6

B. 3,1,5,2,4,6,7

C. 3,5,4,7

D. 2,4,6

E. 5,4,7

12. You have lost all your database control files. To recover them, you are going to use the results of the ALTER DATABASE BACKUP CONTROLFILE TO TRACE command. Your data files and your online redo logs are all intact. Which of the following is true regarding your recovery?

A. You will need to open the database with the RESETLOGS command.

B. All you need to do is execute the trace file from SQL*Plus and it will perform the recovery for you.

C. You will use the RESETLOGS version of the CREATE CONTROLFILE command.

D. You will use the NORESETLOGS version of the CREATE CONTROLFILE command.

E. You will use the trace file to create a backup control file, and then you will recover the database with the RECOVER DATABASE USING BACKUP CONTROLFILE command.

13. Your developers have asked you to restore the development database, which is in NOARCHIVELOG mode, back to last Tuesday the 20th. Your last backup is from Monday the 19th. What do you do?

A. Restore the 19th's backup, restore all archived redo logs, recover the database to the 20th, and open the database.

B. Tell them that their request cannot be met with the current backup strategy.

C. Restore the 19th's backup, apply the online redo logs, and open the database.

D. Switch the database into ARCHIVELOG mode, restore the 19th's backup, restore all archived redo logs, and recover the database to the 20th.

E. Use the RECOVER DATABASE command to roll back the database from today to the 19th of the month.

14. What methods are available to recover lost control files? (Choose all that apply.)

   A. Backup control file

   B. Emergency control file

   C. The `CREATE CONTROLFILE` command

   D. The `RESTORE CONTROLFILE` SQL*Plus command

   E. No backup is required. The database will recreate the control file when it is discovered to be lost.

15. Your ARCHIVELOG-mode database has lost three data files and shut down. One is assigned to the SYSTEM tablespace and two are assigned to the USERS tablespace. You can choose from the following steps to recover your database:

   1. Restore the three database data files that were lost.

   2. Issue the `STARTUP MOUNT` command to mount the database.

   3. Issue the `ALTER DATABASE OPEN` command.

   4. Issue the `ALTER DATABASE OPEN RESETLOGS` command.

   5. Recover the database using the `RECOVER DATABASE` command.

   6. Recover the data files with the `RECOVER DATAFILE` command.

   7. Take the data files offline.

Which is the correct order of these steps in this case?

   A. 1,2,5,3

   B. 2,5,4

   C. 1,2,4,3

   D. 4,7,3,6

   E. 1,2,4,6

16. You have lost all your online redo logs. As a result, your database has crashed. You have tried to restart the database and clear the online redo log files, but when you try to open the database you get the following error:

```
SQL> startup
ORACLE instance started.
Total System Global Area  167395328 bytes
Fixed Size                  1298612 bytes
Variable Size             142610252 bytes
Database Buffers           20971520 bytes
Redo Buffers                2514944 bytes
Database mounted.
ORA-00313: open failed for members of log group 2 of thread 1
```

```
ORA-00312: online log 2 thread 1: '/oracle01/oradata/orcl/redo02a.log'
ORA-27037: unable to obtain file status
Linux Error: 2: No such file or directory
Additional information: 3
ORA-00312: online log 2 thread 1: '/oracle01/oradata/orcl/redo02.log'
ORA-27037: unable to obtain file status
Linux Error: 2: No such file or directory
Additional information: 3
SQL> alter database clear logfile group 2;
alter database clear logfile group 2
*
ERROR at line 1:
ORA-01624: log 2 needed for crash recovery of instance orcl (thread 1)
ORA-00312: online log 2 thread 1: '/oracle01/oradata/orcl/redo02.log'
ORA-00312: online log 2 thread 1: '/oracle01/oradata/orcl/redo02a.log'
```

What steps must you take to resolve the error?

1. Issue the RECOVER DATABASE REDO LOGS command.

2. Issue the STARTUP MOUNT command to mount the database.

3. Restore the last full database backup.

4. Perform a point-in-time recovery, applying all archived redo logs that are available.

5. Restore all archived redo logs generated during and after the last full database backup.

6. Open the database using the ALTER DATABASE OPEN RESETLOGS command.

7. Issue the ALTER DATABASE OPEN command.

A. 2,1,6

B. 5,2,1,6

C. 5,2,1,7

D. 2,1,7

E. 3,5,2,4,6

17. What is the SCN?

   A. The system change number, which represents a point in time relative to transactions within a given database

   B. A number that represents time. Thus, at 1300 hours, the SCN is the same on all databases

   C. The security change number, which represents the security code that is needed to access any database structure

   D. A conversion factor that converts internal database time to external clock time

   E. UTC time in the database, providing a standardized way of tracking time in Oracle

18. You have lost data file 4 from your database, which is in ARCHIVELOG mode. Which is typically the fastest way to restore your database?

   A. Restore and recover the data file.

   B. Restore and recover the tablespace.

   C. Restore and recover the database.

   D. Restore and recover the control file.

   E. Restore and recover the parameter file.

19. You are trying to recover your database in ARCHIVELOG mode. During the recovery process, you receive the following error:

```
ORA-00279: change 5033391 generated at 08/17/2013 06:37:40
needed for thread 1
ORA-00289: suggestion :
/oracle01/fast_recovery_area/ORCL/archivelog/2013_08_17
/o1_mf_1_11_%u_.arc
ORA-00280: change 5033391 for thread 1 is in sequence #11
ORA-00278: log file
'/oracle01/fast_recovery_area/ORCL/archivelog/2013_08_17
/o1_mf_1_10_4bj6wnqm_.arc' no longer needed for this recovery
Specify log: {<RET>=suggested | filename | AUTO | CANCEL}
ORA-00308: cannot open archived log
'/oracle01/fast_recovery_area/ORCL/archivelog/2013_08_17
/o1_mf_1_11_%u_.arc'
ORA-27037: unable to obtain file status
Linux Error: 2: No such file or directory
Additional information: 3
```

How do you respond to this error? (Choose two.)

A. Restore the archived redo log that is missing and attempt recovery again.

B. Recovery is complete, and you can open the database.

C. Recovery needs redo that is not available in any archived redo log. Attempt to apply an online redo log if available.

D. Recover the entire database and apply all archived redo logs again.

E. Recovery is not possible because an archived redo log has been lost.

20. During recovery, you need to know if log sequence 11 is in the online redo logs, and if so, you need to know the names of the online redo logs so you can apply them during recovery. Which view or views would you use to determine this information? (Choose all that apply.)

A. V$LOGFILE

B. V$RECOVER_LOG

C. V$RECOVER_DATABASE

D. V$LOG_RECOVER

E. V$LOG

Chapter

3

Configuring and Backing Up Oracle Databases Using RMAN

ORACLE DATABASE 12c: ADVANCED ADMINISTRATION EXAM OBJECTIVES COVERED IN THIS CHAPTER:

- ✓ Explain Oracle backup and recovery solutions
- ✓ Use the SYSBACK privilege
- ✓ Back up and recover a NOARCHIVELOG database
- ✓ Perform backup and recovery in NOARCHIVELOG mode
- ✓ Use SQL in RMAN
- ✓ Use RMAN stand-alone and job commands
- ✓ Configure and manage RMAN settings
- ✓ Configure persistent settings for RMAN
- ✓ View persistent settings
- ✓ Specify a retention policy
- ✓ Configure the Fast Recovery Area (FRA)
- ✓ Explain the Fast Recovery Area
- ✓ Use various RMAN backup types and strategies
- ✓ Create tape- and disk-based backups
- ✓ Create whole database backups
- ✓ Create consistent and inconsistent backups

✓ **Create backup sets and image copies**

✓ **Create full and incremental backups**

✓ **Use the Oracle-suggested backup strategy (incrementally updated backups)**

✓ **Use techniques to improve backups**

✓ **Create compressed backups**

✓ **Create multisection backups of very large files**

✓ **Create duplexed backup sets**

✓ **Create backups of backup sets**

✓ **Create archival backups**

✓ **Manage backups**

✓ **Configure and monitor block change tracking**

✓ **Create RMAN-encrypted backups**

✓ **Use transparent-mode encryption**

✓ **Use password-mode encryption**

✓ **Use dual-mode encryption**

✓ **Perform backup of non-database files**

✓ **Back up archived redo log files**

Backup and recovery is one of the central themes in the Oracle Database 12*c* OCP exam. In Chapter 1, "Performing Oracle User-Managed Backups," and Chapter 2, "Performing Oracle User-Managed Database Recoveries," we talked about user-managed backup and recovery in Oracle, and now we will move on to what is termed *server-managed* backups, which are managed by RMAN. RMAN is a tool designed to back up and restore Oracle databases easily. RMAN is like SQL*Plus in some ways.

First, RMAN is a client. It connects to the Oracle Database and issues a few commands to the server, and the server actually does the work (hence the term *server-based backups*). The server reports the results to RMAN and RMAN reports those results to you.

In this chapter, we will introduce you to RMAN. We will discuss the features and configuration of RMAN, including configuration of the Fast Recovery Area (FRA). We will also discuss using RMAN to back up your Oracle Database. Later in this book, we will discuss restoring and recovering your backups using RMAN.

Exam objectives are subject to change at any time without prior notice and at Oracle's sole discretion. Please visit Oracle's Training and Certification website (http://www.oracle.com/education/certification/) for the most current exam-objectives listing.

Why Use RMAN?

RMAN has many capabilities to facilitate the backup and recovery process. It comes in both web-based GUI and command-line versions. In general, RMAN performs and standardizes the backup and recovery process, which can reduce mistakes made during this process. The following are just a few of the exciting RMAN features:

- It's free with the Oracle license.
- You can perform full and incremental backups of the entire database, specific tablespaces, and data files. You can also back up control files and archive logs.
- RMAN offers persistent parameter configuration for easy backup and recovery.
- RMAN offers automated backups of control files and spfiles.
- You can validate your database backups without actually recovering your database.

- RMAN offers compression of backup images through various means.
- RMAN offers encryption of database backups.
- RMAN provides various backup reporting capabilities.
- RMAN provides scripting capabilities when you are using a recovery catalog.
- With the Media Management Library (MML) you can integrate easily with third-party tape media software.
- RMAN provides for parallel processing of backups and restores.
- With RMAN, you can create duplicate databases.
- RMAN helps you migrate data files across operating-system platforms.
- With RMAN, you can perform tablespace point-in-time recovery (TSPITR).
- RMAN allows you to recover data files that aren't backed up.
- RMAN will automatically recover tempfiles during a database recovery.

Exploring the RMAN Architecture

One of the nice things about RMAN is that it's part of Oracle. Thus, it can natively use the existing Oracle architecture. Quite a few of the limitations with manual backups are addressed in RMAN. With each release, RMAN has new features that make it even more powerful.

RMAN has a rich feature set, and with each version of Oracle, the feature set becomes even richer. Oracle Database 12*c* offers a very full-featured backup and recovery tool in the form of RMAN.

RMAN is based on a robust architecture consisting of the following main components:

- The RMAN client interface
- The database server
- The database control file
- The optional recovery catalog
- Database pfiles or spfiles
- Backup media and the Media Management Library
- Backup sets and backup set pieces
- RMAN channels
- The snapshot control file

Let's look at each component in a bit more detail:

RMAN Client Interface   The *RMAN command-line interface (RCLI)* provides access to Recovery Manager. This process spawns off-server sessions that connect to the *target database*, which is the database that will be backed up. From the RMAN client interface you will issue RMAN commands to execute RMAN backup, recovery, and restore operations.

Previous versions of this text (and OCP exams) contained significant coverage of Oracle Enterprise Manager (OEM). The Oracle Database 12c OCP exam contains no coverage specific to OEM and much more coverage on user-based backup and recovery. As a result, there is little coverage of OEM within this text.

Database Server   The *database server* is the principal mechanism used to back up the database. Built into the core of the Oracle kernel code are stored packages used by RMAN to back up, restore, and recover the database. RMAN cannot execute backup, restore, or recover operations without having first attached to the database server. Depending on the operation, the database will need to be opened in nomount, mount, or open mode.

Control File   The *database control file* is used to store RMAN-related information for each database. The control file is the principal storage mechanism for all RMAN-related records. All records with respect to database backups, archive-log backups, and control-file backups are stored in the control file.

Control files have limitations with respect to how many RMAN records they can hold, and as a result, certain retention requirements may call for the use of a recovery catalog to augment a control file. RMAN provides an automated means of backing up the control file and restoring it when a control file is not readily available. This method is called a *control-file autobackup*.

Recovery Catalog   The *recovery catalog* is an optional component that stores RMAN-related information inside an Oracle Database. This is similar to the RMAN repository stored in the control file, but the recovery catalog provides some additional features and longer-term storage of RMAN records. The recovery catalog is a special schema that contains backup-related information in a set of tables. During normal database operations, RMAN will synchronize the database control file with the recovery catalog, ensuring that the recovery-catalog schema is in synchronization with the database control file.

Database Pfile or Spfile   You should already be familiar with the *database parameter file (pfile)* and the *server parameter file (spfile)*. These files are critical to RMAN operations because they contain parameters that impact RMAN operations. RMAN can be used to back up and recover an spfile using an option called *autobackup*. Pfiles cannot be backed up with RMAN.

Backup Media and the Media Management Library   Obviously, if RMAN is going to back up your database, it needs to back it up somewhere. RMAN, out of the box, allows you to back up your database to disk. This can be the local disk, or a network-attached disk (in other words, NFS) can be used. RMAN also offers the Media Management Library. The MML is an API set that media vendors (for example, tape-drive vendors) can write to and that allows RMAN to communicate directly with their products.

Backup Sets and Backup Set Pieces   Backup sets are logical entities that consist of one or more backup set pieces. Backup set pieces are physical files that actually store the RMAN backup data.

RMAN Channels   *Channels* are used in RMAN to indicate the device to back up to. They are also used to partition a backup operation, essentially parallelizing the operation. For example, if you had two tape units, you could create two different RMAN channels and stream your backup to the two different tape devices in parallel. This can reduce backup and recovery times significantly.

RMAN offers *automated channel failover* for both backup and recovery operations. With automated channel failover, if a channel in a multichannel backup fails, the other channels will continue to back up the remainder of the database. This can be helpful when, for example, a tape device fails. In addition, Oracle will attempt to back up the data that was supposed to be backed up on the failed channel across the remaining channels.

Snapshot Control File   When RMAN does its business, it bases its knowledge of the database on information in the database control file. That's fine, but if the control file changes during an RMAN operation, what is RMAN to do—use the old information or the new information? The answer to this dilemma is the snapshot control file.

When RMAN performs any operation that requires a consistent view of the control file (such as a backup), it will first create a copy of the control file. This copy is called the *snapshot control file*. The snapshot control file will be used for the duration of that operation and will be overwritten by any subsequent operation. Even related operations (say, during a backup database plus archive-log operation that does an archive log backup, a database backup, and then another archive log backup) will use newly created snapshot control files, one for each operation.

Getting Started with RMAN

Starting RMAN is very easy to do. It has a simple command line interface (as well as an interface through Oracle Cloud Control 12c). In this chapter we will discuss starting RMAN, creating and connecting to an account with the SYSBACKUP privilege. Finally we will look at the command line parameters that you can use with RMAN.

Starting the RMAN Interface

Connecting to the RMAN client is quite simple. RMAN is a command-line tool, so you would want to open a command-line window for your operating system. Once you have done that you will set your ORACLE_HOME environment to the database that you want to connect to. Now you can start RMAN and connect to the target database (or the database that you want to back up and recover). Here is an example of connecting to a database with the RMAN client:

```
C:\oracle\admin\ORCL\wallet>set oracle_sid=orcl
C:\oracle\admin\ORCL\wallet>rman target=/
```

```
Recovery Manager: Release 12.1.0.1.0 -
Production on Thu Feb 20 13:40:41 2014
Copyright (c) 1982, 2013, Oracle and/or its affiliates.
All rights reserved.
connected to target database: ORCL (DBID=1190537904)
```

Sometimes you may need to connect to your target database using Oracle Net connection strings. If you are using a recovery catalog or an auxiliary database, you will normally connect to those using Oracle Net connection strings, as shown in these examples:

```
C:\oracle\admin\ORCL\wallet>rman target=sys/robert@orcl
C:\oracle\admin\ORCL\wallet>rman target=sys/robert@orcl
catalog=rcat_user/robert@rcat
```

The SYSBACKUP Privilege

The Oracle Database has long had special administrative privileges that can be assigned directly to user accounts, such as the SYSDBA privilege. These administrative privileges are different from role-based privileges (such as the DBA role) as they are actually part of the Oracle Kernel, and information on who is granted these privileges is stored in the database password file. This also means that for a database restore, if the password file is not present, you must create one before the restore can begin.

The principle administrative privileges are as follows:

SYSDBA   A very powerful administration privilege that allows almost any database operation. Granting of this privilege should be tightly controlled.

SYSOPER   This privilege provides the DBA with the ability to perform normal administrative tasks such as opening and closing a database, but it does not allow the DBA to look at user data. Therefore, it is more restrictive.

SYSBACKUP   This privilege provides the DBA with the ability to perform RMAN backups of the database. This privilege also provides the ability to perform command line backups of the database.

SYSDG   This privilege is related to Oracle Data Guard administration.

SYSKM   This privilege is related to Oracle Transparent Encryption key management.

On Oracle Database 12*c*, a new privilege called the SYSBACKUP privilege has been introduced. This privilege is designed to provide a more granular approach to granting privileges in the Oracle database, while easing the administrative burden of granting those privileges.

The SYSBACKUP privilege is quite powerful, so it should not be granted without consideration. The Oracle Database Security Guide 12*c* Release 1 (E17607-25) provides a complete list of privileges that are granted with the use of the SYSBACKUP privilege.

The SYSBACKUP privilege is granted by using the grant command as seen in this example:

```
SQL> create user backup identified by backup;
User created.
```

```
SQL> grant sysbackup to backup;
Grant succeeded.
```

The user that is granting the SYSBACKUP privilege must have the ability to use the GRANT SQL command,

When a database is created, a SYSBACKUP account is created with the SYSBACKUP privilege granted to it. The account is locked when it is created. Thus, to use the SYSBACKUP account you would need to unlock it using the ALTER SYSTEM command and then you should change the password using the ALTER SYSTEM command.

Don't Use Default Accounts

It is a best practice to never use default accounts. Never use the SYS account, for example, unless Oracle tells you to. Never use accounts like SYSBACKUP because they are commonly known default account names, and thus subject to hacking attempts. You cannot drop the SYSBACKUP account, so you will want to make sure that you keep it locked at all times.

When you connect to the database using an account that has the SYSBACKUP privilege, you will actually be logged into the database SYS schema as the SYSBACKUP session user. This can be seen via a query to SYS_CONTEXT as seen here:

```
SQL> select sys_context('USERENV', 'CURRENT_SCHEMA') from dual;
sys_context('USERENV','CURRENT_SCHEMA')
---------------------------------------------------------------
SYS
SQL> select sys_context('USERENV', 'SESSION_USER') from dual;
SYS_CONTEXT('USERENV','SESSION_USER')
---------------------------------------------------------------
SYSBACKUP
```

When you use RMAN to connect to an account with SYSBACKUP privileges, you don't need to do anything special from the command line to indicate that you want to use the SYSBACKUP privileges. So, connecting to an account called BACKUP would be as easy as this:

```
C:\Users\Robert>rman target backup/backup
Recovery Manager: Release 12.1.0.1.0 - Production on Sun Jun 1 14:40:31 2014
Copyright (c) 1982, 2013, Oracle and/or its affiliates.  All rights reserved.
connected to target database: ORCL12C (DBID=670264325)
```

The RMAN Command Line

The RMAN command line contains a number of different command-line parameters. You will see many of these in use throughout these next few chapters. Table 3.1 provides an overview of the most commonly used command-line parameters you might use.

 **Real World Scenario**

Putting Files in *ORACLE_HOME* Is Not a Best Practice

You might have noticed that RMAN puts the snapshot control file in an ORACLE_HOME location by default. This is not unusual; Oracle does this for other types of files by default (for example, the FRA defaults to ORACLE_HOME).

In the real world, defaults like this are never acceptable, and we never allow ORACLE_HOME to be the destination for any type of file other than those associated with the Oracle install and certain configuration files (thus its size is fairly static). This is because you do not want the disk space in ORACLE_HOME to unexpectedly become exhausted because Oracle Databases are writing files into it. This becomes even more important as you add more databases to your server and those databases are using the same ORACLE_HOME concurrently. Allowing those databases to write to ORACLE_HOME can cause problems for all databases on the server.

RMAN snapshot control files, files, and directories associated with the Automatic Diagnostic Repository (ADR), database data files, and most other database-related files should be created in directories specific to each database other than ORACLE_HOME. (See Chapter 10, "Managing Database Resources," for more on ADR.)

The real-world solution generally involves the creation of different mount points for database-specific data. These mount points might be shared among different databases, or there might be a unique mount point for each database (or perhaps several mount points for one or more databases). For example, if your database is ORCL, you might have the following mount points/directories created:

- /oracle01/oracle/product/12.1.0/db_1: ORACLE_HOME
- /oracle02/oracle/oradata/orcl (for Oracle Database data files)
- /oracle03/oracle/oradata/orcl (for Oracle Database data files)
- /oracle04/oracle/diag (for the ADR)

For more information, you may want to review Oracle's OFA recommendations. OFA is outside the scope of the OCP exam and this book, but it provides some guidance from Oracle on directory naming and placement for Oracle-related files.

TABLE 3.1   RMAN Command-Line Parameters

Parameter Name	Description
TARGET	Connection string for the target database
CATALOG	Connection string for the recovery catalog database
NOCATALOG	Indicates no recovery catalog is to be used; default
CMDFILE	Name of command file to run
LOG	Name of log file to log RMAN output
TRACE	Name of file for debugging messages
APPEND	Append to log file rather than overwrite
AUXILIARY	The connection string for the auxiliary database

The RMAN Command Prompt

Once you have logged into RMAN, you will be presented the RMAN command prompt that looks like this:

```
RMAN>
```

It is from this command line that we will execute almost all of our RMAN-related operations. Throughout the next several chapters of this book, we will introduce you to many of the RMAN commands that you will call from this prompt.

Calling SQL from the RMAN Command Prompt

One of the handy things that you can do from the RMAN command prompt is to call SQL commands. In Oracle database versions before Oracle Database 12c, you would have to issue an RMAN command called SQL, and then include the SQL command you wanted executed in single quotes. The major drawback to this method of running SQL commands is that you could not see the actual output of the SQL command you were running. Thus, if the command failed, you might not actually know it failed or why, as shown in this example:

```
RMAN> sql 'select * from v$database';
using target database control file instead of recovery catalog
sql statement: select * from v$database
```

Helpful, isn't it?

Oracle Database 12*c* has changed how SQL statements are run (though the old SQL command is still there for backward compatibility). Now you can just run the SQL command from the RMAN command line unaltered, and see the results. Here is an example:

```
RMAN> select name from v$database;
NAME
---------------

ORCL12C
```

Now, that is much more helpful. You can issue pretty much any SQL, DML, or DDL command from the RMAN prompt now. Many SQL commands are supported from the RMAN prompt, but there are some that are not supported. More information on what SQL commands can be used is found in the Oracle Backup and Recovery Reference 12*c* Release 1 (E17631-15) book.

By default, the SQL command will be executed on the target database. You can also execute SQL commands on the recovery catalog database or through a specific assigned channel. In these cases, you need to prefix the command with the RMAN SQL command and then use the catalog or channel_id to indicate where the SQL statement should be executed. Note that you don't need to use single quotes as was required in earlier versions of the Oracle Database.

For example, this executes the SQL command on the catalog database.

```
RMAN> select catalog name from v$database;
NAME
---------------

OCAT
```

You can now also execute anonymous PL/SQL blocks from the RMAN command line parameter. PL/SQL blocks from RMAN do not allow bind variables and no results are returned.

Configuring RMAN

RMAN will work out of the box without any configuration. Unfortunately, this is generally not a good idea. RMAN tends to throw things into ORACLE_HOME if you have not configured the database and RMAN correctly. In this section, we will address configuring RMAN correctly.

In the following sections, we will introduce you to the Fast Recovery Area (FRA) in RMAN. We will then address RMAN persistent configuration settings to allow for streamlined backups followed by using nonpersistent settings when required. Finally, we will cover configuring RMAN for its first use.

The Fast Recovery Area

The Oracle *Fast Recovery Area* was introduced in Oracle Database 10g as the central repository for all files related to Oracle backup and recovery. In this section, we will discuss the Fast Recovery Area. First, we will provide a quick overview of what the FRA is generally used for. Then you'll learn about configuring the FRA for your Oracle Database.

Introducing the FRA

The FRA is the principal store for all Oracle Database backup and recovery–related files. The FRA can be stored on disk or within an ASM instance. It cannot be stored on tape, but files backed up in the FRA can be backed up to tape via the RMAN BACKUP RECOVERY AREA command.

The FRA stores the following types of Oracle Database files:

Backup Set Pieces   Files related to RMAN backups

Archive Log Backups   Files related to backups of online redo logs

Database Archive Logs   Archived redo logs that are not backed-up archived redo logs

Control-File Autobackups   Backups of the control file made by RMAN

Image Copies   Backup of data files made by RMAN that are exact copies of the data files of the database

Database Online Redo Logs   Online redo logs of the Oracle Database

Database Control Files   Control files of the Oracle Database

Flashback Logs   Flashback logs of the database

The FRA supports RMAN's backup and retention policies by automatically removing files when they are no longer needed and when FRA space is required (obsolete RMAN backups to non-FRA locations will not be removed by RMAN automatically).

Configuring the FRA

Configuring the FRA is easy. First, you create the base directory of the FRA from the OS, and then you set the following parameters in any database that will use the FRA:

- DB_RECOVERY_FILE_DEST
- DB_RECOVERY_FILE_DEST_SIZE

The DB_RECOVERY_FILE_DEST parameter defines the FRA base directory location. This is the only directory you will need to create when configuring the FRA. You will need to make sure that this directory is owned by the owner of the Oracle executable so that Oracle can create other subdirectories beneath it.

The DB_RECOVERY_FILE_DEST_SIZE parameter defines the total amount of space this database instance is allowed to consume in the FRA. This is a logical limit, which can be greater than or less than the actual physical limit of space on that device. For example, you may have a file system with 500GB of space available on it. However, you may want to indicate that your database can consume only up to 100GB of space within the FRA while assigning the FRA to the 500GB file system.

You use the ALTER SYSTEM command to configure the FRA. Note that DB_RECOVERY_FILE_DEST is not dynamic, while DB_RECOVERY_FILE_DEST_SIZE is dynamic. To configure the FRA, do the following:

1. Create the base FRA directory:

```
/u01>mkdir /oracle01/fra
```

2. Log into SQL*Plus:

```
C:\oracle\orabackup\orcl>sqlplus sys as sysdba
C:\Users\Robert>sqlplus / as sysdba
SQL*Plus: Release 12.1.0.1.0 Production on Thu Feb 20 13:52:34 2014
Copyright (c) 1982, 2013, Oracle.  All rights reserved.
Connected to:
Oracle Database 12c Enterprise Edition Release 12.1.0.1.0 -
64bit Production
With the Partitioning, OLAP, Advanced Analytics and Real Application Testing
options
SQL>
```

3. Use the ALTER SYSTEM command to set the parameter DB_RECOVERY_FILE_DEST to /oracle01/fra and DB_RECOVERY_FILE_DEST_SIZE to 2GB.

```
sql>alter system set db_recovery_file_dest_size=2GB scope=both;
sql>alter system set db_recovery_file_dest='/oracle01/fra' scope=spfile;
```

4. Shut down and restart the database. Once the database has been restarted, the FRA will become operational.

```
SQL> shutdown immediate
Database closed.
Database dismounted.
ORACLE instance shut down.
SQL> startup
ORACLE instance started.
Total System Global Area  397557760 bytes
Fixed Size                  1333452 bytes
Variable Size             268437300 bytes
Database Buffers          121634816 bytes
Redo Buffers                6152192 bytes
Database mounted.
Database opened.
```

Managing the FRA

Management of the FRA is done principally by Oracle based on backup retention settings for RMAN (see the section "Retention Policies" later in this chapter). Thus, as backups become obsolete and as FRA space is exhausted by an instance, Oracle will remove those obsolete backups automatically. As a result, over time FRA space tends to reach equilibrium, assuming that the database data files do not grow at a great rate.

Real World Scenario

Really Using the FRA

In the real world, it's hard to get things right the first time. Using the FRA is no exception. One of us had a client that had a few problems when they first switched to using the FRA. The databases were not set up correctly, so the FRA would fill up.

Over time, the FRA became more stable as we understood the load profile and its relationship to the creation of archived redo logs and backups. We eventually found the sweet spot with respect to how much disk space we needed to allocate to the FRA. This is actually a good thing because it forced the client to realize that understanding the disk-usage profile of their databases was important.

Monitoring of the FRA is another real-world issue to be aware of. Many companies that are using the FRA are investing some time in scripts to monitor FRA disk-space usage. OEM can be used for this too.

The FRA does require some care and feeding by the DBA, however, particularly at first. Sometimes it's hard to properly estimate the correct setting for the DB_RECOVERY_FILE_DEST_SIZE and you will find the FRA filling up. Archived redo logs are stored in the FRA, so if the FRA fills up, archived redo logs can no longer be written.

If this occurs, Oracle will first try to free space in the FRA by removing obsolete backups. If Oracle cannot free up enough space, then eventually the inability to archive will cause the database to freeze until the out-of-space condition can be rectified. In this case, you can free up space by changing DB_RECOVERY_FILE_DEST_SIZE to a higher value. This parameter is dynamic, so the change can be made immediately.

You can use the V$DB_RECOVERY_FILE_DEST view to determine the state of the FRA. In the following example, we find that the FRA is sized to 2GB and that we have used 251MB in total. We also see that 41MB of that space is reclaimable. In short, this FRA looks pretty good at this point.

```
SQL> select name, space_limit, space_used, space_reclaimable
2 from v$recovery_file_dest;
```

NAME	SPACE_LIMIT	SPACE_USED	SPACE_RECLAIMABLE
c:\oracle\fast_recovery_area	2,147,483,648	251,173,376	41,127,424

> If you manually remove files from the FRA, you will have to let Oracle know that you have done so. By default, Oracle will not detect that the files have been removed. Oracle can detect the file removals by using the RMAN CROSSCHECK and DELETE EXPIRED commands. See Chapter 7, "Performing Oracle Advanced Recovery," for more information on using these commands.

RMAN Persistent Configuration Settings

When RMAN first came out in Oracle version 8.0, you had to manually indicate in each backup where the backup destination was to be, any limits related to the backup (such as the maximum size of backup set pieces), and so on. This required a lot of work and made RMAN a bit archaic-looking and difficult to use.

Oracle Database version 9i introduced the concept of persistent configuration in RMAN. *RMAN persistent configuration settings* are settings that are configured through the RMAN interface, stored in the control file, and automatically used during each backup unless they are overridden.

Oracle Database 12c provides for a number of persistent settings, including the following:

- Backup (database and archive log) retention criteria
- Backup optimization
- Default channel/device configuration
- Control-file autobackup configuration
- Data file and archive log backup-copy configuration
- Default encryption settings
- Default compression settings
- Default location for the snapshot control file

You can see the current settings for all persistent parameters in RMAN by using the RMAN SHOW ALL command, as shown here:

```
RMAN> show all;
using target database control file instead of recovery catalog
RMAN configuration parameters for database with db_unique_name ORCL are:
CONFIGURE RETENTION POLICY TO REDUNDANCY 1; # default
CONFIGURE BACK
UP OPTIMIZATION OFF; # default
CONFIGURE DEFAULT DEVICE TYPE TO DISK; # default
```

```
CONFIGURE CONTROLFILE AUTOBACKUP OFF; # default
CONFIGURE CONTROLFILE AUTOBACKUP FORMAT FOR DEVICE TYPE DISK TO '%F'; #default
CONFIGURE DEVICE TYPE DISK PARALLELISM 1 BACKUP TYPE TO BACKUP SET; # default
CONFIGURE DATAFILE BACKUP COPIES FOR DEVICE TYPE DISK TO 1; # default
CONFIGURE ARCHIVELOG BACKUP COPIES FOR DEVICE TYPE DISK TO 1; # default
CONFIGURE CHANNEL DEVICE TYPE DISK MAXPIECESIZE 100 M;
CONFIGURE MAXSETSIZE TO UNLIMITED; # default
CONFIGURE ENCRYPTION FOR DATABASE OFF; # default
CONFIGURE ENCRYPTION ALGORITHM 'AES128'; # default
CONFIGURE COMPRESSION ALGORITHM 'BASIC'; # default
CONFIGURE COMPRESSION ALGORITHM 'BASIC' AS OF RELEASE 'DEFAULT' OPTIMIZE FOR
LOAD TRUE ; # defaultCONFIGURE RMAN OUTPUT TO KEEP FOR 7 DAYS; # default]

CONFIGURE ARCHIVELOG DELETION POLICY TO NONE; # default
CONFIGURE SNAPSHOT CONTROLFILE NAME TO
 'C:\ORACLE\PRODUCT\11.1.0\DB_1\DATABASE\SNCFORCL.ORA'; # default
```

You can also look at an individual setting by using the SHOW command followed by the setting you are interested in. In this example, we are interested in the retention policy:

```
RMAN> show retention policy;
RMAN configuration parameters for database with db_unique_name ORCL are:
CONFIGURE RETENTION POLICY TO REDUNDANCY 1; # default
```

You can clear configuration settings and reset them to the defaults by using the CONFIGURE CLEAR command, as shown in this example:

```
RMAN>configure device type disk clear;
```

Unique RMAN Configuration Settings

Sometimes you need to do something different. Perhaps you have configured your default channels to go to tape but you want a particular backup to go to disk one time. You can configure unique one-time-only settings in RMAN through the use of a combination of the SET command, a *run block*, and individual keywords available in specific commands. Here is an example of using a run block to override channel defaults. We also use the ALLOCATE CHANNEL command to manually allocate channels. All of these commands are described in more detail later in this chapter:

```
run {
allocate channel c1 device type disk format 'c:\oracle\oraback1\orcl\%U';
allocate channel c2 device type disk format 'c:\oracle\oraback2\orcl\%U';
backup database plus archivelog;
};
```

You can also use options within the backup command to override default settings. For example, by default, RMAN will write backups to the FRA, so the backup command (which we will discuss later in this chapter) is as simple as BACKUP DATABASE PLUS ARCHIVELOG. If you want to write to a directory other than the FRA for a single backup, you would include the FORMAT keyword to override the default setting, as in this example:

```
backup database format 'c:\oracle\backup\backup\%U.bak' plus archivelog
format 'c:\oracle\backup\arch\%U.bak';
```

The RMAN Backup and Recovery Manuals

Oracle provides some great sources of information within the Oracle documentation set. We strongly recommend you acquaint yourself with the Oracle documentation and especially the Oracle RMAN documentation. The place to go for the online Oracle documentation is http://tahiti.oracle.com. For RMAN backup and recovery, look at the following books while you are preparing for your OCP exam:

- *Backup and Recovery Reference* - Part Number E17631-14

- *Backup and Recovery Users Guide* - Part Number E17630-14

And finally, if we may pat our own backs a little bit, a great book on getting to know RMAN is *Oracle Database 11g RMAN Backup & Recovery* by Robert G. Freeman and Matthew Hart (Oracle Press/McGraw-Hill, 2007). It's a comprehensive guide to all things RMAN. The Oracle Database 12*c* version should be available soon.

Preparing RMAN for Use

Before you use RMAN, you will want to customize it to use your preferences. This makes the backup process easy and repeatable with a minimum of effort. In this section, we will discuss a number of configurable features of RMAN:

- The CONTROL_FILE_RECORD_KEEP_TIME parameter
- Backup retention policies
- Backup compression
- Backup encryption
- Specific channel configurations
- Control-file autobackups
- Backup optimization
- Setting the location of the snapshot control file

    Let's look at each of these in some more detail.

Setting the *CONTROL_FILE_RECORD_KEEP_TIME* Parameter

When using RMAN without a recovery catalog (which we discuss in Chapter 5, "Recovering Databases with RMAN"), you will need to make sure that you have set the CONTROL_FILE_ RECORD_KEEP_TIME parameter correctly. This parameter is used to determine how long RMAN-related control-file records are maintained in the control file. Make sure this parameter is set high enough so that it will not interfere with your retention-policy requirements (see the next section for more on retention policies).

You can set the CONTROL_FILE_RECORD_KEEP_TIME (defined in days) parameter using the ALTER SYSTEM command, as shown here:

```
-- Set control_file_record_keep_time to 14 days.
SQL> alter system set control_file_record_keep_time=14
```

This is a dynamic parameter; therefore, you can change it without having to shut down the database.

Setting Retention Policies

RMAN *retention policies* are used to manage how long Oracle will maintain backups. When you're using the FRA, retention policies are used for automated cleanup of unneeded backup sets, which eliminates the need to manually manage space usage. When you're not using the FRA, retention policies can be used to manually manage space usage. In the following sections, you'll learn about the two different kinds of retention policies and how to configure them.

Types of Retention Policies

These are the different types of retention policies that you can set in RMAN:

▪ None

▪ Redundancy (the default)

▪ Recovery window

Let's look at the redundancy and recovery window retention criteria in a bit more detail. Then we will cover how to override the retention criteria with the KEEP operand.

REDUNDANCY RETENTION POLICY

The redundancy retention policy ensures that there will be a certain number of backups available for recovery. Once a backup is no longer needed, Oracle will mark it as obsolete, making it eligible for removal. For example, if the retention criterion is set to redundancy 2, then the following happens as you back up your database:

▪ Backup 1 occurs; when successful, it is considered current.

▪ Backup 2 occurs. Backups 1 and 2 are considered current.

▪ Backup 3 occurs. Backup 1 is marked as obsolete and backups 2 and 3 are considered current.

The default retention setting in RMAN is a redundancy retention policy of one copy.

If an FRA is configured, the backup will be removed when space is needed. If an FRA is not used, you will need to use the RMAN command DELETE OBSOLETE (discussed in Chapter 8, "Understanding Flashback Technology") to remove the backup metadata and physical files.

RECOVERY WINDOW RETENTION POLICY

The recovery retention policy provides the ability to define a recovery window to be applied to your backups in a period of days. For example, if you want to be sure you can restore your database to where it was 14 days ago, you would establish a recovery retention policy of 14 days and earlier. Note that this setting does not impact the lifetime of a specific backup based on when the backup occurred but rather ensures that all backups that are retained can be restored based on the retention policy. This means that backups taken 15, 16, or 30 days ago may remain valid backups, as demonstrated here and in Figure 3.1:

FIGURE 3.1   Recovery-window retention-policy example: 14 days

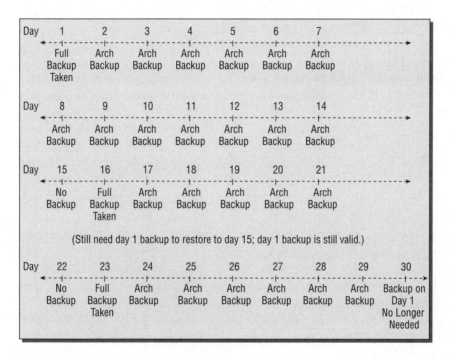

- Your database retention policy is 14 days.

- You perform a full database backup 1 on day 1; it is of course valid.

- Archive log backups are taken on days 1 through 14. Backup 1 is now 15 days old. It remains valid because it is needed to restore the database to days 0 through 14.

▪ Another full database backup 2 is taken on day 16. Database backup 1 is still valid. Why? Because you need database backup #1 to restore the database to day 10, or day 9, since database backup 2 is valid for only day 16 and beyond.

▪ Archive log backups are taken on days 17 through 29. Day 29 would be the 14th day since backup 2 was taken.

▪ On day 29, backup 1 and all the associated archived redo logs are finally eligible for removal.

When the backup is marked obsolete, it is eligible for removal. If it exists in the FRA, then Oracle will remove it automatically (usually when more space is required). If it is not in the FRA, you can use the LIST OBSOLETE command to list those backups subject to removal based on the retention policy and then use the DELETE OBSOLETE command to remove those backups. Here is an example:

```
RMAN> report obsolete;
RMAN retention policy will be applied to the command
RMAN retention policy is set to redundancy 2
Report of obsolete backups and copies
Type                      Key   Completion Time  Filename/Handle
-------------------       ----- ---------------  --------------------
Backup Set                19    05-SEP-
   Backup Piece           36    05-SEP-14        C:\ORACLE\BACKUP\0MJPS3LL_3_1.ORCL
Backup Set                19    05-SEP-14
   Backup Piece           35    05-SEP-14        C:\ORACLE\BACKUP\0MJPS3LL_2_1.ORCL
Backup Set                19    05-SEP-14
   Backup Piece           34    05-SEP-14        C:\ORACLE\BACKUP\0MJPS3LL_1_1.ORCL
Backup Set                20    05-SEP-14
   Backup Piece           37    05-SEP-14        C:\ORACLE\BACKUP\0NJPS3VG_1_1.ORCL
Backup Set                21    05-SEP-14
   Backup Piece           38    05-SEP-14        C:\ORACLE\BACKUP\0OJPS402_1_1.ORCL
Backup Set                22    07-SEP-14
   Backup Piece           39    07-SEP-14        C:\ORACLE\FAST_RECOVERY_AREA\ORCL
\BACKUP SET\2013_09_07\O1_MF_ANNNN_TAG20080907T170612_4D8QMNYR_.BKP
RMAN> delete noprompt obsolete;
RMAN retention policy will be applied to the command
RMAN retention policy is set to redundancy 2
using channel ORA_DISK_1
Deleting the following obsolete backups and copies:
Type                      Key   Completion Time  Filename/Handle
-------------------       ----- ---------------  --------------------
Backup Set                19    05-SEP-14
   Backup Piece           36    05-SEP-14        C:\ORACLE\BACKUP\0MJPS3LL_3_1.ORCL
Backup Set                19    05-SEP-14
   Backup Piece           35    05-SEP-14        C:\ORACLE\BACKUP\0MJPS3LL_2_1.ORCL
```

```
Backup Set              19      05-SEP-14
    Backup Piece        34      05-SEP-14           C:\ORACLE\BACKUP\0MJPS3LL_1_1.ORCL
Backup Set              20      05-SEP-14
    Backup Piece        37      05-SEP-14           C:\ORACLE\BACKUP\0NJPS3VG_1_1.ORCL
Backup Set              21      05-SEP-14
    Backup Piece        38      05-SEP-14           C:\ORACLE\BACKUP\0OJPS402_1_1.ORCL
Backup Set              22      07-SEP-14
    Backup Piece        39      07-SEP-14           C:\ORACLE\FAST_RECOVERY_AREA\ORCL
\BACKUP SET\2013_09_07\O1_MF_ANNNN_TAG20080907T170612_4D8QMNYR_.BKP
deleted backup piece
backup piece handle=C:\ORACLE\BACKUP\0MJPS3LL_3_1.ORCL RECID=36
STAMP=664670185
deleted backup piece
backup piece handle=C:\ORACLE\BACKUP\0MJPS3LL_2_1.ORCL RECID=35
STAMP=664670069
deleted backup piece
backup piece handle=C:\ORACLE\BACKUP\0MJPS3LL_1_1.ORCL RECID=34
STAMP=664669886
deleted backup piece
backup piece handle=C:\ORACLE\BACKUP\0NJPS3VG_1_1.ORCL RECID=37
STAMP=664670208
deleted backup piece
backup piece handle=C:\ORACLE\BACKUP\0OJPS402_1_1.ORCL RECID=38
STAMP=664670216
deleted backup piece
backup piece handle=C:\ORACLE\FAST_RECOVERY_AREA\ORCL
\BACKUP SET\2013_09_07\O1_MF_ANNNN_TAG20080907T170612_4D8QMNYR_.BKP RECID=39
STAMP=664823188
Deleted 6 objects
```

USING THE *KEEP* OPTION

If you have a defined retention policy, you may well want to override it for specific backups. Perhaps you have a policy that says at the end of the year you will make a backup of the database and keep it forever, or perhaps you have a "gold" copy backup that you want to keep for a longer period of time than the default retention policy allows. The KEEP option provides the ability to override the default retention policy. You can define a different retention policy for the specific backup (for example, remove it in 180 days), or you can choose to keep the backup until you decide to obsolete it manually with the UNKEEP command.

For example, if you wanted to create a backup with a retention criterion of 365 days, you would issue the following command:

```
RMAN> backup database plus archivelog delete input
keep until time 'sysdate + 364';
```

Using the KEEP FOREVER option, you could keep the backup indefinitely, as shown here:

```
RMAN> backup database plus archivelog tag=gold_copy
delete input keep forever;
```

A couple of notes about the last two examples: If you are using the FRA, then these examples will fail. This is because you cannot use the KEEP option when storing backup files in the FRA. The FRA has its own retention criteria defined. If you want to use the KEEP option of the BACKUP command you will need to send the backup to a non-FRA location. To do this you would allocate a channel during the backup. Here is an example of what the command would look like:

```
RMAN> backup database plus archivelog delete input format 'c:\backup\%U'keep
until time 'sysdate + 364';
```

Note that the use of the KEEP option does not require that you back up archived redo logs at the same time. Issuing the KEEP command will cause RMAN to back up the archived redo logs needed to restore the backup you are indicating you want to keep. So you could avoid the PLUS ARCHIVELOG option if you wanted, as shown here:

```
RMAN> backup database format 'c:\backup\%U'
keep until time "sysdate+300" tag='DavidW_HeberA_BillJ__DanD';
```

> The KEEP FOREVER option requires that you use a recovery catalog. The KEEP UNTIL TIME option does not require the use of a recovery catalog.

You can use the CHANGE command to subsequently decide to keep a backup or to change the setting on a backup so that the status of the backup is no longer set to keep. For example, you can take a backup with a tag of GOLD_BACKUP that was backed up with the KEEP command and start to enforce the retention criteria on that backup by using the CHANGE NOKEEP command, as shown here:

```
RMAN>backup database plus archivelog tag=gold_copy delete input format
'c:\oracle\backup\%U' keep until time "sysdate+300";
RMAN>change Backup Set tag gold_copy nokeep;
```

> You cannot create backups on which you've used the KEEP option in the FRA. If you want to create backups that have nonstandard retention criteria, you will have to use a non-FRA location to create them. This often requires the use of the FORMAT parameter, as shown in this example:
>
> ```
> backup database format 'c:\oracle\backup\%U' keep until time
> "sysdate+300" ;
> ```

Configuring Retention Policies

Retention policies are configured in RMAN using the `CONFIGURE` command. When configuring a redundancy configuration policy, you will use the `CONFIGURE` command with the `RETENTION POLICY TO REDUNDANCY` keywords, as shown here:

```
RMAN> configure retention policy to redundancy 1 ;
```

To configure a recovery-window retention policy, you use the `CONFIGURE` command with the `RETENTION POLICY TO RECOVERY WINDOW OF DAYS` keywords, as shown here:

```
RMAN> configure retention policy to recovery window of 2 days;
```

To disable the retention policy, use the `CONFIGURE` command with the `RETENTION POLICY TO NONE` keywords, as shown here:

```
RMAN> configure retention policy to none;
```

Compression

RMAN has long offered *white-space compression*. Essentially, this means that blocks in a data file that are not used do not get backed up. White-space compression is quite helpful for a database that is sized quite large but contains little data. It is less helpful for well-packed databases.

In these cases, you will want to take advantage of actual *backup set compression*. This is compression not unlike that available with operating system programs like pkzip, gzip, and compress. Oracle Database 12*c* offers two flavors of compression, zlib and bzip2 (the default). Zlib is designed to compress with a minimum of CPU impact. The result is often a slightly bigger backup image than you get with the bzip2 compression format.

You can configure compression as a default value with the `CONFIGURE COMPRESSION ALGORITHM` command followed by the compression format name, as shown in this example:

```
RMAN> configure compression algorithm 'high';
```

To actually perform a backup with compression, you will need to configure the default device type to use compression, or you will have to use the `AS COMPRESSED` keyword when issuing the `BACKUP` command. Here is an example of configuring the default device type to use compression:

```
RMAN> configure device type disk backup type to compressed Backup Set;
```

And here is an example of using the `AS COMPRESSED` keyword when creating a backup:

```
backup as compressed Backup Set database plus archivelog;
```

Real World Scenario

The Hidden Talents of Compression

Sometimes a product feature has hidden benefits. Compression is one of these. While compression can help reduce the size of your backup sets, there is another potential feature that we look at in the real world, and that is an overall reduction in I/O. With compression enabled, we often see a reduction in backup and recovery times since there is less disk I/O associated with the backup. This can result in reduced backup times, and the backups may have less impact on the overall system.

Everything comes with a price, though, and in this case it's CPU. Compression comes with a high CPU cost. On systems where there was plenty of CPU to go around, we have seen compression significantly reduce backup times and I/O impacts.

Encryption

You can choose to encrypt your backups in Oracle Database 12*c*. Several encryption options are available to you, and they can be found by querying the V$RMAN_ENCRYPTION_ALGORITHMS view. You can use the CONFIGURE command to define the default level of encryption that you want to use. You then use the CONFIGURE command to enable encryption for the entire database or for specific tablespaces.

For example, if you wanted to configure encryption for the entire database, you would use the following commands:

```
RMAN> configure encryption algorithm "AES128";
RMAN> configure encryption for database on;
```

Encryption options for a given tablespace will take precedence over the database global settings. Thus, you can enable global encryption for the database and disable it for a specific tablespace.

There are three different modes of encryption (as opposed to the algorithm used). These are transparent mode, password-based encryption, and dual-mode encryption, which encompasses both modes of encryption. For transparent encryption, you will need to create a wallet, and it must be open. Transparent encryption will then occur automatically after you have issued the CONFIGURE ENCRYPTION FOR DATABASE ON or CONFIGURE ENCRYPTION FOR TABLESPACE ON command.

For password authentication, you will need to use the SET ENCRYPTION IDENTIFIED BY command first to enable password-based authentication. If you are restoring, you will have to use the SET DECRYPTION IDENTIFIED BY command to set the password to decrypt a backup. You can also use the SET command to change the type of encryption for a specific backup or to turn off encryption. Here is an example of the use of the SET ENCRYPTION command:

```
RMAN> set encryption identified by my_pass only on for all tablespaces;
```

Channel Configuration

When you initiate an RMAN backup, RMAN will create one or more channels that connect the database to a backup device. By default, RMAN will create a single channel to back up or recover to or from the FRA. You can override the defaults using the CONFIGURE command. Along with backup locations, the CONFIGURE command allows you to define other settings for your backup channels, including parallelism and backup-set and piece-set sizing. In the following sections, you'll learn about using the CONFIGURE command to define default backup locations, about configuring parallelism, and then about using the CONFIGURE command to set other channel-related parameters.

Configuring Backup Locations

The CONFIGURE DEFAULT DEVICE command is used to configure a backup location other than the default location. If, for example, you wanted to back up to a directory called /oracle01/backup/orcl, you would issue the following command:

```
RMAN> configure channel device type disk format '/oracle01/backup/orcl/%U';
```

RMAN will use this path for future backups. You can configure multiple channels with the CONFIGURE command by specifying each individual channel, as shown here where we have indicated different default backup locations for each channel:

```
RMAN> configure channel 1 device type disk format '/oracle01/backup/orcl/%U';
RMAN> configure channel 2 device type disk format '/oracle02/backup/orcl/%U';
```

You might have wondered about the %U in the backup location format. The %U is an *RMAN backup format specification*. There are a number of different format specifications. %U is the most common because it ensures a unique filename for each backup set piece created by RMAN. Table 3.2 provides a list of the most common format specifications.

TABLE 3.2 Format Options

Option	Description
%a	Specifies the activation ID of the database
%c	Specifies the copy number of the backup piece within a set of duplexed backup pieces
%d	Specifies the name of the database
%D	Specifies the current day of the month from the Gregorian calendar
%e	Specifies the archived log sequence number
%f	Specifies the absolute file number

TABLE 3.2 Format Options *(continued)*

Option	Description
%F	Combines the database ID (DBID), day, month, year, and sequence into a unique and repeatable generated name
%h	Specifies the archived redo log thread number
%I	Specifies the DBID
%M	Specifies the month in the Gregorian calendar in *MM* format
%N	Specifies the tablespace name
%n	Specifies the name of the database, padded on the right with *n* characters to a total length of eight characters
%p	Specifies the piece number within the backup set
%s	Specifies the backup-set number
%t	Specifies the backup-set timestamp
%T	Specifies the year, month, and day in the Gregorian calendar
%u	Specifies an eight-character name constituted by compressed representations of the backup-set or image-copy number
%U	Specifies a system-generated unique filename (this is the default setting)

Configuring Parallelism

Now that you can configure multiple channels, you might want to use them! To do so, you use the CONFIGURE command along with the PARALLELISM keyword, as shown here:

```
RMAN> configure device type disk parallelism 2;
```

This will cause any BACKUP DATABASE command to use two channels, performing the backup in parallel. This can improve performance of your database backup. It can also cause performance to decrease if you overparallelize the backup and consume too much CPU, flood the network, or run out of backup devices.

Note that this, along with the other configuration options, becomes a default option when set. You can manually override these configured default settings for any backup at any time.

Other Channel Configuration Options

You have already seen how to configure channels for alternate backup locations and parallelism, but there are other things you might want to configure for a given channel. In this section, we will discuss the following channel-configuration options, which you will want to be aware of:

- SBT channel configuration
- MAXSETSIZE and MAXPIECESIZE configuration

SBT CHANNEL CONFIGURATION

First, most of our examples in this chapter have identified disk-based locations for backups. You may well want to have your backup go to tape instead. To do so, you will need to install the vendor's interface into RMAN's MML API, following the vendor's instructions. Once you have done so, you then allocate a channel (or more if you want parallel backups) to a device called SBT to send it to the tape device. Here is an example where we use the CONFIGURE command to make the SBT device the default device:

```
configure device type sbt parallelism 2;
```

Or you could configure individual channels like this:

```
RMAN> configure channel 1 device type sbt;
RMAN> configure channel 2 device type sbt;
```

During the backup, you could manually allocate channels to SBT also within a run block:

```
run {
allocate channel c1 device type sbt;
allocate channel c2 device type sbt;
backup database plus archivelog;
};
```

MAXSETSIZE AND *MAXPIECESIZE* CONFIGURATION

You may find that you need to limit the size of your backups. For example, you may find that the OS that you are working on has a maximum file-size limit of 2GB. Thus, you need to make sure your backup set pieces are no larger than 2GB. This is facilitated through the use of the MAXSETSIZE and MAXPIECESIZE operators.

The MAXSETSIZE operator will limit the size of any backup set. The MAXPIECESIZE operator will limit the size of any individual backup set piece. Here is an example of configuring a default channel with a MAXPIECESIZE setting:

```
RMAN> configure channel 1 device type disk maxpiecesize 2g;
```

The main use of the MAXPIECESIZE parameter is to ensure that your backup set pieces do not grow bigger than some OS, file system, or storage device limit. For example, if each of your tapes can hold only 200GB of data, then you would want to limit the size of each backup set piece to 200GB.

MAXSETSIZE has essentially the same purpose, to limit the overall size of one backup set. The downside to using MAXSETSIZE is that if you end up with a data file that is larger than MAXSETSIZE, it will never get backed up since each data file must be backed up within the scope of one backup set.

Control-File Autobackups

When enabled, RMAN will perform automatic control-file autobackups after each backup. Additionally, RMAN/Oracle will automatically create a backup of the control file to disk anytime a database change occurs that impacts the control file and the database physical structure, such as adding a tablespace or data file.

To enable control-file autobackups through RMAN, use the CONFIGURE command with the CONTROLFILE AUTOBACKUP ON keyword, as shown here:

```
RMAN> configure controlfile autobackup on;
```

Control-file autobackups are stored in the FRA if one is configured. You can also use the CONFIGURE command to configure RMAN to create the control-file autobackup in a different location, as shown in this example:

```
configure controlfile autobackup format for device type disk to
'/oracle01/oracle/controfilebackup/%F';
```

In this example, notice the use of the %F format specifier. %F is required when defining the location of the backup control file. This will ensure that the backup control filename is unique each time the backup is created.

Backup Optimization

Sometimes things don't change, like some of our T-shirts (they are older than we are!) and read-only data files. When this happens, you don't need to back them up if they have already been backed up. *Backup optimization* provides the ability to tell RMAN that you don't want to back up a database data file if that backup is not needed. This saves time and effort on the part of RMAN. RMAN still follows all the rules of retention: Backup files are expired when they are set to expire, and if the retention policy calls for two copies of a data file, then the data file will be backed up two times. However, on the third backup of the database, the read-only data file will not be backed up because the two identical copies are sufficient for recovery.

To configure backup optimization, use the CONFIGURE command with the BACKUP OPTIMIZATION ON keyword, as shown here:

```
RMAN> configure backup optimization on;
```

Snapshot Control-File Location

As we mentioned earlier, Oracle places the snapshot control file in the ORACLE_HOME/dbs directory. As a part of the setup of RMAN, you should change the location of the snapshot control file by using the CONFIGURE command, as shown here:

```
configure snapshot controlfile name to '/oracle01/backup/sncf/sncforcl.ora';
```

Note that there needs to be only one snapshot control file at any time. That is why the name of the snapshot control file does not contain any modifier like %U.

Backup Tags

When you create backups, you can optionally tag them. If you do not tag a backup, RMAN will tag it for you. A *tag* is a name that you assign to the backup, such as, for example, Gold Copy (perhaps you recreate your database every day with the backup tagged Gold Copy). You can easily restore and recover the database using the tag as the key for the recovery. We will discuss using tags to recover your database in Chapter 5. Here is an example of performing a backup with a tag included:

```
RMAN> backup database tag 'DPrestwich' plus archivelog
tag='ARCH_GOLD' delete input;
```

You might have noticed that I defined two tags for this backup. That is because this backup is actually two backups in one. The first is the backup of the database, and the second is the backup of the archived redo logs. By default, the tags of both backups will be the same, but you can choose to tag each backup differently.

Duplexing Backups

You may want to create duplicate copies of backup sets when they are created. This is called *duplexing*. Duplexing of backup sets can be configured as a default setting by using the CONFIGURE command, as shown here:

```
RMAN> configure datafile backup copies for device type disk to 2;
```

You can also configure duplexing for archive log backups, as shown here:

```
RMAN> configure archivelog backup copies for device type disk to 2;
```

Duplexing backups has some consequences. Obviously you are doing two backups at the same time, which has system resource implications. Also, duplexing will require more disk space to complete the backup.

Note that you can duplex across similar devices only. So you can duplex across tape devices or across disk devices but not both.

If you want to duplex an individual backup rather than set a persistent configuration setting, you would use the SET BACKUP COPIES command within a RUN block, as in this example:

```
RMAN> run
2> {
3> allocate channel d1 device type disk format 'c:\oracle\backup\%U';
4> set backup copies 2;
5> backup incremental level 0 database plus archivelog delete input;
6> }
```

In Exercise 3.1, you'll configure some RMAN settings.

EXERCISE 3.1

Configuring RMAN

1. Start RMAN from the command line:

```
C:\oracle\admin\ORCL\wallet>rman target=/
Recovery Manager: Release 12.1.0.1.0 - Production on Thu Feb 20 14:38:07 2014
Copyright (c) 1982, 2013, Oracle and/or its affiliates.  All rights reserved.
connected to target database: ORCL (DBID=1190537904)
```

2. Display your RMAN configuration (yours may look different than our output—that's okay):

```
RMAN> show all;
RMAN configuration parameters for database with db_unique_name ORCL are:
CONFIGURE RETENTION POLICY TO REDUNDANCY 1;
CONFIGURE BACKUP OPTIMIZATION ON;
CONFIGURE DEFAULT DEVICE TYPE TO DISK; # default
CONFIGURE CONTROLFILE AUTOBACKUP OFF;
CONFIGURE CONTROLFILE AUTOBACKUP FORMAT FOR DEVICE
TYPE DISK TO '%F'; # default
CONFIGURE DEVICE TYPE DISK PARALLELISM 1 BACKUP
TYPE TO BACKUP SET; # default
CONFIGURE DATAFILE BACKUP COPIES FOR DEVICE TYPE DISK TO 1; # default
CONFIGURE ARCHIVELOG BACKUP COPIES FOR DEVICE TYPE DISK TO 1; # default
CONFIGURE MAXSETSIZE TO UNLIMITED; # default
CONFIGURE ENCRYPTION FOR DATABASE OFF;
CONFIGURE ENCRYPTION ALGORITHM 'AES128';
CONFIGURE COMPRESSION ALGORITHM 'zlib';
CONFIGURE ARCHIVELOG DELETION POLICY TO NONE; # default
CONFIGURE SNAPSHOT CONTROLFILE NAME TO 'C:\ORACLE\PRODUCT\12.1.0\DB_1\
DATABASE\SNCFORCL.ORA'; # default
```

EXERCISE 3.1 *(continued)*

3. Configure the retention policy to redundancy of 2:

```
RMAN> CONFIGURE RETENTION POLICY TO REDUNDANCY 2;
old RMAN configuration parameters:
CONFIGURE RETENTION POLICY TO REDUNDANCY 1;
new RMAN configuration parameters:
CONFIGURE RETENTION POLICY TO REDUNDANCY 2;
new RMAN configuration parameters are successfully stored
```

4. Configure control-file autobackups on:

```
RMAN> CONFIGURE CONTROLFILE AUTOBACKUP on;
old RMAN configuration parameters:
CONFIGURE CONTROLFILE AUTOBACKUP OFF;
new RMAN configuration parameters:
CONFIGURE CONTROLFILE AUTOBACKUP ON;
new RMAN configuration parameters are successfully stored
```

5. Configure for compressed backup sets:

```
RMAN> CONFIGURE DEVICE TYPE DISK PARALLELISM 1 BACKUP
TYPE TO COMPRESSED BACKUP SET;
new RMAN configuration parameters:
CONFIGURE DEVICE TYPE DISK PARALLELISM 1 BACKUP TYPE
TO COMPRESSED BACKUP SET;
new RMAN configuration parameters are successfully stored
```

6. Create a directory to hold the snapshot control file (you will want to use your own directory paths, of course):

```
RMAN> host "mkdir \oracle01";
host command complete
RMAN> host "mkdir \oracle01\snapshot";
host command complete
```

7. Configure RMAN so the snapshot control file will be created in the new directory:

```
RMAN> CONFIGURE SNAPSHOT CONTROLFILE NAME TO 'c:\oracle01\snapshot';
new RMAN configuration parameters:
CONFIGURE SNAPSHOT CONTROLFILE NAME TO 'c:\oracle01\snapshot';
new RMAN configuration parameters are successfully stored
```

8. Exit RMAN:

```
RMAN> exit
Recovery Manager complete.
```

Backing Up Your Database with RMAN

We will discuss backups of your database using RMAN in the following sections. We will first talk about the different types of backups that you can make with RMAN. Then we will discuss what you can back up using RMAN, such as the database, archived redo logs, and so forth.

Using the RMAN Command Line

Like SQL and SQL*Plus, RMAN has its own unique command set. You use these commands to do a number of things:

* Configure RMAN
* Back up database structures (tablespaces, data files, control files, and so on)
* Restore and recover your database
* Produce various reports and lists that contain backup-related information
* Create duplicate databases
* Restore specific tablespaces

This is just a partial list of all the things RMAN can do for you. Table 3.3 describes the RMAN commands you will need to know for the OCP exam.

TABLE 3.3   RMAN Commands

RMAN Command	Description
@	Run a command file.
@@	Run a command file in the same directory as another command file that is currently running. The @@ command differs from the @ command only when run from within a command file.
ALLOCATE CHANNEL	Establish a channel, which is a connection between RMAN and a database instance.
ALLOCATE CHANNEL FOR MAINTENANCE	Allocate a channel in preparation for issuing maintenance commands such as DELETE.
allocOperandList	A subclause that specifies channel control options such as PARMS and FORMAT.
ALTER DATABASE	Mount or open a database.

RMAN Command	Description
archivelogRecord-Specifier	Specify a range of archived redo-log files.
BACKUP	Back up database files, copies of database files, archived logs, or backup sets.
BLOCKRECOVER	Recover an individual data block or set of data blocks within one or more data files.
CATALOG	Add information about a data file copy, archived redo log, or control file copy to the repository.
CHANGE	Mark a backup piece, image copy, or archived redo log as having the status UNAVAILABLE or AVAILABLE; remove the repository record for a backup or copy; override the retention policy for a backup or copy.
completedTimeSpec	Specify a time range during which the backup or copy completed.
CONFIGURE	Configure persistent RMAN settings. These settings apply to all RMAN sessions until explicitly changed or disabled.
CONNECT	Establish a connection between RMAN and a target, auxiliary, or recovery catalog database.
connectStringSpec	Specify the username, password, and net service name for connecting to a target, recovery catalog, or auxiliary database. The connection is necessary to authenticate the user and identify the database.
CONVERT	Convert data file formats for transporting tablespaces across platforms.
CREATE CATALOG	Create the schema for the recovery catalog.
CREATE SCRIPT	Create a stored script and store it in the recovery catalog.
CROSSCHECK	Determine whether files managed by RMAN, such as archived logs, data file copies, and backup pieces, still exist on disk or tape.
datafileSpec	Specify a data file by filename or absolute file number.
DELETE	Delete backups and copies, remove references to them from the recovery catalog, and update their control-file records to status DELETED.

TABLE 3.3   RMAN Commands *(continued)*

RMAN Command	Description
DELETE SCRIPT	Delete a stored script from the recovery catalog.
deviceSpecifier	Specify the type of storage device for a backup or copy.
DROP CATALOG	Remove the schema from the recovery catalog.
DROP DATABASE	Delete the target database from disk and unregister it.
DUPLICATE	Use backups of the target database to create a duplicate database that you can use for testing purposes or to create a standby database.
EXECUTE SCRIPT	Run an RMAN stored script.
EXIT	Quit the RMAN executable.
fileNameConversion-Spec	Specify patterns to transform source to target filenames during BACKUP AS COPY, CONVERT, and DUPLICATE.
FLASHBACK	Return the database to a previous state as defined by a previous time or system change number (SCN).
formatSpec	Specify a filename format for a backup or copy.
HOST	Invoke an operating-system command-line subshell from within RMAN or run a specific operating-system command.
keepOption	Specify that a backup or copy should or should not be exempt from the current retention policy.
LIST	Produce a detailed listing of backup sets or copies.
listObjList	A subclause used to specify which items will be displayed by the LIST command.
maintQualifier	A subclause used to specify additional options for maintenance commands such as DELETE and CHANGE.
maintSpec	A subclause used to specify the files operated on by maintenance commands such as CHANGE, CROSSCHECK, and DELETE.
obsOperandList	A subclause used to determine which backups and copies are obsolete.

RMAN Command	Description
PRINT SCRIPT	Display a stored script.
QUIT	Exit the RMAN executable.
recordSpec	A subclause used to specify the objects on which the maintenance commands should operate.
RECOVER	Apply redo logs and incremental backups to data files restored from backup or data file copies in order to update them to a specified time.
REGISTER	Register the target database in the recovery catalog.
RELEASE CHANNEL	Release a channel that was allocated with an ALLOCATE CHANNEL command.
releaseForMaint	Release a channel that was allocated with an ALLOCATE CHANNEL FOR MAINTENANCE command.
REPLACE SCRIPT	Replace an existing script stored in the recovery catalog. If the script does not exist, then REPLACE SCRIPT creates it.
REPORT	Perform detailed analyses of the content of the recovery catalog.
RESET DATABASE	Inform RMAN that the SQL statement ALTER DATABASE OPEN RESETLOGS has been executed and that a new incarnation of the target database has been created, or reset the target database to a prior incarnation.
RESTORE	Restore files from backup sets or from disk copies to the default or to a new location.
RESYNC	Perform a full resynchronization, which creates a snapshot control file and then copies any new or changed information from that snapshot control file to the recovery catalog.
RUN	Execute a sequence of one or more RMAN commands, which are one or more statements executed within the braces of a RUN block.
SEND	Send a vendor-specific quoted string to one or more specific channels.
SET	Set the value of various attributes that affect RMAN behavior for the duration of a RUN block or a session.

TABLE 3.3   RMAN Commands *(continued)*

RMAN Command	Description
SHOW	Display the current CONFIGURE settings.
SHUTDOWN	Shut down the target database. This command is equivalent to the SQL*Plus SHUTDOWN command.
SPOOL	Write RMAN output to a log file.
SQL	Execute a SQL statement from within RMAN (not required in Oracle Database 12*c* in most cases).
STARTUP	Start up the target database. This command is equivalent to the SQL*Plus STARTUP command.
SWITCH	Specify that a data file copy is now the current data file, that is, the data file pointed to by the control file. This command is equivalent to the SQL statement ALTER DATABASE RENAME FILE as it applies to data files.
UNREGISTER DATABASE	Unregister a database from the recovery catalog.
untilClause	A subclause specifying an upper limit by time, SCN, or log sequence number. This clause is usually used to specify the desired point in time for an incomplete recovery.
UPGRADE CATALOG	Upgrade the recovery-catalog schema from an older version to the version required by the RMAN executable.
VALIDATE	Examine a backup set and report whether its data is intact. RMAN scans all of the backup pieces in the specified backup sets and looks at the checksums to verify that the contents can be successfully restored.

In Oracle Database 12*c*, a new feature has been introduced that simplifies execution of SQL commands from the RMAN command line. You might have noticed the SQL command prompt. In previous versions of RMAN you would need to use the SQL command to execute a SQL statement. The SQL command would be enclosed in single quotes, like this:

```
RMAN> SQL 'alter system archive log current';
```

In Oracle Database 12*c*, RMAN provides the ability to execute SQL statements just as if you are in SQL*Plus. So, you can now execute the same select statement like we just did, but without the SQL command prompt or the single quotes, like this:

```
RMAN> alter system archive log current;
```

Types of RMAN Backups

There are a number of different types of backups in RMAN. First, we will discuss the concept of consistent and inconsistent backups. This is an important fundamental building block to understanding Oracle database backup and recovery operations, should they be RMAN or manual.

Next we will discuss the two principle types of RMAN backups. The first type consists of one or more backup sets. *Backup sets* are a very flexible way of backing up your Oracle Database. The downside is that backup sets are not direct copies of Oracle Database data files. Thus, you need RMAN to put the backup sets back together to restore your database.

Oracle also supports *image copies*. Image copies are direct copies of database data files. Image copies offer faster recovery options but typically take up a great deal more space. In the following sections, we will address these two types of RMAN backups in more detail.

Consistent and Inconsistent Backups

Perhaps the most important concept to understand with backups is the notion of a consistent backup and an inconsistent backup. Oracle does not like anything to be out of order. Because it's so persnickety about this consistency thing, Oracle checks all of the database files, control files, and redo logs when you start the database. It makes sure that they are all consistent to the same point in time. If it finds something amiss, then it will refuse to open the database and the DBA has to figure out what the problem is.

This leads us to the concept of consistent and inconsistent database backups, which are covered in the OCP exam. We will discuss concepts that are related to the idea of a consistent database backup or inconsistent database backup through the next several chapters, so let's take a moment to define what these terms mean.

A *consistent database backup* (sometimes called a cold backup since the database is not running) is one that is taken when the database has been shut down in a normal manner and where the state of the data in the database datafiles is consistent to the point in time of the shutdown of the database. In other words, there is no redo to apply to the database datafiles; it's all "in there."

A consistent backup can be executed through RMAN, but it requires shutting down the database first with the SHUTDOWN, SHUTDOWN IMMEDIATE, or SHUTDOWN TRANSACTIONAL commands. In fact, if the database is in NOARCHIVELOG mode, it will not allow you to perform an inconsistent database backup.

Once you have shut down the database normally, you will then mount the database and issue the appropriate RMAN commands to start the database backup. Consistent database backups are supported when Oracle is in ARCHIVELOG mode and NOARCHIVELOG mode. However, if the database is in NOARCHIVELOG mode, it cannot perform point in time recovery of the database. Instead, you will only be able to restore and recover the database to the time of the actual backup. We will show you examples of inconsistent backups and recoveries later in this and the next chapter.

At almost any point in the lifetime of a running Oracle database, the database datafiles are inconsistent with reality. The newest changes are likely sitting in memory and waiting to get written to disk. When a database is shut down normally, the graceful shutdown of the database flushes the information from memory and writes it to the datafiles. Thus, when the database is shut down normally, everything is in synch. The database datafiles, the online redo logs, and the database control file all "agree" with each other that things are perfectly normal.

However, if you were to issue a SHUTDOWN ABORT command, or pull the plug on the database server and then plug it back in, the database would be in an inconsistent state at that point. The datafiles would all be at different "states." One datafile might reflect the data as it looked an hour ago; another datafile might reflect the state of the data as it looked five minutes ago. It's a good bet that none of them are anywhere near current. In this case, the database is said to be in an inconsistent state. Thus, any backup of this database would be an inconsistent backup.

A consistent backup of a database requires only a copy of the database data files to be recoverable. Though a copy of the online redo logs and the control file would be nice too, they are not required. By definition, a database in NOARCHIVELOG mode must be backed up using a consistent database. We discussed manual consistent backup and restore of Oracle databases in the previous chapters of this book. We will discuss using RMAN to perform consistent backup and recovery in this and the next chapter of this book.

NOARCHIVELOG mode and consistent backups are a bit of a bummer since you have to take the database down to get you want. Thus most organizations put their databases in ARCHIVELOG mode, which may be backed up using a consistent or inconsistent backup. We have already discussed configuring the database for ARCHIVELOG mode operations, so you are halfway to understanding inconsistent backups already.

An *inconsistent backup* is a backup that is taken where either some or all of the database datafiles, the database control files, and the database online redo logs are out of synchronization (which is pretty much all the time when the database is running). An inconsistent backup means that the image being backed up is not going to be consistent to a single point in time.

For example, assume you are backing up a running database. Further assume that the backup of datafile 13 (which contains some HR data) might take place at 2 P.M. The backup of datafile 14 takes place an hour later at at 3 P.M.

In this case, the copy of datafile 13 on the backup media will look like it did at 2 P.M. The copy of datafile 14 will look like it did an hour later. So, those two files are going to represent completely different temporal states of the database. Also keeping in mind that the Oracle database does not immediately write data changes to the datafiles, it's quite possible that the backup image of datafile 13 looks like the database would have looked at noon, while the backup image of datafile 14 is an image of the database as it looked at 1 P.M. In other words, the database datafiles are out of synchronization.

Generally, this situation isn't a problem because Oracle reads the most current data blocks out of memory. It really does not care which copy of the data block is on disk, as long as the most current copy of that data block is in memory. However, when the database is shut down abnormally, the memory is cleared and the result is a bunch of messy database datafiles that are inconsistent. Hence, the name, inconsistent backup.

While this might sound like a terrible situation, the reality is that most database backups are inconsistent backups. The DBA backs up the database datafiles while the database is running. The DBA (using RMAN or the SQL command line) also backs up all of the redo logs generated from the point that the backup started until the time that the backup was completed.

We will discuss the internals of the recovery and restore process associated with incomplete recovery in later chapters in this book, but for now just know that during a recovery from an inconsistent backup, the DBA would restore the database datafiles they backed up, and then simply apply the redo in the backed up redo logs. At the end of the restore, the database is again consistent and ready to open.

RMAN Backup Sets

By default, when you create a backup in RMAN, it writes the backup to physical files. These physical files are called *backup set pieces* (RMAN can also create backups called image copies, which we will discuss later in this section). A given backup may create more than one backup set piece. A collection of related backup set pieces is called a *backup set*. A backup set is a logical entity that is used to maintain the association of independent backup set pieces.

In addition to multiple backup set pieces, you may have more than one backup set. This occurs when you parallelize a backup. Each channel will represent one backup set, each with its own backup set pieces. New backup sets will also be created on a channel if a backup set exceeds the backup set size limitations.

Note that a given data file can span backup set pieces but cannot span backup sets. The ability of a given data file to span backup set pieces is known as *multiplexing*. Multiplexing is another form of parallelization, since it allows RMAN to read from multiple data files in parallel and write them to a single backup set piece. Thus, a given backup set piece may have data from many data files in it.

In the default RMAN configuration, a given tablespace/data file backup may find itself in more than one backup set piece. However, each individual tablespace/data file backup can be associated with only a single RMAN backup set and thus will be backed up by only one channel.

Oracle Database 12*c* has a new feature called multisection backups. *Multisection backups* allow you to parallelize the backup of large data files (bigfile tablespaces or normal tablespaces). You may well find questions on multisection backups on your OCP exam.

Figure 3.2 demonstrates the relationship between backups, backup sets, and backup set pieces.

RMAN Image Copies

RMAN image copies are one-to-one copies of database data files. When you do an image-copy backup of your database, you will receive no benefits of compression, so the disk-space requirement is a one-to-one requirement. Image copies must be made to disk. Figure 3.3 shows the difference between image and regular backups.

The upside to an image copy is that it can be much faster to restore. RMAN will always choose to restore image copies over backup sets if an image copy is available. In fact, using the SWITCH TO COPY command makes it even faster because RMAN will simply switch to the image copy on disk and start using that copy (applying redo as required). To make an image copy, use the BACKUP AS COPY command, as shown in this example:

```
RMAN> Backup as copy database;
```

FIGURE 3.2 Relationship between RMAN backups, backup sets, and backup set pieces

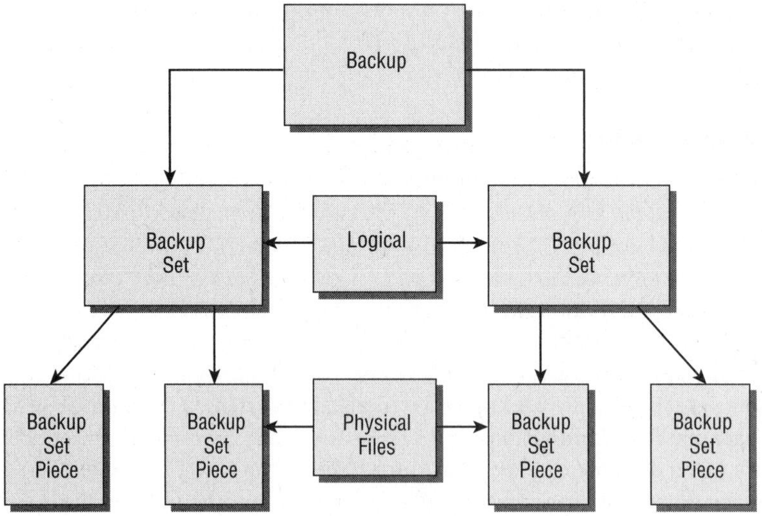

```
                          ┌──────────────┐
                          │   Backup     │
                          └──────────────┘
            ┌────────────────┘      └────────────────┐
            ▼                                         ▼
    ┌──────────┐      ┌──────────┐            ┌──────────┐
    │  Backup  │◄─────│  Logical │───────────►│  Backup  │
    │   Set    │      └──────────┘            │   Set    │
    └──────────┘                              └──────────┘
       ┌───┴────┐                              ┌───┴────┐
       ▼        ▼                              ▼        ▼
  ┌──────┐  ┌──────┐   ┌──────────┐      ┌──────┐  ┌──────┐
  │Backup│  │Backup│   │ Physical │      │Backup│  │Backup│
  │ Set  │◄─│ Set  │◄──│  Files   │─────►│ Set  │  │ Set  │
  │Piece │  │Piece │   └──────────┘      │Piece │  │Piece │
  └──────┘  └──────┘                     └──────┘  └──────┘
```

FIGURE 3.3 Image vs. regular backups

Original Datafile   Regular RMAN Backup Set   Image Copy

You can also make image copies of data files or tablespaces, as shown in these examples:

```
RMAN>backup as copy datafile 4;
RMAN>Backup as copy tablespace users;
```

If you prefer to always use image copies rather than backup sets, you can configure RMAN to do so by default with the CONFIGURE command, as shown here:

```
configure device type disk backup type to copy;
```

RMAN can use a mixture of image copies, incremental backups, and archived redo logs when performing recovery (which we will discuss in more detail in Chapter 4, "Using the RMAN Recovery Catalog"). This can make total recovery of your database, a tablespace, or a data file much quicker.

Don't Confuse Terms

Before we start talking about offline and online backups we wanted to make sure you don't confuse the notion of online and offline backups with consistent and inconsistent backups.

They are two different things. Online or offline backups simply indicate the state of the database (running or not) when the backup occurs.

A consistent or inconsistent backup refers to the temporal state of the data in the database datafiles. An inconsistent backup can occur when the database is running or shut down. A consistent database backup can only occur after the database is shut down normally (e.g., shutdown immediate).

A database in NOARCHIVELOG mode can be backed up only when the database is in a consistent state. As a result, any attempt to restore an inconsistent database backup taken in NOARCHIVELOG mode will fail. A database in ARCHIVELOG mode will be able to recover using either a consistent or inconsistent database backup.

RMAN Offline Backups

We discussed manual offline backups in Chapter 1. Offline backups in RMAN are not much different except that you use the RMAN interface to actually do the backup rather than an OS file-copy utility. You will still need to close the database, but your backup will be done with the database in mount mode rather than completely shut down. No parameter-file adjustments are required for an RMAN offline backup.

We recommend that you configure and use the FRA (discussed earlier in this chapter) even if you are doing offline backups. This makes for a standardized backup location and also allows the Oracle database to manage the overall backup space utilization more efficiently.

To perform an offline backup of your database with RMAN, follow these steps:

1. Start the RMAN client.

2. Shut down the database from the RMAN client, SQL*Plus, or OEM.

   The shutdown should be a consistent shutdown, so use the SHUTDOWN, SHUTDOWN IMMEDIATE, or SHUTDOWN TRANSACTIONAL command.

3. Start up the database in mount mode using the STARTUP MOUNT command.

4. Back up the database with the RMAN BACKUP command:

   ```
   RMAN>backup database;
   ```

5. When the backup is complete, open the database with the ALTER DATABASE OPEN command.

RMAN Online Backups

For online backups in RMAN, the database must be configured in ARCHIVELOG mode (see Chapter 1 for more on configuring the database for ARCHIVELOG-mode operations). Once the database is configured properly and RMAN is configured properly (as discussed earlier in this chapter), you can do online backups.

Online backups with RMAN are easy. You need to make sure the database and the archived redo logs are backed up; thus you issue the command BACKUP DATABASE PLUS ARCHIVELOG. That's it. That command will create a fully recoverable backup of the database, as long as the physical backup set pieces are available to restore from.

Additionally, if you have used the RMAN command CONFIGURE CONTROLFILE AUTOBACKUP ON to configure the automatic backup of control files and SPFILEs, then the database backup is known as a *whole database backup*.

If you want to delete the archived redo logs after the backup, you append the DELETE INPUT clause to the command. Other options are available depending on your needs.

In the following example, we perform an online backup of our database using the BACKUP AS COMPRESSED BACKUP SET DATABASE PLUS ARCHIVELOG DELETE INPUT command. This will create a compressed backup of the database, backing up the archived redo logs and then deleting those backed-up archived redo logs after the backup is complete. Also note that we have configured control-file autobackups.

```
RMAN> backup as compressed Backup Set database plus archivelog delete input;
Starting backup at 05-SEP-13
current log archived
allocated channel: ORA_DISK_1
channel ORA_DISK_1: SID=131 device type=DISK
channel ORA_DISK_1: starting compressed archived log backup set
channel ORA_DISK_1: specifying archived log(s) in backup set
input archived log thread=1 sequence=41 RECID=40 STAMP=664583178
input archived log thread=1 sequence=42 RECID=41 STAMP=664621168
input archived log thread=1 sequence=43 RECID=42 STAMP=664650496
input archived log thread=1 sequence=44 RECID=43 STAMP=664655636
channel ORA_DISK_1: starting piece 1 at 05-SEP-13
channel ORA_DISK_1: finished piece 1 at 05-SEP-13
piece handle=C:\ORACLE\FAST_RECOVERY_AREA\ORCL\BACKUP SET\2013_09_05\
01_MF_ANNNN_TAG20080905T183357_4D3N085C_.BKP tag=TAG20080905T183357
comment=NONE
channel ORA_DISK_1: backup set complete, elapsed time: 00:00:15
channel ORA_DISK_1: deleting archived log(s)
archived log file name=C:\ORACLE\ARCH\ORCL\ARC00041_0662757171.001
RECID=40 STAMP=664583178
archived log file name=C:\ORACLE\ARCH\ORCL\ARC00042_0662757171.001
RECID=41 STAMP=664621168
archived log file name=C:\ORACLE\ARCH\ORCL\ARC00043_0662757171.001
RECID=42 STAMP=664650496
archived log file name=C:\ORACLE\ARCH\ORCL\ARC00044_0662757171.001
RECID=43 STAMP=664655636
Finished backup at 05-SEP-13
```

```
Starting backup at 05-SEP-13
using channel ORA_DISK_1
channel ORA_DISK_1: starting compressed full datafile backup set
channel ORA_DISK_1: specifying datafile(s) in backup set
input datafile file number=00002 name=C:\ORACLE\ORADATA\ORCL\SYSAUX01.DBF
input datafile file number=00001 name=C:\ORACLE\ORADATA\ORCL\SYSTEM01.DBF
input datafile file number=00005 name=C:\ORACLE\ORADATA\ORCL\UNDOTBS02.DBF
input datafile file number=00004 name=C:\ORACLE\ORADATA\ORCL\USERS01.DBF
channel ORA_DISK_1: starting piece 1 at 05-SEP-13
channel ORA_DISK_1: finished piece 1 at 05-SEP-13
piece handle=C:\ORACLE\FAST_RECOVERY_AREA\ORCL\BACKUP SET\2013_09_05\
01_MF_NNNDF_TAG20080905T183432_4D3N0Z0Z_.BKP tag=TAG20080905T183432
comment=NONE
channel ORA_DISK_1: starting piece 2 at 05-SEP-13
channel ORA_DISK_1: finished piece 2 at 05-SEP-13
piece handle=C:\ORACLE\FAST_RECOVERY_AREA\ORCL\BACKUP SET\2013_09_05
\01_MF_NNNDF_TAG20080905T183432_4D3N63Y8_.BKP tag=TAG20080905T183432
comment=NONE
channel ORA_DISK_1: starting piece 3 at 05-SEP-13
channel ORA_DISK_1: finished piece 3 at 05-SEP-13
piece handle=C:\ORACLE\FAST_RECOVERY_AREA\ORCL\BACKUP SET\2013_09_05\
01_MF_NNNDF_TAG20080905T183432_4D3N9PY8_.BKP tag=TAG20080905T183432
comment=NONE
channel ORA_DISK_1: backup set complete, elapsed time: 00:04:48
channel ORA_DISK_1: starting compressed full datafile backup set
channel ORA_DISK_1: specifying datafile(s) in backup set
including current control file in backup set
including current SPFILE in backup set
channel ORA_DISK_1: starting piece 1 at 05-SEP-13
channel ORA_DISK_1: finished piece 1 at 05-SEP-13
piece handle=C:\ORACLE\FAST_RECOVERY_AREA\ORCL\BACKUP SET\2013_09_05\
01_MF_NCSNF_TAG20080905T183432_4D3NBHXS_.BKP tag=TAG20080905T183432
comment=NONE
channel ORA_DISK_1: backup set complete, elapsed time: 00:00:02
Finished backup at 05-SEP-13
Starting backup at 05-SEP-13
current log archived
using channel ORA_DISK_1
channel ORA_DISK_1: starting compressed archived log backup set
channel ORA_DISK_1: specifying archived log(s) in backup set
```

```
input archived log thread=1 sequence=45 RECID=44 STAMP=664655986
channel ORA_DISK_1: starting piece 1 at 05-SEP-13
channel ORA_DISK_1: finished piece 1 at 05-SEP-13
piece handle=C:\ORACLE\FAST_RECOVERY_AREA\ORCL\BACKUP SET\2013_09_05\
01_MF_ANNNN_TAG20080905T183946_4D3NBS89_.BKP tag=TAG20080905T183946
comment=NONE
channel ORA_DISK_1: backup set complete, elapsed time: 00:00:01
channel ORA_DISK_1: deleting archived log(s)
archived log file name=C:\ORACLE\ARCH\ORCL\ARC00045_0662757171.001
RECID=44 STAMP=664655986
Finished backup at 05-SEP-13
```

You can also do backups of tablespaces and data files using the BACKUP command, as shown in these examples:

```
RMAN>Backup tablespace users;
RMAN>Backup datafile 3;
```

In Exercise 3.2, you'll execute an online backup using RMAN.

EXERCISE 3.2

Executing an Online Backup

In this exercise, you will perform an online backup of your ARCHIVELOG mode database. Your database should already be in ARCHIVELOG mode (see Exercise 3.1). Once the database is in ARCHIVELOG mode, you can do this exercise.

1. Log into the database using SQL*Plus:

```
C:\oracle\admin\ORCL\wallet>set oracle_sid=orcl
C:\oracle\admin\ORCL\wallet>sqlplus "/ as sysdba"
SQL*Plus: Release 12.1.0.1.0 Production on Thu Feb 20 14:43:47 2014
Copyright (c) 1982, 2013, Oracle.  All rights reserved.
Connected to:
Oracle Database 12c Enterprise Edition Release 12.1.0.1.0 - 64bit Production
With the Partitioning, OLAP, Advanced Analytics and Real Application Testing
options
```

2. Query the LOG_MODE column of the V$DATABASE view to confirm that the database is in ARCHIVELOG mode. If the database is not in ARCHIVELOG mode, refer to Chapter 1 for information on how to put the database in ARCHIVELOG mode.

```
SQL> Select log_mode from v$database;
LOG_MODE
------------
ARCHIVELOG
```

3. Exit SQL*Plus and start RMAN:

```
SQL> exit
Disconnected from Oracle Database 12c Enterprise Edition Release 12.1.0.1.0 -
64bit Production
With the Partitioning, OLAP, Advanced Analytics and Real Application Testing
options

C:\oracle\admin\ORCL\wallet>rman target=/
Recovery Manager: Release 12.1.0.1.0 - Production on Thu Feb 20 14:46:42 2014
Copyright (c) 1982, 2013, Oracle and/or its affiliates.  All rights reserved.
connected to target database: ORCL (DBID=1190537904)
```

4. Execute the RMAN backup using the BACKUP DATABASE command. Back up the archived redo logs at the same time with the PLUS ARCHIVELOG option. Remove the archived redo logs after they are backed up using the DELETE INPUT option.

```
RMAN> Backup database plus archivelog delete input;
```

5. Review the output and make sure the backup was successful. Here is an example of our output. We bolded the messages that indicate a successful backup.

```
RMAN> Backup database plus archivelog delete input;
Starting backup at 11-SEP-13
current log archived
using target database control file instead of recovery catalog
allocated channel: ORA_DISK_1
channel ORA_DISK_1: SID=128 device type=DISK
channel ORA_DISK_1: starting compressed archived log backup set
channel ORA_DISK_1: specifying archived log(s) in backup set
input archived log thread=1 sequence=87 RECID=86 STAMP=665092065
input archived log thread=1 sequence=88 RECID=87 STAMP=665138962
input archived log thread=1 sequence=89 RECID=88 STAMP=665172239
input archived log thread=1 sequence=90 RECID=89 STAMP=665172313
input archived log thread=1 sequence=91 RECID=90 STAMP=665172466
input archived log thread=1 sequence=92 RECID=91 STAMP=665175694
channel ORA_DISK_1: starting piece 1 at 11-SEP-13
channel ORA_DISK_1: finished piece 1 at 11-SEP-13
piece handle=C:\ORACLE\FAST_RECOVERY_AREA\ORCL
\BACKUP SET\2013_09_11\O1_MF_ANNNN_TAG20080911T190135_4DMHVZFK_.BKP
tag=TAG20080911T190135 comment=NONE
channel ORA_DISK_1: backup set complete, elapsed time: 00:00:07
```

channel ORA_DISK_1: deleting archived log(s)
archived log file name=C:\ORACLE\ARCH\ORCL\
ARC00087_0662757171.001 RECID=86 STAMP=665092065
archived log file name=C:\ORACLE\ARCH\ORCL\
ARC00088_0662757171.001 RECID=87 STAMP=665138962
archived log file name=C:\ORACLE\ARCH\ORCL\
ARC00089_0662757171.001 RECID=88 STAMP=665172239
archived log file name=C:\ORACLE\ARCH\ORCL\
ARC00090_0662757171.001 RECID=89 STAMP=665172313
archived log file name=C:\ORACLE\ARCH\ORCL\
ARC00091_0662757171.001 RECID=90 STAMP=665172466
archived log file name=C:\ORACLE\ARCH\ORCL\
ARC00092_0662757171.001 RECID=91 STAMP=665175694
Finished backup at 11-SEP-13
Starting backup at 11-SEP-13
using channel ORA_DISK_1
channel ORA_DISK_1: starting compressed full datafile backup set
channel ORA_DISK_1: specifying datafile(s) in backup set
input datafile file number=00002
name=C:\ORACLE\ORADATA\ORCL\SYSAUX01.DBF
input datafile file number=00001
name=C:\ORACLE\ORADATA\ORCL\SYSTEM01.DBF
input datafile file number=00005
name=C:\ORACLE\ORADATA\ORCL\UNDOTBS02.DBF
input datafile file number=00004
name=C:\ORACLE\ORADATA\ORCL\USERS01.DBF
channel ORA_DISK_1: starting piece 1 at 11-SEP-13
channel ORA_DISK_1: finished piece 1 at 11-SEP-13
piece handle=C:\ORACLE\FAST_RECOVERY_AREA\ORCL
\BACKUP SET\2013_09_11\O1_MF_NNNDF_TAG20080911T190200_4DMHWM1T_.BKP
tag=TAG20080911T190200 comment=NONE
channel ORA_DISK_1: backup set complete, elapsed time: 00:05:36
Finished backup at 11-SEP-13
Starting backup at 11-SEP-13
current log archived
using channel ORA_DISK_1
channel ORA_DISK_1: starting compressed archived log backup set
channel ORA_DISK_1: specifying archived log(s) in backup set
input archived log thread=1 sequence=93 RECID=92 STAMP=665176062

EXERCISE 3.2 *(continued)*

```
channel ORA_DISK_1: starting piece 1 at 11-SEP-13
channel ORA_DISK_1: finished piece 1 at 11-SEP-13
piece handle=C:\ORACLE\FAST_RECOVERY_AREA\ORCL
\BACKUP SET\2013_09_11\O1_MF_ANNNN_TAG20080911T190742_4DMJ7H29_.BKP
tag=TAG20080911T190742 comment=NONE
channel ORA_DISK_1: backup set complete, elapsed time: 00:00:01
channel ORA_DISK_1: deleting archived log(s)
archived log file name=C:\ORACLE\ARCH\ORCL
\ARC00093_0662757171.001 RECID=92 STAMP=665176062
Finished backup at 11-SEP-13
Starting Control File and SPFILE Autobackup at 11-SEP-13
piece handle=C:\ORACLE\FAST_RECOVERY_AREA\ORCL
\AUTOBACKUP\2013_09_11\O1_MF_S_665176080_4DMJ7SOT_.BKP comment=NONE
Finished Control File and SPFILE Autobackup at 11-SEP-13
```

RMAN Incremental Backups

Incremental database backups are a way to quickly back up your database. In the following sections, we will discuss incremental backups. First, you'll learn about configuring for incremental backups. Next, we will look at the two different kinds of incremental backups that are available, and then you'll learn how to actually do incremental backups.

Configuring for Incremental Backups

Technically, you don't have to configure anything to do an incremental backup. RMAN will perform an incremental backup when you issue the appropriate backup command. However, without any configuration, RMAN must inspect each block and determine whether it has indeed changed since the last backup and if it must go into the backup image.

Optionally you can create a *block-change tracking file* that will keep track of blocks that have changed since the last full or incremental backup. This can significantly reduce the time it takes to perform an incremental backup of your database because it removes the need for Oracle to inspect each data block to determine if it's been changed since the last backup. Figure 3.4 demonstrates the block-change tracking file.

The block-change tracking file can track only a maximum of seven different incremental level-1 backups. After the seventh backup, the initial level-0 backup records will be overwritten in the block-change tracking file. This will result in RMAN having to scan all database blocks on subsequent incremental backups. Thus, you should limit incremental backups without an intervening level 0 to a maximum of seven.

FIGURE 3.4   The block-change tracking file

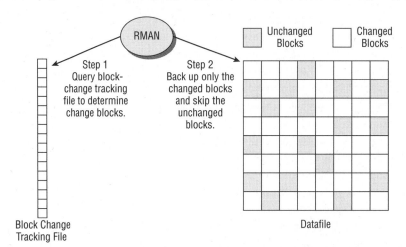

To create the block-tracking file, use the ALTER DATABASE ENABLE BLOCK CHANGE TRACKING command. By default, Oracle will create the block-change tracking file in the location defined by the DB_CREATE_FILE_DEST parameter. If that parameter is not set, Oracle will require that you provide a destination and filename for the block-change tracking file. Here is an example of the creation of a block-change tracking file:

```
SQL> alter database enable block change tracking using file
'c:\oracle\block_change_tracking\orcl_block_change.fil';
```

You can find the location of the current block-change tracking file by looking at the FILENAME column of the V$BLOCK_CHANGE_TRACKING view. You can use the STATUS column of the V$BLOCK_CHANGE_TRACKING view to determine if block-change tracking is enabled.

You should perform a level 0 incremental backup after creating the block-change tracking file. This is because the parent level-0 backup bitmap must be in the block-change tracking file.

Types of Incremental Backups

Two types of incremental backups are available for you to choose from:

- Level-0 incremental backup
- Level-1 incremental backup

The level-0 backup is like a full backup (sometimes it's called a base backup), except that incremental backups can be based on it (they cannot be based on a regular full backup).

The level-1 backup is the incremental backup that backs up changed blocks. There are two different kinds of level-1 backups:

* Differential incremental backup
* Cumulative incremental backup

The *differential incremental backup* will back up all changed blocks since the last level-1 backup. These images are typically smaller. The *cumulative incremental backup* is one where the data backed up is the data that changed since the last level-0 full backup. Thus it is a cumulative backup of all changed blocks since the last level-0 backup. This makes for faster recoveries since you don't have to apply several incremental backups during the database restore. Figure 3.5 provides a visual example of the differences between these types of backups.

FIGURE 3.5   Differential vs. cumulative incremental backups

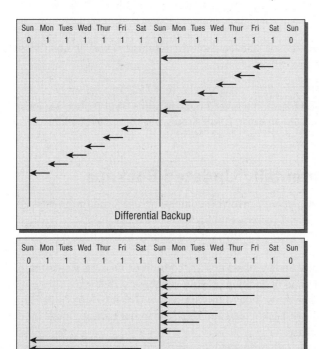

Performing Incremental Backups

Performing incremental backups is almost exactly like performing regular backups except that you include the INCREMENTAL LEVEL option in the BACKUP command. For example, to create a base level-0 backup, you would issue this command:

```
RMAN> Backup as compressed Backup Set incremental level 0 database plus
archivelog delete input;
```

When you are ready to run your first incremental backup you would use the BACKUP command with the incremental level-1 option, as shown here:

```
RMAN> Backup as compressed Backup Set incremental level 1 database plus
archivelog delete input;
```

Differential backups are the default type of incremental backup in Oracle. If you want to perform a cumulative backup, you will need to include the CUMULATIVE keyword, as shown here:

```
RMAN> Backup as compressed Backup Set incremental level 1 cumulative database
plus archivelog delete input;
```

 If you try to do a level-1 backup and a level-0 does not exist, RMAN will not generate an error. It will simply perform a level-0 backup for you instead.

RMAN Incrementally Updated Backups

Incrementally updated backups involve a combination of a full image backup of the database and then subsequent level-1 incremental backups of the database, which are applied to the image-copy backup. An incrementally updated backup makes for a quicker restore but for a bigger backup image.

Oracle incrementally updated backups are considered Oracle's suggested backup strategy. The benefit of this method of backing up your database is that it requires a minimum amount of time to restore it. The down side to this strategy is that it requires a base image copy of the database (as opposed to a backup set) and thus, the initial backup image is equivalent to the size of the target database.

To create an incrementally updated backup, all you need to do is run the following script:

```
RUN { # the recover copy command does not really recover anything.
      # it simply tells RMAN that the incremental to be executed should
      # be applied to the database copy we made above.
      Recover copy of database with tag 'Jacob_Jared_Lizzie';
      Backup incremental level 1
      for recover of copy with tag 'Jacob_Jared_Lizzie' Database; }
```

On the first execution of this script, RMAN will detect that no backup copy exists. Warnings will be generated but no errors. RMAN will proceed to create the initial copy of the database. No incremental copy will be created.

On subsequent executions, RMAN will detect that an image copy does exist, and it will then apply the previous level-1 incremental and then execute another level-1 incremental backup. Note that on the second run, RMAN will detect that no incremental backup exists to apply to the data file copy, and a warning will be raised because of this. That is normal.

This method limits the recovery window for your database to one day. For example, if you executed this script on day 1, day 2, and day 3, after day 3's execution you would not be able to restore your database to any point before day 3's backup.

You could provide for longer recovery windows by including the UNTIL TIME clause. In this example, we allow for a recovery window of five days:

```
run {
  recover copy of database with tag 'lisa' until time 'sysdate - 5';
  backup  incremental level 1 for recover of copy with tag 'lisa' database;
}
```

When configuring incrementally updated backups, you will want to configure the retention policy of the database to a redundancy of 1. This is because the retention policy is not honored in the case of this kind of backup. It is, instead, managed by the use of the UNTIL TIME clause of the RECOVER COPY OF DATABASE command.

RMAN Multisection Backups

Multisection backups were first available in Oracle Database 11*g*. They provide a way to parallelize the backup of a given database data file. Since data files had to be contained wholly within a single backup set, this meant that the backup of that data file was serialized. This can be a bit of a problem if your database consists of one or two huge data files and several smaller data files. Also, if you are using bigfile tablespaces, the lack of inner-file backup parallelization could be a big issue.

You perform multisection backups by using the SECTION SIZE clause in the BACKUP command followed by the desired section size. Here is an example:

```
RMAN> backup section size 40m database;
```

In this example, RMAN will divide up each data file into 40MB chunks, and each allocated channel can process those individual 40MB chunks. Note that if you allocate only one channel, only one chunk at a time will get backed up! Also note that the SIZE parameter does not indicate the size of the resulting backup set piece. Rather, it is the equivalent amount of data within the data file that each RMAN channel will process. The resulting pieces can vary wildly in size.

Previous to Oracle Database 12*c*, multisection backups were available only when performing full backups of the database. Incremental backups and image copies were not supported. Oracle Database 12*c* now supports multisection backups of full backups, incremental backups, and image copies.

RMAN Backup of Archived Redo Logs

Backing up archived redo logs is an important task since it serves to protect the database's principal recovery mechanism, which is redo. Backing up archived redo logs is done via the BACKUP ARCHIVELOG command. This command requires that you include keywords from the ARCHIVELOG SPECIFIER clause, which is used to indicate the archived redo logs that you want to back up. Common keywords that you might use include the following:

ALL   Backs up all archived redo logs currently on disk

SEQUENCE BETWEEN N AND O   Backs up all archived redo logs available on disk between sequence number *n* and sequence number *o*

TIME BETWEEN T1 AND T2   Backs up all archived redo logs available on disk between time *t1* (the earlier time) and time *t2* (the later time)

Be Careful What You Ask For. You Might Just Get It (or Not)

Look at the example where we backed up the archived redo logs for the last 24 hours. The command was as follows:

backup archivelog time between "sysdate-1" and "sysdate";

But guess what happens if you change this command just slightly:

```
RMAN> backup archivelog time between "sysdate" and "sysdate-1";
Starting backup at 05-SEP-2013
using channel ORA_DISK_1
RMAN-00571: ===========================================================
RMAN-00569: =============== ERROR MESSAGE STACK FOLLOWS ===============
RMAN-00571: ===========================================================
RMAN-03002: failure of backup command at 09/05/2013 19:02:56
RMAN-20242: specification does not match any archived log in the
recovery catalog
```

If you didn't know any better, you might just think that there are no archived redo logs to back up and assume the BACKUP ARCHIVELOG command worked fine and dandy. In fact, the command failed because you had the from/to dates in the wrong order. This highlights how important it is to make sure you carefully review the syntax of the command you are getting ready to execute and then review the output of RMAN commands and make sure RMAN did what you thought you told it to do.

Here is an example of backing up all archived redo logs, still on disk, that were generated in the last 24 hours:

```
RMAN> backup archivelog time between "sysdate-1" and "sysdate";
Starting backup at 05-SEP-13
using channel ORA_DISK_1
channel ORA_DISK_1: starting archived log backup set
channel ORA_DISK_1: specifying archived log(s) in backup set
input archived log thread=1 sequence=46 RECID=45 STAMP=664657241
channel ORA_DISK_1: starting piece 1 at 05-SEP-13
channel ORA_DISK_1: finished piece 1 at 05-SEP-13
piece handle=C:\ORACLE\FAST_RECOVERY_AREA\ORCL\BACKUP SET\2013_09_05\
01_MF_ANNNN_TAG20080905T190103_4D3OLO2G_.BKP tag=TAG20080905T190103
comment=NONE
channel ORA_DISK_1: backup set complete, elapsed time: 00:00:01
Finished backup at 05-SEP-13.
```

RMAN Backup of the Spfile and Control Files

We have already discussed control-file autobackups in this chapter. You may find that on occasion you want to do an individual backup of the control file or the spfile.

You have two options in RMAN for control-file backups, using the BACKUP CURRENT CONTROLFILE command or the BACKUP CONTROLFILECOPY command.

The BACKUP AS COPY command will cause the current control file to be backed up. This is a copy of the control file, so it's like a backup control file. Thus, you could just copy the file into place and treat it as a backup control file. By default, the backup will be created in the FRA, as would happen in this example:

```
RMAN> backup as copy current controlfile;
```

Or you can choose to define the location of the output control file, as shown in this example:

```
RMAN>backup as copy current controlfile format
'c:\oracle\controlfilebackup\contrf_backup.ctl';
```

The BACKUP CONTROLFILE COPY command will back up a control-file copy (created with the ALTER DATABASE BACKUP CONTROLFILE TO command or the BACKUP AS COPY CURRENT CONTROLFILE command). Here is an example of the use of the BACKUP CONTROLFILECOPY command:

```
SQL>Alter database backup controlfile to
'c:\oracle\controlfilebackup\contrf_backup.ctl';
RMAN>backup controlfilecopy 'c:\oracle\controlfilebackup\contrf_backup.ctl';
```

You can also back up spfiles with RMAN using the `BACKUP SPFILE` command, as shown in this example:

```
RMAN>Backup spfile;
```

Backing Up RMAN Backup Sets

Often database backups will be initially made to disk, and then later those backups will be backed up to tape. The reason for this is that backing up to disk is generally much faster than backing up to tape. Yet you want to back up to tape so you can offsite the media and because tape tends to be less expensive for longer-term storage (though this is quickly becoming less true).

To back up a backup set, you use the `BACKUP BACKUP SET` command, as shown here:

```
RMAN> backup device type sbt Backup Set all;
```

Backing Up the RMAN FRA

It is not unusual for an enterprise to have a multitiered backup strategy where the most current backups are in the FRA which exists on local disk. However, it is critical to those backup strategies to be able to move copies of those backup sets easily to other media that is not on the local server.

The `BACKUP RECOVERY AREA` RMAN command is used for this situation. This command will take all backup files in the FRA and move them to another disk or SBT location. RMAN will maintain a record of the location of both the files on the FRA and the copies of these files in the tier-two backup location.

The backups in the FRA will be managed by the retention criteria, but the location of the FRA backup files will not be managed by the retention criteria. Thus, you will need to implement separate retention criteria by using `RMAN DELETE OBSOLETE` command.

Here is an example of backing up files from the FRA to a secondary location. We then allocate a maintenance channel to the alternate backup location and delete backups that are older than 31 days old.

NOTE   We have included an alter system command at the top of this example. If you do not configure at least a single LOG_ARCHIVE_DEST_N destination directory to the location USE_DB_RECOVERY_FILE_DEST, then you will find that the backup recovery area command will continue to backup all of the files in the FRA, not just the newly created ones.

```
-- You only need to run the alter system command once.
Alter system set log_archive_dest_10=' LOCATION=USE_DB_RECOVERY_FILE_DEST';
Backup recovery area to destination 'c:\backup_copies';
```

```
Allocate channel for maintenance device type disk format 'c:\backup_copies';
Delete noprompt obsolete recovery window of 31 days;
```

Creating Archival Backups

There may be times when you want a backup to not be subject to a given retention criteria. This might be an end-of-the-year backup, or some backup required for legal reasons. In this case, you will want to perform an archival backup.

An archival backup is a completely self-contained backup of a database. It contains backups of the database datafiles, archived redo logs, and control file required to restore the database to the point in time that it was backed up.

An archival backup is created through the use of the KEEP keyword of the RMAN BACKUP command. You can indicate that the backup should be kept for a specific period of time. For example, you can say KEEP UNTIL TIME 'sysdate+25' to keep the backup for 25 days, as in this example:

```
Backup database keep until time 'sysdate+25' tag test_backup;
```

When the keep time expires, the backup will be considered eligible for removal by the RMAN DELETE OBSOLETE command. Note that the backup will be obsolete after the KEEP time, even if that time is less than the default retention criteria.

You can also indicate that the backup should be kept indefinitely by using the KEEP FOREVER command, as seen here:

```
Backup database keep forever tag test_backup_one;
```

 Any archival backup that uses the KEEP FOREVER will require the use of a recovery catalog, otherwise RMAN will generate an error.

Summary

In this chapter, we introduced you to RMAN, Oracle's backup and recovery tool of choice. We discussed the many features that make RMAN truly a power backup and recovery tool. We discussed the architecture of RMAN, including backup set pieces, which are the critical component of any RMAN backup.

We then talked about how to configure RMAN so that it is easy to use. Persistent configuration parameters are the key to RMAN's ease of use, and understanding what they are and what they do is key to understanding how RMAN works. There are a number of different configuration options to consider, including parallelism, compression, and encryption, and the OCP exam is poised to ask you about all of them.

Finally, we talked about actually backing up your database with RMAN. We talked about the various kinds of backups available to you, from complete database backups to incremental backups. We covered backing up tablespaces and data files and backing up archived redo logs. We even talked about backing up the backups themselves, as if we were not already talking to you in circles enough.

In the following chapters, we will be covering the RMAN recovery catalog, recovering your database with RMAN, reporting from RMAN, and finally, advanced RMAN recovery topics. So there is plenty of fun yet to go. Hang tight—it's going to be a fun ride!

Exam Essentials

Be able to describe the basic RMAN architecture.   Understand what backup sets and backup set pieces are. Understand that backup set pieces are physical files that contain the data that has actually been backed up. Understand what the Fast Recovery Area is, what its benefits are, and what parameters are required to configure it.

Be able to configure RMAN.   Understand what the RMAN CONFIGURE command does and how to use it. Understand how to use the SHOW command to display persistent configuration settings. Understand the use of the different persistent configuration settings, such as compression, encryption, and devices. Know the difference between a disk device and the SBT device (tape). Explain how RMAN retention policies work and how to configure them. Explain what backup optimization is and how it works. Understand how to configure for duplexed backups.

Know how to back up your database with RMAN.   Understand the different kinds of backups available in RMAN. Know what a whole database backup is and how to perform it both with configured settings and using a RUN block. Know how to use the KEEP command to override retention policies. Know what an incremental database backup is and how to perform it. Understand the different kinds of incremental database backups and how to create a block-change tracking file. Know what multisection backups are and how to create them. Know what image copies are and how to create them. Know how to back up archived redo logs, control files, and spfiles. Know how to back up backup sets.

Review Questions

1. How is block-change tracking enabled?

   A. With `ALTER DATABASE ENABLE BLOCK CHANGE TRACKING`

   B. With `ALTER SYSTEM ENABLE BLOCK CHANGE TRACKING`

   C. With an `init.ora` parameter change

   D. With an spfile parameter change

2. What type of backup is stored in a proprietary RMAN format?

   A. Backup set

   B. Image copy

   C. Backup section

   D. Backup group

3. Consider the following command:

   ```
   Backup database plus archivelog delete input;
   ```

   How many backup sets would be created by this command if the following were true:

   * Control-file auto backups were enabled.
   * The size of backup sets was not restricted.
   * One channel was allocated.

   A. 1

   B. 2

   C. 3

   D. 4

   E. 5

4. Which command creates an image copy?

   A. `BACKUP AS COPY`

   B. `BACKUP COPY`

   C. `COPY AS BACKUP`

   D. `COPY BACK`

5. Compressed backups work with which of the following commands?

   A. COPY AS BACKUP

   B. BACKUP AS COPY

   C. BACKUP

   D. COPY

6. Which is the correct command to back up the database, back up the archived redo logs, and then remove the backed-up archived redo logs?

   A. BACKUP DATABASE

   B. BACKUP DATABASE AND ARCHIVELOGS

   C. BACKUP DATABASE PLUS ARCHIVELOGS

   D. BACKUP DATABASE PLUS ARCHIVELOG DELETE INPUT

   E. BACKUP DATABASE AND ARCHIVELOG DELETE INPUT

7. Which of the following best describes a full backup?

   A. All data files of a database

   B. All data files, archive logs, and control files

   C. All data files and control files

   D. All the used blocks in a data file

8. Which type of backup backs up only data blocks modified since the most recent backup at the same level or lower?

   A. Differential incremental backup

   B. Different incremental backup

   C. Cumulative backup

   D. Cumulative incremental backup

9. Which type of backup must be performed first with an incremental backup?

   A. Level 1

   B. Level 0

   C. Level 2

   D. Level 3

10. Which backup option defines a user-defined name for a backup?

   A. FORMAT

   B. NAME

   C. TAG

   D. FORMAT U%

11. Given the following steps, which would be the correct order to create a backup of an Oracle database in NOARCHIVELOG mode?

   a. SHUTDOWN IMMEDIATE from RMAN

   b. Log into RMAN

   c. STARTUP MOUNT from RMAN

   d. BACKUP DATABASE

   e. ALTER DATABASE OPEN

   f. BACKUP DATABASE PLUS ARCHIVELOG DELETE INPUT

   A. b, c ,a, d, e

   B. b, a, c, f, e

   C. a, c, e, d

   D. b, a, c, e, f

   E. b, a, c, d, e

12. Which of the following most closely represents an image copy?

   A. Unix cp command of a file

   B. Bit-by-bit copy of a file

   C. Windows COPY command of a file

   D. All of the above

13. Which dynamic view displays the status of block-change tracking?

   A. V$BLOCK_CHANGE

   B. V$BLOCK_CHANGE_TRACKING

   C. V$BLOCKCHANGE

   D. V$BLOCK_TRACKING

14. What feature comes into play to help ensure the completion of the backup should one of three backup devices fail during a backup that is using three different channels?

   A. Channel failover

   B. Restartable backups

   C. Reschedulable backups

   D. Automatic backup recovery

   E. Channel recovery

15. What command would you use to set a persistent setting in RMAN so that backups are all written to a tape device?

   A. `CONFIGURE DEFAULT DEVICE TYPE TO TAPE MEDIA`

   B. `CONFIGURE DEFAULT DEVICE TYPE TO TAPE`

   C. `CONFIGURE DEFAULT DEVICE TYPE TO SBT`

   D. `CONFIGURE DEFAULT DEVICE TYPE TO SBT_TAPE`

16. The `CONTROL_FILE_RECORD_KEEP_TIME` initialization parameter should be set to what value? (Choose all that apply.)

   A. The initialization parameter should be set to 0 when the RMAN repository is being used.

   B. The initialization parameter should be set to greater than 0 with the RMAN repository utilizing the recovery catalog only.

   C. The initialization parameter should be set to greater than 0 with the RMAN repository utilizing the control file or the recovery catalog.

   D. The initialization parameter should be set to 0 with the RMAN repository utilizing the control file or the recovery catalog.

   E. The initialization parameter should never be set to 0 if you are using RMAN.

17. Given the following steps, which would be the correct order to create a backup of an Oracle database in ARCHIVELOG mode with control-file autobackups enabled?

   a. `BACKUP ARCHIVELOG ALL`

   b. `BACKUP DATABASE ALL`

   c. `BACKUP CONTROLFILE`

   d. `BACKUP ARCHIVELOG, DATABASE, CONTROLFILE DELETE INPUT`

   e. `BACKUP DATABASE PLUS ARCHIVELOG DELETE INPUT`

   A. e

   B. a, b, a, c

   C. d

   D. b, a, c

   E. b, a, c, d, e

18. Which of the following statements are true about the `BACKUP` command? (Choose all that apply.)

   A. The `BACKUP` command cannot be used to make image copies of a data file.

   B. The `BACKUP` command can improve performance by multiplexing backup files.

   C. The `BACKUP` command can take advantage of the block-change tracking capability.

   D. The `BACKUP` command cannot store data in incremental backups.

   E. The `BACKUP` command can store data in cumulative incremental backups only.

19. Which command is used to configure RMAN to perform a compressed backup for every backup executed?

    A. `BACKUP AS COMPRESSED BACKUP SET DATABASE`

    B. `BACKUP AS COMPRESSED COPY OF DATABASE`

    C. `CONFIGURE DEVICE TYPE DISK BACKUP TYPE TO COMPRESSED BACKUP SET`

    D. `CONFIGURE DEVICE TYPE DISK BACKUP TYPE COMPRESS`

    E. `BACKUP DATABASE COMPRESS`

20. You issue the following command:

`RMAN>configure backup optimization on;`

What is the result of this command on your backups?

    A. An incremental backup strategy will be used automatically.

    B. Read-only data files will not be backed up as long as backups of those files already exist and those backups meet established retention criteria.

    C. RMAN will configure itself for maximum performance at the cost of CPU.

    D. RMAN will configure itself for minimal OS/CPU impact at the cost of time to back up the database.

    E. RMAN will automatically compress backups.

Chapter

4

Using the RMAN Recovery Catalog

ORACLE DATABASE 12c: ADVANCED ADMINISTRATION EXAM OBJECTIVES COVERED IN THIS CHAPTER:

✓ **Create and use an RMAN recovery catalog**

  ▫ Configure a recovery catalog

  ▫ Register target databases in a recovery catalog

  ▫ Catalog additional backup files

  ▫ Resynchronize a recovery catalog

  ▫ Use and maintain RMAN stored scripts

  ▫ Upgrade and drop a recovery catalog

✓ **Protect the RMAN recovery catalog**

  ▫ Back up the recovery catalog

  ▫ Recreate an unrecoverable recovery catalog

  ▫ Export and import the recovery catalog

The RMAN recovery catalog is an optional component that you can use with RMAN. The recovery catalog provides an additional place to store RMAN related metadata, such as when backups were taken and where they were stored. In this chapter, we will review the recovery catalog so you will be prepared to answer recovery catalog OCP exam questions. This chapter will contain the information that you need to pass the Oracle OCP exam with respect to the RMAN recovery catalog.

So, let's get on with learning about the recovery catalog!

Exam objectives are subject to change at any time without prior notice and at Oracle's sole discretion. Please visit Oracle's Training and Certification website (http://www.oracle.com/education/certification/) for the most current exam-objectives listing.

Introducing the Recovery Catalog

The *RMAN recovery catalog* is a schema that sits in an Oracle database. This schema is designed to store RMAN-related information. The information stored in the recovery catalog is in large part just like that stored in the control file. Since most RMAN information is stored in the control file of a database, the recovery catalog serves as a backup repository for RMAN information.

Using the recovery catalog has some clear benefits that need to be carefully considered.

- The first is that it acts as a single location to store all your RMAN backup-related information.

- The recovery catalog can store backup-related information for many databases.

- The views of the recovery catalog are well documented, and so you can build reports from those views that will help you to understand the current status of your database backups.

* Another benefit is that the recovery catalog also makes global scripting of RMAN operations much easier.

    You simply store the scripts in the recovery catalog and call them as needed.

* The recovery catalog also enables a few RMAN operations not available without it, like using the KEEP FOREVER option (discussed in Chapter 3, "Configuring and Backing Up Oracle Databases Using RMAN") or keeping RMAN-related records for a period of time greater than a year.

* The recovery catalog can make some recovery operations somewhat easier, such as recreation of a control file.

As you can see, the recovery catalog adds to the overall RMAN architecture nicely. It provides redundancy and additional features that make it very useful. Not all environments will need a recovery catalog. If you have just one or two databases, then a recovery catalog may be more trouble than it's worth. If you have a large environment, though, the recovery catalog can make managing that environment much easier.

Confusing RMAN

Database duplication can cause the recovery catalog all sorts of problems if you are not careful. This is because each database in the recovery catalog is uniquely identified by its database ID, or DBID. If you duplicate a database manually, you must change the DBID of the newly created duplicate database with the Oracle NID utility. If you do not do this and you register the new database in the recovery catalog, RMAN will get confused as to who the individual catalog records belong to. This can put your ability to recover your database with RMAN at risk. Note that when you do an RMAN database duplication, it will change the DBID for you automatically when the duplication is complete.

The recovery catalog provides a number of views (called *recovery catalog views*) into the metadata contained therein. The OCP exam will likely not expect you to memorize these views, but it's still best to be aware of them. All the recovery catalog views start with an RC_ prefix and then end with a descriptive name of the data contained in the view. The following are some more popular recovery catalog views:

* RC_DATABASE
* RC_BACKUP_PIECE
* RC_BACKUP_PIECE_DETAILS
* RC_ARCHIVED_LOG

- RC_BACKUP_ARCHIVELOG_SUMMARY
- RC_BACKUP_SET
- RC_BACKUP_SET_DETAILS
- RC_BACKUP_SPFILE

Creating the Recovery Catalog User and Schema Objects

As we mentioned, the recovery catalog is a schema in an existing Oracle Database. This schema typically will have its own tablespace, where the RMAN recovery catalog schema data will be stored. Creating the recovery catalog user and schema is fairly easy. You use the CREATE USER command to create the database user first. You will then need to create the tablespace that will store the recovery catalog data.

Real World Scenario

To Use the Recovery Catalog or Not to Use the Recovery Catalog; That Is the Question

Adding components to any system has the potential to inject problems into that system. The same is true with the recovery catalog. One database shop implemented the Oracle recovery catalog at the same time they started using RMAN (this was using Oracle Database 10*g*).

Initially things worked great, but over time, backup performance became slower and slower. These performance problems were not seen when the recovery catalog was not in use. In the end, after lots of troubleshooting, they discovered that a couple of queries being issued against the recovery catalog schema were not tuned well and that these queries would slow down a great deal as the catalog schema got larger. They opened a service request with Oracle, and after some time Oracle found the problem and made a patch available.

The moral of this story, in our minds, is to use the KISS (keep it simple, stupid) principle when deciding if you need a recovery catalog or not. If you can justify the additional component because it will provide significant benefit, then by all means use it. Just understand that it's something else that may well break, and things always break at the most inopportune times.

In Exercise 4.1, you'll create a recovery catalog schema.

Metadata Storage Requirements

How much space you will need for the recovery catalog schema is a function of how often you back up the database and how long you retain the RMAN backup database in the recovery catalog. Oracle indicates that for one database with one backup per day and one archive-log backup per day, you can estimate metadata storage requirements of between 15MB and 120MB per year, per database, depending on how many backups (database, archive log, and so on) you do per day. The Oracle documentation provides more guidelines. You will not need to be familiar with these sizing guidelines when taking your OCP exam.

EXERCISE 4.1

Creating a Recovery Catalog Schema

Here are the steps to follow when creating the recovery catalog schema:

1. Open a command-line window. For this example, you will use a database called RCAT. You need to set the ORACLE_SID to RCAT as shown here:

   ```
   C:\Documents and Settings\dstuns>set ORACLE_SID=RCAT
   ```

2. Sign into the database using SQL*Plus:

   ```
   C:\Documents and Settings\Robert>sqlplus sys/robert as sysdba
   ```

   The RCAT database noted in this exercise is a database created by the DBCA. There is nothing different from this Oracle database compared to any other Oracle database except for the new schema and tablespaces you will create in this exercise.

3. Create a tablespace called RCAT_DATA. This tablespace will be used to store the recovery catalog schema data:

   ```
   SQL> create tablespace rcat_data
     2  datafile 'c:\oracle\oradata\rcat\rcat_data_01.dbf' size 60m
     3  autoextend on next 10m maxsize 200m;
   Tablespace created.
   ```

4. Create the user who will store the catalog:

- Use the name RCAT_USER with the password RCAT_USER.

- Make RCAT_DATA the default tablespace (we assume you have a default temporary tablespace already defined).

- Also, you will grant an unlimited quota on RCAT_DATA to RCAT_USER:

```
SQL> create user rcat_user identified by rcat_user
  2  default tablespace rcat_data
  3  quota unlimited on rcat_data;
User created.
```

5. The recovery catalog–owning user requires only a grant to the RECOVERY_CATALOG_OWNER role using the GRANT command:

```
SQL> grant recovery_catalog_owner to rcat_user;
Grant succeeded.
```

6. Test to see whether you can connect to the recovery catalog schema that you have just created:

```
SQL> connect rcat_user/rcat_user
Connected.
```

7. Now you need to create the recovery catalog schema. To do this, use the CREATE CATALOG command, as shown in this example:

```
C:\Documents and Settings\Robert>Rman catalog=rcat_user/rcat_user@rcat
Recovery Manager: Release 12.1.0.1.0 - Production on Sun Feb 23 13:30:59 2014
Copyright (c) 1982, 2013, Oracle and/or its affiliates.  All rights reserved.
connected to target database: ORCL12C (DBID=670264325)
 connected to recovery catalog database
RMAN> create catalog
recovery catalog created
```

Using a Recovery Catalog

Using a recovery catalog is pretty straightforward with RMAN. You simply indicate that you want to connect to the recovery catalog when you start RMAN. You will also have to register the database before your first RMAN operation when connected to the recovery catalog. Most RMAN operations when connected to the recovery catalog are pretty much the same; it's just that RMAN metadata will now be stored in both the control file and the recovery catalog. In the following sections, we will discuss these topics:

- Connecting to the recovery catalog from RMAN
- Registering the database with the recovery catalog
- Unregistering a database from the recovery catalog

Connecting to the Recovery Catalog from RMAN

When you start RMAN, you will need to indicate that you want to connect to a recovery catalog if you want the session to use the recovery catalog. There are a couple of ways of connecting to the recovery catalog. The first is to use the CATALOG RMAN command-line parameter, as shown in this example:

```
C:\Documents and Settings\Robert>Set oracle_sid=orcl
C:\Documents and Settings\Robert>Rman target=sys/Robert
catalog=rcat_user/rcat_user@rcat
Recovery Manager: Release 12.1.0.1.0 - Production on Tue Dec 24 15:19:07 2013
Copyright (c) 1982, 2013, Oracle and/or its affiliates.
All rights reserved.
connected to target database (not started)
connected to recovery catalog database
RMAN>
```

Understanding the connections to the *Target Database* and *Recovery Catalog*

As we first mentioned in Chapter 3, the database you are intending to back up is called the *target database*. In the previous example, you connected directly to the target database with RMAN. At the same time, you connected to the catalog database through Oracle Net. If you desire, you could connect directly to the catalog database and connect to the target database via Oracle Net, or you could connect to both databases via Oracle Net. Since the server itself does the backup work via locally allocated channels, connecting to the server or the recovery catalog through Oracle Net should not impose any undue performance constraints on the performance of your backups.

Another way of connecting to the recovery catalog is to do so from the RMAN command-line prompt using the CONNECT command, as shown in this example:

```
C:\Documents and Settings\Robert>Rman target=sys/Robert
Recovery Manager: Release 12.1.0.1.0 - Production on Tue Dec 24 15:19:07 2013
Copyright (c) 1982, 2013, Oracle and/or its affiliates.
```

```
connected to target database (not started)
RMAN> Connect catalog rcat_user/rcat_user@rcat
connected to recovery catalog database
```

> It should be noted that Oracle Cloud Control supports the creation and management of a RMAN recovery catalog. The OCP exam will not cover the use of Oracle Cloud Control, however, so we cover the manual methods of creating and managing the RMAN recovery catalog in this chapter.

Registering the Target Database with the Recovery Catalog

Once you have connected to the recovery catalog, you will have to register the database with the REGISTER DATABASE command. To be registered, the database must be mounted or open. In this example, you connect to the target database and the recovery catalog and then register the database with the recovery catalog:

```
C:\Documents and Settings\Robert>Rman target=sys/Robert
catalog=rcat_user/rcat_user@rcat
Recovery Manager: Release 12.1.0.1.0 - Production on Tue Dec 24 15:19:07 2013
Copyright (c) 1982, 2013, Oracle and/or its affiliates.
All rights reserved.
connected to target database: ORCL (DBID=1190537904, not open)
connected to recovery catalog database
RMAN> register database;
database registered in recovery catalog
starting full resync of recovery catalog
full resync complete
```

Unregistering a Database

If you are preparing to remove a database, you will want to remove its metadata from the recovery catalog. This is done with the UNREGISTER command, as shown in this example:

```
C:\Documents and Settings\Robert>Rman target=sys/Robert
catalog=rcat_user/rcat_user@rcat
Recovery Manager: Release 12.1.0.1.0 - Production on Tue Dec 24 15:22:07 2013
Copyright (c) 1982, 2013, Oracle and/or its affiliates.
```

```
All rights reserved.
connected to target database: ORCL (DBID=1190537904, not open)
connected to recovery catalog database
RMAN> unregister database;
database name is "ORCL" and DBID is 1190537904
Do you really want to unregister the database (enter YES or NO)? yes
database unregistered from the recovery catalog
```

Unregistering a database from the recovery catalog will cause all recovery catalog–related records to be removed from the recovery catalog. Control-file records for that database will be retained, of course. You might have had older backup records stored in the recovery catalog, though. When you unregister a database, those old records will be lost if the age of the backups exceeds the setting of the CONTROL_FILE_RECORD_KEEP_TIME parameter. Also, any scripts related to the database in the recovery catalog will be lost (we will talk more about scripting next).

Using Scripts in the RMAN Recovery Catalog

One benefit of the recovery catalog is the ability to store RMAN scripts. In the following sections, these topics will be addressed:

- Executing external scripts
- Creating stored scripts
- Replacing stored scripts
- Removing stored scripts
- Executing stored scripts
- Printing stored scripts
- Using script-substitution variables

Executing External Scripts

RMAN provides the ability to execute external scripts. You can do so from the RMAN command line using the CMDFILE option, as shown here:

```
Rman target=/ cmdfile=run_me.rman
```

You can also run an external script from within RMAN using the @ command, as shown here:

```
RMAN> @run_me.rman
```

Creating Stored Scripts

Recovery catalog stored scripts provide the ability to centrally manage your backup and recovery scripts. Using global stored scripts allows you to use common scripts across the entire enterprise.

Use the CREATE SCRIPT RMAN command to store scripts in the recovery catalog. You will assign a name to the stored script when you create it. Stored scripts can be created to do many RMAN operations, including backups, recoveries, and database-maintenance operations. As mentioned earlier, you must be connected to the recovery catalog to be able to create a script.

Here is an example of using the CREATE SCRIPT command to create a script. This script does a backup of the database and the archived redo logs:

```
create script db_backup_script
{ backup database plus archivelog delete input;}
```

Note that if you are using virtual private catalogs (see more on these later in this chapter), you will need to create the script as a global script, as shown here:

```
create global script db_delete_obsolete{ delete obsolete;}
```

Replacing Stored Scripts

The REPLACE SCRIPT command is used to replace stored RMAN scripts. The following example demonstrates the use of the REPLACE SCRIPT command:

```
Replace script db_delete_obsolete
{ delete noprompt obsolete;}
```

Removing Stored Scripts

If you need to remove a stored script permanently, you can use the DELETE SCRIPT command, as shown here:

```
Delete script db_delete_obsolete;
```

Executing Stored Scripts

Once you have created the script, it might be nice to actually run it! To run the script, you will use the EXECUTE SCRIPT command. This command must be run within the confines of an RMAN RUN block, as shown in this example:

```
Run {execute script db_backup_script;}
```

Printing Stored Scripts

The PRINT SCRIPT command will print your script to the standard output device, allowing you to cut and paste its contents. Here is an example of the PRINT SCRIPT command:

```
RMAN> Print script db_delete_obsolete;
printing stored script: db_delete_obsolete
{ delete obsolete;}
```

Using Script Substitution Variables

Oracle Database 12*c* provides for the use of *substitution variables* in RMAN scripts or command files. You define the substitution variables using the ampersand (&) character followed by a number, as shown in this example:

```
Restore database from tag &1;
```

The RMAN executable includes the USING command-line parameter that allows you to define the value of the substitution variable. For example, if the previous RESTORE command were in a file called restore.cmd and you wanted to restore a backup with the tag MINE, you would call RMAN in this manner:

```
Rman target=/ @restore.cmd using MINE
```

You can also use substitution variables with stored scripts. For example, you can create a script to back up your database and use a tag, as shown here:

```
RMAN> create script db_backup_script
2> { backup database tag  '&1' plus archivelog delete input;}
Enter value for 1: test
created script db_backup_script
```

You can then execute the script, setting the variable with the USING command, as shown here:

```
RMAN> Run {execute script db_backup_script using 'TEST';}
```

Maintaining the Recovery Catalog

If you are running the recovery catalog, you will need to know how to synchronize it with the control file of the database. Additionally, you will need to back up the recovery catalog. We briefly cover these two topics next.

Dropping the Recovery Catalog

As you can add a recovery catalog you can drop a recovery catalog. To drop the recovery catalog you simply log into the recovery catalog through RMAN, and then issue the DROP CATALOG RMAN command. There is no need to connect to any target database.

Upgrading the Recovery Catalog

Whenever you upgrade a database, you should also check to see if the recovery catalog database or schema needs to be updated. The recovery catalog database and recovery catalog schema should always be at the highest version of any database supported by that recovery catalog. You would upgrade the recovery catalog database just as you would any other database.

To upgrade the recovery catalog schema, you connect RMAN to a target database that is equal to or greater than the highest version of the databases that are serviced by the recovery catalog. Once you have connected to the recovery catalog you would run the UPGRADE CATALOG command.

When issuing the UPGRADE CATALOG command, you must issue the command twice to confirm that you want to perform the upgrade. Also, you must upgrade the entire recovery catalog. Virtual private catalogs cannot be upgraded separately.

Typically, the recovery catalog schema should be at the same version as the highest database (and RMAN client) version of the database that you will use to connect to the recovery catalog. The Oracle Database Backup and Recovery Reference provides more detailed information on compatibility of the RMAN client versions, the Oracle database version, and the RMAN recovery catalog version.

Synchronizing the Recovery Catalog

Typically during an RMAN operation, the recovery catalog will be synchronized with the control file. New records will be updated or added during this synchronization process. There may be times when you will want to synchronize the recovery catalog yourself manually. You can use the RESYNC CATALOG command to perform manual catalog synchronization. Here is an example of using the RESYNC command:

```
RMAN> resync catalog;
starting full resync of recovery catalog
full resync complete
```

Export and Import the Recovery Catalog

The Oracle RMAN Recovery Catalog fully supports the use of the Oracle Data Pump Export and Import tools. To export the recovery catalog you only need to back-up the recovery catalog schema from a user with sufficient privileges to export the recovery catalog schema. The same is true with importing a Data Pump dumpfile into a new recovery catalog schema.

The only other operations that might be needed are modification of the service for the new recovery catalog database, if that has changed. Otherwise, once the export is complete you can simply import that dump file into a newly created schema that has been granted the RECOVERY_CATALOG_OWNER privilege.

Backing Up the Recovery Catalog

You can actually back up the recovery catalog using RMAN. You would simply use the control file of the recovery catalog to store the backup-related information. You can do online or offline backups and complete or point-in-time restores as your needs dictate. You can also use Oracle's flashback features (see Chapter 8, "Understanding Flashback Technology," for more on Oracle Flashback Database) on the recovery catalog.

 Real World Scenario

Why Resync the Catalog?

You might be asking yourself, "If RMAN resynchronizes the catalog automatically after a backup, why would I ever need to use the RESYNC CATALOG command?" That's a fair question.

One place where one of us was employed had a large number of databases and used RMAN and the recovery catalog. As more and more records were added to the recovery catalog, we found our backups were taking longer. This ended up being because of a bug in RMAN. To work around the problem until Oracle could give us a fix, we did our backups without connecting to the recovery catalog. These made the backups perform much faster. We would then connect to the recovery catalog in a different operation and resync the control file to the recovery catalog.

This corrected the performance problem while still allowing us to use the recovery catalog to store our database backup metadata.

Recreating an Unrecoverable Recovery Catalog

What do you do if you have lost your recovery catalog and you don't have a backup of it. First of all, don't worry too much if you still have the database control file for the target databases. If you do, then a large majority of the information in the recovery catalog will still be intact. Let's look at what needs to be done to recreate an unrecoverable recovery catalog.

Recreating the Recovery Catalog Schema

The first thing we need to do is create a new recovery catalog from scratch. We demonstrated how to do this earlier in this chapter in the section called "Creating the Recovery Catalog User and Schema Objects."

Once the recovery catalog user and schema has been created (or recreated if you prefer), you will need to register each database that is to be stored in the recovery catalog with the newly created recovery catalog. During the registration process, the recovery catalog will be fully synchronized with the target database control file. If you are sure that all of the RMAN backup related metadata is in the control file of the target database then this would be all you need to do to recover a lost recovery catalog.

Cataloging Missing Records in the Recovery Catalog Schema

It's very possible that records that were in the recovery catalog will not be in the control file. They might have been overwritten at some point in time. It's also possible that archival backup records will be missing. There can be many reasons why existing backups stored in the recovery catalog would not be in the target database control file.

In the case where records are missing from the control file and/or the recovery catalog, you can use the RMAN CATALOG command to add additional records to the recovery catalog and the database control file.

The RMAN CATALOG command is very powerful. With the CATALOG command you can catalog these kinds of backup related files:

- database backups
- archive log backups
- and control file backups
- RMAN database image copies
- Non RMAN created database file image copies

When manually add backups using the CATALOG command, you can add backups that are either on disk or that were made through the SBT interface (i.e., tape). You will need to know the name and location of the file that you want to catalog.

If your backup files are on disk (but not the Fast Recovery Act (FRA), then you can simply have RMAN catalog the entire directory full of RMAN files. This is done using the CATALOG command and including the START WITH parameter.

For example, if all of the missing backup set files are in the c:\backup\oldbackups directory, you would first connect to the target database and the recovery catalog. Then you would use the CATALOG command to register these backup files in the recovery catalog, as seen here:

```
RMAN> Catalog start with 'c:\backup\oldbackups' noprompt;
```

If your backup files are on tape, then you will need to know how to properly reference their location when using the CATALOG command. The format you would use is very specific to each vendor that uses the SBT interface. Sometimes it's easier to just copy all of the backup files from tape to a disk device and catalog them from that device, assuming you have enough disk space available. You can then have RMAN move the newly cataloged backup files to tape again (assuming you have the time and network bandwidth).

Another option is if all the files are in the FRA, then you can use the RMAN CATALOG RECOVERY AREA command to re-catalog all files that are contained in the database's FRA.

Another occasion when you will need to use the CATALOG command is if backups were inadvertently deleted from the recovery catalog by the DBA, some wayward script, or an incorrectly set retention criteria. In this case, the backup set pieces might still be available but they will be shown as deleted in the database and in the recovery catalog. In this case, you can simply re-catalog these backups to have them added back to the database and the recovery catalog.

As you can see, the RMAN CATALOG command is a very powerful command and very helpful to have around when you have lost a backup record either in the control file or in the recovery catalog.

Using the RMAN Virtual Private Catalog

You might have noticed that the catalog-schema owner has access to all data in the recovery catalog. In many enterprises there may be hundreds of databases and dozens of people who have administrative access to databases. In these cases, you want to be able to restrict access to database backup records in the recovery catalog to those people who are authorized to have access to those records. In previous versions of the RMAN recovery catalog, this kind of separation would require different recovery catalogs to be created.

Oracle Database 11g introduced the notion of the RMAN virtual private catalog. The Oracle virtual private catalog provides the ability to secure the records in the RMAN recovery catalog on a user-by-user basis. Thus, one user may be able to see all records in the recovery catalog and another user may be able to see only records of a subset of the databases in the catalog.

In the following sections, we will discuss how to create a virtual catalog and how to grant users access to databases contained within it. We will discuss how to create the RMAN virtual private catalog first, and then we will discuss administration of the virtual private catalog.

Creating the RMAN Virtual Private Catalog

If you want to use the *RMAN virtual private catalog (RVPC)*, you start with a regular recovery catalog. The recovery catalog schema should have been created and the databases registered (you can, of course, register databases later), and it can be brand new or already in use.

Now that you have a recovery catalog, let's assume you have registered two databases in the recovery catalog; one is called ORCL and one is called secret. Let's assume you have a DBA named Ed who you don't quite trust (he's a seedy-looking guy with tattoos of the Smurfs all over his arms). Because you don't trust him, you want him to be able to access only the ORCL database RMAN records. The secret database records will remain a mystery to him (you assume, of course, that he does not have SYS access to your recovery catalog, or all is lost!).

To create the RVPC account for Ed, you would execute the following steps:

1. Create the RVPC database account.

First, you create the RVPC database account log in the recovery catalog database as a privileged user (for example, SYS) and issue the CREATE USER command. You will also need to grant the recovery_catalog_owner privilege to the new user.

2. Create the RVPC.

Once the RVPC user has been created, you need to create the virtual catalog. To do this, you log into RMAN as the RVPC user and use the CREATE VIRTUAL CATALOG command, as shown here:

```
Create virtual catalog;
```

3. Grant the RVPC access to the appropriate catalog databases.

4. Now that you have created the RVPC account, you need to indicate to the recovery catalog database which databases this account will have access to. In our case, let's assume we have two different database accounts in ORCL database called rcat_001 and rcat_002. These accounts are granted permission to back up the ORCL database with RMAN.

Since we have implemented VPC with RMAN, we will need to grant permission to access the catalog to these database users. You will use the RMAN GRANT CATALOG command to perform this operation, as shown here, where we grant access to the ORCL database catalog metadata:

```
grant catalog for database orcl to rcat_001;
```

Administering the RMAN Virtual Private Catalog

Once you have set up RVPC, there are other administrative activities you can perform. For example, you can grant the register database privilege to RVPC owners using the RMAN GRANT command, as shown here:

```
RMAN> grant register database to rcat_002;
Grant succeeded.
```

In this case, the rcat_002 user can register the ORCL database with the recovery catalog. The rcat_001 user could not register the database, however, since it does not have the register database privilege.

The REVOKE RMAN command is used to revoke privileges to databases in the RVPC or other privileges, such as the register database privilege, as shown here:

```
RMAN>Revoke catalog for database abc from rcat_002;
```

```
RMAN>Revoke register database from rcat_002;
```

Finally, you can drop the RVPC with the DROP CATALOG command, as shown in this example:

```
RMAN>connect catalog rcat_001/rcat001@rcat;
RMAN> drop catalog;

RMAN> drop catalog;

recovery catalog owner is RVPC
enter DROP CATALOG command again to confirm catalog removal

RMAN> drop catalog;

virtual catalog dropped]
```

After using the DROP CATALOG command, it's safe to drop the RVPC catalog user with the DROP USER SQL command:

```
SQL> drop user rcat_001;
```

Summary

The recovery catalog is an optional but very powerful tool in your RMAN arsenal. It can make your life as a DBA easier by providing a centralized repository for all your RMAN-related data. The recovery catalog is easy to create and maintain. Oracle's new virtual private catalog features make the recovery catalog even more powerful, increasing the security within the catalog.

Exam Essentials

Identify situations that will require the RMAN recovery catalog.   Understand that the recovery catalog is largely optional. A recovery catalog will be needed for storing scripts, and it will be required if you want to store backup records longer than one year or beyond the setting of CONTROL_FILE_RECORD_KEEP_TIME.

Create and use the RMAN recovery catalog.   Understand the process required to create the RMAN recovery catalog. Know how to create the recovery catalog user and what privileges are required. Understand how to register and unregister databases with the recovery catalog and how to create a virtual private catalog and configure users to use it.

Protect the RMAN recovery catalog.   Oracle's virtual private catalog feature of RMAN provides the ability to protect the data within the RMAN recovery catalog. You can isolate database backup–related records in the recovery catalog, configuring users such that they have access only to records they have privileges to.

Review Questions

1. What is the purpose of the RMAN recovery catalog? (Choose all that apply.)

    A. It must be used because all RMAN-related backup and recovery metadata information is contained in it.

    B. It provides a convenient, optional, repository of backup- and recovery-related metadata.

    C. It provides the ability to store RMAN scripts for global use by any database that has access to the repository.

    D. It provides a means of storing all RMAN backup sets physically in an Oracle Database server.

    E. It provides the ability to store backup records for more than a year.

2. What privileges must be granted to allow an account to create the recovery catalog? (Choose all that apply.)

    A. RECOVERY_CATALOG_OWNER

    B. DBA

    C. RESOURCE

    D. SELECT ANY DICTIONARY

    E. CONNECT

3. Which command do you use to create a recovery catalog schema?

    A. CREATE RECOVERY CATALOG

    B. CREATE CATALOG

    C. BUILD CATALOG

    D. CATALOG CREATE

    E. MOUNT CATALOG

4. If you back up a database without connecting to the recovery catalog, which operations will cause the recovery catalog to be updated? (Choose all that apply.)

    A. The next time you back up the database when you are also connected to the recovery catalog and the target database

    B. The next time you are connected to the target database and the recovery catalog database and issue the RESYNC command

    C. The next time you connect RMAN to just the recovery catalog

    D. The next time you connect to the recovery catalog and the target database with RMAN

    E. Connecting to the recovery catalog and issuing the RESYNC ALL DATABASES command

5. You have created a script in the recovery catalog called backup_database. Which of the following commands would successfully execute that script?

A.

```
run {
     open script backup_database;
     run script backup_database
     }
```

B.

```
run {
     engage script backup_database;
     }
```

C.

```
run {
     run script backup_database;
     }
```

D.

```
Run {
     execute script backup_database;
     }
```

E. The name backup_database is an invalid name for an RMAN script. Trying to run it from RMAN would result in an error.

6. In what order would you execute the following steps to create a recovery catalog?

a. Issue the CREATE CATALOG command.

b. Create the recovery catalog database.

c. Create the recovery catalog user.

d. Grant the recovery_catalog_owner privilege to the recovery catalog user.

e. Issue the REGISTER DATABASE command from the target database.

A. a, b, c, d, e

B. b, a, d, c, e

C. b, c, d, a, e

D. b, c, d, e, a

E. b, d, c, a, e

7. How would you grant the RVPC user access to specific RMAN database records in the RMAN virtual private catalog?

   A. Issue the GRANT command from the SYS user (or equivalent) of the target database.

   B. Issue the GRANT command from the SYS user (or equivalent) of the recovery catalog database.

   C. Issue the GRANT command from the recovery catalog–owning schema user account in the recovery catalog.

   D. Issue the GRANT command from RMAN when connected to the recovery catalog–owning schema.

   E. Issue the GRANT command from RMAN when connected to the target database.

8. The RVPC user can do which of the following? (Choose all that apply.)

   A. Register databases if granted the register database privilege.

   B. See all databases in the recovery catalog schema.

   C. See all database-related metadata in the recovery catalog if they are granted access to that database.

   D. Unregister databases from the RVPC catalog that were not granted to the RVPC catalog owner with the GRANT command.

   E. Connect to RMAN using the command-line CATALOG parameter for backup or recovery purposes.

9. Given the script

```
create script db_backup_datafile_script
{backup datafile &1, &2 plus archivelog delete input;}
```

What is the result of running this command?

```
Run {execute script db_backup_datafile_script using 2;}
```

   A. The script will fail since you instructed RMAN to back up only one data file rather than two.

   B. The script will successfully back up datafile 3 without error.

   C. The script will fail since it uses a substitution variable, which is not supported.

   D. The EXECUTE SCRIPT command will prompt for the value of &2 since it's not included in the command.

   E. The script will fail because you cannot use the PLUS ARCHIVELOG command when backing up database data files.

10. Which is the correct way to connect to both the target database and the recovery catalog from the RMAN command line? Assume that the target database is called ORCL and that the recovery catalog database is called RCAT. Also assume that the recovery catalog owner is called RCAT_OWN. Assume the environment is configured for the ORCL database. (Choose all that apply.)

A. RMAN TARGET=/ CATALOG=/@RCAT

B. RMAN TARGET=/ CATALOG=RCAT_OWN/RCAT_OWN

C. RMAN TARGET=/ CATALOG=RCAT_OWN/RCAT_OWN@RCAT

D. RMAN TARGET=SYS/ROBERT@ORCL CATALOG=RCAT_OWN/RCAT_OWN@RCAT

E. You cannot connect to the target database and the recovery catalog at the same time.

Chapter

5

Recovering Databases with RMAN

ORACLE DATABASE 12c: ADVANCED ADMINISTRATION EXAM OBJECTIVES COVERED IN THIS CHAPTER:

✓ Perform complete and incomplete recovery

✓ Use RMAN RESTORE and RECOVER commands

✓ Recover from media failures

✓ Perform complete and incomplete or "point-in-time" recoveries using RMAN

✓ Perform recovery for spfile, password file, control file, redo log files

✓ Perform table recovery from backups

✓ Perform recovery of index, read-only tablespaces, and temp file

✓ Restore a database to a new host

✓ Catalog additional backup files

Database recovery ought to be easy in your mind. You have enough problems when your database has unexpectedly left the building, and those problems should not be made worse by a bad piece of database-backup-and-recovery software. RMAN makes recovery of your database easy as long as you have crafted a solid backup and recovery strategy (discussed in previous chapters). Additionally, the old adage that practice makes perfect very much applies to database recoveries. So take some time and practice a recovery or two before you have to deal with the real thing. All too often, people wait for disaster to strike rather than learning what to do beforehand.

This chapter is about what to do when disaster strikes and you are under the gun to get your backup restored. In this chapter, we will discuss the following topics:

- RMAN database-recovery basics

- Recovering a database in NOARCHIVELOG mode

- Recovering a database in ARCHIVELOG mode

- Recovering data files or tablespaces in ARCHIVELOG mode

- Recovering a database using incomplete recovery

- Using image copies to recover your database

- Other recovery topics

The best way to really learn about backup and recovery is to do it—a lot. The exercises in this chapter along with the examples of the various forms of recovery will certainly get you on your way.

Exam objectives are subject to change at any time without prior notice and at Oracle's sole discretion. Please visit Oracle's Training and Certification website (http://www.oracle.com/education/certification/) for the most current exam-objectives listing.

In this chapter and in Chapter 6, "Tuning and Monitoring RMAN and the Automatic Diagnostic Workflow," we have opted not to use a recovery catalog in our examples. The functionality demonstrated is the same with or without a recovery catalog. Where there are exceptions to this rule, we will note them or provide additional examples.

RMAN Database-Recovery Basics

There is a common theme or pattern when recovering databases in RMAN that you will want to be familiar with. This pattern for recovery is as follows:

Step 1: Put the database in the correct mode.   Putting the database in the proper mode is the first step to recovering it. The proper mode is dependent on the type of recovery you want to be able to make. For example, in NOARCHIVELOG mode your database must always be in MOUNT mode to perform a recovery. We will cover the modes the database should be in for individual recovery in the later sections of this chapter.

RMAN provides commands that you can use to put the database in the mode you want it to be in (you'll find a summary of the RMAN commands in Chapter 3, "Configuring and Backing Up Using RMAN"). If you want the database mounted, then you can use the RMAN STARTUP MOUNT command, for example. RMAN recoveries will occur in almost any mode, NOMOUNT for control-file or spfile recoveries, MOUNT for offline database recoveries, or OPEN for ARCHIVELOG noncritical data file or tablespace recoveries. For the OCP exam, it will be a very good idea if you learn which modes are required for which recovery types.

The RMAN client is full-featured. There should be few times when any recovery operation will require you to use anything other than RMAN. If you do have to use something else, it probably means you have made a mistake, you are having a really bad day, or you have run into a bug (which in and of itself means you are having a really bad day).

Putting the database in the proper mode may also require restoring files required to put it in that mode. For example, if the spfile is missing, you may need to restore it. Perhaps the control file will need to be restored. You will find more information on these kinds of recoveries later in this chapter.

Step 2: Restore the database data files.   After the database has been put in the correct mode for the recovery chosen, you will use the RMAN RESTORE command to begin the database recovery. The RESTORE command will determine which backup set pieces or image copies need to be used to recover the database to the point in time that you direct. By default, RMAN will restore the database to the point of failure if you are running in ARCHIVELOG mode. If you are in NOARCHIVELOG mode, the restore will be to the point of the last backup. Once the data files have been restored, you will be returned to the RMAN prompt so you can issue the RECOVER DATABASE command.

The RESTORE command comes in different flavors, allowing you to restore the entire database, data files, or tablespaces. We understand that a future version will also allow you to restore your broken heart, but that's still in beta.

Step 3: Recover the database.   Once the database data files are restored, the RMAN RECOVER command is used to start the actual recovery process. During the execution of the RECOVER command, RMAN will extract the needed archived redo logs (if running in ARCHIVELOG mode) and apply them as needed. Obviously, during a NOARCHIVELOG-mode recovery, no redo will be applied (and in fact, you will indicate this when you do the recovery, as you will see later in this chapter). Once the RECOVER command has completed its job, you will be returned to the RMAN prompt so you can complete the recovery process by opening the database or bringing the tablespace or data file online.

As with the RESTORE command, the RECOVER command has a number of variations, such as RECOVER DATABASE, RECOVER TABLESPACE, and RECOVER DATAFILE. You will see these demonstrated throughout the rest of this chapter.

Step 4: Complete the recovery.   If your restore and recovery required the database to be in MOUNT mode, then all you need to do is open the database for business and you are the hero of the day. To do so, issue the ALTER DATABASE OPEN command from the RMAN prompt. If you did everything correctly, your database should open and your users will erect a statue in your honor. At one time we had upwards of 15 statues erected in our honor, only to be toppled by DBAs who succeeded us. Statues are, in the end, highly overrated.

Of course, if you didn't get your backup strategy right, your users may well throw another party in your honor—the going-away party, if your boss even allows that. So, you'll want to make sure you get it right the first time and even test it a few times before the real deal comes to town.

If your restore and recovery permitted the database to be open, then you probably had a tablespace or a data file offline. In this case, you will use the RMAN SQL command, embedding the ALTER TABLESPACE ONLINE or ALTER DATAFILE ONLINE command within the confines of that command. With the successful completion of those commands, your recovery will be complete and you can celebrate!

Now that we have shown you the basic pattern for recovering from a downed database, let's talk more specifically about the different kinds of database recoveries you will encounter.

In this chapter the recoveries we are contemplating are on the same hardware platform. In Chapter 6 we will address restoring and recovering databases to a new host, including cross-platform database recoveries.

Recovering a Database in NOARCHIVELOG Mode

Recovering your NOARCHIVELOG-mode database is perhaps the easiest thing you could do. There is no application of redo to worry about, only restoring the database data files and getting the database up and running. One important thing to understand is that your best recovery situation is from a database backup that is consistent. Fortunately, RMAN will force you to do consistent database backups when the database is in NOARCHIVELOG mode, so this isn't a problem. We discussed this situation in detail in Chapter 2, "Performing Oracle User-Managed Database Recoveries," so please make sure you reference that chapter and understand this important concept in backup and recovery. Oftentimes, knowing how something works and why will help you answer an OCP exam question that you otherwise don't really know the answer to.

So, how easy is recovery of your database in NOARCHIVELOG mode? Here are the steps in summary form. We will give you more detail as this chapter progresses:

1. If you have lost your control file or spfile (or database parameter file), you will need to reference the section on recovering your control file or spfile with RMAN, which appears later in this chapter. To start any RMAN recovery, you must have a control file and an spfile (or database parameter file).

2. If you are not already logged into RMAN (for example, if you had to restore your control file), then log into RMAN now. You will see lots of examples of this later in this chapter.

3. Mount your database with the STARTUP MOUNT command.

4. Issue the RMAN RESTORE DATABASE command.

5. Issue the RMAN RECOVER DATABASE command. Because this is a NOARCHIVELOG-mode database recovery, you will need to include the NOREDO keyword to indicate that there is no redo to be applied.

6. Open the database with the ALTER DATABASE OPEN command.

Here is an example of an RMAN restore of a database in NOARCHIVELOG mode:

```
RMAN> connect target /

RMAN> shutdown abort
using target database control file instead of recovery catalog
Oracle instance shut down
RMAN> startup mount
connected to target database (not started)
Oracle instance started
database mounted
Total System Global Area     397557760 bytes
Fixed Size                     1333452 bytes
Variable Size                339740468 bytes
Database Buffers              50331648 bytes
Redo Buffers                   6152192 bytes
RMAN> restore database;
Starting restore at 28-SEP-13
allocated channel: ORA_DISK_1
channel ORA_DISK_1: SID=154 device type=DISK
channel ORA_DISK_1: starting datafile backup set restore
channel ORA_DISK_1: specifying datafile(s) to restore from backup set
```

```
channel ORA_DISK_1: restoring datafile 00002 to
C:\ORACLE\ORADATA\ORCL\SYSAUX01.DBF
channel ORA_DISK_1: reading from backup piece
 C:\ORACLE\FAST_RECOVERY_AREA\ORCL\BACKUPSET\2013_09_22
\O1_MF_NNNDF_TAG20130922T182631_4FJFXXVT_.BKP
channel ORA_DISK_1: piece
handle=C:\ORACLE\FAST_RECOVERY_AREA\ORCL\BACKUPSET\2013_09_22
\O1_MF_NNNDF_TAG20130922T182631_4FJFXXVT_.BKP tag=TAG20130922T182631
channel ORA_DISK_1: restored backup piece 1
channel ORA_DISK_1: restore complete, elapsed time: 00:02:25
channel ORA_DISK_1: starting datafile backup set restore
channel ORA_DISK_1: specifying datafile(s) to restore from backup set
channel ORA_DISK_1: restoring datafile 00001 to
C:\ORACLE\ORADATA\ORCL\SYSTEM01.DBF
channel ORA_DISK_1: restoring datafile 00004 to
C:\ORACLE\ORADATA\ORCL\USERS01.DBF
channel ORA_DISK_1: restoring datafile 00005 to
C:\ORACLE\ORADATA\ORCL\UNDOTBS02.DBF
channel ORA_DISK_1: reading from backup piece
C:\ORACLE\FAST_RECOVERY_AREA\ORCL\BACKUPSET\2013_09_28\
O1_MF_NNNDF_TAG20130928T165801_4G02ZZC7_.BKP
channel ORA_DISK_1: piece
 handle=C:\ORACLE\FAST_RECOVERY_AREA\ORCL\BACKUPSET\2013_09_28
\O1_MF_NNNDF_TAG20130928T165801_4G02ZZC7_.BKP tag=TAG20130928T165801
channel ORA_DISK_1: restored backup piece 1
channel ORA_DISK_1: restore complete, elapsed time: 00:02:55
Finished restore at 28-SEP-13
RMAN> recover database noredo;
Starting recover at 28-SEP-13
using channel ORA_DISK_1
Finished recover at 28-SEP-13
RMAN> alter database open;
database opened
```

Recovering a Database in ARCHIVELOG Mode

If your database is in ARCHIVELOG mode, then your recovery options might include a complete database recovery or an online data file or tablespace recovery. Another option is point-in-time recovery, which we discuss later in this chapter. Other, more advanced options, including tablespace point-in-time recovery, are also available. These are covered in Chapter 6 of this book.

Complete recovery is called for when all or most of the data files of the database have been lost. Tablespace or data file recovery is a better solution if you have lost only a few data files or perhaps all data files of one or two tablespaces. Let's look at each of these recovery methods in more detail next.

Complete Database Recovery in ARCHIVELOG Mode

A *complete* database recovery in ARCHIVELOG mode is required when most or all of the database data files have been lost. In this mode, the database is shut down (if it has not already done so itself because of the loss of data files). It is then mounted and recovered. Here are the steps to follow for a complete database recovery in ARCHIVELOG mode:

1. Shut down the database if it is not already down.

2. If you have lost your control file or spfile, you will need to reference the section "Other Basic Recovery Topics," which appears later in this chapter. To start any RMAN recovery, you must have a control file and an spfile or parameter file.

3. If you are not already logged into RMAN (for example, if you had to restore your control file), then log into RMAN now.

4. Mount your database with the STARTUP MOUNT command.

5. Issue the RMAN RESTORE DATABASE command.

6. Issue the RMAN RECOVER DATABASE command. The command will restore the needed incremental backups and archived redo logs, recovering the database to the point of failure.

7. Open the database with the ALTER DATABASE OPEN command. If you restored your control file, you will need to use the ALTER DATABASE OPEN RESETLOGS command.

Here is an example of a recovery in ARCHIVELOG mode:

```
RMAN> shutdown abort
using target database control file instead of recovery catalog
Oracle instance shut down
RMAN> startup mount
connected to target database (not started)
Oracle instance started
database mounted
Total System Global Area     397557760 bytes
Fixed Size                     1333452 bytes
Variable Size                339740468 bytes
Database Buffers              50331648 bytes
Redo Buffers                   6152192 bytes
RMAN> restore database;
Starting restore at 28-SEP-13
```

```
allocated channel: ORA_DISK_1
channel ORA_DISK_1: SID=154 device type=DISK
channel ORA_DISK_1: starting datafile backup set restore
channel ORA_DISK_1: specifying datafile(s) to restore from backup set
channel ORA_DISK_1: restoring datafile 00002 to
C:\ORACLE\ORADATA\ORCL\SYSAUX01.DBF
channel ORA_DISK_1: reading from backup piece
 C:\ORACLE\FAST_RECOVERY_AREA\ORCL\BACKUPSET\2013_09_22
\O1_MF_NNNDF_TAG20130922T182631_4FJFXXVT_.BKP
channel ORA_DISK_1: piece
handle=C:\ORACLE\FAST_RECOVERY_AREA\ORCL\BACKUPSET\2013_09_22
\O1_MF_NNNDF_TAG20130922T182631_4FJFXXVT_.BKP tag=TAG20130922T182631
channel ORA_DISK_1: restored backup piece 1
channel ORA_DISK_1: restore complete, elapsed time: 00:02:35
channel ORA_DISK_1: starting datafile backup set restore
channel ORA_DISK_1: specifying datafile(s) to restore from backup set
channel ORA_DISK_1: restoring datafile 00001 to
 C:\ORACLE\ORADATA\ORCL\SYSTEM01.DBF
channel ORA_DISK_1: restoring datafile 00004 to
 C:\ORACLE\ORADATA\ORCL\USERS01.DBF
channel ORA_DISK_1: restoring datafile 00005 to
 C:\ORACLE\ORADATA\ORCL\UNDOTBS02.DBF
channel ORA_DISK_1: reading from backup piece
C:\ORACLE\FAST_RECOVERY_AREA\ORCL\BACKUPSET\2013_09_28
\O1_MF_NNNDF_TAG20130928T172015_4G049OQX_.BKP
channel ORA_DISK_1: piece
handle=C:\ORACLE\FAST_RECOVERY_AREA\ORCL\BACKUPSET\2013_09_28
\O1_MF_NNNDF_TAG20130928T172015_4G049OQX_.BKP tag=TAG20130928T172015
channel ORA_DISK_1: restored backup piece 1
channel ORA_DISK_1: restore complete, elapsed time: 00:02:45
Finished restore at 28-SEP-13
RMAN> recover database;
Starting recover at 28-SEP-13
using channel ORA_DISK_1
starting media recovery
media recovery complete, elapsed time: 00:00:03
Finished recover at 28-SEP-13
RMAN> Alter database open;
database opened
```

If you added a data file or a tablespace to the database after your last RMAN backup, RMAN will add that tablespace or data file for you automatically during a restore. Additionally, RMAN will recreate any tempfiles needed during a restore process automatically.

In Exercise 5.1, you'll restore your ARCHIVELOG-mode database with RMAN.

EXERCISE 5.1

Restoring Your ARCHIVELOG-Mode Database with RMAN

This activity builds on the backup done in Exercise 3.2 from Chapter 3. You should have completed Exercise 3.2 prior to executing this activity. Please note that the output you experience from this exercise will probably differ from the output shown in this exercise.

1. Complete Exercise 3.2.

2. Log into the database as SYS using SQL*Plus:

```
C:\oracle>set oracle_sid=orcl
C:\oracle>sqlplus sys as sysdba
SQL*Plus: Release 12.1.0.1.0 Production on Fri Dec 27 10:20:57 2013
Copyright (c) 1982, 2013, Oracle.  All rights reserved.
Enter password:
Connected to:
Oracle Database 12c Enterprise Edition Release 12.1.0.1.0 - 64bit Production
With the Partitioning, OLAP, Advanced Analytics and Real Application Testing
options
SQL>
```

3. Determine the location of the database data files by issuing the SELECT FILE_NAME FROM DBA_DATA_FILES; query:

```
SQL> select file_name from dba_data_files;
FILE_NAME
------------------------------------------------------------------
C:\ORACLE\FAST_RECOVERY_AREA\ORCL\DATAFILE\O1_MF_USERS_4G2Q1YTC_.DBF
C:\ORACLE\ORADATA\ORCL\UNDOTBS01.DBF
C:\ORACLE\ORADATA\ORCL\SYSAUX01.DBF
C:\ORACLE\ORADATA\ORCL\SYSTEM01.DBF
```

4. Shut down the database:

```
SQL> shutdown abort
ORACLE instance shut down.
```

EXERCISE 5.1 *(continued)*

5. Exit SQL*Plus:

```
SQL> quit
Disconnected from Oracle Database 12c Enterprise Edition Release 12.1.0.1.0 –
64bit Production
With the Partitioning, OLAP, Advanced Analytics and Real Application Testing
options
C:\oracle>
```

6. From the operating system prompt, delete all the database data files listed in step 3.

Be careful not to do a wildcard delete because you might delete files in that directory that you do not want to remove, such as the online redo logs or the database control files.

```
C:\oracle>Del C:\ORACLE\FAST_RECOVERY_AREA\ORCL\DATAFILE\O1_MF_
USERS_4G2Q1YTC_.DBF
C:\oracle>Del C:\ORACLE\ORADATA\ORCL\UNDOTBS01.DBF
C:\oracle>Del C:\ORACLE\ORADATA\ORCL\SYSAUX01.DBF
C:\oracle>Del C:\ORACLE\ORADATA\ORCL\SYSTEM01.DBF
```

7. Log into the database as SYS using SQL*Plus:

```
C:\oracle>sqlplus sys as sysdba
SQL*Plus: Release 12.1.0.1.0 Production on Fri Dec 27 10:20:57 2013
Copyright (c) 1982, 2013, Oracle.  All rights reserved. Enter password:
Enter password:
Connected to an idle instance.
```

8. Start the database. Notice the error that you receive:

```
SQL> startup
ORACLE instance started.
Total System Global Area  364081152 bytes
Fixed Size                  1333228 bytes
Variable Size             264243220 bytes
Database Buffers           92274688 bytes
Redo Buffers                6230016 bytes
Database mounted.
ORA-01157: cannot identify/lock data file 1 - see DBWR trace file
ORA-01110: data file 1: 'C:\ORACLE\ORADATA\ORCL\SYSTEM01.DBF'
```

9. Shut down the database:

```
SQL> shutdown abort
ORACLE instance shut down.
```

EXERCISE 5.1 *(continued)*

10. Exit SQL*Plus:

    ```
    SQL> quit
    Disconnected from Oracle Database 12c
    Enterprise Edition Release 12.1.0.1.0 - 64bit Production
    With the Partitioning, OLAP, Advanced Analytics and Real Application Testing
    options
    C:\oracle>
    ```

11. Start RMAN. We will assume you are not using a recovery catalog during this exercise.

    ```
    C:\oracle>rman target=/
    Recovery Manager: Release 12.1.0.1.0 - Production on Fri Dec 27 10:23:32 2013
    Copyright (c) 1982, 2013, Oracle and/or its affiliates.  All rights reserved.
    connected to target database (not started)
    ```

12. Start up the database with the STARTUP MOUNT command from RMAN:

    ```
    RMAN> startup mount
    Oracle instance started
    database mounted
    Total System Global Area    364081152 bytes
    Fixed Size                    1333228 bytes
    Variable Size               264243220 bytes
    Database Buffers             92274688 bytes
    Redo Buffers                  6230016 bytes
    ```

13. Restore the database files with the RESTORE DATABASE command:

    ```
    RMAN> restore database;
    Starting restore at 10/03/2013 00:38:55
    using target database control file instead of recovery catalog
    allocated channel: ORA_DISK_1
    channel ORA_DISK_1: SID=155 device type=DISK
    channel ORA_DISK_1: starting datafile backup set restore
    channel ORA_DISK_1: specifying datafile(s) to restore from backup set
    channel ORA_DISK_1: restoring datafile 00001 to
    C:\ORACLE\ORADATA\ORCL\SYSTEM01.DBF
    channel ORA_DISK_1: restoring datafile 00002 to
    C:\ORACLE\ORADATA\ORCL\SYSAUX01.DBF
    channel ORA_DISK_1: restoring datafile 00003 to
    C:\ORACLE\ORADATA\ORCL\UNDOTBS01.DBF
    channel ORA_DISK_1: restoring datafile 00004 to
    C:\ORACLE\FAST_RECOVERY_AREA\ORCL\DATAFILE\O1_MF_USERS_4G2Q1YTC_.DBF
    ```

```
channel ORA_DISK_1: reading from backup piece
C:\ORACLE\FAST_RECOVERY_AREA\ORCL\BACKUPSET\2013_10_03
\O1_MF_NNNDF_TAG20131003T001928_4GCGCQQ4_.BKP
channel ORA_DISK_1: piece
handle=C:\ORACLE\FAST_RECOVERY_AREA\ORCL\BACKUPSET\2013_10_03
\O1_MF_NNNDF_TAG20131003T001928_4GCGCQQ4_.BKP tag=TAG20131003T001928
channel ORA_DISK_1: restored backup piece 1
channel ORA_DISK_1: restore complete, elapsed time: 00:04:05
Finished restore at 10/03/2013 00:43:02
RMAN>
```

14. Recover the database with the RECOVER DATABASE command:

```
RMAN> recover database;
Starting recover at 10/03/2013 01:43:59
using channel ORA_DISK_1
starting media recovery

media recovery complete, elapsed time: 00:00:04
Finished recover at 10/03/2013 01:44:05
RMAN>
```

15. Open the database with the ALTER DATABASE OPEN command:

```
RMAN> alter database open;
database opened
```

The database is open.

We move back and forth between SQL*Plus and RMAN a lot in our examples. In Oracle Database 12c, you can choose to execute almost all of these queries from the RMAN prompt if you prefer.

Data File or Tablespace Recovery in ARCHIVELOG Mode

If you have lost one or a few database data files, or perhaps all the data files lost are part of a tablespace, you can perform recovery actions specific to those few lost data files rather than to the database as a whole. *Data file recoveries* and *tablespace recoveries* can be far faster than recovering the entire database with a complete recovery.

Some data file and tablespace recoveries require that the database be in MOUNT mode. If you have lost the SYSTEM tablespace or the active UNDO tablespace (or an inactive tablespace that contained transactions when the database was shut down), then your recovery will have to be done with the database mounted.

The best recoveries (if there is really any kind of recovery that is considered good) are those that your users know nothing about. If the data file or tablespace that was lost was not the SYSTEM or active UNDO tablespace, then you can recover that data file or tablespace while the rest of the database is still online. Thus, unless the users need access to the tablespace that is being restored, they will never know that you were in the throes of some form of recovery.

In the following sections, we will address these two kinds of data file and tablespace recoveries. First, we will address recovery of a data file or tablespace when the SYSTEM or active UNDO tablespace is down and the database is not open. We will then address data file and tablespace recoveries when the database is open and running.

Recovering Critical Database Data Files and/or Tablespaces with the Database Down

If the SYSTEM or the active UNDO tablespace, or data files associated with those tablespaces, are lost, then you will have to recover with the database shut down. In fact, if data files associated with these tablespaces are lost, it's likely that the database will have crashed anyway. You can use the RESTORE DATAFILE or RESTORE TABLESPACE RMAN command to restore the lost data files or tablespaces quickly, in turn getting the database recovered as quickly as possible.

To restore a database data file or tablespace with the database shut down, follow these steps.

1. If the database is not already shut down, try to force a checkpoint and then shut down the database as normally as possible.

   It is possible that when you force the checkpoint, the database will crash.

2. If you have lost your control file or spfile, you will need to reference the section "Other Basic Recovery Topics," which appears later in this chapter. To start any RMAN recovery, you must have a control file and an spfile or parameter file.

3. Mount your database with the STARTUP MOUNT command.

4. You will use the RMAN RESTORE command to restore the data files or tablespaces. If you have lost all or most of the data files related to a given tablespace, then issue the RMAN RESTORE TABLESPACE command. If you have lost one or just a few data files, use the RESTORE DATAFILE command. Once the restore is complete, you will be returned to the RMAN prompt.

5. You now need to recover the database with the RMAN RECOVER command. This will apply any incremental backups and any archived redo logs to the data files being restored. If you used the RESTORE TABLESPACE command, recover the tablespace with the RECOVER TABLESPACE command. If you used the RESTORE DATAFILE command, use the RECOVER DATAFILE command to start recovery. Once recovery is complete, you will be returned to the RMAN prompt.

6. Open the database with the ALTER DATABASE OPEN command. If you restored your control file, you will need to use the ALTER DATABASE OPEN RESETLOGS command.

In this example, we will try to start up our database from the RMAN prompt only to find that the SYSTEM tablespace data file is missing for some odd reason:

```
RMAN> startup
Oracle instance started
database mounted
RMAN-00571: ============================================================
RMAN-00569: =============== ERROR MESSAGE STACK FOLLOWS ===============
RMAN-00571: ============================================================
RMAN-03002: failure of startup command at 09/28/2013 17:37:53
ORA-01157: cannot identify/lock data file 1 - see DBWR trace file
ORA-01110: data file 1: 'C:\ORACLE\ORADATA\ORCL\SYSTEM01.DBF'
```

We could, of course, restore the entire database, but the size of the SYSTEM tablespace/ data file is a very small part of the overall size of the database. So we will just restore and recover the SYSTEM tablespace. Note that the SYSTEM tablespace is a critical tablespace; thus, this recovery cannot be done online:

```
RMAN> startup
Oracle instance started
database mounted
RMAN-00571: ============================================================
RMAN-00569: =============== ERROR MESSAGE STACK FOLLOWS ===============
RMAN-00571: ============================================================
RMAN-03002: failure of startup command at 09/28/2013 17:37:53
ORA-01157: cannot identify/lock data file 1 - see DBWR trace file
ORA-01110: data file 1: 'C:\ORACLE\ORADATA\ORCL\SYSTEM01.DBF'
RMAN> restore tablespace system;
Starting restore at 28-SEP-13
using target database control file instead of recovery catalog
allocated channel: ORA_DISK_1
channel ORA_DISK_1: SID=153 device type=DISK
channel ORA_DISK_1: starting datafile backup set restore
channel ORA_DISK_1: specifying datafile(s) to restore from backup set
channel ORA_DISK_1: restoring datafile 00001 to
C:\ORACLE\ORADATA\ORCL\SYSTEM01.DBF
channel ORA_DISK_1: reading from backup piece
C:\ORACLE\FAST_RECOVERY_AREA\ORCL\BACKUPSET\2013_09_28
\O1_MF_NNNDF_TAG20130928T172015_4G049OQX_.BKP
channel ORA_DISK_1: piece
```

```
handle=C:\ORACLE\FAST_RECOVERY_AREA\ORCL\BACKUPSET\2013_09_28
\O1_MF_NNNDF_TAG20130928T172015_4G049OQX_.BKP tag=TAG20130928T172015
channel ORA_DISK_1: restored backup piece 1
channel ORA_DISK_1: restore complete, elapsed time: 00:03:35
Finished restore at 28-SEP-13
RMAN> recover tablespace system;
Starting recover at 28-SEP-13
using channel ORA_DISK_1
starting media recovery
media recovery complete, elapsed time: 00:00:03
Finished recover at 28-SEP-13
RMAN> alter database open;
database opened
```

Restoring Data Files to Different Locations

If during a recovery you need to restore data files to a different location, you will need to use the RMAN SET NEWNAME command to reset the location of each data file that is to be relocated. For example, if you wanted to relocate the USERS01.DBF data file from c:\oracle\oradata\orcl to d:\oracle\oradata\orcl during an RMAN recovery, you would issue this command:

```
set newname for 'c:\oracle\oradata\orcl\users01.dbf' to
'd:\oracle\oradata\orcl\users01.dbf';
```

Note that if you use the SET NEWNAME command, you will have to include it and all restore-and-recovery-related commands within a RUN block, as shown here:

```
run { set newname for datafile 'c:\oracle\oradata\orcl\users01.dbf' to
'c:\oracle\oradata\orcltwo\users01.dbf';
restore database;
recover database; }
```

This section maps to objectives that include restoring index tablespaces.

Recovering Noncritical Database Data Files and/or Tablespaces with the Database Open

When you have lost a data file or a few data files or all the data files of one or several tablespaces, RMAN provides the ability to restore those data files online without having to shut down the database. This is known as an *online data file recovery* or *online tablespace recovery*. Online recoveries allow users to access unaffected tablespaces/data files of the database without knowing that other parts of the database are unavailable. To be sure, anyone who tries to use the parts of the database that are being recovered will know that something is not right, but something working is better than nothing, right?

The SYSTEM and active UNDO tablespaces are considered critical tablespaces and thus are the only tablespaces that will require recovery of the database with the database down (see the previous section for a discussion on recovery of these critical tablespaces). Any other tablespace can be restored with the database running. Let's look at online database recoveries with data files and then tablespaces in the next sections.

 You never need to restore temporary files that are associated with temporary tablespaces. First, RMAN will never back up the temporary tablespace, because it does not need to. All RMAN needs to know is that the temporary tablespace exists, and it knows this by virtue of reading the control file of the database. Knowing what temporary tablespace and what tempfiles are needed, RMAN will simply add the tempfiles to the temporary tablespace after a complete or point-in-time database restore. No data file restore needed!

Preparing to Restore Data Files or Tablespaces Online

It may be that your database is already shut down and will not start because of the missing data files. It may or may not make sense to open the database before starting the restore so users can access unaffected data. To open the database when noncritical data files are missing, follow these steps:

1. From the RMAN prompt, issue the STARTUP command.

   An error will appear indicating the data file that is missing. This will report on just a single missing data file. You can use the REPORT SCHEMA command to report on any other missing data files. Any data file with a size of 0 will be a missing data file and will likely need to be restored. Here is an example of the output from the REPORT SCHEMA command that indicates the USERS01.DBF data file is missing. Note the 0 value in the Size(MB) column:

   ```
   RMAN> report schema;
   Report of database schema for database with db_unique_name ORCL
   List of Permanent Datafiles
   ===========================
   ```

```
File Size(MB) Tablespace          RB segs Datafile Name
---- -------- ------------------- ------- ------------------------
1    700      SYSTEM              ***
C:\ORACLE\ORADATA\ORCL\SYSTEM01.DBF
2    716      SYSAUX              ***
C:\ORACLE\ORADATA\ORCL\SYSAUX01.DBF
4    0        USERS               ***
C:\ORACLE\ORADATA\ORCL\USERS01.DBF
5    30       UNDOTBS2            ***
C:\ORACLE\ORADATA\ORCL\UNDOTBS02.DBF
```

2. From the RMAN prompt, take all the data files or tablespaces to be recovered offline. You do this by using the RMAN SQL command followed by the appropriate ALTER DATABASE DATAFILE OFFLINE command or the ALTER TABLESPACE OFFLINE command.

3. From the RMAN prompt, issue the ALTER DATABASE OPEN command. The database should open without complaining about any missing data files.

Here is a case where we have tried to start our database and the USERS01.DBF data file is not available. We will make sure that this is the only data file that needs to be restored. We then take the data file offline and open the database:

```
RMAN> startup
Oracle instance started
database mounted
RMAN-00571: ===========================================================
RMAN-00569: =============== ERROR MESSAGE STACK FOLLOWS ===============
RMAN-00571: ===========================================================
RMAN-03002: failure of startup command at 09/28/2013 17:50:49
ORA-01157: cannot identify/lock data file 3 - see DBWR trace file
ORA-01110: data file 3: 'C:\ORACLE\ORADATA\ORCL\USERS01.DBF'
-- We use the report schema command here to look at the schema.
-- we will cover this command in the next chapter.
RMAN> report schema;
Report of database schema for database with db_unique_name ORCL
List of Permanent Datafiles
===========================
File Size(MB) Tablespace          RB segs Datafile Name
---- -------- ------------------- ------- ------------------------
1    700      SYSTEM              ***     C:\ORACLE\ORADATA\ORCL\SYSTEM01.DBF
2    716      SYSAUX              ***     C:\ORACLE\ORADATA\ORCL\SYSAUX01.DBF
3    0        USERS               ***     C:\ORACLE\ORADATA\ORCL\USERS01.DBF
5    30       UNDOTBS2            ***     C:\ORACLE\ORADATA\ORCL\UNDOTBS02.DBF
```

```
List of Temporary Files
=======================
File Size(MB) Tablespace       Maxsize(MB) Tempfile Name
---- -------- ---------------- ----------- --------------------
1    20       TEMP             32767       C:\ORACLE\ORADATA\ORCL\TEMP01.DBF
RMAN> sql 'alter database datafile 3 offline';
sql statement: alter database datafile 3 offline
RMAN> alter database open;
database opened
```

Restoring Database Data Files Online

Once the database is up and running or if the database was already running, follow these steps to restore one or more missing data files:

1. From the RMAN prompt, take the data file or data files offline using the RMAN SQL command calling the ALTER DATABASE DATAFILE OFFLINE command. Do this for each data file that you need to take offline.

2. From the RMAN prompt, restore the data files using the RESTORE DATAFILE command. You can restore one or multiple data files in one shot. You will be returned to the RMAN prompt once the restore is complete.

3. Having restored the data files, use the RECOVER DATAFILE command to recover each specific data file. This will apply any incremental backups and archived redo logs to the restored data file. You will be returned to the RMAN prompt once the recovery is complete.

4. Bring the data file(s) back online using the RMAN SQL command to issue the ALTER DATABASE DATAFILE ONLINE SQL command. This will bring each data file online, completing the recovery process.

In this example, the USERS01.DBF data file is already offline (we offlined the data file in the earlier example). We will restore that data file (referring to it by its data file number) and then recover it. Finally, we will bring the data file online so that the database may access it:

```
RMAN> restore datafile 3;
Starting restore at 28-SEP-13
allocated channel: ORA_DISK_1
channel ORA_DISK_1: SID=136 device type=DISK
channel ORA_DISK_1: starting datafile backup set restore
channel ORA_DISK_1: specifying datafile(s) to restore from backup set
channel ORA_DISK_1: restoring datafile 00003 to
C:\ORACLE\ORADATA\ORCL\USERS01.DBF
channel ORA_DISK_1: reading from backup piece
C:\ORACLE\FAST_RECOVERY_AREA\ORCL\BACKUPSET\2013_09_28
\O1_MF_NNNDF_TAG20130928T185206_4G09OW7B_.BKP
channel ORA_DISK_1: piece
```

```
handle=C:\ORACLE\FAST_RECOVERY_AREA\ORCL\BACKUPSET\2013_09_28
\O1_MF_NNNDF_TAG20130928T185206_4G09OW7B_.BKP tag=TAG20130928T185206
channel ORA_DISK_1: restored backup piece 1
channel ORA_DISK_1: restore complete, elapsed time: 00:00:15
Finished restore at 28-SEP-13
RMAN> recover datafile 3;
Starting recover at 28-SEP-13
using channel ORA_DISK_1
starting media recovery
media recovery complete, elapsed time: 00:00:02
Finished recover at 28-SEP-13
RMAN> sql 'alter database datafile 3 online';
sql statement: alter database datafile 3 online
```

Restoring Database Tablespaces Online

If you have lost most or all data files related to one or more tablespaces, it might be easier to recover the entire tablespace rather than individual data files. Of course, a tablespace recovery really is a data file recovery; it just makes RMAN do the extra legwork to figure out which data files need to be restored. Once the database is up and running or if the database was already running, follow these steps to restore one or more tablespaces:

1. From the RMAN prompt, take the tablespace(s) offline using the RMAN SQL command calling the ALTER TABLESPACE OFFLINE command. Do this for each tablespace that you need to take offline.

2. From the RMAN prompt, restore the tablespace using the RESTORE TABLESPACE command.

    You can restore one or multiple tablespaces in one shot. You will be returned to the RMAN prompt once the restore is complete.

3. Having restored the tablespace data files, use the RECOVER TABLESPACE command to recover the tablespace and its associated data files.

    This will apply any incremental backups and archived redo logs to the restored tablespace. You will be returned to the RMAN prompt once the recovery is complete.

4. Bring the data file(s) back online using the RMAN SQL command to issue the ALTER DATABASE DATAFILE ONLINE SQL command.

    This will bring each data file online, completing the recovery process.

Here is an example of a recovery of the USERS tablespace from RMAN (note that if the database was running, we could use the ALTER TABLESPACE OFFLINE command to take the tablespace offline):

```
RMAN> startup
Oracle instance started
database mounted
```

```
RMAN-00571: ===========================================================
RMAN-00569: =============== ERROR MESSAGE STACK FOLLOWS ===============
RMAN-00571: ===========================================================
RMAN-03002: failure of startup command at 09/28/2013 20:01:30
ORA-01157: cannot identify/lock data file 3 - see DBWR trace file
ORA-01110: data file 3: 'C:\ORACLE\ORADATA\ORCL\USERS01.DBF'
RMAN> sql 'alter tablespace users datafile offline';
sql statement: alter tablespace users datafile offline
RMAN> alter database open;
database opened
RMAN> restore tablespace users;
Starting restore at 28-SEP-13
using target database control file instead of recovery catalog
allocated channel: ORA_DISK_1
channel ORA_DISK_1: SID=153 device type=DISK
channel ORA_DISK_1: starting datafile backup set restore
channel ORA_DISK_1: specifying datafile(s) to restore from backup set
channel ORA_DISK_1: restoring datafile 00003 to
C:\ORACLE\ORADATA\ORCL\USERS01.DBF
channel ORA_DISK_1: reading from backup piece
C:\ORACLE\FAST_RECOVERY_AREA\ORCL\BACKUPSET\2013_09_28
\O1_MF_NNNDF_TAG20130928T185206_4G09OW7B_.BKP
channel ORA_DISK_1: piece
handle=C:\ORACLE\FAST_RECOVERY_AREA\ORCL\BACKUPSET\2013_09_28
\O1_MF_NNNDF_TAG20130928T185206_4G09OW7B_.BKP tag=TAG20130928T185206
channel ORA_DISK_1: restored backup piece 1
channel ORA_DISK_1: restore complete, elapsed time: 00:00:15
Finished restore at 28-SEP-13
RMAN> recover tablespace users;
Starting recover at 28-SEP-13
using channel ORA_DISK_1
starting media recovery
media recovery complete, elapsed time: 00:00:02
Finished recover at 28-SEP-13
RMAN> sql 'alter tablespace users online';
sql statement: alter tablespace users online
```

Restoring Read-Only Tablespaces

Restoring read-only tablespaces is done the same way that you restore regular tablespaces. The only difference is that RMAN will skip backups of read-only tablespaces, after they have been backed up and if backup optimization is enabled. The only problem with this is that you will have to keep the backups of that read-only tablespace. This can sometimes be troublesome over the long term. So the message here is to make tablespaces read-only only after you figure out where and how you will store your backups.

The RESTORE DATABASE, TABLESPACE, and DATAFILE commands will restore read-only tablespaces as required.

> If you have read-only tablespaces and you have enabled RMAN optimization so that they are only backed up once, you need to make sure that the backups of those tablespaces don't accidently get deleted. While RMAN is not going to delete them, a human might. Also it's possible that the media management software that controls the media where the backup files are stored will have its own retention criteria. It's no fun to try to restore a tablespace from a backup file that isn't available.

Recovering a Database Using Incomplete Recovery

We discussed *incomplete recovery* or *point-in-time recovery* back in Chapter 3. It is, essentially, restoring the database to some point in time that is not the current point in time. If you are not familiar with what incomplete recovery is, please review Chapter 3 for more details. In the following sections, we will discuss point-in-time recoveries. First, we will discuss the types of recoveries that are available, and then we will discuss the mechanics of such recoveries.

> Remember that point-in-time backups must be consistent. That means you have to restore the whole database to the specific point in time you are aiming for. Oracle offers the ability to do tablespace point-in-time recoveries, which we will discuss in Chapter 7, "Performing Oracle Advanced Recovery."

Types of Point-in-Time Recovery

RMAN supports point-in-time recovery using the UNTIL clause of the RESTORE and RECOVER commands as shown in this example, where we will be restoring to 9/30/2013 at 18:00 hours:

```
Restore database until time '09/30/2013:18:00:00';
Recover database until time '09/30/2013:18:00:00';
```

Real World Scenario

What Happens if the Control File Has Lost the Backup Records

Most RMAN restores are easy and require only the use of the RMAN client. However, we've seen cases where the RMAN client was not enough. In one case, the database site had lost its recovery catalog, and the CONTROL_FILE_RECORD_KEEP_TIME parameter was set to 7 days. Guess what happened to all the RMAN metadata after 7 days when the recovery catalog was lost.

At the same time, we had a need to restore a database to a point in time of perhaps 30 days before to check on the state of some data. Of course, the metadata for the restore was not available. This was clearly a bad day.

There are several ways to address this problem. The Oracle Database 12*c* RMAN CATALOG command provides the ability to catalog backup set pieces in the database (this was not available prior to Oracle Database 10*g*). In the case of the loss listed earlier, we opted to write some PL/SQL and use the PL/SQL packages that RMAN uses itself to restore the backups from tape. RMAN uses a PL/SQL package called dbms_backup_restore to perform most backup and restore operations. Using this package (documented pretty well on Oracle's support site at metalink.oracle.com), we were able to restore a database from an older backup.

The bottom line is that as long as you have the backup set pieces, any RMAN backup can be restored. It just might take some time and effort and perhaps a bit of help from Oracle support.

When using a RUN block, you will use the SET command to set the recovery window for RMAN, as shown in this example:

```
Run {
Set until time until time '09/30/2013:18:00:00';
Restore database;
Recover database;
}
```

You can do point-in-time recovery using the following:

Time   The *time-based point-in-time recovery* method is based on the timestamps in the online redo logs. RMAN will restore the database to the closest possible timestamp listed in the command. You can find the timestamp ranges contained in specific online redo logs by querying the FIRST_TIME column of the V$LOG_HISTORY view for each redo log. In this example, RMAN will restore the database to 9/29/2013 at 15:00:00:

```
restore database until time '09/29/2013:15:00:00';
recover database until time '09/29/2013:15:00:00';
alter database open resetlogs;
```

SCN   The *SCN-based point-in-time recovery* method is based on recovery to a specific SCN in the database. You can determine the current SCN of the database from the CURRENT_SCN column of the V$DATABASE view. You can determine the SCN range contained within a given redo log by querying the FIRST_CHANGE# and NEXT_CHANGE# columns of the V$LOG_HISTORY view. Here is an example of an SCN-based point-in-time recovery:

```
restore database until SCN 12345;
recover database until SCN 12345;
alter database open resetlogs;
```

Log Sequence Number   The *log sequence number point-in-time recovery* method is based on recovery up to and including a specific log sequence number. Log sequence numbers for individual redo logs can be found in the V$LOG_HISTORY and V$LOG views. Here is an example of a point-in-time recovery based on a log sequence number:

```
restore database until sequence 12345;
recover database until sequence 12345;
alter database open resetlogs;
```

In Exercise 5.2, you'll perform a point-in-time recovery with RMAN.

EXERCISE 5.2

Perform a Point-in-Time Recovery with RMAN

This activity builds on the backup done in Exercise 4.2 in Chapter 4, "Using the RMAN Recovery Catalog." You should have completed Exercise 4.2 prior to executing this activity. Please note that the output you experience from this exercise will probably differ from the output shown in this exercise.

1. Complete Exercise 4.2.

2. Set the NLS_DATE_FORMAT environment variable from the operating system.

   In Unix (may vary based on the shell you are using):

   ```
   export NLS_DATE_FORMAT='mm/dd/yyyy hh24:mi:ss'
   ```

   In DOS:

   ```
   set NLS_DATE_FORMAT=mm/dd/yyyy hh24:mi:ss
   ```

EXERCISE 5.2 *(continued)*

3. Start RMAN. We will assume you are not using a recovery catalog during this exercise.

```
C:\oracle>rman target=/
Recovery Manager: Release 12.1.0.1.0 - Production on Fri Dec 27 10:23:32 2013
Copyright (c) 1982, 2013, Oracle and/or its affiliates.  All rights reserved.
connected to target database (not started)
```

4. Start up the database with the STARTUP FORCE MOUNT command from RMAN:

```
RMAN> startup force mount
Oracle instance started
database mounted
Total System Global Area      364081152 bytes
Fixed Size                      1333228 bytes
Variable Size                 264243220 bytes
Database Buffers               92274688 bytes
Redo Buffers                    6230016 bytes
```

5. Determine the current backups that are available for restore with the LIST BACKUP OF DATABASE SUMMARY command (to be discussed in Chapter 6):

```
RMAN> list backup of database summary;
List of Backups
===============
Key     TY LV S Device Type Completion Time      #Pieces #Copies Compressed Tag
------- -- -- - ----------- -------------------- ------- ------- ---------- ---
6        B  F  A DISK        09/29/2013 14:07:23 1       1       NO
SILVER_COPY
11       B  F  A DISK        10/02/2013 00:46:25 1       1       YES
GOLD_COPY
17       B  F  A DISK        10/03/2013 00:25:19 1       1       YES
TAG20131003T001928
```

6. From the output generated in step 5, choose the date and time of the most current backup (in our case, it's 10/03/2013 at 00:25:19). We will restore the database to 10 minutes after this date and time (in our case, 10/03/2013 at 00:35:19).

7. Issue the RESTORE DATABASE UNTIL TIME command to restore the database to the date and time selected. In our case, the command will be RESTORE DATABASE UNTIL TIME '10/03/2013:00:35:19'; your command will have a different date and time (unless you have reset the clock so precisely that you got the same date!).

```
RMAN> restore database until time '10/03/2013:00:35:19';
Starting restore at 10/03/2013 01:57:31
```

```
allocated channel: ORA_DISK_1
channel ORA_DISK_1: SID=155 device type=DISK
channel ORA_DISK_1: starting datafile backup set restore
channel ORA_DISK_1: specifying datafile(s) to restore from backup set
channel ORA_DISK_1: restoring datafile 00001 to
C:\ORACLE\ORADATA\ORCL\SYSTEM01.DBF
channel ORA_DISK_1: restoring datafile 00002 to
C:\ORACLE\ORADATA\ORCL\SYSAUX01.DBF
channel ORA_DISK_1: restoring datafile 00003 to
C:\ORACLE\ORADATA\ORCL\UNDOTBS01.DBF
channel ORA_DISK_1: restoring datafile 00004 to
C:\ORACLE\FAST_RECOVERY_AREA\ORCL\DATAFILE\O1_MF_USERS_4G2Q1YTC_.DBF
channel ORA_DISK_1: reading from backup piece
C:\ORACLE\FAST_RECOVERY_AREA\ORCL\BACKUPSET\2013_10_03
\O1_MF_NNNDF_TAG20131003T001928_4GCGCQQ4_.BKP
channel ORA_DISK_1: piece
handle=C:\ORACLE\FAST_RECOVERY_AREA\ORCL\BACKUPSET\2013_10_03
\O1_MF_NNNDF_TAG20131003T001928_4GCGCQQ4_.BKP tag=TAG20131003T001928
channel ORA_DISK_1: restored backup piece 1
channel ORA_DISK_1: restore complete, elapsed time: 00:07:15
Finished restore at 10/03/2013 02:04:47
```

8. Recover the database with the RECOVER DATABASE UNTIL TIME command. Our com-mand would be RECOVER DATABASE UNTIL TIME '10/03/2013:00:35:19'; your com-mand will have a different date and time.

```
RMAN> recover database until time '10/03/2013:00:35:19';
Starting recover at 10/03/2013 02:06:01
using channel ORA_DISK_1
starting media recovery
media recovery complete, elapsed time: 00:00:03
Finished recover at 10/03/2013 02:06:05
```

9. Open the database with the ALTER DATABASE OPEN RESETLOGS command:

```
RMAN> alter database open resetlogs;
Statement processed
```

The database is open. You would want to perform a complete backup after this recovery.

What Can I Recover To?

You may want to make sure you can actually recover to the point in time that you are interested in before you haul off and try the recovery. Nothing makes for a worse day than trying to do a point-in-time restore, after having removed the existing data files, and then finding out that you can't do the restore.

The RESTORE VALIDATE command can come in handy here. You can use this command to make sure that all of the backup set pieces you will need to restore your database are available, without actually restoring the database. This command checks both backup sets for data file backups and archived redo logs as well as any data file image copies. Here is an example of the RESTORE VALIDATE command for a point-in-time database recovery:

```
RMAN> restore database until time 'sysdate -1/24' validate;
Starting restore at 28-SEP-13
using channel ORA_DISK_1
channel ORA_DISK_1: starting validation of datafile backup set
channel ORA_DISK_1: reading from backup piece
C:\ORACLE\FAST_RECOVERY_AREA\ORCL\BACKUPSET\2013_09_28
\01_MF_NNNDF_TAG20130928T185206_4G09OW7B_.BKP
channel ORA_DISK_1: piece
handle=C:\ORACLE\FAST_RECOVERY_AREA\ORCL\BACKUPSET\2013_09_28
\01_MF_NNNDF_TAG20130928T185206_4G09OW7B_.BKP tag=TAG20130928T185206
channel ORA_DISK_1: restored backup piece 1
channel ORA_DISK_1: validation complete, elapsed time: 00:00:25
Finished restore at 28-SEP-13
```

Point-in-Time Recovery Mechanics

Regardless of the type of point-in-time recovery you are going to do, the mechanics are the same. During a point-in-time recovery, the database must be in MOUNT mode. There is no online point-in-time recovery for an entire Oracle database (though RMAN does offer tablespace point-in-time recovery, which can be done online).

Once the point-in-time recovery is complete, you will open the database with the ALTER DATABASE OPEN RESETLOGS command. This will reset (or recreate if need be) the online redo logs of the database and open it for business. The end result is a new incarnation of the database (see Chapter 2 for more on database incarnations), which can impact future backups. Oracle Database 12c and RMAN will be able to use the same backup to restore the database (as well as any old and new archived redo logs). Still, it's probably a good idea to perform another backup of your database, because it just makes things cleaner and easier.

Here is a list of the RMAN commands needed to perform a time-based point-in-time recovery to September 29, 2013, at 15:00 hours:

```
shutdown abort
startup mount
restore database until time '09/29/2013:15:00:00';
recover database until time '09/29/2013:15:00:00';
alter database open resetlogs;
```

And here is the result of the execution of those commands:

```
C:\Documents and Settings\Robert>rman target=/
Recovery Manager: Release 12.1.0.1.0 -
Production on Wed Oct 1 22:30:48 2013
Connected to:
Oracle Database 12c
Enterprise Edition Release 12.1.0.1.0 - 64bit Production
With the Partitioning, OLAP, Advanced Analytics and Real Application Testing
options
connected to target database: ORCL (DBID=1194488809)
RMAN> shutdown abort
Oracle instance shut down
RMAN> startup mount
connected to target database (not started)
Oracle instance started
database mounted
Total System Global Area     364081152 bytes
Fixed Size                     1333228 bytes
Variable Size                239077396 bytes
Database Buffers             117440512 bytes
Redo Buffers                   6230016 bytes
RMAN> restore database until time '09/29/2013:15:00:00';
Starting restore at 10/01/2013 22:32:44
allocated channel: ORA_DISK_1
channel ORA_DISK_1: SID=151 device type=DISK
channel ORA_DISK_1: starting datafile backup set restore
channel ORA_DISK_1: specifying datafile(s) to restore from backup set
channel ORA_DISK_1: restoring datafile 00001 to
C:\ORACLE\ORADATA\ORCL\SYSTEM01.DBF
channel ORA_DISK_1: restoring datafile 00002 to
C:\ORACLE\ORADATA\ORCL\SYSAUX01.DBF
channel ORA_DISK_1: restoring datafile 00003 to
```

```
C:\ORACLE\ORADATA\ORCL\UNDOTBS01.DBF
channel ORA_DISK_1: restoring datafile 00004 to
C:\ORACLE\FAST_RECOVERY_AREA\ORCL
\DATAFILE\O1_MF_USERS_4G2Q1YTC_.DBF
channel ORA_DISK_1: reading from backup piece
C:\ORACLE\FAST_RECOVERY_AREA\ORCL
\BACKUPSET\2013_09_29\O1_MF_NNNDF_SILVER_COPY_4G2DQT1Y_.BKP
RMAN> recover database until time '09/29/2013:15:00:00';
Starting recover at 10/02/2013 00:09:47
using channel ORA_DISK_1
starting media recovery
archived log for thread 1 with sequence 5 is already on disk as file
C:\ORACLE\PRODUCT\12.1.0\DB_1\RDBMS\ARC00005_0666708076.001
archived log for thread 1 with sequence 6 is already on disk as file
C:\ORACLE\FAST_RECOVERY_AREA\ORCL\ARCHIVELOG\2013_09_30
\O1_MF_1_6_4G4QPYYR_.ARC
archived log file name=
C:\ORACLE\PRODUCT\12.1.0\DB_1\RDBMS\ARC00005_0666708076.001
thread=1 sequence=5
media recovery complete, elapsed time: 00:00:14
Finished recover at 10/02/2013 00:10:03
RMAN> alter database open resetlogs;
database opened
```

You could also have executed this restore using the following commands:

```
shutdown abort
startup mount
run {
set until time '09/30/2013:18:00:00';
restore database;
recover database;
}
sql 'alter database open resetlogs';
```

One time when you might need to perform point-in-time recovery is during a database recovery after a complete loss of the online redo logs of the database. This might include cases when just the online redo logs were lost or cases when the entire database was lost, including the online redo logs. While it is possible to save your database data in the event of such a loss (see Chapter 2 for more information on such a case), it is likely that you will have to perform a point-in-time recovery to get your database operational again. This will, of course, result in some data loss.

You can also restore databases using tags. A tag allows you to choose a specific backup image that you want to use for the restore. You can also use a tag during a recovery to indicate specific incremental backups that you want to use for a restore. When you use tags, Oracle will still do a complete recovery unless you use the UNTIL TIME parameter to indicate that you want to recover to a specific point in time.

Here is an example where we are restoring the database using the tag gold_copy:

```
shutdown immediate
startup mount
restore database from tag 'gold_copy';
recover database from tag 'gold_copy';
alter database open;
```

 We discussed database incarnations in Chapter 2. Sometimes for specific types of RMAN recoveries you will need to reset the database incarnation. We will cover this in more detail in Chapter 7.

Using Image Copies to Recover Your Database

Recall that an *image copy* is an exact copy of a given database data file. You can use image copies to restore your database. This can provide for quick database recovery, though the image copies will require much more storage than a compressed backup set piece.

Oracle provides the SWITCH command to use in place of the RESTORE command. This will essentially change the control file so it will point to the data file copy(ies). You then would call the RECOVER command to apply any incremental backups and archived redo logs to restore the data file(s) or tablespace(s). You can switch the entire database, tablespaces, or specific data files depending on your needs. Here is an example where we are restoring data file 4:

```
Sql 'alter database datafile 4 offline';
Switch datafile 4 to copy '/oracle/backup/users_01.dbf';
Recover datafile 4;
Sql 'alter database datafile 4 online';
```

Note that if you are making image copies and backup-set copies, RMAN will determine which to use during a normal restore operation. This includes image copies that are updated with incremental backups (discussed in Chapter 3). So, with image copies you really have two options for restore and recovery:

RESTORE **command**   Use the RESTORE command to have RMAN copy the image copies to the original location of the database data files. This will not result in any changes to data file locations in the database control file.

SWITCH **command**   Use the SWITCH command to cause RMAN to instantly start using the image copy of the data file in its current location. This will cause the database control file to be changed with the old database datafile locations being changed to the locations of the new database data files.

Other Basic Recovery Topics

There are other recovery-related topics you will need to be aware of. In the following sections, we will cover some of those, and in Chapter 7 we will cover other, more advanced recovery topics. In this section, we will discuss block media recovery and recovering from lost control files and lost spfiles with RMAN.

Block Media Recovery

Sometimes one or a few blocks will become corrupt. It's rare, but it happens. RMAN provides the ability to do online block media recovery. With *block media recovery*, RMAN will recover the corrupted blocks online. The only user impact will be to those users who want to access the corrupt blocks, and they will have been impacted anyway.

In Oracle Database 12*c*, you use the RECOVER command with the DATAFILE ... BLOCK option to perform block media recovery. To use the RECOVER BLOCK command, the following requirements must be met:

- The database must be in ARCHIVELOG mode.
- The database must be mounted or open.
- There must be a current database control file in place.
- All redo logs must be accessible.
- Only blocks marked as MEDIA_CORRUPT can be recovered.

For example, sometimes you will issue a DML or DDL statement and get an error such as the one found here:

```
ORA-01578: ORACLE data block corrupted (file # 6, block # 55)
ORA-01110: data file 6: '/oracle/oradata/trgt/users01.dbf'
```

In this case, you could issue the RECOVER DATAFILE command using the BLOCK parameter, as shown in this example:

```
Recover datafile 6 block 55;
```

In some cases, you may want to repair a range of blocks, as shown here:

```
Recover datafile 6 block 55 to 105;
```

You can also recover a range of blocks and several data files at one time:

```
Recover datafile 6 block 55 to 105 datafile 7 block 27 to 44;
```

You can also run the BACKUP DATABASE VALIDATE command to determine if any blocks are media corrupt. Any blocks that are corrupt will be listed in the V$DATABASE_BLOCK_CORRUPTION view. The column CORRUPTION_TYPE will indicate if they are media corrupt.

You can attempt to recover all corrupted blocks listed in the V$DATABASE_BLOCK_CORRUPTION view by using the RECOVER command with the CORRUPTION LIST parameter from RMAN, as shown in this example:

```
RMAN> recover corruption list;
Starting recover at 28-OCT-13
using target database control file instead of recovery catalog
allocated channel: ORA_DISK_1
channel ORA_DISK_1: SID=153 device type=DISK
starting media recovery
media recovery complete, elapsed time: 00:00:01
Finished recover at 28-OCT-13
```

Recovering the Control File

One recovery that you need to be prepared for is the recovery of a lost control file. Two different situations come into play here. The first is recovering the control file from a control-file autobackup; the second is recovering a control file if you are not using control-file autobackups. Let's look at each of these methods in more detail.

Recovering Control Files with Control-File Autobackups

We talked about RMAN *control-file autobackups* in Chapter 3. They are a way of automating the backup of database control files. Recovering the control file is quite easy if you are using control-file autobackups. There are two different situations that you will deal with when using control-file autobackups: one when you are using the Fast Recovery Area (FRA) and the other when you are not using the FRA. Let's look at these in a bit more detail.

Control-File Backups Using the FRA

If you are using the FRA and have enabled control-file autobackups, then restoring the current control file is easy. Simply do the following:

1. Start the database instance with the STARTUP NOMOUNT command.
2. Issue the RESTORE CONTROLFILE FROM AUTOBACKUP command. RMAN will proceed to restore the control file from the latest automated control-file backup on disk.
3. Mount the database after the restore is complete.
4. Recover the database with the RMAN RECOVER command.
5. Open it using the ALTER DATABASE OPEN RESETLOGS command.

Here is an example of the RMAN code:

```
RMAN> Startup nomount;
connected to target database (not started)
Oracle instance started
Total System Global Area      535662592 bytes
Fixed Size                      1334380 bytes
Variable Size                 369099668 bytes
Database Buffers              159383552 bytes
Redo Buffers                    5844992 bytes
RMAN> Restore controlfile from autobackup;
Starting restore at 28-SEP-13
allocated channel: ORA_DISK_1
channel ORA_DISK_1: SID=153 device type=DISK
channel ORA_DISK_1: looking for AUTOBACKUP on day: 20130928
channel ORA_DISK_1: AUTOBACKUP found:
c:\oracle\controlfilebackup\c-437680418-20130928-00
channel ORA_DISK_1: restoring control file from AUTOBACKUP
 c:\oracle\controlfilebackup\c-437680418-20130928-00
channel ORA_DISK_1: control file restore from AUTOBACKUP complete
output file name=C:\ORACLE\ORADATA\RCAT\CONTROL01.CTL
output file name=C:\ORACLE\ORADATA\RCAT\CONTROL02.CTL
output file name=C:\ORACLE\ORADATA\RCAT\CONTROL03.CTL
Finished restore at 28-SEP-13
RMAN> alter database mount;
database mounted
released channel: ORA_DISK_1
RMAN> recover database;
Starting recover at 28-SEP-13
allocated channel: ORA_DISK_1
channel ORA_DISK_1: SID=153 device type=DISK
starting media recovery
archived log for thread 1 with sequence 13 is already on disk as file
C:\ORACLE\ORADATA\RCAT\REDO01.LOG
archived log for thread 1 with sequence 14 is already on disk as file
C:\ORACLE\ORADATA\RCAT\REDO02.LOG
archived log file name=C:\ORACLE\ORADATA\RCAT\REDO01.LOG thread=1 sequence=13
archived log file name=C:\ORACLE\ORADATA\RCAT\REDO02.LOG thread=1 sequence=14
media recovery complete, elapsed time: 00:00:01
Finished recover at 28-SEP-13
```

```
RMAN> alter database open resetlogs;
Statement processed
```

When you use the RESTORE CONTROLFILE FROM AUTOBACKUP command, Oracle will start searching for the most current control-file autobackup by default. If you have used the SET UNTIL command to perform a point-in-time recovery, RMAN will start searching for the most current control file starting with that day/time and moving backward.

The RESTORE CONTROLFILE command also comes with the MAXSEQ and MAXDAYS parameters to further control how much effort is used to search for a backup control file.

The MAXSEQ Parameter   Each control-file backup on a given day is assigned a sequence number. That number increments by one for each additional control-file autobackup, until the next day when the sequence resets itself. The maximum sequence number is 256 and the minimum number is 0. RMAN will always search for the highest sequence number (or the most current file) first. The MAXSEQ parameter indicates to RMAN which sequence number it should start with when looking for the correct control-file autobackup. This allows you to skip certain sequence numbers if you know you do not want to use them. Here is an example of using MAXSEQ:

```
Restore controlfile from autobackup maxseq 200;
```

The MAXDAYS Parameter   By default, RMAN will look back 7 days (from the current date or the set until date) to find the correct control-file autobackup. If you want to change this default setting, use the MAXDAYS parameter when calling the RESTORE CONTROLFILE FROM AUTOBACKUP command. You can search from 0 to 366 days for the current control-file autobackup. Here is an example of using MAXDAYS where we will go back 30 days to find the correct control-file autobackup:

```
Restore controlfile from autobackup maxdays 30;
```

The MAXDAYS and MAXSEQ parameters also apply to spfile autobackup restore operations, and both parameters can be used in one command.

Control-File Backups Not Using the FRA

If you are not using the FRA but have enabled control-file autobackups, you will need to determine the database ID (DBID) of the database. Each database has a DBID, which uniquely identifies it. You should maintain a list of DBIDs for each of your databases if you are not using the FRA but want to use control-file autobackups. You can find the DBID in the DBID column of the V$DATABASE view, as seen in this query:

```
SQL> select dbid from v$database;
      DBID
----------
437680418
```

The database DBID is included in the filename of the control-file auto-backup backup set pieces (if you're not using the FRA). Thus, in a worst-case situation, you can determine the DBID for your database by looking at these files and determining the DBID from the filenames. If you are not using the FRA, this is one very good reason to put control-file autobackups in different directories for different databases!

Now that you have the DBID, you are ready to restore the database control file. To do so, follow these steps:

1. Start up the database in NOMOUNT mode. This will start the database and load the database parameter file. The FRA parameters will be set at this point.

2. Issue the SET DBID command to set the database DBID that RMAN will look for.

3. Set the control-file autobackup location with the SET CONTROLFILE AUTOBACKUP FOR-MAT command.

4. Restore the control file with the RESTORE command.

5. Mount the database for recovery.

6. Issue the RECOVER DATABASE command.

7. Open the database using the ALTER DATABASE OPEN RESETLOGS command.

Here is an example of recovering a control file when the FRA is not in use:

```
RMAN> startup force nomount;
Oracle instance started
Total System Global Area     535662592 bytes
Fixed Size                     1334380 bytes
Variable Size                369099668 bytes
Database Buffers             159383552 bytes
Redo Buffers                   5844992 bytes
RMAN> Set dbid 437680418;
executing command: SET DBID
RMAN> set controlfile autobackup format for device type
disk to 'c:\oracle\controlfilebackup\%F';
executing command: SET CONTROLFILE AUTOBACKUP FORMAT
RMAN> Restore controlfile from autobackup;
Starting restore at 28-SEP-13
using channel ORA_DISK_1
channel ORA_DISK_1: looking for AUTOBACKUP on day: 20130928
channel ORA_DISK_1: AUTOBACKUP found:
c:\oracle\controlfilebackup\c-437680418-20130928-04
channel ORA_DISK_1: restoring control file from AUTOBACKUP
c:\oracle\controlfilebackup\c-437680418-20130928-04
```

```
channel ORA_DISK_1: control file restore from AUTOBACKUP complete
output file name=C:\ORACLE\ORADATA\RCAT\CONTROL01.CTL
output file name=C:\ORACLE\ORADATA\RCAT\CONTROL02.CTL
output file name=C:\ORACLE\ORADATA\RCAT\CONTROL03.CTL
Finished restore at 28-SEP-13
RMAN> Alter database mount;
database mounted
released channel: ORA_DISK_1
RMAN> Recover database;
Starting recover at 28-SEP-13
allocated channel: ORA_DISK_1
channel ORA_DISK_1: SID=153 device type=DISK
starting media recovery
archived log for thread 1 with sequence 1 is already on disk as file
C:\ORACLE\ORADATA\RCAT\REDO01.LOG
archived log for thread 1 with sequence 2 is already on disk as file
C:\ORACLE\ORADATA\RCAT\REDO02.LOG
archived log file name=C:\ORACLE\ORADATA\RCAT\REDO01.LOG thread=1 sequence=1
archived log file name=C:\ORACLE\ORADATA\RCAT\REDO02.LOG thread=1 sequence=2
media recovery complete, elapsed time: 00:00:02
Finished recover at 28-SEP-13
RMAN> alter database open resetlogs;
Statement processed
```

You can also use the RESTORE CONTROLFILE command to restore a control file to a different location and filename using the TO keyword, as shown in this example:

```
Restore controlfile to '/tmp/orcl.ctl' from autobackup;
```

Recovering Control Files When Not Using Control-File Autobackups

If you have not enabled control-file autobackups, you need to use the recovery catalog to restore a control file (there are other ways—see the sidebar "Emergency Control-File Recoveries"). Simply follow these steps:

1. Start RMAN and connect to the recovery catalog.
2. Use the STARTUP FORCE NOMOUNT command to start the database instance.
3. Issue the RESTORE CONTROLFILE command and RMAN will restore the control file.
4. Mount the database with the ALTER DATABASE MOUNT command.
5. Issue a RECOVER DATABASE command.
6. Open the database with the ALTER DATABASE OPEN RESETLOGS command.

Here is an example of the commands you would use to perform a control-file restore using the recovery catalog:

```
Startup force nomount
restore controlfile;
alter database mount;
recover database;
Alter database open resetlogs;
```

You can also use the RESTORE CONTROLFILE command to restore a control file to a different location and filename using the TO keyword, as shown in this example:

```
Restore controlfile to '/tmp/orcl.ctl';
```

Emergency Control-File Recoveries

If you are not using control-file autobackups and you are not using a recovery catalog, what are you to do when you lose your control file? You can always recreate the control file with the CREATE CONTROLFILE command (see Chapter 1, "Performing Oracle User-Managed Backups," for more on this command). You can then use the CATALOG command to catalog the backup set pieces. One complication may occur if you are backing up to tape. In this case, you may have to restore your backups from tape to local disk before you can run the CATALOG command.

It is not a fun exercise to have to create your own CREATE CONTROLFILE command from scratch, and we strongly recommend that you configure control-file autobackups instead.

Recovering the Spfile

If you have enabled control-file autobackups, then RMAN will back up the current spfile each time a control-file autobackup occurs. To restore your spfile, you will first need to start the database from RMAN without a parameter file of any sort. Simply type in **STARTUP NOMOUNT** and the database will start using default parameter settings. This positions the database to be able to restore the spfile from the autobackup. RMAN will display a message when it's using default parameter settings, as shown in this output:

```
RMAN> startup nomount
connected to target database (not started)
startup failed: ORA-01078: failure in processing system parameters
LRM-00109: could not open parameter file
'C:\ORACLE\PRODUCT\12.1.0\DB_1\DATABASE\INITORCL.ORA'
```

```
starting Oracle instance without parameter file for retrieval of SPFILE
Oracle instance started
Total System Global Area      159019008 bytes
Fixed Size                      1331852 bytes
Variable Size                  67112308 bytes
Database Buffers               83886080 bytes
Redo Buffers                    6688768 bytes
```

The restore process for an spfile differs a bit depending on whether you have been using the FRA or not. We will look into these two different options in the next sections.

Restoring the Spfile When Using the FRA

Restoring the spfile when using the FRA is a bit more complex than restoring the control file. First, you will need to start the database instance, as demonstrated previously. Then you will need to configure the FRA location. Because the FRA parameter DB_RECOVERY_FILE_DEST is not dynamic, you need to create a temporary pfile based on the current memory settings and then update it with the correct FRA location.

You create the temporary pfile from the in-memory settings using the SQL command CREATE PFILE FROM MEMORY. This command will create a database parameter file that you will edit. The parameter settings in this file will be based on the default, in-memory settings used when RMAN started the database. Here is an example of the creation of the pfile from memory:

```
RMAN> sql 'create pfile from memory';
using target database control file instead of recovery catalog
sql statement: create pfile from memory
```

Note that you must create a pfile and not an spfile. This is because you cannot restore over an existing spfile that is in use. Using your editor of choice, edit the pfile you just created. The pfile will typically be created in ORACLE_HOME/database in Windows and $ORACLE_HOME/dbs in Linux.

You will want to set the DB_RECOVERY_FILE_DEST parameter to the location of the FRA and DB_RECOVERY_FILE_DEST_SIZE to the size of the FRA. When setting the DB_RECOVERY_FILE_DEST_SIZE parameter, don't worry about how big to size it because this is just a temporary parameter setting for the spfile restore. The real value of the parameter will be set after the spfile has been restored. Here is an example of what those parameters would look like in a pfile:

```
db_recovery_file_dest='c:\oracle\fast_recovery_area'
db_recovery_file_dest_size=10g
```

Once the parameter has been set correctly, save the file and restart the database using the temporary pfile, as shown here:

```
C:\Documents and Settings\Robert>rman target=/
Recovery Manager: Release 12.1.0.1.0 -
```

```
Production on Sun Sep 28 14:56:38 2013
Connected to:
Oracle Database 12c Enterprise Edition
Release 12.1.0.1.0 - 64bit Production
With the Partitioning, OLAP, Advanced Analytics
and Real Application Testing options
connected to target database (not started)
RMAN> startup force nomount pfile=?/database/initorcl.ora
Oracle instance started
Total System Global Area     163213312 bytes
Fixed Size                     1331852 bytes
Variable Size                 71306612 bytes
Database Buffers              79691776 bytes
Redo Buffers                  10883072 bytes
```

Using ? in the Pfile Command

Did you see how we used the ? placeholder in the PFILE command? The ? placeholder represents the location for ORACLE_HOME.

You can now restore the spfile backed up in the last control-file autobackup using the RESTORE SPFILE FROM AUTOBACKUP command, as shown here:

```
RMAN> restore SPFILE from autobackup;
Starting restore at 28-SEP-13
using target database control file instead of recovery catalog
allocated channel: ORA_DISK_1
channel ORA_DISK_1: SID=98 device type=DISK
recovery area destination: c:\oracle\fast_recovery_area
database name (or database unique name) used for search: ORCL
channel ORA_DISK_1: AUTOBACKUP
C:\ORACLE\FAST_RECOVERY_AREA\ORCL\AUTOBACKUP\2013_09_28
\O1_MF_S_666628278_4FZTDYVC_.BKP found in the recovery area
AUTOBACKUP search with format "%F" not attempted because DBID was not set
channel ORA_DISK_1: restoring SPFILE from AUTOBACKUP
C:\ORACLE\FAST_RECOVERY_AREA\ORCL\AUTOBACKUP\2013_09_28
\O1_MF_S_666628278_4FZTDYVC_.BKP
channel ORA_DISK_1: SPFILE restore from AUTOBACKUP complete
Finished restore at 28-SEP-13
```

Now all you need to do is shut down and start up the database (assuming further restore and/or recovery operations are not required) or use the STARTUP FORCE command, as shown here:

```
RMAN> startup force
Oracle instance started
database mounted
database opened
Total System Global Area      397557760 bytes
Fixed Size                      1333452 bytes
Variable Size                 335546164 bytes
Database Buffers               54525952 bytes
Redo Buffers                    6152192 bytes
```

Just to summarize the steps needed to perform this recovery, here they are:

1. Issue the STARTUP NOMOUNT command to start up the database from RMAN.

2. Issue the CREATE PFILE FROM MEMORY command from SQL*Plus or using the SQL RMAN command.

3. Edit the pfile so that it contains the correct setting for the parameter DB_RECOVERY_FILE_DEST and the parameter DB_RECOVERY_FILE_DEST_SIZE.

4. Shut down and restart the database instance using the newly created pfile.

5. Use the RESTORE SPFILE FROM AUTOBACKUP command to restore the spfile.

6. Restart the database using the STARTUP FORCE command.

Restoring the Spfile When Not Using the FRA

If you are not using the FRA, the procedure to restore the spfile from an autobackup is actually slightly easier. First, you have already started the database instance. You will have to set two RMAN parameters. The first parameter identifies the DBID of the database (discussed earlier in this chapter). You use the SET DBID command to do this, as shown here:

```
RMAN> Set dbid= 437680418
executing command: SET DBID
```

Now you need to use the SET command with the CONTROLFILE AUTOBACKUP FORMAT parameter to indicate where the control-file autobackups can be found, as shown here:

```
RMAN> SET CONTROLFILE AUTOBACKUP FORMAT FOR DEVICE TYPE DISK TO
2> 'c:\oracle\controlfilebackup\%F';
executing command: SET CONTROLFILE AUTOBACKUP FORMAT
using target database control file instead of recovery catalog
```

All that remains is the restore of the spfile:

```
RMAN> Restore SPFILE from autobackup;
Starting restore at 28-SEP-13
allocated channel: ORA_DISK_1
channel ORA_DISK_1: SID=98 device type=DISK
channel ORA_DISK_1: looking for AUTOBACKUP on day: 20130928
channel ORA_DISK_1: AUTOBACKUP found:
c:\oracle\controlfilebackup\c-437680418-20130928-00
channel ORA_DISK_1: restoring SPFILE from AUTOBACKUP
c:\oracle\controlfilebackup\c-437680418-20130928-00
channel ORA_DISK_1: SPFILE restore from AUTOBACKUP complete
Finished restore at 28-SEP-13
```

You can also include the SET commands within the confines of a RUN block, as shown here:

```
RUN
{
  SET CONTROLFILE AUTOBACKUP FORMAT FOR DEVICE TYPE DISK TO
   'c:\oracle\controlfilebackup\%F';
  RESTORE CONTROLFILE FROM AUTOBACKUP MAXSEQ 100;
}
```

You can now open the database with the STARTUP FORCE command, as shown here:

```
RMAN> startup force
Oracle instance started
database mounted
database opened
Total System Global Area     535662592 bytes
Fixed Size                     1334380 bytes
Variable Size                369099668 bytes
Database Buffers             159383552 bytes
Redo Buffers                   5844992 bytes
```

To summarize the steps for this recovery, here they are:

1. Start up the database in NOMOUNT mode.
2. Set the database DBID.
3. Use the SET command to set the RMAN parameter CONTROLFILE AUTOBACKUP FORMAT to point to the correct control-file autobackup location.
4. Restore the SPFILE with the RESTORE SPFILE FROM AUTOBACKUP command.
5. Recycle the database to reread the newly recovered spfile parameter file.

Recovering the Database Password File

The database password file is a critical file that stores the credentials for users granted non-role-based privileges. The privileges stored in the password file are those granted for:

- SYSDBA
- SYSBACKUP
- SYSOPER
- SYSDG
- SYSKM
- SYSASM (for ASM instances)

The password file is created (or recreated) using the orapwd utility. Here is an example of the creation of a password file:

```
orapwd FILE='+DATA_DG/orcl/orapworcl' ENTRIES=10 DBUNIQUENAME='orcl'
```

In this example, we have created a password file for the database orcl. The password file will be created in the ASM disk group called +DATA_DG. This password file is called orapworcl, which follows the standard naming convention of password files for Oracle databases. The password file standard naming convention is orapw, followed by the name of the database assigned to that password file—in this case orcl. The DBUNIQUENAME parameter is required for ASM to ensure that the password file name will not conflict with that of another password file.

The view V$PWFILE_USERS is provided so that you can look at the users in the database password file and what privileges they have been granted. It's a good idea to print a report showing the users and the privileges they have been granted in case you need to recreate the password file.

You can backup the password file at any time. You can also restore the password file from that backup. Additionally, you can recreate the password file using the orapwd utility. In this case, you would also need to re-grant users the permissions that they previously had.

Clearing Redo Logs

Once in a great while something happens to an online redo log and the database just seems to get stuck. Now, there are many reasons for this. It might be that the FRA has filled up and you need to add additional space to it. Another rare possibility is that the online redo log has become corrupted somehow. If might be that the logfile can't be archived for some reason (perhaps it was accidently deleted, in which case the database might well just hang instead of crashing).

In cases like this, you can use the ALTER DATABASE CLEAR LOGFILE command to reinitialize the bad online redo log file. Further, you may need to indicate that the bad log file should not be archived, in which case you would issue the ALTER DATABASE CLEAR UNARCHIVED LOGFILE to indicate that it should not be archived. This is common in cases where the online redo log file has accidently been deleted and the ARCH*n* process is not able to process that missing online redo log file.

If you have to use the ALTER DATABASE CLEAR LOGFILE command (especially if you use the UNARCHIVED option), you should always immediately perform a full backup of your database because any previous backups are going to be unusable past the point that you issued the ALTER DATABASE CLEAR LOGFILE command. Here is an example of using the ALTER DATABASE CLEAR LOGFILE command:

```
Alter database clear unarchived logfile '/u01/oradata/orcl/redolog01a.log';
```

Summary

As you can see, there are several ways to recover a database with RMAN. From database recoveries to tablespace recoveries to data file recoveries and beyond, there is a lot that can go wrong—and a number of different ways to fix what may go wrong.

For your OCP exam, you will want to be familiar with the different kinds of database restores and recoveries that are possible. In this chapter we have provided you with the information you need to successfully answer the RMAN-recovery-oriented questions.

We strongly recommend that you practice these recovery techniques before you take the test. This is particularly important if you have not had any experience with RMAN restore and recovery operations. You might use the exercises in this chapter to give you more experience with recovery of your database and to better prepare you for the exam.

Backup and recovery are the lifeblood of being a DBA. Truly there is nothing more important than knowing not only how to recover your database but also how to craft an overall backup and recovery strategy for your database.

Exam Essentials

Describe the basic process used when performing an RMAN database restore and recovery. Understand the essentials behind RMAN backup and recovery. Know what might be required to prepare for an RMAN recovery. Understand the basic steps of a typical RMAN recovery and what they are for.

Know how to use the RESTORE **command.**   Understand the use of the RESTORE command. Know the different options of the RESTORE command, such as RESTORE DATABASE, RESTORE TABLESPACE, and RESTORE DATAFILE. Understand what happens when you call the RESTORE command.

Know how to use the RECOVER **command.**   Understand and be able to successfully use the RECOVER command. Know the different options of the RECOVER command, such as RECOVER

DATABASE, RECOVER TABLESPACE, and RECOVER DATAFILE. Understand what happens when you call the RECOVER command.

Understand point-in-time recovery.   Understand and be able to perform point-in-time recovery with RMAN. Know how to use the UNTIL TIME parameter of the RECOVER and RESTORE commands to perform a point-in-time recovery. Know how to use the SET UNTIL TIME command to perform a point-in-time recovery.

Understand how to perform other recoveries.   Understand how to recover from loss of a control file. Understand how to recover from loss of an spfile.

Review Questions

1. What command would you issue to enable automated backups of control files?

   A. ALTER DATASE CONTROLFILE AUTOBACKUP ON

   B. ALTER SYSTEM CONTROLFILE AUTOBACKUP ON

   C. CONFIGURE CONTROLFILE AUTOBACKUP ON

   D. ENABLE CONTROLFILE AUTOBACKUP

2. Given the following RMAN commands, choose the option that reflects the order required to restore your currently operational ARCHIVELOG-mode database.

   a. RESTORE DATABASE;

   b. RECOVER DATABASE;

   c. SHUTDOWN IMMEDIATE

   d. STARTUP

   e. RESTORE ARCHIVELOG ALL;

   f. ALTER DATABASE OPEN

   A. a, b, c, d, e, f

   B. c, b, a, d, e, f

   C. c, b, a, d, f

   D. c, a, b, d

   E. c, a, e, b, d, f

3. Which commands are used for RMAN database recovery? (Choose all that apply.)

   A. RESTORE

   B. REPAIR

   C. COPY

   D. RECOVER

   E. REPLACE

4. Given a complete loss of your database, in what order would you need to perform the following RMAN operations to restore it?

   a. RESTORE CONTROLFILE

   b. RESTORE DATABASE

   c. RESTORE SPFILE

   d. RECOVER DATABASE

   e. ALTER DATABASE OPEN

   f. ALTER DATABASE OPEN RESETLOGS

   A. b, a, c, d, e

   B. a, c, b, d, f

   C. c, a, b, d, e

   D. c, a, b, d, f

   E. e, a, b, d, c

5. If you lost your entire database, including the database spfile, control files, online redo logs, and database data files, what kind of recovery would be required with RMAN?

   A. Complete database recovery.

   B. Incomplete database recovery.

   C. Approximate database recovery.

   D. Archived database recovery.

   E. The database could not be recovered with RMAN.

6. Which command will restore all data files to the date 9/30/2013 at 18:00 hours?

   A. RESTORE DATAFILES UNTIL TIME '09/28/2013:21:03:11';

   B. RESTORE DATABASE FILES UNTIL TIME '09/28/2013:18:00:00';

   C. RESTORE DATABASE UNTIL TIME '09/28/2013:18:00:00';

   D. RECOVER DATABASE UNTIL TIME '09/28/2013:18:00:00';

   E. RECOVER DATABASE UNTIL TIMESTAMP '09/28/2013:18:00:00';

7. What is the end result of these commands if they are successful?

```
RMAN> show retention policy;
RMAN configuration parameters for database with db_unique_name ORCL are:
CONFIGURE RETENTION POLICY TO REDUNDANCY 1; # default
Backup database tag='gold_copy' plus archivelog
tag='gold_copy' delete input;
Backup database tag='silver_copy' plus archivelog
tag='silver_copy' delete input;
```

    A. Attempting to restore silver_copy will fail.

    B. Attempting to restore gold_copy will fail.

    C. Both backups will be available for restore without question.

    D. Attempting to restore gold_copy may or may not succeed.

    E. You will not be able to restore either gold_copy or silver_copy.

8. You are using RMAN to backup your ARCHIVELOG mode database. You have enabled control-file autobackups. Which files are not backed up during the RMAN backup?

    A. Database data files

    B. Database control files

    C. Online redo logs

    D. Archived redo logs

    E. The database spfile

    F. None of the above; all these files are backed up

9. True or false: RMAN offers the equivalent of the SQL command ALTER DATABASE BACKUP CONTROLFILE TO TRACE.

    A. True

    B. False

10. You need to restore your database to 9/30/2013 at 18:00. In what order would you run the following commands to compete this task?

    a. `RESTORE CONTROLFILE UNTIL TIME'09/30/2013:18:00:00';`

    b. `RESTORE DATABASE UNTIL TIME'09/30/2013:18:00:00';`

    c. `RESTORE SPFILE UNTIL TIME'09/30/2013:18:00:00';;`

    d. `RECOVER DATABASE UNTIL TIME'09/30/2013:18:00:00';`

    e. `ALTER DATABASE OPEN RESETLOGS;`

    f. `ALTER DATABASE OPEN;`

    A. b, d, e

    B. b, d, f

    C. c, a, b, d, e

    D. c, a, b, d, f

    E. a, b, d, e

11. What is the correct order of the following commands if you wanted to restore data file 4, which was accidentally removed from the file system?

    a. `SQ; 'ALTER DATABASE DATAFILE 4 ONLINE';`

    b. `RESTORE DATAFILE 4;`

    c. `RECOVER DATAFILE 4;`

    d. `SQL 'ALTER DATABASE DATAFILE 4 OFFLINE';`

    e. `STARTUP`

    f. `SHUTDOWN`

    A. a, c, b, d

    B. d, b, c, a

    C. f, d, b, c, a, e

    D. c, a, b, d, f

    E. a, b, d, e

12. Your database is up and running and one of your three control files is accidentally erased. You start RMAN and run the following command:

```
RESTORE CONTROLFILE FROM AUTOBACKUP;
```

Which of the following statements is true? (Choose all that apply.)

    A. The command restores only the missing control file.

    B. The command restores all the control files.

    C. The command fails because the database is running.

    D. This is the correct way to address this problem.

    E. This is not the correct way to address this problem.

13. Which of the following are valid `UNTIL` command options when attempting point-in-time recovery in RMAN? (Choose all that apply.)

    A. `UNTIL TIME`

    B. `UNTIL CHANGE`

    C. `UNTIL SEQUENCE`

    D. `UNTIL SCN`

    E. `UNTIL COMMIT`

14. Which of the following does the `RECOVER` command not do?

    A. Restore archived redo logs

    B. Apply archived redo logs

    C. Restore incremental backups

    D. Apply incremental backups

    E. Restore data file images

15. You have a database with the following tablespaces: `SYSTEM`, `SYSAUX`, `UNDO`, `USERS`, `TEMP`. You want to roll back the data in the `USERS` tablespace to the way it looked yesterday. Which tablespaces do you need to perform a point-in-time restore operation on in order to complete this task? (Choose all that apply.)

    A. `SYSTEM`

    B. `SYSAUX`

    C. `UNDO`

    D. `USERS`

    E. `TEMP`

    F. This restore is not possible.

16. You have backed up your database using image copies. You have lost the `SYSTEM` tablespace and need to restart your database as quickly as possible. What is the correct solution?

    A. Restore the `SYSTEM` tablespace from the last backup set and then recover the database.

    B. Restore the `SYSTEM` tablespace image copy using the `RESTORE` command and then restore the database.

    C. Use the `SWITCH DATAFILE` command to instantly switch to the data file copy, recover the tablespace, and open the database.

    D. The database is not recoverable in this situation with image copies.

    E. Manually copy the data file image copy to the correct location and then manually restore the database from SQL*Plus.

17. If you find errors in the view V$DATABASE_BLOCK_CORRUPTION with a status of MEDIA_CORRUPT, what RMAN command would you run to correct the problem?

    A. RECOVER LOST BLOCKS;

    B. RECOVER CORRUPT BLOCKS;

    C. RECOVER MEDIA CORRUPT BLOCKS FROM LIST;

    D. RECOVER CORRUPT BLOCKS FROM LIST;

    E. RECOVER CORRUPTION LIST;

18. What will be the end result of this set of RMAN commands?

    ```
    shutdown abort
    startup mount
    restore datafile 4 until time '09/30/2013:15:00:00';
    recover datafile 4 until time '09/29/2013:15:00:00';
    alter database open resetlogs;
    ```

    A. Data file 4 will be recovered until 9/30/2013 at 15:00 and the database will open.

    B. The RESTORE command will fail.

    C. The RECOVER command will fail.

    D. The ALTER DATABASE OPEN RESETLOGS command will fail.

    E. All these commands will fail because they must be in the confines of a RUN block.

19. Which of the following represents the correct way to perform an online recovery of data file 4, which is assigned to a tablespace called USERS?

    A. SHUTDOWNRESTORE DATAFILE 4;RECOVER DATAFILE 4;ALTER DATABASE OPEN;

    B. SQL 'ALTER DATABASE DATAFILE 4 OFFLINE';RESTORE DATAFILE 4;RECOVER DATAFILE 4;ALTER DATABASE OPEN;

    C. SQL 'ALTER DATABASE DATAFILE 5 OFFLINE';RESTORE DATAFILE 4;SQL 'ALTER DATABASE DATAFILE 4 ONLINE';

    D. SQL 'ALTER DATABASE DATAFILE 4 OFFLINE';RESTORE DATABASE DATAFILE 4;RECOVER DATABASE DATAFILE 4;SQL 'ALTER DATABASE DATAFILE 4 ONLINE';

    E. SQL 'ALTER DATABASE DATAFILE 4 OFFLINE';RESTORE DATAFILE 4;RECOVER DATAFILE 4;SQL 'ALTER DATABASE DATAFILE 4 ONLINE';

20. David managed to accidentally delete the data files for database called DSL. He called Heber, and Heber tried to help but he managed to delete the control files of the database. Heber called Bill, and Bill saved the day. They are using a recovery catalog for this database. What steps did Bill perform to recover the database and in what order?

   a. He restored the control file with the RMAN RESTORE CONTROLFILE command.

   b. He mounted the DSL instance with the ALTER DATABASE MOUNT command.

   c. He restored the data files for the DSL database with the RMAN RESTORE command.

   d. He opened the DSL database with the ALTER DATABASE OPEN RESETLOGS command.

   e. He recovered the data files for the DSL database with the RMAN RECOVER command.

   f. He started the DSL instance.

   g. He connected to the recovery catalog with RMAN.

   A. a, b, c, d, e, f, g

   B. b, c, d, g, f, e, a

   C. g, f, a, b, c, e, d

   D. c, a, d, b, f, e, g

   E. g, f, a, b, e, c, d

Chapter

6

Tuning and Monitoring RMAN and the Automatic Diagnostic Workflow

ORACLE DATABASE 12*c*: ADVANCED ADMINISTRATION EXAM OBJECTIVES COVERED IN THIS CHAPTER:

✓ Manage backups

✓ Report on backups using LIST and REPORT commands

✓ Manage backups using CROSSCHECK and DELETE commands

✓ Describe the Automatic Diagnostic Workflow

✓ Use the Automatic Diagnostic Workflow

✓ Use ADRCI

✓ Find and interpret message output and error stacks

Overview of the RMAN Report and List Commands

RMAN provides a wealth of reporting with respect to backups, the database, and other various RMAN-related information. In the following sections, we will discuss the RMAN REPORT command and the RMAN LIST command. You will need to be familiar with both commands.

Exam objectives are subject to change at any time without prior notice and at Oracle's sole discretion. Please visit Oracle's Training and Certification website (http://www.oracle.com/education/certification/) for the most current exam-objectives listing.

Using the RMAN *REPORT* Command

First, we will cover the RMAN REPORT command. We will describe the purpose of the REPORT command in RMAN, and then we will provide several examples of its use.

Introducing the RMAN *REPORT* Command

The RMAN REPORT command provides information on records within the database control file or the RMAN recovery catalog. The REPORT command provides the following information:

- Database, tablespace, or data files that need to be backed up
- Obsolete backups. These are backups that do not meet the retention criteria and can be removed with the DELETE OBSOLETE commands
- Objects in the database that need to be backed up because of unrecoverable SQL operations
- Information on the database schema

Let's look at some examples of how to use the REPORT command.

Seeing the RMAN *REPORT* Command in Action

Now we will show a number of examples of the use of the RMAN REPORT command. First, we will show the REPORT BACKUP command, and then we will show the REPORT SCHEMA command.

Example of the *REPORT NEED BACKUP* Command

If you wanted to know which data files need to be backed up in your database based on the retention criteria, you could use the REPORT NEED BACKUP command:

```
RMAN> report need backup;
RMAN retention policy will be applied to the command
RMAN retention policy is set to redundancy 1
Report of files with less than 1 redundant backups
File #bkps Name
---- ----- -------------------------------------------
5    0     C:\ORACLE\ORADATA\ORCL\MY_DATA_01.DBF
```

In this example you see that data file 5 is in need of backup with respect to the retention policy. You also see that it has 0 backups (in the #bkps column). In this case, this is a new data file that has never been backed up.

You can use various options with the REPORT NEED BACKUP command to customize the report. For example, you could say that you want to see a report of all files that have not been backed up in the last three days. The report would look like this:

```
RMAN> report need backup days 3;
Report of files whose recovery needs more than 3 days of archived logs
File Days  Name
---- ----- ------------------------------------------------------
1    6     C:\ORACLE\ORADATA\ORCL\SYSTEM01.DBF
2    6     C:\ORACLE\ORADATA\ORCL\SYSAUX01.DBF
3    6     C:\ORACLE\ORADATA\ORCL\UNDOTBS01.DBF
4    6     C:\ORACLE\ORADATA\ORCL\USERS01.DBF
```

There are other reporting options besides days:

Incremental   Maximum number of incrementals to apply.

Recovery window of   Indicates the recovery-window criteria to apply. This can be handy when trying to determine the impacts of changing the recovery-window retention policy.

Redundancy   Indicates the level of backup redundancy for data files. This can be handy when trying to determine the impacts of changing the redundancy retention policy.

Example of the *REPORT OBSOLETE* Command

The REPORT OBSOLETE command is used to list backup sets that are marked as obsolete in the control file or the recovery catalog. Depending on your configuration, you might look at the REPORT OBSOLETE command output and ensure that the backups listed in that command are supposed to be deleted. If so, you could remove them with the DELETE OBSOLETE command (discussed later in this chapter).

In this example, you can see that several backup set pieces are obsolete and no longer needed. If these were present in a Fast Recovery Area (FRA), then Oracle would automatically delete the backup set pieces when space was needed or when you ran the DELETE OBSOLETE command. If you were not using the FRA, you would need to run the DELETE OBSOLETE command to remove those pieces.

```
RMAN> report obsolete;
RMAN retention policy will be applied to the command
RMAN retention policy is set to redundancy 1
Report of obsolete backups and copies
Type                   Key    Completion Time    Filename/Handle
-------------------- ------ ------------------ --------------------
Backup Set             424    11-OCT-13
  Backup Piece         432    11-OCT-13
C:\ORACLE\FAST_RECOVERY_AREA\ORCL\BACKUPSET\
2013_10_11\01_MF_ANNNN_TAG20131011T142547_4H22YY00_.BKP
Backup Set             426    11-OCT-13
  Backup Piece         434    11-OCT-13
C:\ORACLE\FAST_RECOVERY_AREA\ORCL\BACKUPSET\
2013_10_11\01_MF_NCSNF_TAG20131011T142622_4H23CVNJ_.BKP
Backup Set             429    11-OCT-13
  Backup Piece         437    11-OCT-13
C:\ORACLE\FAST_RECOVERY_AREA\ORCL\AUTOBACKUP\
2013_10_11\01_MF_S_667838162_4H23KXWB_.BKP
Backup Set             430    12-OCT-13
  Backup Piece         438    12-OCT-13
C:\ORACLE\FAST_RECOVERY_AREA\ORCL\AUTOBACKUP\
2013_10_12\01_MF_S_667915771_4H4HCM7L_.BKP
```

Example of the *REPORT SCHEMA* Command

The REPORT SCHEMA command provides information on the tablespaces and related data files (and tempfiles) in the database. Displayed by the REPORT SCHEMA command are the data file ID, the size of the data file, and the tablespace that the data file is associated with. An example of the use of the REPORT SCHEMA command is shown here:

```
RMAN> report schema;
using target database control file instead of recovery catalog
Report of database schema for database with db_unique_name ORCL

List of Permanent Datafiles
===========================
File Size(MB) Tablespace        RB segs Datafile Name
---- -------- ----------------- ------- ------------------------
1    680      SYSTEM            ***     C:\ORACLE\ORADATA\ORCL\SYSTEM01.DBF
2    612      SYSAUX            ***     C:\ORACLE\ORADATA\ORCL\SYSAUX01.DBF
```

```
3    25       UNDOTBS1      ***     C:\ORACLE\ORADATA\ORCL\UNDOTBS01.DBF
4    5        USERS         ***     C:\ORACLE\ORADATA\ORCL\USERS01.DBF
5    50       MY_DATA       ***     C:\ORACLE\ORADATA\ORCL\MY_DATA_01.DBF
List of Temporary Files
=======================
File Size(MB) Tablespace          Maxsize(MB) Tempfile Name
---- -------- ------------------- ----------- --------------------
1    20       TEMP                32767       C:\ORACLE\ORADATA\ORCL\TEMP01.DBF
```

Note that the report header indicates that the control file is being used instead of the recovery catalog.

Example of the *REPORT UNRECOVERABLE* Command

Certain types of SQL operations can make an object unrecoverable. This is because these operations do not produce redo, in an effort to make the process more performant. Since there is no redo, there is no recovering the object, and what you end up with after a recovery is a shell of an object with no data in it. Here is an example.

First, you log into RMAN and issue the command REPORT UNRECOVERABLE DATABASE:

```
RMAN> report unrecoverable database;
starting full resync of recovery catalog
full resync complete
Report of files that need backup due to unrecoverable operations
File Type of Backup Required Name
---- ----------------------- -----------------------------------
```

 You might have noticed the message "full resync complete" in some of our output. This simply means that we are connected to a recovery catalog, and the control file and the recovery catalog are being synchronized.

Next, you create an object in the SCOTT schema and load it with data:

```
SQL> create table unrecover_table (id number);
SQL> begin
  2  for dd in 1..50
  3  loop
  4  insert into unrecover_table values (dd);
  5  end loop;
6* end;
  7  /
```

```
PL/SQL procedure successfully completed.

SQL>commit;
```

Now you will create a table based on the UNRECOVER_TABLE. You will make the operation an unrecoverable operation:

```
SQL> Create table test_norecover nologging as select * from unrecover_table;
```

The RMAN REPORT UNRECOVERABLE command indicates that your USERS tablespace needs a backup:

```
RMAN> report unrecoverable database;
Report of files that need backup due to unrecoverable operations
File Type of Backup Required Name
---- ----------------------- -----------------------------------
4    full or incremental     C:\ORACLE\ORADATA\ORCL\USERS01.DBF
```

To fix this problem, you back up the USERS tablespace, as shown here:

```
RMAN> backup tablespace users;
Starting backup at 18-OCT-13
allocated channel: ORA_DISK_1
channel ORA_DISK_1: SID=134 device type=DISK
channel ORA_DISK_1: starting datafile copy
input datafile file number=00004 name=C:\ORACLE\ORADATA\ORCL\USERS01.DBF
output file name=C:\ORACLE\FAST_RECOVERY_AREA\ORCL\DATAFILE\
O1_MF_USERS_4HM3CGQX_.DBF tag=TAG20131018T011646 RECID=1
STAMP=668395023
channel ORA_DISK_1: datafile copy complete, elapsed time: 00:00:03
Finished backup at 18-OCT-13
Starting Control File and SPFILE Autobackup at 18-OCT-13
piece handle=C:\ORACLE\FAST_RECOVERY_AREA\ORCL\AUTOBACKUP\2013_10_18\
O1_MF_S_668395027_4HM3CWNZ_.BKP comment=NONE
Finished Control File and SPFILE Autobackup at 18-OCT-13
RMAN> report unrecoverable database;
Report of files that need backup due to unrecoverable operations
File Type of Backup Required Name
---- ----------------------- -----------------------------------
```

In Exercise 6.1, you will get to experiment with the REPORT command.

Using the REPORT Command

1. Log into RMAN, connecting to your recovery catalog.

```
C:\>rman target=/ catalog=rcat_user/rcat_user@rcat
Recovery Manager: Release 12.1.0.1.0 -
Production on Sat Jan 4 20:01:34 2014
Copyright (c) 1982, 2013, Oracle and/or its affiliates.  All rights reserved.
connected to target database: ORCL (DBID=1195614221)
connected to recovery catalog database
```

2. Just type in the command **REPORT;**. Review the output. Notice how RMAN prompts you for the syntax it is expecting. For example, in this case it's expecting something akin to report device, report need, report obsolete, and so on.

```
RMAN> report;
RMAN-00571: ===========================================================
RMAN-00569: =============== ERROR MESSAGE STACK FOLLOWS ===============
RMAN-00571: ===========================================================
RMAN-00558: error encountered while parsing input commands
RMAN-01009: syntax error: found ";": expecting one of:
"device, need, obsolete, schema, unrecoverable"
RMAN-01007: at line 1 column 7 file: standard input
```

3. See what data files and tempfiles are in the database by using the REPORT SCHEMA command:

```
RMAN> report schema;
Report of database schema for database with db_unique_name ORCL
List of Permanent Datafiles
===========================
File Size(MB) Tablespace        RB segs Datafile Name
---- -------- ----------------- ------- ------------------------
1    680      SYSTEM            YES     C:\ORACLE\ORADATA\ORCL\SYSTEM01.DBF
2    631      SYSAUX            NO      C:\ORACLE\ORADATA\ORCL\SYSAUX01.DBF
3    25       UNDOTBS1          YES     C:\ORACLE\ORADATA\ORCL\UNDOTBS01.DBF
4    5        USERS             NO      C:\ORACLE\ORADATA\ORCL\USERS01.DBF
5    50       MY_DATA           NO      C:\ORACLE\ORADATA\ORCL\MY_DATA_01.DBF
List of Temporary Files
=======================
File Size(MB) Tablespace        Maxsize(MB) Tempfile Name
---- -------- ----------------- ----------- --------------------
1    20       TEMP              32767       C:\ORACLE\ORADATA\ORCL\TEMP01.DBF
```

EXERCISE 6.1 *(continued)*

4. See what backups in the database have become obsolete because they do not meet the retention criteria. To do so, you will use the REPORT OBSOLETE command:

```
RMAN> report obsolete;
RMAN retention policy will be applied to the command
RMAN retention policy is set to redundancy 1
Report of obsolete backups and copies
Type                    Key    Completion Time     Filename/Handle
-------------------- ------ ------------------ --------------------
Archive Log             926    18-OCT-13
C:\ORACLE\PRODUCT\11.1.0\DB_1\RDBMS\ARC00022_0667833490.001
Backup Set              978    18-OCT-13
  Backup Piece          980    18-OCT-13
C:\ORACLE\FAST_RECOVERY_AREA\ORCL\AUTOBACKUP\2013_10_18
\O1_MF_S_668446569_4HNOPMRF_.BKP
Backup Set              1252   18-OCT-13
  Backup Piece          1260   18-OCT-13              C:\ORACLE\FAST_RECOVERY_AREA\
ORCL\BACKUPSET\2013_10_18
\O1_MF_ANNNN_TAG20131018T153543_4HNOP6OH_.BKP.OLD
Backup Set              1253   18-OCT-13
  Backup Piece          1261   18-OCT-13              C:\ORACLE\FAST_RECOVERY_AREA\
ORCL\BACKUPSET\2013_10_18\
O1_MF_NNNDF_TAG20131018T152908_4HNO9DX9_.BKP.OLD
```

5. Log out of RMAN and log into the database with SQL*Plus:

```
RMAN> quit
Recovery Manager complete.
C:\Documents and Settings\Robert>sqlplus "/ as sysdba"
SQL*Plus: Release 12.1.0.1.0 Production on Sat Jan 4 20:05:34 2014
Copyright (c) 1982, 2013, Oracle.  All rights reserved.
Connected to:
Oracle Database 12c Enterprise Edition Release 12.1.0.1.0 - 64bit Production
With the Partitioning, OLAP, Advanced Analytics
and Real Application Testing options
SQL>
```

6. Add a tablespace to the database, and then log out of SQL*Plus. You may want to put your tablespace in a different location; this is fine.

```
SQL> create tablespace testtbs
  2  datafile 'c:\oracle\oradata\orcl\testtbs.dbf' size 20m;
Tablespace created.
```

```
SQL> exit
Disconnected from Oracle Database 11g Enterprise Edition
Release 11.1.0.6.0 - Production
With the Partitioning, OLAP, Data Mining and
Real Application Testing options
```

7. Log into RMAN, connecting to your recovery catalog:

```
C:\>rman target=/ catalog=rcat_user/rcat_user@rcat
Recovery Manager: Release 12.1.0.1.0 -
Production on Sat Jan 4 20:01:34 2014
Copyright (c) 1982, 2013, Oracle and/or its affiliates.  All rights reserved.
connected to target database: ORCL (DBID=1195614221)
connected to recovery catalog database
```

8. Now generate a report of data files that need to be backed up with the REPORT NEED
   BACKUP command. You will see that the new data file shows up as needing a backup.
   Note that as long as you have the archived redo logs that were generated since the data
   file was created, you can still recover this data file and any data in it.

```
RMAN> report need backup;
RMAN retention policy will be applied to the command
RMAN retention policy is set to redundancy 1
Report of files with less than 1 redundant backups
File #bkps Name
---- ----- ------------------------------------------
6    0     C:\ORACLE\ORADATA\ORCL\TESTTBS.DBF
```

Using the RMAN *LIST* Command

The RMAN LIST command provides information on backups in your Oracle database. The
LIST command has the following functionality:

- Listing expired backups
- Listing the database incarnation
- Listing database restore points
- Listing scripts
- Listing information on database backups and image copies

Additionally, information can often be listed in two formats, detail and summary, as
you will see in the following sections.

Seeing the *LIST EXPIRED BACKUP* Command in Action

When you run the CROSSCHECK command (discussed later in this chapter), any missing backup files will be marked as EXPIRED, meaning that they are no longer on the media where they are expected to be. The LIST EXPIRED command will show you the backups that are expired. You can review this list and then use the DELETE command to mark the backup files as deleted in the control file and the recovery catalog. Here is an example of the LIST EXPIRED BACKUP command in use:

```
RMAN> list expired backup of database;
List of Backup Sets
===================
BS Key  Type LV Size        Device Type Elapsed Time Completion Time
------- ---- -- ---------- ----------- ------------ ---------------
425     Full    176.72M    DISK        00:06:02     11-OCT-13
BP Key: 433    Status: EXPIRED  Compressed: YES  Tag: TAG20131011T142622
Piece Name: C:\ORACLE\FAST_RECOVERY_AREA\ORCL\BACKUPSET\2013_10_11\
O1_MF_NNNDF_TAG20131011T142622_4H22ZOMK_.BKP
  List of Datafiles in backup set 425
  File LV Type Ckp SCN    Ckp Time  Name
  ---- -- ---- ---------- --------- ----
  1       Full 903859     11-OCT-13 C:\ORACLE\ORADATA\ORCL\SYSTEM01.DBF
  2       Full 903859     11-OCT-13 C:\ORACLE\ORADATA\ORCL\SYSAUX01.DBF
  3       Full 903859     11-OCT-13 C:\ORACLE\ORADATA\ORCL\UNDOTBS01.DBF
  4       Full 903859     11-OCT-13 C:\ORACLE\ORADATA\ORCL\USERS01.DBF
```

In this case, we have one backup set that is expired. Each backup set has its own unique backup-set key that you will find in many reports. In this report, the backup-set key 425 is missing. This backup includes backups of four data files. Since it's expired, this essentially means it's missing from the database. Expired backups will not show up on this report until the CROSSCHECK command detects that they are missing. You can find more information on the CROSSCHECK command later in this chapter. If you want to mark these as deleted in the recovery catalog, you can use the DELETE EXPIRED command. You can find more information on the DELETE EXPIRED command later in this chapter.

Seeing the *LIST INCARNATION* Command in Action

The LIST INCARNATION command provides information related to database incarnation from the control file or the recovery catalog. You can use this command to guide you in situations in which you need to reset the database incarnation for certain types of database recoveries (see Chapter 5, "Recovering Databases with RMAN," for more on this topic).

The LIST INCARNATION command output is slightly different depending on whether you are connected to a recovery catalog or the database control file. For example, here is some sample output from the LIST INCARNATION command when we were connected to the control file of the database:

```
RMAN> list incarnation;
List of Database Incarnations
DB Key  Inc Key DB Name  DB ID             STATUS  Reset SCN  Reset Time
------- ------- -------- ----------------- ------- ---------- ----------
1       1       ORCL     1195614221        PARENT  1          15-OCT-13
2       2       ORCL     1195614221        CURRENT 886308     11-OCT-13
```

Note that there are two records here, and the DBID for each record is the same. When you execute the same command from the recovery catalog, you may get different results; our results are shown here:

```
RMAN> list incarnation;
List of Database Incarnations
DB Key  Inc Key DB Name  DB ID             STATUS  Reset SCN  Reset Time
------- ------- -------- ----------------- ------- ---------- ----------
1       15      ORCL     1194488809        PARENT  1          15-OCT-13
1       16      ORCL     1194488809        PARENT  886308     29-SEP-13
1       17      ORCL     1194488809        ORPHAN  907851     02-OCT-13
1       2       ORCL     1194488809        PARENT  953055     02-OCT-13
1       270     ORCL     1194488809        CURRENT 988211     02-OCT-13
321     335     ORCL     1195614221        PARENT  1          15-OCT-13
321     322     ORCL     1195614221        CURRENT 886308     11-OCT-13
```

This is a case where we have two databases called ORCL in our recovery catalog. Notice that each of those databases has a different DBID. Oracle will be able to separate the databases based on this unique ID, but both databases show up in the report because the report is generated based on the database name, not the DBID.

Seeing the *LIST RESTORE POINT* Command in Action

Database restore points are a function of Oracle Flashback Database technologies (see Chapter 8, "Understanding Flashback Technology," for more information on Oracle Flashback Database). You can set restore points from the SQL prompt with the CREATE RESTORE POINT command. In this example, we use the LIST RESTORE POINT ALL command to list all restore points:

```
RMAN> list restore point all;
SCN             RSP Time  Type       Time      Name
--------------- --------- ---------- --------- ----
1219891                              18-OCT-13 ROBERT
```

You could also list a specific restore point, as in this example:

```
RMAN> list restore point robert;
SCN              RSP Time  Type       Time       Name
---------------- --------- ---------- ---------- ----
1219891                               18-OCT-13 ROBERT


RMAN> list restore point davep;
SCN              RSP Time  Type       Time       Name
---------------- --------- ---------- --------- ----
```

Seeing the *LIST ALL SCRIPT NAMES* Command in Action

The LIST ALL SCRIPT NAMES command generates a report with the names of all scripts in the recovery catalog. This command is available for use only when you are connected to the recovery catalog. Here is an example of the LIST ALL SCRIPT NAMES command where you find one script in the recovery catalog called db_backup_script:

```
RMAN> list all script names;
List of Stored Scripts in Recovery Catalog
    Scripts of Target Database ORCL
        Script Name
        Description
        -----------------------------------
        db_backup_script
```

Examples of Listing Backup-Related Information

DBAs will, from time to time, want to know what backups have been made on their database. The LIST command provides all sorts of information on database backups. For example, if you want to see what full backups of your database are available, then you can run the LIST BACKUP OF DATABASE command:

```
RMAN> list backup of database;
List of Backup Sets
===================
BS Key  Type LV Size       Device Type Elapsed Time Completion Time
------- ---- -- ---------- ----------- ------------ ---------------
2       Full    176.72M    DISK        00:06:02     11-OCT-13
        BP Key: 2   Status: EXPIRED  Compressed: YES  Tag: TAG20131011T142622
        Piece Name: C:\ORACLE\FAST_RECOVERY_AREA\ORCL\BACKUPSET\2013_10_11\
O1_MF_NNNDF_TAG20131011T142622_4H22ZOMK_.BKP
  List of Datafiles in backup set 2
```

```
   File LV Type Ckp SCN    Ckp Time  Name
   ---- -- ---- ---------- --------- ----
    1      Full 903859     11-OCT-13 C:\ORACLE\ORADATA\ORCL\SYSTEM01.DBF
    2      Full 903859     11-OCT-13 C:\ORACLE\ORADATA\ORCL\SYSAUX01.DBF
    3      Full 903859     11-OCT-13 C:\ORACLE\ORADATA\ORCL\UNDOTBS01.DBF
    4      Full 903859     11-OCT-13 C:\ORACLE\ORADATA\ORCL\USERS01.DBF


BS Key  Type LV Size       Device Type Elapsed Time Completion Time
------- ---- -- ---------- ----------- ------------ ---------------
11      Full    186.89M    DISK        00:04:43     18-OCT-13
        BP Key: 11   Status: AVAILABLE  Compressed: YES  Tag: TAG20131018T032019
        Piece Name: C:\ORACLE\FAST_RECOVERY_AREA\ORCL\BACKUPSET\2013_10_18\
O1_MF_NNNDF_TAG20131018T032019_4HMBLT5V_.BKP
   List of Datafiles in backup set 11
   File LV Type Ckp SCN    Ckp Time  Name
   ---- -- ---- ---------- --------- ----
    1      Full 1195239    18-OCT-13 C:\ORACLE\ORADATA\ORCL\SYSTEM01.DBF
    2      Full 1195239    18-OCT-13 C:\ORACLE\ORADATA\ORCL\SYSAUX01.DBF
    3      Full 1195239    18-OCT-13 C:\ORACLE\ORADATA\ORCL\UNDOTBS01.DBF
    4      Full 1195239    18-OCT-13 C:\ORACLE\ORADATA\ORCL\USERS01.DBF
    5      Full 1195239    18-OCT-13 C:\ORACLE\ORADATA\ORCL\MY_DATA_01.DBF


BS Key  Type LV Size       Device Type Elapsed Time Completion Time
------- ---- -- ---------- ----------- ------------ ---------------
15      Full    187.63M    DISK        00:05:37     18-OCT-13
        BP Key: 15   Status: AVAILABLE  Compressed: YES  Tag: TAG20131018T134250
        Piece Name: C:\ORACLE\FAST_RECOVERY_AREA\ORCL\BACKUPSET\2013_10_18\
O1_MF_NNNDF_TAG20131018T134250_4HNH25TC_.BKP
   List of Datafiles in backup set 15
   File LV Type Ckp SCN    Ckp Time  Name
   ---- -- ---- ---------- --------- ----
    1      Full 1218699    18-OCT-13 C:\ORACLE\ORADATA\ORCL\SYSTEM01.DBF
    2      Full 1218699    18-OCT-13 C:\ORACLE\ORADATA\ORCL\SYSAUX01.DBF
    3      Full 1218699    18-OCT-13 C:\ORACLE\ORADATA\ORCL\UNDOTBS01.DBF
    4      Full 1218699    18-OCT-13 C:\ORACLE\ORADATA\ORCL\USERS01.DBF
    5      Full 1218699    18-OCT-13 C:\ORACLE\ORADATA\ORCL\MY_DATA_01.DBF
```

Of course, when you read the output of the previous example, you probably said to yourself, "Wow! That's a lot more output than I needed!" You can use the SUMMARY keyword to produce summary output, which is often all you need, as shown in this example:

```
RMAN> list backup of database summary;
List of Backups
===============
Key     TY LV S Device Type Completion Time #Pieces #Copies Compressed Tag
------- -- -- - ----------- --------------- ------- ------- ---------- ---
2       B  F  X DISK        11-OCT-13       1       1       YES
TAG20131011T142622
11      B  F  A DISK        18-OCT-13       1       1       YES
TAG20131018T032019
15      B  F  A DISK        18-OCT-13       1       1       YES
TAG20131018T134250
```

Now that's a lot easier to read! Here you see that there are three backups of the database, when they were taken, the type, and other interesting information on the backups.

You can get the following details on the various types of backups that you might be taking with RMAN:

- Lists of all backups
- Lists of backup-set backups
- Lists of archive-log backups
- Lists of image copies
- Lists of control-file backups
- Backups of specific tablespaces or data files

For example, here is a list of the backups of all archive logs. Note that the LIST BACKUP OF ARCHIVELOG command provides the ability to list specific archive logs based on numerous criteria, such as a log-sequence number range, time range, and SCN range, or you can just list them all, as we do in this example:

```
RMAN> list backup of archivelog all summary;
List of Backups
===============
Key     TY LV S Device Type Completion Time #Pieces #Copies Compressed Tag
------- -- -- - ----------- --------------- ------- ------- ---------- ---
1       B  A  A DISK        11-OCT-13       1       1       YES
TAG20131011T142547
4       B  A  A DISK        11-OCT-13       1       1       YES
TAG20131011T143308
5       B  A  A DISK        11-OCT-13       1       1       NO
TAG20131011T143528
```

```
10     B  A  A DISK          18-OCT-13          1          1          YES
TAG20131018T031922
12     B  A  A DISK          18-OCT-13          1          1          YES
TAG20131018T032513
14     B  A  A DISK          18-OCT-13          1          1          YES
TAG20131018T134136
16     B  A  A DISK          18-OCT-13          1          1          YES
TAG20131018T134839
```

In Exercise 6.2, you will get to experiment with the LIST command.

EXERCISE 6.2

Using the LIST Command

1. Log into RMAN, connecting to your recovery catalog:

```
C:\>rman target=/ catalog=rcat_user/rcat_user@rcat
Recovery Manager: Release 12.1.0.1.0 -
Production on Sat Jan 4 20:01:34 2014
Copyright (c) 1982, 2013, Oracle and/or its affiliates.  All rights reserved.
connected to target database: ORCL (DBID=1195614221)
connected to recovery catalog database
```

2. You can see what backups are available by calling the LIST BACKUP OF DATABASE SUMMARY command:

```
RMAN> list backup of database summary;
List of Backups
===============
Key  TY LV S Device Type Completion Time #Pieces #Copies Compressed Tag
---- -- -- - ----------- --------------- ------- ------- ---------- ---
1253 B  F  A DISK         18-OCT-13          1          1          YES
TAG20131018T152908
1342 B  F  A DISK         18-OCT-13          1          1          YES
TAG20131018T163034
```

3. To look at both of these backups in more detail, call the LIST BACKUP command:

```
RMAN> list backup of database;
List of Backup Sets
===================
BS Key  Type LV Size       Device Type Elapsed Time Completion Time
------- ---- -- ---------- ----------- ------------ ----------------
```

EXERCISE 6.2 *(continued)*

```
1253    Full    187.77M    DISK         00:00:00    18-OCT-13
        BP Key: 1261    Status: AVAILABLE  Compressed: YES
Tag: TAG20131018T152908
    Piece Name: C:\ORACLE\FAST_RECOVERY_AREA\ORCL\BACKUPSET\2013_10_18
\O1_MF_NNNDF_TAG20131018T152908_4HNO9DX9_.BKP.OLD
List of Datafiles in backup set 1253
File LV Type Ckp SCN    Ckp Time  Name
---- -- ---- ---------- --------- ----

1       Full 1222465    18-OCT-13 C:\ORACLE\ORADATA\ORCL\SYSTEM01.DBF
2       Full 1222465    18-OCT-13 C:\ORACLE\ORADATA\ORCL\SYSAUX01.DBF
3       Full 1222465    18-OCT-13 C:\ORACLE\ORADATA\ORCL\UNDOTBS01.DBF
4       Full 1222465    18-OCT-13 C:\ORACLE\ORADATA\ORCL\USERS01.DBF
5       Full 1222465    18-OCT-13 C:\ORACLE\ORADATA\ORCL\MY_DATA_01.DBF


BS Key  Type LV Size        Device Type Elapsed Time Completion Time
------- ---- -- ---------- ----------- ------------ ---------------

1342    Full    187.87M    DISK         00:56:47    18-OCT-13
        BP Key: 1348    Status: AVAILABLE  Compressed: YES
Tag: TAG20131018T163034
    Piece Name: C:\ORACLE\FAST_RECOVERY_AREA\ORCL\BACKUPSET\2013_10_18
\O1_MF_NNNDF_TAG20131018T163034_4HNRWKVC_.BKP
List of Datafiles in backup set 1342
File LV Type Ckp SCN    Ckp Time  Name
---- -- ---- ---------- --------- ----

1       Full 1224452    18-OCT-13 C:\ORACLE\ORADATA\ORCL\SYSTEM01.DBF
2       Full 1224452    18-OCT-13 C:\ORACLE\ORADATA\ORCL\SYSAUX01.DBF
3       Full 1224452    18-OCT-13 C:\ORACLE\ORADATA\ORCL\UNDOTBS01.DBF
4       Full 1224452    18-OCT-13 C:\ORACLE\ORADATA\ORCL\USERS01.DBF
5       Full 1224452    18-OCT-13 C:\ORACLE\ORADATA\ORCL\MY_DATA_01.DBF
```

4. Next, simulate the loss of a backup set piece by using the HOST command and deleting the backup set piece.

In this case, you will remove the backup set piece called 01_MF_NNNDF_
TAG20131018T163034_4HNRWKVC_.BKP, which showed up in the report in step 3. Your backup set piece will probably be named differently.

```
RMAN> Host 'del C:\ORACLE\FAST_RECOVERY_AREA\ORCL\BACKUPSET\2013_10_18
\O1_MF_NNNDF_TAG20131018T163034_4HNRWKVC_.BKP';
```

5. Now you need to use the CROSSCHECK command so that RMAN will detect that you have deleted the backup set piece. Note that the backup set piece you removed is now marked as expired.

```
RMAN> crosscheck backup;
allocated channel: ORA_DISK_1
channel ORA_DISK_1: SID=122 device type=DISK
crosschecked backup piece: found to be 'AVAILABLE'
backup piece handle=C:\ORACLE\FAST_RECOVERY_AREA\ORCL\AUTOBACKUP\
2013_10_18\01_MF_S_668446569_4HNOPMRF_.BKP RECID=29 STAMP=668446579
crosschecked backup piece: found to be 'AVAILABLE'
backup piece handle=C:\ORACLE\FAST_RECOVERY_AREA\ORCL\BACKUPSET\
2013_10_18\01_MF_ANNNN_TAG20131018T153543_4HNOP6OH_.BKP.OLD RECID=31
STAMP=668449007
crosschecked backup piece: found to be 'AVAILABLE'
backup piece handle=C:\ORACLE\FAST_RECOVERY_AREA\ORCL\BACKUPSET\
2013_10_18\01_MF_NNNDF_TAG20131018T152908_4HNO9DX9_.BKP.OLD RECID=32
STAMP=668449009
crosschecked backup piece: found to be 'EXPIRED'
backup piece handle=C:\ORACLE\FAST_RECOVERY_AREA\ORCL\BACKUPSET\
2013_10_18\01_MF_NNNDF_TAG20131018T163034_4HNRWKVC_.BKP RECID=33
STAMP=668449841
crosschecked backup piece: found to be 'AVAILABLE'
backup piece handle=C:\ORACLE\FAST_RECOVERY_AREA\ORCL\AUTOBACKUP\
2013_10_18\01_MF_S_668453268_4HNW82VT_.BKP RECID=34
STAMP=668453282
crosschecked backup piece: found to be 'AVAILABLE'
backup piece handle=C:\ORACLE\FAST_RECOVERY_AREA\ORCL\AUTOBACKUP\
2013_10_19\01_MF_S_668533219_4HQBBXCQ_.BKP RECID=35 STAMP=668533245
Crosschecked 6 objects
```

6. Now issue the LIST EXPIRED BACKUP command to get a report of expired RMAN backup set pieces:

```
RMAN> list expired backup;
List of Backup Sets
===================

BS Key  Type LV Size       Device Type Elapsed Time Completion Time
------- ---- -- ---------- ----------- ------------ ---------------
1342    Full    187.87M    DISK        00:56:47     18-OCT-13
```

```
BP Key: 1348   Status: EXPIRED  Compressed: YES Tag: TAG20131018T163034
        Piece Name: C:\ORACLE\FAST_RECOVERY_AREA\ORCL\BACKUPSET\2013_10_18
\O1_MF_NNNDF_TAG20131018T163034_4HNRWKVC_.BKP
  List of Datafiles in backup set 1342
  File LV Type Ckp SCN  Ckp Time  Name
  ---- -- ---- -------- --------- ----
    1      Full 1224452  18-OCT-13 C:\ORACLE\ORADATA\ORCL\SYSTEM01.DBF
    2      Full 1224452  18-OCT-13 C:\ORACLE\ORADATA\ORCL\SYSAUX01.DBF
    3      Full 1224452  18-OCT-13 C:\ORACLE\ORADATA\ORCL\UNDOTBS01.DBF
    4      Full 1224452  18-OCT-13 C:\ORACLE\ORADATA\ORCL\USERS01.DBF
    5      Full 1224452  18-OCT-13 C:\ORACLE\ORADATA\ORCL\MY_DATA_01.DBF
```

7. Finally, mark the backup set piece as deleted by using the DELETE EXPIRED BACKUP command. You will need to respond when prompted to verify that you want to delete the backup set piece:

```
RMAN> delete expired backup;
using channel ORA_DISK_1
List of Backup Pieces
BP Key  BS Key  Pc# Cp# Status      Device Type Piece Name
------- ------- --- --- ----------- ----------- ----------
1348    1342    1   1   EXPIRED     DISK        C:\ORACLE\FAST_RECOVERY_AREA\
ORCL\BACKUPSET\2013_10_18
\O1_MF_NNNDF_TAG20131018T163034_4HNRWKVC_.BKP
Do you really want to delete the above objects (enter YES or NO)? yes
deleted backup piece
backup piece handle=C:\ORACLE\FAST_RECOVERY_AREA\ORCL\BACKUPSET\
2013_10_18\O1_MF_NNNDF_TAG20131018T163034_4HNRWKVC_.BKP RECID=33
STAMP=668449841
Deleted 1 EXPIRED objects
```

Monitoring, Administering, and Tuning RMAN

For the OCP exam, you will be expected to know a little bit about how to monitor RMAN operations. The exam will also test your knowledge of RMAN administration and tuning options. In the following sections, we will address all of these items.

Monitoring RMAN Operations

More often than not, RMAN works just fine. However, there are times when you will want to be able to monitor RMAN operations. In the next sections, we will discuss RMAN tuning, including enabling asynchronous I/O and monitoring RMAN operations with data dictionary views.

Configuring for Asynchronous I/O

In most cases, your operating system (OS) will already support asynchronous I/O operations natively. In these cases, no special configuration is required.

If your OS does not support native asynchronous I/O operations, then you may want to consider configuring your database, and RMAN, to simulate asynchronous I/O. Oracle provides Oracle slave I/O processes, which are individual processes that Oracle starts that are used to simulate asynchronous I/O.

You can enable these asynchronous I/O processes by configuring the parameter DBWR_IO_SLAVES. This parameter indicates to Oracle how many I/O slaves should be started when the database is started. When this parameter is zero, simulated asynchronous I/O is disabled. When the parameter is greater than zero, Oracle will automatically start four backup I/O slaves.

When using I/O slaves to simulate asynchronous I/O, you will also want to configure the large pool using the LARGE_POOL_SIZE parameter. RMAN will use the large pool, if configured, instead of the shared pool. If the large pool is allocated when you're using I/O slaves but insufficient memory exists, then RMAN will generate an error and will not use asynchronous I/O. If the large pool is not allocated and I/O slaves are enabled, RMAN will use the shared pool and try to simulate asynchronous I/O operations. If the large pool is not allocated and there is not enough shared-pool memory, then Oracle will use the PGA. In this case, simulated asynchronous I/O operations will not occur.

Using the *V$SESSION_LONGOPS* View to Monitor RMAN

Oracle provides the V$SESSION_LONGOPS view as a means to monitor long-running processes within the Oracle Database. Since RMAN uses internal database calls, records for long-running RMAN operations will appear in V$SESSION_LONGOPS. This view can be useful when you're trying to determine just how long a database backup or restore is likely to take. In this example, you first start an RMAN backup in one session. And as the backup is running, you will query the V$SESSION_LONGOPS view with this query:

```
SQL> Select sid, serial#, opname, time_remaining
  2  From v$session_longops
  3  Where sid in (select sid from v$session
  4                       Where program like '%rman%')
  5  And time_remaining > 0;
       SID    SERIAL# OPNAME                              TIME_REMAINING
---------- ---------- ----------------------------------- --------------
       129        415 RMAN: aggregate input                          188
       121        269 RMAN: full datafile backup                     161
```

In the output from this example, it appears that the overall time for the RMAN backup in question is about 188 seconds (the aggregate input figure is the one to use here). Keep in mind that these figures are just for the individual backup operation that is currently running. The output is not cumulative for the entire BACKUP command.

For example, if you executed a backup using a command like BACKUP AS COMPRESSED BACKUPSET DATABASE PLUS ARCHIVELOG DELETE INPUT, the output displayed would be only for the database backup or the archived redo-log backup. Keep in mind that the BACKUP DATABASE PLUS ARCHIVELOG command can show a series of backups. These would include two individual archive-log backups, the database backup, and then the control-file auto-backup. Each of these operations will appear in the V$SESSION_LONGOPS view differently. Notice in the previous example that OPNAME is displayed as full data file backup. The value for OPNAME would be different for different stages in the RMAN backup operation.

Real World Scenario

Tuning RMAN: It's the Little Things That Count

In the real world, tuning RMAN can make a huge difference. RMAN works fine as it is out of the box, but very often there is a lot you can do to make things run faster. Sometimes even the smallest things can make a huge difference. One place where one of us worked had limited tape drives for performing backups.

The problem was that individual DBAs were scheduling their backups for each of their individual databases and there wasn't a lot of coordination of schedules going on. We started getting complaints because backups were taking a long time.

It turned out that everyone was hitting the tape drives at the same time. The tape drives would be working a specific backup, and all the other backups would sit and wait for a tape device to become available. Once we worked out a reasonable schedule, the backups started working better and everyone was much happier!

Using the *V$SESSION* and *V$SESSION_WAIT_HISTORY* Views to Troubleshoot RMAN Problems

Trouble. We hate trouble. Sometimes you get into problems with RMAN and are not sure what the trouble is. The V$SESSION and V$SESSION_WAIT views can be a big help in your troubleshooting efforts. These views can help identify the cause of RMAN processes that are not running as fast as you would like. In this example, we have an RMAN backup running, and rather slowly at that. We query the V$SESSION view to determine the total number of waits that the session has experienced and the wait event that the session is currently experiencing:

```
SQL> Select sid, serial#, event, seconds_in_wait
  2  From v$session
```

```
 3  Where sid in (select sid from v$session
 4                Where program like '%rman%');
      SID    SERIAL# EVENT                            SECONDS_IN_WAIT
---------- ---------- ------------------------------ ---------------
      121        269 RMAN backup & recovery I/O                    2
      129        415 SQL*Net message from client                  63
      130        270 SQL*Net message from client                   8
```

Here you see that the backup-and-recovery I/O on SID 121 appears to be a problem. It's been waiting 2 seconds, which is a long time for an I/O request. Note that the two other wait events are considered idle waits and are likely not a problem. Later we might run the query again and see something like this:

```
      SID    SERIAL# EVENT                            SECONDS_IN_WAIT
---------- ---------- ------------------------------ ---------------
      121        269 control file sequential read                  3
      129        415 SQL*Net message from client                   3
      130        270 SQL*Net message from client                   3
```

The control-file sequential read is now the main wait.

The V$SESSION view lists waits that are occurring at that moment. We could query V$SESSION_WAIT_HISTORY and find out all waits for the session since it started, as shown here:

```
SQL> Select sid, event, wait_time
  2  From v$session_wait_history
  3  Where sid in (select sid from v$session
  4                Where program like '%rman%')
  5 And wait_time>0;
      SID EVENT                            WAIT_TIME
---------- ------------------------------ ----------
      121 RMAN backup & recovery I/O              11
      129 SQL*Net message from client              1
      129 SQL*Net message from client              2
      129 SQL*Net message from client              2
      130 SQL*Net message from client            400
      130 SQL*Net message from client            200
      130 SQL*Net message from client            100
      130 SQL*Net message from client            766
```

This gives us the cumulative wait times for a given session. We might wait for a few moments and run the query again. Perhaps we would get these results:

```
      SID EVENT                            WAIT_TIME
---------- ------------------------------ ----------
      121 RMAN backup & recovery I/O              85
```

```
121 RMAN backup & recovery I/O          47
129 SQL*Net message from client          1
129 SQL*Net message from client          2
129 SQL*Net message from client          2
130 SQL*Net message from client       1000
130 SQL*Net message from client       1000
130 SQL*Net message from client       1000
130 SQL*Net message from client       1000
130 SQL*Net message from client       1000
```

The difference in session 121's wait titled RMAN backup & recovery I/O might indicate a problem with the disk subsystem that we are backing up to (which is quite correct in this situation, since we ran this on a slow computer).

Administering RMAN Operations

For the OCP exam, you will be expected to know how to administer RMAN. The principal commands used to administer RMAN are the DELETE command, the CROSSCHECK command, the CATALOG command, and finally, the RESYNC command.

Using the *DELETE* Command

The DELETE command is used to mark backup set pieces, image copies, or archived redo logs as deleted if they have been previously marked as expired (missing) or obsolete (retention criteria–related). Previously in this chapter, you saw the LIST EXPIRED command used to indicate which backup set pieces were expired. After running the LIST EXPIRED command, we would use the DELETE EXPIRED BACKUP command to mark those as permanently deleted from the control file and the recovery catalog.

When the DELETE EXPIRED command is executed, all records for those backup set pieces in the control file and/or the recovery catalog are marked as deleted. When the DELETE OBSOLETE command is executed, that command will mark the records for the backup set pieces as deleted in the control file and recovery catalog. The DELETE OBSOLETE command will also remove any physical-backup set pieces present on the backup media.

Here is an example where we list the expired (missing) backup set pieces and then delete them:

```
RMAN> list expired backup;
List of Backup Sets
===================

BS Key  Type LV Size       Device Type Elapsed Time Completion Time
------- ---- -- ---------- ----------- ------------ ---------------
425     Full    176.72M    DISK        00:06:02     11-OCT-13
        BP Key: 433   Status: EXPIRED  Compressed: YES  Tag: TAG20131011T142622
        Piece Name: C:\ORACLE\FAST_RECOVERY_AREA\ORCL\BACKUPSET\2013_10_11
```

```
\01_MF_NNNDF_TAG20131011T142622_4H22ZOMK_.BKP
  List of Datafiles in backup set 425
  File LV Type Ckp SCN    Ckp Time  Name
  ---- -- ---- ---------- --------- ----
   1       Full 903859    11-OCT-13 C:\ORACLE\ORADATA\ORCL\SYSTEM01.DBF
   2       Full 903859    11-OCT-13 C:\ORACLE\ORADATA\ORCL\SYSAUX01.DBF
   3       Full 903859    11-OCT-13 C:\ORACLE\ORADATA\ORCL\UNDOTBS01.DBF
   4       Full 903859    11-OCT-13 C:\ORACLE\ORADATA\ORCL\USERS01.DBF
RMAN> delete expired backup;
Allocated channel ORA_DISK_1
Channel ORA_DISK_1: SID=186 device type=DISK
List of Backup Pieces
BP Key  BS Key  Pc# Cp# Status      Device Type Piece Name
-------  -------  --- --- ----------- ----------- ----------
433     425     1   1   EXPIRED     DISK
C:\ORACLE\FAST_RECOVERY_AREA\ORCL\BACKUPSET\2013_10_11
\01_MF_NNNDF_TAG20131011T142622_4H22ZOMK_.BKP
Do you really want to delete the above objects (enter YES or NO)? yes
deleted backup piece
backup piece handle=C:\ORACLE\FAST_RECOVERY_AREA\ORCL\BACKUPSET\2013_10_11\
01_MF_NNNDF_TAG20131011T142622_4H22ZOMK_.BKP RECID=2 STAMP=667837589
Deleted 1 EXPIRED objects
```

One important thing to note is that once you have marked a backup set with a DELETED status, that status cannot be changed. Thus, if you ever needed to restore that backup set piece, you would have to use the CATALOG command to reimport it into the database control file and recovery catalog (assuming it was still available).

Using the *CROSSCHECK* Command

The CROSSCHECK command is used to validate RMAN records in the database control file and the recovery catalog against what is physically on the backup media. The CROSSCHECK command can be used on both disk backups and tape backups. In this example, we are using it to validate that all the backup set pieces recorded in the control file of our database are actually on the media where they are supposed to be:

```
RMAN> crosscheck backup of database;
using channel ORA_DISK_1
crosschecked backup piece: found to be EXPIRED'
backup piece handle=C:\ORACLE\FAST_RECOVERY_AREA\ORCL\BACKUPSET\2013_10_18
\01_MF_NNNDF_TAG20131018T152908_4HNO9DX9_.BKP RECID=27 STAMP=668446156
Crosschecked 1 objects
```

In this case, we had some bad news because one of our backup set pieces is marked EXPIRED, or missing. If we know that it's permanently gone, we can use the DELETE EXPIRED command (discussed earlier in this chapter) to mark it as deleted. Sometimes the backup set piece is expired just because the backup media is offline (for example, a bad disk cable). Once the backup media is back online, you would rerun the CROSSCHECK command and the backup set piece would be marked as AVAILABLE once it is again accessible by RMAN.

As with other administration commands, you can cross check the gambit of backups. From database backups and archive-log backups to image copies, the CROSSCHECK command covers them all.

Using the *CATALOG* Command

The CATALOG command is used to import one or more backup set pieces, image copies, control-file copies, or archived redo logs into the recovery catalog. For example, say we had executed a CROSSCHECK of our database backups and then deleted the expired backup set pieces with the DELETE EXPIRED command. That would mark the expired backup set piece as deleted in our control file and recovery catalog. This is okay until the missing backup set piece reappears (say we restore it from a tape backup). In this case, we would have to use the CATALOG command to reregister the backup set piece in the control file and recovery catalog. Here is an example of the use of the CATALOG command:

```
RMAN> crosscheck backup of database;
using channel ORA_DISK_1
crosschecked backup piece: found to be 'EXPIRED'
backup piece handle=C:\ORACLE\FAST_RECOVERY_AREA\ORCL\BACKUPSET\2013_10_18
\O1_MF_NNNDF_TAG20131018T152908_4HNO9DX9_.BKP RECID=27 STAMP=668446156
Crosschecked 1 objects
RMAN> catalog backuppiece
'C:\ORACLE\FAST_RECOVERY_AREA\ORCL\BACKUPSET\2013_10_18
\O1_MF_NNNDF_TAG20131018T152908_4HNO9DX9_.BKP';
cataloged backup piece
backup piece handle=C:\ORACLE\FAST_RECOVERY_AREA\ORCL\BACKUPSET\2013_10_18
\O1_MF_NNNDF_TAG20131018T152908_4HNO9DX9_.BKP RECID=30 STAMP=668447953
```

The CROSSCHECK command can also import complete directories, as shown in this example:

```
RMAN> catalog start with
'C:\ORACLE\FAST_RECOVERY_AREA\ORCL\BACKUPSET\2013_10_18\';
searching for all files that match the pattern
C:\ORACLE\FAST_RECOVERY_AREA\ORCL\BACKUPSET\2013_10_18\
List of Files Unknown to the Database
=====================================
File Name: C:\ORACLE\FAST_RECOVERY_AREA\ORCL\BACKUPSET\2013_10_18\
O1_MF_ANNNN_TAG20131018T153543_4HNOP6OH_.BKP.old
```

```
File Name: C:\ORACLE\FAST_RECOVERY_AREA\ORCL\BACKUPSET\2013_10_18\
O1_MF_NNNDF_TAG20131018T152908_4HNO9DX9_.BKP.old
Do you really want to catalog the above files (enter YES or NO)? yes
cataloging files...
cataloging done
List of Cataloged Files
=======================
File Name: C:\ORACLE\FAST_RECOVERY_AREA\ORCL\BACKUPSET\2013_10_18\
O1_MF_ANNNN_TAG20131018T153543_4HNOP6OH_.BKP.old
File Name: C:\ORACLE\FAST_RECOVERY_AREA\ORCL\BACKUPSET\2013_10_18\
O1_MF_NNNDF_TAG20131018T152908_4HNO9DX9_.BKP.old
RMAN> list backup of database summary;
List of Backups
===============
Key     TY LV S Device Type Completion Time #Pieces #Copies Compressed Tag
------- -- -- - ----------- --------------- ------- ------- ---------- ---
1253    B  F  A DISK        18-OCT-13       1       1       YES
TAG20131018T152908
```

The `CATALOG` command can come in quite handy during disaster-recovery exercises when all you have are backup set pieces and an Oracle Database instance. You can create the instance, catalog the backup set pieces (including control-file autobackups), and then restore your database. The `CATALOG` command works only with disk devices, so in disaster-recovery cases you might first have to restore data files from tape before you can catalog them.

Using the *RESYNC* Command

The `RESYNC` command is used to synchronize the recovery catalog with the control file. RMAN will often perform automatic resync operations, but there may be times when you will want to perform a manual resync operation. Simply issue the `RESYNC CATALOG` command and the catalog will be synchronized with the recovery catalog, as shown in this example:

```
RMAN> resync catalog;
starting full resync of recovery catalog
full resync complete
```

Tuning RMAN Operations

The final topic in this section is how to tune RMAN operations. Of course, standard Oracle tuning methodologies apply here; use enough backup devices to get good I/O performance. Allocate enough memory to the database, and make sure your CPUs can handle the load.

Another method of tuning your RMAN operations is through parallel channel operations. Recall that using channels is the method that RMAN uses to write backup-related information from the database to the backup device. If you can create multiple channels to different backup devices (say two channels to two different disk drives or tape devices), then you can speed up the performance of your backups in many cases.

Oracle also provides the DURATION parameter associated with the BACKUP command, which allows you to indicate to Oracle how much overall impact it should allow the backup to have on the database as a whole. When using the DURATION parameter, you indicate the overall duration that you want the backup to run. If it runs over that (say 5 hours), then RMAN will terminate the backup. The data files already backed up will still be valid, but there may be data files that are not backed up. RMAN will prioritize any missed data file backups on the subsequent backup operation.

Incomplete Backups

If a backup does not complete after the amount of time identified in the DURATION parameter, then the whole backup will be considered to have failed. Other backup operations within a RUN block will not be executed as a result. You can use the PARTIAL keyword to indicate to RMAN that it should consider the backup to have been successful and not return an error. This will allow subsequent commands (like archive-log backups) to execute. Here is an example of the use of the PARTIAL keyword:

```
RMAN> Backup as compressed backupset duration 1:00
partial minimize load database ;
```

If you use the DURATION MINIMIZE LOAD parameter when performing a backup, then you will be indicating to Oracle that you want it to reduce the load that the backup has on the database as a whole. When MINIMIZE LOAD is used, Oracle will try to spread the backup over the entire time identified in the DURATION parameter. This will result in slower backup times but improved overall database performance. Here is an example of the use of the DURATION parameter in the BACKUP command:

```
RMAN> Backup as compressed backupset duration 1:00 minimize load database;
```

The Oracle Database Fault Diagnostic Framework

One of the objectives listed in the Oracle 12*c* OCP exam is knowledge of the Oracle Automatic Diagnostic Workflow. To understand this feature in Oracle, you first need to understand the architecture that underlies this workflow. This architecture is called the Oracle Database Fault Diagnostic Framework.

The Oracle Database Fault Diagnostic Framework (and the associated Automatic Diagnostic Workflow) was introduced in Oracle Database 11g and has been improved upon with the advent of Oracle Database 12c. In this section, we will discuss the Oracle Database Fault Diagnostic Framework as follows:

* Overview of the Oracle Database Fault Diagnostic Framework

* The Oracle Advanced Diagnostic Repository (ADR)

* Problems and incidents

* Oracle Database Fault Diagnosability components

Overview of the Oracle Database Fault Diagnostic Framework

The purpose of the Oracle Database Fault Diagnostic Framework is to make it easier for database problems to be captured when they occur. Additionally, the Framework will collect diagnostic data related to problems that occur in the database. This information is packaged into a single file to be sent to Oracle Support. This relieves the DBA of the tedious work of collecting this diagnostic information themselves.

Oracle describes the goals of the Fault Diagnostic Framework as follows:

* First-failure diagnosis

* Problem prevention

* Limiting damage and interruptions after a problem is detected

* Reducing problem diagnostic time

* Reducing problem resolution time

* Simplifying customer interaction with Oracle Support

These goals, when implemented in the enterprise, provide many benefits including the following:

* Automated capture of diagnostic information when a failure occurs. This can save the DBA tremendous amounts of time.

* Quick problem resolution, reducing the time it takes to address problems and thus reducing downtime and outages.

* Integration with other Oracle Database technologies and with My Oracle Support (MOS) from Enterprise Manager. This streamlines the problem-resolution workflow and reduces the overall time to resolve a problem.

* A suite of proactive diagnostic health checks that can also be run on demand. These health checks can be run to detect problems before they become a serious issue impacting the database. Also, these health checks can be run when problems occur to help diagnose and provide potential resolutions to the problem.

The Fault Diagnosability Framework is supported by an underlying infrastructure called the Fault Diagnosability Infrastructure (the FDI—No need to fear; the FDI is not collecting your email information in this case!). The FDI comprises a set of technologies that are described in Table 6.1.

TABLE 6.1 Technologies Used as a Part of the FDI

Technology Name	Description
Automatic capture of diagnostic data upon first failure	Perhaps the most exciting part of this Framework is the fact that critical database errors (such as ORA-0600 errors) are automatically trapped when they occur. When errors are trapped, Oracle will quickly collect all the diagnostic files that were created as a result of the failure. These files are stored in an area called the Automatic Diagnostic Repository (ADR), which we will discuss later in this chapter.
Standardized trace formats	Oracle has standardized the location and format of Oracle-generated trace files. This makes for easier problem resolution.
Health checks	Oracle has created a number of health checks that run on the Oracle Database. These checks run on a regular basis and also when a critical database error occurs. You can also run the health checks manually and review the results from OEM or through V$ views in the database.
Incident Packaging Service (IPS) and incident packages	When a critical error is detected, Oracle will create an incident package related to that failure. This incident package will contain all of the relevant information that Oracle will need to diagnose the problem. This reduces the workload of the DBA in that they no longer need to look for files related to the critical problem that occurred.
Data Recovery Advisor	Integrated into the Fault Diagnostic Framework is the Data Recovery Advisor. This tool is integrated into the Oracle Database RMAN backup and recovery tool as well as the database health checks. The Data Recovery Advisor can then be used to analyze database recovery issues and recommend correct recovery actions.
SQL Test Case Builder	In cases where the issue is a SQL problem, the SQL Test Case Builder provides a way to produce a SQL test case and send the results of that test case to Oracle Support.

This Framework and its associated infrastructure can create a large number of files. These files need to be stored somewhere in a logical storage structure. This storage structure is provided through the auspices of the Automatic Diagnostic Repository. Let's discuss that topic next.

The fact that the ADR can grow quite large implies that some space management may be required from time to time. This would be something you would consider as a part of the various maintenance processes to be implemented on an active database system.

The Oracle ADR

The ADR is a standardized set of directories that are functionally defined within the ADR framework. This means that each directory location has a specific purpose and stores specific types of files. The root directory of the ADR is called the ADR_BASE. This location is defined by the database parameter DIAGNOSTIC_DEST. The DIAGNOSTIC_DEST parameter is set in one of the following ways:

- By directly setting the DIAGNOSTIC_DEST parameter in the database parameter file. This will cause the directories related to ADR to be created under the directory defined in the DIAGNOSTIC_DEST directory. The name of the root directory will be DIAGNOSTIC_DEST/diag.

- By setting the Oracle OS environment variable ORACLE_BASE. In this case, the DIAGNOSTIC_DEST directory will be created under the ORACLE_BASE directory. The name of the root directory will be $ORACLE_BASE/diag.

- If ORACLE_BASE is not set, then DIAGNOSTIC_DEST will be located under ORACLE_HOME (i.e., $ORACLE_HOME/diag).

The location where the DIAGNOSTIC_DEST is assigned is known as the ADR BASE directory. All other ADR directories are created and written to under this ADR BASE directory.

Under ADR BASE, there is a series of directories that are predefined and are used to store specific types of data. The standardized ADR directory structure is shown in Figure 6.1.

For example, let's say you have set the DIAGNOSTIC_DEST parameter in your database to the location /u01/app/oracle. The ADR directory structure that Oracle would create would begin at /u01/app/oracle, which would become the ADR_BASE.

Under the ADR_BASE, there will be several ADR_HOME directories. Each of these ADR_HOME directories is specific to a given component that writes into that structure. For example, assume that you have created a database called orcl. Further, assume that this is an RAC database and that there are two instances, orcl1 and orcl2. In this case, there are essentially two unique ADR_HOME directories that will be defined. Thus, you have two different defined locations for your orcl RAC database, as shown in Table 6.2.

TABLE 6.2 ADR Directory Locations

Name	Location
ADR_BASE	/u01/app/oracle
ADR_HOME	/u01/app/oracle/diag/rdbms/orcl/orcl1

FIGURE 6.1 The Oracle ADR directory structure

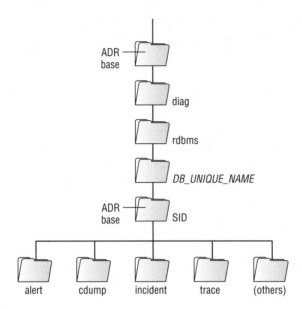

In this case, the ADR_BASE is the directory structure /u01/app/oracle. Note that Oracle created all the directories including the ADR_BASE directory itself and all of the directories under that directory.

Under the ADR_BASE directory is the main directory of the ADR, which is called diag. Under the diag directory you will see a number of directories that have been created. Each of these directories represents an Oracle component. For example, the rdbms directory represents the Oracle database component.

Under the rdbms directory will be additional directories that represent the database and instance that the underlying data belongs to.

Then, under the instance directory, there are a number of directories that represent different types of files that the database will create at various times and places. For example, the database alert log, trace files, and various diagnostic data are stored in the various directories. As an example, the following directory is used to store trace files for the orcl1 instance of the orcl database:

```
C:\APP\ORACLE\diag\rdbms\orcl12c\orcl12c\trace
```

As you can see in the code example that is printed below. Also in that code output you can see the various ADR locations by using the V$DIAG_INFO view, as shown in the following example. Note that this example demonstrates the ADR locations for a single-instance Oracle database; therefore it has only one ADR_HOME:

```
SELECT * FROM V$DIAG_INFO;
```

INST_ID	NAME	VALUE	CON_ID
1	Diag Enabled	TRUE	0
1	ADR Base	C:\APP\ORACLE	0
1	ADR Home	C:\APP\ORACLE\diag\rdbms\orcl12c\orcl12c	0
1	Diag Trace	C:\APP\ORACLE\diag\rdbms\orcl12c\orcl12c\trace	0
1	Diag Alert	C:\APP\ORACLE\diag\rdbms\orcl12c\orcl12c\alert	0
1	Diag Incident	C:\APP\ORACLE\diag\rdbms\orcl12c\orcl12c\incident	0
1	Diag Cdump	C:\app\oracle\diag\rdbms\orcl12c\orcl12c\cdump	0
1	Health Monitor	C:\APP\ORACLE\diag\rdbms\orcl12c\orcl12c\hm	0
1	Default Trace File	C:\APP\ORACLE\diag\rdbms\orcl12c\orcl12c\trace\orcl12c_ora_6276.trc	0
1	Active Problem Count	1	0
1	Active Incident Count	1	0

As you see, the ADR is a complex set of directory structures that are specific to individual technology components such as the database, the listener, and so on. Each technology component then has its own ADR HOME directory. This ADR_HOME directory, then, is a logical separation of the ADR-related files, by technology.

For example, the database ADR_HOME will be something like DIAGNOSTIC_DEST/diag/rdbms. From this directory, each database and each database instance will have its own unique ADR home directory. In certain cases you will need to set the ADR_HOME directory when working with ADR files. We will demonstrate how to do that shortly.

The main time you will need to be concerned about what ADR HOME you are in is if you are using the ADRCI interface with ADR, which we will discuss later in this chapter. The only other time you will probably need to be concerned about it is when you take your OCP exam! We will talk more about the ADR_HOME directory shortly when we discuss the ADRCI command-line interface.

Problems and Incidents

Recall that one of the jobs of the FDI is to automatically detect critical database faults, such as ORA-0600 errors. When these faults are detected, the database will collect all of the trace files and other information related to the error. It will take all of this information and pack it into a compressed archive file and store that file in the ADR. (As an aside, we have no idea if the FDI ships these files to the NSA and if the NSA shares them with the CIA or MI5; certainly you can choose to share them with ORCL if you like.)

At the same time, the database will create some metadata to help track the issue. If this is the first time the problem has occurred, Oracle will create a master record for that problem in the ADR repository. This master record is called a *problem*. Each problem is unique to a specific error and any related error codes.

Once the problem is created, an incident will be created. The incident is a record of a specific occurrence of the problem. If the same error occurs five times, then one problem and five incidents will be created. Each time an incident occurs, the related troubleshooting files are collected, and each individual collection of this information is associated with a specific incident.

Sometimes a given problem may occur so frequently that creating an incident for each occurrence would impact database performance. Thus, Oracle flood controls the creation of incidents. The thresholds for flood control are fixed and cannot be modified. The thresholds are as follows:

- 5 incidents for the same problem in one hour are flood controlled until the next day.

- 50 incidents for the same problem in one hour are flood controlled and future incidents of the problem will no longer be recorded.

- 25 incidents for the same problem in one hour are flood controlled until the next day.

- 250 incidents for the same problem in one day are flood controlled and future incidents of the problem will no longer be recorded.

The Automatic Diagnostic Workflow—Managing Problems and Incidents

To streamline the process of problem management, the Fault Diagnostic Framework provides a general workflow that offers a way of tracking problems, incidents, and related service requests. This relieves a large amount of work that the DBA previously had to do in order to deal with a database-related problem. The workflow reduces the burden on the DBA by

- Automatically collecting diagnostic information related to the failure. This seriously reduces the time the DBA must spend trying to manually collect this information.

- Automatically (optional) opening the support ticket with MOS. This reduces the time the DBA must spend filling out SR-related tickets.

- Tracking the status of service requests (SRs) in a single pane of glass. This keeps SRs fresh and helps to avoid having an SR "fall through the cracks."

- Providing more accountability and efficiency. Management can review the status of all SRs in the enterprise.

The general workflow from the time that a problem/incident occurs and when that problem/incident is resolved is shown in Figure 6.2.

As you can see, the DBA's activity begins after the error is surfaced by the database, which will typically be through Oracle Enterprise Manager and the Support Workbench. It should be noted that you can manually create a problem/incident for any error that you wish to have Oracle Support assist you with. Manual creation is supported through the Support Workbench or ADRCI (discussed later in this chapter).

FIGURE 6.2   Workflow to resolve a problem

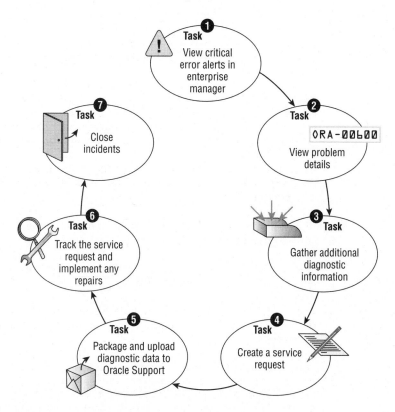

The DBA then reviews the problem and gathers details related to that problem (though most details have actually already been collected). The DBA will then open a service request, typically through the Support Workbench.

After opening the SR, the DBA will upload the incident package to Oracle. If additional information is requested, the DBA can collect this information and add it to the incident package that was created when the incident occurred. The DBA can then send the incident package to Oracle automatically via the Support Workbench.

The DBA can then track the incident through the Support Workbench and apply corrective action. Finally, once the problem has been resolved, the incident can be closed.

Components Related to the Fault Diagnosability Framework

We have discussed the purpose of the Fault Diagnosability Framework, the ADR, and the concept of problems and incidents. All that is left to do now is discuss the components that are part of this overall Framework. Table 6.3 lists the different components of the Fault Diagnosability Framework and their purpose.

TABLE 6.3   Components of the Fault Diagnosability Framework

Component	Purpose
ADR	The ADR is a file-based repository. The ADR was covered earlier in this chapter.
Alert log	The alert log is a text-based file, and there is also an XML-based file that contains various database messages that indicate errors, information on database events, and other output used for database administration and problem diagnosis.
Trace files	Each server process writes to a trace file, which is a diagnostic file. Trace files are stored in the ADR. SQL Tracing also creates trace files.
Dump files	Diagnostic files that are used to troubleshoot database problems. These are stored in the ADR.
Core files	Diagnostic files that are used to troubleshoot database problems. These are stored in the ADR.
Other ADR content	Additional files that are stored in the ADR include health monitor reports, data repair records, SQL test cases, incident packages, and more.
Enterprise Manager Support Workbench (EMSW)	Contained in Oracle Enterprise Manager, the Support Workbench provides the ability to investigate and report on problems. Some problems can be repaired with the Support Workbench. The Support Workbench automates much of the work of managing the Fault Diagnosability Framework.
ADRCI command-line utility	An alternative to the Support Workbench, the ADRCI command-line utility provides a way to manually interact with and manage the Fault Diagnosability Framework.

Enterprise Manager Support Workbench

We introduced you to the Enterprise Manager Support Workbench in the previous section. This is a component of Oracle Enterprise Manager, and it simplifies managing the technology associated with the Fault Diagnosability Framework. The EMSW is an easy-to-use graphical interface that provides the ability to manage the AWR repository, problems, incidents, and related support tickets.

Normally, we try to provide exercises within our books to familiarize you with the topics. However, the various tutorials that you would need to complete to fully understand the OEM Support Workbench and other components would make the page count of this book way too high (and it's pretty hefty as it is now).

So, for items related to the Fault Diagnosability Framework, we are going to point you to some tutorials that are available online from Oracle.

Oracle offers a number of tutorials on various subjects, including the OEM Support Workbench. The tutorial I'd like to point you to is a good introductory tutorial that demonstrates how the OEM Support Workbench can analyze and detect a database problem, in this case, data dictionary corruption.

The tutorial then walks you through reviewing the incident, packaging it up for sending to Oracle Support (which you wouldn't do, of course, since it is a tutorial). I'd strongly suggest that you run through this Oracle tutorial on OEM Support Workbench. It takes about 30 minutes to complete and it can be found by searching on the Web for the terms "Oracle support workbench data dictionary corruption." The title of the tutorial is "Analyzing Data Dictionary Corruption Using Support Workbench."

> We don't like to provide URLs in our books because web pages tend to change all the time. However, the search terms for the specific pages we will be suggesting rarely change. Thus, we use search terms to point you to the tutorial we are recommending.

The ADRCI Command-Line Utility

We mentioned the Automatic Diagnostic Repository Command Interpreter (ADRCI) previously. It is an alternative method of managing the functionality of the Fault Diagnosability Framework components and infrastructure. It provides a command-line-driven means of doing most of the tasks that Support Workbench does graphically. If you are not using Oracle Enterprise Manager Cloud Control, you will have to use ADRCI. This is because Enterprise Manager Express does not have an interface to ADRCI built into it.

ADRCI provides the ability to

* Review the data that is contained in the ADR

* Review Health Monitor reports

* Work on problems and packaging incidents and send those incidents to MOS

ADRCI is not unlike SQL*Plus in that you can issue commands and even create ADRCI scripts to run. ADRCI is protected based on what user you are logged in as and the permissions of the files on the operating system. As a result, there is no password required to use ADRCI.

Starting ADRCI

ADRCI is easy to use. Simply enter **adrci** at the OS prompt to start the interface, as shown here:

```
C:\Users\rfreeman>adrci
ADRCI: Release 12.1.0.1.0 - Production on Sun Jan 5 12:27:58 2014
Copyright (c) 1982, 2013, Oracle and/or its affiliates.  All rights reserved.
```

```
ADR base = "C:\app\oracle"
adrci>
```

Note here that the current ADR base is listed. It is possible on some systems that you might have more than one ADR base (for example, if you have more than one version of Oracle installed).

The ADRCI command line has a number of commands available for you to use. The command list is long, so we are not going to attempt to repeat it here. There are a few basic commands that you will want to be aware of, and these are listed in Table 6.4. Many other commands and functionality exist through the use of the ADRCI interface.

TABLE 6.4 Commonly Used ADRCI Commands

Command	Description
Exit	Exit ADRCI.
Quit	Quit ADRCI.
Help	Display the ADRCI help screen. You can add the command name to the end of the Help command and help will be provided for that specific command.
Set	Provides the ability to set various internal variables in ADRCI.
Show homes	Displays the available ADRCI homes.
Set homepath	By default, HOMEPATH is set to NULL. Thus if you run an ADRCI inquiry, the results will come from all ADR homes under the current ADR base directory. Use the set homepath command to further refine the ADR home that you wish to pull information from.
	For example, assume that you have the following directory structures in AWR:
	/u01/oracle/diag/rdbms/orcl/orcl1
	/u01/oracle/diag/rdbms/orcl/orcl2
	In this case, by default both directories are ADR homes. So if you request information from the ADR, it will return information from both instances. You can use the set homepath command to indicate that you want just one of the directories to be considered the ADR home for the purposes of the ADRCI commands you intend on running.
Show alert	Displays the alert log contents. Includes the optional parameter -tail n, which allows you to tail the last n number of rows, and tail -f, which feeds constant output as it is written to the output file.

Summary

In some ways, this is the most important chapter when it comes to RMAN overall. In previous chapters we have shown you that typical backup and recovery is usually not a very complex task in RMAN. When things go wrong, however, RMAN can become a bit trickier. Of course, things tend to go wrong just when the stress is the highest and the need to get your database up and running is the highest.

To help you with these difficult moments and prepare you for the OCP exam, we covered RMAN reporting, tuning, and monitoring. Reporting is quite important because you need to be able to see what backups are available (for example, to determine what types of incomplete recovery are actually available).

Tuning is important because you want your backups and your recoveries to go as fast as possible. The longer they take, the more impact they have on the system. Of course, everyone wants restores to go fast. That's where strategies like parallelism come in handy.

Monitoring is important too because you need to be able to look at backup or restore operations as they are happening and determine if they are proceeding normally. Monitoring gives you that ability. It's important to know what is normal for your backups and your recoveries so that when the time comes, you will be able to understand what is not normal and how deviant a statistic actually is from the norm. Then you can address the problem.

We have covered a lot of RMAN material and there is more to come. Questions on RMAN will be a significant portion of your OCP exam, which is why we have really hit it hard in this book. Study it thoroughly, and practice backup and recovery (both RMAN and user-managed) several times before you take your test. If you do so, we suspect you will do well on your exam.

We also introduced you to the Fault Diagnosability Framework and workflow. This is new in the Oracle Database 12c exam. If you are a new DBA or even an old pro, it is well worth taking the time to learn this fairly new feature (since Oracle Database 11g) of Oracle. Questions on this feature likely will appear on your exam.

Exam Essentials

Be able to use the `LIST` **and** `REPORT` **commands.** Understanding the `LIST` and `REPORT` commands is very important to RMAN operations and to being successful on your OCP exam. They allow you to review metadata contained within the database control file and recovery catalog, understand backups that have been taken, and take corrective action when certain conditions arise.

Be able to administer the RMAN environment. Understanding how to administer RMAN is quite important. Knowing how to use commands like `CATALOG`, `DELETE`, and `CROSSCHECK` is critical to properly administering the RMAN environment. These commands will come in especially handy after disaster recovery when you need to get your database up and running quickly.

Be able to performance-tune your RMAN operations.   Understanding how parallelism can make your database backups and restores perform faster is critical to making RMAN performant. Understand how to control the duration of a backup and how to reduce the overall I/O load with the DURATION command.

Understand the Automatic Diagnostic Workflow.   Understand the basic framework that surrounds the Fault Diagnosability Framework. Understand the ADR and what is stored in the ADR. Understand the framework of technology that feeds data into the ADR and makes it possible to send failure information to Oracle Support. Understand the tools that support the ADR such as the ADRCI and the Support Workbench.

Review Questions

1. Which command would you use to determine what database backups are currently available for restore?

    A. LIST DATABASE BACKUP;

    B. REPORT DATABASE BACKUP;

    C. LIST BACKUP OF DATABASE;

    D. LIST SUMMARY BACKUP;

    E. REPORT BACKUP OF DATABASE;

2. What command would you use to ensure that backup records in the control file are pointing to actual physical files on the backup media?

    A. CROSSCHECK

    B. LIST BACKUP

    C. CONFIRM

    D. RESYNC

    E. BACKUP VALIDATE

3. You have backed up your database twice without connecting to the recovery catalog. What command do you issue to transfer the control-file metadata to the recovery catalog?

    A. SYNCH CATALOG

    B. RESYNC CATALOG

    C. REPLICATE CATALOG

    D. UPDATE CATALOG

    E. RESTORE CATALOG

4. You want to make sure that your database backup does not exceed 10 hours in length. What command would you issue that would meet this condition?

    A. BACKUP DATABASE PLUS ARCHIVELOG;

    B. BACKUP DATABASE PLUS ARCHIVELOG UNTIL TIME '10:00';

    C. BACKUP DATABASE PLUS ARCHIVELOG TIMEOUT '10:00';

    D. BACKUP DATABASE PLUS ARCHIVELOG DURATION '10:00';

    E. BACKUP DATABASE PLUS ARCHIVELOG TIMEOUT 10:00;

5. You have lost all your RMAN backup set pieces due to a disk failure. Unfortunately, you have an automated cross-check script that also does a DELETE EXPIRED BACKUPSET command. You have restored all the backup set pieces from tape. What command would you use to get those backup set pieces registered in the recovery catalog and the control file of the database again?

    A. REGISTER DATABASE

    B. RECOVER CATALOG

    C. LOAD BACKUPSET

    D. SYNCH METADATA

    E. CATALOG START WITH

6. You run the following commands:

    ```
    RMAN> list expired backup;
    RMAN> delete expired backup;
    ```

    What will happen to the backup set pieces associated with the backups that appear in the LIST EXPIRED BACKUP command?

    A. They will be renamed.

    B. Nothing will happen to them. The backup set pieces do not exist.

    C. They will be deleted immediately since they are not in the fast recovery area.

    D. You will need to manually remove the physical files listed in the output of the commands.

    E. They will become hidden files and removed 10 days later.

7. Why would you run the DELETE OBSOLETE command? (Choose all that apply.)

    A. To remove missing backup set pieces physically from disk

    B. To remove metadata related to backup set pieces in the control file and the recovery catalog

    C. To mark as deleted records in the control file and the recovery catalog associated with obsolete backup sets

    D. To delete backup set pieces associated with backups that are no longer needed due to retention criteria

    E. To remove old versions of RMAN backups

8. What does it mean if a backup is expired?

   A. The backup set has exceeded the retention criteria set in RMAN and is eligible for removal.

   B. The backup set has one or more invalid blocks in it and is not usable for recovery.

   C. The backup set contains one or more tablespaces no longer in the database.

   D. The backup set contains one or more missing backup set pieces.

   E. The backup set is from a previous version of RMAN and was not upgraded.

9. If a backup set is expired, what can you do to correct the problem?

   A. Change the retention criteria.

   B. Make the lost backup set pieces available to RMAN again and rerun the CROSSCHECK command.

   C. Run the CROSSCHECK command to correct the location for the backup set piece contained in the metadata.

   D. Nothing. The backup set piece is lost forever.

   E. Call Oracle Support. Their assistance is required.

10. How long will this backup be allowed to run?

    ```
    Backup as compressed backupset duration 2:00 minimize load database ;
    ```

    A. 2 minutes

    B. 2 hours

    C. 2 days

    D. The command will generate an error.

    E. This backup is not constrained by any time limitation.

11. What is the impact of the following backup if it exceeds the duration allowance? (Choose all that apply.)

    ```
    Backup as compressed backupset duration 2:00 partial minimize load database ;
    ```

    A. The entire backup will fail. It will not be usable for recovery.

    B. The entire backup will fail, but any data file successfully backed up will be usable for recovery.

    C. If this backup fails, subsequent backups will prioritize data files not backed up.

    D. If this backup fails, an error will be raised and any other commands will not be executed.

    E. If this backup fails, no error will be raised and any other commands will be executed.

12. In what view are you likely to see the following output?

```
    SID     SERIAL# EVENT                             SECONDS_IN_WAIT
---------- ---------- ----------------------------- ----------------
    121       269 RMAN backup & recovery I/O                      2
    129       415 SQL*Net message from client                    63
    130       270 SQL*Net message from client                     8
```

   A. V$SESSION_EVENT

   B. V$SESSION

   C. V$WAITS

   D. V$WAITSTAT

   E. V$SYSSTAT

13. What view might you use to try to determine how long a particular backup will take?

   A. V$SESSION_EVENT

   B. V$SESSION

   C. V$WAITS

   D. V$WAITSTAT

   E. V$SESSION_LONGOPS

14. What is the impact of the output of the following command?

```
RMAN> report unrecoverable database;
Report of files that need backup due to unrecoverable operations
File Type of Backup Required Name
---- ---------------------- -----------------------------------
4    full or incremental    C:\ORACLE\ORADATA\ORCL\USERS01.DBF
```

   A. There are no backup sets with any backups of the users01.dbf data file.

   B. The users01.dbf data file has had unrecoverable operations occur in it. It will need to be backed up or some data loss is possible during a recovery.

   C. The users01.dbf data file is corrupted.

   D. The users01.dbf data file backup exceeds the retention criteria.

   E. The last backup of the users01.dbf data file failed and must be rerun.

15. What does the output on this report indicate?

```
RMAN> report need backup;
RMAN retention policy will be applied to the command
RMAN retention policy is set to redundancy 1
Report of files with less than 1 redundant backups
File #bkps Name
---- ----- -------------------------------------------
5    0     C:\ORACLE\ORADATA\ORCL\MY_DATA_01.DBF
```

   A. The my_data_01.dbf data file is corrupted and needs to be restored.

   B. The my_data_01.dbf data file has not yet been backed up. This report does not imply that the data in the data file cannot be recovered.

   C. The my_data_01.dbf data file has not yet been backed up. This report implies that the data in the data file cannot be recovered.

   D. The my_data_01.dbf data file no longer meets the retention criteria for backups.

   E. Data file 5 is missing.

16. What does the `MINIMIZE LOAD DATABASE` parameter mean when backing up a database?

   A. RMAN will attempt to make the backup run as fast as possible without any I/O limitations.

   B. RMAN will automatically restrict the number of channels in use to one.

   C. RMAN will spread the backup I/O over the total duration stated in the `BACKUP` command.

   D. RMAN will skip any data file that currently is involved in an I/O operation. RMAN will retry backing up the data file later and an error will be raised at the end of the backup if the data file cannot be backed up.

   E. Data files will be backed up; those having the lowest current number of I/O operations will be backed up first.

17. What is the result of this command?

```
RMAN> Report need backup days 3;
```

   A. Lists all data files created in the last three days that are not backed up.

   B. Lists all data files not recoverable based on the current retention criteria.

   C. Lists all data files not backed up in the last three days. The data file is not recoverable.

   D. Lists all data files that need to be backed up due to unrecoverable operations.

   E. Lists all data files not backed up in the last three days. It does not imply that the data file is not recoverable.

18. Which tool would you need to use to review the contents of the ADR repository?

    A. Oracle ADR Monitor

    B. ADDM

    C. ADRCI

    D. ADR Manager

    E. No tool exists

19. Which of the following are components of the Fault Diagnosability Framework? (Choose all that apply.)

    A. ADR

    B. Oracle Resource Manager

    C. Alert log

    D. Trace files

    E. Database parameter files

20. Which of the following are functions provided by the Fault Diagnosability Framework? (Choose all that apply.)

    A. The ability to open SRs

    B. Collection of problem and incident data related to SRs

    C. Automatic responses to tablespace out-of-space conditions

    D. Suspend database operations in the event that ORA-0600 errors occur, and then restart the database after the error is corrected

    E. Suspend database archiving if there is insufficient disk space

Chapter

7

Performing Oracle Advanced Recovery

ORACLE DATABASE 12c: ADVANCED ADMINISTRATION EXAM OBJECTIVES COVERED IN THIS CHAPTER:

✓ Use various RMAN backup types and policies

✓ Employ best practices for data warehouse backups

✓ Perform backup of non-database files

✓ Back up ASM diskgroup metadata

✓ Recover files using RMAN

✓ Perform table recovery from backups

✓ Restore a database to a new host

✓ Configure and use Oracle Secure Backup

✓ Create proxy copies

✓ Choose a technique for duplicating a database

✓ Duplicate a database from an active database, connected to the target and auxiliary instances

✓ Duplicate a database from backup, connected to the target and auxiliary instances

✓ Duplicate a database from backup, connected to the auxiliary instance, not connected to the target, but with recovery catalog connection

✓ Duplicate a database with RMAN

✓ Perform backups of a CDB and PDBs

✓ Recover PDB from PDB datafile loss

✓ Duplicate PDBs using RMAN

✓ **Use Data Pump**

✓ **Use the Data Recovery Advisor**

✓ **Perform complete and incomplete or "point-in-time" recoveries using RMAN**

We have already discussed the basics of recovering your Oracle database. You now know how to use the RESTORE and RECOVER commands to recover your database to the point of failure. In this chapter, we will cover more advanced recovery topics. First, we will cover RMAN incarnations, and then we will introduce you to RMAN database duplication. After that, we will discuss tablespace point-in-time recovery and disaster recovery of your Oracle database. Finally, we will discuss configuring and using Oracle Secure Backup (OSB), which is a new objective in the Oracle Database 12c OCP exam.

Switching between RMAN Incarnations

We introduced you to the idea of RMAN incarnations in Chapter 2 and have talked about incarnations in several other chapters. A *database incarnation* is the measure of the logical lifetime of an Oracle database. A database's first incarnation begins when it is created and ends whenever the RESETLOGS option is used to open the database. The next incarnation starts at the point of the RESETLOGS operation and ends at the point of the next RESETLOGS operations and so on. When a new incarnation is started, the log sequence numbers are reset, the online redo logs are flushed, and the database literally has a new future.

Sometimes when performing RMAN operations it is necessary to reset to a previous database incarnation. This is pretty rare and is typically done in cases where you have restored your database using point-in-time recovery. After such cases, if you need to perform another restore and that restore needs to be to an SCN that is before the current resetlog SCN, then you will have to reset the database incarnation.

For example, look at this output of this LIST INCARNATION command:

```
RMAN> list incarnation;
using target database control file instead of recovery catalog
List of Database Incarnations
```

DB Key	Inc Key	DB Name	DB ID	STATUS	Reset SCN	Reset Time
1	1	ORCL	1194923408	PARENT	1	10/15/2012 10:08:59
2	2	ORCL	1194923408	PARENT	886308	10/03/2013 13:24:36
3	3	ORCL	1194923408	CURRENT	904361	10/03/2013 14:05:15

If you wanted to restore the database to a point in time before 10/03/2013 at 14:05:15 (or SCN 904361), you would need to reset the database to one of the previous incarnations. If, however, you wanted to restore the database to the resetlog time/SCN or after that time, then you would not need to reset the database incarnation.

To reset the database incarnation, you first need to mount the database. Then you use the RESET DATABASE TO INCARNATION command. You include the incarnation number that you want to switch to in the command. This number comes from the INC KEY column displayed in the LIST INCARNATION command output. Here is an example of switching the database to incarnation 2:

```
RMAN> shutdown immediate
database closed
database dismounted
Oracle instance shut down
RMAN> startup mount
connected to target database (not started)
Oracle instance started
database mounted
Total System Global Area      364081152 bytes
Fixed Size                      1333228 bytes
Variable Size                 239077396 bytes
Database Buffers              117440512 bytes
Redo Buffers                    6230016 bytes
RMAN> Reset database to incarnation 2;
database reset to incarnation 2
```

Figure 7.1 provides a graphic example of database incarnations. In this graphic, the database crashes at SCN 40000 (shown in point A in the figure). We restore the database from a backup taken at SCN 10000 (shown in point B in the figure) and recover it to SCN 25000 (shown in point C). Perhaps we have lost the redo logs needed to restore the database beyond SCN 25000, and so we open the database at SCN 25000 with the ALTER DATABASE OPEN RESETLOGS command. This creates a new incarnation of the database. Note that the SCNs are greater than 40000 (because the SCN does not change), but notice that there is a new timeline with which the changes are being recorded (the tangent line heading to the northeast in the figure). This is the new incarnation of the database (demonstrated in point D). It's a completely new life for the database, and everything that happened in the database in the previous life after the previous SCN 25000 is as if it had never happened. There are now actually two SCN 25000s in the redo stream.

FIGURE 7.1   Example of an Oracle incarnation

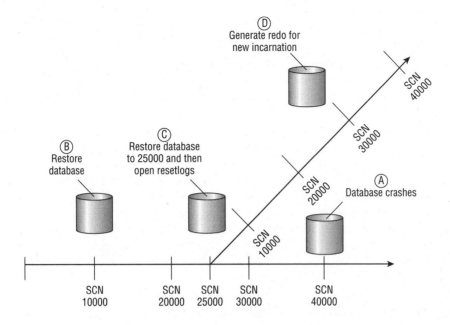

Overview of RMAN Database Duplication

One frequent use of RMAN is to duplicate an existing database. *Database duplication* can be used for a number of different purposes, such as creating development and test databases from production databases or creating a database to test upgrades. In the following sections, we will discuss RMAN duplication basics. Then we will cover how to use the RMAN DUPLICATE DATABASE command to duplicate a database. We will first look at how to prepare to duplicate the database. We will then walk you through actually duplicating the database, and finally we will discuss things to do afterward.

RMAN Database Duplication Basics

The host from which the database is being duplicated is the *source host*. The host to which the database is being duplicated is the *destination host*. The source host and destination host can be the same computer or a different computer, depending on your needs. One requirement is that the source and destination host must be on the same platform. The target or source database is the database that you will be duplicating from. You will be duplicating to a database instance that will be associated with the new database. This instance is called the *auxiliary instance*.

Two types of database duplication exist:

Active Database Duplication Active database duplication duplicates the live target database to the auxiliary instance over the network. As a result, no backup of the target database is required, and the destination host need not have access to the RMAN backup set pieces.

Backup-Based Database Duplication Backup-based database duplication requires that a backup of the database being duplicated be available. This backup can be an RMAN backup set or image copy. The target host must have access to these backup sets in order to complete the database duplication.

Database duplication takes place over the auxiliary channel. This channel is created during the duplication process and is a server process associated with the auxiliary instance.

When you connect to RMAN to start a database duplication, you will connect to both the target database and the auxiliary instance. This implies that network connectivity to the auxiliary instance is available, and as you will see, getting the auxiliary instance up and running is one prerequisite to starting a database-duplication operation.

There are several different techniques, based on various permutations of choices that are available when duplicating a database. Which technique you use depends on the conditions that exist when you are duplicating your database. Table 7.1 lists the different permutations of techniques and when you should use them.

TABLE 7.1 RMAN database duplication options

Option	Duplication Type	Connect to Target/Catalog/Aux Instance?	When you would use this option
1	Active	Yes/Optional/Yes	When you want to duplicate from an open database without needing access to the backup files or if there is no backup.
2	Backup	Yes/No/Yes	Normal duplication based on the target database control file.
3	Backup	No/Yes/Yes	Used if the target database is not available but the backup files are available.
4	Backup	No/No/Yes	Duplication when there is no recovery catalog and the target database is not available. In this case, you will use the BACKUP LOCATION parameter of the DUPLICATE RMAN command to indicate the location of the backup files.
5	Backup	Yes/Yes/Yes	Normal database duplication with recovery catalog.

Each of the cases listed before have used cases that are associated with them, but the basic mechanism of performing the duplication is still the same. We will cover how to perform these duplications next.

Performing an RMAN Database Duplication

Duplicating a database is an operation that many DBAs perform. RMAN provides the DUPLICATE DATABASE command to help ease the database-duplication process. As you saw previously, there are different ways to do a duplication, but most of them have to do with how you connect to RMAN to do the duplication (for example, if there is or is not a recovery catalog to connect to) and the type of duplication you need to perform (for example, active database duplication vs. backup based database duplication).

With respect to the actual procedures that you follow, they will only differ, for the most part, depending on if you are doing an active database duplication or a backup-based database duplication. In the next sections, we will discuss the steps needed to perform these kinds of duplications.

Preparing to Duplicate Your Database

Preparing to duplicate your database requires a few steps:

1. Backing up the target database (backup-based database duplication only)

2. Making backup images available to the destination host (backup-based database duplication only)

3. Deciding where to put the duplicate database-related files

4. Preparing the auxiliary instance for the duplication

Let's look at each of these steps in more detail.

Backing up the target database is not required if you are using active database duplication. If you are doing backup-based duplication, you will need a complete backup of the target database. Follow the steps outlined in Chapter 3 to perform an RMAN backup of your database. The database can be in NOARCHIVELOG or ARCHIVELOG mode.

Making backup images available to the destination host is not required if you are using active database duplication. If you are doing backup-based duplication, you will need to make the backup set pieces associated with the backup of the target database and all associated archived redo logs available to the destination host. This is so they can be read by RMAN during the duplication process. You can make everything available to the destination host by putting the backup set pieces on shared devices (such as Network File System, or NFS) or some other shared disk environment. You could also manually copy the needed files to the destination host via Secure File Transfer Protocol (SFTP) or some equivalent file-copy protocol.

You will need to decide where you want to put the database files that will be associated with the newly duplicated database. Files like the control files, the online redo logs, and the database data files need a home, and you have to know where that will be before you start the duplication process. In the next step, you will use this information to configure the auxiliary instance for duplication.

Before you can begin the duplication process, you must configure the auxiliary instance so that it will start. To do so, follow these steps:

1. Configure any OS-specific requirements.

   Different operating systems require that certain prerequisites be completed before you can start a database instance. For example, in Windows you must create the Windows service, and in most Unix flavors you will need to configure shared memory. You will need to make sure that these preconfiguration steps are complete before you can start the auxiliary instance and begin the duplication process.

2. Configure the database password file for the auxiliary instance.

   The auxiliary instance will require a password file. Use the ORAPWD command (see Chapter 3 for more on ORAPWD) to create the password file. If you prefer, you can instruct Oracle to copy the password file from the target database to the duplicated database when you issue the DUPLICATE command.

3. Configure Oracle networking for the auxiliary instance.

   If you will be executing the DUPLICATE command from a host other than the destination host, or if you are going to use active database duplication, you will have to configure Oracle networking so that you can connect to the auxiliary instance via Oracle Net. You can use the Oracle Net Configuration Assistant to configure both the database listener and the tnsnames.ora file for naming resolution.

4. Configure the database parameter file for the auxiliary instance.

   Configuring the database parameter file correctly can ensure successful database duplication. Incorrectly configuring the parameter file can be a frustrating exercise in futility. The parameter file must be configured to be able to start the auxiliary instance. The parameters listed in Table 7.2 are available for use during the database-duplication process. You may not need to use all of the parameters listed in Table 7.2 when duplicating databases. In some cases these parameters can also be defined on the RMAN command line as parameters of the DUPLICATE command.

TABLE 7.2   Auxiliary database parameters related to database duplication

Parameter Name	Purpose
DB_NAME	The name of the duplicated database. This same name will be used in the RMAN DUPLICATE command. This name should be unique for databases on a given host. This parameter is a required parameter for any database duplication.

Parameter Name	Purpose
CONTROL_FILES	Identifies the location of the control files for the auxiliary instance. This parameter is required unless you are using OMF.
DB_BLOCK_SIZE	Block size of the database to be created. This parameter is required if the same parameter has been defined on the source database.
DB_FILE_NAME_CONVERT	Contains pairs of strings that indicate the conversion path for database files from the source database to the target database. For example, if the parameter were set to '/ora01/oracle/ oradata','/ora02/oracle/oradata', all files contained in / ora01/oracle/oradata would be recreated on the duplicate database in /ora02/oracle/oradata. This parameter can also be defined as part of the call to the RMAN DUPLICATE command.
LOG_FILE_NAME_CONVERT	Contains pairs of strings that indicate the conversion path for database redo-log files from the source database to the target database. For example, if the parameter were set to '/ora01/ oracle/oradata','/ora02/oracle/oradata', all online redo-log files contained in /ora01/oracle/oradata would be recreated on the duplicate database in /ora02/oracle/oradata. This parameter can also be defined as part of the call to the RMAN duplicate command.

5. Start the auxiliary instance.

The auxiliary instance should be ready to start at this time. To start it, simply connect to the auxiliary instance from SQL*Plus and issue the STARTUP NOMOUNT command. Once you are able to get the auxiliary instance started, you are ready to duplicate to it.

Duplicating Your Database

As mentioned previously, there are two different modes of database duplication: active database duplication and backup-based database duplication. Both duplication methods are achieved via the DUPLICATE DATABASE command. Let's examine the DUPLICATE DATABASE command. Following that we will look at both database-duplication modes in more detail.

Connecting to RMAN for a Database Duplication

Before starting database duplication, you will need to start RMAN and connect to the correct databases. When starting RMAN, you will need to connect to the following:

- The target database
- The auxiliary database

Typically you will connect to the target database locally and connect to the auxiliary database via Oracle Net, but this is not a requirement. Here is an example of connecting to RMAN to perform a database duplication. In this example, we are connecting to a local target database called `orcl`. We use the auxiliary command-line parameter to indicate that we are connecting to an auxiliary database. In this case, it is the database pointed to by the net service name of mydb.

```
set oracle_sid=orcl
rman target=/ auxiliary=sys/password@mydb
```

You could also use these variations to connect with RMAN for a database duplication:

```
rman target=sys/robert auxiliary=sys/password@mydb
rman target=sys/robert@orcl auxiliary=sys/password@mydb
```

 You might have noticed that we don't use SYSDBA when connecting to RMAN. That is because all connections from RMAN to any database are always with SYSDBA privileges.

The RMAN *DUPLICATE DATABASE* Command

The RMAN `DUPLICATE DATABASE` command is used when performing either mode of database duplication. The command comes with a number of different options that give you the ability to complete the following operations:

- Copy the source spfile to the auxiliary instance.
- Change specific parameters when copying a source spfile to the auxiliary instance.
- Indicate the location that the duplicated files should be copied to using the database filename conversion options `DB_FILE_NAME_CONVERT` and `LOG_FILE_NAME_CONVERT`.
- Create a standby database environment on the auxiliary instance.
- Open the duplicated database in a restricted session.
- Use the password file from the target database to create the password file on the auxiliary instance (active database duplication only).
- Skip read-only tablespaces.
- Include or exclude specific tablespaces.
- Restore to a specific restore point or use the `UNTIL` clause to restore to a specific time, SCN, or log sequence number (backup-based database duplication only).

During the duplication process, RMAN will automatically create the needed tempfiles for any temporary tablespaces. Here is an example of the RMAN `DUPLICATE` command:

```
Duplicate target database to neworcl nofilenamecheck spfile;
```

You can use the DUPLICATE command to exclude tablespaces, as shown here:

```
Duplicate target database to neworcl nofilenamecheck spfile skip tablespace users;
```

You can also define a restore point, as shown in this example:

```
Duplicate target database to neworcl nofilenamecheck spfile skip
tablespace users to restore point 'Test';
```

You can have Oracle open the duplicated database in restricted mode by adding the OPEN RESTRICTED parameter, as follows:

```
Duplicate target database to neworcl nofilenamecheck spfile open restricted;
```

 As with pretty much everything else Oracle, the DUPLICATE command is well documented. We strongly recommend that you review the Oracle Database Backup and Recovery Reference (Oracle part number B28273-02) for more information on all RMAN-related commands.

Active Database Duplication

When you perform standard RMAN database duplication, the server where the new database is going to be created must have access to the RMAN backup set files of the target database. This can be problematic if the systems do not have a way to share storage or if security restrictions make maintaining NFS mounts impractical. Also, if the target database has not yet been backed up, then you would not be able to duplicate it (this is a much less frequent situation).

In cases like this, you can use an RMAN feature called Active Database Duplication. Active Database Duplication sources the duplicate database creation from the target database itself rather than from RMAN backup sets. Active Database Duplication uses the network to move the data from the target database to the duplicate database being created (thus, a network connection must be able to be established between the servers where the target and duplicated database reside).

Active database duplication is started by issuing the RMAN DUPLICATE DATABASE command and including the FROM ACTIVE DATABASE parameter. Active database duplication is not the default.

When you perform active database duplication, Oracle will create the auxiliary channel to the auxiliary database. An additional target-database RMAN channel will also be required. If you have configured automated channels, this should be sufficient. If not, you will need to allocate a channel manually with the ALLOCATE CHANNEL command.

Finally, the UNTIL and TO RESTORE POINT clauses are not valid when doing an active database duplication. Here is an example of the RMAN DUPLICATE command performing an active database duplication:

```
duplicate target database to neworcl from active database nofilenamecheck
spfile set control_files 'c:\oracle\oradata\neworcl\control01.ctl',
```

```
'c:\oracle\oradata\neworcl\control02.ctl'
set db_file_name_convert 'c:\oracle\oradata\orcl','c:\oracle\oradata\neworcl'
set log_file_name_convert
'c:\oracle\oradata\orcl', 'c:\oracle\oradata\neworcl';
```

Backup-Based Database Duplication

Using the DUPLICATE DATABASE command without the FROM ACTIVE DATABASE parameter starts backup-based database duplication. The auxiliary channel will be allocated automatically. No additional channel is required with backup-based database duplication.

When executing a backup-based database duplication, RMAN will determine the last archived redo log available. RMAN will then restore the duplicate database to the point of that last available archived redo log by default. You can use the UNTIL or TO RESTORE POINT parameter to change this behavior. Here is an example of the RMAN DUPLICATE command performing a backup-based database duplication:

```
duplicate target database to neworcl
spfile
set control_files 'c:\oracle\oradata\neworcl\control01.ctl',
'c:\oracle\oradata\neworcl\control02.ctl'
set db_file_name_convert 'c:\oracle\oradata\orcl','c:\oracle\oradata\neworcl'
set log_file_name_convert 'c:\oracle\oradata\orcl',
'c:\oracle\oradata\neworcl';
```

After the Duplication

Once the database duplication is complete, the duplicated database will be opened and operational. You can use the RESTRICTED SESSION parameter of the DUPLICATE command to indicate that RMAN should open the database in a restricted session only. You should, of course, consider backing up the newly created database on a regular basis.

In Exercise 7.1, you'll be duplicating a database using backup-based database duplication.

EXERCISE 7.1

Duplicating a Database Using Backup-Based Duplication

In this exercise, you will use backup-based duplication to create a database on the same system that the target database resides on. For this exercise, your database should be running in ARCHIVELOG mode and all networking to the target database should be already configured.

1. Back up your database as shown in Exercise 3.2 in Chapter 3.

2. Start RMAN and confirm that you have a valid backup with the LIST BACKUP OF DATABASE SUMMARY command and with the RESTORE DATABASE VALIDATE command. Note that your output will likely look very different from ours:

```
C:\Documents and Settings\Robert>rman target=/
Recovery Manager: Release 12.1.0.1.0 -
Production on Sat Jan 4 20:01:34 2014
Copyright (c) 1982, 2013, Oracle and/or its affiliates.  All rights reserved.
connected to target database: ORCL (DBID=1194923408)
RMAN> list backup of database summary;
using target database control file instead of recovery catalog
List of Backups
===============
Key     TY LV S Device Type Completion Time #Pieces #Copies Compressed
------- -- -- - ----------- --------------- ------- ------- ----------
Tag
---
2       B  F  A DISK        03-OCT-13       1       1       YES
TAG20131003T135426
RMAN> restore database validate;
Starting restore at 04-OCT-13
allocated channel: ORA_DISK_1
channel ORA_DISK_1: SID=127 device type=DISK
channel ORA_DISK_1: starting validation of datafile backup set
channel ORA_DISK_1: reading from backup piece C:\ORACLE\FLASH_RECOVERY_AREA\
ORCL\BACKUPSET\2013_10_03
\O1_MF_NNNDF_TAG20131003T135426_4GDY3S9H_.BKP
channel ORA_DISK_1: piece handle=C:\ORACLE\FLASH_RECOVERY_AREA\ORCL\
BACKUPSET\2013_10_03
\O1_MF_NNNDF_TAG20131003T135426_4GDY3S9H_.BKP tag=TAG20131003T135426
channel ORA_DISK_1: restored backup piece 1
channel ORA_DISK_1: validation complete, elapsed time: 00:01:36
Finished restore at 04-OCT-13
RMAN>exit
```

3. If you are running in Windows, create the service for the new database with ORADIM. In this example, you are creating a new database instance called neworcl:

```
C:\>oradim -new -sid neworcl
Instance created.
```

If there are any other OS-specific operations required to create a database instance, complete them now.

EXERCISE 7.1 *(continued)*

4. Create the password file for the neworcl instance:

   ```
   C:\>orapwd file=c:\oracle\product\12.1.0\db_1\database\pwdneworcl.ora
   Enter password for SYS:
   ```

5. Create a temporary pfile for the neworcl auxiliary instance using your editor of choice. The pfile should be contained in the ORACLE_HOME\database directory of the auxiliary instance and should be named initneworcl.ora. The pfile should contain these parameters:

   ```
   db_name=neworcl
   memory_target=300m
   control_files='c:\oracle\oradata\neworcl\control01.ctl',
   'c:\oracle\oradata\neworcl\control02.ctl'
   ```

   You will do the actual file-location conversions during the duplication.

6. Create the directory c:\oracle\oradata\neworcl:

   ```
   mkdir c:\oracle\oradata\neworcl
   ```

7. Start up the auxiliary instance:

   ```
   C:\oracle\product\11.1.0\db_1\database>set oracle_sid=neworcl
   C:\oracle\product\11.1.0\db_1\database>sqlplus "/ as sysdba"
   SQL*Plus: Release 11.1.0.6.0 - Production on Sat Oct 4 23:09:52 2013
   Copyright (c) 1982, 2012, Oracle.  All rights reserved.
   Connected to an idle instance.
   SQL> startup nomount
   ORACLE instance started.
   Total System Global Area  313860096 bytes
   Fixed Size                  1332892 bytes
   Variable Size             192940388 bytes
   Database Buffers          113246208 bytes
   Redo Buffers                6340608 bytes
   ```

8. Configure service name resolution for your new auxiliary database. The method of this configuration will vary based on your site. In our case, we created an entry in the tnsnames.ora file on our server that looked like this:

   ```
   NEWORCL =
     (DESCRIPTION =
       (ADDRESS = (PROTOCOL = TCP)(HOST = 192.168.2.2)(PORT = 1521))
       (CONNECT_DATA =
   ```

```
      (SERVER = DEDICATED)
      (SERVICE_NAME = neworcl)
   )  )
```

9. Now you need to hard-code the instance name into the listener.ora file until the duplication of the database has been completed or you will get network errors. An example of the entry in our listener.ora is as follows:

```
SID_LIST_LISTENER =
  (SID_LIST =
    (SID_DESC =
        (ORACLE_HOME=C:\oracle\product\12.1.0\db_1)
        (SID_NAME=neworcl)
    )  )
LISTENER =
  (DESCRIPTION_LIST =
    (DESCRIPTION =
      (ADDRESS = (PROTOCOL = TCP)(HOST = 192.168.2.2)(PORT = 1521))
      (ADDRESS = (PROTOCOL = IPC)(KEY = EXTPROC1521))
    )  )
```

10. Test the network connectivity to the auxiliary instance:

```
C:\Documents and Settings\Robert>sqlplus sys/Robert@neworcl
SQL*Plus: Release 12.1.0.1.0 Production on Sat Jan 4 20:05:34 2014
Copyright (c) 1982, 2013, Oracle.  All rights reserved.
Connected to:
Oracle Database 12c Enterprise Edition Release 12.1.0.1.0 - 64bit Production
With the Partitioning, OLAP, Advanced Analytics
and Real Application Testing options
SQL> select instance_name from v$instance;
INSTANCE_NAME
----------------
neworcl
```

If the connection fails, review the network configuration and ensure that the new auxiliary instance is running.

11. Start RMAN, connecting to the target and the auxiliary databases:

```
C:\oracle\product\12.1.0\db_1\database>Set oracle_sid=orcl
C:\oracle\product\12.1.0\db_1\database>Rman target=/ auxiliary=sys/Robert@
neworcl
```

```
Recovery Manager: Release 12.1.0.1.0 -
Production on Sat Jan 4 20:01:34 2014
Copyright (c) 1982, 2013, Oracle and/or its affiliates.  All rights reserved.
connected to target database: ORCL (DBID=1194923408)
connected to auxiliary database: NEWORCL (not mounted)
```

12. You are now ready to start the database duplication. Issue the DUPLICATE DATABASE command, as shown here:

```
duplicate target database to neworcl nofilenamecheck
spfile set control_files=
'c:\oracle\oradata\neworcl\control01.ctl',
'c:\oracle\oradata\neworcl\control02.ctl'
set db_file_name_convert 'c:\oracle\oradata\orcl',
'c:\oracle\oradata\neworcl'
set log_file_name_convert 'c:\oracle\oradata\orcl',
'c:\oracle\oradata\neworcl';
```

This command does the following:

- It starts the duplication process.

- The SPFILE parameter causes the target database spfile to be copied to the dupli-cate database. The duplicate database will use this spfile.

- The SET commands (SET CONTROL FILES, SET DB_FILE_NAME_CONVERT, and SET LOG_FILE_NAME_CONVERT) modify or add parameters to the spfile being copied to the duplicate database.

This DUPLICATE command will result in a great deal of output, which we have decided not to include here because it seems a great waste of a perfectly good tree. Here is the output that you hopefully will see at the end of the database duplication:

```
database opened
Finished Duplicate Db at 04-OCT-13
```

13. Connect to the duplicated database to verify that it is open:

```
C:\oracle\product\12.1.0\db_1\database>set oracle_sid=neworcl
C:\oracle\product\12.1.0\db_1\database>sqlplus sys/Robert as sysdba
SQL*Plus: Release 12.1.0.1.0 Production on Sat Jan 4 20:05:34 2014
Copyright (c) 1982, 2013, Oracle.  All rights reserved.
Connected to:
```

```
Oracle Database 12c Enterprise Edition Release 12.1.0.1.0 - 64bit Production
With the Partitioning, OLAP, Advanced Analytics
and Real Application Testing options
SQL> select name, open_mode from v$database;
NAME          OPEN_MODE
---------     ----------
NEWORCL       READ WRITE
```

If you want to run this exercise again after the first successful run, you will need to perform these steps:

1. Shut down the auxiliary instance (now it's a new database!).

2. Remove the spfile assigned to the auxiliary instance.

3. Start up the auxiliary instance with STARTUP NOMOUNT.

4. Run this exercise again starting at step 11.

Performing an RMAN Tablespace Point-in-Time Recovery

As you may recall, when you do a point-in-time recovery of an Oracle database, you have to restore the entire database to the point in time selected. There are times when you may want to restore a specific tablespace to a specific point in time. DBAs have been doing this type of recovery manually for a long time. Simply, they restore a backup to another database on the same or a different server to the point in time they want to restore the tablespace to. They then export the objects they want to restore (or use transportable tablespaces) to the original database.

Of course, this is a lot of manual work. RMAN automates *tablespace point-in-time recovery (TSPITR)* for you, making recovery much easier to perform. In this section, we will address TSPITR. We will first look at the TSPITR-related prerequisites and considerations and then look at the aftereffects of a TSPITR. We will then look into setting up for and executing a TSPITR.

Setting the `NLS_DATE_FORMAT`

For the `UNTIL TIME` commands shown in this chapter, we set `NLS_DATE_FORMAT` at the Windows OS level to a value of mm/dd/yyyy hh24:mi:ss, as shown in this example:

```
Set nls_date_format=mm/dd/yyyy hh24:mi:ss
```

How you set the `NLS_DATE_FORMAT` OS LEVEL parameter will vary by platform.

If you are using a different date format, you will need to change the date/time in the commands to that format. You can also use the `to_date` function to format the date, as shown in this example:

```
recover tablespace users
until time "to_date('10/06/2013:22:42:00','mm/dd/yyyy:hh24:mi:ss')"
auxiliary destination 'c:\oracle\auxiliary';
```

TSPITR Overview

RMAN provides the ability to do a full TSPITR on a given tablespace or set of tablespaces with minimal user interaction. This is known as fully automated TSPITR. You may want to exercise more granular control over TSPITR, in which case you might want to choose to perform customized RMAN TSPITR where you have more control over the creation of the auxiliary instance and other aspects of the operation. For the purposes of this book, we will be concerned with only fully automated TSPITR.

1. Before starting TSPITR, decide on the location of the files associated with the database.

   Since TSPITR creates an auxiliary-instance database, it needs to know where you want to put the files associated with that database. For automated TSPITR, you are going to use the `AUXILIARY DESTINATION` parameter of the `RECOVER TABLESPACE` command (discussed shortly); then you will need to create the directory associated with the auxiliary destination before executing the TSPITR.

2. Start TSPITR.

   You will start TSPITR using the RMAN command `RECOVER TABLESPACE`. Special syntax (which we will cover shortly) that you will include in the body of the command will indicate to RMAN that this is a tablespace TSPITR rather than a normal tablespace recovery. Here is an example of the use of the `RECOVER TABLESPACE` command to start a TSPITR recovery:

```
recover tablespace users
until time '10/06/2013:22:42:00'
auxiliary destination 'c:\oracle\auxiliary';
```

In this case, we are executing a TSPITR of the USERS tablespace. We want to recover the entire USERS tablespace to 10/6/2013 at 22:42:00 hours. The AUXILIARY DESTINATION clause, discussed earlier, indicates where we want RMAN to create the auxiliary instance database files—in this case, the directory c:\oracle\auxiliary.

Now that you have executed the RECOVER TABLESPACE command, what happens next?

3. Create the TSPITR auxiliary instance.

   TSPITR requires the use of an auxiliary instance just as database duplication does. The *auxiliary instance* (in RMAN output, it's called an *automatic instance*) is the database that will be used to perform the TSPITR. It is a transient database, used just long enough to restore the tablespaces, export the database, and finish the TSPITR. The main difference here is that once RMAN is done with the TSPITR, the auxiliary instance is no longer needed.

4. Check the TSPITR transport set.

   When you start the TSPITR with the RECOVER TABLESPACE command, RMAN will check that the tablespace you want to recover can actually be recovered. It does this by checking the transport set to ensure that it's wholly self-contained. See the next section, "Checking the Transport Set," for more information on this process and why it's needed.

5. Create the auxiliary instance.

   Once RMAN confirms that the tablespace set can be transported, it will create the auxiliary instance, start it, and connect to it. This is nice because you will not have to create the auxiliary instance. You can opt to create the auxiliary instance yourself if there are specific reasons to do so. RMAN will create a control file for the auxiliary instance.

6. Take the target database tablespaces offline.

   Once the auxiliary instance has been created, the tablespaces on the target database to be moved will be taken offline. This implies that the data in these databases will not be available to users until the tablespaces are brought back online. Since you are restoring these tablespaces to a different point in time, the data the users will see the next time the tablespaces are brought back online will possibly be very different. Keep this in mind when doing a TSPITR: You are impacting the entire tablespace or set of tablespaces. If someone is not aware of what you are doing, you might get a very nasty phone call.

7. Transport the source tablespaces.

   Now that the tablespace(s) has been taken offline, RMAN will restore the recovery set and the auxiliary set from the target database to the auxiliary instance. The *recovery set* is the set of tablespaces that you are going to recover with TSPITR. The *auxiliary set* is the set of data files that are required to get the auxiliary instance running. This includes files for the SYSTEM tablespace, the UNDO tablespace, and the SYSAUX tablespace and tablespace tempfiles.

8. Recover the auxiliary-instance database.

   Once the auxiliary set and the recovery set are restored, RMAN will proceed to recover the auxiliary-instance database to the point in time identified when the RMAN RECOVER command was issued. Once the restore is complete, the auxiliary-instance database will be opened.

9. Transport the tablespace set.

   TSPITR uses transportable tablespaces to facilitate the movement of the tablespace data files from the auxiliary database instance to the target database instance. To perform this action, RMAN will first export needed metadata from the auxiliary database instance. It will then shut down the auxiliary database instance. On the target system, RMAN SWITCH commands are executed to cause the data file locations in the target database control file to be switched to the newly recovered data files. Finally, the backed-up metadata will be restored to the target database so the data in the restored tablespaces will be accessible to the target database.

10. Complete the operation.

    The auxiliary database files will be removed after the operation is completed. The target database tablespaces will be offline. You should back up those tablespaces, and then you will need to bring those tablespaces online manually. Once you do, you will find that the tablespaces contain the data in the version it existed in at the restore time indicated in the RECOVER command.

    TSPITR does not restore the point-in-time statistics for the objects contained in the restored tablespaces. Thus, you should analyze the objects in the tablespaces after completing the TSPITR.

Checking the Transport Set

When you perform a TSPITR, you want a transport set that is self-contained. This means that the tablespaces in the transport set do not have external object references; that is, they don't refer to objects that are not in the transport set. For example, suppose you are transporting the USERS tablespace, and a table in that tablespace has an index in the INDEX tablespace. In this case, you will not be able to transport the USERS tablespace unless you also transport the INDEX tablespace. When you transport both the USERS and INDEX tablespaces, you are transporting a wholly self-contained transport set.

RMAN will determine if the transport set is fully self-contained, but you may want to check beforehand to save some time. You can query the TS_PITR_CHECK view. In our example, USERS and INDEX_TBS are self-contained. If USERS is not transported with INDEX_TBS, then the TSPITR will error out. To determine if USERS and INDEX_TBS are self-contained, you would issue this query:

```
SQL> SELECT ts1_name, ts2_name, reason
  2  FROM SYS.TS_PITR_CHECK
  3  WHERE (
  4          TS1_NAME IN ('USERS','INDEX_TBS')
  5          AND TS2_NAME NOT IN ('USERS','INDEX_TBS')
  6        )
  7  OR    (
  8          TS1_NAME NOT IN ('USERS','INDEX_TBS')
```

```
 9            AND TS2_NAME IN ('USERS','INDEX_TBS')
 10*         )
SQL> /
no rows selected
```

If you were to plan to transport only the USERS tablespace, then you would see the following error:

```
SQL> SELECT ts1_name, ts2_name, reason
  2   FROM SYS.TS_PITR_CHECK
  3   WHERE (
  4            TS1_NAME IN ('USERS')
  5            AND TS2_NAME NOT IN ('USERS')
  6         )
  7   OR    (
  8            TS1_NAME NOT IN ('USERS')
  9            AND TS2_NAME IN ('USERS')
 10*         )
SQL> /

TS1_NAME    TS2_NAME
----------  ----------
REASON
----------------------------------------------------------------------
USERS       INDEX_TBS
Tables and associated indexes not fully contained in the recovery set
```

Lost Objects

When you perform a TSPITR recovery, it is possible that you will lose objects in the tablespace that were created after the point in time to which you restore the tablespace. You can export these objects before the TSPITR with Oracle Data Pump and then import them after the TSPITR has completed.

By querying the view TS_PITR_OBJECTS_TO_BE_DROPPED, you can determine which objects will be lost, as shown in this example:

```
SQL> SELECT OWNER, NAME, TABLESPACE_NAME,
  2          TO_CHAR(CREATION_TIME, 'YYYY-MM-DD:HH24:MI:SS')
  3          FROM TS_PITR_OBJECTS_TO_BE_DROPPED
  4   WHERE TABLESPACE_NAME IN ('USERS')
  5   AND CREATION_TIME >
  6   TO_DATE('07-OCT-13:22:35:30','YY-MON-DD:HH24:MI:SS')
  7   ORDER BY TABLESPACE_NAME, CREATION_TIME;
```

```
OWNER                            NAME
------------------------------   ---------------------------
TABLESPACE_NAME                  TO_CHAR(CREATION_TI
------------------------------   -------------------
SCOTT                            TESTTABLE
USERS                            2013-10-07:19:34:39
```

Rules, Rules, and More Rules

Finally, TSPITR involves a few rules you need to be aware of:

▪ The target database must be in ARCHIVELOG mode.

▪ You must have a backup that was taken before the point in time that you want to perform the TSPITR.

▪ You must have all archived redo logs generated since the last backup (complete or incremental) up to the point to which you want to restore the transport set.

▪ If you rename a tablespace, you cannot perform a TSPITR to any point in time before that rename operation occurred.

▪ If you have tables in tablespace_1 that have associated constraints in tablespace_2, then you must transport both tablespaces.

▪ If a tablespace contains the following objects, then that tablespace cannot be used during a TSPITR:

  ▪ Replicated master tables.

  ▪ Incomplete tables; you must transport complete tables, including all partitions of a partitioned table.

  ▪ Any tables that contain VARRAY columns, nested tables, or external tables.

  ▪ Snapshot-related objects (snapshot logs and snapshots).

  ▪ Tablespaces with UNDO or rollback segments.

  ▪ Any tablespace with objects owned by the SYS schema.

TSPITR Aftereffects

Some interesting things happen after a TSPITR:

▪ If a data file was added to the tablespace on the target database after the point in time for the recovery, then the resulting tablespace after the TSPITR process will have an empty data file restored.

▪ Once the TSPITR is complete, all backups associated with tablespaces in the transport set taken before the point in time that you restored the tablespaces to are no longer valid. You should run a backup after the TSPITR.

- Once a TSPITR is complete, you will not be able to run another TSPITR on that tablespace to any time before the point to which you restored the tablespace.
- Once a TSPITR is complete, you will not be able to use the control file to restore any part of the database to any point in time before the time that you restored the tablespaces to during the TSPITR.

In Exercise 7.2, you'll perform a tablespace point-in-time recovery with RMAN.

EXERCISE 7.2

Performing a Tablespace Point-in-Time Recovery

In this exercise, you will perform a tablespace point-in-time recovery of the USERS tablespace.

1. Log into the scott account in the database with SQL*Plus:

```
C:\Documents and Settings\Robert>set oracle_sid=orcl
C:\Documents and Settings\Robert>sqlplus scott/tiger
SQL*Plus: Release 12.1.0.1.0 Production on Sat Jan 4 20:05:34 2014
Copyright (c) 1982, 2013, Oracle.  All rights reserved.
Connected to:
Oracle Database 12c Enterprise Edition Release 12.1.0.1.0 - 64bit Production
With the Partitioning, OLAP, Advanced Analytics
and Real Application Testing options
SQL>
```

2. Create a table called TSPITR for this exercise. It will be created in the USERS tablespace (create the USERS tablespace if required):

```
SQL> create table tspitr (id number, the_date date)  tablespace users;
Table created.
```

3. Exit SQL*Plus and start RMAN. Back up the database with RMAN:

```
RMAN> backup as compressed backupset database plus archivelog delete input;
```

4. Exit RMAN and connect to the scott schema again with SQL*Plus:

```
RMAN> exit
Recovery Manager complete.
C:\Documents and Settings\Robert>sqlplus scott/tiger
Recovery Manager: Release 12.1.0.1.0 -
Production on Sat Jan 4 20:01:34 2014
Copyright (c) 1982, 2013, Oracle and/or its affiliates.  All rights reserved.
connected to target database
SQL>
```

EXERCISE 7.2 *(continued)*

5. Insert a record into the TSPITR table and commit:

```
SQL> insert into tspitr values (1,sysdate);
1 row created.
SQL> commit;
Commit complete.
SQL>
```

6. Wait a minute and insert another record into TSPITR. Commit the record:

```
SQL> insert into tspitr values (2,sysdate);
1 row created.
SQL> commit;
Commit complete.
SQL>
```

7. Select from the TSPITR table. Record the time/date of both records for a later step:

```
SQL> select * from tspitr;

        ID THE_DATE
---------- -------------------
         1 10/09/2013 22:09:02
         1 10/09/2013 22:10:04
```

8. Exit SQL*Plus.

9. From the operating system, create a directory for the auxiliary database files. In our case, we are using c:\oracle\auxiliary.

```
c:>mkdir c:\oracle\auxiliary
```

10. Start RMAN. Connect to the target database:

```
C:\Documents and Settings\Robert>rman target=/
Recovery Manager: Release 12.1.0.1.0 -
Production on Sat Jan 4 20:01:34 2014
Copyright (c) 1982, 2013, Oracle and/or its affiliates.  All rights reserved.
connected to target database: ORCL (DBID=1194923408)
RMAN>
```

11. Perform a tablespace point-in-time recovery of the USERS tablespace to a point in time between insert #1 and insert #2.

```
RMAN> recover tablespace users
2> until time '10/09/2013:22:09:20' auxiliary destination 'c:\oracle\auxiliary';
< we have decided to remove the output here to save a few trees.>
```

EXERCISE 7.2 *(continued)*

12. Back up the USERS tablespace:

```
RMAN> backup tablespace users;
Starting backup at 10/09/2013 22:28:51
using channel ORA_DISK_1
channel ORA_DISK_1: starting full datafile backup set
channel ORA_DISK_1: specifying datafile(s) in backup set
input datafile file number=00004
name=C:\ORACLE\ORADATA\ORCL\USERS01.DBF
channel ORA_DISK_1: starting piece 1 at 10/09/2013 22:28:58
channel ORA_DISK_1: finished piece 1 at 10/09/2013 22:28:59
piece handle=C:\ORACLE\FLASH_RECOVERY_AREA\ORCL\BACKUPSET\2013_10_09
\O1_MF_NNNDF_TAG20131009T222851_4GXPJB5V_.BKP
tag=TAG20131009T222851 comment=NONE
channel ORA_DISK_1: backup set complete, elapsed time: 00:00:01
Finished backup at 10/09/2013 22:28:59
Starting Control File and SPFILE Autobackup at 10/09/2013 22:28:59
piece handle=C:\ORACLE\FLASH_RECOVERY_AREA\ORCL\AUTOBACKUP\2013_10_09
\O1_MF_S_667693739_4GXPJMNZ_.BKP comment=NONE
Finished Control File and SPFILE Autobackup at 10/09/2013 22:29:14.
```

13. Connect to SYS with SQL*Plus:

```
C:\Documents and Settings\Robert>sqlplus sys/robert as sysdba
SQL*Plus: Release 12.1.0.1.0 Production on Sat Jan 4 20:05:34 2014
Copyright (c) 1982, 2013, Oracle.  All rights reserved.
Connected to:
Oracle Database 12c Enterprise Edition Release 12.1.0.1.0 - 64bit Production
With the Partitioning, OLAP, Advanced Analytics
and Real Application Testing options
```

14. Bring the USERS tablespace online:

```
SQL> alter tablespace users online;
Tablespace altered.
```

15. Select from the TSPITR table. Notice that only the first record is now in the table. This concludes this exercise.

```
SQL> select * from tspitr;

        ID THE_DATE
---------- -------------------
         1 10/09/2013 22:09:02
```

Restoring a Database to a New Host

In the previous several chapters, we discussed user-based backup and recovery and RMAN-based (or server-based) backup and recovery.

When we think about restoring databases to other hosts, we might think about a number of situations. One might be disaster recovery where we have to start from the bottom up and where all we have are (hopefully) some backup tapes somewhere.

Other cases might involve a refresh process where new systems are being moved into your data center and you need to move your database over to that new system. Perhaps your other host is a development system and you just want to restore a copy of your production database over there. There are a number of different possibilities.

There are several ways to approach this requirement, and the method you would use really depends on what is required. If you are restoring to a bare metal machine, then you would need to make sure that the operating system was installed, the Oracle software was installed, and so on.

With respect to moving an Oracle database, there are many things to consider, including the following:

- The size of the database
- The platform you are moving from
- The platform you are moving to
- How long you can take the databases down to make the move
- Network speed
- Disk speed
- Impacts on other users and systems
- And so on...

So, moving a database to a new host is not usually a simple "just do it" kind of operation.

There are different methods that can be employed to perform these database moves. The following list provides a summary of those methods:

- RMAN
- Oracle Data Pump
- Oracle GoldenGate
- Oracle Data Guard

Of course, there is also the consideration of what to do in a complete disaster. Let's look at these options in a bit more detail next:

Using RMAN to Move a Database

We have already discussed the RMAN DUPLICATE DATABASE command. If the new host is connected to the old host via the network then RMAN duplication of a database may well be the easiest way to restore a database to a new host.

As we have already mentioned, RMAN comes with a DUPLICATE DATABASE command. Using the DUPLICATE DATABASE command provides a way to quickly move a database between two different hosts that are running the same operating system. It also is a great way to produce copies of existing databases on a different host, and it can also be used to create standby databases on another host. Again, all of these need to be on the same platform.

With active database duplication, the process is even easier because RMAN does not need to access the database backup files of the database. Instead it simply scoops the data from the database datafiles and duplicates them over the network to the new host. Again, the same platform is required.

Note in these previous cases that the resulting database copy is logically a different database, with a different database ID. So, while the data in the database might be the same, the database itself is a logically different entity.

In Oracle Database 12c RMAN introduced a feature called cross-platform transportable database. This provides the ability to transport the entire database and, in this case, the resulting database is logically consistent with the source database. This is because along with all the tablespaces that are moved over (as would occur with transportable tablespaces) the SYSTEM tablespace is also moved over. This preserves the system related metadata such as object_IDs and so on. This method of database movement does not provide for movement across platforms with different byte formats.

Note that the cross-platform transport of databases can use image copies or RMAN backup sets. Which one is more efficient will depend on a number of different factors, such as CPU speed, memory availability, and network speed.

There are two different kinds of byte formats you will need to deal with as a DBA. These are called endian byte formats. One is known as little endian and the other is known as big endian. Until Oracle Database 12c, the only way to move a complete database between platforms with different byte formats was to use Oracle Data Pump to logically move the data between the two platforms. This process could be complex and take much more time than restoring an RMAN backup

RMAN now provides the ability to transport databases across the different byte formats. A new command called CONVERT provides the ability to convert the files to the new byte format on the target platform. You can convert the files on the source or destination server, which allows you to control which machine is impacted by the conversion process.

The CONVERT process can be used with specific datafiles or tablespaces, or when moving an entire database across platforms. Again, the use of image copies or RMAN backup sets are both supported.

The problem with using RMAN in this case is that it will take time to move the data between the source and destination hosts. This could impact the database performance and network bandwidth. Also, you will have to take the source database offline for a while as you synchronize the new database with the target database. The other problem is that the move is almost an all-or-nothing type of decision. Rolling back the move, once you have opened the database, can be time consuming and frustrating.

There are other solutions to moving databases to different hosts that reduce the downtime and provide for testing before you actually open the new database up for users to use. Let's look at those options for a moment.

Oracle Data Pump, Oracle GoldenGate and Oracle Data Guard

Oracle Data Pump is a logical backup and restore solution provided by Oracle. This solution is typically slower than using an RMAN solution. Before cross-platform movement of data via RMAN was possible, Oracle Data Pump was the only option. Now, it is perhaps the last option as the speed of Data Pump is usually much slower than RMAN. Also, RMAN preserves much more of the meta structure of the underlying database than Oracle Data Pump. This might not be important in most cases, but there can be those cases where this might be important.

Oracle provides other tools such as Data Guard and GoldenGate that provide the ability to instantiate the remote database on the other host, and keep it in synch with the original database. This will allow you to move the database and then test it before actually opening it up to the world. Additionally, the time required to switch over to the new database host is substantially reduced.

Complete Disaster

So what happens if there is a complete disaster and you lose everything? You need to plan for such an event. Taking backups and moving them offsite is the first step. You need to make sure not only that you have backups of your database offsite but that you have copies of the Oracle software available offsite too. Any parameter files that are not backed up by RMAN (say, your tnsnames.ora or your listener.ora files) should be backed up offsite.

We thought we would close this section of the chapter with a review of what you would need to do if you had to recover from offsite backups following a disaster. If you are using RMAN and you find you need to do a complete database recovery, you would follow the steps listed here. Chapter 5 provides more detail on the individual RMAN recovery steps and how to execute them:

1. Restore the OS.

2. Restore the Oracle software.

3. Configure Oracle networking.

4. Ensure that you have access to the RMAN backup set pieces that you need.

5. Restore the database spfile from the control-file autobackup. We assume that if you are doing control-file autobackups to disk, you will move those backups to tape and offsite them.

6. Once the database spfile is restored, you can mount the database and restore the control files of the database from the autobackups.

7. Once the database control file is restored, you can begin the restore and recovery of the database proper.

This would complete your disaster-recovery operation. If you needed to restore database files to a different location, you would use the SET NEWNAME RMAN command as discussed in Chapter 6.

8. After you have completed the restore and recovery of the database data files, you would open the database with the ALTER DATABASE OPEN RESETLOGS command.

If you are doing user-managed backup and recovery, the process is not all that different, as you can see here:

1. Restore the OS.

2. Restore the Oracle software.

3. Configure Oracle networking.

4. Ensure that you have access to the database backups that you will be restoring.

5. Restore the database parameter file or spfile from your backup media.

6. Once the database parameter file or spfile is restored, you can mount the database with the ALTER DATABASE MOUNT command.

7. Use a backup control file or the CREATE CONTROLFILE command to recreate the control file of the database.

8. Once the database control file is restored, move the backups of the database data files from the backup media.

   If you are restoring the database data files to a different location, you will need to rename them in the database control file.

9. Use the ALTER DATABASE RENAME FILE command for this operation.

10. Restore the needed archived redo logs from the backup media.

11. Use the RECOVER DATABASE command to complete the database recovery.

   You will need to perform an incomplete recovery, since the online redo logs are not available. See Chapter 3 for more on incomplete user-managed recoveries.

12. Once the RECOVER DATABASE command has completed its work, open the database with the ALTER DATABASE OPEN RESETLOGS command.

Backup Best Practices for Data Warehouses

Oracle has a set of best practices that offer a guide with respect to how you should perform your database backups. RMAN is part of that solution. Another part of that solution offers a set of best practices for how to best use RMAN to backup large databases, such as data warehouses.

The best practice calls for the use of one full backup, and then incrementally backing up that backup image over time. This has the effect of only requiring that one full backup of the database ever be taken. Subsequent backups then just back up the incremental changes. This kind of backup is called an incrementally updated backup and it can save you a great deal of time when backing up your database, space to store these backups, and save you lots of time when restoring these backups.

All of this is done through the auspices of a two RMAN commands as seen here:

```
Run {
RECOVER COPY OF DATABASE
WITH TAG 'incremental_update';
BACKUP
  INCREMENTAL LEVEL 1
  FOR RECOVER OF COPY WITH TAG 'incremental_update' DATABASE;
}
```

These commands are run as a set, the first being a predicate to the second. These commands might look a bit different than your regular RMAN BACKUP commands, and they are. Let's look at what's happening in a bit more detail.

The First Execution of the Command

When these set of commands are run the first time, the RECOVER COPY OF DATABASE will cause RMAN to lookup and find any incremental backup that might need to be applied to the base backup of the database that was taken.

At the beginning of the first execution there will be no backups for the command to find at all, since none have been taken (using this tag, presumably) to this point. This is expected and while a message will appear, no error really occurs.

Note the use of the TAG parameter and that the tags are the same in both commands. This is important since it provides a way for RMAN to find the correct backups to update in later executions.

The BACKUP command on this first execution will create a complete image copy of the database. Note that this is an image copy, and not a backup set, so the resulting size of the backup files will be the same as the size of the database and likely much larger than normal RMAN database backups. However, this format, and the strategy we are discussing now, is the absolute fastest way to restore a large database.

So, let's say that this backup takes place on June 1. If we looked at the FRA on June 1, after the backup, what we would find is a copy of all of the database datafiles sitting in the FRA. We would also find, if we looked around, that we forgot to back up the archived redo logs, which would be a problem since they will be needed to be able to actually recover this database completely. We will fix this problem by modifying our script as follows:

```
Run {
RECOVER COPY OF DATABASE
```

```
WITH TAG 'incremental_update';
BACKUP
  INCREMENTAL LEVEL 1
  FOR RECOVER OF COPY WITH TAG 'incremental_update' DATABASE  PLUS ARCHIVELOG
DELETE INPUT;
}
```

The Second Execution of the Command

During the second execution of the RECOVER COPY OF DATABASE command, RMAN will find the previously created full backup, with the tag name applied. However, there will be no incremental backups found to apply to that backup since we have not made an incremental backup yet. So, the RECOVER COPY OF DATABASE command still has no real function. As a result, the command simply does nothing but send a notification messages.

The BACKUP command in this case will perform a level 1 incremental backup, since there is already a level 0 base copy available. So, after the second execution of the command, we will have one full image copy and one incremental RMAN backup of the database. Also, since we told it to back up the archived redo logs, they will be backed up as well.

One thing we should make clear is the distinction between the first full backup of the database and the subsequent incremental backup. The first full backup of the database is an image copy, as we mentioned previously. The subsequent incremental backups will be RMAN incremental backups, and as such, they are stored in RMAN backup sets. Thus, they can take advantage of RMAN features such as compression as seen in this example:

```
Run {
RECOVER COPY OF DATABASE
WITH TAG 'incremental_update';
BACKUP AS COMPRESSED BACKUPSET
  INCREMENTAL LEVEL 1
  FOR RECOVER OF COPY WITH TAG 'incremental_update' DATABASE
  PLUS ARCHIVELOG DELETE INPUT;
}
```

The Third Execution of the Command

The third execution of this set of commands is where the real magic happens, and it also requires us to do a little bit of thinking.

The third execution of this set of commands, by default, will cause the last incremental backup to be restored and applied to the image copy of the database that was originally taken. Thus, the image copy of the database now looks like the database looked on the second day, and it no longer looks like the database did on the first day. This is where we need to start to do a little thinking.

The keyterm is *retention*, or, how long do we need to be able to go back in time and restore the database (or a copy of the database) for business purposes. Currently, our script offers us pretty much no retention criteria. As soon as we run it, the ability to restore the database to the previous day with RMAN is no longer possible.

So, you need to determine what the requirements for point-in-time recovery actually are. For example, if your SLA requires that you be able to restore your database to any point in time within the last 30 days, you need to consider how to implement this requirement. In many environments, there is a need to take a copy of a database and make several other copies of that database for various purposes, such as development. However, in some cases, they might want to be able to restore the database to the point in time that it looked seven days ago. This could be another consideration with respect to your backup planning.

Another possibility is that there may be some legal requirement to be able to restore your database back to a point in time 30 days ago, or six months ago. At the end of the day, you will have to figure out the number of days to which you need to be able to recover your database.

Once you have determined your retention requirements, you would configure these retention requirements via RMAN, since it controls retention automatically within the FRA, and you can manually control that retention if you have used non-FRA locations. With incrementally updated backups, RMAN's automatic retention policies are not applied. Also, looking for obsolete backups manually does not work since your backups are being wrapped into the complete backup.

So, how do we provide for a recovery window, making it possible to restore the database to some number of days in the past? We simply need to add the retention criteria into the backup command itself. Here is an example where we have defined a retention criteria of seven days:

```
Run {
RECOVER COPY OF DATABASE
WITH TAG 'incremental_update'
UNTIL TIME 'SYSDATE-7';            ←——— Retain.
BACKUP AS COMPRESSED BACKUPSET
  INCREMENTAL LEVEL 1
  FOR RECOVER OF COPY WITH TAG 'incremental_update' DATABASE
  PLUS ARCHIVELOG DELETE INPUT;
}
```

The effect of adding the UNTIL TIME clause is that the incremental backups will not be wrapped into the image copies of the database until seven days has passed. This results in more incremental backups being stored on media to support the required recovery point.

Table 7.3 provides a quick look at the progress of a backup and its backup files given the previous command.

TABLE 7.3 Recovery timelines when using incrementally updated backups data-pump should be Data Pump

Day #	Mirror Backup Taken	Incremental Merged	Incremental Created	Incremental Deleted	Farthest day you can recover to
1	Y	N	N	N	1
2	N	N	Y	N	1
3	N	N	Y	N	1
4	N	N	Y	N	1
5	N	N	Y	N	1
6	N	N	Y	N	1
7	N	N	Y	N	1
8	N	Y (day #2)	Y	Y (day #2)	2
9	N	Y (day #3)	Y	Y (day #3)	3

Obviously, as your retention requirement increases, your storage space requirements will increase (since you are storing more incremental backups). However, since these backups can be compressed, you might be able to mitigate the space usage.

Restoring from Incrementally Updated Backups

There is nothing special about restoring from incrementally updated backups. RMAN will detect which recovery strategy will be the most efficient and act accordingly. If it finds that there is an incrementally updated backup, then it will use that backup for restore and recovery automatically.

Performing Table and Partition Recovery from Backups

Until Oracle Database 12c, there were limited options available for the restore of individual tables and partitions or a set of tables and partitions. In the past, restores like these were problematic and time consuming. Often the restore would require that you restore the entire database and then roll it forward in its entirety. You would then need to export the objects (or use transportable tablespaces) and import them into the database you were trying to recover.

Of course, if you had a Data Pump logical backup of the database, and it was taken at the point in time when you needed to restore the database to, then you could use that option. There are several problems with this choice though, including the fact that it is not possible to roll the data backed up in the Data Pump export forward in time after it's restored. Thus, if your export was taken at 4 P.M. three days ago, then that is the image of the data that you're going to see when you restore the export file to the database.

Oracle Database 12c and RMAN now make it much easier to restore a given table or table partition (singular or plural). Now you can use the RMAN RECOVER TABLE command to indicate to RMAN what table (or tables) you wish to restore.

In this section, we will discuss the following:

- Things to check before trying to restore and recover database tables and partitions
- Restrictions when restoring and recovering database tables and partitions
- Options to consider when performing table or table partition restores
- An example of using RMAN to restore and recover a database table

Things to Check Before Trying to Restore and Recover Database Tables and Partitions

Individual table and table partition restores are done using the RMAN interface. As with everything else, there are some prerequisites that need to be met, including the following:

- The database must have been in ARCHIVELOG mode when it was backed up.
- After the backup, the database must have remained in ARCHIVELOG mode until the point that you want to restore the database to.
- You will need all the archived redo logs generated from the point in time when the database backup started and the point in time to which you wish to restore the table or partition.
- For partition recovery, the COMPATIBLE parameter must be set to 11.1.0 or later.
- A complete RMAN backup of the SYSTEM, SYSAUX, UNDO, and SYSEXT tablespaces must be available (full backup or a base and subsequent incrementals).
- You must have a backup of the tablespace(s) that contain the objects that you want to restore. All of these backups must have been completed before the point in time to which you want to restore the objects.
- All tablespaces in the restore set must be restored to the same point in time.
- The database you are restoring to (the target database) must be open in read-write mode.
- The target database must be in ARCHIVELOG mode.

As with any point-in-time recovery, you will need to know the time, log sequence number, or SCN that you want to restore the table or partitions to. If you've met these prerequisites, you are ready to perform a restore of tables or table partitions using RMAN. Now let's look at some of the restrictions related to the restore of tables and table partitions.

Restrictions When Restoring and Recovering Database Tables and Partitions

There are some restrictions related to table and partition-level recoveries. These include the following:

* You cannot restore tables that belong to the SYS schema.
* Tables that are stored in the SYSTEM and SYSAUX tablespaces cannot be restored.
* Tables and table partitions in standby databases cannot be restored.
* If a table to be restored has a NOT NULL constraint assigned to it, then you can't use the REMAP option of the RECOVER TABLE command.

Next, we will discuss the various options that you can use when restoring tables or table partitions.

Options to Consider When Performing Table or Table Partition Restores

When you issue the commands to restore a table or a partition, you will want to take advantage of various options. Table 7.4 provides a list of these parameters and their use.

TABLE 7.4   RMAN Parameters Used When Restoring Tables

Parameter Name	Purpose
AUXILIARY DESTINATION	Location used to create the auxiliary instance-related files.
DUMP FILE	The name of the Data Pump export file.
DATAPUMP DESTINATION	The directory where the Data Pump export file should be created. This directory should have been created in the database using the CREATE DIRECTORY command.
NOTABLEIMPORT	Indicates that the export file should be created. However, the contents should not be imported into the target database.
REMAP TABLE	Renames the table in the target database when it's created.
REMAP TABLESPACE	Creates the tables in a different tablespace of the target database.

An Example of Using RMAN to Restore and Recover a Database Table

In this example, we will use a database called ORCL. We will assume that you already have an RMAN backup of that database and that all of the database's archived redo logs are either backed up by RMAN or are available on disk. In this example, we will restore the tables owned by the HR schema using the RMAN RESTORE FILE command after making some changes to these tables. These tables are EMP, DEPT, SALGRADE, and BONUS. First, let's look at the current time before any changes were made:

```
SQL> alter session set nls_date_format='mm/dd/yyyy hh24:mi:ss';

Session altered.
SQL> select sysdate, current_scn from v$database;

SYSDATE             CURRENT_SCN
------------------- -----------
03/27/2013 10:24:29  2074999
```

Developers are using the HR schema in our database. The HR schema has four tables, as shown in this query:

```
SQL> select table_name from user_tables;
TABLE_NAME
--------------------------------------------------------------------------
DEPT
EMP
BONUS
SALGRADE
```

The row counts in the table are shown here:

```
SQL> select count(*) from DEPT;
  COUNT(*)
----------
     4

SQL> select count(*) from EMP;
  COUNT(*)
----------
    14

SQL> select count(*) from BONUS;
```

```
  COUNT(*)
----------
     0


SQL> select count(*) from SALGRADE;
  COUNT(*)
----------
     5
```

During testing, something terribly bad happens. Instead of individual rows being deleted, the new bulk update application, lacking an appropriate WHERE clause in the DELETE statement, managed to remove all the records in all the tables instead of unique ones. After the application ran, the row counts looked like this:

```
SQL> select count(*) from DEPT;
  COUNT(*)
----------
     0
SQL> select count(*) from EMP;
  COUNT(*)
----------
     0
SQL> select count(*) from BONUS;
  COUNT(*)
----------
     0
SQL> select count(*) from SALGRADE;
  COUNT(*)
----------
     0
```

It's a shame, but the developers also forgot to export their test schema before the test. It's not a good day for the developers. The developers are upset about the loss of their data and the knowledge that the whole database will probably have to be restored instead of just the HR schema. Lots of good and important data exists in other schemas.

They call you, their DBA, and ask how they can get their data restored. Fortunately for you, the database is running Oracle Database 12c. You tell them to hang tight and you will take care of the problem. After asking them what time they started their testing, you tell them you will restore HR to the second before testing and get back to them when you have finished. One important bit of information that the developers were able to give you was the specific point in time that you need to restore the table objects to. We will assume it's the same time and date that the query against V$DATABASE gave us earlier in this section.

Sitting down at your laptop you set your Oracle environment for the correct database and start RMAN. Now you use the RMAN RESTORE command to restore the tables in the HR schema. Note that you can't recover a specific schema, only the tables in it, so your RECOVER command will specify the schema and table names of the tables you need to restore.

 When you restore a table, the restore will fail if that table already exists. In this case, you need to either rename the table in the database or drop it. Another option is to remap the table name to something different than the original table or remap the table to a new schema.

Before you start the restore, you need to decide where you want the auxiliary database-related files to be stored. In this case, we have chosen to use the directory /u01/app/oracle/aux. Once you confirm that the directory exists, you log into RMAN and start the restore:

```
[oracle@server12c ~]$ rman target=/
recover table hr.emp, hr.dept, hr.bonus, hr.salgrade
until time "to_date('03/27/2013 10:24:29','mm/dd/yyyy hh24:mi:ss')"
auxiliary destination '/u01/app/oracle/aux';
```

When you press Enter, RMAN will start the restore. The output of the restore is quite lengthy, so we decided not to include it here. In summary, you will see the following in the output:

- Allocation of channels
- The creation of the auxiliary instance
- Restore of the control file for the auxiliary instance
- A list of data files that will be restored, followed by their restore and recovery in the auxiliary instance
- Export of tables from the auxiliary instance via Oracle Data Pump
- Import of tables, constraints, indexes, and other dependent objects into the target database from the Data Pump export file
- Cleanup of the auxiliary instance

ASM-Related Backups

Automatic Storage Management (ASM) has become very commonly used in Oracle Database architectures to manage the disks that are used by the database. With respect to ASM, there are some backup considerations that you will need to be aware of for your OCP exam. We will address these in this section as follows:

1. Quick overview of ASM
2. ASM diskgroup metadata backups
3. Restore ASM disk groups

Quick ASM Overview

Automatic Storage Management (ASM) provides a centralized way to manage Oracle Database disk storage. ASM is designed to simplify Oracle database storage administration. Database environments have become more and more complex, with large numbers of (and larger) datafiles, storage area networks (SANs), and high-availability requirements. ASM is somewhat like a logical volume manager, allowing you to reduce the management of Oracle files into ASM disk groups.

ASM also provides redundancy configurations, rebalancing operations, and, when installed on top of clusterware, the ability to share database-related files.

ASM stores files in *disk groups*, which are logical entities made up of one or more physical disk drives. ASM is good for more than just storing database datafiles. In an ASM instance, you can store database datafiles, online redo logs, archived redo logs, backup files, and data-pump dumpfiles as well as change-tracking files and control files of one or several Oracle databases.

ASM can also be used to store regular files through the support of Oracle database options that provide the ability to mount an ASM disk group as a sharable file system. Oracle DBFS or ACFS both provide these options and work in concert with the Oracle database. You can create an Oracle DBFS or ACFS database, and after configuring the environment correctly, you can then share out the space allocated to that database in the form of a OS file system.

While ASM does not require backing up (this occurs when you back up the databases using ASM), it's still not a bad idea to back up metadata related to ASM. In the most severe cases, it's possible that ASM metadata could get lost, and as a result, attributes related to disk groups might end up being lost, or even the disk groups themselves. Obviously, you can recreate the disk groups pretty easily, but since disk groups can have attributes customized, backing up the metadata and being able to restore it is a nice thing to have.

What are some of the things stored in the ASM metadata? How about the following:

- The disks that belong to that disk group
- The amount of space that is available in that disk group
- All of the file names of the files in that disk group
- The location of disk group data file extents
- A log file that provides information about changing metadata blocks. This is much like a redo log file
- Oracle ADVM volume information

As you can see, ASM metadata is rich in information and it certainly needs to be protected. Let's see how we do that.

ASM Diskgroup Metadata Backups

To back up ASM diskgroup metadata, you will use the ASM command line administration tool called asmcmd. To use asmcmd, you would set your environment for the ASM instance (which should be using a GRID_HOME location that is separate from your ORACLE_HOME location. So, starting asmcmd might look like this:

```
/opt/oracle>export ORACLE_SID=+ASM1
/opt/oracle>asmcmd
```

The asmcmd tool provides a great deal of functionality, as seen in Table 7.5 below:

TABLE 7.5   ASMCMD commands

Command	Purpose	Example
Cd	Changes ASM directory.	cd +group1
du	Gets disk use.	du
find	Finds directory or file.	find + rob11g
help	Displays the help screen.	help
ls	Lists files in directory.	ls -l
lsct	Lists all clients using the ASM instance.	lsct
lsdg	Lists information on disk groups in the ASM instance.	lsdg
lsdsk	Lists ASM visible disks. Supported only in Unix.	lsdsk -k -d DATA *
mkalias	Creates an ASM alias for a given ASM filename.	mkalias +cooked_dgroup1/11gDB/ controlfile/Current.258.613087119 +cooked_dgroup1/control01.ctl
Mkdir	Creates an ASM directory.	mkdir old
md_backup	Backs up ASM metadata.	md_backup -b /tmp/dgbackup070222 -g dgroup1 -g dgroup2
md_restore	Restores ASM metadata.	md_restore -t full -g dgroup1 -i / tmp/dgbackup070222
pwd	Locates where you are on the ASM directory tree.	pwd
remap	Remaps a range of physical blocks on disk.	remap data data_0003 6000-8000

Command	Purpose	Example
rm	Removes an ASM directory or file.	rm Current.258.613087119
	rm current*	
	rm -r current*	
rmalias	Removes an ASM alias.	rmalias +cooked_dgroup1/11gDB/data-file/alias_tbs_01.dbf

For the purposes of the OCP exam, we are interested in the md_backup and md_restore commands. The md_backup command provides a way to back up the ASM diskgroup metadata, as seen here:

```
md_backup -b /tmp/dgbackup070222 -g dgroup1 -g dgroup2
```

In this case, we are backing up the ASM metadata from two disk groups, dgroup1 and dgroup2. This backup will be stored in the file system /tmp/dgbackup070222.

Restoring ASM Disk Groups

Restoring ASM disk group metadata is seemingly simple, as you would just use the asmcmd command md_restore, as seen here:

```
md_restore -t full -g dgroup1 -i /tmp/dgbackup070222
```

In this case, we are restoring the metadata for dgroup1 from the backup we took previously. However, it should be said that before attempting such an operation, it's a very good idea to talk to Oracle Support and make sure that this step is truly required.

If you have a normal ASM configuration, it's likely that you don't really need to have backups of the ASM metadata. However, if you have configured unique property definitions, then a backup of the ASM disk group would be worthwhile.

Configuring and Using Oracle Secure Backup

In the previous chapters where we discussed RMAN backup and restores, we discussed how RMAN interfaces with tape devices. We mentioned that to send backups to tape you use the Oracle SBT library API to communicate with the vendor table software, which then manages the movement of the backup data to tape. This architecture works great, but there are some inherent problems with it, such as having to pay vendors additional vendor license fees. To solve these problems, Oracle offers a product called Oracle Secure Backup.

In this section, we will introduce you to Oracle Secure Backup (OSB) and provide you with the information you need to answer the questions you will find on your OCP exam with respect to Oracle Secure Backup. Please note that Oracle Secure Backup has a lot of features and details that we will not cover in this book. Otherwise, the book would probably have to be dedicated to OSB. If you want more detailed information on OSB beyond what you will need for the Oracle OCP exam, we suggest a book coauthored by one of us, Robert Freeman, with Matthew Hart, called *Oracle RMAN 11g Backup and Recovery*. It contains information on OSB and RMAN well beyond what is required for your OCP exam.

> You might consider that reading this book and passing your OCP exam will grant you your bachelor's degree. Reading the *Oracle Database 11g Backup and Recovery* handbook is something like getting your master's in Oracle Database backup studies. That's my story and I'm sticking with it.

In this section, we will discuss the following:

- What is OSB?
- How does OSB interface with RMAN?
- The OSB architecture
- Installing and configuring OSB

tape backup

What Is OSB?

- OSB is a complete tape backup solution provided by Oracle. Previously, if you wanted to back up a database to a vendor tape system, you needed to interface with the vendor libraries. This additional layer of abstraction was often a cause of frustration and confusion because it could be difficult to set up and configure. You were also dependent on the vendor to correctly write their interface into the Oracle SBT media interface.
- OSB offers an all-in-one solution, providing a tape backup management solution that is centralized and enterprise ready.
- OSB comes in two flavors. The first is the standard OSB, and the second is called OSB-XE. OSB-XE is a limited product that is bundled with Oracle Database and provides a basic version of this product that is limited to a single tape device. OSB-XE does not require any license other than the Oracle Database license to operate legally.
- The full-fledged OSB enterprise version requires a license and comes with a number of features, including the following:

  - Support for many different operating systems
  - Integration with Oracle Enterprise Manager

- The ability to back up databases easily through RMAN
- Support for OS file system backups, including OCFS file systems (OCFS is deprecated in Oracle Database 12*c* but is still available.)
- Support for all major tape drives and SAN tape libraries
- Full support for fiber-attached devices as well as Gigabit Ethernet, SCSI, and Infini-Band environments
- Support for all commonly used Internet protocols
- The ability to do incremental backups, duplexing of backups, and backups that span more than one volume
- Support for compression and encryption of backups
- Reduction in the number of support contacts that are required to deal with backup-related issues

• As you can see, OSB provides a large number of features that help reduce the demands on the DBA and provide the best architecture for the enterprise. In this book, we are mostly concerned with databases and how OSB supports database backups. So, let's discuss that next.

How Does OSB Interface with RMAN?

The nice thing about OSB is that if you are already using a vendor tape API to back up or restore your databases (called the SBT interface, as we have mentioned in several chapters), OSB uses the same interface. So, if you are backing up to tape devices, your backup commands will not change. You will still use the SBT library to connect. Thus, a basic BACKUP command might look like this:

```
backup database device type SBT;
```

Notice that the DEVICE TYPE SBT part of the command indicates that you want Oracle to use the MML interface to connect to some existing tape vendor. So, in changing over to OSB, your backup scripts need not change at all if you already use the SBT device.

The one exception to this is if you are including specific commands that need to be sent to the vendor software. In this case, you will probably need to remove those commands from your backup scripts.

The OSB Architecture

The OSB architecture contains a number of different components. These components are logically connected together through the OSB domain, and OSB operations are managed by various OSB daemons. OSB administration is effected through OSB accounts that are secured through the definition of OSB classes and rights. In the next sections, we will discuss each of these components in more detail so you will understand the architecture of OSB.

The OSB Components

The OSB architecture consists of four main components:

The Administrative Server   This server is responsible for starting and stopping backup or recovery jobs within a defined domain. The administrative server software can run on a host where other applications are running; it is not required to have a dedicated server.

The Media Server   This server houses the libraries that you will be backing up to, including tape drives or tape libraries.

The Client   The client consists of one or more hosts where data will be backed up. The client may or may not have Oracle Database running on it.

The Hosts   Any physical server that is running the administrative server, a media server, or a client is considered a host.

The OSB Domain

The OSB domain is a logical collection of hosts that is defined for the purposes of OSB. Each domain is a logically separated entity. For example, you might have a test domain and a production domain that are separated logically, even if they share common physical infrastructures. The test domain cannot access the hosts in the production domain. Thus, depending on the configuration of the domain, you would likely not be able to restore backups from the production domain to the test domain.

A typical OSB domain might consist of an administrative server, a media server with a tape drive attached, and three clients, for a total of five individual hosts.

The OSB Daemons

Various daemon processes will be running on the hosts within the OSB domain, as shown in Table 7.6.

TABLE 7.6   OSB daemons and their descriptions

Daemon Name	Description
Service daemon	This daemon provides general services to OSB on the different hosts in the OSB domain.
Schedule daemon	This daemon supports the OSB scheduler on the administrative server.
Index daemon	This daemon manages the backup catalog on the administrative server.

Daemon Name	Description
Web server daemon	This daemon provides the web interface to OSB for administrative purposes. It runs only on the administrative server.
NDMP daemon	This daemon provides communication services between the different hosts in the domain.
Robot daemon	This daemon provides tape manipulation services to OSB.
Proxy daemon	This daemon runs on clients to validate user access.

OSB Accounts

Two different account types are associated with OSB:

- OSB user accounts
- Operating system accounts

The accounts associated with OSB itself provide access to the OSB interface, allowing you to schedule backups and restores, execute these functions on demand, and execute a number of other functions.

Operating system accounts are used to locate OSB-related software, run the OSB programs, and perform other OSB-related activities. Operating system accounts and OSB accounts are considered to be in different namespaces; thus, an OSB user account and an OSB operating system account can have the same name or different names.

OSB Security

OSB security is managed by OSB classes and OSB rights. An OSB class is created and then assigned OSB rights. Users are then assigned to those OSB classes. You can assign more than one OSB class to a given user, so you can have a hierarchy of OSB rights—perhaps one for backups, one for restores, and another for administrative purposes.

Installing and Configuring OSB

Installing OSB is not difficult. First, you must make sure that the proposed OSB domain conforms to certain requirements. Next, you install OSB. Finally, you configure OSB. You can then use OSB to perform backups.

We'll look at these three steps in installing and configuring OSB in more detail.

OSB comes with an optional OSB cloud module, which provides the ability to do OSB backups to the cloud (such as Amazon cloud services). You will need to download the OSB cloud module separately from Oracle.

OSB Requirements

There are some requirements that you need to meet on each host that will be associated with the individual OSB host installs:

- Each host must be running TCP/IP on the domain.
- Each IP address must be statically assigned, or the DHCP server should be configured to assign the same address to the hosts in the domain.
- Within the OSB domain to be defined, the hostnames must be unique.
- If you are running on Linux systems, then the SCSI generic driver needs to be installed.
- You will need to install OSB on each node of any RAC cluster.

OSB Install

Installing OSB involves the following high-level steps:

1. Download the software.
2. Install the administrator software.
3. Install the media server software.
4. Install the clients.

You can download the OSB software from Oracle's download site quite easily. No license is required to download or install the software.

1. Create a directory in which to install OSB, and then download the software into that directory.
2. Uncompress the download images into the install directory you created.
3. Run the setup command to start the setup process.

   The setup program will then start the installob program, which is the main program that is used to install OSB.

   The setup program will ask you a number of questions to define the various configuration settings. These include passwords, what components to install (you could install all of the components on the same host if you want), the encryption key, and any tape libraries that you might want to connect to.

   Once you've answered the prompts, OSB will be installed on the selected host.
4. When first installing OSB in your environment, install the server first so you can get access to the OSB web tool, which will allow you to configure OSB.

OSB Configuration

Once the administrative server is installed, you should be able to connect to the associated administrative server with your web browser at the web location indicated during the install. Within the web server interface, you can create OSB users, add hosts, configure backups, configure OEM for OSB usage, and define OSB targets.

Once you have configured OSB, you can then proceed to schedule OSB backups of both Oracle Database and the operating system file system. You will need to install the OSB client on any host that you wish to back up with OSB before you can use OSB on that host.

Oracle Database 12*c* Multitenant Architecture and RMAN

Oracle Database 12*c* introduces a complete new architecture called Oracle Multitenant. We will cover the basics of Oracle Multitenant in Chapter 12 of this book. However, in this chapter, it seemed to make sense to include RMAN and backup and recovery operations related to Oracle Multitenant. We also include coverage on using Data Pump with the multitenant architecture in this chapter.

Architecture Overview

Chapter 12 provides a complete overview of Oracle Multitenant, but we felt that a quick overview was important since we will be dealing with some concepts of Oracle Multitenant in this section.

With Oracle Multitenant there are two principal concepts to understand: CDB and PDB. Let's quickly take a look at each of these.

Oracle Multitenant CDB

In previous versions of Oracle, a given database instance would be associated with one, and only one, Oracle database. Oracle Multitenant has turned that principle on its head. Now, the Oracle database instance can service more than one Oracle database.

This new architecture contains three layers, two of which are somewhat new to you:

- The container database (CDB)
- The pluggable database (PDB)
- The underlying schemas in the PDB

The CDB is the top layer. Think of it as the root of the new database architecture. In a way, all of the other databases, the PDBs, are contained in a tree structure that starts underneath the owning CDB.

The CDB contains tablespaces and schemas, and it manages the control files and online redo logs. The CDB is purely administrative in nature, so you should never create objects in the CDB. Connecting to a CDB is like connecting to a non-multitenant database. You simply set the `ORACLE_SID` to the name of the CDB and then you can connect via SQL*Plus. You can also use Oracle Net service naming to connect to the CDB just as you always have.

The logging mode of the entire database is determined at the CDB level. As with a non-multitenant database, the CDB can be in ARCHIVELOG mode or NOARCHIVELOG mode. The functionality of the multitenant database in both modes is unchanged.

The CDB contains a great deal of critical information about the CDB itself and all of the PDBs that are plugged into the CDB. Because of the information contained in the CDB, it must be backed up just like any other Oracle database, even though you don't store objects there. Restoring the CDB is not like restoring a lost control file. You can't simply restore it by issuing a SQL statement. You have to do a physical database restore.

When you create an Oracle multitenant database, you are creating the CDB as well as some PDBs. Now that we have discussed the CDB, let's look at the PDBs and what they do.

Oracle Multitenant PDB

The Oracle PDB (also called a container) is very similar to a non-multitenant Oracle database. The PDB is a named entity that contains tablespaces (and thus physical data files), schemas, schema objects, and the like. A PDB also has its own UNDO tablespace. A PDB does not have its own online redo logs or its own control files.

A PDB is owned by a CDB. A CDB can own one or more PDBs. Thus, if you have three Oracle databases—one for HR (HR), one for Payroll (PAY), and one for Accounts Payable (AP)—you can take each of those databases and plug them into a container database called the CDB. Now, instead of three databases and three instances, you have three databases and one instance. This makes for much more efficient use of memory and other system resources.

While you can connect to an Oracle CDB by setting the ORACLE_SID environment variable, in most cases, you need to connect to a PDB through an Oracle Net service name. When the PDB is created, a service will be created for that PDB with the listener that the CDB is registered with. You will need to update the network naming resolution methods (i.e., tnsnames .ora) to be able to access that service, or you can use the Oracle EZCONNECT string.

PDBs can be plugged in (or installed) or unplugged (removed) from the CDB. Thus, it's easy to move or duplicate databases within a CDB or across CDBs. You simply unplug the database from one CDB and plug it into another CDB. In the process, you might need to move those files, but it's still very simple. You can also easily duplicate a PDB from within a CDB with a very simple process.

We mentioned that when a CDB is created, some PDBs are created at that time. These PDBs include the root container (which is really a CDB but it looks like a PDB) and the seed PDB. See Chapter 12 for more information on the PDBs that are created when the CDB is created and for more information on moving or duplicating PDBs.

What we want to talk about in this chapter is backing up and restoring CDBs and PDBs. We will also discuss using Oracle Data Pump with CDBs and PDBs. With that in mind, let's continue.

Backing Up CDBs with RMAN

We have already discussed using RMAN to backup non-multitenant Oracle databases. Using RMAN with CDBs and PDBs is not very different. In this section, we will briefly discuss backing up CDBs with RMAN.

You are already familiar with backups using RMAN from the last few chapters. When you are working with a multitenant Oracle database, the procedures you will use to back up CDBs are not much different.

When you use RMAN to back up your multitenant database, you use the RMAN BACKUP DATABASE command just as you would when backing up a non-multitenant database. You will also use the same backup database options (such as PLUS ARCHIVELOG DELETE INPUT) as you always have.

In contrast, if you issue a BACKUP TABLESPACE or BACKUP DATAFILE command while connected to the CDB, then the tablespaces or data files of the root CDB are backed up. Tablespaces and data files of all of the PDBs are not backed up. You need to connect directly to the PDB in order to back up specific PDB tablespaces and data files. We will discuss this in the next section.

Here is an example of a full backup of a CDB:

```
C:>set ORACLE_SID=mycdb
rman target=/
backup database plus archivelog delete input;
```

Nothing looks all that different, does it? First, we set the ORACLE_SID to the name of the CDB, which is called mycdb. This is the same thing we do with regular Oracle databases. The result of this backup is that the CDB is backed up and all of the underlying PDBs are also backed up.

Note that in this backup we assumed that the CDB was in ARCHIVELOG mode. If the CDB was in NOARCHIVELOG mode, then we would need to shut down and mount the CDB before starting the backup. We would then need to reopen the CDB and all of the PDBs after the backup was complete.

We simply had RMAN log into the CDB itself. By doing so, when we execute a backup it backs up the entire database. That includes the CDB and all of the PDBs. You can use pretty much all of the RMAN backup features when backing up a CDB. These include things like compressed backups, incremental backups, multisection backups, adding tags, and so on.

Backing Up PDBs with RMAN

Now that we have discussed backing up the CDB with RMAN, the next step is backing up the PDBs. Backing up the individual PDBs is similar to backing up the CDB. In this section, we will discuss backing up the root container, which is part of the overall CDB. We will then discuss backing up individual PDBs in the database with RMAN.

Keep in mind that the normal way to back up the PDBs in the database is to back up everything at the CDB level. Backing up a PDB should not be considered a normal way of backing up an entire CDB.

Recall that a PDB (or a container) is the equivalent of a database. It makes sense, then, that you will need to have a way to back up your PDBs. Typically, your backup process will back up the CDB and all of the subordinate PDBs at the same time.

There may be cases where you will wish to back up specific PDBs. For example, you might have just created or plugged in a PDB and you want to quickly back it up. Or perhaps you have a very active PDB that you want to back up more frequently.

The root container contains critical metadata about the entire CDB. Therefore it makes sense that the root container needs to be backed up. While you typically back up the root container with a complete CDB backup, you may want to back up the root container individually. This is easy to do, as shown in this example:

```
C:>set ORACLE_SID=mycdb
rman target=/
backup database root plus archivelog delete input;
```

Note that we connected directly to the CDB and then used the BACKUP DATABASE command, adding the name of the container we wanted to back up—in this case, the root container.

To back up other PDBs, we will change the BACKUP command slightly, using the BACKUP PLUGGABLE DATABASE command. We still log into the CDB as before, as shown here:

```
C:>set ORACLE_SID=mycdb
rman target=/
backup pluggable database mypdb plus archivelog delete input;
```

The result will be a complete backup of the mypdb database. You can back up more than one PDB at a time, as follows:

```
C:>set ORACLE_SID=mycdb
rman target=/
backup pluggable database mypdb, newpdb plus archivelog delete input;
```

You may want to perform a tablespace or data file backup of a given PDB. To do so you will need to connect to the PDB with RMAN and then execute the backup. Here is an example of backing up the USERS tablespace from the newpdb PDB that is contained within the newcdb database:

```
rman target sys/robert@mypdb
RMAN> backup tablespace users;
```

In this case, we have connected to the mypdb PDB and we are backing up just the USERS tablespace in that PDB. Note that the PDB must be open to perform this operation.

Recovering CDBs and PDBs with RMAN

Recovery of a CDB or a PDB pretty much follows the same steps as recovery of a non-multitenant database. You can perform a recovery of the entire CDB or recover tablespaces or data files specific to the CDB or any PDB. For example, if you wanted to restore an entire CDB from RMAN, you would issue this command from RMAN while connected to the CDB:

```
C:>set ORACLE_SID=mycdb
rman target=/
```

```
restore database;
Recover database;
Alter database open;
```

Looks just the same, doesn't it? You can also restore a specific PDB from RMAN using the RESTORE PLUGGABLE DATABASE command, as shown in this example of restoring the mypdb PDB:

```
C:>set ORACLE_SID=mycdb
rman target=/
Rman>Alter pluggable database mypdb close;
Rman>restore pluggable database mypdb;
Rman>Recover pluggable database mypdb;
Rman>Alter pluggable database mypdb open;
```

Note that you have to close the PDB and then perform the restore using the RESTORE PLUGGABLE DATABASE RMAN command. Then you recover the pluggable database followed by opening the PDB.

You can also perform a point-in-time restore and recovery of an individual PDB using the RESTORE PLUGGABLE DATABASE command, as shown here:

```
C:>set ORACLE_SID=mycdb
rman target=/
Rman>Alter pluggable database mypdb close;
Rman>restore pluggable database mypdb until time 'sysdate-1/24';
Rman>Recover pluggable database mypdb until time 'sysdate-1/24';
Rman>Alter pluggable database mypdb open;
```

Additionally, you can restore specific tablespaces and data files associated with a specific PDB by logging into the PDB and using the RESTORE TABLESPACE, RECOVER TABLESPACE, RESTORE DATAFILE, and RECOVER DATAFILE commands. Here is an example of restoring a tablespace called USERS. You first take the tablespace offline and then restore it. You then recover the tablespace to apply the online redo logs and finally bring it online. Note that the PDB must be open before you can do this.

```
rman target sys/robert@mypdb
Rman>Alter tablespace users offline;
Rman>restore tablespace users;
Rman>Recover tablespace users;
Rman>Alter tablespace users online;
```

Duplicating a PDB with RMAN

The RMAN DUPLICATE command, which we have already discussed, works the same way with a container database. The only thing you need to do is add the

`ENABLE_PLUGGABLE_DATABASE=YES` parameter to the auxiliary instance parameter file. The auxiliary instance that will be created will be a CDB (and thus must be created as a CDB).

With RMAN you can duplicate the entire CDB, a single PDB, or several PDBs. When you duplicate a PDB, the root and seed PDBs are automatically copied over as well. Thus, the duplicated database is a fully functional CDB able to plug in, unplug, and copy PDBs.

The RMAN `DUPLICATE` command provides some additional options when duplicating PDBs:

* `PLUGGABLE DATABASE`—Duplicates the specified PDBs.

* `SKIP PLUGGABLE DATABASE`—Duplicates all PDBs except the PDBs that are listed.

* `TABLESPACE`—Duplicates specific tablespaces within the PDB listed in the option.

* `SKIP TABLESPACE`—Indicates that all tablespaces in the CDB should be duplicated except those listed by PDB.

Here are some examples of commands used to duplicate PDBs. In this first example, we are duplicating the PDB `mypdb1` to the CDB called `mycdb`:

```
DUPLICATE DATABASE TO mycdb PLUGGABLE DATABASE mypdb1;
```

In this example, we will duplicate all PDBs in `mycdb` except the PDB called `skippdb`:

```
DUPLICATE DATABASE TO mycdb SKIP PLUGGABLE DATABASE skippdb;
```

Finally, we can duplicate more than one PDB by using a command similar to this one:

```
DUPLICATE DATABASE TO mycdb PLUGGABLE DATABASE mypdb1,mypdb3;
```

Oracle Data Pump and Oracle Multitenant

Oracle Data Pump fully supports operations in a CDB, but this is quite rare. In most cases, when using Data Pump, you will need to connect directly to the PDB that you wish to export from. Data Pump does not support exporting all PDBs when logged into the root of the CDB. Data Pump will return an error if you attempt that operation.

To properly export a PDB, you must log into the PDB that you want to export and then export that PDB individually. Here is an example where we are exporting the content of the `mypdb` PDB:

```
expdp 'sys/robert@mypdb as sysdba' directory=ROBERT full=y
```

Note that with the exception of needing to log into the PDB specifically, the way you export or import data into a PDB is no different than it is with a non-CDB Oracle database. For example, here we are exporting the `SCOTT` schema. Note that the expdp command is really no different:

```
expdp 'sys/robert@mypdb as sysdba' directory=ROBERT schemas=scott
dumpfile=test.dmp
```

We can import the resulting dumpfile using Data Pump import, as shown here:

```
impdp 'sys/robert@mypdb as sysdba' directory=ROBERT schemas=scott
dumpfile=test.dmp table_exists_action=truncate
```

As you can see, Data Pump supports CDB databases and the PDBs within the CDBs quite nicely.

The Data Recovery Advisor

The Data Recovery Advisor is a feature in Oracle Database 12c that is designed to help you find solutions when a database needs to be restored. The Data Recovery Advisor works with both Multitennant Oracle databases and Oracle databases that are not Multitennant. Let's look at how the Data Recovery Advisor works.

Using the Data Recovery Advisor

When you start a database, you hope that it will just do its thing and magically open. Oracle databases do that so often that the need to restore and recover from a backup is pretty rare. As a result, many new DBAs are not that practiced at restore and recovery. The Data Recovery Advisor can help the new DBA to figure out what the problem is, and what the solution is, when a database fails to start up.

For example, assume we have a multitenant database (this could also just be a regular database and if it were, nothing would be different) called mycdb. When we try to start up the database, we get the following error:

```
SQL> startup
ORACLE instance started.
Total System Global Area 2555445248 bytes
Fixed Size                   2405904 bytes
Variable Size              671091184 bytes
Database Buffers          1862270976 bytes
Redo Buffers                19677184 bytes
Database mounted.
ORA-01157: cannot identify/lock data file 12 - see DBWR trace file
ORA-01110: data file 12:
'C:\APP\ORACLE\ORADATA\MYCDB\7FB9FCBC34324645B4750F9C5FC71A24\DATAFILE\O1_MF_
USERS_9KKGRXH1_.DBF'
```

It appears that the database won't open because we have a problem with a missing data file. If you were a very junior DBA, you might not know exactly what to do in this case. You can use the Data Recovery Advisor to provide the answers that you need.

The Data Recovery Advisor runs from RMAN or from Oracle Enterprise Manager. For the purposes of this book, we will use the RMAN interface to the Data Recovery Advisor.

There are three main steps to process a failure though RMAN:

- Identify the failure with the LIST FAILURE command.
- Use the ADVISE FAILURE command to analyze the failure.
- Repair the failure as recommended by the results generated by the ADVISE FAILURE command.

Once you have executed these three steps, you should be able to open the database. Let's look at an example.

Using the Data Recovery Advisor to Repair a Failure

We just mentioned that when we tried to open our database, we got an error. The error indicated that a data file was probably missing. To use the Data Recovery Advisor, we need to connect the database to RMAN, as shown here:

```
set oracle_sid=mycdb
rman target=/
```

Note that at this point the database is mounted. When the failure occurred, the database instance had been started and the database had completed the mount stage—mounting the control file. With a failure of the type we experienced in this example, the database will stay up in mount mode. This is okay, because we need the database to be mounted to use the Data Recovery Advisor. If you had shutdown the database after the failure, then you would need to re-open it with the STARTUP MOUNT command from RMAN or SQL*Plus.

Now, from the RMAN prompt, we will use the Data Recovery Advisor to see what the failure is. To do so, we will use the LIST FAILURE command, as follows:

```
RMAN> list failure;
using target database control file instead of recovery catalog
Database Role: PRIMARY


List of Database Failures
=========================

Failure ID Priority Status    Time Detected Summary
---------- -------- --------- ------------- -------
822        CRITICAL OPEN      06-MAR-14     System datafile 7: 'C:\APP\ORACLE\
ORADATA\MYCDB\F0C1AB908C5349DD93E43CE41D6A4188\DATAFIL
E\O1_MF_SYSTEM_9KKF33GZ_.DBF' needs media recovery
8          HIGH     OPEN      08-MAR-14     One or more non-system
datafiles are missing
825        HIGH     OPEN      06-MAR-14     One or more non-system datafiles
need media recovery
```

This output pretty much confirms what we already know: we are missing a data file. To find out what to do about that problem we use the ADVISE FAILURE command from RMAN. This command can take a little while to run because it has to analyze the failure and the options that are available to correct the failure. Here is the complete output from the ADVISE FAILURE command that we ran for our test situation:

```
RMAN> advise failure;
Database Role: PRIMARY
List of Database Failures
=========================

Failure ID Priority Status    Time Detected Summary
---------- -------- --------- ------------- -------
822        CRITICAL OPEN      06-MAR-14     System datafile 7:
'C:\APP\ORACLE\ORADATA\MYCDB\F0C1AB908C5349DD93E43CE41D6A4188\DATAFIL
E\01_MF_SYSTEM_9KKF33GZ_.DBF' needs media recovery
8          HIGH     OPEN      08-MAR-14     One or more non-system
atafiles are missing
825        HIGH     OPEN      06-MAR-14     One or more non-system
atafiles need media recovery

analyzing automatic repair options; this may take some time
allocated channel: ORA_DISK_1
channel ORA_DISK_1: SID=5 device type=DISK

analyzing automatic repair options complete
Mandatory Manual Actions
========================
no manual actions available

Optional Manual Actions
=======================
1. If you restored the wrong version of data file C:\APP\ORACLE\ORADATA\MYCDB\
F0C1AB908C5349DD93E43CE41D6A4188\DATAFILE\01_MF_SYSTEM_9KKF33GZ_.DBF, then
replace it with the correct one

2. If file C:\APP\ORACLE\ORADATA\MYCDB\7FB9FCBC34324645B4750F9C5FC71A24\
DATAFILE\01_MF_USERS_9KKGRXH1_.DBF was unintentionally renamed or moved, restore
it

3. If you restored the wrong version of data file C:\APP\ORACLE\ORADATA\MYCDB\
F0C1AB908C5349DD93E43CE41D6A4188\DATAFILE\01_MF_SYSAUX_9KKF33GZ_.DBF, then
replace it with the correct one
```

```
4. If you restored the wrong version of data file C:\APP\ORACLE\ORADATA\MYCDB\
F0C1AB908C5349DD93E43CE41D6A4188\DATAFILE\O1_MF_USERS_9KKF4Z7O_.DBF, then
replace it with the correct one

Automated Repair Options
========================
Option Repair Description
------ ------------------

1      Restore and recover datafile 12; Recover datafile 7; Recover datafile 8;
...
Strategy: The repair includes complete media recovery with no data loss
Repair script: C:\APP\ORACLE\diag\rdbms\mycdb\mycdb\hm\reco_2067260308.hm
```

There are several things to notice in this output:

1. First is the repeated output of the LIST FAILURE command.

2. Next, RMAN begins to review the errors and generate recovery actions.

3. Then RMAN displays the manual recovery actions that are available.

   For example, if the data file were there but just offline, the manual action might be to bring the data file back online. In our case, there are no manual actions available because the data file is missing.

4. Next, you will see some optional manual actions.

   In this case, these actions are there for us to perform in case we accidently renamed the file or copied the wrong file into place. None of these is the case here.

5. Finally, you see the Automated Repair Options section.

   This section provides you with the actions needed to restore and recover the missing data file. In this case, we are being told to restore three data files (12, 7, and 8). Note that the output also includes a repair script, which contains the commands needed to restore and recover the database. The repair script is the place to check for all of the commands that need to be used.

At this point, we could manually run the RMAN commands to restore and recover the data files in question. If we wanted to further exercise the Data Recovery Advisor, we could then use the REPAIR FAILURE command, as shown here (we have removed the output of the actual repair since it isn't important to the overall concept we are trying to teach):

```
RMAN> repair failure;
Strategy: The repair includes complete media recovery with no data loss
Repair script: C:\APP\ORACLE\diag\rdbms\mycdb\mycdb\hm\reco_3183092618.hm
contents of repair script:
   # recover datafile
   sql 'MYPDB' 'alter database datafile 7, 8, 9 offline';
   recover datafile 7, 8, 9;
   sql 'MYPDB' 'alter database datafile 7, 8, 9 online';
```

```
Do you really want to execute the above repair (enter YES or NO)? YES
executing repair script
```

Once the restore is complete, all we need to do is open the PDB:

```
RMAN> alter pluggable database mypdb open;
Statement processed
```

Note that the actions you take to restore a database will differ based on the nature of the failure. However the Data Recovery Advisor will take into account the nature of the failure, the type of database you are running (ARCHIVELOG, NOARCHIVLOG, CDB, non-CDB) and perform the type of restore that would be required for that database and the failure that was experienced.

Summary

WHEW! This is a long chapter and we have covered quite a bit of material. I think now is a good time to grab a drink and just mull over everything that you have read. I'd even suggest something sweet to get your blood sugar level up a little bit because this has been heavy, skull crushing, reading.

In this chapter, we talked about some advanced RMAN recovery concepts. First, we talked about changing database incarnations. You will want to know how to change incarnations of your database because this provides the ability to restore your database from previous incarnations in certain cases.

The ability of RMAN to duplicate databases is very powerful. The Oracle OCP exam will include questions about this functionality, and we strongly suggest you go through the exercise of performing database duplication. The first few times, it can be a frustrating exercise, but it's well worth the experience.

Oracle Database 12*c* offers a number of different options with respect to database duplication, so make sure you understand what these different options are and when they can, or should, be used.

Tablespace point-in-time recovery is an RMAN feature that makes recovering tablespaces to specific points in time easy to do. We covered the basics of TSPITR, which you will need to know for your OCP exam, but we encourage you to do further research into more customized methods of doing TSPITR that might meet your unique needs.

Also in this chapter, we discussed disaster recovery. This is the end game of backup and recovery (or as one person once told us, it should be called recovery and backup since *recovery* is the really important part). We gave you an outline of the process to follow to get your database back up to speed should you lose the whole database server.

We also took that discussion a bit further and addressed ways to copy a database to a new host. We dealt with byte semantic incompatibility issues, database duplication, backup and restore with RMAN, and other methods that might be used in different cases.

We discussed Oracle's strategy for data warehouse backups. This strategy provides the ability to just perform one full database backup and then forever after you perform incremental backups of the database, which are used to update the database backup itself.

We also talked about Oracle Secure Backup, which is a new topical area in the Oracle Database 12c OCP exam. We discussed downloading, installing, and configuring OSB.

We also discussed tablespace point-in-time recovery, which is a very powerful feature provided by Oracle RMAN.

Oracle 12c provides the ability to recover tables and partitions from RMAN backups. We discussed that in detail in this chapter. This feature alone might well remove the need to have regular Data Pump exports of your database for backup purposes.

We then moved on to discuss backup considerations of ASM metadata. We showed you how to back up and restore the ASM metadata. We also discussed Oracle's Data Recovery Advisor, which can help you to figure out the best way to restore and recover your database.

Finally, we discussed Oracle Multitenant and some of the considerations that you need to understand with respect to backup and recovery through RMAN. We also discussed Oracle Data Pump with respect to Oracle Multitenant.

Exam Essentials

Describe database incarnations.   Understand how to use the SET DATABASE INCARNATION command. Know what a database incarnation is and when a given incarnation changes.

Describe database duplication.   There are two kinds of database duplication, active and backup-based. Understand that when you use backup-based duplication: the backup set pieces must be available on the host to which you are duplicating. Understand that active database duplication occurs over the network. Know how to set up for database duplication.

Describe tablespace point-in-time recovery.   Be able to list the benefits of tablespace point-in-time recovery. Understand how to perform a tablespace point-in-time recovery and what the restrictions are.

Describe disaster-recovery basics.   Understand how to restore a system from a complete disaster using both RMAN-based backup sets and user-managed recovery.

Describe Oracle Database 12c multitenant operations with respect to backup and recovery. Understand how to use RMAN to back up and restore Oracle Database 12c multitenant databases including CDBs and individual PDBs.

Duplicate multitenant databases with RMAN.   Understand how to duplicate an entire CDB or one or more PDBs to another CDB using RMAN.

Describe Oracle Database 12c multitenant operations with respect to Oracle Data Pump. Understand how to use Oracle Data Pump to export PDBs and how to use Oracle Data Pump to import into PDBs.

Review Questions

1. True or false: RMAN supports duplication of only the entire CDB to another CDB.

   A. True

   B. False

2. Which command is used to begin a tablespace point-in-time recovery?

   A. RESTORE TABLESPACE

   B. RECOVER TABLESPACE

   C. TABLESPACE RECOVER

   D. RECOVER TO TIME

   E. RECOVER DATAFILE

3. When you're performing active database duplication, a backup of what kind is required?

   A. A current RMAN backup-set backup is required.

   B. No backup is required.

   C. An RMAN image backup is required.

   D. A manual backup is required.

   E. A duplicate preparatory backup is required.

4. Which of the following commands will perform an active database duplication of the ORCL database to the ORCL2 database?

   A.

```
Set oracle_sid=orcl
rman target=sys/robert auxname=sys/Robert@orcl2
create duplicate target database to neworcl from
active database nofilenamecheck
spfile set control_files 'c:\oracle\oradata\neworcl\control01.ctl',
'c:\oracle\oradata\neworcl\control02.ctl'
set db_file_name_convert
'c:\oracle\oradata\orcl','c:\oracle\oradata\neworcl'
set log_file_name_convert
'c:\oracle\oradata\orcl','c:\oracle\oradata\neworcl';
```

   B.

```
Set oracle_sid=orcl
rman target=sys/robert auxname=sys/Robert@orcl2
```

```
duplicate target database nofilenamecheck
spfile set control_files 'c:\oracle\oradata\neworcl\control01.ctl',
'c:\oracle\oradata\neworcl\control02.ctl'
set db_file_name_convert
'c:\oracle\oradata\orcl','c:\oracle\oradata\neworcl'
set log_file_name_convert
'c:\oracle\oradata\orcl','c:\oracle\oradata\neworcl';
```

C.

```
Set oracle_sid=orcl
rman target=sys/robert auxname=sys/Robert@orcl2
duplicate target database to neworcl nofilenamecheck
spfile set control_files 'c:\oracle\oradata\neworcl\control01.ctl',
'c:\oracle\oradata\neworcl\control02.ctl'
set db_file_name_convert
'c:\oracle\oradata\orcl','c:\oracle\oradata\neworcl'
set log_file_name_convert
'c:\oracle\oradata\orcl','c:\oracle\oradata\neworcl';
```

D.

```
Set oracle_sid=orcl
rman target=sys/robert auxname=sys/Robert
duplicate target database to neworcl from active database
nofilenamecheck
spfile set control_files 'c:\oracle\oradata\neworcl\control01.ctl',
'c:\oracle\oradata\neworcl\control02.ctl'
set db_file_name_convert
'c:\oracle\oradata\orcl','c:\oracle\oradata\neworcl'
set log_file_name_convert
'c:\oracle\oradata\orcl','c:\oracle\oradata\neworcl';
```

E.

```
Set oracle_sid=orcl
rman target=sys/robert auxname=sys/Robert@orcl2
duplicate target database to neworcl from active database
nofilenamecheck
spfile set control_files 'c:\oracle\oradata\neworcl\control01.ctl',
'c:\oracle\oradata\neworcl\control02.ctl'
set db_file_name_convert
'c:\oracle\oradata\orcl','c:\oracle\oradata\neworcl'
set log_file_name_convert
'c:\oracle\oradata\orcl','c:\oracle\oradata\neworcl';
```

5. How many database instances are used during a database-duplication process?

   A. One

   B. Two

   C. Three

   D. Four

   E. Five

6. What command is used to reset a database to a previous incarnation?

   A. `RESET INCARNATION`

   B. `INCARNATION RESET`

   C. `RESET DATABASE TO INCARNATION`

   D. `RESET DATABASE INCARNATION`

   E. `RESET DATABASE INCARNATION NUMBER`

7. What view would you use to determine if a given tablespace is fully self-contained for the execution of a tablespace point-in-time recovery?

   A. `TS_CHECK`

   B. `TPITR_CHECK`

   C. `TS_PITR_CHECK`

   D. `CHECK_TSPITR`

   E. `PITR_TS_CHECK`

8. Which of the following is true with respect to multitenant backups?

   A. You cannot use RMAN to restore a PDB.

   B. You cannot use Oracle Data Pump if the source database is a PDB.

   C. Oracle Data Pump can export from only a single PDB at a time.

   D. You cannot use RMAN to back up an entire CDB database.

   E. All of the above are false statements.

9. When performing a database duplication, which `DUPLICATE DATABASE` parameter would you set to ensure that the online redo logs are created in the correct location?

   A. `LOG_FILE_NAME_CONVERT`

   B. `CONVERT_LOG_FILE_NAME`

   C. `FILE_NAME_CONVERT_LOG`

   D. `REDO_LOG_FILE_NAME_CONVERT`

   E. `LOGFILE_CONVERT_DIRECTORY`

10. Which command would correctly start a TSPITR of the USERS tablespace?

    A.

    ```
    recover tablespace users
    until time '10/06/2013:22:42:00' auxiliary 'c:\oracle\auxiliary';
    ```

    B.

    ```
    recover tablespace users
    time '10/06/2013:22:42:00' auxiliary destination 'c:\oracle\auxiliary';
    ```

    C.

    ```
    recover tablespace users
    to point-in-time '10/06/2013:22:42:00'
    auxiliary destination 'c:\oracle\auxiliary';
    ```

    D.

    ```
    recover tablespace users
    except time '10/06/2013:22:42:00'
     auxiliary destination 'c:\oracle\auxiliary';
    ```

    E.

    ```
    recover tablespace users
    until time '10/06/2013:22:42:00'
    auxiliary destination 'c:\oracle\auxiliary';
    ```

11. True or false: You can perform an active database duplication when the database is in NOARCHIVELOG mode.

    A. True

    B. False

12. When running the tablespace point-in-time RECOVER command

    ```
    recover tablespace users
    until time '10/06/2013:22:42:00'
    auxiliary destination 'c:\oracle\auxiliary';
    ```

    you receive the following error:

    ```
    RMAN-00571: ===========================================================
    RMAN-00569: =============== ERROR MESSAGE STACK FOLLOWS ===============
    RMAN-00571: ===========================================================
    RMAN-03002: failure of recover command at 10/08/2013 16:00:30
    RMAN-20202: Tablespace not found in the recovery catalog
    RMAN-06019: could not translate tablespace name "USERS"
    ```

What is the likely cause of the error?

A. The database is in ARCHIVELOG mode.

B. There is no current backup of the database available.

C. The USERS tablespace has dependent objects in other tablespaces and cannot be a part of a TSPITR alone.

D. The USERS tablespace is not eligible for TSPITR because it has invalid objects.

E. The RECOVER TABLESPACE command is incorrect and generates the error.

13. Which of the following restrictions are not true with respect to tablespace point-in-time recovery? (Choose all that apply.)

A. The target database must be in NOARCHIVELOG mode.

B. No backup is required of the database before you perform a TSPITR.

C. You must have all archived redo logs generated since the last backup up to the point to which you want to restore the transport set.

D. If you rename a tablespace, you can not perform a TSPITR to any point in time before that rename operation occurred.

E. If you have tables in tablespace_1 that have associated constraints in tablespace_2, then you must transport both tablespaces.

14. If you are going to run a TSPITR recovery, which view will help you to determine which objects will be lost during the TSPITR?

A. TS_OBJECTS_TO_BE_DROPPED

B. TS_PTTR_OBJECT_DROPPED

C. TS_PITR_OBJECTS_TO_BE_DROPPED

D. TS_OBJECTS_DROPPED

E. TS_DROPPED_OBJECTS

15. You're performing tablespace point-in-time recovery on a tablespace called USERS. If an object in that tablespace has a foreign key constraint owned by another object in the INDEX_TBS, which statement is true?

A. You cannot perform the TSPITR with the constraints enabled.

B. You must perform the TSPITR recovery of both tablespaces for it to be successful.

C. You can perform TSPITR only on the USERS tablespace.

D. RMAN will determine if the INDEX_TBS tablespace must also be duplicated and will duplicate it automatically.

E. The TSPITR will be successful only if the constraint is enabled.

16. When issuing the DUPLICATE DATABASE command, you use the parameter DB_FILE_ NAME_CONVERT. For what purpose do you use this parameter?

    A. To indicate the location of the auxiliary-instance online redo logs.

    B. To indicate the location of the target database data files.

    C. To indicate the location of the auxiliary-instance control file and online redo logs.

    D. To indicate the location of the auxiliary-instance database data files.

    E. This is not a valid parameter when duplicating a database.

17. What is the end result of the following commands?

```
recover tablespace users
until time '10/06/2013:22:42:00'
auxiliary destination 'c:\oracle\auxiliary';
sql 'alter tablespace users online';
recover tablespace users
until time '10/06/2013:20:40:00'
auxiliary destination 'c:\oracle\auxiliary';
sql 'alter tablespace users online';
```

    A. The commands will be successful. The USERS tablespace will be recovered until 10/06/2013 at 20:40.

    B. The first RECOVER TABLESPACE command will fail because the syntax is incorrect.

    C. The first ALTER TABLESPACE USERS ONLINE command will fail because the tablespace will already be online after the RECOVER command.

    D. The second RECOVER TABLESPACE command will fail because it will be unable to complete the recovery.

    E. The second ALTER TABLESPACE USERS ONLINE command will fail because you cannot perform two TSPITRs in a row without backing up the database between the first and the last recovery.

18. Which of the following is not a valid method of duplicating a database?

    A. Connect to target, connect to auxiliary, do not connect to catalog and perform active database duplication.

    B. Connect to auxiliary, don't connect to target, don't connect to the catalog and perform an active database duplication.

    C. Connect to auxiliary, connect to the catalog and perform a normal database duplication.

    D. Connect to the target in ARCHIVELOG mode, connect to the auxiliary and connect to the catalog database and perform an active database duplication.

    E. All of the above are valid options.

19. Which of the following is a capability of Oracle Secure Backup? (Choose all that apply.)

   A. Directly connects to vendor tape devices

   B. Still uses SBT RMAN channels

   C. Provides the ability to perform OS backups

   D. Provides a function to allow for the creation of a database that uses Oracle copy on write technologies

   E. Provides an interface into Oracle Support that allows you to directly submit Oracle Database support tickets

20. Which command do you use to generate a report of database incarnations?

   A. `LIST INCARNATION OF DATABASE`

   B. `REPORT INCARNATION OF DATABASE`

   C. `LIST DATABASE INCARNATION`

   D. `DATABASE INCARNATION LIST`

   E. `REPORT DATABASE INCARNATION`

Understanding Flashback Technology

ORACLE DATABASE 12*c*: ADVANCED ADMINISTRATION EXAM OBJECTIVES COVERED IN THIS CHAPTER:

✓ **Using Flashback Technologies**

- ▪ Describe the Flashback technologies
- ▪ Use Flashback to query data
- ▪ Perform Flashback Table operations
- ▪ Describe and use Flashback Data Archive

✓ **Using Flashback Database**

- ▪ Perform Flashback Database

If you have been working through this book chapter by chapter, you should have a pretty firm grasp of Oracle backup and recovery methods available through RMAN. For the most part, RMAN works in the physical realm. It provides recovery from physical problems such as physical block corruption, failed hardware, missing files, and so on. It is vital for a database administrator to be able to recover from these types of problems, and RMAN is definitely the tool for the job.

But database administrators must also have tools to deal with *logical corruption* in the database. Logical corruption, for the most part, is synonymous with the term *user error.* Rather than having a physical problem with your database, you have a problem with the data in your database. Here are some examples:

- A developer accidentally drops a table.
- A programming bug causes data updates to populate the wrong records.
- The DBA is purging data and accidentally deletes the wrong rows.
- An inadvertent table TRUNCATE takes place.

Logical corruption is far more common than physical corruption. And although RMAN could certainly be used to recover from logical corruption, a full-blown recovery effort is time-consuming and generally involves database downtime.

In these situations, Flashback technology provides the solution. It allows dropped objects to be recovered. It allows queries to view data as it existed at a point in time in the past, and it allows queries to view a history of changes made to data. It even allows returning the entire database to a point in time or system change number (SCN). Having a thorough understanding of the many Flashback options will not only help you pass your OCP exam; it will help you to be a better DBA.

This chapter offers a detailed explanation of the functionality provided by Flashback technology as it exists in Oracle Database 12*c* (Oracle 12*c*).

Initially, we will provide a brief overview of Flashback functionality and where it fits in the database administrator's arsenal. We will also examine Automatic Undo Management, the cornerstone upon which key Flashback technologies rely. Next, we will examine the various Flashback options:

- Flashback Drop and the Recycle Bin
- Flashback Query
- Flashback Version Query
- Flashback Transaction

- Flashback Temporal Validity Query
- Flashback Table
- Flashback Data Archive
- Flashback Database

For each of these options, we will discuss the requirements, capabilities, and limitations in detail.

Describe the Flashback Technologies

Oracle Flashback technology consists of Oracle Database features that let you view database objects as they were at a previous point in time or return objects to a prior state without performing point-in-time media recovery. Flashback technology was first introduced in Oracle Database 9*i*. Since then, it has been steadily improved with each successive Oracle release. In Oracle Database 12*c*, it represents a mature and time-tested technology.

Flashback technology consists of a set of tools that allow users to recover from logical data errors without resorting to a database recovery. However, Flashback can do much more.

Recycle Bin   The Recycle Bin allows dropped objects to persist in the database, and the Flashback Drop option allows the objects to be restored.

Flashback Query   The Flashback Query option allows the user to query tables as they looked at a specific point in the past.

Flashback Version Query   The Flashback Version Query option allows the user to retrieve a historical view of data as it changed over time. In other words, if a column had been updated multiple times, Flashback Version Query could provide a list of each of the values and the date and time that they were changed.

Flashback Transaction Query   Flashback Transaction Query is a useful diagnostic tool that allows the user to retrieve detailed transaction information for previously executed transactions. It can run for a single transaction or for all transactions that occurred during a specified time frame.

Flashback Table   Flashback Table allows point-in-time recovery (recovering one or more tables to a specified point in the past) without the need to take any part of the database offline. This offers a very desirable alternative to performing a full-blown point-in-time recovery.

Flashback Database   Flashback Database is best used as a replacement for incomplete recovery of the entire database. The main benefit of Oracle Flashback Database over incomplete database recovery is that Flashback Database is much quicker and more efficient. Flashback Database is not based on undo data but on flashback logs. It is best suited to recovering from errors such as truncating a large table, an incomplete batch job, or a dropped user.

As you can see, Flashback offers a wide variety of tools for the DBA. However, these options are not exclusive to the DBA. In fact, one of the key advantages to the various

Flashback technologies is that they do not require DBA-level privileges. Users and developers can utilize them to recover from their own errors without DBA intervention (except for Flashback Database).

Managing Undo Automatically

Before we can delve too deeply into Flashback technologies, it is important to understand that all of the Flashback options covered in this chapter, except for Flashback Database and Flashback Drop, work in conjunction with Oracle's undo functionality. Without undo, there would be no Flashback. In fact, without undo, transaction processing as we know it would not exist.

The topics of undo and undo management should not be new to you and will not be covered in depth here. However, we believe that a brief overview of the subject will be helpful in better understanding Flashback technologies and how they work.

In the following sections, you will take a look at undo and *Automatic Undo Management (AUM)*. First, we will define undo and its purpose. You will discover how Oracle can automatically manage undo on your behalf. Then you will learn how undo sizing and undo record retention play a key role in Flashback technologies.

Uncovering Undo

So what exactly is "undo" and why does it need to be managed? Undo is a key component of the Oracle database that stores a record of every change made to data in the database. This record contains the data necessary to undo the change (in other words, roll back the transaction) and restore the data to its previous condition. For example, when a row in a table is updated, Oracle will create an undo record that stores the data that was changed. If a new row is inserted into a table, an undo record will be created that will effectively delete the row.

Maintaining undo records serves multiple purposes in the database:

- Transaction processing
- Failed-transaction recovery
- Read consistency
- Flashback functionality

Let's look at each of these individually.

Processing Transactions

Transaction processing allows SQL statements to be grouped into discrete units of work that can be committed or rolled back as one. The classic example is that of woman walking into a bank and asking to transfer $500 from her checking account to her savings account. Behind the scenes, two SQL statements are executed: one that subtracts $500 from her checking-account balance and one that adds $500 to her savings-account balance.

Now, suppose the bank's computer system crashed after completing the first statement but not the second. The money would be gone from her checking account but never added to her savings account. She would be out $500 on the deal. Instead, the two statements must be treated as a single, logical unit of work (in other words, a transaction). Only when both statements have completed successfully should the changes be committed. If either fails, they must both be rolled back.

When a user changes data in a table (via insert, update, or delete), the change does not occur immediately. The user must either commit the change (finalize it) or roll it back (undo it). Until they do, the database must keep track of both versions of the data (before the change and after the change).

In order to meet this requirement, the database will modify the data in the table to reflect the change and create an *undo record* in the undo tablespace that contains any data needed to undo the change.

Although the transaction remains in limbo (neither committed nor rolled back), other users who query the table will see the data as it looked prior to the change. If the user decides to roll back the transaction, the undo information is used to modify the table data to revert it to its previous value. If the user decides to commit the transaction, the change becomes permanent.

From strictly a transaction-processing standpoint (allowing a transaction the option of committing or rolling back), the undo records for a transaction are useless after the transaction finishes. They have served their purpose and could be deleted. However, by retaining undo information for a period of time after a commit, many new options become available to us.

As you will see as you continue through this chapter, the whole host of Flashback options becomes available by the simple act of retaining undo records for a period of time after they have been committed.

Recovering Failed Transactions

A failed transaction is a transaction that never completes; that is, it never commits or rolls back. This can happen for a variety of reasons, but they all boil down to a session closing with a transaction still in progress.

Since most (if not all) Oracle clients are designed to either commit or roll back automatically when a session is closed, simply forgetting to finish a transaction before exiting will rarely result in a failed transaction. In general, a failed transaction occurs because of an abnormal server shutdown (because of hardware failure, loss of power, or even a shutdown abort).

When a failed transaction is discovered (generally at startup time following an abnormal shutdown), Oracle will undo the transaction automatically using the data stored in the undo tablespace.

Maintaining Read Consistency

When a user issues a query, the database is required to process the query and return the data as it looked at the moment the query started. In other words, if you kicked off a long-running query at 10 a.m. and it finished at 10:15 a.m., the data should not reflect changes (committed or uncommitted) made by other users in the interim.

To fulfill this requirement, Oracle must retain undo records after their associated transaction has been committed. The length of time that it chooses to retain this data is governed by the undo retention period, which will be covered later in this chapter.

Flashback functions allow users to view elements of the database as they appeared at a certain point in time. These functions will be described in much more detail later in this chapter.

Much like the read-consistency requirements, Flashback requires that undo records be retained for a period of time after the associated transaction has completed.

In short, the undo feature creates and maintains records of all transactions that occur in the database and stores the data necessary to undo them. By maintaining these records throughout the life of a transaction, undo provides transaction management and read-consistency capabilities. By maintaining these records after the transaction has been committed, undo provides read-consistency and Flashback options.

Working with Automatic Undo Management

Undo data is temporary. In that respect, the undo tablespace is similar to a temporary tablespace. Information is written there to fulfill a temporary need. As soon as the information is no longer needed, it can be removed to make room for new undo data. Keeping things running smoothly requires a considerable amount of management. Luckily, Oracle offers the Automatic Undo Management feature.

Automatic Undo Management (AUM) is a feature whereby Oracle will handle all undo management tasks without interaction from the DBA. AUM is not a new feature in Oracle Database 12*c*; beginning with Oracle Database 11*g*, AUM is enabled by default. In prior Oracle versions, manual undo management was the default setting.

When creating a new database with the Database Configuration Assistant (DBCA), Oracle will perform the following actions:

1. Create an undo tablespace named UNDOTBS1.

2. Configure the undo tablespace to autoextend.

3. Add an UNDO_MANAGEMENT=AUTO initialization parameter.

These three steps ensure that Oracle will automatically manage the undo needs for the database.

Automatic Undo Management must ensure that Oracle can store undo information for all new transactions as they occur. This means that adequate space must be available in the undo tablespace.

By creating an autoextending undo tablespace, Oracle can extend the size as needed to maintain adequate undo information.

So how long should Oracle retain committed undo information? The simple answer is, long enough to satisfy the undo retention period. The undo retention period represents the minimum amount of time that Oracle will attempt to retain committed undo information before allowing it to be overwritten.

In Oracle Database 12*c*, if the UNDO_MANAGEMENT initialization parameter is set to NULL or omitted, the database will default to AUTO. Please note that it is still possible to run the database in manual undo management mode. This can be done by changing the initialization parameter to UNDO_MANAGEMENT=MANUAL. However, Oracle strongly advises against it.

Preserving Data with Undo Retention

The undo functionality of Oracle Database 12*c* is governed by a setting known as the undo retention period. The undo retention period represents the minimum time (expressed in seconds) that committed undo information should be retained in the undo tablespace.

To ensure read consistency, the undo retention period should be set to a value larger than the runtime of your longest-running query. If your longest-running query takes 60 minutes to run and you retain undo information for 65 minutes, your system should not encounter any ORA-01555 Snapshot too old errors.

To make sure that undo data is available for Flashback operations, the undo retention period should be set long enough to retain adequate data to support your Flashback needs. For example, if you want to always maintain a 4-hour window in which to undo data changes, then the setting should be at least 14400 (4 hours expressed in seconds).

It is important to understand that the undo retention setting is actually a target for AUM to achieve; it does not guarantee that data will actually be retained for the entire time. There are circumstances under which AUM may choose to violate the undo retention period, for example, if the undo tablespace is a fixed size and is not large enough to accommodate committed transaction data for the retention period.

Undo data is considered to be in one of three possible states at any given time: uncommitted, unexpired, or expired.

Uncommitted State   Uncommitted data is undo data corresponding to a transaction that has been neither committed nor rolled back. Undo data in this state will remain in the undo tablespace indefinitely. It will never be removed based on the retention period.

Unexpired State   Once data has been committed, it enters the unexpired state. This effectively starts the timer running on the retention-period clock. It will remain in this state until the retention period has elapsed.

Expired State   When the retention period has elapsed, the data will enter the expired state, meaning the data has been retained for the requested amount of time. The expired state tells Oracle that the data is now eligible to be purged from the undo tablespace to make room for new data.

By keeping track of the state of all undo data, AUM can manage the space and ensure adequate space for new transactions. But suppose a new transaction begins when the undo tablespace is full and none of the undo data is expired? Oracle will attempt to extend the tablespace (if it is enabled) to make more space. If autoextend is not possible (because it is not enabled or it has reached the MAXSIZE), Oracle must make a choice. It can either forego the retention period by removing unexpired data or honor the retention period, thereby causing the new transaction to fail. By default, Oracle will choose to sacrifice the unexpired data to make room for the new transaction.

In the following sections, you will learn how an undo retention period can be established and what effect it will have. You will also learn about the power and the pitfalls of guaranteeing undo retention.

Establishing an Undo Retention Period

As part of its management duties, AUM monitors system activity and available undo space to derive an optimum undo retention time. This setting may change over time as activity and available space change. Since AUM takes care of this, there is no action required by the DBA to establish an undo retention period.

However, AUM will also allow you to specify the retention period yourself. It can be done by setting the UNDO_RETENTION initialization parameter, as shown here:

```
SQL> ALTER SYSTEM SET UNDO_RETENTION=14400
    SCOPE=BOTH;


System altered
```

When AUM encounters a manual undo retention setting, it will honor the setting only if it is using an autoextending tablespace. If AUM is configured with a fixed-size tablespace, it will ignore the setting and will instead follow its default behavior of dynamically setting the retention time based on system activity and available disk space.

Because of this behavior, it is highly recommended that you allow AUM to use an autoextending undo tablespace. If you are concerned that an errant long-running query could cause it to extend too much, use the MAXSIZE option to limit its growth.

Guaranteeing Retention

As mentioned previously, Oracle will violate the undo retention period if it is required to prevent transactions from failing. For most users, it is a fair trade-off. However, there may be situations where it is more important to guarantee the retention period, even at the expense of failed transactions. This can be accomplished by specifying the RETENTION GUARANTEE clause on the undo tablespace. This can be done either when initially creating the tablespace or by altering the tablespace, as shown here:

```
SQL> ALTER TABLESPACE UNDOTBS1 RETENTION
    GUARANTEE;


Tablespace altered.
```

When the clause is invoked on the undo tablespace, Oracle will never remove unexpired data from the undo tablespace, even if it means allowing new transactions to fail.

Using the RETENTION GUARANTEE option is a mixed blessing and one that must be carefully considered. On the one hand, you ensure that undo records necessary for all of your Flashback and read-consistency needs will be retained. On the other hand, if space runs out and the undo tablespace cannot be extended, Oracle will stubbornly enforce the guarantee and allow new transactions to fail.

To summarize, these sections offered you a brief overview of undo and AUM. First, you learned about undo and its purpose. You saw how Oracle automatically manages undo on your behalf. And you learned how undo sizing and undo record retention play a key role in Flashback technologies. But what exactly are Flashback technologies? You are about to find out.

Employing Flashback Technologies

In the following sections, we will explore each of the various Flashback options and provide examples of how they can be used in the real world. First, we will discuss the Flashback Drop option and the Recycle Bin and how the two work together to recover dropped objects in the database. Next, we will use the Flashback Query option to view data as it existed at a point in the past.

We will continue on to discuss Flashback Version Query, and you'll learn how to retrieve a historical view of changes made to the database. We will show how to use the Flashback Transaction Query option to retrieve information about past transactions and then show how to use the Flashback Transaction functionality to reverse those transactions.

Recovering Tables and Objects with Flashback Drop and the Recycle Bin

In Oracle Database 10g, the *Recycle Bin* feature was added to the Oracle database. This feature enabled tables (and their associated objects) to persist in the database after they were dropped. Oracle 10g also introduced the Flashback Drop feature, which allows objects to be recovered from the Recycle Bin. These features remain largely unchanged in Oracle Database 12c.

The Recycle Bin is a logical container for dropped tables and their associated objects (indexes, constraints, triggers, nested tables, large-object [LOB] segments, and LOB index segments).

When a table is dropped in Oracle Database 12c, it is not actually removed from the database. Instead, it is moved into the Recycle Bin. These objects remain in the Recycle Bin until they are purged explicitly or due to space pressure (permanently removed) or restored via the Flashback Drop feature.

In this section, we will cover the usage of the Recycle Bin, including how to use it, how to purge objects from it, how to enable and disable it, and how to recover objects from it using *Flashback Drop*.

Because the Recycle Bin is a logical container, as opposed to a physical container, there is no Recycle Bin tablespace or data file into which the dropped objects are moved. Instead, the objects remain in their original tablespace and are simply renamed using a special naming convention. This naming convention ensures that database objects with the same name will not be assigned duplicate identifiers when they are moved into the Recycle Bin.

Demonstrating How the Recycle Bin Works

To demonstrate how objects interact with the Recycle Bin, this section will provide a series of examples showing how a dropped table is represented in the Recycle Bin. We will use the HR sample schema provided with the 12*c* database and grant DBA privileges to the HR schema to simplify the execution of the examples. To begin, we first must drop a table, as shown here:

```
SQL> drop table job_history;

Table dropped.
```

Once the table has been dropped, our next step is to view the contents of the Recycle Bin to verify that the table is truly there. One simple way to do this is to use the SHOW RECYCLEBIN command, as shown here:

```
SQL> show recyclebin
ORIGINAL NAME    RECYCLEBIN NAME                 OBJECT TYPE  DROP TIME
---------------- ------------------------------ ------------ --------------------
JOB_HISTORY      BIN$2siLENifTmCBmAu0+mXAuQ==$0 TABLE        2013-09-16:12:45:37
```

For a table to be recoverable using Flashback Drop, it can't reside in the SYSTEM tablespace, and the tablespace in which it resides must be locally managed.

The SHOW RECYCLEBIN command confirms that our table now resides in the Recycle Bin, as expected. It also provides several other pieces of useful information. These are described in Table 8.1.

TABLE 8.1 SHOW RECYCLEBIN Columns

Column Name	Description
ORIGINAL NAME	This column stores the original name of the object (at the time when it was dropped).

Column Name	Description
RECYCLEBIN NAME	This column shows the system-assigned name of the object. This is the object's unique identifier within the Recycle Bin.
OBJECT TYPE	This column shows the type of the object (TABLE, INDEX, and so on).
DROP_TIME	This column shows the timestamp corresponding to the dropping of the object.

Next, we will create a new table named JOB_HISTORY, insert some data, and then drop it. We will then look in the Recycle Bin to verify that both tables are there, even though both tables had the same name.

```
SQL> create table job_history (job_id number) tablespace users;

Table created.

SQL> insert into job_history values(1);

1 row created.

SQL> commit;

Commit complete.

SQL> drop table job_history;

Table dropped.

SQL> show recyclebin
ORIGINAL NAME    RECYCLEBIN NAME                 OBJECT TYPE  DROP TIME
---------------  ------------------------------  -----------  -------------------


JOB_HISTORY      BIN$2siLENifTmCBmAu0+mXAuQ==$0 TABLE         2013-09-16:12:45:37
JOB_HISTORY      BIN$NIaEC81/SJ24Dqr+fTvqTQ==$0 TABLE         2013-09-16:12:55:11

SQL>
```

As promised, Oracle assigned the second version of the JOB_HISTORY table a unique identifier (RECYCLEBIN NAME). This ensures that either version of the table could be restored if required.

Besides the SHOW RECYCLEBIN command, Oracle also offers views named USER_RECYCLEBIN and DBA_RECYCLEBIN, which can be used to query objects in the Recycle Bin. These views offer much more information than the simple SHOW RECYCLEBIN command. For example, look at the following query:

```
SQL> select original_name, object_name, type, droptime from user_recyclebin;

ORIGINAL_NAME
-----------------------------------------------------------------

OBJECT_NAME
-----------------------------------------------------------------

TYPE                      DROPTIME
------------------------- -------------------
JOB_HISTORY
BIN$2siLENifTmCBmAu0+mXAuQ==$0
TABLE                     2013-09-16:12:45:37

JHIST_DEPT_IX
BIN$oNMhLpjfQDKANxMqxyNTQg==$0
INDEX                     2013-09-16:12:45:37

JHIST_JOB_IX
BIN$4ef0bWg/RSqQwyRilF8B7w==$0
INDEX                     2013-09-16:12:45:37

JHIST_EMP_ID_PK
BIN$Yy7yGm0/ScmYjpB8SfX9oQ==$0

INDEX                     2013-09-16:12:45:37

JHIST_EMPLOYEE_IX
BIN$39LSAx7mSACzu4agKkRYKQ==$0
INDEX                     2013-09-16:12:45:37

JOB_HISTORY
BIN$NIaEC81/SJ24Dqr+fTvqTQ==$0
TABLE                     2013-09-16:12:55:11
```

```
6 rows selected.
SQL>
```

On first glance, you might have assumed that this query would have returned the exact same results as the SHOW RECYCLEBIN command. Instead we see four additional rows showing the indexes that were moved to the Recycle Bin when we dropped the first JOB_HISTORY table.

The SHOW RECYCLEBIN command shows only tables that reside in the Recycle Bin. It filters out the dependent objects such as indexes and constraints. Furthermore, the DBA_RECYCLEBIN view also offers many other columns, as listed in Table 8.2.

TABLE 8.2   DBA_RECYCLEBIN Columns

Column Name	Description
OWNER	The original owner of the dropped object.
OBJECT_NAME	The system-assigned name of the object. This is the object's unique identifier within the Recycle Bin.
ORIGINAL_NAME	The original name of the object (at the time when it was dropped).
OPERATION	The type of operation that occurred to move the object into the Recycle Bin (in other words, DROP, TRUNCATE). Currently, only dropped objects can be restored.
TYPE	The type of object (TABLE, INDEX, and so on).
TS_NAME	The name of the tablespace where the object resides.
CREATETIME	Timestamp reflecting when the object was created.
DROPTIME	Timestamp reflecting when the object was dropped.
DROPSCN	The system change number (SCN) corresponding to the dropping of the object.
PARTITION_NAME	If the dropped object was partitioned, the name of the partition.
CAN_UNDROP	This object can be undropped (restored) using the Flashback Drop option. This is true only for table objects. Dependent objects can be restored but not by themselves. They will be restored only if their related table is restored.
CAN_PURGE	This object can be purged from the Recycle Bin.
RELATED	Object number of the parent object.

TABLE 8.2 DBA_RECYCLEBIN Columns *(continued)*

Column Name	Description
BASE_OBJECT	Object number of the base object (in other words, the original table that was dropped).
PURGE_OBJECT	Object number of the current Recycle Bin object. This is the object number that will be purged.
SPACE	Number of blocks used by the object.

Tables residing in the Recycle Bin can be queried directly, just like any other table. The only caveat is that they cannot have any Data Definition Language (DDL) or Data Manipulation Language (DML) statements performed on them. Any attempt to do so will result in an error.

To query a table currently residing in the Recycle Bin, simply use the system-assigned name (OBJECT_NAME), not the original name. Also, since this name consists of mixed-case characters, you must enclose the name in double quotes in your SELECT statement. Here's an example—please note, failure to enclose the object name in double quotes will result in an ORA-00933: SQL command not properly ended error:

```
SQL> select * from "BIN$NIaEC81/SJ24Dqr+fTvqTQ==$0";


    JOB_ID
----------
         1
```

Purging the Recycle Bin

As was mentioned previously, objects are never physically moved into the Recycle Bin. Therefore, there is no tablespace associated with it. Instead, the objects remain in their respective tablespaces but are no longer listed in the data dictionary. So, they appear to have been dropped, yet they are still available for recovery.

However, this poses a problem for a user who is dropping tables to reclaim space in a tablespace. Or perhaps you have a temporary table that you have no further need for and will never need to restore. For situations like these, the purge option should be used. Purging objects from the Recycle Bin will remove them permanently and release the storage space that they were occupying. However, it also means that they cannot be restored.

Purging can be accomplished in several ways. The first is by adding the PURGE option to the command, as shown here:

```
SQL> drop table employees purge;
Table dropped
```

By adding PURGE to the end of the DROP command, you make the table drop bypass the Recycle Bin altogether. It will not be recoverable, so proceed with caution.

To purge objects that already reside in the Recycle Bin, you have several options. First, you can purge a specific table, as shown:

```
SQL> purge table employees;
```

```
Table purged.
```

When purging a single table, you can reference the table by using either the original table name or the system-assigned name. If you use the system-assigned name, be sure to use double quotes around the name.

You can also purge all objects from a specific tablespace by using the TABLESPACE option, as shown:

```
SQL> purge tablespace user_data;
```

```
Tablespace purged.
```

You can also purge the entire Recycle Bin (all objects you have dropped, regardless of tablespace), as shown here:

```
SQL> purge recyclebin;
```

```
Recyclebin purged.
```

This command will purge all of the objects from the Recycle Bin. By the same token, a DBA can purge all of the objects from all users' Recycle Bins at once using the following:

```
SQL> purge dba_recyclebin;
```

```
DBA Recyclebin purged.
```

There may also be times when Oracle itself will purge objects from the Recycle Bin. This will occur when Oracle can no longer allocate new extents in a tablespace where the dropped objects reside without extending the tablespace. This is referred to as *space pressure*. Before extending the tablespace, Oracle will choose to purge Recycle Bin objects.

When space pressure occurs, Oracle will purge the oldest objects first, and it will purge dependent objects (in other words, indexes and triggers) before purging the table itself.

Because of the threat of space pressure, objects in the Recycle Bin are not guaranteed to be recoverable.

In Exercise 8.1, you'll purge a table from the Recycle Bin.

Purging a Table from the Recycle Bin

To purge a table from the Recycle Bin, do the following:

1. Create a table and add rows of data.

    ```
    SQL> create table foo (x number, y varchar2(10)) tablespace users;
    Table created.

    SQL> insert into foo values (1,'test1');
    1 row created.
    SQL> insert into foo values (2,'test2');
    1 row created.
    SQL> insert into foo values (3,'test3');
    1 row created.
    SQL> commit;
    Commit complete.
    ```

2. Drop the table.

    ```
    SQL> drop table foo;
    Table dropped.
    ```

3. Verify that the table exists in the Recycle Bin.

    ```
    SQL> show recyclebin
    ORIGINAL NAME    RECYCLEBIN NAME                 OBJECT TYPE  DROP TIME
    ---------------- ----------------------------- ------------ -------------------


    FOO              BIN$3xVo45MkQpyced0i7/2Jgg==$0 TABLE        2013-09-16:12:59:28
    ```

4. Purge the table from the Recycle Bin.

    ```
    SQL> purge table foo;
    Table purged.
    ```

5. Verify that the table is no longer in the Recycle Bin.

    ```
    SQL> show recyclebin;
    SQL>
    ```

Disabling and Enabling the Recycle Bin

It is important to understand that even though the Recycle Bin is extremely useful, its use is entirely optional. Though it is enabled by default, it can be turned off at either the system or session level to suit the users' needs. For instance, if you work in an environment that is very tight on space, the Recycle Bin might be more of a hindrance than a help.

The Recycle Bin feature is governed by an initialization parameter named RECYCLEBIN. As with other initialization parameters, it can be set in the INIT.ORA file as shown:

```
RECYCLEBIN=OFF
```

For a database using spfiles, the same thing can be accomplished, as shown here:

```
SQL>  alter system set recyclebin = off scope=spfile;

System altered.
```

You can't dynamically enable or disable the Recycle Bin at a system level for existing sessions, but you can for future sessions:

```
SQL> show parameter recyclebin
NAME                                 TYPE          VALUE
------------------------------------ -----------   -----------------------------
recyclebin                           string        on
SQL> alter system set recyclebin=off;
alter system set recyclebin=off
                          *
ERROR at line 1:
ORA-02096: specified initialization parameter is not modifiable with this
option


SQL>
SQL>  alter system set recyclebin = off DEFERRED;

System altered.
```

Enabling the Recycle Bin can also occur at the session level, as shown in the following example:

```
SQL>  alter session set recyclebin = off;

Session altered.
```

And, as you can probably guess, the Recycle Bin feature can be reenabled by all the same methods; just substitute ON for OFF.

> The ALTER SYSTEM ... DEFERRED statement applies the global value to future sessions that connect to the database but does not modify the value for existing sessions.

Restoring Objects with Flashback Drop

Now that you've seen how the Recycle Bin works, it's time to use the Flashback Drop feature to restore objects from it. The syntax for the Flashback Drop command is as follows:

```
FLASHBACK TABLE table_name
TO BEFORE DROP
[RENAME TO new_table_name];
```

By default, a Flashback Table operation will restore the table using the same name it had originally. The optional RENAME clause allows you to restore the table under a different name. This may be required if an object with the original name already exists in your schema.

Let's take a look at how it all works. In this example, we will restore the JOB_HISTORY table and rename it JOB_HIST:

```
SQL> flashback table job_history to before drop rename to job_hist;

Flashback complete.
```

Now we'll query the restored table, as shown here:

```
SQL> select * from job_hist;

    JOB_ID        1
```

As you can see, the Flashback Drop feature was successful in restoring the table. However, we had two different versions of the JOB_HISTORY table in the Recycle Bin. Why did Oracle choose to restore this one instead of the other one? The answer is that Oracle will always choose to restore the most recently dropped version of the table (if it has two identically named tables).

To recover the previous version of the JOB_HISTORY table, we have two options. Since we already recovered the first one, we can simply execute the Flashback Drop command again to restore the second version (however, we must rename one of them). However, a better alternative is to use the system-assigned object name whenever you want to recover a specific version of a table. Here's an example:

```
SQL> flashback table "BIN$NIaEC81/SJ24Dqr+fTvqTQ==$0" to before drop;

Flashback complete.
```

By specifying the system-assigned object name in your Flashback Drop, you avoid duplicate-name issues and ensure that only the specific table that you've selected (and the specific version of that table) will be restored.

Flashback Drop functionality offers a simple way to recover from logical corruption caused when a table has been dropped in error. It is simple, fast, and works well. But there are other types of logical corruption that you must also be able to deal with, and those will require different tools. In the next section, we will introduce you to the next one: Flashback Query.

Regarding the Behavior of Dependent Objects after Undropping

When you recover a table from the Recycle Bin, the triggers, constraints, and indexes are also brought back; however, the names of the dependent objects remain as they were in the Recycle Bin. For example, if table T has an index IN_T, a primary key constraint PK_T, and a trigger named TR_T and the table is dropped and later flashed back, all of these dependent objects will revert back to table T but with different names:

```
SQL> select trigger_name from user_triggers where table_name = 'T';
 TRIGGER_NAME
----------------------------
BIN$VJSEhlG2cMngQA4KH2h7+A==$0
 SQL> select index_name from user_indexes where table_name = 'T';
 INDEX_NAME
----------------------------
BIN$VJSEhlG0cMngQA4KH2h7+A==$0
BIN$VJSEhlG1cMngQA4KH2h7+A==$0
 SQL> select constraint_name from user_constraints where table_name = 'T';
 CONSTRAINT_NAME
----------------------------
BIN$VJSEhlGzcMngQA4KH2h7+A==$0
```

You will need to explicitly rename these objects to their former names, if you so choose. Additionally, the following statements are true:

- Some constraints, such as FK, can't be flashed back; they are lost.

- Bitmap join indexes are not flashed back.

- Materialized view logs are not placed in the Recycle Bin, so they are lost.

- It's possible that some indexes may have been erased from the Recycle Bin, even when the table remained (typically under space pressure). So, it's not guaranteed that all the indexes will be reverted when the table is flashed back before drop.

Use Flashback to Query Data

In the previous section you learned how to restore tables that had been dropped by accident. But oftentimes logical corruption issues are not as blatant as a dropped table. It is much more common that a user will make a mistake on a data-entry form, delete a row by accident, or make any of a number of other mistakes. When a problem like this occurs, wouldn't it be nice to be able to go back in time to fix it? Flashback Query allows you to do just that—in a manner of speaking.

Flashback Query provides a method of viewing data as it existed at a prior point in time. So when a user makes a mistake, you can just go back in time and fix it.

Flashback Query is implemented through the AS OF clause of the SELECT statement. The AS OF clause is used to specify a particular point in time (either a timestamp or an SCN for one or more tables in the query. When the query is executed, Flashback Query will return the data exactly as it existed at a specified point in time. It is important to note that Flashback Query will return only committed data. It will never return uncommitted data. So if the query happens to specify a point in time that falls in the middle of a transaction, Flashback Query will ignore the transaction and simply return the committed data.

As you can imagine, Flashback Query can be used in many situations encountered by a DBA in the course of their duties:

- Recovering from data changes that were committed by mistake

- Comparing current data values to past values

- Simplifying certain programming tasks by alleviating the need to store certain types of temporary data

- Allowing users to correct their own mistakes

In the past, these types of problems could be addressed only through a costly and time-consuming recovery process. With Flashback Query, they can be handled with ease. Also, Flashback Query functionality is not limited to the DBA. Any user who has been granted SELECT and FLASHBACK privileges can take advantage of it.

Let's take a look at Flashback Query in action. To begin with, we will look at the JOB_HISTORY table in the HR schema:

```
SQL> select * from hr.job_history;


EMPLOYEE_ID START_DAT END_DATE  JOB_ID     DEPARTMENT_ID
----------- --------- --------- ---------- -------------
        102 13-JAN-01 24-JUL-06 IT_PROG               60
        101 21-SEP-97 27-OCT-01 AC_ACCOUNT           110
        101 28-OCT-01 15-MAR-05 AC_MGR               110
        201 17-FEB-04 19-DEC-07 MK_REP                20
        114 24-MAR-06 31-DEC-07 ST_CLERK              50
        122 01-JAN-07 31-DEC-07 ST_CLERK              50
        200 17-SEP-95 17-JUN-01 AD_ASST               90
        176 24-MAR-06 31-DEC-06 SA_REP                80
```

```
      176 01-JAN-07 31-DEC-07 SA_MAN                   80
      200 01-JUL-02 31-DEC-06 AC_ACCOUNT               90
10 rows selected.
```

Now, let's simulate a user accidentally dropping a row:

```
SQL> delete from job_history where employee_id = 102;

1 row deleted.

SQL> commit;

Commit complete.
```

You can see that the row has indeed been deleted:

```
SQL> select * from job_history;

EMPLOYEE_ID START_DAT END_DATE  JOB_ID     DEPARTMENT_ID
----------- --------- --------- ---------- -------------
        101 21-SEP-97 27-OCT-01 AC_ACCOUNT           110
        101 28-OCT-01 15-MAR-05 AC_MGR               110
        201 17-FEB-04 19-DEC-07 MK_REP                20
        114 24-MAR-06 31-DEC-07 ST_CLERK              50
        122 01-JAN-07 31-DEC-07 ST_CLERK              50
        200 17-SEP-95 17-JUN-01 AD_ASST               90
        176 24-MAR-06 31-DEC-06 SA_REP                80
        176 01-JAN-07 31-DEC-07 SA_MAN                80
        200 01-JUL-02 31-DEC-06 AC_ACCOUNT            90
9 rows selected.
```

Now, we can use Flashback Query to view the data that existed prior to the delete, as shown here:

```
SQL> select *
2 from job_history as of timestamp(
3 to_timestamp('23-AUG-2013 11:50:00','DD-MON-YYYY HH24:MI:SS'))
4 where employee_id = 102;

EMPLOYEE_ID START_DAT END_DATE  JOB_ID     DEPARTMENT_ID
----------- --------- --------- ---------- -------------
        102 13-JAN-01 24-JUL-06 IT_PROG               60
```

The Flashback Query successfully returned the missing row, but we have only displayed it. We haven't actually recovered it. To do so, we can simply run the same query but wrap it inside an INSERT statement, as shown here:

```
SQL> insert into job_history
2 (select * from job_history
3 as of timestamp(
4 to_timestamp('23-AUG-2013 11:50:00','DD-MON'))
5 where employee_id = 102);

1 row created.

SQL> commit;

Commit complete.

SQL> select * from job_history;

EMPLOYEE_ID START_DAT END_DATE  JOB_ID     DEPARTMENT_ID
----------- --------- --------- ---------- -------------

        102 13-JAN-01 24-JUL-06 IT_PROG               60
        101 21-SEP-97 27-OCT-01 AC_ACCOUNT           110
        101 28-OCT-01 15-MAR-05 AC_MGR               110
        201 17-FEB-04 19-DEC-07 MK_REP                20
        114 24-MAR-06 31-DEC-07 ST_CLERK              50
        122 01-JAN-07 31-DEC-07 ST_CLERK              50
        200 17-SEP-95 17-JUN-01 AD_ASST               90
        176 24-MAR-06 31-DEC-06 SA_REP                80
        176 01-JAN-07 31-DEC-07 SA_MAN                80
        200 01-JUL-02 31-DEC-06 AC_ACCOUNT            90

10 rows selected.
```

We have now successfully recovered from the accidental deletion and, as you can see, the effort was minimal.

In the example, our Flashback Query pulled data only from a single table and at a single point in time. Flashback Query is not limited to such simple queries. It can be used in multitable join queries as well. It can also be mixed and matched with tables that are not flashed back as well as tables that are flashed back to a different point in time. Look at the following example:

```
SQL> select e.last_name, d.department_name, j.job_title
  2  from employees as of timestamp(to_timestamp('23-AUG-2013 11:50:00',
```

```
3    'DD-MON-YYYY HH24:MI:SS')) e, departments as of timestamp(
4    to_timestamp('23-AUG-2013 11:53:00','DD-MON-YYYY HH24:MI:SS')) d, jobs j
5    where e.department_id = d.department_id
6    and e.job_id = j.job_id
7*   and e.employee_id = 200;
```

```
LAST_NAME  DEPARTMENT_NAME        JOB_TITLE
---------- --------------------   ------------------------
Whalen     Administration         Administration Assistant
```

This query joined a total of three tables. Two of these tables were flashed back to different points in time. The third table was not flashed back at all. This demonstrates the flexibility of Flashback Query. In fact, a single table could even be joined multiple times, each join flashed back to a different point in time. As has been discussed before, the only limitation is how far back in time you can flash back, and that is determined by the undo retention period.

It is important to understand that the data present in the undo segment governs the ability to flash back to a point in time. Undo retention is only a guideline.

In this section, you've seen a sample of what Flashback Query can do and what a powerful tool it can be in a DBA's arsenal. It allows you to look into the past to view data as it existed at a specific point in time. But what if you're not sure exactly when a change was made? Or suppose you wanted to see all the changes that were made to a column over a period of time. Those are different types of problems and require a different type of tool—Flashback Version Query.

In Exercise 8.2, you'll practice using the Flashback Query feature.

EXERCISE 8.2

Using Flashback Query

To practice using the Flashback Query feature, perform the following:

1. Create a table, insert rows of data, and commit.

   ```
   SQL> create table foo (x number, y varchar2(10));
   ```

   ```
   Table created.
   ```

   ```
   SQL> insert into foo values (1,'test1');
   ```

   ```
   1 row created.
   ```

```
SQL> insert into foo values (2,'test2');

1 row created.

SQL> insert into foo values (3,'test3');

1 row created.

SQL> commit;

Commit complete.
```

2. Select the system time.

```
SQL> select sysdate from dual;

SYSDATE
----------18-AUG-13 22:24:11
```

3. Insert more rows of data into the table, and commit.

```
SQL> insert into foo values (4,'test4');

1 row created.

SQL> insert into foo values (5,'test5');

1 row created.

SQL> commit;

Commit complete.
```

EXERCISE 8.2 *(continued)*

```
SQL> select * from foo;


      X Y
----- ------        1 test1
      2 test2
      3 test3
      4 test4
      5 test5
```

4. Select all rows from the table prior to the system time returned in step 3.

```
SQL> select * from foo as of timestamp(to_timestamp(
'18-AUG-13 22:24:11','DD-MON-YY HH24:MI:SS'));
      X Y
----- ------        1 test1
      2 test2
      3 test3
SQL>
```

Recovering Data with Flashback Version Query

Flashback Version Query allows you to query a table and retrieve all of the versions of the data that have existed between two specific points in time (specified by a timestamp or an SCN). What's more, Flashback Version Query offers a host of metadata columns that can also be included in your query, allowing you to view details regarding each change, such as the date/time that the change took place and the SCN that governed the change.

Like Flashback Query, Flashback Version Query returns only the committed occurrences of the data. Uncommitted data will be ignored. Also just like Flashback Query, Flashback Version Query works by retrieving data from the undo tablespace and is therefore limited by the undo retention period. It also requires the same privileges as Flashback Query: SELECT and FLASHBACK.

Flashback Version Query is implemented by adding a VERSIONS BETWEEN clause to a SELECT statement. Just like the AS OF clause in Flashback Query, the VERSIONS BETWEEN clause allows the starting point in time to be expressed as either a timestamp or an SCN.

Let's look at Flashback Version Query in action. First, we will update a single row in our table several times to simulate changes that may have occurred over time:

```
SQL> update employees
    set salary=salary*1.03
    where employee_id = 193;
```

```
1 row updated.

SQL> commit;

Commit complete.

SQL> update employees
     set salary=salary*1.05
     where employee_id = 193;

1 row updated.

SQL> commit;

Commit complete.

SQL> update employees
     set salary=salary/2
     where employee_id=193;

1 row updated.

SQL> commit;

Commit complete.
```

As you can see, our sample employee received a 3 percent raise, a 5 percent raise, and then had his salary cut in half. Next, we will query the table using the VERSIONS BETWEEN clause to view the history of changes:

```
SQL> select salary
  from employees
  versions between scn minvalue and maxvalue
  where employee_id = 193;

    SALARY
----------
   2108.93
   4217.85
      4017
      3900
```

The results show us, from most to least recent, the history of our employee's salary changes. He started off at a salary of $3,900, his 3 percent raise boosted him to $4,017, and his 5 percent raise boosted him to $4,217.85. Finally, our hapless employee's salary was cut in half, to $2,018.93 (presumably after he was unable to quickly restore the rows his boss deleted since he didn't know about Flashback technologies).

You will also notice that the sample query used the clause between scn minvalue and maxvalue to identify the range of versions to select. This construct allows the user to quickly select all versions that are available in the undo tablespace. This is a much cleaner solution than using artificially low and high date ranges such as BETWEEN TIMESTAMP TO_TIMESTAMP('01-JAN-1700', 'DD-MON-YYYY')

AND

TO_TIMESTAMP('31-DEC-2999', 'DD-MON-YYYY').

As mentioned earlier, there are several pseudocolumns available in conjunction with Flashback Version Query that can be used to identify when and how the changes were originally made. These columns are identified in Table 8.3.

TABLE 8.3   Flashback Version Query Pseudocolumns

Column Name	Description
VERSIONS_STARTTIME	The timestamp of the first version of the rows returned from the query.
VERSIONS_ENDTIME	The timestamp of the last version of the rows returned from the query.
VERSIONS_STARTSCN	The SCN of the first version of the rows returned from the query.
VERSIONS_ENDSCN	The SCN of the last version of the rows returned from the query.
VERSIONS_XID	The unique transaction ID under which the data was originally changed. In Oracle 12c and 11g this is a raw value, whereas in 10g it was a character value.
VERSIONS_OPERATION	The type of operation that caused the change. Valid values are as follows:
	I – Insert
	U – Update
	D – Delete

In our next example, we will use some of these pseudocolumns to create a simple history report covering the salary changes of our sample employee. The query is shown here:

```
SQL> select to_char(versions_starttime,'DD-MON HH:MI') "START DATE",
    to_char (versions_endtime, 'DD-MON HH:MI') "END DATE",
    versions_operation,
    employee_id,
    salary
    from employees
    versions between scn minvalue and maxvalue
    where employee_id = 193;


START DATE      END DATE       V EMPLOYEE_ID SALARY
-----------     -----------    - ----------- ----------

13-MAY 09:13                   U         193    2108.93
13-MAY 09:12 13-MAY 09:13      U         193    4217.85
13-MAY 09:08 13-MAY 09:12      U         193       4017
13-MAY 08:15 13-MAY 09:08      I         193       3900
```

This simple query has produced a comprehensive report showing a wealth of information regarding this employee's salary history. By reading from the bottom up, you can see the date and time that the employee was first inserted into the EMPLOYEES table (presumably the day he was hired), as well as his starting salary.

The next lines show the dates, times, amounts, and durations of each salary change for the employee. You will notice that the last line (the top one) has no value for END DATE. This shows that this value still represents the current salary for the employee.

 The Flashback Version Query can also be used in DDL and DML subqueries.

So, in conclusion, Flashback Version Query allows you to see into the past to view the history of data changes in the database. It takes the power of Flashback Query a step further and provides you with additional metadata to identify changes in more detail. It even allows you to identify the specific transaction that made the change.

But wouldn't it be nice if you could drill down even further, to see specific details about that transaction? Unfortunately, Flashback Version Query does not allow you to do that. Instead, you need to move ahead to the next section and learn about the tool that *will* allow you to do that: Flashback Transaction Query.

Detecting Changes with Flashback Transaction Query

Flashback Transaction Query is a diagnostic tool used to identify changes made to the database at the transaction level. Much like Flashback Version Query, Flashback Transaction Query allows you to identify all changes made between two specific points in time. But

Flashback Transaction Query goes a step further, allowing you to perform transactional recovery of tables. In other words, it provides you with the SQL that could be used to undo the transaction.

Before you can begin using Flashback Transaction Query functionality, there are two configuration steps that must be completed.

1. Ensure that the database is running with version compatibility = 10.0 or higher.

2. Enable supplemental logging (in other words, ALTER DATABASE ADD SUPPLEMENTAL LOG DATA;).

In addition to these system-wide settings, users who want to take advantage of this feature must be granted the SELECT ANY TRANSACTION privilege. They must also be granted the FLASHBACK privilege on the specific tables they want to flash back, or they must have the broader FLASHBACK ANY TABLE privilege.

Flashback Transaction Query is implemented through the use of the FLASHBACK_TRANSACTION_QUERY view. The data in this view allows analysis of a specific transaction to identify what changes were made to the data. This view can be large, so it is helpful to use a filter when querying the view. This will generally be the transaction identifier (XID column).

Be sure to note that the transaction identifier is stored as a raw value in Oracle 12c. This is a change from Oracle 10g, which stored it as a character value. Because of this, you can't simply pass in a string representation of a transaction identifier; you must provide a raw value. You can use Flashback Version Query to provide it for you. For example, let's use the FLASHBACK_TRANSACTION_QUERY view to analyze the transactions that created the changes we viewed in the previous section. To do this, we will join a Flashback Version Query with the FLASHBACK_TRANSACTION_QUERY view, as shown here:

```
SQL> select table_name, operation, undo_sql
from flashback_transaction_query t,
(select versions_xid as xid
 from employees versions between scn minvalue and maxvalue
 where employee_id = 123) e
where t.xid = e.xid
and operation = 'UPDATE';


TABLE_NAME OPERATION UNDO_SQL
----- ----- --------------------
EMPLOYEES  UPDATE    update "HR"."EMPLOYEES" set "SALARY" =
                     '2108.93' where ROWID =
                     'AAARAgAAFAAAABYABd';
EMPLOYEES  UPDATE    update "HR"."EMPLOYEES" set "SALARY" =
                     '4217.85' where ROWID =
                     'AAARAgAAFAAAABYABd';
EMPLOYEES  UPDATE    update "HR"."EMPLOYEES" set "SALARY" =
                     '4017' where ROWID =
```

```
                        'AAARAgAAFAAAABYABd';
```

`3 rows selected.`

This query shows you the three update transactions we ran earlier to modify our employee's salary. It also provides you with a SQL statement that could be run to effectively offset the transaction.

The example query selected only a few of the columns available in the view. Table 8.4 shows the complete list.

TABLE 8.4   FLASHBACK_TRANSACTION_QUERY View Columns

Column Name	Description
XID	Transaction identifier.
START_SCN	Current SCN at start of transaction.
START_TIMESTAMP	Timestamp at start of transaction.
COMMIT_SCN	SCN at commit of transaction. This is the SCN associated with the transaction.
COMMIT_TIMESTAMP	Timestamp at commit of transaction.
LOGON_USER	User who executed the transaction.
UNDO_CHANGE#	Link to the related undo information.
OPERATION	DML operation performed by the transaction.
TABLE_NAME	Name of the table to which the DML is being applied.
TABLE_OWNER	Owner of the table to which the DML is being applied.
ROW_ID	Row ID of the row modified by the DML.
UNDO_SQL	SQL to undo the transaction.

If you've ever used Oracle Log Miner, the columns listed in Table 8.4 may look familiar to you. In fact, Flashback technology offers functionality that is very similar to Log Miner but is much simpler to use. It allows you to drill down to the transactional level to analyze data changes. It also provides the SQL necessary to undo any transaction, provided the necessary undo records still exist in the undo tablespace.

Perform Flashback Table Operations

All of the previous Flashback options we've covered in this chapter have allowed you to view and correct specific data elements within a table. They have not affected the table as a whole. Flashback Table is a little different in that regard.

Flashback Table is a Flashback technology that allows you to recover an entire table (or set of tables) to a specific point in time without the hassle of performing an incomplete recovery. This means that rather than rolling back a single transaction, the entire table will be rolled back. If the table has dependent objects associated with it, they are also rolled back automatically.

So why would you choose to use Flashback Table instead of performing an incomplete recovery? There are several reasons:

Speed It is much faster than incomplete recovery.

Simplicity It is much easier than incomplete recovery.

Availability Flashback Table does not impact the availability of the database. Unlike other recovery methods, the database remains available, and the tablespace remains online the entire time.

Accessibility Users can flash back their own tables, so DBA involvement is not required.

Like other Flashback technologies, Flashback Table is limited only by the availability of undo data. Flashback Table also uses RETENTION GUARANTEE in the same manner as the previously discussed Flashback options.

There are two main clauses that are used with the Flashback Table:

- The TO SCN clause can recover the Flashback Table to a certain SCN.
- The TO TIMESTAMP clause can recover the Flashback Table to a certain point in time.

> To flash back a table, the table must have ROW MOVEMENT enabled. This can be accomplished with the following command: ALTER TABLE *tablename* ENABLE ROW MOVEMENT.

It is important to get the current SCN from the database. The current SCN can be identified by querying the CURRENT_SCN column in the V$DATABASE view. To show that Flashback Table is recovered, you can create a change to the data. In the following example, you will update the SALARY value for an employee and commit the transaction. Then you will perform a Flashback Table operation to recover the table to its state prior to the update. This change will be missing if the table is recovered to an SCN before the change is introduced.

Let's walk through performing a Flashback Table operation with SCN:

1. Enable row movement on the employees table:

```
SQL> alter table employees enable row movement;

Table altered.
```

2. Retrieve the current SCN from the database. This is for reference, so make a note of it:

```
SQL> select current_scn from v$database;

CURRENT_SCN
-------      623411
```

3. Query the employees table to verify the current salary for the employee with an employee_id = 110:

```
SQL> select employee_id, salary
from employees
where employee_id = 110;

EMPLOYEE_ID SALARY
------ ------
110              8200
```

4. Update the employees table as shown. Be sure to commit the change too:

```
SQL> update employees set salary=4000 where
    employee_id = 110;

1 row updated.

SQL> commit;

Commit complete.
```

5. Query the employees table to verify the new salary for our sample employee:

```
SQL> select employee_id, salary
from employees
where employee_id = 110;

EMPLOYEE_ID SALARY
----------- ----------
110              4000
```

6. Perform a Flashback Table operation to recover the table to the SCN retrieved in step 2:

```
SQL> flashback table employees
        to scn 623411;
```

7. Query the employees table again to verify that the change was eliminated because of the Flashback Table operation:

```
SQL> select employee_id, salary
from employees
where employee_id = 110;


EMPLOYEE_ID SALARY
----------- ----------
110                8200
```

As the example shows, the table has been recovered to its previous state, as it existed back at SCN 623411. Also, if any dependent objects such as indexes existed on the table, they would have also been recovered to maintain consistency.

If a table contains triggers, however, there are some special rules that apply when a Flashback Table operation is performed. All triggers are disabled during a Flashback Table operation. By default, they will remain disabled after the operation is complete, regardless of whether the trigger was previously enabled or not.

If a table has one or more enabled triggers and you want them to remain enabled after the Flashback Table operation is complete, you can add the ENABLE TRIGGERS clause to the statement, as shown here:

```
SQL> flashback table employees
  to scn 623411
    enable triggers;
```

When you specify the ENABLE TRIGGERS option, all triggers that were previously enabled will be reenabled after the operation is complete. Note that the trigger did not remain enabled during the Flashback Table operation. As stated before, all triggers are disabled during the operation (they will not fire in conjunction with the recovery operation). They are then reenabled only after the operation is complete.

As you can see, the Flashback Table operation is a valuable recovery method. Now when a user updates a table using an incorrect WHERE clause, you can simply undo the change using Flashback Table. They could even do it themselves. And, best of all, the availability of the database is not impacted by the operation. Please keep in mind that more complex flashback operations may be required, depending on the number of objects and relations impacted.

In Exercise 8.3, you'll practice using the Flashback Table feature; continue using the table created in Exercise 8.2.

EXERCISE 8.3

Using Flashback Table

To practice using the Flashback Table feature, continue using the table created in Exercise 8.2, and perform the following:

1. Select all rows from the table.

```
SQL> alter table foo enable row movement;
Table altered.
SQL> select * from foo;


       X Y
---------- ----------
         1 test1
         2 test2
         3 test3
         4 test4
         5 test5
```

2. Verify the system time at which the last two rows were inserted as part of the previous exercise.

3. Flash back the table to the system time verified in step 2:

```
SQL> flashback table foo to timestamp to_timestamp (
'18-AUG-13 22:24:11','DD-MON-YY HH24:MI:SS');


Flashback complete.


SQL> select * from foo;


       X Y
---------- ----------
         1 test1
         2 test2
         3 test3
```

Describe and Use Flashback Data Archive

The *Flashback Data Archive* allows you to retain and track all transactional changes to a record over its lifetime. This eliminates the need to write custom programs to archive all transactional changes to data. The uses of the Flashback Data Archive are many, but auditing and compliance are two key areas where this technology can be useful.

To utilize the Flashback Data Archive capabilities, create one or more tablespaces as an archive. You can create multiple archives in a tablespace. Each archive has a retention time that determines how long data is retained within it. The DBA can designate a default Flashback Data Archive for the database.

Once you have created a Flashback Data Archive, you can enable flashback data archiving on a per-table basis. By default, flashback archiving is turned off.

Configuring the Flashback Data Archive

Setting up the Flashback Data Archive is straightforward. Simply name the archive and assign an existing tablespace, an optional space quota, and the retention time:

```
SQL> create flashback archive audit_flash_archive
tablespace audit_archive quota 20g retention 7 year;

SQL> create flashback archive audit_flash_archive_2
Tablespace audit_archive quota 10m retention 90 day;
```

To establish a default Flashback Data Archive, simply add the `default` keyword in the create clause:

```
SQL> create flashback archive default default_flash_archive
Tablespace audit_archive quota 10m retention 90 day;
```

After you've created a Flashback Data Archive, you may want to alter it. As DBA, you may alter the storage quota and retention time and add, drop, or modify tablespaces in a data archive using the `ALTER FLASHBACK ARCHIVE` command. Here are a few examples:

```
SQL> alter flashback archive default_flash_archive
Modify tablespace audit_archive quota 100m;
SQL> alter flashback archive default_flash_archive
Modify retention 180 day;
SQL>
SQL> alter flashback archive default_flash_archive
Remove Tablespace audit_archive;
SQL>
```

To clean up or purge data to an SCN or timestamp from a Flashback Data Archive, use the ALTER command with the purge clause:

```
SQL> alter flashback archive default_flash_archive
Purge before SCN 979271;
SQL>
SQL> alter flashback archive default_flash_archive
Purge before timestamp (SYSDATE - 180);
SQL>
```

And if you have established a deletion policy for archives, you can drop an archive, including the default archive, quite easily, with no warning from the system:

```
SQL> drop flashback archive audit_flash_archive2;
SQL>
```

Using the Flashback Data Archive

Once the Flashback Data Archive is created, you can begin archiving data from specific tables. To enable archiving for an existing table, use the ALTER TABLE command with the FLASHBACK ARCHIVE clause:

```
SQL> alter table employee_history flashback archive audit_flash_archive;
SQL>
```

If you have created a default flashback archive and want to use it, then you don't need to specify the name of the archive.

Equally straightforward, create a new table with the archive feature to utilize the default Flashback Data Archive:

```
SQL> create table shipments (ship_id number(9),
shipper number(9), ship_date date)
flashback archive;
SQL>
```

Now that you have established all the structures, query the base table to retrieve archive data using the AS OF TIMESTAMP clause:

```
SQL> select * from shipments AS OF TIMESTAMP TO_TIMESTAMP
('2013-02-01 12:00:00', 'YYYY-MM-DD HH24:MI:SS');
SQL>
```

To disable archiving for a table, simply alter the table using the NO FLASHBACK ARCHIVE clause:

```
SQL> alter table shipments no flashback archive;
SQL>
```

Certain DDL is not allowed on archived tables: TRUNCATE, DROP, and RENAME as well as ALTER commands that drop, rename, or modify a column, change a long raw to a LOB, perform a partition or subpartition operation, or use the UPGRADE TABLE clause.

Monitoring the Flashback Data Archive

The Flashback Data Archive process, FBDA, archives the historical rows of tables enabled for archiving to the Flashback Data Archive. FBDA writes a pre-image of a row and metadata on current rows into the flashback archive when a transaction that changes data commits. FBDA manages the Flashback Data Archive retention and space.

Several views are available for monitoring the Flashback Data Archive. See Table 8.5 for a description of the views.

TABLE 8.5 Flashback Data Archive Views

View Name	Description
DBA_FLASHBACK_ARCHIVE	Information about Flashback Data Archive
DBA_FLASHBACK_ARCHIVE_TS	Tablespaces used for Flashback Data Archive
DBA_FLASHBACK_ARCHIVE_TABLES	Tables that are enabled for archive

Perform Flashback Database Operations

Flashback Database was introduced in Oracle 10g. There is one main difference between the other Flashback technologies and Flashback Database: Flashback Database relies on the flashback logs as opposed to undo tablespaces.

Flashback Database allows you to flash the entire database back to a specific point in time. This is extremely useful to recover from errors such as truncating a large table, not completing a batch job, or dropping a user. Flashback Database recovery is also the best choice for logical corruptions such as a bad complex transaction that gets propagated throughout the database.

Before you can use Flashback Database, you must set up the *fast recovery area*. Please refer to Chapter 2, "Performing Oracle User-Managed Database Recoveries," for an introduction to the fast recovery area, and refer to Chapter 3, "Configuring and Backing Up Using RMAN," to learn how to configure it.

One major technological benefit of Flashback Database is that it allows you to reverse user errors or logical corruption much more quickly than performing a traditional incomplete recovery or using the Oracle Log Miner utility. The reason Flashback Database recovery is much quicker than traditional recovery operations is that recovery is no longer impacted by the size of the database. The mean time to recovery (MTTR) for traditional recovery is dependent on the size of the data files and archive logs that need to be restored and applied. Using Flashback Database recovery, recovery time is proportional to the number of changes that need to be backed out of the recovery process, not the size of data files and archive logs. This makes the Flashback Database recovery process the most efficient recovery process in most user-error or logical-corruption situations.

The Flashback Database architecture consists of the recovery writer *RVWR* background process and Flashback Database logs. When the Flashback Database is enabled, the RVWR process is started. *Flashback Database logs* are a new type of log file that contain a "before" image of physical database blocks. The RVWR writes the Flashback Database logs in the fast recovery area. Enabling the fast recovery area is a prerequisite to using Flashback Database because the Flashback Database logs are written to the fast recovery area.

In the following sections, you will learn how to configure, monitor, and perform Flashback Database operations.

Configuring Flashback Database

The database must have multiple features configured prior to configuring Flashback Database. The database must have ARCHIVE LOG enabled. As mentioned earlier, the fast recovery area must be configured to store the Flashback Database logs.

First, make sure the database is shut down. Next, the database must be started in mount mode. Then, the database parameter DB_FLASHBACK_RETENTION_TARGET can be set to the desired value, which is based on minutes. This value determines how far back in time you can flash back the database. This is like a baseline for Flashback Database. Next, Flashback Database can be enabled with the ALTER DATABASE FLASHBACK ON command. Finally, the database can be opened for normal use.

Let's walk through these steps in more detail:

1. Start the database in mount mode:

```
SQL> connect / as sysdba
SQL> startup mount
ORACLE instance started.
Total System Global Area  535662592 bytes
Fixed Size                  1334380 bytes
Variable Size             171967380 bytes
Database Buffers          356515840 bytes
Redo Buffers                5844992 bytes
Database mounted.
```

2. Set the `DB_FLASHBACK_RETENTION_TARGET` parameter to the desired value. This value is in minutes, which equates to three days:

```
SQL> alter system set db_flashback_retention_target=4320 scope=both;
```

3. Enable the Flashback capability:

```
SQL> alter database flashback on;
```

4. Now the database can be opened for normal use:

```
SQL> alter database open;
```

As you can see, enabling Flashback Database is fairly simple. A key point for you to know is how far back in time you need to be able to flash back from, or know the `DB_FLASHBACK_RETENTION_TARGET` parameter value. The `DB_FLASHBACK_RETENTION_TARGET` value will determine how far you can flash back the database in minutes. In the preceding example, we specified the value of 4,320, which is for three days; the default value is 1,440, or one day.

Monitoring Flashback Database

The Flashback Database can be monitored by using a few dynamic views: `V$DATABASE`, `V$FLASHBACK_DATABASE_LOG`, and `V$FLASHBACK_DATABASE_STAT`. These views provide some valuable information regarding the status of the Flashback Database and the supporting operations.

The `V$DATABASE` view displays whether the Flashback Database is on or off. This tells you whether the Flashback Database is enabled or not.

Let's query the `V$DATABASE` view and see the results:

```
SQL> select flashback_on from v$database;


FLASHBACK_ON
------------
YES
SQL>
```

Query the `V$FLASHBACK_DATABASE_LOG` to determine the amount of space required in the recovery area to support the flashback activity generated by changes in the database. The values in the `OLDEST_FLASHBACK_SCN` and `OLDEST_FLASHBACK_TIME` columns give you information regarding how far back you can use Flashback Database. This view also shows the size of the flashback data in the `FLASHBACK_SIZE` column. The column `ESTIMATED_FLASHBACK_SIZE` can be used to identify the estimated size of flashback data that you need for your current target retention. Shown next is an example of querying the `V$FLASHBACK_DATABASE_LOG`:

```
SQL> select
  2  oldest_flashback_scn,
```

```
  3   oldest_flashback_time,
  4   retention_target,
  5   estimated_flashback_size
  6   from v$flashback_database_log;


OLDEST_FLASH_SCN OLDEST_FLASH_TIME RET_TARGET EST_FLASHBACK_SIZE
---------------- ----------------- ---------- ------------------
    979720           20-JUL-13        4320         298967040

SQL>
```

The V$FLASHBACK_DATABASE_STAT view is used to monitor the overhead of maintaining the data in the Flashback Database logs. This view allows you to make estimates regarding future Flashback Database operations. This is done by coming up with an estimate about potential required space.

Let's look at the V$FLASHBACK_DATABASE_STAT view:

```
SQL> select * from v$flashback_database_stat;


BEGIN_TIM END_TIME  FLASHBACK_DATA    DB_DATA   REDO_DATA
--------- --------- --------------- ---------- ----------

ESTIMATED_FLASHBACK_SIZE CON_ID
------------------------ 

20-JUL-13 20-JUL-13        61784064   35880960   99203072
                      0     3
SQL>
```

As you can see, the V$FLASHBACK_DATABASE_STAT dynamic view shows the utilization of the Flashback Database log. This is determined by the begin and end times.

Performing Flashback Database Operations

The Flashback Database can be used with SQL*Plus to perform recoveries. Once the database is configured for the Flashback Database, you just need to start the database in mount mode, and you are ready to perform a Flashback Database recovery. You also need to get either OLDEST_FLASHBACK_SCN or OLDEST_FLASHBACK_TIME from the V$FLASHBACK_DATABASE_LOG view. This will allow you to utilize the TO SCN or TO TIME clause in the FLASHBACK DATABASE clause. If you have established a *restore point*, you can recover to it if it is newer than the OLDEST_FLASHBACK_SCN.

Let's walk through performing a Flashback Database recovery to an SCN:

1. First, query the V$FLASHBACK_DATABASE_LOG view to retrieve the OLDEST_FLASHBACK_SCN:

```
SQL> select oldest_flashback_scn, oldest_flashback_time
  2   from v$flashback_database_log;
```

```
OLDEST_FLASHBACK_SCN OLDEST_FLASHBACK_TIME
-------------------- ---------------------
              979720 20-JUL-13

SQL>
```

2. Next, shut down and start the database in mount mode:

```
SQL> shutdown immediate
Database closed.
Database dismounted.
ORACLE instance shut down.
SQL>
SQL> startup mount
ORACLE instance started.
Total System Global Area  535662592 bytes
Fixed Size                  1334380 bytes
Variable Size             171967380 bytes
Database Buffers          356515840 bytes
Redo Buffers                5844992 bytes
Database mounted.
SQL>
```

3. Next, issue the Flashback Database recovery command to an SCN that is associated with a restore point newer than the OLDEST_FLASHBACK_SCN discussed previously:

```
SQL> flashback database to scn 979721;
Flashback complete.
SQL>
```

4. Finally, open the database with the RESETLOGS option, because you recovered to a time prior to the current database:

```
SQL> alter database open resetlogs;
Database altered.
SQL>
```

As you can see, the Flashback Database recovery is a fairly simple process. The V$FLASHBACK_DATABASE_LOG dynamic view is useful for both TO SCN and TO TIME recoveries. The Flashback Database recovery is a quick and efficient method for recovering from user errors or logical corruptions in the database. This is a great alternative to performing a traditional incomplete recovery.

Flashback Database recovery can also be performed in SQL*Plus with the FLASHBACK DATABASE command as well as with RMAN.

Real World Scenario

Real-World Scenario: Limitations with the Flashback Database

Flashback Database recovery cannot recover from some common occurrences such as resizing a data file to a smaller size or deleting a data file. In these cases, the data file would need to be restored with traditional methods to a point in time prior to the deletion or resizing of the data file. Then you could use Flashback Database recovery to recover the rest of the database.

Flashback Database is a nice substitute for incomplete recovery for logical corruption and user errors. However, there are some limitations to Flashback Database that you should be aware of:

- You cannot resolve media failure with Flashback Database. You will still need to restore data files and recover archived redo logs to recover from media failure.

- You cannot undo the resizing of data files to a smaller size, also called shrinking data files, with Flashback Database.

- You cannot use Flashback Database if the control file has been restored or recreated.

- You cannot drop a tablespace and recover it through reset logs.

- You cannot flash back the database to an SCN prior to the earliest available SCN in the flashback logs.

Summary

In this chapter, you learned about Flashback technologies and their dependence on Oracle's undo functionality. You learned about Automatic Undo Management (AUM) and how it aids the DBA in managing undo information.

We discussed the Recycle Bin in detail, and you learned how dropped objects are moved to the Recycle Bin. We showed you how to query the contents of the Recycle Bin and how to recover objects using the Flashback Drop feature.

Next, you learned about Flashback Query and its ability to show you data as it appeared at a specific time in the past.

The next section discussed the Flashback Version Query, which retrieves all versions of the rows that existed between two specific points in time.

You then used the Flashback Transaction Query to view transactional changes in data. You saw examples of how you can use this tool to perform transactional analysis, including producing SQL statements that will undo the transaction.

You used Flashback Table to recover a table to a specific point in time without performing an incomplete recovery. You also learned how all dependent objects are recovered when using Flashback Table.

The Flashback Database command is best used to recover from logical corruption and user error. This is an alternative to incomplete recovery or the Log Miner utility. The Flashback Database command can be enabled and configured fairly easily. You must have the fast recovery area enabled to implement Flashback Database.

The last Flashback technology discussed in this chapter was the Flashback Data Archive, which can be used to track all DML changes to a table and keep the changes for a specific retention period.

Exam Essentials

Know how to restore dropped tables from the Recycle Bin.   Make sure that you understand how the Recycle Bin handles dropped objects. You should be able to locate objects in the Recycle Bin. You should be able to perform a Flashback Drop recovery of a dropped object.

Know how to perform a Flashback Query.   You must understand how Flashback Query works. Know which options are available in the AS OF clause (timestamp and SCN). Be able to execute a Flashback Query and understand what the results represent.

Know how to use Flashback Transaction Query.   Know how to use Flashback Transaction Query to expose transactional information relating to changes in the database. Be sure that you are familiar with the contents of the FLASHBACK_TRANSACTION_QUERY view. Be able to access the undo SQL required to roll back a transaction.

Understand how to perform Flashback Table operations.   Understand the basics of how Flashback Table works. Know how to perform a Flashback Table operation with a timestamp or an SCN. Be aware of how undo data is used in Flashback Table and how to protect this data.

Understand the Flashback Database architecture.   Make sure you are aware of the components that make up the Flashback Database architecture. Understand the Flashback Database logs and RVWR background-process functionality.

Understand how to enable and disable the Flashback Database.   Know how to configure the Flashback Database. Understand the fast recovery area and how it is configured.

Know how to monitor the Flashback Database.   Know the dynamic views that monitor the Flashback Database. Understand what each view contains.

Know how to create and use a Flashback Data Archive.   Know the syntax to create a Flashback Data Archive in a tablespace, alter the storage and retention parameters, purge and drop, archive a table, and query the results.

Review Questions

1. Which of the following Oracle features utilize the undo tablespace? (Choose all that apply.)

   A. Flashback Query

   B. Flashback Drop

   C. Flashback Table

   D. Flashback Database

   E. Transaction Processing

   F. Recycle Bin

2. Which of the following statements are true regarding the Recycle Bin? (Choose all that apply.)

   A. The Recycle Bin is a physical storage area for dropped objects.

   B. The Recycle Bin is a logical container for dropped objects.

   C. The Recycle Bin stores the results of a Flashback Drop operation.

   D. The objects in the Recycle Bin are stored in the tablespace in which they were created.

3. Over the course of a day, a department performed multiple DML statements (inserts, updates, deletes) on multiple rows of data in multiple tables. The manager would like a report showing the time, table name, and DML type for all changes that were made. Which Flashback technology would be the best choice to produce the list?

   A. Flashback Drop

   B. Flashback Query

   C. Flashback Transaction Query

   D. Flashback Version Query

   E. Flashback Table

4. A user named Arren is executing this query:

```
select table_name, operation, undo_sql
    from
    flashback_transaction_query t,
     (select versions_xid as xid
  from employees versions between scn minvalue
  and maxvalue
     where employee_id = 123) e
     where t.xid = e.xid;
```

When the query runs, he receives an ORA-01031: insufficient privileges error. Since the user owns the employees table, you know that it is not the problem. Which of the following SQL statements will correct this problem?

A. GRANT SELECT ANY TRANSACTION TO ARREN;

B. GRANT SELECT ON FLASHBACK_TRANSACTION_QUERY TO ARREN;

C. GRANT SELECT_ANY_TRANSACTION TO ARREN;

D. GRANT FLASHBACK TO ARREN;

E. GRANT SELECT ANY VIEW TO ARREN;

5. AUM has been retaining about 15 minutes' worth of undo. You want to double the retention period but not at the expense of new transactions failing. You decide to alter the system to set the parameter UNDO_RETENTION=18000. However, AUM still retains only about 15 minutes' worth of undo. What is the problem? (Choose the best answer.)

A. You need to alter the undo tablespace to add the RETENTION GUARANTEE setting.

B. You need to increase the size of the undo tablespace.

C. The undo tablespace is not set to autoextend.

D. You need to alter the Recycle Bin to add the RETENTION GUARANTEE setting.

6. In order to perform Flashback Transaction Query operations, which of these steps are required? (Choose all that apply.)

A. Ensure that the database is running with version 10.1 or greater compatibility.

B. Enable Flashback Logging.

C. Enable Supplemental Logging.

D. Ensure that the database is running with version 10.0 compatibility.

E. Ensure that the database is in archive log mode.

7. Users notify you that their application is failing every time they try to add new records. Because of poor application design, the actual ORA error message is unavailable. What might be the problem? (Choose the best answers.)

   A. The application user has exceeded their undo quota.

   B. The FLASHBACK GUARANTEE option is set on the undo tablespace.

   C. The table is currently being queried by a Flashback Transaction Query operation.

   D. The table is currently being queried by a Flashback Version Query operation.

   E. The RETENTION GUARANTEE option is set on the undo tablespace.

   F. The application was coded by an idiot.

8. Which of the following statements best describes Flashback Version Query?

   A. Flashback Version Query is used to make changes to multiple versions of data that existed between two points in time.

   B. Flashback Version Query is used to view all version changes on rows that existed between the time the query was executed and a point in time in the past.

   C. Flashback Version Query is used to view version changes and the SQL to undo those changes on rows that existed between two points in time.

   D. Flashback Version Query is used to view all version changes on rows that existed between two points in time.

9. Which pseudocolumn could you use to identify a unique row in a Flashback Version Query?

   A. XID

   B. VERSIONS_PK

   C. VERSIONS_XID

   D. VERSIONS_UNIQUE

10. Which of the following can be used in conjunction with a Flashback Version Query to filter the results? (Choose all that apply.)

   A. A range of SCN values

   B. A list of SCN values

   C. Starting and ending timestamps

   D. Minimum and maximum sequence values

   E. A list of sequence values

11. At the request of a user, you issue the following command to restore a dropped table:

```
flashback table "BIN$F2JFfMq8Q5unbC0ceE9eJg==$0" to
before drop;
```

Later, the user notifies you that the data in the table seems to be very old and out of date. What might be the problem?

A. Because a proper range of SCNs was not specified, the wrong data was restored.

B. A proper range of timestamps was not specified, so the wrong data was restored.

C. A previous Flashback Drop operation had been performed, resulting in multiple versions of the table being stored in the Recycle Bin.

D. Either option A or B could be correct. Not enough information was provided to determine which.

E. None of the above

12. Which of the following statements is true regarding the VERSIONS BETWEEN clause?

A. The VERSIONS BETWEEN clause may be used in DML statements.

B. The VERSIONS BETWEEN clause may be used in DDL statements.

C. The VERSIONS BETWEEN clause may not be used to query past DDL changes to tables.

D. The VERSIONS BETWEEN clause may not be used to query past DML statements to tables.

13. Which of the following statements is true regarding implementing a Flashback Table recovery?

A. An SCN is never used to perform a Flashback Table recovery.

B. If a significant number of changes have been made to the table, row movement must be enabled.

C. The tablespace must be offline before performing a Flashback Table recovery.

D. Flashback Table recovery is completely dependent on the availability of undo data in the undo tablespace.

14. You have just performed a Flashback Table operation using the following command:

```
flashback table employees
to scn 123456;
```

The employees table has triggers associated with it. Which of the following statements is true regarding the state of the triggers during the Flashback Table operation?

A. All of the triggers are disabled.

B. All of the triggers are enabled by default.

C. Enabled triggers remain enabled and disabled triggers remain disabled.

D. Triggers are deleted when a Flashback Table operation is performed.

15. Which method could be utilized to identify both DML operations and the SQL statements needed to undo those operations for a specific schema owner? (Choose all that apply.)

    A. Query `DBA_TRANSACTION_QUERY` for `TABLE_NAME`, `OPERATION`, and `UNDO_SQL`. Limit rows by `START_SCN` and `TABLE_OWNER`.

    B. Query `FLASHBACK_TRANSACTION_QUERY` for `TABLE_NAME`, `OPERATION`, and `UNDO_SQL`. Limit rows by `START_SCN` and `TABLE_OWNER`.

    C. Query `FLASHBACK_TRANSACTION_QUERY` for `TABLE_NAME`, `OPERATION`, and `UNDO_SQL`. Limit rows by `START_TIMESTAMP` and `TABLE_OWNER`.

    D. Query `DBA_TRANSACTION_QUERY` for `TABLE_NAME`, `OPERATION`, and `UNDO_SQL`. Limit rows by `START_TIMESTAMP` and `TABLE_OWNER`.

16. Flashback Database relies on which technologies to recover to a point in time?

    A. Flashback Data Archive

    B. Flashback logs in the fast recovery area

    C. Undo tablespace

    D. RMAN command line

    E. None of the above

17. The _____ writes the Flashback Database logs in the fast recovery area.

    A. FLSH

    B. FLDB

    C. RVWR

    D. RVRW

    E. FBDA

18. Which of these are valid Flashback Database recovery point parameters? (Choose all that apply.)

    A. SCN

    B. Timestamp

    C. Named recovery point

    D. Transaction ID

    E. Session ID

19. When setting up the Flashback Data Archive, which of these key parameters are required? (Choose all that apply.)

   A. Tablespace name

   B. Storage quota

   C. Retention

   D. Table name

   E. A default archive

20. To clean up old records that are in a Flashback Data Archive and are past the retention period, what must the DBA do?

   A. Truncate the archive table.

   B. Drop the Flashback Data Archive.

   C. Nothing; expired rows are automatically removed.

   D. Nothing; expired rows are moved to an archive table.

   E. Delete entries from the archive where the metadata date retained is greater than the retention period.

Chapter

9

Diagnosing the Database and Managing Performance

ORACLE DATABASE 12c: ADVANCED ADMINISTRATION EXAM OBJECTIVES COVERED IN THIS CHAPTER:

✓ **Diagnosing Failures**

  ▪ Describe the Automatic Diagnostic Workflow

  ▪ Handle block corruption

✓ **Managing Performance**

  ▪ Monitor operations and performance in a CDB and PDBs

  ▪ Manage allocation of resources between PDBs and within a PDB

  ▪ Perform Database Replay

This chapter is divided into two sections; the first section is dedicated to tools that help the database administrators diagnose problems in the database, and the second part is dedicated to tools that assist with detecting and resolving performance issues.

In the first part, we describe the Automatic Diagnostic Repository, the central repository for all database diagnostic information, and the Support Workbench, which the DBA uses for problem recognition, reporting, and resolution. Together these represent the diagnostic workflow. We also discuss and demonstrate block media recovery.

In the second part, we describe how to monitor operations and performance in the 12*c* multitenant architecture, with a brief introduction to container databases (CDBs) and pluggable databases (PDBs), and how to manage allocation of resources between PDBs and within a PDB using the SQL Tuning Advisor and the SQL Access Advisor. We also teach you the fundamentals of Database Replay. Database Replay allows the DBA to capture a workload on a production system and replay it on a different system, simulating the behavior of the production application in a different environment.

Exam objectives are subject to change at any time without prior notice and at Oracle's sole discretion. Please visit Oracle's Training and Certification website (http://www.oracle.com/education/certification/) for the most current exam-objectives listing.

Diagnosing Failures

One of the most important day-to-day tasks of the DBA is to monitor system activity and diagnose, report, and repair problems. The Automatic Diagnostic Repository was introduced in Oracle 11*g* and provides a central location for storing problem- and incident-related information. We will describe and demonstrate the diagnostic process and workflow and include an introduction to the Automatic Diagnostic Repository Command Interpreter (ADRCI). Block media recovery improvements in 12*c* make it easier for the DBA to recognize and recover from a data-corruption incident.

Setting Up the Automatic Diagnostic Repository

The Automatic Diagnostic Repository (ADR) is a hierarchical, file-based, system-wide and system-managed repository for storing and organizing dump files, trace files, alert logs, health monitor reports, network tracing, and all other error diagnostic data. In Oracle 12c, ADR is the diagnostic data repository for Automatic Storage Management (ASM), the database, and many other Oracle server products.

The ADR stores information in files outside the database so the information is available whether or not the database is up. The files are stored in a directory structure that includes a home directory for each instance of each product.

ADR Initialization Parameters

Since the Oracle 12c ADR provides a single repository location for the alert log and all dump files and trace files, there is no longer a need for the BACKGROUND_DUMP_DEST, CORE_DUMP_DEST, and USER_DUMP_DEST initialization parameters. They are deprecated and ignored. Now you use the initialization parameter DIAGNOSTIC_DEST to designate the location of the ADR.

```
SQL> show parameter diag
NAME                                 TYPE        VALUE
------------------------------------ ----------- ---------
diagnostic_dest                      string      C:\ORACLE
```

The default value for DIAGNOSTIC_DEST is $ORACLE_BASE. If the ORACLE_BASE environment variable is not set, then $ORACLE_HOME/log is used for DIAGNOSTIC_DEST. The value of DIAGNOSTIC_DEST is referred to as the *ADR base* or *ADR root*.

Directory Structure of the Automatic Diagnostic Repository

Within the DIAGNOSTIC_DEST directory, Oracle builds the hierarchy of directories to support the ADR. This is the basic pattern:

```
<diagnostic_dest>/diag/rdbms/<dbname>/<instname>
```

For the examples used in this chapter, the following represents the correct *ADR home*:

```
C:\oracle\diag\rdbms\orcl\orcl
```

These are some important directories that you need to know about:

Incident   Each incident gets its own subdirectory within the incident directory.

Alert   The alert log is written to the alert directory.

cdump   Core dumps are written to this directory.

Trace   Trace files are written to the trace directory.

See Figure 9.1 for an example directory structure, which shows other subdirectories of the ADR home that store information such as incident packages, health monitor reports, the DDL log, and the debug log.

FIGURE 9.1 Folders within the ADR home directory

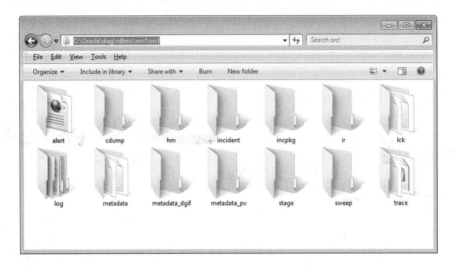

 The DBA can set the value of DIAGNOSTIC_DEST on each instance in Real Application Clusters. The recommendation from Oracle is for each instance in a cluster to have the same value for DIAGNOSTIC_DEST.

In Exercise 9.1, you'll set the diagnostic destination.

EXERCISE 9.1

Setting the Diagnostic Destination

To set the value for the diagnostic destination, do the following:

1. Verify the current setting for DIAGNOSTIC_DEST.

```
SQL> show parameter diag
```

```
NAME                                 TYPE        VALUE
------------------------------------ ----------- ---------
diagnostic_dest                      string      C:\ORACLE
```

2. Determine the new destination. Check the new destination for security, access, and sufficient space. In this example, we're moving the diagnostic destination from c:\oracle to c:\temp.

3. Use the ALTER SYSTEM command to change the value of DIAGNOSTIC_DEST:

```
SQL> alter system set diagnostic_dest="c:\temp";
```

4. Verify that the directory structure has been created. Oracle creates the diag directory under the diagnostic_dest directory and creates the directory tree under the diag directory:

```
SQL> host

c:\temp>cd diag

c:\temp\diag>tree
Folder PATH listing for volume CPACK042
Volume serial number is 8656-F008
C:.
rdbms
    orcl
        orcl
            alert
            cdump
            hm
            incident
            incpkg
            ir
            lck
                log
                    ddl
                    debug
                    test
            metadata
            metadata_dgif
            metadata_pv
            stage
            sweep
            trace


c:\temp\diag>
```

Using the Support Workbench

The Oracle Enterprise Manager Cloud Control 12*c* (OEM12c) Support Workbench is a central location for the DBA to see reported problems, investigate the problems, report the problem to Oracle support, and follow up through problem resolution. This is a vast improvement over previous versions, where there was no central location and no defined process for reporting, tracking, and resolving problem incidents.

You can access the Support Workbench from multiple places. For this task, we will start from the Enterprise Manager Cloud Control 12*c* home page, click the Enterprise menu, from the drop-down choose the Monitoring menu item, and then click the Support Workbench menu item.

Fundamental Tasks of the Support Workbench

The Support Workbench provides a framework for problem resolution: investigate, report, and resolve a problem. The following are the basic tasks within the Support Workbench:

1. View critical error alerts.

2. View problem details.

3. Gather additional diagnostic information.

4. Create a service request.

5. Package and upload diagnostic data to Oracle Support.

6. Track the service request and implement any repairs.

Task 1: View Critical Error Alerts

In most cases, you'll discover a critical alert on the Enterprise Manager home page and then work your way to the Support Workbench page. On the EM Database home page, critical-error alerts and warnings will be displayed in the Incidents and Problems section. A red *X* in the Severity column and an incident in the Type column indicate a critical-error alert. See Figure 9.2 for an example.

Task 2: View Problem Details

Under Incidents and Problems, when you select the Summary link, EM will direct you to the Incident Details page, General tab, shown in Figure 9.3. This page shows the general information about the incident but also has tabs that give you greater detail about the incident.

Click the Events tab, and you'll see the event details, as shown in Figure 9.4. We see one event associated with this incident. In Oracle 12*c*, a *problem* is a critical error in the database. An *incident* is a single occurrence of a *problem*. By default, incidents of a problem that have occurred within the last 24 hours are displayed on the Incident Manager home page.

Task 3: Gather Additional Diagnostic Information

With many problems, the DBA needs to generate additional dumps and test cases before engaging Oracle Support, as noted at the top of the Problem Details subpage. Now would be a good time to perform self-service. In the Investigate And Resolve section on the Self Service tab, select Run Checkers.

FIGURE 9.2   Alerts on the Enterprise Manager Database home page

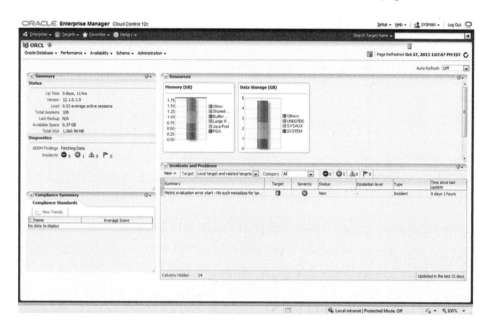

FIGURE 9.3   Incident Manager: Incident Details

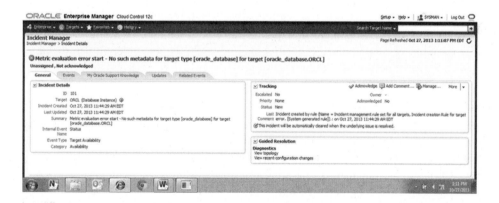

Task 4: Create a Service Request

If you would like to open a service request with Oracle Support, click the Go To Metalink button in the Investigate And Resolve section; your browser will take you to Oracle's Metalink home page. From there, you can open a service request and then return to EM.

FIGURE 9.4   Incident Manager: Events

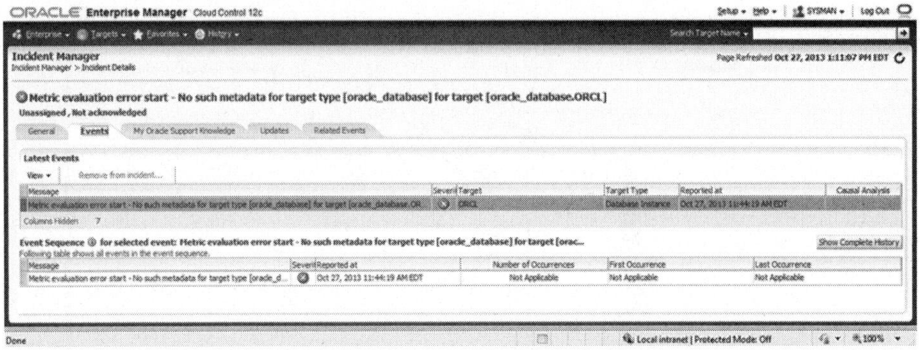

Task 5: Package and Upload Diagnostic Data to Oracle Support

The Support Workbench has solved one very annoying problem for the active DBA: packaging all of the related data for an incident and getting it to Oracle. In the past, we searched for relevant files, compressed them, batched them, and either FTPed them to Oracle Support or attached the files to the Technical Assistance Request (TAR). Oracle 12*c* Incident Packaging Service (IPS) makes it easy. It identifies all files associated with a critical error and adds them to a zip file so you can easily send it to Oracle Support.

IPS is built into the Support Workbench and is meant to make the DBA more productive and help Oracle Support to receive a complete set of data before advising on action steps.

The next steps are to open Support Workbench and proceed through creating a user-reported problem. Start by opening the Support Workbench; Figure 9.5 shows the Support Workbench home page.

1. Click the Create User-Reported Problem link, and you'll see the screen in Figure 9.6. Then click Continue With Creation Of Problem.

2. To package and upload the problem and send it to Oracle Support, start the quick packaging process, as shown in Figure 9.7.

3. Enter your package description, and if you intend to send it to Oracle Support, provide your Oracle Support credentials and customer-support identifier. If you do not intend to send the package to Oracle Support, select the No radio button.

4. Click Next, and processing will continue, as shown in Figure 9.8.

5. Next, view the contents of the package, as shown in Figure 9.9.

6. Click the Next button to see the View Manifest screen, shown in Figure 9.10, which displays the package information that will be sent to Oracle Support.

7. After you verify that the information is correct, click Next to proceed to the Schedule screen, as shown in Figure 9.11, where you can immediately submit or schedule the job that will submit the information to Oracle Support.

FIGURE 9.5   Support Workbench

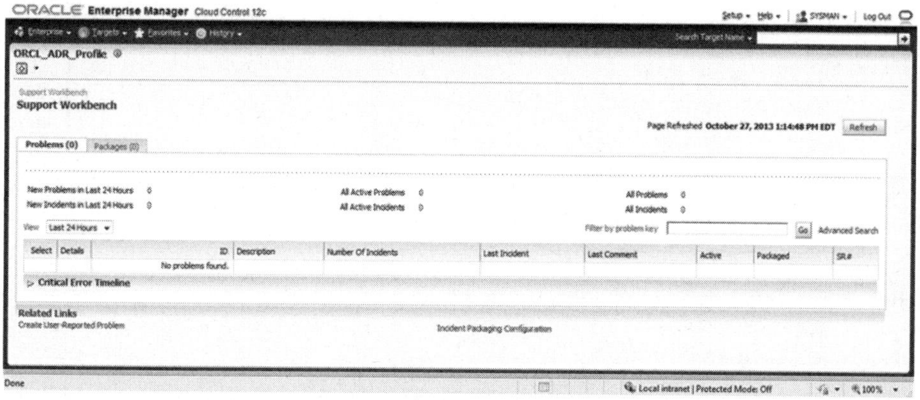

FIGURE 9.6   Create User-Reported Problem

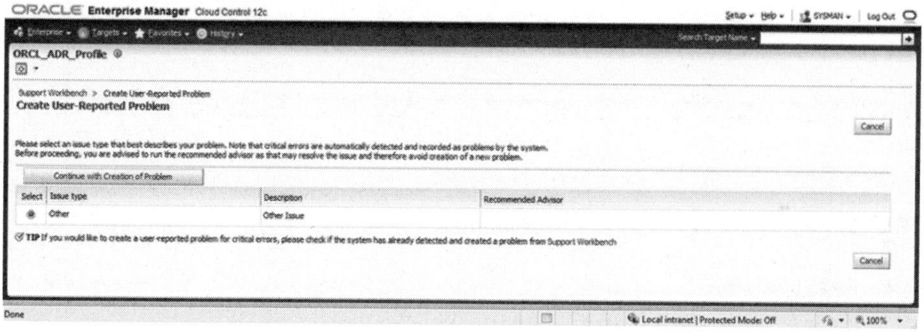

FIGURE 9.7   Quick Packaging: Create New Package

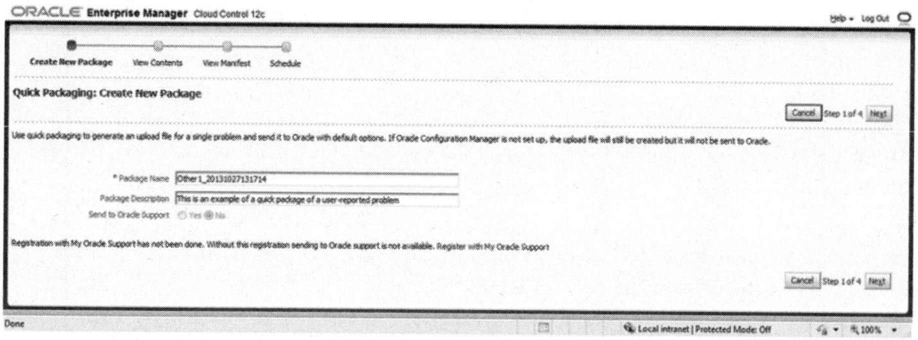

FIGURE 9.8 Processing: Quick Package

FIGURE 9.9 Quick Packaging: View Contents

FIGURE 9.10 Quick Packaging: View Manifest

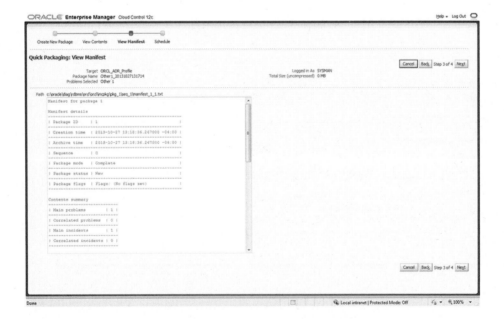

8. Once you verify the job send time, click the Submit button, and you'll see the packaging process in Figure 9.12 and upload confirmation in Figure 9.13.

9. Then click the OK button to return to the Problem Details page, as shown in Figure 9.14.

FIGURE 9.11   Quick Packaging: Schedule

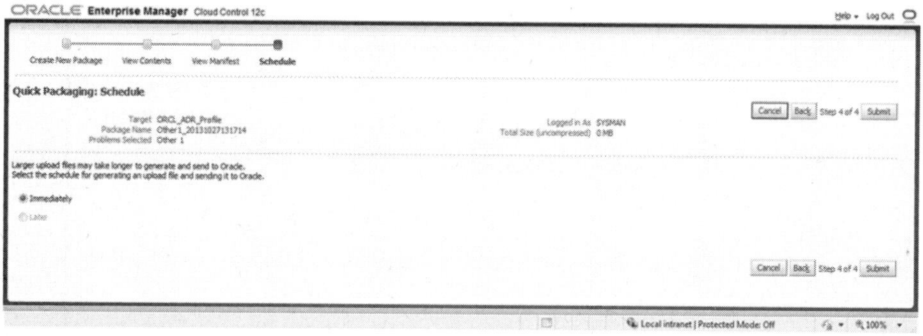

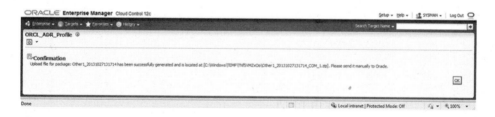

FIGURE 9.12   Quick Packaging: Generating Upload File for Package

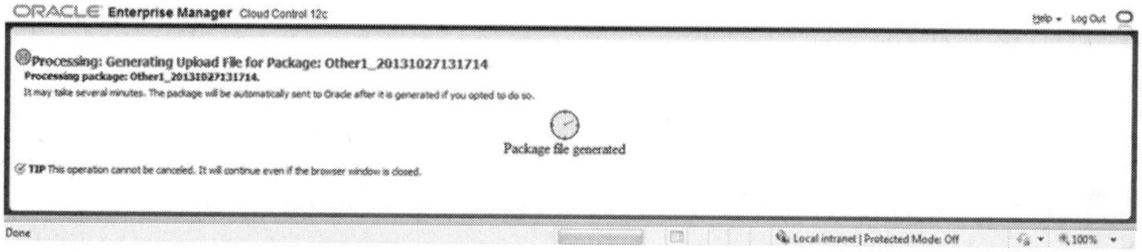

FIGURE 9.13   Confirmation screen

Task 6: Track the Service Request and Implement Any Repairs

From the Support Workbench page, view the current status of any activities performed in response to this problem, as shown in Figure 9.15.

FIGURE 9.14   Support Workbench Problem Details page

FIGURE 9.15   Support Workbench Problems

ADR Command Interpreter

The ADR Command Interpreter (ADRCI) is a command-line alternative utility to the Support Workbench, which enables the DBA to perform many of the same functions as the Support Workbench.

To run the ADRCI, enter the following command at the OS command prompt (remember that on Unix variants the command is case-sensitive):

```
C:\>adrci
```

The utility starts and displays the following prompt:

```
adrci>
ADRCI: Release 12.1.0.1.0 - Production on Mon Oct 14 19:36:24 2013

Copyright © 1982, 2013, Oracle and/or its affiliates. All Rights reserved.
ADR base = "C:\temp"
```

As mentioned, this is an introduction to the ADRCI, so we will not go into the great detail of the individual command-line statements; however, there are a few fundamental commands that are important to learn. In Exercise 9.2, you'll become familiar with the ADRCI interface.

EXERCISE 9.2

Using the ADRCI

This activity is designed to familiarize you with the ADRCI command interface by guiding you through the following tasks:

1. Start the ADRCI command line from the OS.

2. Show help.

3. Show the ADR home.

4. View the alert log.

5. Show incidents.

6. Exit ADRCI.

```
c:\>ADRCI
adrci>
ADRCI: Release 12.1.0.1.0 - Production on Mon Oct 14 19:36:24 2013

Copyright © 1982, 2013, Oracle and/or its affiliates. All Rights reserved.
ADR base = "C:\temp"
adrci> HELP
 HELP [topic]
   Available Topics:
        CREATE REPORT
        ECHO
```

EXERCISE 9.2 *(continued)*

```
            EXIT
            HELP
            HOST
            IPS
            PURGE
            RUN
            SET BASE
            SET BROWSER
            SET CONTROL
            SET ECHO
            SET EDITOR
            SET HOMES | HOME | HOMEPATH
            SET TERMOUT
            SHOW ALERT
            SHOW BASE
            SHOW CONTROL
            SHOW HM_RUN
            SHOW HOMES | HOME | HOMEPATH
            SHOW INCDIR
            SHOW INCIDENT
            SHOW LOG
            SHOW PROBLEM
            SHOW REPORT
            SHOW TRACEFILE
            SPOOL


    There are other commands intended to be used directly by Oracle, type
    "HELP EXTENDED" to see the list

adrci>
adrci> SHOW HOMES
ADR Homes:
diag\clients\user_CPACK\host_19681201
diag\clients\user_SYSTEM\host_19681201
diag\rdbms\orcl\orcl
diag\tnslsnr\CPACK042\listener
adrci>
adrci> SHOW ALERT
```

Choose the home from which to view the alert log:

```
1: diag\clients\user_CPACK\host_19681201
2: diag\clients\user_SYSTEM\host_19681201
3: diag\rdbms\orcl\orcl
4: diag\tnslsnr\CPACK042\listener
Q: to quit
```

Please select option:3
Output the results to file: C:\temp\AppData\Local\Temp\alert_8924_6016_orcl_1.ado

```
                      //launches the default text editor
                      //and displays the alert log
```

Please select option: Q
adrci>
adrci> SHOW INCIDENTS

```
ADR Home = c:\TEMP\diag\clients\user_CPACK\host_19681201:
****************************************************************************
0 rows fetched


ADR Home = c:\TEMP\diag\clients\user_SYSTEM\host_19681201:
****************************************************************************
0 rows fetched


ADR Home = c:\TEMP\diag\rdbms\orcl\orcl:
****************************************************************************
INCIDENT_ID         PROBLEM_KEY
 CREATE_TIME
-------------------- --------------------------------------------------------
 ---------------------------------------
12257               ORA 445
 2013-10-07 09:51:32.874000 -04:00
29377               ORA 600 [kpdbModAdminPasswdInRoot: not CDB]
 2013-10-13 19:17:30.154000 -04:00
```

```
ADR Home = c:\TEMP\diag\tnslsnr\CPACK042\listener:
**********************************************************************
0 rows fetched

adrci> EXIT              //or QUIT
```

 You can use the ADRCI utility PURGE command to manually purge expired diagnostic data.

Performing Block Media Recovery

Block media recovery (BMR) is used to repair corrupt blocks within a data file. It allows you to recover corrupt blocks while keeping the data file online, as opposed to data file media recovery, which requires taking the file offline during the restore and recovery operation. You can perform BMR only on blocks that are identified as corrupt. Block media recovery requires the Enterprise Edition of Oracle Database 12*c*.

Advantages of Block Media Recovery

The advantages of block media recovery are straightforward:

- The mean time to recovery (MTTR) is reduced.
- Data files remain online while corrupt blocks are repaired.

These advantages are related to recovery performance and returning the customer to normal operating mode.

Detecting Block-Level Corruption

Data-block corruption can occur because of memory corruption that is written to disk or because of I/O errors. Corruption is detected by dbv, SQL that accesses corrupt blocks, RMAN, ANALYZE operations, and any other operation that attempts to read data from a corrupt block, including DBMS_REPAIR.CHECK_OBJECT. Once a corrupt block is detected, the database will not allow access to that block until it is repaired.

Physical and logical block corruption are recorded in V$DATABASE_BLOCK_CORRUPTION. Physical block corruption occurs when the database does not recognize the block because the block header is damaged, the checksum is invalid, or the block contains all zeros. This is often due to disk hardware or OS failures and often is not acknowledged as corruption by the OS or underlying storage devices. Logical block corruption occurs when the contents of the block are logically inconsistent, sometimes the result of an Oracle internal error. Logical block corruption checking is performed by using the RMAN BACKUP, RESTORE, RECOVER, or VALIDATE command with the CHECK LOGICAL clause. Logical block corruption is not repairable by BMR.

 Real World Scenario

Identify Data File Corruption using the DBV Utility Program

To aid the DBA in diagnosis of data file corruption, Oracle provides the dbv "DB Verify" OS utility program. The dbv program takes, for example, a database filename as a command-line parameter, performs an analysis of the structure and contents of the file, and determines if there is any block corruption. At the command line, execute dbv to see the following help screen:

```
C:\>DBV
```

```
DBVERIFY: Release 12.1.0.1.0 - Production on Mon Oct 14 20:07:43 2013

Copyright (c) 1982, 2013, Oracle and/or its affiliates.  All rights reserved.

Keyword      Description                      (Default)
----------------------------------------------------------------
FILE         File to Verify                   (NONE)
START        Start Block                      (First Block of File)
END          End Block                        (Last Block of File)
BLOCKSIZE    Logical Block Size               (8192)
LOGFILE      Output Log                       (NONE)
FEEDBACK     Display Progress                 (0)
PARFILE      Parameter File                   (NONE)
USERID       Username/Password                (NONE)
SEGMENT_ID   Segment ID (tsn.relfile.block)   (NONE)
HIGH_SCN     Highest Block SCN To Verify      (NONE)
             (scn_wrap.scn_base OR scn)

C:\>
```

Performing Block Media Recovery

Oracle 12c can restore prior uncorrupted versions of the corrupt block from the flashback logs, improving recovery performance over restore from tape or disk backups. In previous versions of the database, block media recovery required restoring the uncorrupted blocks from a backup and then applying any necessary archive logs. A gap in archive logs meant the end of the recovery process. In Oracle 12c, if BMR encounters a gap in archive logs, it will continue to search for newer versions of the corrupted blocks. If a newer version is available, the restore and recovery can continue. If there are no uncorrupted newer versions of the block, the operation will fail.

To perform BMR, the database must be open or mounted and in archive log mode and must have a current, usable control file. The database must not be a standby database. You must use level 0 or full backups for the restore. All of the required archived redo logs must be available for the recovery process.

If you have enabled Flashback Database and logging, then RMAN will search the flashback logs for uncorrupted versions of the required blocks.

The steps to recover blocks using BMR are fairly simple. From SQL*Plus, determine which blocks need recovery by viewing the alert log or querying the V$DATABASE_BLOCK_CORRUPTION view:

```
SQL> SELECT FILE#, BLOCK#, BLOCKS, CORRUPTION_TYPE "TYPE"
FROM V$DATABASE_BLOCK_CORRUPTION;
```

FILE#	BLOCK#	BLOCKS	CORRUPTION_CHANGE#	TYPE
1201	1968	2		PHYSICAL

Now that you have the blocks required for recovery, connect to the target database with RMAN and begin the recovery:

```
RMAN> RECOVER DATAFILE 1201 BLOCK 1968;
```

RMAN also allows you to recover all corrupt blocks in a database using BMR. Query the V$DATABASE_BLOCK_CORRUPTION view to measure the extent of the damage; then launch RMAN to perform the recovery:

```
RMAN> RECOVER CORRUPTION LIST;
```

When a block is repaired, it is removed from the V$DATABASE_BLOCK_CORRUPTION view.

Block media recovery will fail if there is physical corruption in the redo logs that results in a checksum failure.

Managing Database Performance

In the following sections, you will learn how to monitor operations and performance in a container database (CDB) and pluggable databases (PDBs) and manage allocation of resources between PDBs and within a PDB. To accomplish these tasks in the Oracle 12*c* multitenant database environment, we will use the SQL Tuning Advisor, the SQL Access Advisor, and Database Replay.

Each of these tools can be used by the DBA to analyze and improve database performance. The Advisors operate directly on the database you wish to tune, while the Database Replay feature allows you to test a production workload on a test system to determine ways to improve performance without directly impacting the production system.

Chapter 10, "Managing Database Resources," is dedicated to the topics of managing memory and disk space resources.

Using the SQL Tuning Advisor

The SQL Tuning Advisor is a tool that you can use to analyze the performance of one or more SQL statements. To improve SQL performance, the Advisor may suggest new or modified indexes, new SQL profiles, restructuring your SQL statements, or gathering statistics. The SQL Tuning Advisor runs in one of two modes, automatic or manual. The Automatic Tuning Advisor is scheduled to run during the maintenance window, finds ways to improve high-load SQL statements, and automatically takes action.

In the multitenant Oracle Database 12*c* environment, Automatic SQL Tuning Advisor data is stored in the CDB root and has these characteristics:

- Data may include SQL statements executed in a PDB that were analyzed by the Tuning Advisor. These results are not included if the PDB is unplugged.

- Results are visible only to a *common user* whose current container is the root, not when the current container is a PDB.

Use the SQL Tuning Advisor in manual mode to analyze collections of SQL statements or individual SQL statements. In manual mode, the SQL Tuning Advisor is used to analyze a collection of SQL statements called a SQL Tuning Set.

You can run the SQL Tuning Advisor in manual mode in the multitenant environment to tune SQL statements in one or more PDBs.

Multiple PDBs   To tune an SQL statement that runs in multiple PDBs, run the SQL Tuning Advisor manually as a *common user* whose current container is the root. The results are stored in the root.

The Current PDB   To tune an SQL statement only in the current PDB, run the SQL Tuning Advisor manually as a user whose current container is the PDB. The results are stored in the PDB and are included if the PDB is unplugged. The same SQL statement running in other PDBs will not be tuned.

A common user must have the SET CONTAINER privilege to run SQL Tuning Advisor for SQL statements from a PDB, as well as the privileges to run the SQL statements in the PDB.

Chapter 11, "Creating Oracle Multitenant Databases," describes container databases and pluggable databases in detail. At this point, you need to know that a CDB may contain zero or more PDBs, and a PDB is a collection of schemas, schema objects, and non-schema objects that would appear to be an independent database. Also, a *common user* is a database user that has the same identity in the root container and in every PDB in a CDB.

Manual SQL Tuning Advisor

It is common for SQL statements to not meet performance expectations, so the DBA will need to intervene to improve performance. Use the SQL Tuning Advisor when a performance situation occurs to determine how to improve the performance of the SQL statements. To run the SQL Tuning Advisor on demand, we will utilize the Tuning Advisor in Enterprise Manager.

1. From the database home page in EM, select Performance ➤ SQL ➤ SQL Tuning Advisor, as shown in Figure 9.16, and you'll see the page in Figure 9.17, where you are asked to schedule the Tuning Advisor to begin SQL tuning.

2. On the SQL Tuning Advisor page, input the parameters for collecting SQL statement information, including scheduling information for task-data collection.

3. Click the SQL Tuning Sets link in the Overview section, or click the spyglass next to the SQL Tuning Set text box to take you to the SQL Tuning Sets page, shown in Figure 9.18.

   If there are no defined SQL tuning sets, then you have the opportunity to create a new one.

FIGURE 9.16   Navigating to the SQL Tuning Advisor home page

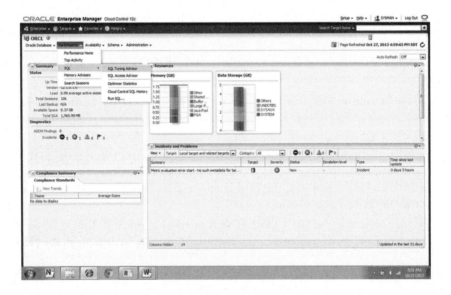

FIGURE 9.17   Schedule SQL Tuning Advisor page

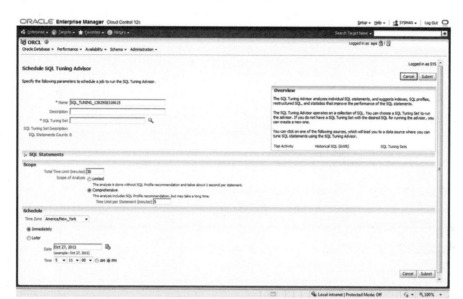

FIGURE 9.18   SQL Tuning Sets

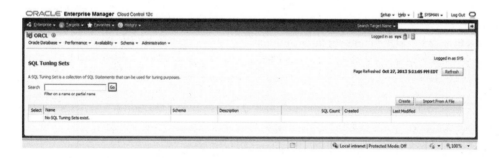

4. Click the Create button; this will begin the process to create a new SQL tuning set.

   a. Step 1 is to type a name for your tuning set, the schema owner, and a description, as shown in Figure 9.19. Then click Next to continue.

   b. Step 2 is to choose the load methods; in this case, as shown in Figure 9.20, specify a duration of 24 hours with samples taken at 5-minute intervals. Then click Next.

   c. In step 3 you set criteria for SQL statements to include in the tuning set, as shown in Figure 9.21. The drop-down menu allows you to select from a predefined list to add additional filter attributes. For this example we would like to see all of the SQL statements, so do not apply filter conditions. Then click Next.

FIGURE 9.19   Creating a new SQL tuning set

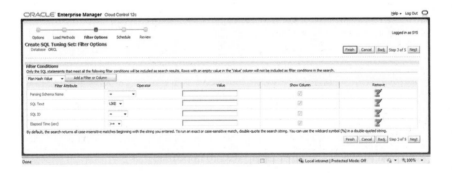

FIGURE 9.20   SQL tuning set load methods

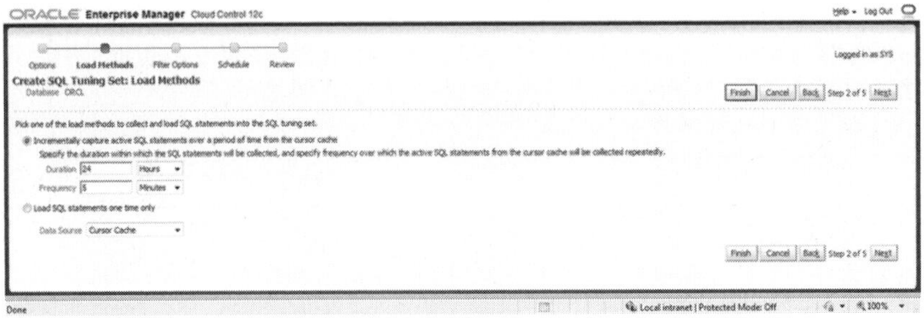

FIGURE 9.21   SQL tuning set filter options

d. In step 4 (Figure 9.22), you finalize the parameters to create and schedule the job to collect the SQL statement information and load it into a SQL tuning set. We want to start collecting immediately for this example. Click Next for the final review.

FIGURE 9.22   SQL tuning set schedule

e. In step 5 you review the options you entered, confirm the data, and click Submit
    to begin collecting SQL statement information for the tuning set, as shown in
    Figure 9.23.

FIGURE 9.23   SQL tuning set review

The Confirmation page, shown in Figure 9.24, indicates that the SQL tuning set and
collection job have been successfully created.

FIGURE 9.24   SQL tuning set confirmation

5. Return to the SQL Tuning Sets page and select the name of the SQL tuning set you wish to investigate.

   You should receive quick confirmation that SQL collection is in progress—the SQL statements count will increase.

6. After you have collected SQL statements in a set, you can run the SQL Tuning Advisor using the tuning set. In Figure 9.25, we identify which SQL tuning set to process.

FIGURE 9.25 SQL tuning set selection

7. Select a tuning set, and you will be taken to the SQL Tuning Set results page.

8. You can filter the results to a manageable amount that you can review by selecting Search For SQL Within Tuning Set, as shown in Figure 9.26.

FIGURE 9.26 SQL Tuning Advisor results

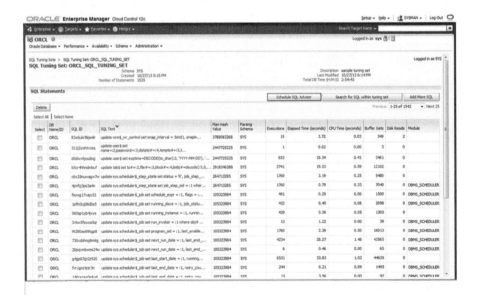

9. To reduce the number of SQL statements in the result set, choose to filter by Schema name = 'SCOTT'. The Advisor shows us the SQL statements that are potential opportunities for tuning, as shown in Figure 9.27. From the result set, choose a SQL statement to review.

10. We selected the first query that looked suspicious to us, a multi-table join that did not have a WHERE clause (select * from dept,emp,bonus,salgrade), and on the details page, shown in Figure 9.28; the Advisor indicates that we have a Merge Join Cartesian operation in the execution plan, which could present a potential tuning opportunity.

FIGURE 9.27   SQL Tuning Advisor recommendations for a SQL statement

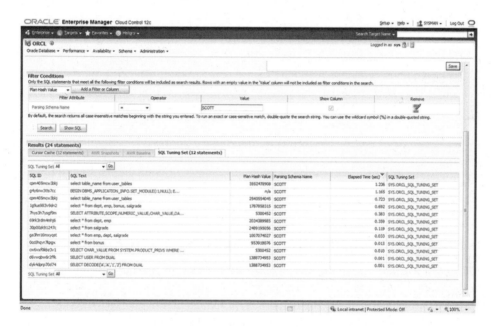

SQL Tuning Advisor Supplied Package and Views

Oracle 12*c* includes the DBMS_SQLTUNE package to manually execute the SQL Tuning Advisor. Instead of pointing and clicking from Oracle EM, you can manually configure the steps from SQL*Plus or another SQL front end.

Oracle also provides SQL tuning informational views, if you prefer to use them instead of EM:

- DBA_ADVISOR_*
- DBA_SQLTUNE_*
- DBA_SQLSET_*
- DBA_SQL_PROFILES

FIGURE 9.28 SQL Tuning Advisor recommendations: SQL statement original explain plan

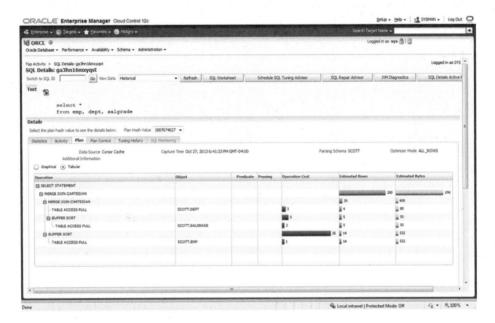

Using the SQL Access Advisor to Tune a Workload

The SQL Access Advisor is a tuning tool that assists the DBA by offering recommendations for indexes, partitioning, and materialized view logs for a workload.

Indexing recommendations may include B-tree, bitmap, and function-based indexes. The SQL Access Advisor may recommend partitioning tables, new partitioned indexes, and new partitioned materialized views. It also provides recommendations on how to improve the performance of materialized views by using Fast Refresh and Query Rewrite.

You can manually execute the SQL Access Advisor functions and procedures included in the DBMS_ADVISOR package. For this exercise, we will use Enterprise Manager.

1. From the database home page in EM, select Performance ≻ SQL ≻ SQL Access Advisor, as shown in Figure 9.29.

2. From the Initial Options page, shown in Figure 9.30, choose the Recommend New Access Structures option. Click Continue.

3. First, select the workload source. We'll use the current and recent SQL activity that is in the cache, shown in Figure 9.31. Click Next to continue.

4. Next, choose the depth and breadth of recommendation options, shown in Figure 9.32. For this exercise, we just want to view index recommendations, so select the Indexes box.

The Advanced Options link allows you to select workload categorization (scope and volatility), space restrictions, tuning prioritization, default storage schema and tablespace names for indexes and materialized views, and tablespace names for materialized view logs and partitions.

FIGURE 9.29 Launching the SQL Access Advisor

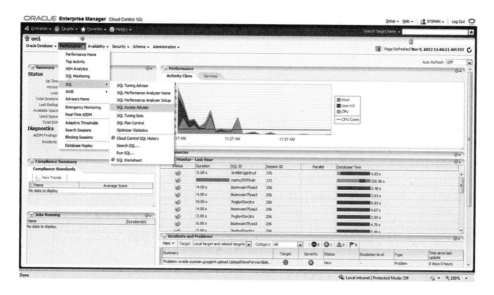

FIGURE 9.30 SQL Access Advisor: Initial Options

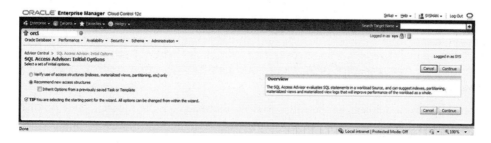

5. In step 3, schedule the SQL Access Advisor task, as shown in Figure 9.33.

6. In step 4, you need to review and verify the information you have provided and click Submit, as shown in Figure 9.34.

Once the task is submitted, you receive confirmation that the task was submitted successfully. You can monitor the task through completion from the Advisor Central home page, shown in Figure 9.35.

FIGURE 9.31 Choose the workload source for SQL Access Advisor.

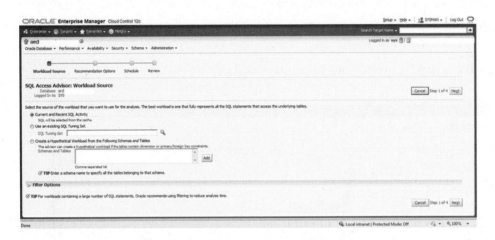

FIGURE 9.32 Recommendation options for SQL Access Advisor task

7. Once the task is complete, in the Advisor Tasks section, click the Results Name link to view the detailed recommendations for the task.

   The results of our task are shown in Figure 9.36.

   For this simplified example, there were numerous recommendations.

8. Click the SQL Statements tab to display the recommendations to improve SQL statements, as shown in Figure 9.37.

   With larger tables and more SQL statements to work with, we would see a greater number of legitimate recommendations.

FIGURE 9.33   Schedule the SQL Access Advisor task.

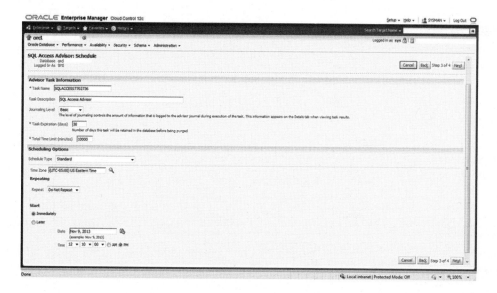

FIGURE 9.34   Review and submit the SQL Access Advisor task.

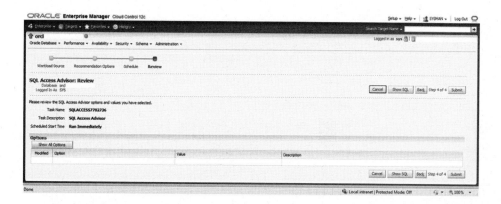

9. To implement the recommendations, select the recommended items and then click the Schedule Implementation button.

   Figure 9.38 shows the Schedule Implementation page.

10. Click the Submit button to implement the recommendations.

    The confirmation note will appear on the Results page, shown in Figure 9.39.

FIGURE 9.35 Monitor the SQL Access Advisor task.

FIGURE 9.36 Results for SQL Access Advisor task

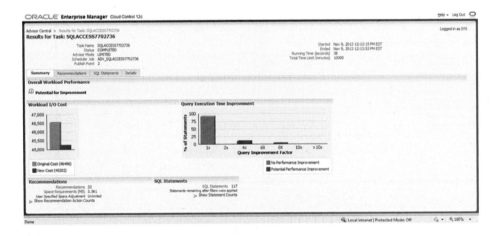

When implementing recommendations in SQL Access Advisor, be aware that certain operations will take time to complete. Partitioning an existing large table may take a long time, so keep that in mind before implementing it. The partitioning process creates a copy of the existing unpartitioned table, so make sure you have sufficient disk space for the operation.

FIGURE 9.37   Recommendations for the SQL Access Advisor task

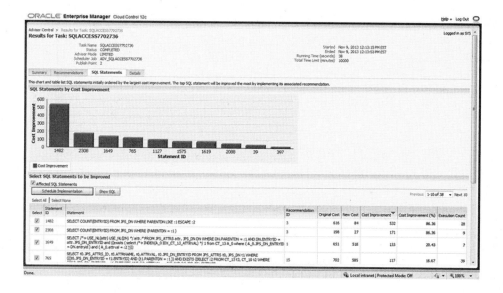

FIGURE 9.38   Implement recommendations for the SQL Access Advisor task.

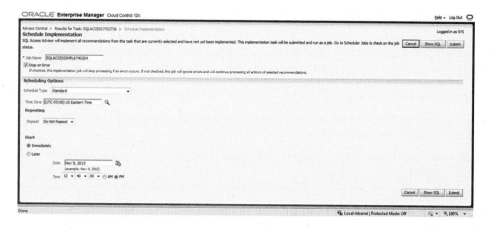

In Exercise 9.3, you will run the SQL Access Advisor on your database instance and determine which tuning steps should be applied.

FIGURE 9.39   Results confirmed for the SQL Access Advisor task

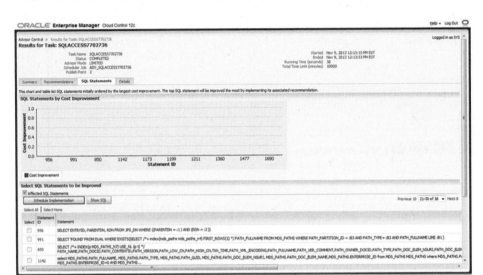

EXERCISE 9.3

Using the SQL Access Advisor

In this exercise, you will utilize the SQL Access Advisor to tune a workload. Since the workload is highly dependent on your database configuration, you will need to provide a workload, execute the advisor, and take the recommended actions.

1. Select a workload that you've already created, or create a new workload.

2. For the depth and breadth of recommendation options, you want to review only indexing recommendations.

3. Review the recommendations. If they make sense to you for your database, then implement them.

Perform Database Replay

One of the most difficult tasks for the professional DBA is setting up and conducting valid workload performance tests. It's easy to test the performance of a single query but often very challenging to test how an entire workload will perform in a different environment. For many organizations, the cost to test a platform migration is prohibitive, but the risk of not testing is significant. Organizations need to know how infrastructure changes will affect database application performance and if there's any impact to service-level agreements.

Database Replay allows the DBA to capture a workload on one database and replay it on another. Database Replay is platform independent, so it is very useful when planning a hardware or operating-system change to understand how workload performance might also change. If you have multiple platforms or components available to test, you can conduct a valid and repeatable performance comparison. The DBA and team can utilize Database Replay to identify performance bottlenecks in the workload; determine if storage, CPU, memory, or OS changes can remove the bottlenecks; and then run additional comparisons after the changes are made.

These are the basic steps of Database Replay:

1. Capture the database workload.

2. Preprocess the workload.

3. Replay the workload.

4. Analyze the workload replay results.

Let's look at each of these individually.

Capturing a Workload

Make sure you have a replay database that is similar in data content to the capture system. You can accomplish this by using Oracle or third-party tools to keep the data synchronized close to the capture start time. Consider RMAN, a standby database, or export/import.

Oracle recommends a clean shutdown and restart of the capture database before beginning workload capture. Start the database instance in restricted mode, start the capture, and the instance will automatically switch to unrestricted. If a database instance restart is not feasible, then quiesce the database or verify that there are no transactions running at the time the workload capture begins.

Define either inclusion or exclusion workload filters to include or exclude specific user sessions. The default is to capture all user sessions; you can use include or exclude filters but not both.

Set up a capture at the operating system level, and make sure it's empty and has plenty of space. The workload capture will stop if it runs out of space.

We start by capturing all the external client requests performed against a database and writing the information to a platform-independent binary capture file. The workload capture contains the following client request info:

- SQL text

- Bind variable values

- Information about transactions

Workload capture can be initiated from Oracle Enterprise Manager or through the DBMS_WORKLOAD_CAPTURE package. For this text, we will focus on EM.

At the Enterprise Manager database home page, click the Performance tab. From the page shown in Figure 9.40, choose the Database Replay menu item.

Note that EM provides an overview and lists the typical steps to perform a database replay, as shown in Figure 9.41. You can click the Expand All link to show the detail steps:

1. Start a workload capture by first clicking Capture Production Workload to expand this task; then on the Capture Workload row click the Go To Task icon in the rightmost column. Acknowledge that the prerequisites have been met (see Figure 9.42).

FIGURE 9.40 Launching Database Replay

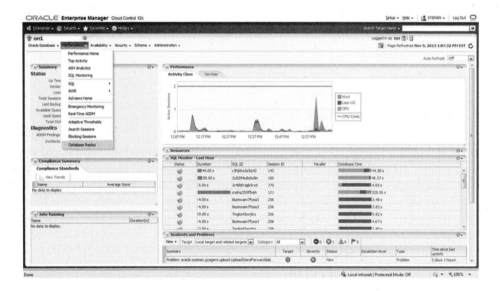

FIGURE 9.41 Database Replay home page

FIGURE 9.42   The Capture Workload: Plan Environment screen

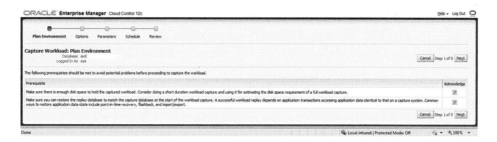

Restrictions and Limitations of Workload Capture

The following are restrictions and limitations on workload capture:

* Only one workload capture can run at a time.

* Distributed transactions will be replayed as local transactions.

The following are not captured:

* Background activities and database scheduler jobs

* Direct path load of data from external files using utilities such as SQL*Loader

* Shared server requests (Oracle MTS)

* Oracle streams

* Advanced replication streams

* Non-PL/SQL-based Advanced Queuing (AQ)

* Flashback queries

* Object navigations based on Oracle Call Interface (OCI)

* Non-SQL-based object access

* Remote DESCRIBE and COMMIT operations

---

2. Choose to restart the database and select workload filters, as shown in Figure 9.43.

3. Specify the name of the capture file, the directory object, and the database-instance shutdown and startup options, as shown in Figure 9.44.

   If the directory doesn't exist, you can create it using an OS program and then click the Create Directory Object button to assign the directory to a directory object. Figure 9.44 shows confirmation that the directory object was created successfully.

Workload Capturing in an Oracle Real Application Cluster

In an Oracle Real Application Cluster (RAC) database, workload capture is for the database, not for a single instance. Following Oracle's recommendation to capture a clean workload, you will need to shut down and restart all instances in this manner:

1. Shut down all instances associated with the database.

2. Start one of the instances.

3. Begin the workload capture.

4. Start the remaining instances.

FIGURE 9.43   The Capture Workload: Options screen

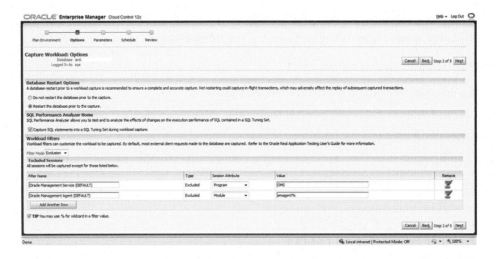

4. Specify the job schedule, parameters, and credentials in step 4, shown in Figure 9.45.

5. Perform a final review and acknowledgement, as shown in Figure 9.46.

6. Click the Submit button to begin the workload capture.

   You will be asked to confirm that you wish to restart the database and begin the capture.

7. If you wish to continue, click the Yes button.

   After you click Yes, you will be directed to an information page (see Figure 9.47) while the database is restarted.

FIGURE 9.44   The Capture Workload: Parameters screen

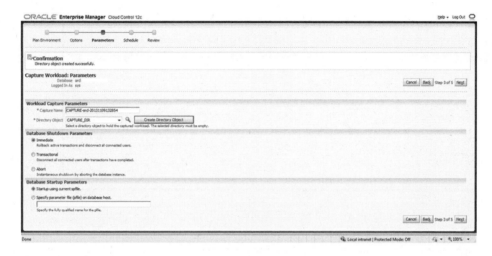

FIGURE 9.45   The Capture Workload: Schedule screen

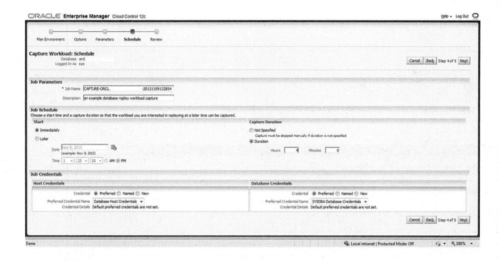

8. Click Refresh to log on to the database after it has restarted.

When you log on, you will be directed to the View Workload Capture screen, shown in Figure 9.48, where you can observe the capture in progress.

FIGURE 9.46   The Capture Workload: Review screen

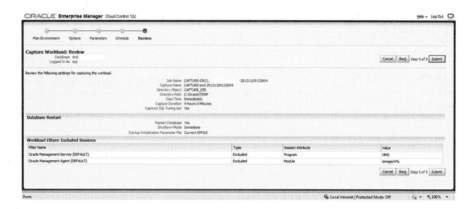

FIGURE 9.47   Database restarting Confirmation screen

FIGURE 9.48   The View Workload Capture screen

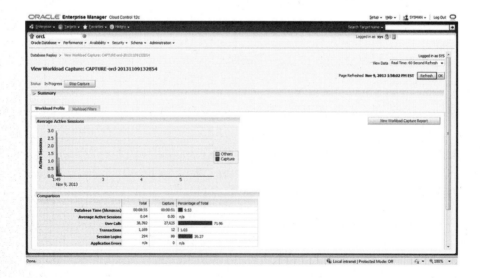

9. Click the Summary button to change the view.

10. Click the View Workload Capture Report button to see the detailed workload capture report.

11. Click Stop Capture to end the workload capture.

    You will be asked to acknowledge before the capture is stopped. Once you stop the capture, you will be presented with the option to export the workload to the AWR workload directory. If you choose not to save the AWR data at this time, you may do so later.

12. Click the OK button to return to the Database Replay page.

For this example, we used the general-purpose database supplied with Oracle 12c. We inserted rows and ran queries from three SQL*Plus sessions.

Preprocess a Captured Workload

The next task is to preprocess the captured workload. Launch the task by expanding the Prepare For Replay task name and then clicking the Go To Task icon at the end of the Preprocess Workload row (see Figure 9.49).

To preprocess a captured workload, follow these steps:

1. Locate a workload by using an existing workload directory on the host, as shown in Figure 9.50.

FIGURE 9.49   Database Replay preprocess

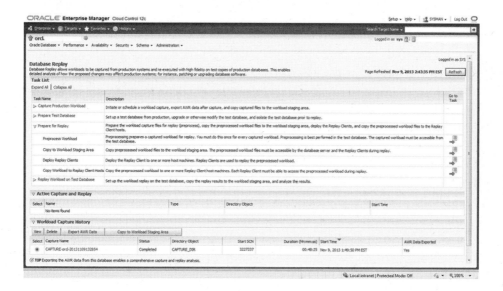

FIGURE 9.50   The Preprocess Captured Workload: Locate Workload screen

2. Click Next and step 2 will be skipped.

   The next screen is shown in Figure 9.51.

FIGURE 9.51   The Preprocess Captured Workload: Select Directory screen

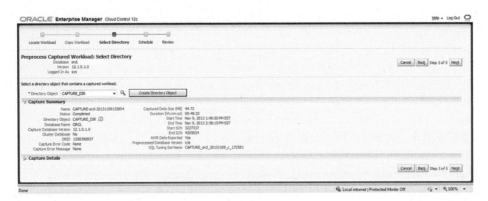

3. Locate and select a workload directory object, and the relevant data will be populated to the EM screen. Once you have acknowledged that you have the correct workload, click Next.

4. Schedule the preprocess job, as shown in Figure 9.52.

   For this exercise, we will start immediately upon completion of these steps. You will need to provide host OS credentials for the host machine where the Database Replay capture directory object resides.

5. Review the preprocess job and submit it, as shown in Figure 9.53.

When the job is submitted, you will be returned to the Database Replay screen and will receive confirmation that the preprocess job has been submitted, as shown in Figure 9.54.

6. Click the Refresh button and verify that the job has completed successfully, as indicated at the bottom of the Database Replay home page in the Workload Capture History section, Capture Name and Status columns, as shown in Figure 9.55.

FIGURE 9.52　　The Preprocess Captured Workload: Schedule screen

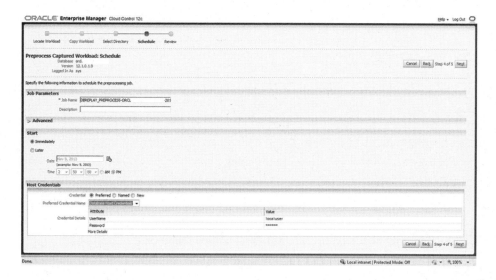

FIGURE 9.53　　The Preprocess Captured Workload: Review screen

FIGURE 9.54 The Confirmation screen

FIGURE 9.55 Workload Capture History status

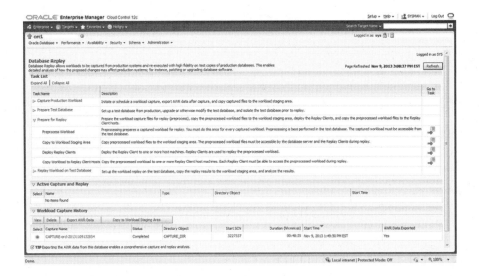

Replay a Captured Workload

To replay a workload, you need a test database that has data that's similar to the data in the capture database. We created a general-purpose database named STDB using the Database Configuration Assistant, and it is basically the same as the ORCL database we used to capture the workload.

You can perform Workload Replay using the DBMS_WORKLOAD_REPLAY supplied package, but for this example, we will use EM:

1. From the EM home page, choose the target database home page, choose the Performance menu item, and then click Database Replay.

   The next page presented is the Database Replay page.

2. In this example, expand the task Replay Workload On Test Database and choose Replay Workload, as shown in Figure 9.56.

FIGURE 9.56 Database Replay home page: Replay Workload On Test Database expanded

3. As you did during workload capture, locate a workload, shown as step 1 in the process in Figure 9.57, and use an existing workload directory on this host. In the previous workload capture example, we utilized the C:\Oracle\Temp directory and created the CAPTURE_DIR directory object. Select the directory object in step 2 and then click OK.

FIGURE 9.57 Replay Workload: Locate Workload screen

4. Once you have selected the workload from a directory and confirmed it in step 3 of the process, shown in Figure 9.58, click Next to review the initialize options, shown in Figure 9.59.

FIGURE 9.58 Replay Workload: Select Directory page

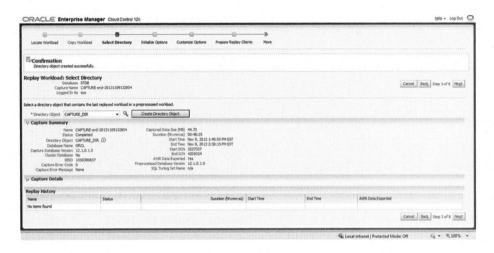

FIGURE 9.59 Replay Workload: Initialize Options page

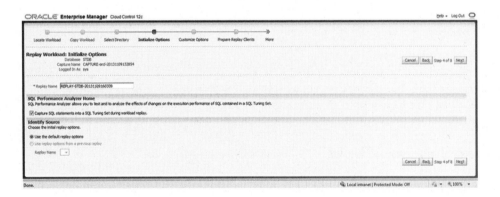

5. On the Initialize Options page (step 4), shown in Figure 9.59, in the Identify Source section, select Use The Default Replay Options; then click Next to proceed.

   There will be a brief preparation before moving to the next screen.

6. In step 5, you can customize the connection mappings on the first page, shown in Figure 9.60, and choose the replay parameters on the second page, shown in Figure 9.61. For this example we will use the default connection mappings and replay parameters.

FIGURE 9.60   Replay Workload: Customize Connection Mappings page

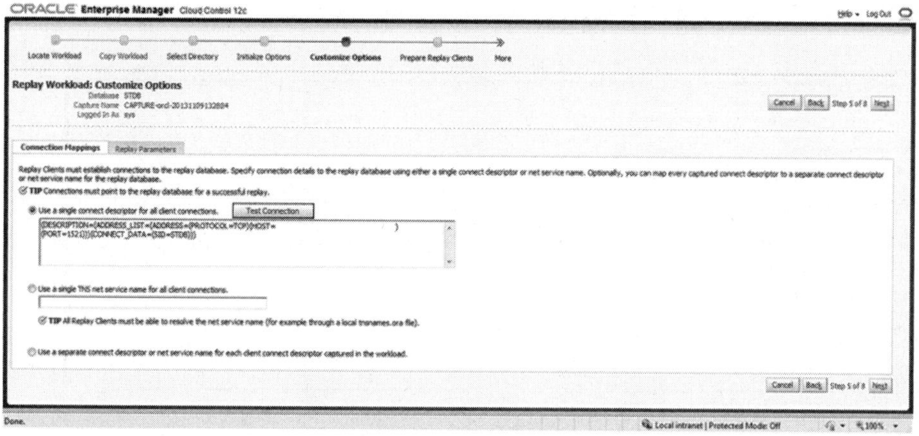

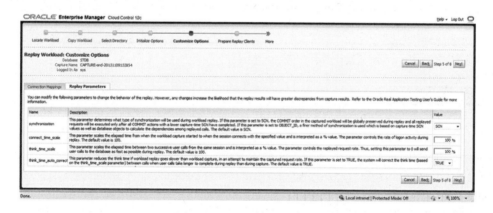

FIGURE 9.61   Replay Workload: Customize Replay Parameters page

On the Connection Mappings page, you can designate a connect descriptor and test it, use a single TNS net service name for each client, or use separate connect descriptors for each client.

7. Next, in step 6, you can prepare replay clients, as shown in Figure 9.62.

In this example we're choosing one replay client, since we had only one capture database session. If you had more than one capture session, adjust the number of replay sessions to match.

You will run the replay clients from the OS, not within Enterprise Manager, so now is a good time to make sure you're ready to run the clients (see Figure 9.63).

8. Open an OS command window and change directories to the replay directory.

FIGURE 9.62   Replay Workload: Prepare Replay Clients page

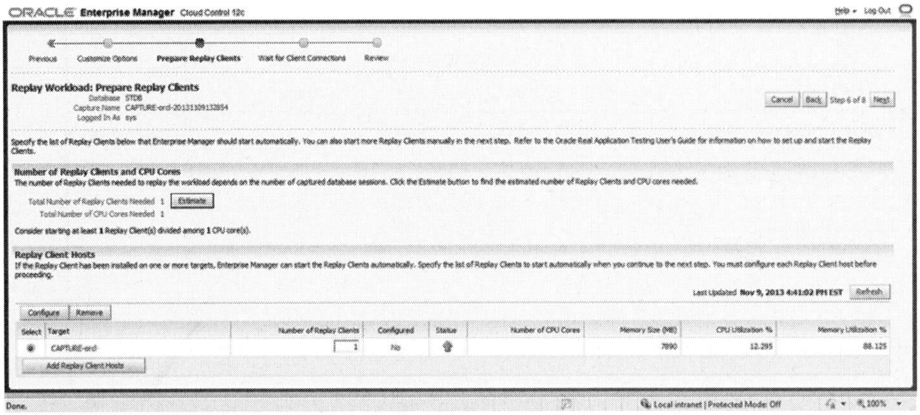

FIGURE 9.63   Waiting for the Database Replay client

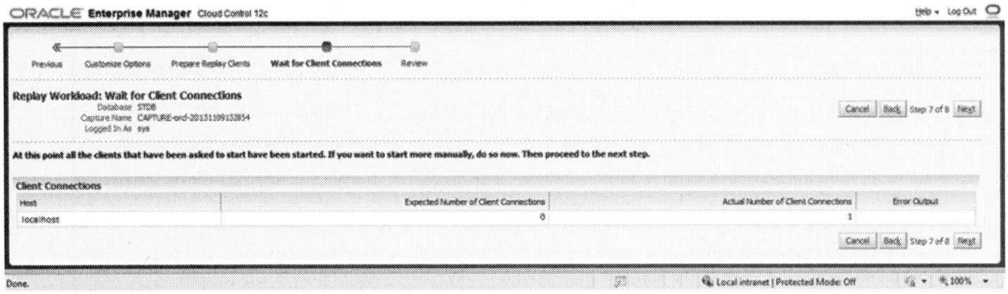

9. To start a replay client, you'll need to execute the $ORACLE_HOME\bin\wrc program with the appropriate parameters (see Figure 9.64). For this basic exercise, pass the username and password parameters, but there's no need to indicate the replay directory since you navigated to that directory prior to executing the command.

```
c:\oracle\bin\wrcsystem/system@stdb replaydir=c:\Oracle\temp\
Workload Replay Client: Release 12.1.0.1.0 - Production on Mon Oct 14
20:31:04 2013


Copyright (c) 1982, 2013, Oracle and/or its affiliates.  All rights reserved.
Wait for the replay to start (20:31:04)
```

10. Once the client or clients have connected, as indicated by the actual number of client connections, click Next to continue.

FIGURE 9.64   Database Replay client executing

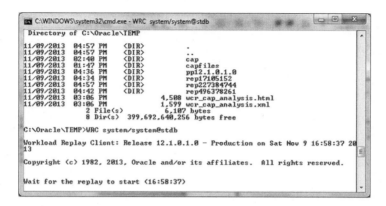

11. On the Review page, shown in Figure 9.65, you are instructed to reset the system time on the test database server to match the start time of the workload capture. Begin the replay by clicking the Submit button.

FIGURE 9.65   Replay Workload: Review page

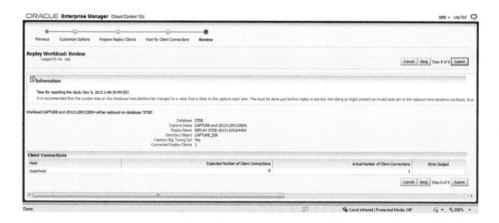

Once the replay has begun, you can confirm that the workload replay has started, as shown in Figure 9.66, and monitor the replay progress, as shown in Figure 9.67. At the OS prompt where you ran the wc command, you'll notice an acknowledgement that the replay has started.

When the replay is complete, the command window will indicate the replay completion time. If you choose to manually stop the replay by pressing the Stop Replay button on the View Workload Replay screen, the command window will indicate that the replay was cancelled. You can then view the report and analyze the results.

FIGURE 9.66   Replay Workload: View Workload Replay screen

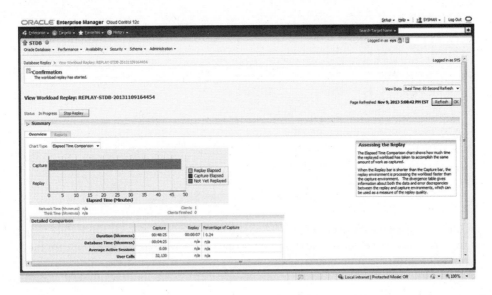

FIGURE 9.67   Replay Workload: monitoring workload replay

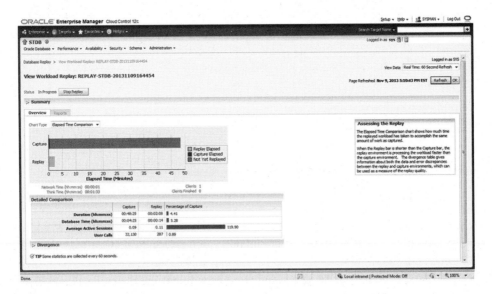

Analyze the Workload Replay Results

The basic steps to analyze the results are to view the capture report, view the replay report, and compare the results. You can view the reports from the Database Replay page in EM after the replay is complete:

1. Select the report of your choice from the View Workload Replay screen, as shown in Figure 9.68.

FIGURE 9.68   Database Replay: View Workload Replay summary

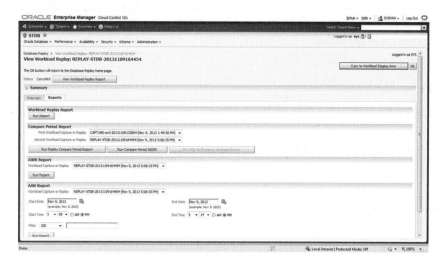

2. We will not go into a detailed analysis of the report, but there are a few key sections of the report to review:

- Workload Captured
- Workload Not Captured
- SQL Text
- Workload Filters

3. Key items to look for in the replay report are top SQL statements, performance divergence, data divergence, and error divergence.

Performance divergence is usually due to infrastructure or configuration differences between the capture and replay environments. In Figure 9.67 we can see that for the limited amount of the captured workload that was replayed, the replay time was greater than the capture time. Given this information, we need to further investigate to determine the bottlenecks in the test system. Data divergence occurs when the DML and SQL statement results in the replay system and capture system do not match. Error divergence occurs when the errors do not match.

In Exercise 9.4, you will capture a Database Replay workload on a source database and replay it on a destination database.

EXERCISE 9.4

Performing Database Replay

In this exercise, you will use the Database Replay feature to compare workload performance between a source database and a destination database.

1. Create a replay database as a copy of the capture database. One method is to use RMAN to make a clone. You could also use the DBCA to create a new capture database and a replay database.

2. Capture a workload on the source database.

3. Preprocess the workload capture.

4. Replay the workload on the destination database.

5. Analyze the results.

Summary

In this chapter, you learned about tools that help the DBA diagnose problems in the database and tools that assist with detecting and resolving performance issues.

In the first part, we introduced the Automatic Diagnostic Repository (ADR), the new central repository for storing all database diagnostic information, and the Support Workbench, which the DBA uses for problem recognition, reporting, and resolution. The Support Workbench improves DBA productivity by providing a process and web pages to report, analyze, and send diagnostic information to Oracle Support for problem resolution.

Block media recovery (BMR) is used to repair corrupt blocks within a data file while keeping the data file online. Block media recovery requires Enterprise Edition.

In the second part, we introduced the SQL Tuning Advisor, the SQL Access Advisor, and Database Replay. To help improve the performance of SQL statements, the SQL Tuning Advisor recommends new or modified indexes, SQL profiles, rewriting your SQL statements, or using statistics. The SQL Access Advisor looks at workgroups and recommends indexes, partitioning, and materialized views to improve the performance of a workload. Database Replay is an extremely useful tool that allows the DBA to capture and replay a workload to compare the performance of one system to another.

Exam Essentials

Know how to set up the Automatic Diagnostic Repository.   Make sure you understand the new initialization parameter for ADR, which parameters are deprecated, and the basic directory structure of the ADR.

Know how to use the Support Workbench to report an incident.   Know the steps required to open a service request with Oracle Support. Know how to package and submit the files related to a problem incident.

Know how to perform block media recovery.   Know how to discover corrupt data blocks, what causes data corruption, and how to repair corrupt data blocks. Know what can contribute to faster recoveries. Know what is required to perform block media recovery.

Understand automatic and manual SQL tuning.   Understand the differences between automatic and manual SQL tuning using the Tuning Advisor. Understand the advantages and potential dangers of automatic SQL tuning. Understand how to use the SQL Tuning Advisor in manual mode. Understand the scope differences between CDBs and PDBs when using the SQL Tuning Advisor in automatic and manual modes.

Understand the SQL Access Advisor.   Know what types of changes and types of indexes the SQL Access Advisor may recommend. Understand the impact of implementing recommendations.

Know when to use Database Replay.   Know the purpose and uses for Database Replay. Know what is required to set up and perform Database Replay. Know how to compare results from the production workload and the replay workload.

Review Questions

1. Which of the following initialization parameters have been deprecated in Oracle 12*c* because of the introduction of the Automatic Workload Repository? (Choose all that apply.)

   A. BACKGROUND_DUMP_DEST

   B. FOREGROUND_DUMP_DEST

   C. CORE_DUMP_DEST

   D. USER_DUMP_DEST

   E. DIAGNOSTIC_DEST

   F. All of the above

2. Which of the following statements is true regarding the initialization parameter DIAGNOSTIC_DEST?

   A. The default value is the value of the environment variable $ORACLE_HOME; if $ORACLE_HOME isn't set, then the default is set to $ORACLE_BASE.

   B. The default value is the value of the environment variable $ORACLE_BASE; if $ORACLE_BASE isn't set, then it is set to $ORACLE_HOME.

   C. DIAGNOSTIC_DEST is always equal to $ORACLE_HOME.

   D. DIAGNOSTIC_DEST is always equal to $ORACLE_BASE.

3. Which of these formats represents the correct hierarchy for the ADR?

   A. <diagnostic_dest>/rdbms/diag/<dbname>/<instname>

   B. <diagnostic_dest>/diag/rdbms/<instname>/<dbname>

   C. <diagnostic_dest>/diag/rdbms/<dbname>/<instname>

   D. None of the above

4. Which of the following are not fundamental tasks of the Support Workbench? (Choose all that apply.)

   A. View long-running SQL workloads.

   B. View problem details.

   C. Gather additional diagnostic information.

   D. Create a service request.

   E. Clean up incident data after upload to Oracle Support.

5. Which of the following tasks does the tool Incident Packaging Service (IPS) perform?

    A. Clean up the ADR by deleting files not associated with an incident uploaded to Oracle Support.

    B. Identify all files associated with a critical error and add them to a zip file to be sent to Oracle Support.

    C. Automatically open a service request with Oracle Support for each critical error and send all relevant files.

    D. Display a high-level view of critical errors on the database home page.

6. Choose the correct order to package and upload data for an incident to Oracle Support.

    A. Schedule, create new package, view manifest, view contents

    B. Create new package, view manifest, view contents, schedule

    C. Schedule, create new package, view contents, view manifest

    D. Create new package, view contents, view manifest, schedule

    E. None of the above

7. Which of the following is *not* an advantage of block media recovery (BMR)?

    A. Reduced MTTR.

    B. Data files remain offline while corrupt blocks are repaired.

    C. Data files remain online while corrupt blocks are repaired.

    D. A and C

8. Which of the following methods can be used to detect block corruption?

    A. ANALYZE operations

    B. dbv

    C. SQL queries that access the potentially corrupt block

    D. RMAN

    E. All of the above

9. Which of the following are correct about block media recovery? (Choose all that apply.)

    A. Physical and logical block corruption is recorded automatically in V$DATABASE_BLOCK_CORRUPTION.

    B. Logical corruptions are repairable by BMR.

    C. Physical corruptions are repairable by BMR.

    D. RMAN can use any backup for a BMR restore.

    E. Archive log mode is not required if you have both a full and incremental backup for restore.

10. While querying the EMPLOYEES table, you receive an ORA-01578 message indicating block corruption in File# 1201 and Block# 1968. You analyze the table and the corruption is verified. Which RMAN command do you use to perform BMR and repair the corrupt block? (Choose all that apply.)

    A. RECOVER FILE=1201 BLOCK=1968;

    B. RECOVER CORRUPTION LIST;

    C. RECOVER DATAFILE 1201 BLOCK 1968;

    D. RECOVER BLOCK CORRUPTION LIST;

    E. None of the above

11. To view the results of the most recent Automatic SQL Tuning Advisor task, which sequence should you follow?

    A. EM Database home page ➢ Software And Support ➢ SQL Advisors ➢ Automatic SQL Tuning Advisor.

    B. EM Database home page ➢ Software And Support ➢ Advisor Central ➢ SQL Advisors ➢ Automatic SQL Tuning Advisor.

    C. EM Database home page ➢ Software And Support ➢ Support Workbench ➢ Advisor Central ➢ SQL Advisors ➢ Automatic SQL Tuning Advisor.

    D. Either B or C

    E. All of the above

12. When creating a SQL tuning set, which of the following steps allows the DBA to reduce the size of the SQL set by selecting specific operators and values?

    A. Filter versions

    B. Filter loads

    C. Filter tasks

    D. Filter options

13. To view the results of a manual SQL Tuning Advisor task, which steps should the DBA take?

    A. From the Advisor Central home page, select the Tuning task from the Advisor Tasks section.

    B. From Advisor Central, choose SQL Advisors ➢ SQL Tuning Advisors ➢ Manual Tuning Task Results.

    C. From Advisor Central, choose SQL Advisors ➢ Manual SQL Tuning Advisors ➢ Tuning Task Results.

    D. Either B or C

14. Which of these appropriately describes the results of a manual SQL Tuning Advisor task?

    A. A list of SQL statements and recommendations for tuning

    B. A list of SQL statements that have been tuned by the Advisor, with before and after metrics

    C. Graphs showing the actual performance improvement made by the Advisor after it implemented the recommended changes

    D. All of the above

15. Which of the following is a potential performance tuning recommendation from the SQL Access Advisor?

    A. Create new indexes.

    B. Modify existing indexes.

    C. Implement partitioning on a nonpartitioned table.

    D. Create materialized views.

    E. All of the above

16. Which statement most accurately describes the implementation of a SQL Access Advisor recommendation?

    A. SQL Access Advisor recommendations are automatically implemented.

    B. Individual SQL Access Advisor recommendations can be scheduled for implementation.

    C. All SQL Access Advisor recommendations for a specific task must be implemented at the same time.

    D. SQL Access Advisor recommendations are automatically scheduled for implementation during the maintenance window.

    E. None of the above

17. Which of the following represents the correct sequence of events for Database Replay?

    A. Capture, analyze, preprocess, replay

    B. Capture, preprocess, analyze, replay

    C. Capture, preprocess, replay, analyze

    D. Analyze, capture, preprocess, replay

    E. None of the above

18. Which of these recommendations should be followed before capturing a workload? (Choose all that apply.)

   A. Make sure your replay database has the same structure as the capture database, except without data.

   B. Make sure the replay and capture databases are similar in data content.

   C. Perform a clean shutdown and restart of the capture database before beginning a workload capture.

   D. Start the capture database in unrestricted mode; then start the capture.

   E. Define inclusion and exclusion filters.

19. Which is true concerning Database Replay in an Oracle Real Application Cluster (RAC) database?

   A. Workload capture is per instance.

   B. You need to restart only one instance to begin workload capture.

   C. Specifically in RAC, you shut down all instances, restart them individually, and begin workload capture with the last instance started.

   D. RAC does not support workload capture, but it does support workload replay.

   E. None of the above.

20. Performance divergence indicated in the Workload Replay report is most likely due to what?

   A. DML and SQL statement results that do not match between the capture and replay systems

   B. When errors that occur in the capture system don't occur in the replay system

   C. Top SQL statements

   D. Infrastructure or system-configuration differences

   E. Time-of-day differences between capture and replay systems

Chapter

10

Managing Database Resources

ORACLE DATABASE 12c: ADVANCED ADMINISTRATION EXAM OBJECTIVES COVERED IN THIS CHAPTER:

✓ **Managing Storage in a CDB and PDBs**

- Manage permanent and temporary tablespaces in CDB and PDBs

In this chapter, we will discuss how to most effectively manage database storage resources. For space management, we will discuss resumable space allocation, transportable tablespaces and databases, and shrinking segments.

We'll cover two features (resumable space allocation and shrinking segments) for managing the efficient utilization of space resources and two features (transportable tablespaces and transportable databases) for managing large-scale data movement. The resumable space allocation feature allows you to efficiently utilize space resources and prevent transaction aborts when space limitations are encountered. Shrinking segments allow you to eliminate white space in a segment in place while the segment remains online and available for application use. For large-scale movement of tablespaces from one database to another, the DBA can use the transportable tablespaces feature. To move an entire database, even to another platform, you can use the transportable database feature.

We will discuss storage resource management in the Oracle 12*c* multitenant architecture, specifically how permanent and temporary tablespaces are managed in CDBs and PDBs.

Exam objectives are subject to change at any time without prior notice and at Oracle's sole discretion. Please visit Oracle's Training and Certification website (http://www.oracle.com/education/certification/) for the most current exam-objectives listing.

Managing Storage

In the following sections, we will explore resumable space allocation, transportable tablespaces, transportable databases, and shrinking segments. Resumable space allocation allows you to temporarily suspend operations that run out of space while you correct the space issue without aborting the operation. With the transportable tablespace feature, you can copy a set of tablespaces from a source database to a destination database. With the transportable database feature, you can copy an entire database from one platform to another. And finally, you'll learn how to shrink segments dynamically.

Managing Resumable Space Allocation

If the Oracle database encounters a space problem during the execution of an operation, it can suspend the operation and then later resume the operation. This feature is called *resumable space allocation*, and it allows the DBA to fix a problem prior to the database returning an error message to the user process. Once you've fixed the problem, the database automatically resumes the suspended operation.

Enabling resumable space allocation is simple: You can set the initialization parameter RESUMABLE_TIMEOUT to a value greater than zero, or you can issue the ALTER SESSION ENABLE RESUMABLE statement.

Understanding Resumable Space Allocation

A resumable statement suspends when an object runs out of space, it reaches the maximum number of extents, or a space quota is exceeded. An object running out of space or reaching maximum extents applies to tables, indexes, temporary segments, undo segments, large objects (LOBs), clusters, and table or index partitions. When a resumable statement is suspended, an error is reported in the alert log and the system issues the resumable session suspended alert, and if an AFTER SUSPEND trigger is in place, it will be executed. When the statement is suspended, the transaction will be suspended and all transaction resources held until rolled back or the suspend operation is resumed to completion. When the suspend condition is resolved, it will automatically resume and the associated resumable session suspended alert is cleared; of course, the original error message logged in the alert log remains.

In a distributed transaction, the remote RESUMABLE_TIMEOUT initialization parameter applies to the remote part of the transaction, and the remote session resumable setting applies. Also, local resumable settings do not apply to the remote part of the distributed transactions.

Resumable Space Operations

Specific Data Definition Language (DDL), Import/Export, Data Manipulation Language (DML), and query statements are candidates for resumable executions:

- SELECT statements that run out of sort area temporary space
- INSERT, UPDATE, DELETE, and INSERT INTO...SELECT
- Export/import and SQL*Loader
- The following DDL statements:

```
CREATE TABLE AS SELECT
CREATE INDEX
ALTER TABLE MOVE PARTITION
ALTER TABLE SPLIT PARTITION
ALTER INDEX REBUILD
ALTER INDEX REBUILD PARTITION
ALTER INDEX SPLIT PARTITION
CREATE MATERIALIZED VIEW
CREATE MATERIALIZED VIEW LOG
```

For parallel operations, each process is handled independently. If one suspends, an error is logged and the associated AFTER SUSPEND trigger, if any, is executed. Meanwhile, the other parallel processes continue. However, if one aborts, the parallel operation aborts. As with all resumable processing, when a suspend condition is repaired, it will continue and join up with the others.

Enabling and Disabling Resumable Operations

You enable resumable operations and configure the suspend time-out for the instance and for a session. For the instance, configure the initialization parameter RESUMABLE_TIMEOUT. For the session, set the session parameter RESUMABLE_TIMEOUT to a numeric value greater than zero, or issue the ALTER SESSION command.

Enabling and Disabling Resumable Operations for an Instance

To enable resumable operations for the instance, alter the instance parameter RESUMABLE_TIMEOUT to a numeric value greater than zero. The default value is 0, which in effect initially disables resumable operations for all sessions. This represents the number of seconds that an operation may suspend while you take corrective action. After the time-out is reached, the operation will abort. In this example, we alter the system RESUMABLE_TIMEOUT from 1 minute to 10 minutes:

```
SQL> show parameter resumable

NAME                                 TYPE          VALUE
------------------------------------ -----------   -------
resumable_timeout                    integer       60
SQL> alter system set resumable_timeout=600 scope=both;

System altered.
```

Enabling and Disabling Resumable Operations for a Session

Before you can enable or disable resumable operations at the session level, the user must have been granted the RESUMABLE system privilege. Once that's granted, resumable operations are enabled within a session when the following command is issued:

```
SQL> alter session enable resumable;

Session altered.
```

If you do not set a specific value for RESUMABLE_TIMEOUT for the instance or when enabling resumable for a session, the default value for a session is 7,200 seconds. To disable resumable operations within a session, issue the following command:

```
SQL> alter session disable resumable;

Session altered.
```

Additionally, the user session can control the suspend time-out in one of three ways: by altering the RESUMABLE_TIMEOUT parameter for the session, by executing the DBMS_RESUMABLE.SET_TIMEOUT procedure (covered later, in the section "The DBMS_RESUMABLE Supplied Package"), or by appending to the ALTER SESSION ENABLE RESUMABLE command as follows:

```
SQL> alter session set resumable_timeout=3600;

Session altered.

SQL> show parameter resumable;

NAME                                 TYPE         VALUE
------------------------------------ ----------- -----
resumable_timeout                    integer      3600
SQL>

SQL> alter session enable resumable timeout 7200;

Session altered.
SQL> show parameter resumable;

NAME                                 TYPE         VALUE
------------------------------------ ----------- -----
resumable_timeout                    integer      3600
SQL>
```

The ALTER SESSION ENABLE RESUMABLE TIMEOUT *NNNN* command does not alter the value of the session-initialization parameter RESUMABLE_TIMEOUT.

Procedurally, you can also enable resumable operations for a session with a logon trigger.

Identifying Resumable Sessions

By default, if a session is enabled for resumable space allocation, the session is identified in the NAME column of the DBA_ and USER_RESUMABLE views by the username, session ID, and instance number, as follows:

```
SQL> select name from user_resumable;


NAME
------------------------------------
User SYS(0), Session 108, Instance 1


SQL>
```

You can alter the session identifier by issuing the ALTER SESSION command and adding the NAME clause, as follows:

```
SQL> alter session enable resumable name 'LNE test';
Session altered.
SQL> select name from user_resumable;
NAME
----------------------------------------------------
LNE test
SQL>
```

This changed name remains in effect until it's altered by the ENABLE RESUMABLE NAME command, until resumable is disabled by the session, or until the session ends.

Working with Resumable Operations

Once you've enabled resumable operations, you'll need to monitor and take action on suspended resumable operations. You'll monitor specific views to determine the status of resumable operations, and you'll write AFTER SUSPEND triggers and utilize the DBMS_RESUMABLE supplied package to take action within a session when a suspend occurs.

Additionally, Enterprise Manager reports resumable alerts and provides the mechanism for resolving resumable space issues.

Views for Monitoring Resumable Space Allocation

The DBA_RESUMABLE and USER_RESUMABLE views contain rows for suspended resumable statements as well as those that are executing as normal. The key information columns are described in Table 10.1. The USER_ID column is not included in the USER_RESUMABLE view, and as with all USER_ views, only the current session information is shown.

The DBA can also use the V$SESSION_WAIT view to catch suspended resumable operations. The EVENT column will contain a statement indicating that the operation is suspended and waiting for the error to be cleared.

TABLE 10.1 DBA_RESUMABLE Columns

Column Name	Description
USER_ID	User ID number of the resumable statement owner
SESSION_ID	Session identifier of the resumable statement
INSTANCE_ID	Instance number of the resumable statement
COORD_INSTANCE_ID	Instance number on which the parallel coordinator is running
COORD_SESSION_ID	Session identifier of the parallel coordinator
STATUS	Status of the RESUMABLE statement: RUNNING, SUSPENDED, TIMEOUT, ERROR, or ABORTED
TIMEOUT	Time-out value of the resumable statement
START_TIME	Start time of the resumable statement
SUSPEND_TIME	The last time the resumable statement was suspended
RESUME_TIME	The last time the statement resumed
SQL_TEXT	The resumable statement
ERROR_NUMBER	The error number of the last error logged or this resumable statement. If no errors, the value will be NULL
ERROR_PARAMETER*n*	Error parameter columns 1 through 5
ERROR_MSG	The error message associated with the ERROR_NUMBER

Monitoring Resumable Space Alerts with Enterprise Manager

Oracle Enterprise Manager will display alerts on the database home page when there are resumable space suspends. In the example shown in Figure 10.1, we have created a suspend condition by attempting to insert into a table that is in a space-constrained tablespace.

On the database alerts page, shown in Figure 10.2, click the error message Summary link to see the details of the error.

Now from the alert page, under the Guided Resolution section, click the Edit Tablespace link, shown in Figure 10.3, to display the tablespace details.

For the constrained tablespace, shown in Figure 10.4, choose to add a new data file to the tablespace or edit the data file and increase the size.

FIGURE 10.1 Tablespace space alert on database home page

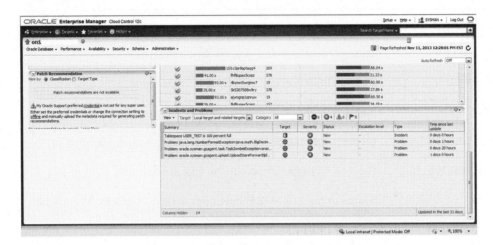

FIGURE 10.2 Database alerts page

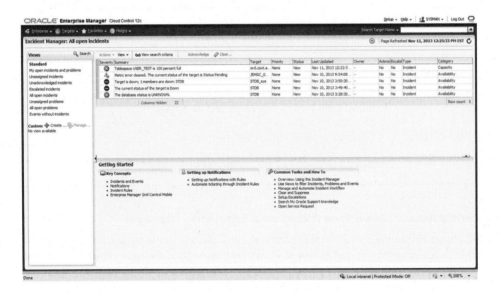

FIGURE 10.3   Tablespaces

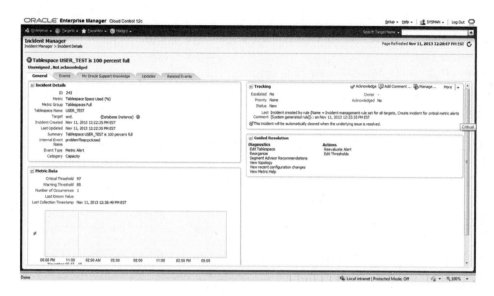

FIGURE 10.4   Tablespaces data file details

For this example, we will click the link on the data file name, and we can either increase the size of the data file or change the data file to AUTOEXTEND ON to resolve the suspend issue.

The *DBMS_RESUMABLE* Supplied Package

The DBMS_RESUMABLE package allows you to get and set time-out parameters for a session, abort a suspended resumable session, and query the error stack for specific resumable space errors. Table 10.2 describes the package functions and subprograms.

TABLE 10.2 DBMS_RESUMABLE Package Programs

Program Name	Description
ABORT	Procedure that allows you to abort a suspended resumable operation
GET_SESSION_TIMEOUT	Function that when passed the session ID returns the current resumable time-out
GET_TIMEOUT	Function that returns resumable time-out for the current session
SET_SESSION_TIMEOUT	Procedure that when passed the session ID and time-out value sets the time-out for a session
SET_TIMEOUT	Procedure that sets the time-out for the current session
SPACE_ERROR_INFO	Function that allows you to search the error stack on error_type, object_type, object_owner, object_name, sub_object_name, and table_space_name

In the following code, you see an example that enables resumable for the session; gets the session time-out value; changes the value; queries the value; disables resumable; and then queries, modifies, and enables it. You'll note that the resumable time-out value is retained by the session even though resumable was disabled. Also note that the default time-out for an enabled session is 7,200 seconds.

```
SQL> alter session enable resumable;

Session altered.

SQL> select dbms_resumable.get_timeout from dual;

GET_TIMEOUT
-----------
       7200

SQL> exec dbms_resumable.set_timeout (9600);
```

```
PL/SQL procedure successfully completed.

SQL> select dbms_resumable.get_timeout from dual;

GET_TIMEOUT
-----------
       9600

SQL> alter session disable resumable;

Session altered.

SQL> select dbms_resumable.get_timeout from dual;

GET_TIMEOUT
-----------
       9600

SQL> alter session enable resumable timeout 7200;

Session altered.

SQL> select dbms_resumable.get_timeout from dual;

GET_TIMEOUT
-----------
       7200
```

Triggered Events to Respond to Suspends

Oracle has created the AFTER SUSPEND trigger to help you resolve suspend conditions program-matically. By registering an AFTER SUSPEND trigger on the database as user SYS using the ON DATABASE clause, you can take action regardless of who owns the resumable operation. Here's an example:

```
SQL> CREATE OR REPLACE TRIGGER resumable_default_timeout
AFTER SUSPEND
ON DATABASE
BEGIN
DBMS_RESUMABLE.SET_TIMEOUT(14400);
END;
/
```

Managing Transportable Tablespaces

The transportable tablespace feature allows you to copy or move a tablespace from one database to another. Using transportable tablespaces is faster than copying rows or using export/import or unload/load. With Oracle 10g or higher, it is possible to transport tablespaces across some but not all platforms. Transportable tablespaces are useful for, but not limited to, the following:

- Database migrations
- Sharing tablespaces with other database users (for example, remote customers)
- Tablespace point-in-time recovery (TSPITR)
- Archiving data from one database to another
- Exporting and importing partitions

Transporting a tablespace is straightforward, but there are caveats and limitations. You can use Enterprise Manager, or you can use SQL*Plus and the OS command line. We will take you through the basic process and list the major considerations.

The first step is to determine what will be transported. If your intent is to transport objects that exist in only one tablespace and have no dependencies in other tablespaces, then the process is simplified. If, however, you intend to transport a set of objects that are spread across multiple tablespaces or have dependencies on objects in other tablespaces, then the task becomes slightly more complex.

Transportable Tablespace Sets

A transportable tablespace set is a self-contained group of tablespaces that encapsulate the objects that you wish to transport from one database to another. For example, if you wish to transport several tables that reside in different tablespaces, then you would include each of the tablespaces in the tablespace set. If you wish to transport a partitioned table and the different partitions are in different tablespaces, then you would need to include each of the tablespaces in the tablespace set.

We'll discuss tablespace sets in detail and show examples a bit later.

Manually Transporting a Tablespace

In this section, we will demonstrate how to manually transport a tablespace using a combination of SQL*Plus, the OS command line, and Oracle Data Pump.

The basic steps are as follows:

1. Check compatibility and endian format.
2. Choose the transportable tablespace set.
3. Generate the transportable tablespace set.
4. Transport the tablespace set.
5. Import the tablespace set.

Requirements of Transportable Tablespaces

Transportable tablespaces can be locally managed or dictionary managed and must meet the following requirements:

- In Oracle 9*i* or higher, the transported tablespace does not have to be the same block size as the target database's standard block size. However, the target database must have a DB_*n*K_CACHE_SIZE initialization parameter set, where *n* is the block size of the transportable tablespace.

- The tablespace must be placed in read-only mode during the transport process.

- Starting with Oracle 11*g*, Oracle Data Pump is used instead of export/import to move the metadata from the source to the target.

- You can't import a transported tablespace that has the same name as an existing tablespace in the target database. You can rename the transported tablespace as part of the import process.

- In order for an object to be transportable, all of the partitions that contain its dependent objects such as indexes, materialized views, and partitioned tables must be included in the tablespace set.

- Tablespaces that do not use block encryption but have tables that have encrypted columns are not transportable.

- You can't transport the SYSTEM tablespace or objects owned by the SYS user.

- Tablespaces with 8.0-compatible advanced queues with multiple recipients are not transportable.

- If you're transporting across platforms, RAW, BFILE, and AnyTypes are not converted from one endian type to another as part of the transport process.

Step 1: Check Compatibility and Endian Format

If the source and target are different versions of the database, you'll need to verify the minimum compatibility for transportable tablespaces. When you create a transportable tablespace set, Oracle determines the minimum compatibility level for the target. Oracle throws an error if the target database's compatibility level is lower than the minimum compatibility. If you're transporting a tablespace to the same platform, the minimum compatibility must be 8.0 for both the source and target. Both source and target must have a minimum compatibility of 9.0 if the transportable tablespace's block size is different than the target's standard block size. For different platforms, the minimum compatibility must be 10.0 for both source and target.

Database Requirements for Transportable Tablespaces

To utilize the transportable tablespace feature, you must make sure the database meets the following criteria:

■ To create a transportable tablespace set, the source database must be Oracle 8*i* or later, and it must be Enterprise Edition.

■ To import a tablespace set from the same platform, the target database can be any edition of Oracle 8*i* or higher.

■ To create a transportable tablespace set for import into a database on a different platform, the source database must have compatibility set to 10.0 or higher.

■ To import a transportable tablespace set from a different platform, both the source and target databases must have compatibility set to 10.0 or higher.

■ The source and target database must have the same character set and national character set.

If your source and target are different platforms, it will be necessary to check for endian compatibility. If the source and target are not directly compatible—for example, the source is big endian and the target is little endian—then you will need to use RMAN to convert the copy of each tablespace data file on either the source or target platform. To determine which platforms you can transport to, run this query:

```
SQL> select * from v$transportable_platform order by PLATFORM_ID;
PLATFORM_ID PLATFORM_NAME                        ENDIAN_FORMAT   CON_ID
----------- ---------------------------------    -------------   --------------
          1 Solaris[tm] OE (32-bit)              Big                          0
          2 Solaris[tm] OE (64-bit)              Big                          0
          3 HP-UX (64-bit)                       Big                          0
          4 HP-UX IA (64-bit)                    Big                          0
          5 HP Tru64 UNIX                        Little                       0
          6 AIX-Based Systems (64-bit)           Big                          0
          7 Microsoft Windows IA (32-bit)        Little                       0
          8 Microsoft Windows IA (64-bit)        Little                       0
          9 IBM zSeries Based Linux              Big                          0
         10 Linux IA (32-bit)                    Little                       0
         11 Linux IA (64-bit)                    Little                       0
         12 Microsoft Windows x86 64-bit         Little                       0
         13 Linux x86 64-bit                     Little                       0
```

```
    15 HP Open VMS                            Little               0
    16 Apple Mac OS                           Big                  0
    17 Solaris Operating System (x86)         Little               0
    18 IBM Power Based Linux                  Big                  0
    19 HP IA Open VMS                         Little               0
    20 Solaris Operating System (x86-64)      Little               0
    21 Apple Mac OS (x86-64)                  Little               0
20 rows selected.
SQL>
```

If you want to see only target platforms that are endian-compatible with the source platform, run this query at your source database:

```
SQL> COL "Source" FORM A32
SQL> COL "Compatible Targets" FORM A32
SQL> BREAK ON "Source"

SQL> select d.platform_name "Source", t.platform_name
 "Compatible Targets", endian_format
 from v$transportable_platform t, v$database d
 where t.endian_format = (select endian_format
                          from v$transportable_platform t,
                          v$database d
                          where d.platform_name =
                          t.platform_name)
SQL> /

Source                          Compatible Targets
          ENDIAN_FORMAT
------------------------------- -------------------------
------ --------------


Source                          Compatible Targets                  ENDIAN_FORMAT
------------------------------- ----------------------------------- --------------


Microsoft Windows x86 64-bit    Microsoft Windows IA (32-bit)       Little
                                Linux IA (32-bit)                   Little
                                HP Tru64 UNIX                       Little
                                Linux IA (64-bit)                   Little
                                HP Open VMS                         Little
                                Microsoft Windows IA (64-bit)       Little
```

```
                        Linux x86 64-bit                        Little
                        Microsoft Windows x86 64-bit            Little
                        Solaris Operating System (x86)          Little
                        HP IA Open VMS                          Little
                        Solaris Operating System (x86-64)       Little
                        Apple Mac OS (x86-64)                   Little

12 rows selected.

SQL>
```

If the source and target have the same endian format, no RMAN conversion is necessary. If they are different, you will need to use RMAN to convert the tablespace data files in the transportable set to the correct endian format.

Step 2: Choose the Transportable Tablespace Set

In order for a tablespace set to be transportable, it must be self-contained; that is, objects in the tablespace set must have no dependencies in tablespaces outside the tablespace set. Here are some basic rules:

- The tablespace set must contain all of the partitions of a partitioned table if any of the table's partitions are included in the tablespace set.
- If an index is included in a tablespace set, its corresponding table must also be included in the tablespace set.
- If you choose to include referential integrity constraints in the tablespace set, then all tablespaces required to support the constraints must be included in the set.
- If you have tables with LOB columns in the set, the tablespace that contains the LOBs must be included.

The easy way to determine if the set of tablespaces is self-contained is to execute the DBMS_TTS.TRANSPORT_SET_CHECK procedure, supplying the list of tablespaces in the tablespace set, as in this example:

```
SQL> create table scott.foo_1 (x number, y varchar2(20)) tablespace users;
Table created.
SQL> create index scott.foo_1_indx on scott.foo_1 (x) tablespace user_data;
Index created.
SQL> SET SERVEROUTPUT ON
SQL> exec dbms_tts.transport_set_check ('USER_DATA');
PL/SQL procedure successfully completed.
SQL> SELECT * FROM TRANSPORT_SET_VIOLATIONS;
VIOLATIONS
ORA-39907: Index SCOTT.FOO_1_INDX in tablespace USER_DATA points to table
SCOTT.FOO_1 in tablespace USERS.
SQL>
```

This simple verification showed that the index foo_1_indx was built in the USER_DATA tablespace but the corresponding foo_1 table is in the USERS tablespace, which is not included in the transportable tablespace set. You must remedy this situation before you can transport tablespace USER_DATA.

It is important at this time to discuss the concept of referential integrity constraints relative to transportable tablespace sets. By default, referential integrity constraints are not required to be included in the transportable set; however, you can test for constraint containment with the DBMS_TTS.TRANSPORT_SET_CHECK procedure. For the following example, we have created the table FOO in the USER_DATA tablespace and checked the transportability. We then add an index on FOO in the USERS tablespace and create a primary key constraint on the indexed column. We check the transportability of the USER_DATA tablespace as follows:

```
SQL> exec dbms_tts.transport_set_check ('USER_DATA',TRUE);
PL/SQL procedure successfully completed.

SQL> SELECT * FROM TRANSPORT_SET_VIOLATIONS;
no rows selected
SQL>
SQL> CREATE INDEX SCOTT.FOO_INDX
  2  ON SCOTT.FOO (X)
  3  TABLESPACE USERS;
Index created.
SQL> ALTER TABLE SCOTT.FOO ADD (PRIMARY KEY (x));
Table altered.
SQL> exec dbms_tts.transport_set_check ('USER_DATA',TRUE);
PL/SQL procedure successfully completed.
SQL> SELECT * FROM TRANSPORT_SET_VIOLATIONS;

VIOLATIONS
-----------------------------------------------------------

ORA-39908: Index SCOTT.FOO_INDX in tablespace USERS
 enforces primary constraints
of table SCOTT.FOO in tablespace USER_DATA.
SQL>
```

Before we can transport the USER_DATA tablespace, we need to resolve this constraint issue by including the USERS tablespace, by rebuilding the index into the USER_DATA tablespace, by dropping the primary key constraint, or by deciding not to include constraints in the transportable set.

The SYSAUX tablespace is not transportable. Also, if the SYSTEM tablespace is locally managed, you can plug in a dictionary-managed tablespace, but it will be read-only and cannot be made writable.

Step 3: Generate the Transportable Tablespace Set

As introduced earlier, a transportable tablespace set is a self-contained group of tablespaces that encapsulate the objects that you wish to transport from one database to another. The transportable set must include all data files for each of the tablespaces to transport. The remaining component of the transportable set is a Data Pump export file that contains metadata about the transportable set. Here are the basic steps required to generate the transportable set:

1. Make all of the tablespaces in the transportable set read-only.

2. Use Data Pump on the source system to specify which tablespaces are included in the transportable set.

3. If converting to a different endian format, use the RMAN CONVERT command to convert the files in a temporary location on the source system.

With these basic steps, we can show you a straightforward example. Remember, the tablespaces are placed in read-only mode and remain read-only until the files have been copied to the target or to their temporary location for endian conversion.

You must have the EXP_FULL_DATABASE role to export a transportable tablespace. You must use a valid DIRECTORY in your Data Pump export command.

First, place the tablespaces in the transportable set in read-only mode:

```
SQL> alter tablespace user_data read only;
Tablespace altered.
```

Now exit or "host" to the command line and execute the Data Pump export command:

```
SQL> host
C:\>expdp dumpfile=expdat.dmp DIRECTORY=DATA_PUMP_DIR
ORA-39123: Data Pump transportable tablespace job aborted
ORA-39187: The transportable set is not self-contained, violation list is

ORA-39908: Index SCOTT.FOO_INDX in tablespace USERS enforces primary constraints
   of table SCOTT.FOO in tablespace USER_DATA.]
 TRANSPORT_TABLESPACES= user_data

Export: Release 12.1.0.1.0 - Production on Monday, 21 October, 2013 20:40:19
```

```
Copyright (c) 1982, 2013, Oracle.  All rights reserved.

Username: sys as sysdba
Password:

Connected to: Oracle Database 12c Enterprise Edition
 Release 12.1.0.1.0 - 64bit Production
With the Partitioning, OLAP, Advanced Analytics and Real Application Testing
options
Starting "SYS"."SYS_EXPORT_TRANSPORTABLE_01":
sys/******** AS SYSDBA dumpfile=e
xpdat.dmp DIRECTORY=EXP_DIR TRANSPORT_TABLESPACES= user_data
Processing object type TRANSPORTABLE_EXPORT/PLUGTS_BLK
Processing object type TRANSPORTABLE_EXPORT/TABLE
Processing object type TRANSPORTABLE_EXPORT/INDEX
Processing object type TRANSPORTABLE_EXPORT/CONSTRAINT/CONSTRAINT
Processing object type TRANSPORTABLE_EXPORT/INDEX_STATISTICS
Processing object type TRANSPORTABLE_EXPORT/TABLE_STATISTICS
Processing object type TRANSPORTABLE_EXPORT/POST_INSTANCE/PLUGTS_BLK
Master table "SYS"."SYS_EXPORT_TRANSPORTABLE_01" successfully loaded/unloaded
**************************************************************************
Dump file set for SYS.SYS_EXPORT_TRANSPORTABLE_01 is:
  C:\TEMP\EXPDAT.DMP
**************************************************************************
Datafiles required for transportable tablespace USER_DATA:
  C:\ORACLE\ORADATA\ORCL\USER_DATA01.DBF
Job "SYS"."SYS_EXPORT_TRANSPORTABLE_01" successfully completed at 20:41:47
```

Once the export is complete, if no endian conversion is required you can move on to the step of transporting the tablespace set. If endian conversion is required and you want to run the conversion on the target system, move on to that step. Otherwise, endian conversion is required locally and you'll need to invoke RMAN on the source system as follows:

```
C:\>RMAN TARGET /
RMAN> convert tablespace user_data
2> to platform 'Solaris[tm] OE (32-bit)'
3> format 'c:\temp\%U';

Starting conversion at source at 21-OCT-13
using channel ORA_DISK_1
channel ORA_DISK_1: starting datafile conversion
input datafile file number=00006 name=C:\ORACLE\ORADATA\ORCL\USER_DATA01.DBF
converted datafile=C:\TEMP\DATA_D-ORCL_I-1190467526_TS-
```

```
USER_DATA_FNO-6_3RJRNU8G
channel ORA_DISK_1: datafile conversion complete, elapsed time: 00:00:01
Finished conversion at source at 21-OCT-13

RMAN>
```

At this point you can exit from RMAN and return to SQL*Plus; you have a transportable set that consists of the export dump file and the converted tablespace data file on the local source system. You can exit to SQL*Plus and return the tablespaces in the transportable set to read-write mode:

```
SQL>alter tablespace user_data read write;
Tablespace altered.
SQL>
```

Step 4: Transport the Tablespace Set

Now you will need to copy the export dump file and data files in the tablespace set to the target system. If the data files didn't need endian conversion or if you converted the data files using RMAN on the source system, copy the data files from the source to the target destination using an operating-system copy utility or FTP binary mode, RMAN, or the DBMS_FILE_TRANSFER package. If the files require target-side conversion, copy the files into the temporary staging directory on the target.

Once you have copied the data files from the source system, you can return to SQL*Plus on the source and return the tablespaces in the transportable set to read-write mode:

```
SQL>alter tablespace user_data read write;
Tablespace altered.
SQL>
```

If the files do not need conversion, move on to step 5 at this time. If the data files require target-side endian conversion, invoke RMAN to perform the conversion, as in this example:

```
RMAN> CONVERT DATAFILE
'/orastage/user_data01.dbf'
TO PLATFORM="Solaris[tm] OE (32-bit)"
FROM PLATFORM="Microsoft Windows IA (32-bit)"
DB_FILE_NAME_CONVERT="/oracle/oradata/LNEB/";
```

Now that the data files are converted locally and in the correct target destination, you can move on to step 5.

Step 5: Import the Tablespace Set

As mentioned in an earlier note, either the transportable tablespace's block size must match the standard block size of the target database or the target database must have a cache configured for the same block size as the transportable set.

In the previous target-side endian conversion example, we copied the tablespace data file and converted it into the /oracle/oradata/LNEB directory. Make sure that you have a DIRECTORY created for the target database and that you have copied the export metadata file referenced by DUMPFILE into that location. Now we'll import the data files:

```
IMPDP DUMPFILE=expdat.dmp DIRECTORY=imp_dir
TRANSPORT_DATAFILES=/oracle/oradata/LNEB/user_data01.dbf
```

If the schema owner on the source does not exist on the target, you must either create the schema owner on the target or use the REMAP_SCHEMA import clause to specify a new schema owner. You must use a valid DIRECTORY object in your Data Pump import command.

Once you have verified that the import completed successfully, it would be a good time to verify that the source tablespaces are in read-write mode.

In Exercise 10.1, you will see how to export a transportable tablespace set.

EXERCISE 10.1

Exporting a Transportable Tablespace Set

To export a transportable tablespace set, do the following:

1. Check source and destination compatibility.

2. Select the tablespaces for the transportable tablespace set and verify that the set is self-contained.

3. Generate the transportable tablespace set.

Using Enterprise Manager to Transport a Tablespace

In this section, we will show you how to transport a tablespace using Enterprise Manager. From the Enterprise Manager database home page, click the Schema menu; then click the Database Export/Import menu item and then Transport Tablespaces, as shown in Figure 10.5.

From the Transport Tablespaces page, select the Generate A Transportable Tablespace Set option, provide the host credentials, and then click the Continue button, as shown in Figure 10.6.

Now, in the screen shown in Figure 10.7, add the tablespaces required in the transportable tablespace set, and choose Self or Full under Containment Type. For self-contained, determine if you need to include constraints. You can also check containment at this time.

Once you have checked containment, you will be given the opportunity to select the destination database platform and character set, as shown in Figure 10.8.

FIGURE 10.5   The Transport Tablespaces link in Enterprise Manager

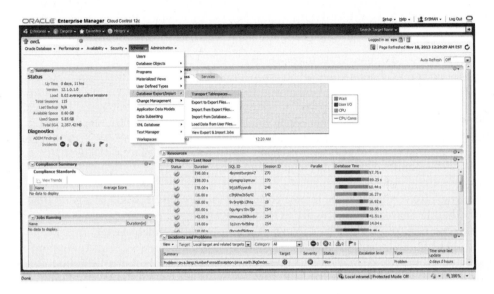

FIGURE 10.6   Transport tablespaces using Enterprise Manager

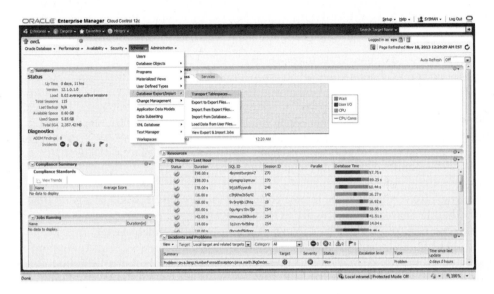

FIGURE 10.7   Generate Transportable Tablespaces: Select Tablespaces

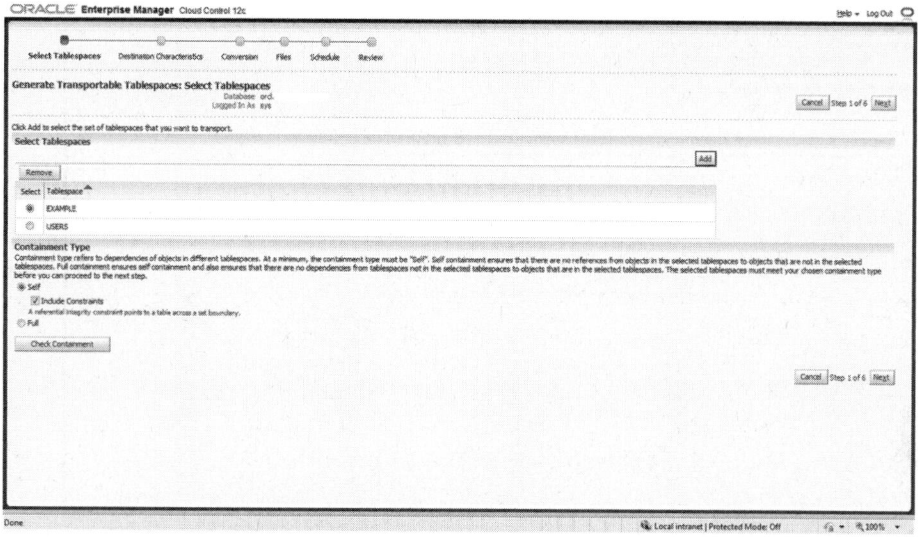

FIGURE 10.8   Generate Transportable Tablespaces: Destination Characteristics

The next step is to choose the conversion process, either convert at destination or convert at source, as shown in Figure 10.9. For this exercise, you'll choose to convert at the source.

FIGURE 10.9 Generate Transportable Tablespaces: Conversion

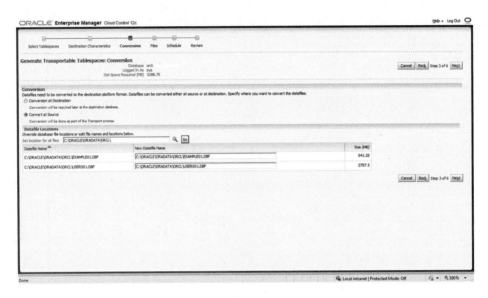

Now choose the dump file directory and dump file name, as shown in Figure 10.10.

FIGURE 10.10 Generate Transportable Tablespaces: Files

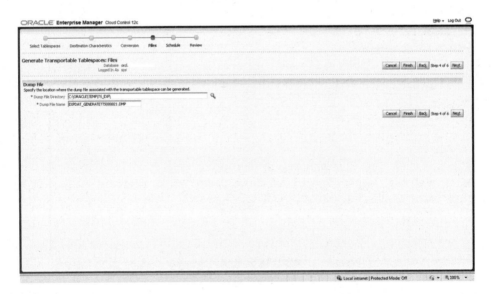

Now you can schedule the export and conversion and then review, as shown in Figure 10.11.

FIGURE 10.11   Generate Transportable Tablespaces: Review

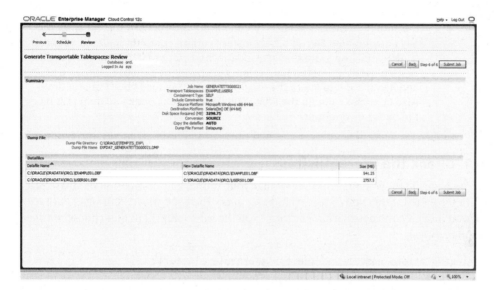

Submit the job. You will be returned to the Data Movement home page, and you can view the job details if you choose. At this point, you have a transportable tablespace set that you can import into a target database using Enterprise Manager or the command line.

Managing Transportable Databases

Transportable Database (TDB) allows you to migrate an entire database from one platform to another as long as the source and destination platforms have the same endian format. You must use a tool other than TDB for database migration if the source and destination are not of the same endian format.

TDB utilizes RMAN to convert all data files from the source to the destination platform. You can use TDB to create a copy of the database on the source system in the format of the destination system and then copy the files to the destination, or you can copy the source files to the destination system into a staging area and then use RMAN to convert the data files and copy them to their intended final destination.

The basic steps for TDB to migrate a database to a new platform are as follows:

1. Verify the prerequisites.

2. Identify all external files and directories.

3. Start the source database in read-only mode.

4. Verify that the source database is ready for migration.

5. Run RMAN CONVERT DATABASE.

6. Move files to the destination system.

7. Complete the migration.

> A large amount of the time required to complete the migration will be spent writing files, with RMAN converting files and transferring files from the source to the destination. If you have a time constraint, consider manually copying files across a LAN instead; utilize your storage area network (SAN)–attached storage, network attached storage (NAS), or network file system (NFS)–mounted file systems to speed the process. Allowing source and destination to share the staging area will reduce your transfer time. Also consider running the RMAN CONVERT process on the system that has the better throughput.

Step 1: Check the Prerequisites

Before you begin TDB, you'll need to verify that your source and destination database platforms are supported. From your source database, query the V$DB_TRANSPORTABLE_PLATFORM view. If you don't see the destination platform, you'll need to skip TDB and choose another migration method.

```
SQL> select platform_name from v$db_transportable_platform;

PLATFORM_NAME
------------------------------

Microsoft Windows IA (32-bit)
Linux IA (32-bit)
HP Tru64 UNIX
Linux IA (64-bit)
HP Open VMS
Microsoft Windows IA (64-bit)
Linux x86 64-bit
Microsoft Windows x86 64-bit
Solaris Operating System (x86)
HP IA Open VMS
Solaris Operating System (x86-64)
Apple Mac OS (x86-64)

12 rows selected.

SQL>
```

The query results show that you can transport the database on this server to any of those platforms listed.

The remaining prerequisite steps are as follows:

1. Verify that there are no restrictions or limitations that the source or destination database may encounter.

2. Verify that the destination and source systems have the same Oracle version, critical patch updates, patch-set version, and patch-set exceptions. Verify using the OPatch utility.

3. Determine if you will use the source or destination system to perform the conversion.

Step 2: Identify All External Files and Directories

Verify that you have created all necessary directories on the destination system as well as determined which external database files, such as BFILES and external tables, need to migrate to the destination. Query DBA_DIRECTORIES to report file system locations. Execute the supplied function DBMS_TDB.CHECK_EXTERNAL to identify external tables, directories, and BFILES that you'll need to move as part of the migration. Here's an example:

```
SQL> set serveroutput on
SQL> declare
        tdb_check boolean;
    begin
        tdb_check := dbms_tdb.check_external();
    end;
/
The following external tables exist in the database:
SYS.OPATCH_XML_INV, SH.SALES_TRANSACTIONS_EXT
The following directories exist in the database:
SYS.ORACLE_HOME, SYS.ORACLE_BASE, SYS.OPATCH_LOG_DIR, SYS.OPATCH_SCRIPT_DIR,
SYS.XSDDIR, SYS.DATA_PUMP_DIR, SYS.ORACLE_OCM_CONFIG_DIR,
SYS.ORACLE_OCM_CONFIG_DIR2, SYS.ORACLECLRDIR, SYS.DATA_FILE_DIR, SYS.MEDIA_DIR
The following BFILEs exist in the database:
PM.PRINT_MEDIA]

PL/SQL procedure successfully completed.

SQL>
```

Once you start the migration, don't create any new external objects in the source database.

Step 3: Start the Source Database in Read-Only Mode

When you're ready to start the migration, you'll need to shut down the source database and open it in read-only mode.

```
SQL> shutdown immediate;
SQL> startup mount;
SQL> alter database open read only;
```

At this point, you have not started the migration to the destination system, and you haven't made any changes to the source system. If you run into problems and need to return to normal operations in the source system, this would be your "rollback" point.

Step 4: Verify That the Database Is Ready for Migration

Now you need to verify that the source database is in fact ready for migration to the destination. Execute the DBMS_TDB.CHECK_DB function, providing the destination system PLATFORM_NAME exactly as shown in the V$DB_TRANSPORTABLE_PLATFORM view. If the CHECK_DB function returns an error condition, you must fix it before you can continue the migration.

```
SQL> set serveroutput on
SQL> declare
        tdb_check boolean;
     begin
        tdb_check := dbms_tdb.check_db
        ('Linux IA (64-bit)',dbms_tdb.skip_none);
     end;
/
Database is not open in READ-ONLY mode. Open the database
 in READ-ONLY mode and retry.
PL/SQL procedure successfully completed.
```

The results show that you didn't start the database in read-only mode, so you must fix that and rerun the PL/SQL block before moving to the next step.

> If you're using a physical standby database for the migration source, run the DBMS_TDB.CHECK_DB function on the standby, not the primary. Follow this general rule for the remainder of this section unless otherwise indicated. If you're migrating from a physical standby database, use the physical standby, not the primary database, wherever we refer to the source.

Step 5: Run RMAN *CONVERT DATABASE*

With the RMAN conversion, you'll run either a source-system or destination-system conversion. We'll describe the process for both, starting with the source-system and then the destination-system approach.

Database Conversion on the Source System

To create the converted copy of the source database on the source system, connect to RMAN on the source system and execute the CONVERT DATABASE command. In this example, we converted the small orcl sample database on a Windows 32-bit system to Linux 64-bit. The database files are converted and placed into the c:\temp\stage directory on the source system, and the transport script and the init.ora file are placed in the c:\temp directory.

```
RMAN> convert database
2> transport script 'c:\temp\transport_db_orclnx.sql'
3> new database 'orclnx'
4> to platform 'Linux IA (64-bit)'
5> parallelism 4
6> format 'c:\temp\%d%f'
7> db_file_name_convert 'c:\oracle\oradata\orcl\','c:\temp\stage\';

Starting conversion at source at 21-OCT-13
using target database control file instead of recovery catalog
allocated channel: ORA_DISK_1
channel ORA_DISK_1: SID=417 device type=DISK
allocated channel: ORA_DISK_2
channel ORA_DISK_2: SID=299 device type=DISK
allocated channel: ORA_DISK_3
channel ORA_DISK_3: SID=358 device type=DISK
allocated channel: ORA_DISK_4
channel ORA_DISK_4: SID=418 device type=DISK

External table SYS.OPATCH_XML_INV found in the database
External table SH.SALES_TRANSACTIONS_EXT found in the database

Directory SYS.ORACLE_HOME found in the database
Directory SYS.ORACLE_BASE found in the database
Directory SYS.OPATCH_LOG_DIR found in the database
Directory SYS.OPATCH_SCRIPT_DIR found in the database
Directory SYS.XSDDIR found in the database
Directory SYS.DATA_PUMP_DIR found in the database
Directory SYS.ORACLE_OCM_CONFIG_DIR found in the database
Directory SYS.ORACLE_OCM_CONFIG_DIR2 found in the database
Directory SYS.ORACLECLRDIR found in the database
Directory SYS.DATA_FILE_DIR found in the database
Directory SYS.MEDIA_DIR found in the database
Directory SYS.LOG_FILE_DIR found in the database
Directory SYS.XMLDIR found in the database
```

```
Directory SYS.SS_OE_XMLDIR found in the database
Directory SYS.SUBDIR found in the database
Directory SYS.TSPITR_DIROBJ_DPDIR found in the database

BFILE PM.PRINT_MEDIA found in the database

User SYS with SYSDBA and SYSOPER privilege found in password file
User SYSDG with SYSDG privilege found in password file
User SYSBACKUP with SYSBACKUP privilege found in password file
User SYSKM with SYSKM privilege found in password file
channel ORA_DISK_1: starting datafile conversion
input datafile file number=00002 name=C:\APP\ORACLE\ORADATA\ORCL\EXAMPLE01.DBF
channel ORA_DISK_2: starting datafile conversion
input datafile file number=00003 name=C:\APP\ORACLE\ORADATA\ORCL\SYSAUX01.DBF
channel ORA_DISK_3: starting datafile conversion
input datafile file number=00001 name=C:\APP\ORACLE\ORADATA\ORCL\SYSTEM01.DBF
channel ORA_DISK_4: starting datafile conversion
input datafile file number=00005 name=C:\APP\ORACLE\ORADATA\ORCL\UNDOTBS01.DBF
converted datafile=C:\TEMP\STAGE\EXAMPLE01.DBF
channel ORA_DISK_1: datafile conversion complete, elapsed time: 00:00:08
channel ORA_DISK_1: starting datafile conversion
input datafile file number=00004 name=C:\APP\ORACLE\ORADATA\ORCL\USERS02.DBF
converted datafile=C:\TEMP\STAGE\USERS02.DBF
channel ORA_DISK_1: datafile conversion complete, elapsed time: 00:00:01
channel ORA_DISK_1: starting datafile conversion
input datafile file number=00006 name=C:\APP\ORACLE\ORADATA\ORCL\USERS01.DBF
converted datafile=C:\TEMP\STAGE\USERS01.DBF
channel ORA_DISK_1: datafile conversion complete, elapsed time: 00:00:01
converted datafile=C:\TEMP\STAGE\SYSAUX01.DBF
channel ORA_DISK_2: datafile conversion complete, elapsed time: 00:00:13
converted datafile=C:\TEMP\STAGE\SYSTEM01.DBF
channel ORA_DISK_3: datafile conversion complete, elapsed time: 00:00:13
converted datafile=C:\TEMP\STAGE\UNDOTBS01.DBF
channel ORA_DISK_4: datafile conversion complete, elapsed time: 00:00:12
Edit init.ora file C:\TEMP\INIT_ORCLNX4294967295.ORA. This PFILE will be used to
 create the database on the target platform
Run SQL script C:\TEMP\TRANSPORT_DB_ORCLNX.SQL on the target platform to create
database
To recompile all PL/SQL modules, run utlirp.sql and utlrp.sql on the target plat
form
```

```
To change the internal database identifier, use DBNEWID Utility

Finished conversion at source at 21-OCT-13

RMAN>
```

 Verify the accuracy of the filenames and directories in the script files before you run them and attempt to start up your new destination database.

Database Conversion on the Destination System

To create the converted copy of the source database on the destination system, run RMAN on the destination system and execute the CONVERT DATABASE ON DESTINATION PLATFORM command. The command produces the convert script necessary to convert the database files on the destination system, the pfile, and a transport script.

```
rman connect target=/
RMAN> convert database on destination platform
2>convert script '/tmp/convert_orclnx.rman'
3>transport script '/tmp/transport_orclnx.sql'
4>new database 'orclnx'
5>format '/tmp/orclnx%U'
6>db_file_name_convert '/ora100/oradata/orclnx/datafile','/tmp/stage/';
```

Step 6: Move Files to the Destination System

If you converted the data files at the source, you should now copy them to the destination system. If you used your SAN, NAS, or NFS storage, now's the time for the destination system to take ownership of the database files. Copy the transport SQL script, pfile, external table files, and BFILES to the destination.

If you chose to convert the files at the destination, you will now need to copy the convert script to the destination and move the unconverted data files to the staging area. Again, SAN, NAS, and/or NFS storage should be made read/write for the destination at this time.

Step 7: Complete the Migration

If you converted the data files at the destination, you'll need to run the RMAN convert script on the destination system.

Whether you converted at the source or at the destination, review and modify the pfile as required. Now review the transport script created by the RMAN CONVERT DATABASE command. Verify that the directory locations are correct for the pfile, data files, log files, and tempfile. After you make corrections and verify, execute the transport script and check for any error messages.

Shrinking Segments

As with the files on the hard drive in your personal computer, the data within Oracle database segments can become fragmented with use. Data Manipulation Language (DML) operations—namely delete, update, and insert—can cause fragmentation of data and free space. Fragmentation of free space leads to wasted free space as well as performance issues such as the following:

Cache Utilization   Sparsely populated (fragmented) data blocks in memory require more reads to get the same amount of data as densely populated (defragmented) data blocks.

Table Scans   A full segment scan of fragmented data blocks requires more physical reads than a scan of defragmented blocks, so full table scans must read more fragmented blocks than defragmented blocks to get the same results.

There are two methods to defragment a segment online; use either table redefinition, also referred to as *reorganization*, or segment shrink. Table redefinition copies a table to a new location and consolidates the data. This operation requires space for the new copy of the table and its dependent objects. Also worth mentioning is the method to deallocate unused space above the high-water mark by issuing the DEALLOCATE UNUSED command. See Table 10.3 for a comparison of these methods.

TABLE 10.3   Comparing Space-Reclamation Methods

Method	Reclamation Method
Segment shrink	Reclaims space above and below the high-water mark without using additional space
Reorganization	Moves rows to a new physical location, resetting the high-water mark but using additional space during the operation
Deallocate unused	Deallocates space above the high-water mark that is currently not in use

For segments in dictionary-managed tablespaces or for locally managed tablespaces with manual segment space management, segment reorganization is the only permitted operation for reclaiming fragmented free space.

Online segment shrink compacts the segment in place and does not require additional space to perform the operation. Segment shrink can be performed on the dependent objects like indexes and partitions. Segment shrink works on the following objects:

- Heap tables
- Index-organized tables and their overflow segments

- LOBs and LOB indexes
- Materialized views and materialized view logs
- Indexes
- Partitions and subpartitions

To be eligible for segment shrink, the segment must have row movement enabled and reside in a tablespace that is locally managed and utilizes Automatic Segment Space Management (ASSM). The following objects in an ASSM tablespace are not eligible for segment shrink:

- SecureFile LOBs
- Index-organized table-mapping tables
- Tables that have ROWID-based materialized views
- Tables with function-based indexes

To enable row movement for a table, issue the ALTER TABLE … ENABLE ROW MOVEMENT command.

Performing an Online Segment Shrink Operation

Because segment shrink moves rows and changes the ROWIDs, before you perform the online segment shrink operation, you will need to do the following:

- Enable row movement.
- Disable any ROWID-based triggers defined on the object.
- Determine if the application uses any ROWID-based DML or queries.

By default, online segment shrink performs the following:

- Compacts the segment
- Resets the high-water mark
- Releases the reclaimed free space

Since segment shrink is an online operation, DML and queries can continue as normal. There is a brief block of concurrent DML operations on the segment when the space is released at the end of the shrink operation. Indexes remain usable throughout the operation.

Here's an example of shrinking a table:

```
SQL> ALTER TABLE HR.EMPLOYEES SHRINK SPACE;
ALTER TABLE HR.EMPLOYEES SHRINK SPACE
*
ERROR at line 1:
ORA-10636: ROW MOVEMENT is not enabled
SQL> ALTER TABLE HR.EMPLOYEES ENABLE ROW MOVEMENT;
Table altered.
```

```
SQL> ALTER TABLE HR.EMPLOYEES SHRINK SPACE;
Table altered.
```

There are two optional clauses with the SHRINK SPACE command: COMPACT and CASCADE. The COMPACT clause defragments and compacts but does not reset the high-water mark or return the free space. Execute the SHRINK SPACE command without the COMPACT clause at a later time to complete the task.

The CASCADE clause performs the Shrink Space operation on all dependent objects, as reported by the DBMS_SPACE.OBJECT_DEPENDENT_SEGMENTS procedure.

Partitions in a partitioned table are automatically shrunk with the SHRINK SPACE command, so you don't need to specify the CASCADE clause.

Here's an example of a small sample table called HR.EMPLOYEES_HIST, built as a copy of the Oracle-provided HR.EMPLOYEE table. We've inserted rows until we've allocated 40 blocks, then deleted about 70 percent of the rows. The shrink operation should reduce the number of blocks to 16. We'll perform the two-step COMPACT process and CASCADE so that you can see how they work:

```
SQL> SELECT COUNT(1) from hr.employees_hist;


  COUNT(1)
----------
      2943


SQL> SELECT SEGMENT_NAME, BLOCKS FROM DBA_SEGMENTS
WHERE OWNER = 'HR' and SEGMENT_NAME LIKE 'EMPL%';


SEGMENT_NAME                 BLOCKS
------------------------ ----------

EMPLOYEES                       8
EMPLOYEES_HIST                 40
EMPLOYEES_HIST_IX              16


SQL> ALTER TABLE HR.EMPLOYEES_HIST SHRINK SPACE COMPACT;
Table altered.
SQL> SELECT SEGMENT_NAME, BLOCKS FROM DBA_SEGMENTS
WHERE OWNER = 'HR' and SEGMENT_NAME LIKE 'EMPL%';


SEGMENT_NAME                 BLOCKS
------------------------ ----------

EMPLOYEES                       8
EMPLOYEES_HIST                 40
```

```
EMPLOYEES_HIST_IX                16

SQL> ALTER TABLE HR.EMPLOYEES_HIST SHRINK SPACE;
Table altered.
SQL> SELECT SEGMENT_NAME, BLOCKS FROM DBA_SEGMENTS
WHERE OWNER = 'HR' and SEGMENT_NAME LIKE 'EMPL%';

SEGMENT_NAME                 BLOCKS
----------------------- ----------
EMPLOYEES                         8
EMPLOYEES_HIST                   16
EMPLOYEES_HIST_IX                16

SQL> ALTER TABLE HR.EMPLOYEES_HIST SHRINK SPACE CASCADE;
Table altered.
SQL> SELECT SEGMENT_NAME, BLOCKS FROM DBA_SEGMENTS
WHERE OWNER = 'HR' and SEGMENT_NAME LIKE 'EMPL%';

SEGMENT_NAME                 BLOCKS
----------------------- ----------
EMPLOYEES                         8
EMPLOYEES_HIST                   16
EMPLOYEES_HIST_IX                 8

SQL> SELECT COUNT(1) from hr.employees_hist;

  COUNT(1)
----------
       910

SQL>
```

Using Enterprise Manager Segment Space Advisor to Perform an Online Segment Shrink Operation

After repopulating and deleting from the test table HR.EMPLOYEES_HIST, you want to use EM to shrink the segment.

1. From the Enterprise Manager database home page, select the Performance menu ⇨ Advisors Home ⇨ Segment Advisor.

2. From the Segment Advisor: Scope page, shown in Figure 10.12, choose Schema Objects and then click Next.

FIGURE 10.12 The Automatic Segment Advisor: Scope page

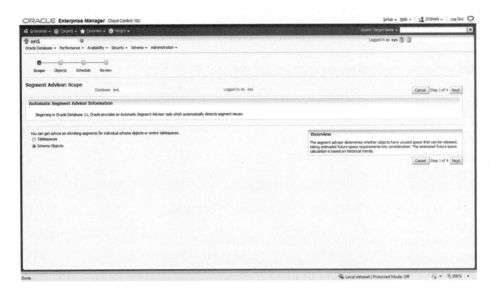

3. On the Schema Objects page, select the HR schema, and choose the objects to add to the advisor by clicking the check box in the Select column next to the object name, as shown in Figure 10.13

FIGURE 10.13 The Automatic Segment Advisor: Schema Objects page

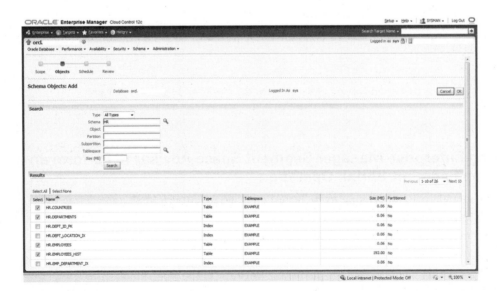

4. You have the option to set the time limit for analysis by expanding the Show Advanced Options link on the page shown in Figure 10.14.

FIGURE 10.14   The Automatic Segment Advisor: Schema Objects page

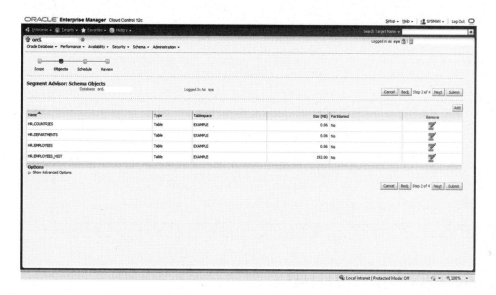

5. Once you set the schedule and review it, return to the Advisor Central page to monitor the Auto Space Advisor task results.

For the example, the Segment Space Advisor chose not to shrink our HR.EMPLOYEES_HIST table.

6. To be really persistent about shrinking this table, from the EM database home page go to the Schema page, click Database Objects and then Tables, enter the schema and object information for HR.EMPLOYEES_HIST, and then click the Go button.

The basic information for the object will be displayed, as in Figure 10.15.

Figure 10.16 shows that we chose the Shrink Segment operation from the Actions drop-down menu.

7. Under Shrink Segment: Options, choose to compact segments only or to compact segments and release the freed space. Click the Implement button and you will see the Shrink Segment: Schedule screen, as shown in Figure 10.17.

8. Schedule a job to shrink the table by clicking the Submit button then submit the job.

You can see in Figure 10.18 that the job completed successfully, and you can view the SQL statement executed to shrink the segment.

FIGURE 10.15   Selecting a table

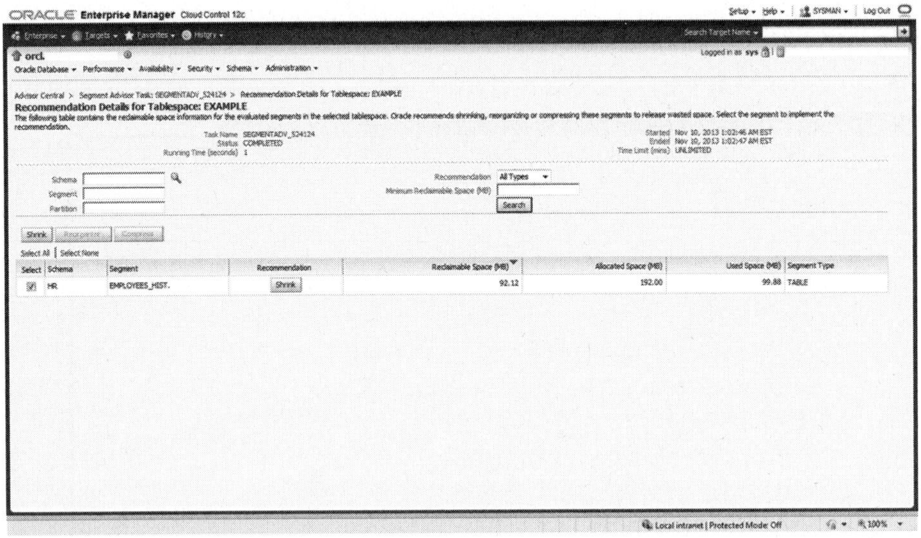

FIGURE 10.16   Selecting the shrink operation

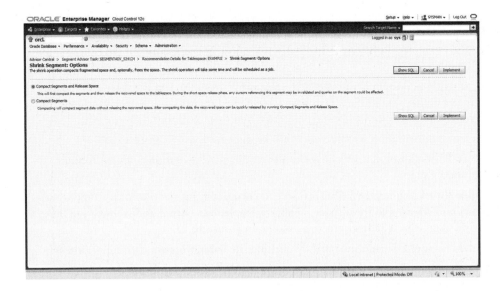

FIGURE 10.17   Selecting the shrink options

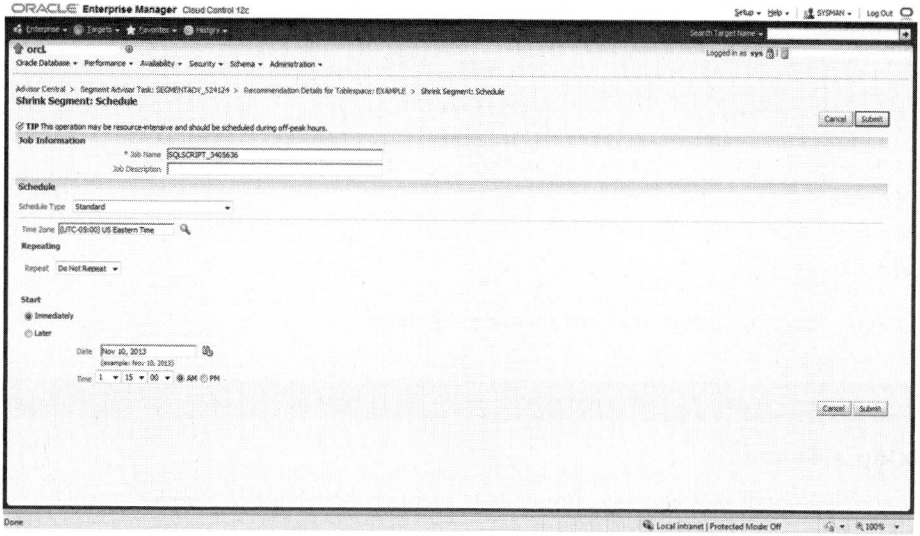

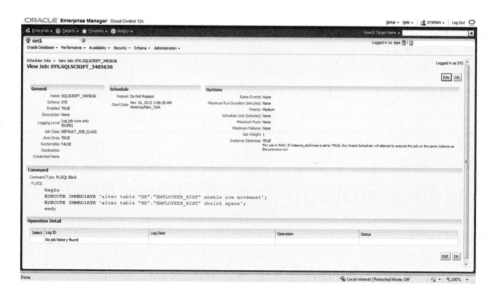

FIGURE 10.18   Viewing the shrink job

9. To verify that the operation was successful, in SQL*Plus run the query you ran before to validate the results:

```
SQL> SELECT SEGMENT_NAME, BLOCKS FROM DBA_SEGMENTS
WHERE OWNER = 'HR' and SEGMENT_NAME LIKE 'EMPL%';


SEGMENT_NAME                BLOCKS
------------------------ ----------
EMPLOYEES                       8
EMPLOYEES_HIST                 16
EMPLOYEES_HIST_IX               8
```

In Exercise 10.2, you'll learn how to shrink a segment.

EXERCISE 10.2

Shrinking a Segment

For this exercise, you'll create a table, populate it, delete rows, and then shrink the table segment:

1. Create a table named shrink_test with two columns: a NUMBER column named X and a VARCHAR2 (10) column named Y. Enable row movement for the table.

2. Insert two rows with a unique value for X for each row.

3. Now, using the INSERT INTO SHRINK_TEST SELECT * FROM SHRINK_TEST SQL statement repeatedly, grow the table to 1 million rows (or more), and commit.

4. Query DBA_SEGMENTS to determine the size of the segment.

5. Delete half the rows from the table, using one of the values of X as the delete criteria.

6. Now shrink the segment online, and verify that the number of blocks decreases.

Managing Storage in a CDB and PDBs

In the Oracle 12*c* multitenant architecture, storage resources as data files and tablespaces are allocated and managed somewhat differently than in previous versions of the RDBMS since you now have the option to operate with a CDB and PDBs. For the CDB and for individual PDBs, you can create, modify, and drop tablespaces. For the CDB and for each PDB, you can create a default temporary tablespace. You can also specify a default tablespace and default tablespace type for the root (CDB). The root has its out-of-the-box tablespaces like SYSTEM and SYSAUX, and each PDB has its own tablespaces.

The root and each PDB have their own data files. Individual PDBs can have their own temporary tablespaces.

 Chapter 12, "Managing Oracle Multitenant Databases," describes container databases (CDBs) and pluggable databases (PDBs) in detail. At this point, you need to know that a CDB may contain zero or more PDBs, and a PDB is collection of schemas, schema objects, and non-schema objects that would appear to be an independent database. Also, a common user is a database user who has the same identity in the root container and in every PDB in a CDB.

Manage Permanent and Temporary Tablespaces in CDB and PDBs

To manage tablespaces in a CDB you use the ALTER DATABASE statement, using the following guidelines:

- A permanent tablespace may be associated with only one container.
- When a tablespace is created in a container it is associated with that container.
- A CDB can have only one active UNDO tablespace.
- Each instance of an Oracle RAC CDB can have only one active UNDO tablespace.
- A CDB has one default temporary tablespace. The root and PDBs can use it.
- A PDB can have its own temporary tablespaces.

Use the STORAGE clause in a CREATE PLUGGABLE DATABASE or ALTER PLUGGABLE DATABASE statement to assign the data file size for a PDB.

Managing Permanent Tablespaces in the CDB and PDBs

A permanent tablespace may be associated with only one container: the root or a PDB. Containers may not share default permanent tablespaces; each must have its own. A user who does not have an assigned default tablespace will use the container's default tablespace.

Changing the Default Permanent Tablespace for the Root

To set the default tablespace for the root, connect to the target and enter the following command, making sure the tablespace already exists in the root.

```
SQL> ALTER DATABASE DEFAULT TABLESPACE root_tablespace;

System altered.
```

Now a user whose current container is the root that is not explicitly assigned a tablespace uses the root_tablespace as the default permanent tablespace.

Managing Temporary Tablespaces in CDB and PDBs

A temporary tablespace is used to improve the performance of sort operations. You can't create a permanent schema object in a temporary tablespace, and when your session is over, any data that was stored in the temporary tablespace for your use goes away. Also, the underlying file type for temporary tablespaces is a temp file, which is different from a common database data file used for permanent tablespaces.

The default configuration for a CDB is to have a single default temporary tablespace named TEMP that is used by each PDB. You must be connected to the root to create a default temporary tablespace for the CDB. There is one default temporary tablespace for a CDB. Additional temporary tablespaces can be created in the root, and users can be assigned to the additional temporary tablespaces.

For a PDB, you may create a local temporary tablespace and then set it as the default. Additional temporary tablespaces can be created in a PDB, and users in that PDB can be assigned to the additional temporary tablespaces. When you unplug a PDB from a CDB, its temporary tablespaces are also unplugged.

Changing the Default Temporary Tablespace for the Root

To use a different default temporary tablespace, enter the following command:

```
SQL> ALTER DATABASE DEFAULT TEMPORARY TABLESPACE temp_tablespace;


System altered.
```

The tablespace or tablespace group specified must exist in the root. This tablespace or tablespace group is also the default temporary tablespace for PDBs, unless you have explicitly assigned a default temporary tablespace for a PDB, for example:

```
SQL> ALTER SESSION SET CONTAINER = pdb1;


Session altered.
SQL> ALTER PLUGGABLE DATABASE pdb1 DEFAULT TEMPORARY TABLESPACE temp_
tablespace_19681201;


System altered.
```

Summary

In this chapter, you learned about resumable space operations, transportable tablespaces, transportable databases, and segment shrink operations.

You learned about resumable space allocations and how to configure, detect, and remedy suspended transactions. You learned about transportable tablespaces and transportable databases. With transportable tablespaces, you can convert a tablespace set to run on a different platform with a different endian-ness using the RMAN CONVERT clause. You cannot transport an entire database to a different endian format, but you can convert it to run on a different platform with the same endian-ness.

The segment shrink feature can be used to reclaim space both above and below the high-water mark while a segment remains online and in use.

You learned the basics of tablespace management in the new Oracle 12c multitenant architecture, understanding that the root default temporary tablespace can be utilized by each PDB and that each PDB can have its own default temporary tablespace.

Exam Essentials

Understand how to configure resumable space allocation. Know that if the Oracle database encounters a space problem during the execution of an operation, it can suspend the operation and then later resume the operation.

Describe the concepts of transportable tablespaces and databases. Know how to copy tablespaces from one database to another and how to transport tablespaces and databases from one platform to another.

Understand how to shrink segments. Understand that segments can become fragmented and that wasted space due to fragmentation can be defragmented.

Understand how to manage temporary and permanent tablespaces in a CDB and PDBs. Know how to alter the database to use a different default temporary tablespace for an entire CDB. Know how to alter a PDB to use a different default temporary tablespace.

Review Questions

1. To enable resumable space allocation for the instance, which of the following initialization parameters should you set to a nonzero value?

   A. RESUMABLE_SPACE_TIME

   B. RESUMABLE_SPACE

   C. RESUMABLE_TIME

   D. RESUMABLE_TIMEOUT

   E. TIME_RESUMABLE

2. Which of the following describes how a distributed resumable transaction behaves?

   A. The resumable setting on the initiating session determines the resumable conditions for the entire distributed transaction.

   B. The resumable setting for the initiating instance determines the resumable conditions for the entire distributed transaction.

   C. The resumable setting on the initiating session controls only that part of the transaction that occurs within the local instance; remote resumable settings determine the behavior of the distributed parts of the transaction.

   D. None of the above

3. Which of these components, in order, correctly identify the unique value of the NAME column in the DBA_RESUMABLE view?

   A. Username, instance number, session ID

   B. Instance number, username, session ID

   C. Instance number, session ID, username

   D. Username, session ID, instance number

   E. None of the above

4. Which of the following are included in a transportable tablespace set? (Choose all that apply.)

   A. The data files that make up a self-contained group of tablespaces required for copy

   B. The system tablespace

   C. An export of the tablespace metadata

   D. The spfile

   E. All of the above

5. The following query will provide what information about transportable tablespaces for the current database? (Choose all that apply.)

```
select d.platform_name "Source", t.platform_name
 "Compatible Targets", endian_format
 from v$transportable_platform t, v$database d
 where t.endian_format = (select endian_format
    from   v$transportable_platform t,
                        v$database d
                where d.platform_name =
                    t.platform_name);
```

A. The list of target platforms having the same endian format as the source database

B. The list of target platforms requiring endian conversion

C. The list of target platforms that will not require endian conversion

D. The list of all target platforms that can receive transportable tablespaces from the source database

E. None of the above

6. When exporting metadata for the transportable tablespaces, what is the correct next step after confirming endian format?

A. Export the tablespaces using Data Pump.

B. Determine if the transportable set is self-contained.

C. Convert the data files using RMAN.

D. Copy the data files from source to destination.

7. Which of the following are prerequisite steps to transport a database? (Choose all that apply.)

A. Query the V$TRANSPORTABLE_PLATFORMS view in the source database to determine if the intended destination is listed.

B. Verify that there are no restrictions or limitations that the source or destination database may encounter.

C. Verify that the source and destination have the same Oracle version, critical updates, patch-set version, and patch-set exceptions.

D. Determine if you will perform the conversion on the source or destination platform.

E. None of the above

8. Which of the following supplied functions is used to identify external tables, directories, and BFILES?

   A. DBMS_TDB.CHECK_DIRECTORIES

   B. DBMS_TDB.CHECK_EXTERNAL

   C. DBMS_TDB.CHECK_BFILE

   D. DBMS_TDB.CHECK_EXT

9. Which of the following is a prerequisite for running DBMS_TDB.CHECK_DB to a successful completion?

   A. The database must be in read-write mode.

   B. The database must have no external files.

   C. The database must open in read-only mode.

   D. The database must be mounted but not opened.

10. Which of the following options describes segment shrink?

    A. Reclaims space above and below the high-water mark without using additional space

    B. Moves rows to a new physical location, resetting the high-water mark, but uses additional space during the operation

    C. Deallocates space above the high-water mark that is currently not in use

    D. None of the above

11. For which of the following can you use segment shrink? (Choose all that apply.)

    A. Heap tables

    B. Tables with function-based indexes

    C. Indexes

    D. Partitions and subpartitions

    E. None of the above

12. When shrinking a table segment, you choose to shrink all the indexes for that table using the SHRINK SPACE command. Which clause should you use?

    A. INCLUDING DEPENDENCIES

    B. INCLUDING DEPENDENCIES CASCADE

    C. COMPACT

    D. CASCADE

    E. None of the above

13. Which is true regarding the default temporary tablespace?

    A. Each CDB in a PDB can have its own default temporary tablespace.

    B. Each CDB and PDB must have its own default temporary tablespace.

    C. A PDB may have only one temporary tablespace.

    D. A PDB may use the CDB's default temporary tablespace or have its own.

    E. There is only one default temporary tablespace allowed for a CDB and all of its PDBs.

14. Which of these system privileges must be granted to a user for resumable operations to work at a session level?

    A. RESUMABLE

    B. RESUME

    C. SYSTEM RESUMABLE

    D. SESSION RESUMABLE

    E. None of the above

15. Which of the following are not true regarding transportable tablespaces?

    A. In order for an object to be transportable, all of the partitions that contain its dependent objects such as indexes, materialized views, and partitioned tables must be included in the tablespace set.

    B. Tablespaces that do not use block encryption but have tables that have encrypted columns are not transportable.

    C. You can't transport the SYSTEM tablespace or objects owned by the SYS user.

    D. None of the above

    E. All of the above

16. Which of the following are true statements about transportable tablespaces? (Choose all that apply.)

    A. The tablespaces can be locally managed or dictionary managed.

    B. In Oracle 9i or higher, the transported tablespace does not have to be the same block size as the target database's standard block size. However, the target database must have a DB_nK_CACHE_SIZE initialization parameter set, where n is the block size of the transportable tablespace.

    C. The tablespace must be placed in read-write mode during the transport process.

    D. Tablespaces with 8.0-compatible advanced queues with multiple recipients are transportable.

    E. None of the above

17. Shrinking segments is a good practice for which of the following reasons?

   A. Full table scans of fragmented data blocks require more physical reads.

   B. Each defragmented block takes up less space on disk.

   C. Each defragmented block takes up less space in cache.

   D. Shrinking segments should not be considered because of the requirement to drop and recreate any indexes to prevent corruption.

   E. None of the above

18. Which of the following options allows you to migrate a database from one platform to another?

   A. Transportable Database, for any source or target platform

   B. Transportable Tablespace, for any source or target platform

   C. Transportable Database, but only if the source and target have the same endian format

   D. Transportable Tablespace, and only for big endian format source and target

   E. None of the above

19. Use the `DBMS_TDB.CHECK_EXTERNAL` supplied function to identify which of the following?

   A. External tables

   B. Directories

   C. BFILES

   D. All of the above

   E. None of the above

20. In the multitenant environment, is it true that you can create a permanent tablespace that can be used by multiple containers?

   A. True, common users can share objects in different PDBs that share the same permanent tablespace.

   B. False, a permanent tablespace can be associated with only one container.

   C. True, common and local users can share the same permanent tablespaces across multiple PDBs

   D. True, common users create common tablespaces in the root that are shared to all PDBs.

   E. None of the above

Chapter

11

Creating Oracle Multitenant Databases

ORACLE DATABASE 12*c*: ADVANCED ADMINISTRATION EXAM OBJECTIVES COVERED IN THIS CHAPTER:

- ✓ Multitenant Container and Pluggable Database Architecture

- ✓ Describe the multitenant architecture

- ✓ Explain pluggable database provisioning

- ✓ Creating Multitenant and Pluggable Databases

- ✓ Configure and create a CDB

- ✓ Create a PDB using different methods

- ✓ Unplug and drop a PDB

- ✓ Migrate pre-12.1 non-CDB database to CDB

This chapter is divided into two sections; the first section is an introduction to the concepts of the Oracle multitenant architecture, new to Oracle Database 12*c*. The second—and larger—section is an introduction to creating multitenant container databases (CDBs) and pluggable databases (PDBs).

In the first section we will describe the components, advantages, and fundamentals of the multitenant architecture and explain at a high level how to provision new pluggable databases.

In the second section we will introduce and demonstrate the different methods used to create CDBs and PDBs. You should already be familiar with the tools used to create CDBs and PDBs, since they're the same as for creating non-CDBs, but they've been updated to work with the multitenant architecture. We'll also discuss unplugging and dropping PDBs, as well as migrating Oracle databases that were created in a previous version into the new multitenant architecture.

Exam objectives are subject to change at any time without prior notice and at Oracle's sole discretion. Please visit Oracle's Training and Certification website (http://www.oracle.com/education/certification/) for the most current exam-objectives listing.

Multitenant Container and Pluggable Database Architecture

New to Oracle 12*c*, the Oracle multitenant architecture is designed to allow an Oracle database to host multiple Oracle databases within one overall structure. The multitenant container database (CDB) can include zero, one, or many DBA-created pluggable databases (PDBs). From a client connection perspective, a PDB looks like a traditional Oracle database and comprises schemas, schema objects, and non-schema objects. Oracle databases prior to Oracle 12*c* were non-CDBs.

Describing the Multitenant Architecture

The basic components of the multitenant architecture are the multitenant container database (CDB) and its zero to many DBA-created pluggable databases (PDBs). Consider the CDB the host for zero to many PDBs. In the multitenant architecture, a PDB doesn't have the necessary structures to stand independently as an Oracle database: it must reside within a CDB.

I like to visualize the multitenant architecture, a container database, and its pluggable databases as a recreational vehicle campground. The campground provides water, electricity, services and common areas, whereas each RV is portable and can migrate to other campgrounds.

About the Multitenant Architecture

Beginning with Oracle Database 12*c*, you have the option to create a database as either a CDB or non-CDB. A database created in a previous version of Oracle is considered a non-CDB. It is possible to plug a non-CDB into a CDB as a PDB. You must use Oracle Data Pump if you want to move a PDB to a non-CDB.

Containers in a CDB

? CDB ?

A container is either the root container (the root) or a PDB. The root is a collection of schemas, schema objects, and non-schema objects to which all PDBs belong. Every CDB has the following containers:

✔ One root, named CDB$ROOT

✔ One seed PDB, named PDB$SEED

▪ Zero or more DBA-created PDBs

The root contains common users and Oracle-supplied metadata. Common users are database users that span all containers in a CDB. The common user SYS can manage the CDB$ROOT and all PDBs. The source code for Oracle-supplied PL/SQL packages is an example of metadata stored in the root.

Within a CDB, the PDB$SEED system-supplied template can be used to create new PDBs. You cannot modify, add, or delete objects in PDB$SEED.

A PDB is a DBA-created container that organizes the objects required to support a specific application, group of applications, or set of features, for example, schemas to support the Oracle WebCenter application, Oracle Spatial and Graph option, or a custom application that requires one or more dedicated schemas. PDBs do not exist at the time the CDB is first created. The DBA adds PDBs as needed.

The Relationship between CDBs and PDBs

Simply put, the CDB is a host for multiple PDBs. The CDB manages the interaction with the physical server or servers, while each PDB contains the schemas and objects that end users and applications will connect to and interact with.

The Container Database   A container database is a collection of zero, one, or many DBA-created pluggable databases. When the CDB is started up, background server processes are associated with the CDB, similar to the way non-CDBs functioned in prior versions of the database.

The Pluggable Database   The PDB is a collection of schemas and non-schema objects. The PDB can't operate without a CDB.

Advantages and Benefits of the Multitenant Architecture

The purpose of the multitenant architecture is to consolidate databases to conserve or fully utilize physical server resources. The multitenant architect is designed to help the DBA eliminate unnecessary overhead and fully utilize hardware by consolidating multiple databases from multiple computers into a single container database on a single computer. Benefits of the multitenant architecture include the following:

- Overall reduction in hardware requirements, since you can run more databases on the same server.
- More efficient management and movement of data and code.
- Simpler management of the database.
- Differentiation in duties between PDB administrators and CDB administrators: PDB administrators can focus on the specific application and users they manage; CDB administrators can focus on the system, performance, backups, and overall security.

Benefits of PDBs include these:

- Provisioning of a new PDB is simple.
- Moving an existing PDB to another platform is easily accomplished by unplugging and plugging in.
- It's easier to patch or upgrade all the PDBs in a CDB as one instead of separately.
- The DBA can also unplug a PDB and plug it into a newer version CDB.
- A server can run one CDB with multiple PDBs more efficiently than running multiple non-CDBs.

 From a licensing perspective, Oracle Multitenant is an option that you purchase in addition to the base license. At the time of this writing the base Oracle license will allow you to create a container database with one pluggable database in it, referred to as single-tenant. If you configure more than one pluggable database in your container database, then you will need to purchase the Oracle Multitenant option. For current licensing information, check the Oracle Database 12*c* Licensing document included in the Oracle Database 12*c* Documentation Library, found at http://docs.oracle.com.

In an environment with multiple databases and various platforms, the multitenant environment offers a destination in which the DBA can consolidate and manage systems that were previously required to exist independently. Using pluggable database technology, the DBA can consolidate databases onto servers that offer greater CPU and memory density, higher throughput, lower operational cost, lower overall energy consumption, fewer storage and network connections, and higher degrees of transportability.

Database consolidation reduces DBA workload and cost through easier overall management. Managing 1 SGA on 1 server, even if it has 100 PDBs, is simpler than managing

50 SGAs on multiple servers, possibly running several different operating systems and versions of Oracle Database.

Explaining Pluggable Database Provisioning

In Oracle Database 12*c*, the DBA has the option to create a new database as a container database, a pluggable database that exists within a CDB, or a non-container database. The non-container database is conceptually the same as databases created in versions prior to Oracle Database 12.1.

In this section we will explain the concepts fundamental to creating a CDB and then discuss the concepts behind creating PDBs.

Concepts of CDB Creation

As mentioned previously, the CDB is the building block for PDBs, so the DBA needs to create a CDB prior to plugging in or creating new PDBs. The initial planning steps for the CDB are the same as for traditional non-CDBs. That is, you'll need the base software, sufficient storage to build, and sufficient memory and CPU to run a CDB. Consider that your CDB will most likely host multiple PDBs, so sufficient server resources are critical to planning a successful multitenant implementation.

Methods to Create a CDB

In the next section we will go into detail about how to create CDBs and PDBs using different methods. For now, you need to know that the same tools used to create non-CDBs are used to create CDBs. At the command line, SQL*Plus is the primary tool used to create a new CDB. The preferred GUI method is to use the Database Configuration Assistant (DBCA). Oracle recommends that you use the DBCA to create and configure CDBs, PDBs, and non-CDBs. Also, the DBA can create a new CDB using Enterprise Manager Cloud Control 12*c* (EM12*c*).

Methods to Create a PDB

As with CDBs and non-CDBs, the tools used to create PDBs are fundamentally the same: SQL*Plus at the command line and the DBCA. But with PDBs you can also create new PDBs from different sources:

- Using the seed database in the CDB: PDB$SEED
- Cloning an existing PDB
- Plugging an unplugged PDB into a CDB
- Creating a PDB by moving a non-CDB into a PDB

Also, the DBA can create a new PDB using EM12*c*.

Creating Multitenant Container Databases and Pluggable Databases

In the following sections, you will learn how to configure and create multitenant CDBs and PDBs. You will learn the different tools and methods for creating CDBs and PDBs. We will teach you how to unplug and drop a PDB, and we will teach you how to migrate non-CDB databases to CDBs. Remember, all databases created prior to version 12.1 are considered non-CDBs.

As mentioned before, the tools available to create CDBs and PDBs are familiar: SQL*Plus, the Database Creation Assistant (DBCA), and EM12c.

Creating and Configuring a CDB

The method to create a CDB is almost identical to the one for creating a non-CDB, so if you're familiar with previous versions of Oracle Database, there's not a completely new set of commands and concepts to learn. As with all new database installations, planning for growth and overall performance is key to the success of the implementation.

In this chapter we will not go into great detail about how to create a new database. We will focus on the differences associated with creating CDBs and PDBs in the multitenant architecture. The examples in this chapter were performed with Oracle Database 12c 64-bit on Windows 7 64-bit.

Creating a CDB Using the DBCA

From the Windows Start menu, navigate to the Oracle 12c folder and then the Configuration and Migration folder.

1. Select the Database Configuration Assistant. The DBCA GUI launches, and you will be placed on the Database Operation screen, as shown in Figure 11.1.

2. On the Database Operation screen, choose the first item, Create Database. Familiarize yourself with the other options, and notice that the last item allows you to use the DBCA to manage pluggable databases.

3. Click Next and you will progress to the Creation Mode screen, which allows you to specify the details of the new database, as shown in Figure 11.2.

   On the Creation Mode screen, enter the name of the new database, storage type, file locations, character set, and the administrative password for the SYS account.

4. For this lesson, we're most interested in the Create As Container Database option. Check this box, and enter the name of your first DBA-created pluggable database.

FIGURE 11.1 DBCA Database Operation screen

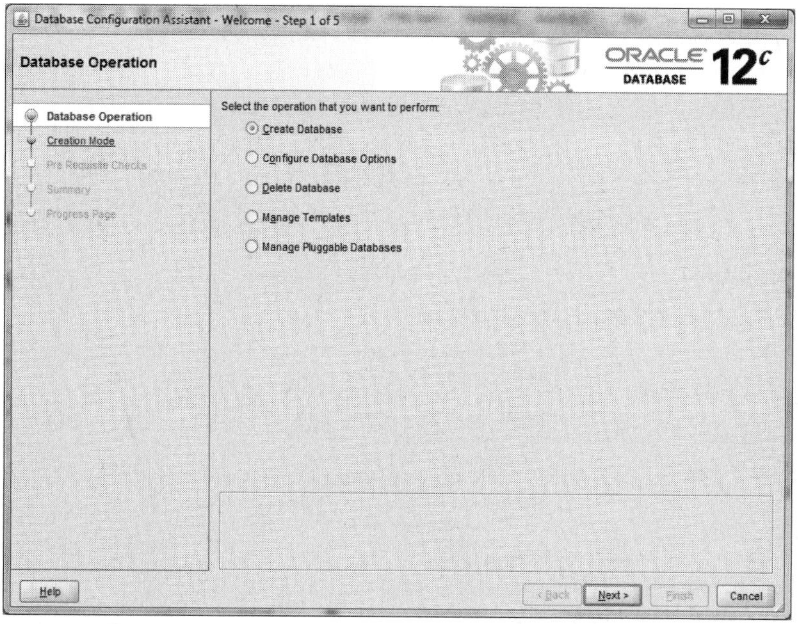

FIGURE 11.2 DBCA Creation Mode screen

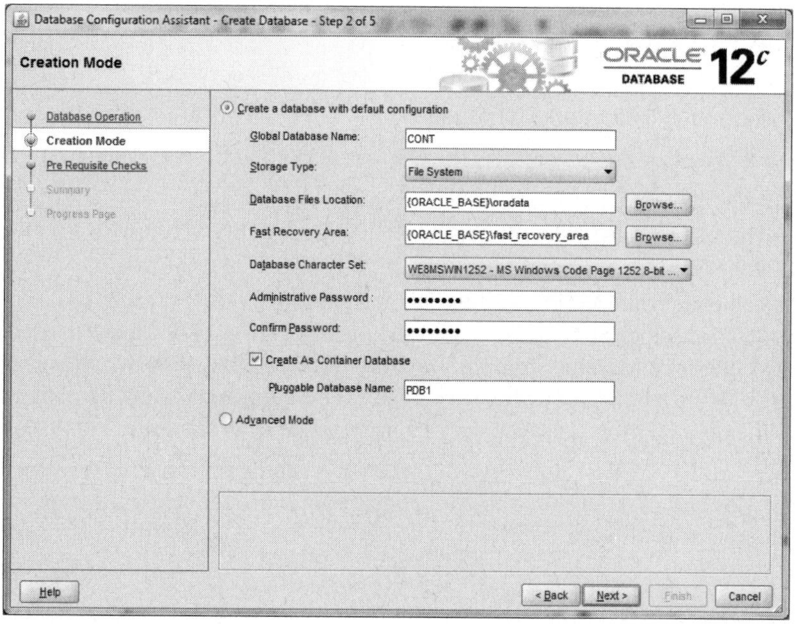

5. Once you've entered the configuration data, click Next to complete the prerequisite checks; then progress to the Create Database - Summary page, as shown in Figure 11.3.

FIGURE 11.3   DBCA Summary screen

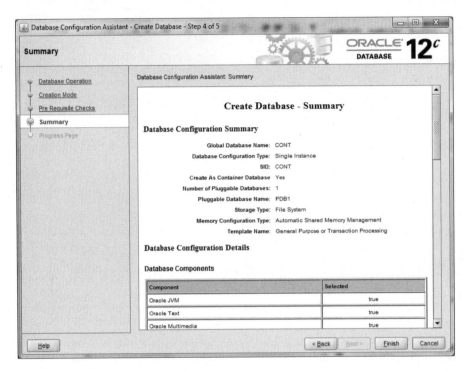

Here's your opportunity to confirm that the information is correct.

6. Click Finish to start creating the database.

7. Now you can monitor the progress as the DBCA creates the CDB and the first PDB, as shown in Figure 11.4.

   Note that you can view the Activity Log or the Alert Log and monitor the detailed steps of the operation.

   Once you complete construction of the CDB and the first PDB, a pop-up screen will display the specifics of the new CDB, as shown in Figure 11.5. Please note that the Oracle Enterprise Manager Express Database Edition URL is shown; this is the replacement for Database Control that you can use to manage the new database. You also have the opportunity to unlock specific user accounts at this time.

8. Before you click Exit, please note that you will not have the opportunity to return to this screen, so take a screen shot and confirm that you have unlocked the user accounts of your choice at this time.

FIGURE 11.4   DBCA Progress Page

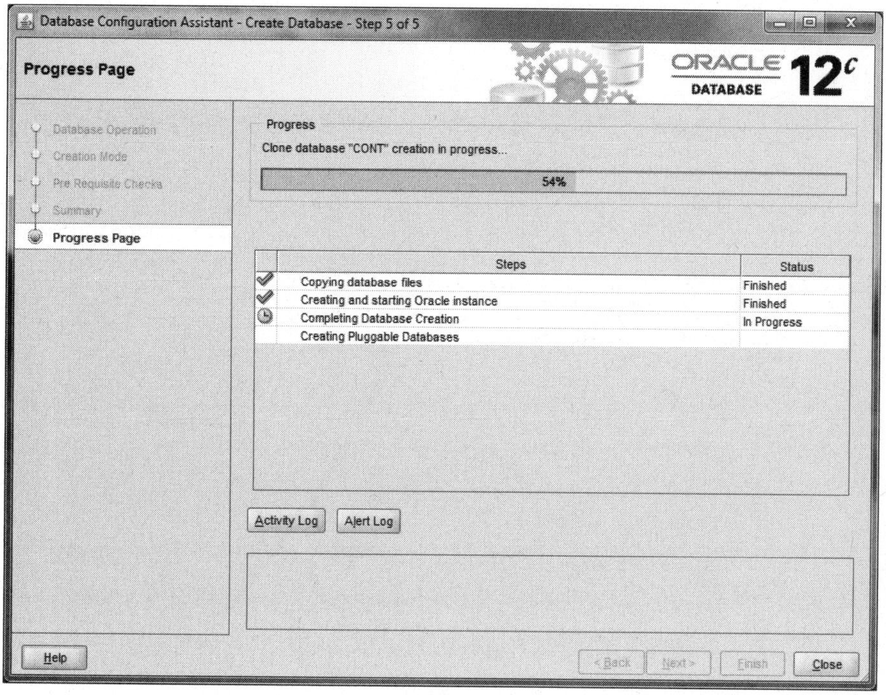

FIGURE 11.5   Database Configuration Assistant completion screen

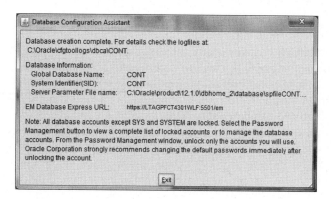

9. Click Exit.

You're returned to the Progress Page, shown in Figure 11.6; at this point your options are to review the Activity Log, review the Alert Log, or close the DBCA.

FIGURE 11.6   DBCA Progress Page final screen

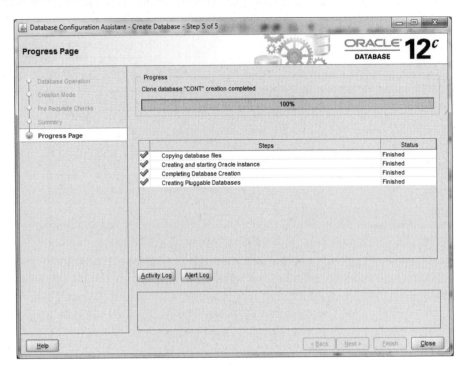

Now that you have created your CDB and first PDB, you can access the CDB through the command line via SQL*Plus or by using Oracle Enterprise Manager Database Express Edition at the URL provided.

Creating a CDB Using SQL* Plus

Oracle strongly recommends that you utilize the DBCA to create new databases, including CDBs. However, you can utilize SQL*Plus to create a new CDB manually.

To create a new CDB, use the CREATE DATABASE ... ENABLE PLUGGABLE DATABASE SQL statement. If you do not include the ENABLE PLUGGABLE DATABASE clause, the new database is created as a non-CDB and can never host PDBs.

In Exercise 11.1, we will walk you through the steps to create a CDB using SQL*Plus.

EXERCISE 11.1

Creating a New CDB Using SQL*Plus

In this exercise you will create a new CDB on a Windows 7 server, using Oracle Managed Files. This is meant to be a simplified example and does not include all available parameters and features. We will follow the basic steps outlined in the Database Administrators Guide:

1. Specify an instance identifier (SID) unique to this server and database domain.

   ```
   C:\ set ORACLE_SID=NDLNE
   ```

2. Set the required environment variables. ORACLE_HOME is required on some operating systems.

   ```
   C:\ set ORACLE_HOME=C:\Oracle\product\12.1.0\dbhome_2
   ```

3. Determine the database administrator authentication method. By default, in the Windows OS the user who installed the Oracle RDBMS software is automatically added to the Administrators group, so no additional steps are necessary.

4. Create the initialization parameter file (init.ora) and database directory folders. In the admin\<ORACLE_SID>\pfile directory for the new database, create the init.ora file. Here's an example of an Oracle-supplied init.ora file:

   ```
   ###########################################################################
   # Copyright (c) 1991, 2013 by Oracle Corporation
   ###########################################################################

   ########################################
   # Cache and I/O
   ########################################
   db_block_size=8192


   ########################################
   # Cursors and Library Cache
   ########################################
   open_cursors=300


   ########################################
   # Database Identification
   ########################################
   db_domain=""
   db_name="NDLNE"
   ```

```
##########################################
# File Configuration
##########################################
db_create_file_dest="C:\Oracle\oradata"
db_recovery_file_dest="C:\Oracle\fast_recovery_area"
db_recovery_file_dest_size=6930m

##########################################
# Miscellaneous
##########################################
compatible=12.1.0.0.0
diagnostic_dest=C:\Oracle
enable_pluggable_database=true

##########################################
# Processes and Sessions
##########################################
processes=300

##########################################
# SGA Memory
##########################################
sga_target=2366m

##########################################
# Security and Auditing
##########################################
audit_file_dest="C:\Oracle\admin\NDLNE\adump"
audit_trail=db
remote_login_passwordfile=EXCLUSIVE

##########################################
# Shared Server
##########################################
dispatchers="(PROTOCOL=TCP) (SERVICE=CONTXDB)"

##########################################
# Sort, Hash Joins, Bitmap Indexes
```

EXERCISE 11.1 *(continued)*

```
############################################
pga_aggregate_target=788m

############################################
# System Managed Undo and Rollback Segments
############################################
undo_tablespace=UNDOTBS1

control_files=("C:\ORACLE\ORADATA\NDLNE\CONTROLFILE\O1_MF_980KX1CY_.CTL", "C:\
ORACLE\FAST_RECOVERY_AREA\NDLNE\CONTROLFILE\O1_MF_980KX1N8_.CTL")
```

5. In Windows create an instance as a service. Run this one-line command as administrator from the command line:

```
C:\ oradim -NEW -SID NDLNE -STARTMODE MANUAL -PFILE C:\Oracle\admin\NDLNE\
init.ora
Instance created.
```

6. Connect to the instance:

```
C:\ sqlplus /nolog
SQL> CONNECT / AS SYSDBA
Connected to an idle instance.
```

7. Create a server parameter file (spfile):

```
SQL> create spfile from pfile= 'C:\Oracle\admin\NDLNE\pfile\init.ora';
File created.
```

8. Start the instance:

```
SQL> STARTUP NOMOUNT
ORACLE instance started.


Total System Global Area 2471931904 bytes
Fixed Size                   2405664 bytes
Variable Size              671091424 bytes
Database Buffers           1778384896 bytes
Redo Buffers                20049920 bytes
SQL>
```

EXERCISE 11.1 *(continued)*

9. Issue the CREATE DATABASE statement:

```
SQL> CREATE DATABASE NDLNE
USER SYS IDENTIFIED BY system
USER SYSTEM IDENTIFIED BY system
EXTENT MANAGEMENT LOCAL
DEFAULT TABLESPACE users
DEFAULT TEMPORARY TABLESPACE temp
UNDO TABLESPACE undotbs1
ENABLE PLUGGABLE DATABASE
SEED
SYSTEM DATAFILES SIZE 125M AUTOEXTEND ON NEXT 10M MAXSIZE UNLIMITED
SYSAUX DATAFILES SIZE 100M;
Database created.


SQL>
```

10. Create additional tablespaces as needed, based on the requirements of the CDB and PDBs.

11. Run scripts to build data dictionary views:

```
@%ORACLE_HOME%\RDBMS\ADMIN\catalog.sql
@%ORACLE_HOME%\RDBMS\ADMIN\catproc.sql


Connect as SYSTEM and run
@%ORACLE_HOME%\SQLPLUS\ADMIN\pupbld.sql
```

12. Run the catcdb.sql SQL script. This script installs the components required by a CDB.

```
@%ORACLE_HOME%\RDBMS\ADMIN\catcdb.sql
```

13. Verify that all supplied PL/SQL packages are valid. Compile any that are not. This is a standard practice when manually building a database using SQL*Plus.

```
SELECT object_name, object_type FROM dba_objects
WHERE status = 'INVALID';
```

You can also generate a script to recompile the invalid objects by spooling the results of this query:

```
select 'alter '||object_type||' '||owner||'.'||object_name||' compile;'
from dba_objects where status = 'INVALID'
/
```

Now run the script as SYS until there are no more invalid objects returned by the first query.

14. Run scripts to install additional options, depending on the additional features and options required for this CDB.

15. Back up the database.

16. Enable automatic instance startup. Here's the Windows way to do it:

```
ORADIM –EDIT –SID NDLNE –STARTMODE AUTO –SRVCSTART SYSTEM –SPFILE
```

Specify –SPFILE if you want the instance to read the spfile on auto-startup.

Now that you've created a CDB using SQL*Plus, you can add PDBs using the methods described in the upcoming sections.

At the time of this writing, catcdb.sql and catcdb_int.sql were omitted from the 12.1.0.1.0 release. The files can be downloaded as part of a patch from Oracle Support. Also confirm that Perl is in your path. If you are unable to create the CDB using SQL*Plus, take advantage of the DBCA to accomplish the same task.

Creating a PDB Using Different Methods

In the upcoming sections we will demonstrate how to create PDBs using SQL*Plus and the DBCA. Also, we will further discuss the different sources of PDBs that you may be required to use to create a PDB, for example:

- Using the seed database in the CDB: PDB$SEED
- Cloning an existing PDB
- Plugging an unplugged PDB into a CDB
- Creating a PDB by moving a non-CDB into a PDB

We will demonstrate creating a PDB from the PDB$SEED using both the DBCA and the SQL*Plus command line.

Creating a PDB Using the DBCA

As mentioned earlier, you can use the DBCA to create CDBs and PDBs. In this section you'll use the DBCA to create a PDB in an existing CDB, using the PDB$SEED database as your starting point.

1. Launch the DBCA, and in Step 1, on the first screen, select the last item, Manage Pluggable Databases, as shown in Figure 11.7.

FIGURE 11.7 Managing pluggable databases using the DBCA

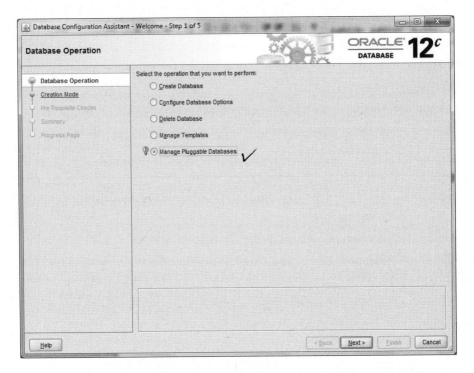

2. For Step 2, from the Manage Pluggable Databases screen, shown in Figure 11.8, choose Create A Pluggable Database; then click Next.

3. In Step 3, to create a PDB you'll need to select a host CDB from the list of available databases, as shown in Figure 11.9, and provide the logon credentials for a common user with SYSDBA privileges. Please note that all databases on the host server are listed, some of which may be non-CDBs.

If you select a non-CDB and click Next, the DBCA will inform you that you have chosen a non-CDB (shown in Figure 11.10) and return you to the Database List screen.

FIGURE 11.8 Creating a PDB using the DBCA

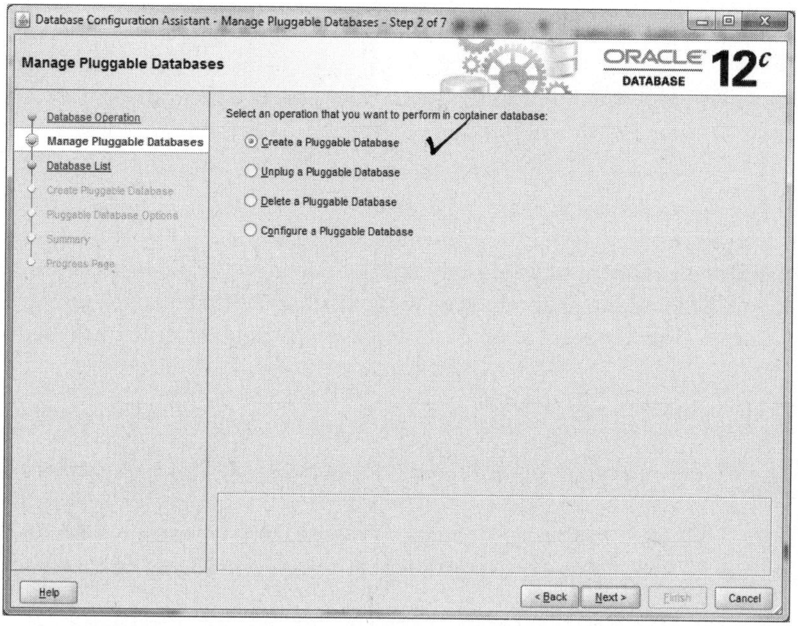

FIGURE 11.9 DBCA Database List

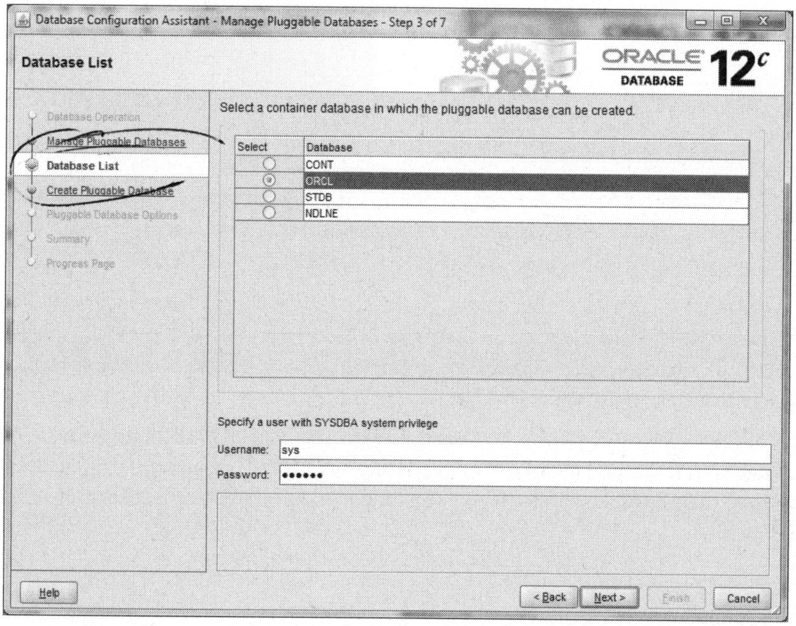

FIGURE 11.10 Selected database is a non-CDB.

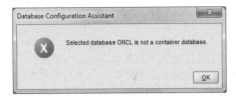

4. From the Database List screen, choose a valid CDB, as shown in Figure 11.11, enter the username and password, then click Next. The DBCA will validate the CDB, and in Step 4, you'll choose the method to create the PDB. For this lesson, choose the first option, Create A New Pluggable Database, as shown in Figure 11.12. Click Next.

FIGURE 11.11 Select a valid CDB.

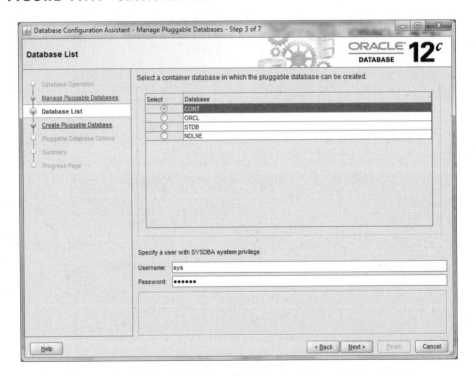

5. In Step 5, shown in Figure 11.13, enter the PDB name, select the file options, indicate whether to create a default user tablespace, and enter the PDB administrator username and password. Your screen may vary based on the Oracle storage options chosen. Click Next to continue.

FIGURE 11.12 Create a new pluggable database.

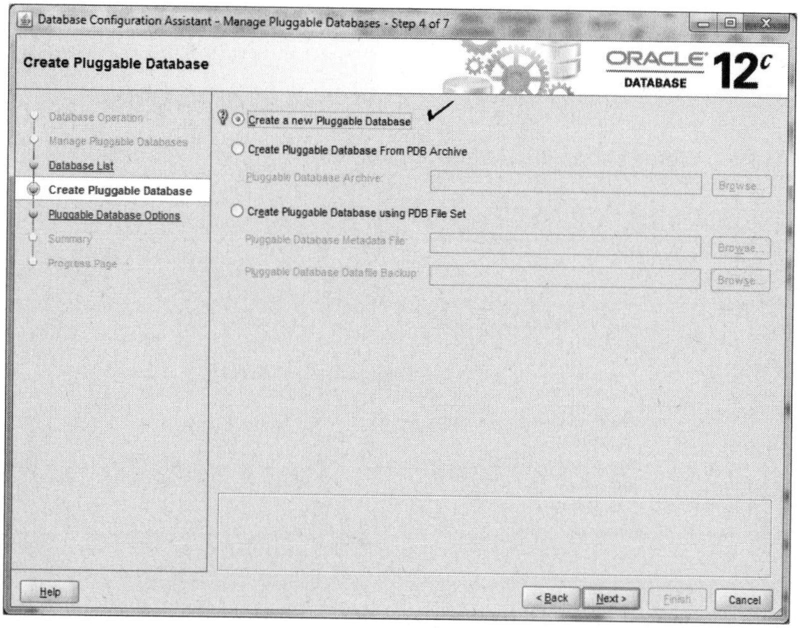

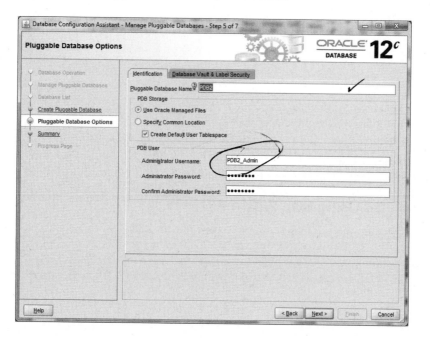

FIGURE 11.13 Pluggable Database Options screen

If you entered a PDB name that is already in use in this CDB, the DBCA will display an error window and return you to Step 5.

6. In Step 6, the Summary screen (shown in Figure 11.14), you need to review and verify the information, and then click Finish if the information is correct and you wish to proceed and create the PDB.

FIGURE 11.14 Create Pluggable Database: Summary

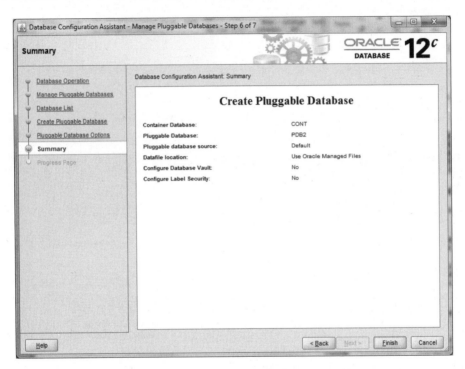

7. In Step 7, you monitor the progress, shown in Figure 11.15, and have the options to review the Activity Log and the Alert Log (shown in Figure 11.16).

Creating a PDB is quick work for the DBCA, and when it's complete, you'll see the success screen shown in Figure 11.17.

Once the PDB is created, click Close to exit the DBCA.

Creating a PDB Using SQL Plus

To create a PDB from the SQL*Plus command line, use the CREATE PLUGGABLE DATABASE SQL statement. This PDB is created from the PDB$SEED database and includes the full data dictionary, which includes internal links to system-supplied root objects and metadata. You can create a PDB within a CDB, but not from within a non-CDB or from within another PDB.

FIGURE 11.15 Monitor the PDB creation.

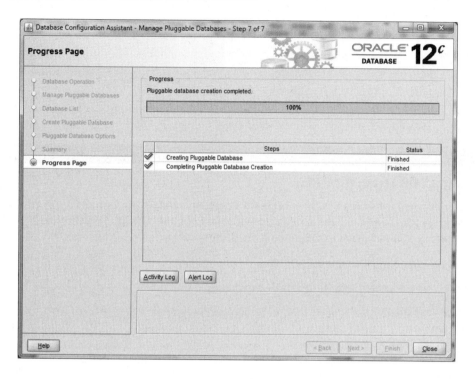

FIGURE 11.16 The Alert Log

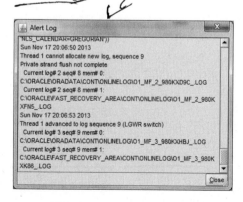

If you've been following along in the previous examples and have created the CONT CDB and pluggable databases PDB1 and PDB2, you can move forward with Exercise 11.2 and create the new pluggable database PDB3 at the SQL*Plus command line.

FIGURE 11.17 Success screen

EXERCISE 11.2

Creating a PDB Using SQL*Plus

In this exercise, you will utilize SQL*Plus to create a pluggable database in a container database, using the PDB seed database and Oracle Managed Files (the default). This exercise assumes that you already have a CDB running on the host server.

1. From the command line, launch SQL*Plus.

2. Connect as a common user with SYSDBA privileges.

3. Create the PDB:

```
C:\>sqlplus sys@CONT as sysdba


SQL*Plus: Release 12.1.0.1.0 Production on Sun Nov 17 20:49:57 2013


Copyright (c) 1982, 2013, Oracle.  All rights reserved.


Enter password:


Connected to:
Oracle Database 12c Enterprise Edition Release 12.1.0.1.0 - 64bit Production
With the Partitioning, OLAP, Advanced Analytics and Real Application Testing
options


SQL>
SQL> CREATE PLUGGABLE DATABASE pdb3
  2  ADMIN USER pdb3_admin IDENTIFIED BY system03
  3  /
```

```
Pluggable database created.


SQL>
```

After you create a PDB using SQL*Plus, open the new PDB (in read/write mode) to complete the integration of the new PDB into the CDB. Once the database is open and control is returned at the command prompt, the new PDB is ready to use.

```
SQL> connect sys/system@CONT as sysdba
Connected.
SQL>
SQL>



SQL> alter pluggable database pdb3 open;

Pluggable database altered.

SQL>
```

Creating a PDB from a Clone

In this section we will demonstrate two methods for creating a clone of a PDB. The first option is to create a PDB clone locally, or within the existing CDB. The second option is to create a PDB as a clone of a remote PDB, or a PDB from another CDB. The CREATE PLUGGABLE DATABASE statement copies the source PDB files to a new location and creates the target PDB.

Creating a Clone PDB Using a Local PDB

While there are options to this method, it is incredibly simple in its base form. Verify that the source PDB is open in read-only mode, and then issue the CREATE PLUGGABLE DATABASE command:

```
SQL> alter pluggable database pdb1 open read only;
Pluggable database altered.
SQL> create pluggable database lne1 from pdb1;
Pluggable database created.
```

This assumes, of course, that LNE1 doesn't already exist within the current CDB and that PDB1 does.

Creating a Clone PDB Using a Remote PDB

There are options to this method as well, and it is also incredibly simple in its base form. Verify that the source PDB is open in read-only mode, and then issue the CREATE PLUGGABLE DATABASE command. In this example, CONT is the remote or source CDB, and NDLNE is the local or target CDB:

```
SQL> create database link CONT
  2   connect to system identified by system
  3   using 'CONT';

Database link created.


SQL> connect sys/system@CONT
Connected.
SQL> alter pluggable database pdb1 open read only;
Pluggable database altered.
SQL> connect sys/system@NDLNE as sysdba
Connected.
SQL>
SQL> create pluggable database lne4 from pdb1@CONT;
Pluggable database created.
```

This assumes that LNE4 doesn't already exist within the current CDB and that PDB1 does exist in the remote database.

Plugging an Unplugged PDB into a CDB

For this example we'll use an unplugged PDB from one CDB and plug it into another CDB as a PDB with a new name. Consider using this method to quickly copy an unplugged PDB from a development database to a test database:

1. In Step 1, shown in Figure 11.18, launch the DBCA and from the Database Operation screen, choose Managed Pluggable Databases; then click Next.

2. In Step 2, choose Create A Pluggable Database; then click Next, as shown in Figure 11.19.

3. In Step 3, choose the target CDB that you want to plug the new PDB into. Enter the credentials for a user in the target database who has SYSDBA privileges, and then click Next, as shown in Figure 11.20.

4. In Step 4, since you're using an unplugged database from another CDB, you'll choose to create the PDB from a PDB file set, as shown in Figure 11.21. Click the Browse button to select the files that have been previously unplugged from other CDBs on the local system. Click Next when you have selected the correct XML file, and the associated DFB filename will be filled in for you.

FIGURE 11.18   Creating a PDB from an unplugged PDB: Step 1

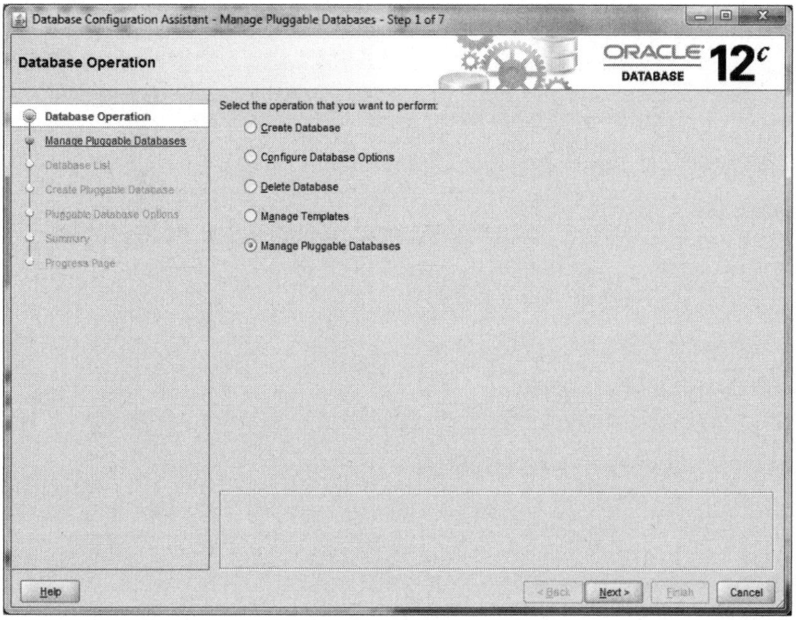

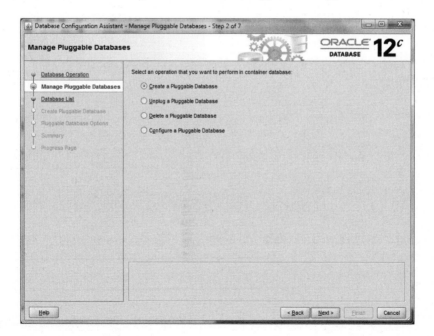

FIGURE 11.19   Creating a PDB from an unplugged PDB: Step 2

FIGURE 11.20 Creating a PDB from an unplugged PDB: Step 3

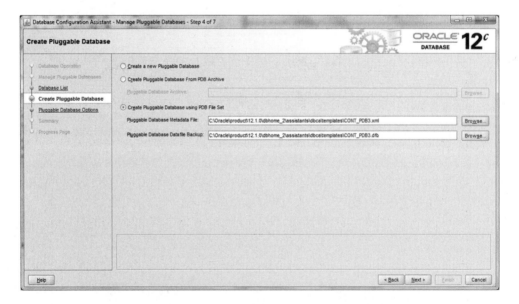

FIGURE 11.21 Creating a PDB from an unplugged PDB: Step 4

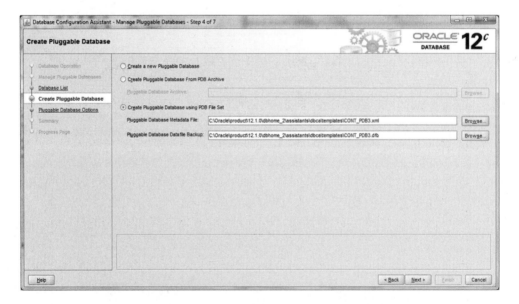

5. As shown in Figure 11.22, in Step 5 you will enter the name of the new PDB in the target CDB. In this example we'll use Oracle Managed Files and default settings.

6. Click Next to continue on to Step 6. Review the Summary page, as shown in Figure 11.23, and then click Finish to complete the task.

FIGURE 11.22   Creating a PDB from an unplugged PDB: Step 5

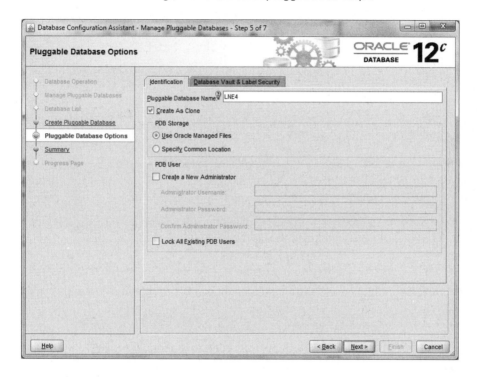

7. Monitor the progress in Step 7, shown in Figure 11.24. When the task is complete, you'll see the successful completion pop-up window shown in Figure 11.25.

Creating a PDB by Moving a Non-CDB into a PDB

We'll use SQL*Plus in this example demonstrating one method to copy an Oracle 12c database that was created as a non-CDB into a new PDB inside an existing CDB. Again, the non-CDB must be an Oracle 12c database, created as a non-CDB. The fundamental steps are listed here, followed by the OS command-line and SQL*Plus command-line steps:

1. Start up the source non-CDB in read-only mode.

2. After you've created the appropriate operating system directory, use the DBMS_PDB package to generate an XML metadata file. In the example that follows, we'll call it ncdb.xml.

FIGURE 11.23 Creating a PDB from an unplugged PDB: Step 6

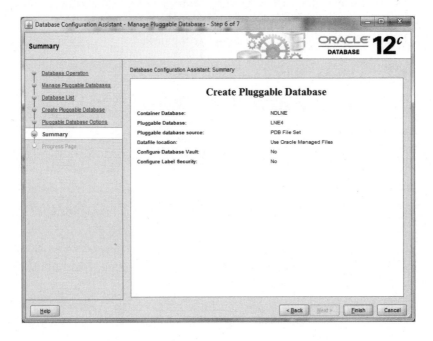

FIGURE 11.24 Creating a PDB from an unplugged PDB: Step 7

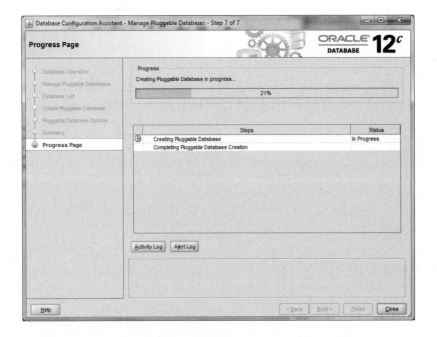

FIGURE 11.25   Creating a PDB from an unplugged PDB: Success

3. Shut down the source non-CDB.

4. Create the target PDB data file directory that will be used in the FILE_NAME_CONVERT clause.

5. Connect to the CDB (NDLNE in the sample).

6. Create the new PDB from the non-CDB, using the COPY and FILE_NAME_CONVERT key terms.

7. Connect to the new PDB and complete the PDB provisioning.

```
C:\> set ORACLE_SID=ORCL
C:\> set ORACLE_HOME=C:\Oracle\product\12.1.0\dbhome_2
C:\> sqlplus / as sysdba
SQL*Plus: Release 12.1.0.1.0 Production on Sun Nov 24 23:08:37 2013
Copyright (c) 1982, 2013, Oracle.  All rights reserved.
Connected to an idle instance.
SQL> startup mount
ORACLE instance started.

Total System Global Area 5027536896 bytes
Fixed Size                   2412928 bytes
Variable Size              704646784 bytes
Database Buffers          4311744512 bytes
Redo Buffers                 8732672 bytes
Database mounted.
SQL>
SQL> alter database open read only;
Database altered.
SQL> BEGIN
  2      DBMS_PDB.DESCRIBE(
  3      pdb_descr_file => 'c:\oracle\temp\ncdb.xml');
  4  END;
  5  /
PL/SQL procedure successfully completed.
```

```
SQL> shutdown immediate;
Database closed.
Database dismounted.
ORACLE instance shut down.
SQL> exit
Disconnected from Oracle Database 12c Enterprise Edition Release 12.1.0.1.0
- 64bit Production
With the Partitioning, OLAP, Advanced Analytics and Real Application Testing
options
```

The command to create the PDB does not create the directories on the file system, so using your preferred file system manager or the command line, create the target directory for the PDB data files. Now update your environment variables to switch to the target CDB and log on to SQL*Plus as SYSDBA. Once you're connected, plug in the non-CDB as a PDB.

```
C:\>mkdir C:\oracle\oradata\NDLNE\LNE2\DATAFILE
C:\>set ORACLE_SID=NDLNE

C:\>sqlplus / as sysdba

SQL*Plus: Release 12.1.0.1.0 Production on Mon Nov 25 20:58:10 2013

Copyright (c) 1982, 2013, Oracle.  All rights reserved.


Connected to:
Oracle Database 12c Enterprise Edition Release 12.1.0.1.0 - 64bit Production
With the Partitioning, OLAP, Advanced Analytics and Real Application Testing
options

SQL> CREATE PLUGGABLE DATABASE LNE2 USING 'c:\oracle\temp\ncdb.xml'
COPY
FILE_NAME_CONVERT = ('c:\oracle\oradata\ORCL\', 'c:\oracle\oradata\NDLNE\LNE2\
DATAFILE\');

Pluggable database created.
```

Now connect to the new PDB and run the %ORACLE_HOME%\rdbms\admin\noncdb_to_pdb .sql script. You must run this script before the PDB can be opened for the first time. The script will SET ECHO ON, open the new PDB, make its changes, and then close the PDB. Once it's complete, alter the PDB to open it and begin using it. (The output is truncated here.)

```
SQL> alter session set container=LNE2;

Session altered.
```

```
SQL> @%ORACLE_HOME%\RDBMS\ADMIN\noncdb_to_pdb.sql

SQL>
SQL> alter pluggable database LNE2 open;

Pluggable database altered.
```

Following the creation of a PDB using SQL*Plus and running the necessary script, confirm that the PDB is in a usable state. Before running the noncdb_to_pdb.sql script, the LNE2 PDB looks like this:

```
SQL> col pdb_name form a20
SQL> SELECT PDB_NAME, STATUS FROM DBA_PDBS;


PDB_NAME                STATUS
-------------------- -------------

LNE1                    NORMAL
PDB$SEED                NORMAL
PDB3                    NORMAL
LNE4                    NORMAL
LNE2                    NEW
```

After running the noncdb_to_pdb.sql script, the LNE2 PDB looks like this:

```
        SQL> SELECT PDB_NAME, STATUS FROM DBA_PDBS;


PDB_NAME                STATUS
-------------------- -------------

LNE1                    NORMAL
PDB$SEED                NORMAL
PDB3                    NORMAL
LNE4                    NORMAL
LNE2                    NORMAL


SQL>
```

Unplugging and Dropping a PDB

In this section we'll discuss the primary methods for unplugging and dropping a PDB, using the DBCA and SQL*Plus. But first we need to explain the difference between unplugging a PDB and dropping a PDB. Unplugging a PDB removes the associations between a PDB and its host CDB. Unplug a PDB when you want to make it unavailable or move it to another CDB. Unplugging removes the PDB from the CDB but retains the data files and metadata. When you unplug a PDB you can easily plug it back into the CDB or into another CDB.

Dropping or deleting a PDB completely removes the PDB from the CDB. The DROP PLUGGABLE DATABASE statement drops a PDB and modifies the control file of the CDB to eliminate all references to the PDB. The clause INCLUDING DATAFILES removes the PDB data files from disk. The default is KEEP DATAFILES, which does not remove the data files. Regardless, the TEMP files are removed. Archived redo log files and backups associated with the PDB are not removed. If you want to remove those files, use Oracle Recovery Manager (RMAN), as described in Chapter 6, "Reporting, Monitoring, and Tuning with RMAN."

> A PDB must have been opened at least once prior to unplugging or dropping it. In SQL*Plus from the CDB, issue the ALTER PLUGGABLE DATABASE pdb_name OPEN; command.

Unplugging a PDB Using the DBCA

In this section we'll discuss and demonstrate how to unplug a PDB using the Database Configuration Assistant. The DBCA simplifies the operation and is the preferred method to unplug a PDB.

1. Launch the DBCA, and from the Database Operations page (Step 1), choose the Manage Pluggable Databases option; then click Next.

2. In Step 2, select Unplug A Pluggable Database, as shown in Figure 11.26; then click Next.

3. Choose the CDB that hosts the PDB you wish to unplug, as shown in Step 3, Figure 11.27. Enter the credentials for the common user with SYSDBA privileges.

4. In Step 4, select the PDB that you want to unplug from the drop-down list. For this example, choose the most recently created PDB, PDB3. You'll also choose to generate a pluggable database file set, allowing the defaults as shown in Figure 11.28.

   Click Next to continue to the Summary page, Step 5, shown in Figure 11.29.

5. Once you've confirmed that this is the correct PDB to unplug, click Finish to begin Step 6, the unplugging, and monitor the progress, as shown in Figure 11.30.

   If the selected PDB has not been opened prior to this, then you'll receive an error message, as in Figure 11.31.

   Once the database is unplugged successfully, you'll see the pop-up window indicating success, as in Figure 11.32.

FIGURE 11.26 Manage Pluggable Databases: Unplug a PDB

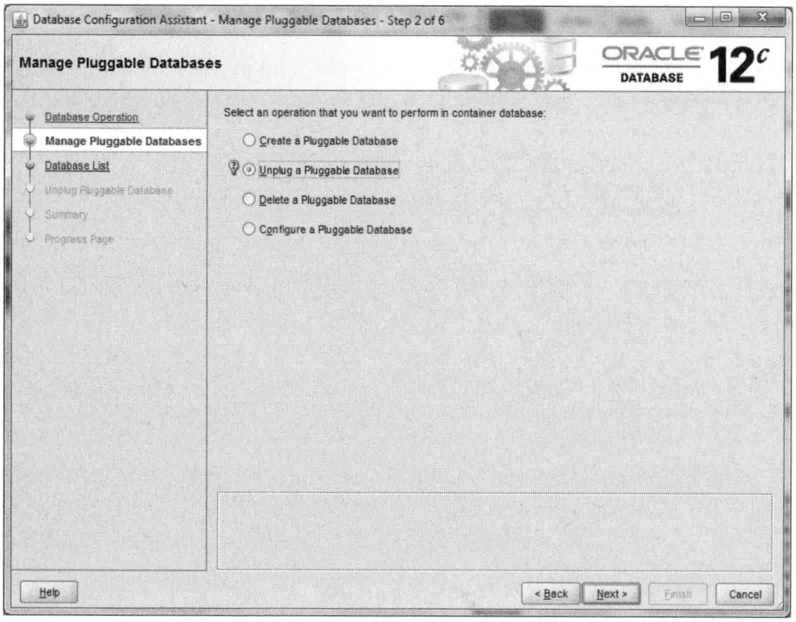

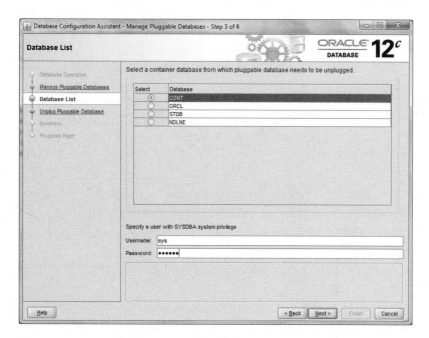

FIGURE 11.27 Unplug a PDB: Choose the CDB

FIGURE 11.28 Unplug a PDB: Choose the PDB

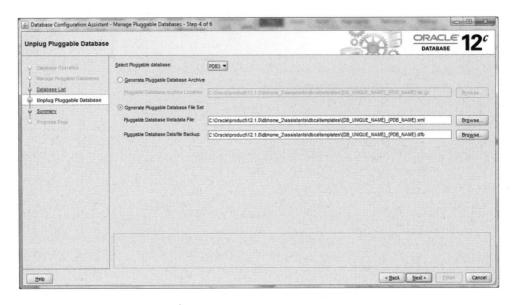

FIGURE 11.29 Unplug a PDB: Summary

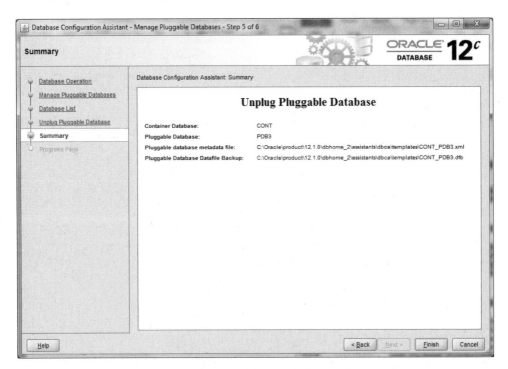

FIGURE 11.30 Unplug a PDB: Progress Page

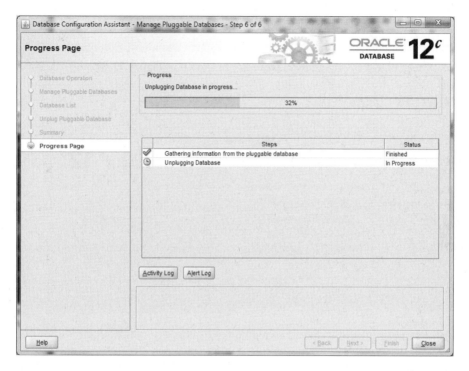

FIGURE 11.31 Unplug a PDB: Failure pop-up

FIGURE 11.32 Unplug a PDB: Success pop-up

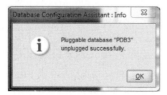

Dropping a PDB Using the DBCA

Now that you've successfully unplugged a PDB, the next logical step to learn is how to drop or delete a PDB:

1. To drop a PDB, launch the DBCA, and select Manage Pluggable Databases.

2. In Step 2 select Delete A Pluggable Database, as shown in Figure 11.33.

FIGURE 11.33   Delete a PDB

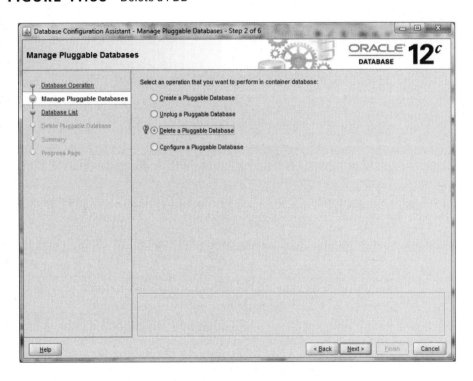

3. In Step 3, shown in Figure 11.34, choose the CDB that contains the PDB you wish to delete, and provide the credentials for the user account with SYSDBA privileges. Click Next to continue.

You'll see the list of PDBs available for deletion, as shown in Step 4, Figure 11.35.

Notice that the previously unplugged PDB3 is missing from the list of available PDBs.

4. Choose to delete PDB1. Click Next to continue, and you're taken to Step 5, the Delete Pluggable Database Summary page, shown in Figure 11.36.

5. Confirm the name of the PDB you're about to delete. If you change your mind, click the Back button and choose another PDB. Click Finish to delete the PDB.

6. Monitor the progress of the delete in Step 6, shown in Figure 11.37. The DBCA moves quickly to delete the PDB, and the success pop-up is shown in Figure 11.38, confirming that PDB1 has been deleted.

FIGURE 11.34   Delete a PDB: CDB database list

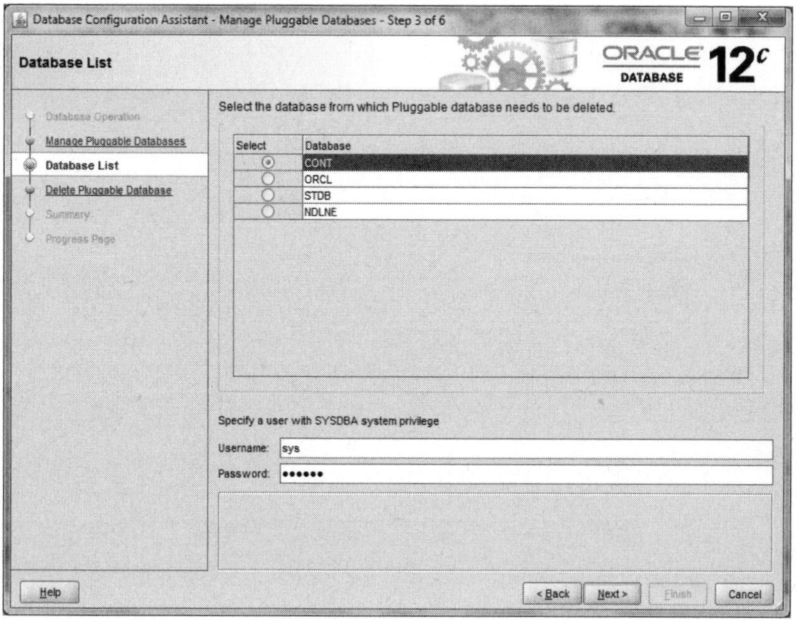

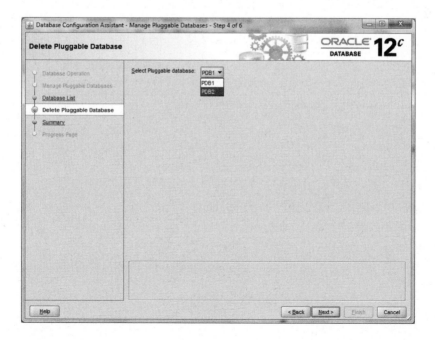

FIGURE 11.35   Delete a PDB: PDB database list

FIGURE 11.36 Delete a PDB: Summary page

FIGURE 11.37 Delete a PDB: Progress page

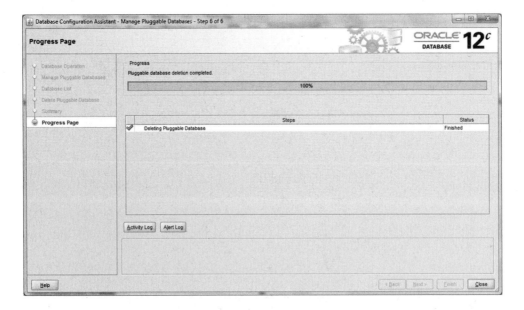

FIGURE 11.38 Delete a PDB: Success pop-up

You have the opportunity to review the Activity Log and Alert Log.

7. Click Close to end the DBCA session.

Unplugging a PDB Using SQL* Plus

If you've been following along, we're down to one PDB (PDB2) in our CDB. We'll use SQL*Plus to demonstrate unplugging PDB2. To unplug a PDB using SQL*Plus, you must be connected as a user as SYSDBA or SYSOPER, either commonly granted or locally granted in the PDB.

```
SQL> connect sys/system@CONT as sysdba
Connected.
SQL> ALTER PLUGGABLE DATABASE pdb2 UNPLUG INTO 'C:\Oracle\TEMP\pdb2.xml';
ALTER PLUGGABLE DATABASE pdb2 UNPLUG INTO 'C:\Oracle\TEMP\pdb2.xml'
*
ERROR at line 1:
ORA-65025: Pluggable database PDB2 is not closed on all instances.


SQL> ALTER PLUGGABLE DATABASE pdb2 close;

Pluggable database altered.

SQL> ALTER PLUGGABLE DATABASE pdb2 UNPLUG INTO 'C:\Oracle\TEMP\pdb2.xml';

Pluggable database altered.

SQL>
```

Please note that the PDB must be closed prior to issuing the UNPLUG command.

Dropping a PDB Using SQL* Plus

Dropping the PDB is quite simple. Issue the DROP PLUGGABLE DATABASE command and the SQL*Plus prompt, keeping in mind that you must have the SYSDBA or SYSOPER privileges as previously described:

```
SQL> DROP PLUGGABLE DATABASE pdb2;

Pluggable database dropped.

SQL>
```

Notice that the DBCA and SQL*Plus do not exhibit the same behaviors. When you unplug a PDB using the DBCA, it doesn't show up on the database list of available PDBs to delete. When you unplug a PDB in SQL*Plus, it doesn't automatically delete the PDB; you'll have to enter the SQL*Plus command to drop the PDB.

Migrating a Pre-12.1 Non-CDB Database to a CDB

In this section we will discuss how to take a non-CDB database created in a previous version of Oracle Database and migrate it into a CDB. Basically there are two options. Either upgrade the non-CDB to Oracle 12c and plug the 12c non-CDB into a CDB as a new PDB, or use a migration tool to move the contents of the non-CDB into a CDB as a new PDB.

Since there is no direct upgrade from a pre-12.1 non-CDB to a CDB, the first option would be to upgrade the non-CDB from a prior version to 12c and then move the new non-CDB into a PDB as described in previous sections. The second option, which we will focus on for the remainder of this section, is to use Oracle Data Pump to move content directly from the pre-12.1 non-CDB into a new PDB (see Exercise 11.3).

> Performing an upgrade on a pre-12.1 non-CDB will result in a 12c non-CDB. To migrate the contents of a pre-12.1 non-CDB, you will need to create a new 12c CDB, and migrate the pre-12.1 non-CDB into a new PDB in the CDB.

Using Data Pump to Migrate a Non-CDB to a CDB

For this method we will use Oracle Data Pump to define a data set on a non-CDB from a previous Oracle Database release, for example, Oracle Database 11g. We will create an empty PDB in a CDB and then use Oracle Data Pump to import the data set into the PDB.

We will create a complete copy of the non-CDB as a Full Transportable Export using Oracle Data Pump, which exports all objects and data.

The Full Transportable dump file contains all objects in the database and is available beginning with Oracle Database 11g Release 2 (11.2.0.3). You can then use this dump file to import into Oracle Database 12c.

You can use Data Pump to migrate the following:

- All or part of a non-CDB into a PDB
- Between PDBs within the same or different CDBs
- From a PDB into a non-CDB

A Few Words about Data Pump

Data Pump does not support any CDB-wide operations in Oracle Database 12*c* Release 1 (12.1). If you are connected to CDB$ROOT or PDB$SEED and attempt to utilize Data Pump, you'll get an error message, as shown here:

```
ORA-39357: WARNING: Oracle Data Pump operations are not typically needed when
connected to the root or seed of a container database.
```

 Another option is to use a product such as Oracle GoldenGate to replicate the non-CDB to a new PDB.

EXERCISE 11.3

Using Data Pump to Migrate a Non-CDB into a PDB

In this exercise you will use the Data Pump to export a non-CDB database that is in a version prior to Oracle 12*c* and use the Data Pump import process to move the content into a PDB.

1. Create a new CDB target, or utilize an existing CDB.

2. Create a new PDB.

3. Start up the source non-CDB. Alter the non-system tablespaces to read-only mode.

4. Begin the Data Pump export process. In this example, our source database is also 12*c*.

   ```
   Set DATA_PUMP_DIR=c:\temp
   expdp sys FULL=y DUMPFILE=ncdb_expdat.dmp DIRECTORY=data_pump_dir
   TRANSPORTABLE=always VERSION=12.0 LOGFILE=export.log
   ```

5. Complete the Data Pump import process. In the previous command you exported the full database. Here you will import part of the database into a PDB:

   ```
   impdp hr@LNE5 DIRECTORY=data_pump_dir DUMPFILE=ncdb_expdat.dmp SCHEMAS=hr
   ```

Summary

In this chapter, you learned about the Oracle Database 12*c* multitenant architecture, its primary components, advantages of the multitenant architecture, and use-cases for the option. You saw how to provision pluggable databases and how to create the multitenant container database environment.

You learned how to create container databases using the Database Configuration Assistant and SQL*Plus. You discovered how to create pluggable databases using various methods and various sources: from the seed database, from non-CDBs, and from existing PDBs.

You also learned how to unplug and drop existing PDBs using different tools. You were introduced to migrating pre-Oracle Database 12*c* (non-CDB databases) into a CDB environment using Oracle Data Pump.

Exam Essentials

Know the fundamental components of the Oracle Database 12*c* multitenant architecture. Make sure you understand what makes the multitenant architecture unique and what differentiates a CDB from a non-CDB.

Know how to explain the advantages of the Oracle multitenant architecture.   Know the technical and administrative advantages of the multitenant architecture over the basic single-tenant architecture.

Know the different methods to provision pluggable databases.   Know the different sources and methods used to create a new PDB.

Demonstrate how to create a CDB.   Understand the prerequisites to creating a container database. Know how to create a CDB using the DBCA or SQL*Plus.

Understand how to create a PDB.   Know what methods are available to create a PDB and what nuances exist when creating PDBs from different sources.

Know how to unplug and delete a PDB.   Know the difference between unplugging and dropping a PDB. Know what to do once you've unplugged a PDB and want to clean up the residual files.

Know how to migrate pre-12.1 non-CDB databases.   Remember that all databases created in previous versions of the database are referred to as non-CDBs. Know how to migrate non-CDBs forward using Data Pump and the techniques described earlier to create CDBs and PDBs.

Review Questions

1. In the Oracle 12*c* multitenant architecture, which of the following accurately describes the relationship between PDBs and CDBs?

    A. A PDB can exist across multiple CDBs.

    B. Many CDBs can exist across multiple PDBs.

    C. Many CDBs can exist in a single PDB.

    D. Many PDBs can exist in a single CDB.

    E. All of the above.

2. Which of the following statements is true regarding the number of user-created pluggable databases per CDB?

    A. A maximum of 252 user-created PDBs per CDB

    B. A maximum of 253 user-created PDBs per CDB

    C. A maximum of 252 CDBs per user-created PDB

    D. A maximum of 253 CDBs per user-created PDB

3. Which of these formats represents the correct command to create a PDB using SQL*Plus?

    A. `CREATE PDB DATABASE pdb3 ADMIN USER pdb3_admin IDENTIFIED BY system03;`

    B. `CREATE PLUGGABLE DATABASE pdb3 ADMIN USER pdb3_admin IDENTIFIED BY system03;`

    C. `CREATE PLUGGABLE DATABASE pdb3 SYSTEM USER pdb3_admin IDENTIFIED BY system03;`

    D. None of the above

4. Which of the following statements is true concerning the Oracle multitenant architecture?

    A. It is available beginning with Oracle 11*g* and expanded in Oracle 12*c*.

    B. It supports multiple PDBs within one CDB that spans multiple platforms.

    C. It allows the DBA to shut down a CDB but keep tenant PDBs active.

    D. It allows the DBA to host multiple releases of the Oracle Database within one CDB.

    E. None of the above.

5. Which of the following are components of the multitenant container database? (Choose all that apply.)

    A. CDB$SEED

    B. PDB$SEED

    C. PDB$ROOT

    D. Zero or more PDBs

    E. CDB$ROOT

6. Which of the following CDB containers is used as a system-supplied template to create new containers within the CDB?

    A. PDB$SPEED

    B. CDB$SEED

    C. PDB$SYS

    D. PDB$SEED

    E. None of the above.

7. Which of the following are advantages of the multitenant architecture? (Choose all that apply.)

    A. Reduced hardware requirements

    B. Efficient management of data and code

    C. Simpler management of the database

    D. Platform independence

8. Which of the following describes a non-CDB? (Choose all that apply.)

    A. A PDB

    B. All Oracle databases created in Oracle 12*c* Release 1

    C. All Oracle databases created prior to Oracle 12*c* Release 1

    D. A container database that contains only one PDB

    E. An Oracle 12*c* database that was not created with the multitenant option

9. Which of the following are viable methods to provision a PDB? (Choose all that apply.)

    A. By using the seed database in the CDB

    B. By cloning an existing PDB

    C. By plugging in an unplugged PDB

    D. By moving a non-CDB into a PDB

    E. By moving a CDB into a PDB

10. While creating a new Oracle 12*c* database using the CREATE DATABASE command, which of the following clauses is required to build the database as a CDB?

    A. CREATE PLUGGABLE DATABASE

    B. ENABLE CONTAINER DATABASE

    C. CREATE CONTAINER DATABASE

    D. ENABLE PLUGGABLE DATABASE

    E. None of the above

11. To update a non-CDB to a CDB in Oracle Database 12*c*, which command does the common user enter?

    A. ALTER DATABASE CREATE PLUGGABLE DATABASE

    B. ALTER DATABASE ENABLE CONTAINER DATABASE

    C. ALTER DATABASE CREATE CONTAINER DATABASE

    D. ALTER DATABASE ENABLE PLUGGABLE DATABASE

    E. None of the above

12. When you manually create an Oracle 12*c* database using SQL*Plus, which of the following scripts must be executed to enable the CDB and enable the creation of PDBs?

    A. catpdb.sql

    B. catcdb.sql

    C. pupcdb.sql

    D. None of the above

13. When using the Database Configuration Assistant, which is the correct sequence to unplug a PDB?

    A. Manage pluggable databases, unplug a pluggable database, choose the CDB, choose the PDB.

    B. Manage pluggable databases, choose the CDB, unplug a pluggable database, choose the PDB.

    C. Manage pluggable databases, choose the CDB, choose the PDB, unplug a pluggable database.

    D. Choose the CDB, choose the PDB, manage pluggable databases, unplug a pluggable database.

14. Which of these SQL*Plus commands creates a PDB?

    A. create pluggable database lne1201;

    B. create pluggable database lne1201 from pdb1;

    C. create pluggable database lne1201 from PDB$SEED;

    D. All of the above

15. Which of the following commands creates a local PDB from a PDB in a remote CDB?

    A. create pluggable database lne1201 using pdb1@CONT;

    B. create pluggable database lne1201 from pdb1@CONT;

    C. create pluggable database lne1201 from PDB$SEED@CONT;

    D. All of the above

16. Which are valid options to migrate a non-CDB into a CDB? (Choose all that apply.)

    A. Oracle GoldenGate.

    B. Oracle Data Pump.

    C. Use SQL*Plus and the DBMS_PDB.MIGRATE supplied procedure.

    D. Use SQL*Plus and the DBMS_PDB.DESCRIBE supplied procedure.

    E. None of the above.

17. Which of the following are not necessary steps to migrate a non-CDB into a PDB? (Choose all that apply.)

    A. Start up the source non-CDB in read-only mode.

    B. Use the DBMS_PDB package to generate an XML file.

    C. Create a temporary PDB in the non-CDB.

    D. Shut down the source non-CDB.

    E. Create the PDB in the target CDB.

18. After creating a PDB from a non-PDB, which are necessary steps? (Choose all that apply.)

    A. Shut down the target CDB.

    B. Make the target PDB read-only.

    C. Run the noncdb_to_pdb.sql script.

    D. Open the PDB.

    E. All of the above.

19. To unplug a PDB, which of these steps are required? (Choose all that apply.)

    A. The PDB must have been opened at least once.

    B. You must specify an INTO clause and a valid XML target file.

    C. The PDB must be closed.

    D. The PDB must be in read-only mode.

    E. None of the above.

20. To drop a pluggable database, what steps are required? (Choose all that apply.)

    A. The PDB must have been opened at least once.

    B. You must specify an INTO clause and a valid XML target file.

    C. The PDB must be closed.

    D. The PDB must be in read-only mode.

    E. None of the above.

Chapter

12

Managing Oracle Multitenant Databases

ORACLE DATABASE 12c: ADVANCED ADMINISTRATION EXAM OBJECTIVES COVERED IN THIS CHAPTER:

✓ Managing a CDB and PDBs

✓ Establish connections to CDB/PDB

✓ Start up and shut down a CDB and open and close PDBs

✓ Evaluate the impact of parameter value changes

In this chapter, we will explore how to manage the multitenant database environment that is based on the Oracle Database 12*c* multitenant architecture. We will differentiate between multitenant container databases (CDBs) and pluggable databases (PDBs).

The first topic of conversation is how to connect to CDBs and PDBs, and similarities to and differences from establishing connections to non-CDBs. We will demonstrate establishing connections through various exercises.

The second topic focuses on starting up and shutting down CDBs and then on opening and closing PDBs. We will discuss the startup and shutdown options, as well as the open and close options, and demonstrate use cases for each.

The third topic explores the impact of initialization parameter value changes on the CDB and PDBs. We will list and discuss which parameters have an impact on the operation of the multitenant environment.

 Exam objectives are subject to change at any time without prior notice and at Oracle's sole discretion. Please visit Oracle's Training and Certification website (http://www.oracle.com/education/certification/) for the most current exam-objectives listing.

Establishing Connections to CDB/PDB

New to Oracle 12*c*, the Oracle multitenant architecture is designed to allow an Oracle database to host multiple Oracle databases within one overall structure. The multitenant container database can includes zero, one, or many DBA-created pluggable databases. From a client-connection perspective, a PDB looks like a traditional Oracle database and is composed of schemas, schema objects, and non-schema objects. Oracle databases prior to Oracle 12*c* were non-CDBs.

Because the intent is for a PDB to appear as a non-CDB to the client connection, but in reality the PDB exists in a host CDB, there are a few underlying differences that the DBA must be aware of when establishing connections to the CDB and PDBs, starting up and shutting down instances, and configuring initialization parameters.

In this section, we will discuss the ways to connect to a CDB and the various methods for connecting to a PDB. We will discuss the types of accounts in a CDB, the common users, and PDB users. Connecting to the CDB$ROOT should be an activity reserved for administrators and system accounts. All users and custom applications should connect to PDBs. For a user connecting to a database, a PDB should appear to be just the same as a non-CDB.

Before we establish connections, let's discuss users and containers in the multitenant environment.

Chapter 11, "Creating Oracle Multitenant Databases," demonstrates how to create CDBs and PDBs. The exercises in this chapter assume that you have created a CDB and PDBs.

User Accounts in a CDB

In the multitenant environment, a user is either a common user, which has access to all containers in the CDB, or a local user, which has access only to the PDB in which it was created.

The Common Users in a CDB

In the context of a CDB, the word *common* is used to indicate that some entity is common to all containers. In context, *local* means that an entity is restricted to exactly one container.

A common user is a CDB user that has the same identity in CDB$ROOT and in all PDBs and can connect to and perform operations in the root and in any PDB where it has CREATE SESSION privileges. Examples of common users that are created with each CDB are SYS and SYSTEM. The ability to create, modify, or delete CDB-wide attributes of a common user or role is restricted to a common user connected to the root. A common user with appropriate privileges can switch between containers and administer PDBs from the root. A DBA-created common user has the following characteristics:

- Username begins with the characters c## or C##.
- Username contains only ASCII or EBCDIC characters.
- Resides in the root and uses the same identity to connect to every PDB.
- The schema associated with a common user can be different in each PDB.

It is not essential for a common user to have the same privileges in every PDB. In Exercise 12.1, we will demonstrate how to create a common user in an existing CDB.

The Local Users in a CDB

The local user is not a common user but is local to a specific PDB and can operate in only a single PDB. A user who has the CREATE USER role or greater within a PDB, including common users, can create a local user. A local user has the following characteristics:

- Username may not begin with the characters c## or C##.
- Is unique and specific to a particular PDB and owns a schema in the same PDB.
- Can't be created in the root.
- Can't log on to another PDB or to the root.
- If granted, can access objects in a common-user schema in the same PDB.

In Exercise 12.2, we will demonstrate how to create a local user in an existing PDB.

The *CONTAINER* Clause

When you create a new user, the CONTAINER clause differentiates the local user from the common user. If you want to create a common user, make sure your current container is CDB$ROOT and use CONTAINER = ALL when issuing the CREATE USER statement. This is the default if you're logged into CDB$ROOT.

If you want to create a local user in a PDB, set your current container to the PDB and use the CONTAINER = CURRENT clause. This is the default if you're logged into a PDB.

When creating a common user the DEFAULT TABLESPACE, TEMPORARY TABLESPACE, QUOTA, and PROFILE specified must exist in all the containers belonging to the CDB.

The Current Container

The current container is where the current session is running, and each session can have only one current container at any point in time. It can be the root for common users or a PDB for local and common users. Each container has a separate data dictionary, so the current container data dictionary is used for privilege authorization and name resolution.

Chapter 14, "Oracle Security in CDBs and PDBs," goes into greater detail about users, roles, and privileges in CDBs and PDBs.

Establishing Connections to a CDB

This section describes using SQL*Plus to access the root of a CDB. You can connect to a CDB by starting SQL*Plus with a connect string to the CDB, using the SQL*Plus CONNECT command if you're already logged on, or you can switch from a PDB to the CDB$ROOT by using the ALTER SESSION SET CONTAINER = CDB$ROOT SQL statement.

Clients access the root through a database service that has the same name as the database name. With the service name, you can access the CDB$ROOT using the easy connect syntax or the net service name configured in the tnsnames.ora file. When you create a new database using the DBCA, it creates a new listener service handler, and a service name is created in the local tnsnames.ora file. Oracle Net Services must be configured for you to connect to the CDB$ROOT using a net service name.

The SESSIONS initialization parameter limits the total number of sessions that may be established in a CDB and its PDBs. If you reach the SESSIONS limit, you will not be able to log on.

Connecting to a CDB Using SQL*Plus

In Exercise 12.1, we will establish connections to a CDB and its DBA-created PDBs. This exercise assumes that you have created a CDB and PDBs on your local machine and that the CDB has been started.

EXERCISE 12.1

Connecting to a CDB Using SQL*Plus

In this exercise, you will connect to an existing CDB on a Windows 7 server and SQL*Plus at the command line. For this CDB, the database name, Oracle SID, and Oracle net service name are all CONT.

1. Launch a command-line window:

    a. From the Windows 7 Start menu, search for "CMD," or press the Windows command button and the R key simultaneously; then enter CMD.

    b. At the C:\> prompt, specify an instance identifier (SID), unique to this server and database domain, for the container database you wish to connect to:

    C:\ set ORACLE_SID=CONT

2. Set the required environment variables. ORACLE_HOME is required on some operating systems:

    C:\ set ORACLE_HOME= C:\Oracle\product\12.1.0\dbhome_2

3. Connect to the root of the CDB specified by the ORACLE_SID, with user SYS as SYSDBA, using OS authentication. Use the SQL*Plus command SHOW CON_NAME to show the name of the current container for the session:

    C:\>sqlplus / as sysdba

    SQL*Plus: Release 12.1.0.1.0 Production on Fri Nov 29 12:36:18 2013

    Copyright (c) 1982, 2013, Oracle. All rights reserved.

    Connected to:
    Oracle Database 12c Enterprise Edition Release 12.1.0.1.0 - 64bit Production
    With the Partitioning, OLAP, Advanced Analytics and Real Application Testing
    options

    SQL> SHOW USER
    USER is "SYS"
    SQL> SHOW CON_NAME

    CON_NAME

    CDB$ROOT
    SQL> EXIT
    Disconnected from Oracle Database 12c Enterprise Edition Release 12.1.0.1.0 -
    64bit Production

With the Partitioning, OLAP, Advanced Analytics and Real Application Testing options

C:\>

4. Connect to the CDB root as SYS using DB authentication:

C:\>sqlplus sys/system as sysdba

SQL*Plus: Release 12.1.0.1.0 Production on Fri Nov 29 12:40:42 2013

Copyright (c) 1982, 2013, Oracle. All rights reserved.

Connected to:
Oracle Database 12c Enterprise Edition Release 12.1.0.1.0 - 64bit Production
With the Partitioning, OLAP, Advanced Analytics and Real Application Testing options

SQL> SHOW USER
USER is "SYS"
SQL> SHOW CON_NAME

CON_NAME

CDB$ROOT
SQL> EXIT
Disconnected from Oracle Database 12c Enterprise Edition Release 12.1.0.1.0 - 64bit Production
With the Partitioning, OLAP, Advanced Analytics and Real Application Testing options

C:\>

5. Connect to the CDB root as user SYSTEM using a net service name connection:

C:\>tnsping CONT

TNS Ping Utility for 64-bit Windows: Version 12.1.0.1.0 - Production on 29-NOV-2013 12:49:57

Copyright (c) 1997, 2013, Oracle. All rights reserved.

Used parameter files:
C:\Oracle\product\12.1.0\dbhome_2\network\admin\sqlnet.ora

Used TNSNAMES adapter to resolve the alias
Attempting to contact (DESCRIPTION = (ADDRESS = (PROTOCOL = TCP)(HOST = localhost)(PORT = 1521)) (CONNECT_DATA = (SERVER = DEDICATED) (SERVICE_NAME = CONT)))

OK (10 msec)

C:\>sqlplus system/system@CONT

SQL*Plus: Release 12.1.0.1.0 Production on Fri Nov 29 12:43:35 2013

Copyright (c) 1982, 2013, Oracle. All rights reserved.

Connected to:
Oracle Database 12c Enterprise Edition Release 12.1.0.1.0 - 64bit Production
With the Partitioning, OLAP, Advanced Analytics and Real Application Testing
options

```
SQL> SHOW USER
USER is "SYSTEM"
SQL> SHOW CON_NAME

CON_NAME
---------
CDB$ROOT
SQL>
```

6. Since you're here, create a new common user, grant connect to the user, and then
   connect to the CDB root as the user via the net service name:

```
SQL> CREATE USER c##cdbuser IDENTIFIED BY common
  2  DEFAULT TABLESPACE users
  3  QUOTA UNLIMITED ON users
  4  CONTAINER = ALL;

User created.

SQL> GRANT CONNECT TO C##cdbuser;

Grant succeeded.

SQL> CONNECT c##cdbuser/common@CONT
Connected.
SQL> SHOW USER
USER is "C##CDBUSER"
SQL> SHOW CON_NAME

CON_NAME
---------
CDB$ROOT
SQL>
```

Connecting to a CDB Using the SQL*Plus *ALTER SESSION* Command

Once you've established a connection to a CDB, switching to the CDB$ROOT container is accomplished by issuing the ALTER SESSION command. In the next section we will connect to PDBs and further demonstrate how to switch between containers.

```
SQL> ALTER SESSION SET CONTAINER = CDB$ROOT;

Session altered.

SQL>
```

Ensure that each service name, listener, and CDB combination are unique on a computer. When you run two or more CDBs on the same computer and you have more than one PDB with the same service name using the same listener, an attempted connection that specifies this service name will connect randomly to one of the PDBs with the non-unique service name. To prevent this condition, either configure separate listeners for the CDB and PDBs that conflict or use unique service names for all PDBs on the computer system.

Establishing Connections to a PDB

This section describes using SQL*Plus to access the PDBs in a CDB. You can connect to a PDB by starting SQL*Plus with a connect string to the PDB, using the SQL*Plus CONNECT command if you're already logged on, or you can switch to a PDB from the CDB$ROOT by using the ALTER SESSION SET CONTAINER SQL statement.

Clients access a PDB through a database service that has the same name as the PDB name. With the service name, you can access the PDB using the easy connect syntax or a net service name configured in the tnsnames.ora file. When you create a new PDB using the DBCA, it does create a new listener service handler, but it does not create a service name in the local tnsnames.ora file, so you must create a new entry in tnsnames.ora if you intend to use tnsnames to resolve connections. Oracle Net Services must be configured for you to connect to the PDB using a net service name.

The SESSIONS initialization parameter limits the total number of sessions that may be established in a CDB and its PDBs. If you reach the SESSIONS limit, you will not be able to log on.

Connecting to a PDB Using SQL*Plus

In Exercise 12.2 you will establish connections to a DBA-created PDB. This exercise assumes that you have created a CDB and PDBs on your local machine and that the CDB has been started.

> **EXERCISE 12.2**

Connecting to a PDB Using SQL*Plus

In this exercise, you will create a new PDB user and connect to an existing PDB on a Windows 7 server, using SQL*Plus at the command line.

1. Set the required environment variables. ORACLE_HOME is required on some operating systems. Launch a command-line window and set the variable:

   ```
   C:\>set ORACLE_HOME= C:\Oracle\product\12.1.0\dbhome_2
   ```

2. Confirm that the net service name exists and is valid for the target PDB.

   By default, when you create a PDB using the DBCA or SQL*Plus, Oracle does not automatically create an entry in the tnsnames.ora file. If you are using TNSNAMES to resolve service names, confirm that a valid entry exists in %ORACLE_HOME% \network\ admin\tnsnames.ora, for example:

   ```
   PDB1 =
     (DESCRIPTION =
       (ADDRESS = (PROTOCOL = TCP)(HOST = localhost)(PORT = 1521))
       (CONNECT_DATA =
         (SERVER = DEDICATED)
         (SERVICE_NAME = PDB1)
       )
     )
   ```

3. If you're connecting to a local system, confirm that the listener is up and that the target service is available. Also verify the connection to the PDB using tnsping:

   ```
   C:\>lsnrctl stat

   LSNRCTL for 64-bit Windows: Version 12.1.0.1.0 - Production on 29-NOV-2013 13:11:14

   Copyright (c) 1991, 2013, Oracle.  All rights reserved.

   Connecting to (DESCRIPTION=(ADDRESS=(PROTOCOL=IPC)(KEY=EXTPROC1521)))
   STATUS of the LISTENER
   ------------------------
   Alias                     LISTENER
   Version                   TNSLSNR for 64-bit Windows: Version 12.1.0.1.0 -
   Produ
   ction
   Start Date                24-NOV-2013 12:29:35
   Uptime                    5 days 0 hr. 41 min. 39 sec
   ```

EXERCISE 12.2 *(continued)*

```
Trace Level              off
Security                 ON: Local OS Authentication
SNMP                     OFF
Listener Parameter File  C:\Oracle\product\12.1.0\dbhome_2\network\admin\
listen
er.ora
Listener Log File        C:\Oracle\diag\tnslsnr\LOCALHOST\listener\alert\
log.xml
Listening Endpoints Summary...
  (DESCRIPTION=(ADDRESS=(PROTOCOL=ipc)(PIPENAME=\\.\pipe\EXTPROC1521ipc)))
  (DESCRIPTION=(ADDRESS=(PROTOCOL=tcp)(HOST=LOCALHOST)(PORT=1521)))
  (DESCRIPTION=(ADDRESS=(PROTOCOL=tcps)(HOST=LOCALHOST)(PORT=5501)))
(Security=(my_wallet_directory=C:\ORACLE\admin\CONT\xdb_wallet))
(Presentation=HTTP)(Session=RAW))
Services Summary...
Service "CLRExtProc" has 1 instance(s).
  Instance "CLRExtProc", status UNKNOWN, has 1 handler(s) for this service...
Service "CONT" has 1 instance(s).
  Instance "cont", status READY, has 1 handler(s) for this service...
Service "CONTXDB" has 1 instance(s).
  Instance "cont", status READY, has 1 handler(s) for this service...
Service "pdb1" has 1 instance(s).
  Instance "cont", status READY, has 1 handler(s) for this service...
Service "pdb2" has 1 instance(s).
  Instance "cont", status READY, has 1 handler(s) for this service...
Service "pdb3" has 1 instance(s).
  Instance "cont", status READY, has 1 handler(s) for this service...
The command completed successfully

C:\>tnsping pdb1

TNS Ping Utility for 64-bit Windows: Version 12.1.0.1.0 - Production on
29-NOV-2013 13:11:20

Copyright (c) 1997, 2013, Oracle.  All rights reserved.

Used parameter files:
C:\Oracle\product\12.1.0\dbhome_2\network\admin\sqlnet.ora

Used TNSNAMES adapter to resolve the alias
Attempting to contact (DESCRIPTION = (ADDRESS = (PROTOCOL = TCP)(HOST =
localhost)(PORT = 1521)) (CONNECT_DATA = (SERVER = DEDICATED) (SERVICE_NAME =
PDB1)))
```

```
OK (0 msec)

C:\>
```

4. At the prompt, specify the service name of the PDB you wish to connect to: the instance identifier (SID) unique to this server and database domain:

```
C:\> set ORACLE_SID=pdb1
```

5. Connect to the PDB specified in the ORACLE_SID with user SYS as SYSDBA using database authentication:

```
C:\>sqlplus sys/system@pdb1 as sysdba

SQL*Plus: Release 12.1.0.1.0 Production on Fri Nov 29 14:28:34 2013

Copyright (c) 1982, 2013, Oracle.  All rights reserved.

Connected to:
Oracle Database 12c Enterprise Edition Release 12.1.0.1.0 - 64bit Production
With the Partitioning, OLAP, Advanced Analytics and Real Application Testing
options

SQL> SHOW USER
USER is "SYS"
SQL>
SQL> SHOW CON_NAME

CON_NAME
---------
PDB1
SQL>
```

6. While you're here, create a new local user, grant connect to the user, and then connect to the PDB as the user via the net service name:

```
SQL> CREATE USER testpdb IDENTIFIED BY password
CONTAINER = current;
User created.
SQL> GRANT CONNECT TO testpdb;

Grant succeeded.

SQL> connect testpdb/password@pdb1
Connected.
SQL>
```

Connecting to a PDB Using the SQL*Plus *ALTER SESSION* Command

In addition to using the CONNECT SQL*Plus command, you can alter the session to switch to a different current database, whether it's the CDB or any other PDB that you have access to in the CDB. To switch from the current CDB to a PDB, use the ALTER SESSION command:

```
SQL> connect testpdb/password@pdb1
Connected.
SQL> ALTER SESSION SET CONTAINER=CDB$ROOT;
ERROR:
ORA-01031: insufficient privileges


SQL> SHOW USER
USER is "TESTPDB"
SQL>
```

As you can see, the locally created user testpdb does not have sufficient privileges to connect to CDB$ROOT. To connect to the CDB$ROOT, you must connect as a common user, such as SYS or SYSTEM, for example. Connect as SYS and then switch from the current CDB to a PDB, using the ALTER SESSION command:

```
SQL> CONNECT SYS/SYSTEM@CONT AS SYSDBA
Connected.
SQL> SHOW CON_NAME

CON_NAME
------------------
CDB$ROOT
SQL>
SQL> ALTER SESSION SET CONTAINER = pdb1;

Session altered.

SQL> SHOW CON_NAME

CON_NAME
------------------
PDB1
```

While you're here, create a new tablespace specifically for the PDB1 database, and make it the default tablespace for user testpdb. By switching from the CDB$ROOT to PDB1, you've made PDB1 the current scope database, so adding a new tablespace here will make it available only to PDB1:

```
SQL> create tablespace pdb1_users
  2  datafile 'pdb1_users_01.dbf'
  3  size 10m autoextend on;

Tablespace created.

SQL> alter user testpdb default tablespace pdb1_users;

User altered.

SQL> GRANT UNLIMITED TABLESPACE TO testpdb;

Grant succeeded.
```

Now switch back to CDB$ROOT:

```
SQL> ALTER SESSION SET CONTAINER=CDB$ROOT;

Session altered.

SQL> SHOW CON_NAME

CON_NAME
------------------
CDB$ROOT
SQL>
```

You can switch between the root and PDBs by using the ALTER SESSION command with a valid PDB name. The PDB does not have to be open to establish a connection.

```
SQL> COL pdb_name FORM a20
SQL> SELECT pdb_name, status FROM dba_pdbs;

PDB_NAME              STATUS
-------------------- -------------
PDB1                 NORMAL
PDB$SEED             NORMAL
PDB2                 NEW
PDB3                 NEW
```

```
SQL> ALTER SESSION SET CONTAINER=pdb$seed;

Session altered.

SQL> ALTER SESSION SET CONTAINER=pdb2;

Session altered.

SQL>
```

Start Up and Shut Down a CDB and Open and Close PDBs

In this section, we will discuss the methods to start up and shut down a CDB and the methods to open and close PDBs within a CDB. In Oracle Database 12c, the DBA starts up a CDB in basically the same way as a non-CDB; however, there is a new set of commands to start up a PDB that exists within a CDB. To shut down a CDB, the DBA uses the same commands that would be used to shut down a non-CDB, but there is a new set of commands to shut down a PDB.

Starting Up the CDB Using SQL*Plus

To start up the CDB using SQL*Plus, start a SQL*Plus session and connect to a CDB as a user with administrator privileges; then issue the STARTUP command. A user with the SYSDBA, SYSOPER, SYSBACKUP, SYSDG, or SYSKM system privileges may start up a CDB. By default, users SYS and SYSTEM may start up a CDB.

Starting Up a CDB Instance

To start up a CDB instance, the current user must have sufficient privileges and must be a common user whose current container is the root. When you open a CDB, its PDBs are by default mounted but not opened, but this can be changed with a trigger. The startup options are the same for non-CDBs and CDBs:

FORCE   Performs a SHUTDOWN ABORT and then STARTUP. Can be used to force the instance to start after there was a problem with either a previous startup attempt or shutdown.

MOUNT   Mounts the database after the instance is started but does not open it for general access, allowing for certain DBA activities such as enabling or disabling archiving.

NOMOUNT   Starts the instance but does not mount the database. This option is used during database creation and to re-create the control files.

OPEN   Starts the instance, mounts the database, and opens it for general access. This is the default.

OPEN RECOVER   Starts the instance and begins complete media recovery.

RESTRICT   Starts the instance but prevents general access and allows access only for users with RESTRICTED SESSION privileges.

Starting Up a CDB Instance: Examples

As mentioned previously, to start up a CDB you'll need to connect to the idle instance and issue the STARTUP command. In this example, you'll use STARTUP RESTRICT and then open the database for general access:

```
C:\>set ORACLE_SID=CONT
C:\>sqlplus / as sysdba

SQL*Plus: Release 12.1.0.1.0 Production on Fri Nov 29 14:28:34 2013

Copyright (c) 1982, 2013, Oracle.  All rights reserved.

Connected to an idle instance.

SQL> STARTUP RESTRICT
ORACLE instance started.

Total System Global Area 2471931904 bytes
Fixed Size                   2405664 bytes
Variable Size              671091424 bytes
Database Buffers          1778384896 bytes
Redo Buffers                20049920 bytes
Database mounted.
Database opened.
SQL>
SQL> select name, open_mode from v$pdbs;

NAME                         OPEN_MODE
---------------------------- ----------
PDB$SEED                     READ ONLY
PDB1                         MOUNTED
PDB2                         MOUNTED
```

```
PDB3                              MOUNTED

SQL>
```

At this point, the CDB is open in read-write mode and RESTRICTED, but the DBA-created PDBs are in the MOUNT state. Attempting to alter a pluggable database to open it at this time is not allowed. Attempting to connect as a common user who does not have RESTRICTED SESSION privileges will result in a failed logon.

```
C:\>sqlplus c##cdbuser/common

SQL*Plus: Release 12.1.0.1.0 Production on Sat Nov 30 16:23:01 2013

Copyright (c) 1982, 2013, Oracle.  All rights reserved.

ERROR:
ORA-01035: ORACLE only available to users with RESTRICTED SESSION privilege

Enter user-name:
```

Issuing the ALTER DATABASE DISABLE RESTRICTED SESSION command will allow general access to the CDB:

```
SQL> ALTER SYSTEM DISABLE RESTRICTED SESSION;

System altered.

SQL> exit
C:\>sqlplus c##cdbuser/common

SQL*Plus: Release 12.1.0.1.0 Production on Sat Nov 30 16:29:13 2013

Copyright (c) 1982, 2013, Oracle.  All rights reserved.

Last Successful login time: Fri Nov 29 2013 15:18:37 -05:00

Connected to:
Oracle Database 12c Enterprise Edition Release 12.1.0.1.0 - 64bit Production
With the Partitioning, OLAP, Advanced Analytics and Real Application Testing
options

SQL>
```

Shutting Down the CDB

The DBA can shut down a database instance with SQL*Plus by connecting as a user with SYSOPER, SYSDBA, SYSBACKUP, or SYSDG privileges and then issuing the SHUTDOWN command. When the shutdown is complete, control is returned to the session that issued the database SHUTDOWN command. If a user attempts to connect while a shutdown is in progress, an error message similar to this will be returned:

```
SQL> connect c##cdbuser/common
ERROR:
ORA-01089: immediate shutdown or close in progress - no operations are permitted
Process ID: 0
Session ID: 0 Serial number: 0

SQL>
```

The valid modes to shut down a database are normal, transactional, immediate, and abort. SHUTDOWN NORMAL waits for all users to disconnect. SHUTDOWN TRANSACTIONAL waits for users to complete either by committing or rolling back pending transactions before shutting down. SHUTDOWN IMMEDIATE rolls back any pending transactions prior to shutting down. SHUTDOWN ABORT stops all processes immediately.

SHUTDOWN NORMAL CDB Instance

SHUTDOWN NORMAL is the default, so the NORMAL clause is optional. Issuing SHUTDOWN NORMAL disallows new connections and waits for all current connections to disconnect from the database. Just be aware that the database will not shut down until all users disconnect. If you're in a hurry or need to run a scheduled task with the database down, then SHUTDOWN NORMAL is probably not the right command option at this time:

```
SQL> shutdown
Database closed.
Database dismounted.
ORACLE instance shut down.
SQL>
```

The next time you start up the database, it will not require instance recovery.

SHUTDOWN IMMEDIATE CDB Instance

For a DBA, SHUTDOWN IMMEDIATE is a very useful command that safely brings the database down as quickly as possible. Use the IMMEDIATE option in the following situations:

* When you need to start a cold backup
* When server maintenance, a restart, or power down is required and the databases need to be brought offline
* When you need to restart the database because the database is functioning abnormally

```
SQL> shutdown immediate;
Database closed.
Database dismounted.
ORACLE instance shut down.
SQL>
```

Immediate database shutdown disallows new connections. Active transactions are rolled back, and all connected users are disconnected.

The next time you start up the database it will not require instance recovery.

SHUTDOWN TRANSACTIONAL CDB Instance

SHUTDOWN TRANSACTIONAL is a compromise between SHUTDOWN NORMAL and IMMEDIATE. Use SHUTDOWN TRANSACTIONAL when you want to allow active transactions to complete prior to taking the database down. When you issue the command, new connections and new transactions are disallowed. As transactions complete, the associated client sessions are disconnected:

- After a transaction completes, if the client is still connected to the instance, it will be disconnected.

- After all transactions complete and sessions are disconnected, the database shutdown will proceed.

 If there are pending transactions in the CDB$ROOT container, the SHUTDOWN TRANSACTIONAL command will wait until the transactions are committed or rolled back, and then the shutdown will continue. Issuing the SHUTDOWN TRANSACTIONAL command from the CDB$ROOT will roll back any pending transactions in PDBs and discard any changes that are not committed.

A transactional shutdown prevents clients from losing work as they would during a SHUTDOWN IMMEDIATE but does not wait for users to disconnect as during a SHUTDOWN NORMAL.

The next time you start up the database it will not require instance recovery.

SHUTDOWN ABORT CDB Instance

SHUTDOWN ABORT brings the instance down immediately. The database is not closed and it is not dismounted. This action is a controlled method to take the database offline, just one step shy of killing the server processes, losing power, or otherwise crashing the server. Perform a SHUTDOWN ABORT only in the following situations:

- SHUTDOWN IMMEDIATE did not work.

- Instantaneous shutdown is required, for example, when you disconnect users immediately and recover the database.

- There were problems when you tried to start up a database.

SHUTDOWN ABORT disallows new connections, disallows new transactions, and terminates current SQL statements. Current user connections are disconnected.

```
SQL> SHUTDOWN ABORT
ORACLE instance shut down.
SQL>
```

Notice that there is no indication that the database was closed or dismounted. The next time you start up the database, it will require automatic instance recovery. Uncommitted transactions will be rolled back when the instance restarts.

```
SQL> STARTUP
ORACLE instance started.

Total System Global Area 2471931904 bytes
Fixed Size                   2405664 bytes
Variable Size              671091424 bytes
Database Buffers          1778384896 bytes
Redo Buffers                20049920 bytes
Database mounted.
Database opened.
SQL>
```

Here's an example of what that looks like in the alert log:

```
ALTER DATABASE OPEN
Sat Nov 30 17:43:33 2013
Beginning crash recovery of 1 threads
 parallel recovery started with 3 processes
Sat Nov 30 17:43:33 2013
Started redo scan
Sat Nov 30 17:43:33 2013
Completed redo scan
 read 321 KB redo, 114 data blocks need recovery
Sat Nov 30 17:43:34 2013
Started redo application at
 Thread 1: logseq 22, block 5188
Sat Nov 30 17:43:34 2013
Recovery of Online Redo Log: Thread 1 Group 1 Seq 22 Reading mem 0
  Mem# 0: C:\ORACLE\ORADATA\CONT\ONLINELOG\O1_MF_1_980KX74L_.LOG
  Mem# 1: C:\ORACLE\FAST_RECOVERY_AREA\CONT\ONLINELOG\O1_MF_1_980KX9PB_.LOG
Sat Nov 30 17:43:34 2013
Completed redo application of 0.24MB
```

```
Sat Nov 30 17:43:34 2013
Completed crash recovery at
 Thread 1: logseq 22, block 5830, scn 2457361
 114 data blocks read, 114 data blocks written, 321 redo k-bytes read
```

Opening a PDB

When you start up and open a CDB, the DBA-created PDBs are mounted but not opened. The PDB$SEED database is open in read-only mode, however. To start a PDB instance, the CDB must be open for general access.

There are basically three ways to open a PDB in SQL*Plus. The first option is to connect to the PDB instance and start it as you would a CDB. The second method is to alter the PDB as a common user with DBA privileges and open the PDB. And the third method is to use an after-startup trigger on the CDB.

Starting Up a PDB Instance

To start up the PDB using SQL*Plus, start a SQL*Plus session and connect to the CDB as a user with administrator privileges; then alter the session to make the target PDB the current container and issue the STARTUP command. A user with the SYSDBA, SYSOPER, SYSBACKUP, SYSDG, or SYSKM system privileges may start up a PDB. By default, users SYS and SYSTEM may start up a PDB. You can also connect directly to the target PDB as a common user with these privileges and issue the STARTUP command. STARTUP opens the PDB by default in read-write mode.

Use STARTUP FORCE to close an open PDB before reopening it in read-write mode; it is not a requirement that the PDB be in an open status when issuing this command. STARTUP FORCE is mutually exclusive from other STARTUP options. Use STARTUP RESTRICT to enable only users with the RESTRICTED SESSION system privilege in the PDB to access the PDB. Use STARTUP UPGRADE only when upgrading a PDB or applying specific initialization parameter changes. Here are a few examples:

```
C:\>set ORACLE_SID=PDB1

C:\>sqlplus sys/system@PDB1 as sysdba

SQL*Plus: Release 12.1.0.1.0 Production on Sat Nov 30 18:21:28 2013

Copyright (c) 1982, 2013, Oracle.  All rights reserved.


Connected to:
Oracle Database 12c Enterprise Edition Release 12.1.0.1.0 - 64bit Production
```

```
With the Partitioning, OLAP, Advanced Analytics and Real Application Testing
options

SQL>
SQL> startup restrict
Pluggable Database opened.
SQL>
SQL> startup force
Pluggable Database opened.
SQL>

SQL> connect sys/system@CONT as sysdba
Connected.
SQL> show con_name

CON_NAME
------------------------------
CDB$ROOT
SQL> ALTER SESSION SET CONTAINER=pdb1;

Session altered.

SQL> SHOW CON_NAME

CON_NAME
------------------------------
PDB1
SQL> SELECT NAME, OPEN_MODE FROM v$pdbs;

NAME                           OPEN_MODE
------------------------------ ----------
PDB1                           MOUNTED

SQL> STARTUP
Pluggable Database opened.
SQL> SELECT NAME, OPEN_MODE FROM v$pdbs;

NAME                           OPEN_MODE
------------------------------ ----------
PDB1                           READ WRITE
```

Opening a PDB

The next option is to use the ALTER PLUGGABLE DATABASE statement to open one or more PDBs. You can open one or more PDBs as a common user with privileges previously described:

```
SQL> ALTER SESSION SET CONTAINER=CDB$ROOT;

Session altered.
SQL> SHOW USER
USER is "SYS"
SQL>
SQL> ALTER PLUGGABLE DATABASE pdb1 OPEN;
Pluggable database altered.
SQL> ALTER PLUGGABLE DATABASE pdb2 OPEN READ ONLY;
Pluggable database altered.


SQL> select name, open_mode from v$pdbs;

NAME                           OPEN_MODE
------------------------------ ----------
PDB$SEED                       READ ONLY
PDB1                           READ WRITE
PDB2                           READ ONLY
PDB3                           MOUNTED
SQL>
```

The default open mode is read-write. Specify READ ONLY after you have opened the PDB at least once prior in read-write mode. Read-write is the default when RESTRICT is not specified. To issue the ALTER PLUGGABLE DATABASE command when the current container is a PDB, the current user must have SYSDBA, SYSOPER, SYSBACKUP, or SYSDG administrative privilege, which must be either commonly granted or locally granted in the PDB. The user must connect using AS SYSDBA, AS SYSOPER, AS SYSBACKUP, or AS SYSDG. The PDB must be mounted before opening unless the OPEN FORCE option is used.

Shutting Down or Closing a PDB

As with starting up a PDB, you can use the SHUTDOWN command in SQL*Plus or alter the PDB and CLOSE it. The same privileges and scope apply as with starting up a PDB.

Shutting Down a PDB

You can shut down a PDB using the SHUTDOWN command, similar to the way you would shut down a CDB; however, the scope would be local, shutting down only the local PDB. If you attempt to close a PDB with the SHUTDOWN command, no new connections will be allowed to the PDB. NORMAL, IMMEDIATE, TRANSACTIONAL, and ABORT rules apply as in the CDB:

```
SQL> SHOW CON_NAME

CON_NAME
------------------------------
PDB1
SQL> select name, open_mode from v$pdbs;

NAME                            OPEN_MODE
------------------------------- ----------
PDB1                            READ WRITE

SQL> SHUTDOWN IMMEDIATE
Pluggable Database closed.
SQL> select name, open_mode from v$pdbs;

NAME                            OPEN_MODE
------------------------------- ----------
PDB1                            MOUNTED

SQL>
```

If there are pending transactions or any sessions connected to the current PDB container, the SHUTDOWN TRANSACTIONAL command will wait until the transactions are committed or rolled back and wait for the sessions to disconnect, and then SHUTDOWN will continue.

Closing a PDB

If you attempt to close the local PDB with the ALTER PLUGGABLE DATABASE CLOSE command while users are connected to the PDB, the command will disallow new connections and wait for existing sessions to disconnect. This is similar in function to the SHUTDOWN NORMAL command. ALTER PLUGGABLE DATABASE CLOSE IMMEDIATE behaves much like SHUTDOWN IMMEDIATE, will end any sessions in the local PDB, and will shut down the PDB:

```
SQL> SHOW CON_NAME

CON_NAME
------------------------------
PDB1
```

```
SQL> select name, open_mode from v$pdbs;

NAME                            OPEN_MODE
------------------------------ ----------
PDB1                            READ WRITE

SQL> ALTER PLUGGABLE DATABASE pdb1 CLOSE IMMEDIATE;
Pluggable database altered.
SQL> select name, open_mode from v$pdbs;

NAME                            OPEN_MODE
------------------------------ ----------
PDB1                            MOUNTED

SQL>
```

Evaluate the Impact of Parameter Value Changes

In this section, we will discuss initialization parameters that influence the behavior of the multitenant environment. Where appropriate, we present the range of valid values, the default values, and any potential impact on the CDB and PDBs. Where relevant, we also discuss the impact on non-CDBs.

Initialization parameters that have an impact on the behavior of CDBs and PDBs are listed in alphabetic order in the following sections.

AUDIT_FILE_DEST

When the AUDIT_TRAIL initialization parameter is set to os, xml, or "xml, extended", the AUDIT_FILE_DEST parameter indicates the operating system directory where the audit trail is written. The audit records will be written in XML format if AUDIT_TRAIL is set to xml or "xml, extended". If the AUDIT_SYS_OPERATIONS initialization parameter is set to TRUE, audit records for users connected as SYSDBA or SYSOPER are written to AUDIT_FILE_DEST.

In a CDB, the scope of the settings for AUDIT_FILE_DEST is the CDB. The audit trail is provided per PDB in a CDB, but AUDIT_FILE_DEST is not configurable for individual PDBs.

AUDIT_SYS_OPERATIONS

Boolean, default value FALSE, when set to TRUE enables the auditing of SQL statements directly issued by users connected as SYSDBA or SYSOPER. SQL statements run within PL/SQL functions or procedures are not written to the audit trail.

In a CDB, the scope of the settings for AUDIT_SYS_OPERATIONS is the CDB. The audit trail is provided per PDB in a CDB but AUDIT_SYS_OPERATIONS is not configurable for individual PDBs.

AUDIT_SYSLOG_LEVEL

The AUDIT_SYSLOG_LEVEL parameter, which is a string value with no default, writes SYS and standard OS audit records to the system audit log using the SYSLOG OS utility. There are multiple possible values for this parameter, and you can enter multiple occurrences of this parameter in the init.ora file.

If AUDIT_SYSLOG_LEVEL is set and AUDIT_SYS_OPERATIONS = TRUE, then it overrides the AUDIT_TRAIL parameter and SYS audit records are written to the system audit log. If AUDIT_SYSLOG_LEVEL is set and AUDIT_TRAIL = os, then standard audit records are written to the system audit log.

In a CDB, the scope of the settings for AUDIT_SYSLOG_LEVEL is the CDB. The audit trail is provided per PDB in a CDB, but AUDIT_SYSLOG_LEVEL is not configurable for individual PDBs.

AUDIT_TRAIL

The AUDIT_TRAIL parameter enables or disables database auditing. Values can be NONE, OS, DB, "DB, EXTENDED", XML, or "XML, EXTENDED".

NONE   This is the default if you created the database using a method other than the DBCA, for example, manually.

OS   This is the Oracle-recommended value it and writes audit records to an operating system file.

DB   This is the default if you created the database using Database Configuration Assistant, and it writes audit records to the SYS.AUD$ table, except for those records that are always written to the OS audit trail.

"DB, EXTENDED"   This is the same as AUDIT_TRAIL=DB plus the SQL bind and SQL text CLOB-type columns of the SYS.AUD$ table when available. If the AUDIT_TRAIL parameter was set to DB, EXTENDED and the database was started in read-only mode, the AUDIT_TRAIL is internally set to OS.

XML   This writes in XML format to the OS audit file and writes all elements of the AuditRecord node except Sql_Text and Sql_Bind.

"XML, EXTENDED"   This includes AUDIT_TRAIL=XML plus SQL text and SQL bind information.

SQL AUDIT   This overrides the AUDIT_TRAIL setting.

In a CDB, the scope of the settings for AUDIT_TRAIL is the CDB. The audit trail is provided per PDB in a CDB, but AUDIT_TRAIL is not configurable for individual PDBs.

ENABLE_PLUGGABLE_DATABASE

ENABLE_PLUGGABLE_DATABASE must be set in init.ora before creating a CDB. ENABLE_PLUGGABLE_DATABASE is a Boolean bootstrap initialization parameter that, when set to TRUE, indicates that the DB is to be created as a CDB. When set to the default FALSE, the database is created as a non-CDB.

LDAP_DIRECTORY_ACCESS

The LDAP_DIRECTORY_ACCESS initialization parameter is a string value and has no default; valid options are SSL, PASSWORD, or NONE. All the PDBs in a CDB use the Oracle Internet Directory (OID) authentication specified by the parameter. You use the DBCA to register Oracle databases (including PDBs) with OID.

MAX_STRING_SIZE

The MAX_STRING_SIZE initialization parameter defaults to STANDARD, and a valid alternative is EXTENDED. When set to STANDARD, the length limits of 4000 bytes for VARCHAR2 and NVARCHAR2 and 2000 bytes for RAW apply. When set to EXTENDED and the COMPATIBLE initialization parameter is set to 12.0.0.0 or higher, the 32,767-byte limit introduced in Oracle Database 12c applies.

You can change the value of MAX_STRING_SIZE from STANDARD to EXTENDED, but you can't change it from EXTENDED to STANDARD. To take advantage of the increased column sizes in a PDB, do the following:

1. Shut down the PDB, and then restart it with the STARTUP UPGRADE command.

2. Change MAX_STRING_SIZE in the PDB to EXTENDED by issuing the ALTER SYSTEM SET MAX_STRING_SIZE=EXTENDED command.

3. Connect AS SYSDBA and run the $ORACLE_HOME\rdbms\admin\utl32k.sql script in the PDB.

4. Restart the PDB.

NONCDB_COMPATIBLE

The NONCDB_COMPATIBLE Boolean parameter, default value FALSE, indicates that SQL executed in a PDB will default to normal CDB behavior. If you have a specific case where SQL commands executed in a PDB need to function as they do in a non-CDB, then set this value to TRUE. Specifically, if you have code that causes ORA-65040 in the PDB, then setting NONCDB_COMPATIBLE to TRUE may be required.

There are some `ALTER DATABASE` and `ALTER SYSTEM` statements that fail in a PDB if `NONCDB_COMPATIBLE=FALSE`, but they will succeed if `NONCDB_COMPATIBLE` is set to `TRUE`.

PDB_FILE_NAME_CONVERT

When you're creating a pluggable database as a copy or clone of another PDB or non-CDB, the `PDB_FILE_NAME_CONVERT` parameter is used to map directory names of source files to the directory name of new target files when using the `CREATE PLUGGABLE DATABASE` command. Also this parameter is used when the `CREATE DATABASE ENABLE PLUGGABLE DATABASE` command is issued, when Oracle Managed Files is not enabled, and if the `FILE_NAME_CONVERT_CLAUSE` is not used. Do not use filenames or directories that use Oracle Managed Files. The parameter values need to be a string that includes valid directory names. There is no default value.

Here's an example

```
PDB_FILE_NAME_CONVERT = 'C:\oradata\dbs\s1\','C:\oradata\dbs\t1\', 'C:\oradata\
dbs\s2\','C:\oradata\dbs\t2\'
```

where source and target alternate.

RESOURCE_MANAGER_PLAN

In a non-CDB, `RESOURCE_MANAGER_PLAN` specifies the top-level resource plan to use for the instance.

In the CDB$ROOT of a CDB, `RESOURCE_MANAGER_PLAN` specifies the resource plan for the CDB, which allocates resources among PDBs. You create a CDB resource plan with the `DBMS_RESOURCE_MANAGER.CREATE_CDB_PLAN` and `CREATE_CDB_PLAN_DIRECTIVE` procedures.

A common user must be logged into CDB$ROOT and use the `ALTER SYSTEM` command to change the `RESOURCE_MANAGER_PLAN` for a CDB, for example:

```
SQL> ALTER SYSTEM SET RESOURCE_MANAGER_PLAN = mycdb_resource_plan;
SQL> ALTER SYSTEM SET RESOURCE_MANAGER_PLAN = '';
```

In a PDB, `RESOURCE_MANAGER_PLAN` indicates the PDB resource plan to use for this PDB. A session must have its current container set to the PDB to enable or disable a PDB resource plan for this PDB. The following limitations apply to PDB resource plans:

- They cannot have subplans.
- They can have a maximum of eight consumer groups.
- They can't have a multiple-level scheduling policy.

The CDB resource plan should contain policies regarding resource allocation among PDBs.

SESSIONS

The `SESSIONS` initialization parameter specifies the maximum number of sessions that can be created in the CDB. This parameter determines the maximum number of concurrent users in the CDB. Set this parameter to the number of background processes, plus your estimate of the maximum number of concurrent users, plus 10 percent for recursive sessions.

The default values of the TRANSACTIONS parameters are derived from SESSIONS. If you increase the value of SESSIONS, you should also increase the value for TRANSACTIONS.

In a CDB, the root container's SESSIONS parameter specifies the total number of sessions for the multitenant CDB and associated PDBs. The SESSIONS parameter for a PDB indicates the maximum number of sessions that can utilize that PDB, and by default, it is the same value as for the CDB root. If the maximum number of sessions is reached for a PDB, the next attempt to connect will throw an ORA-00018 error.

The SESSIONS parameter for a PDB can't exceed the CDB SESSIONS value and can be modified only by the PDB.

Summary

In this chapter, you learned more about the Oracle Database 12*c* multitenant architecture, how to manage a CDB and PDBs, how to establish connections to a CDB and PDBs, how to shut down and start up a CDB, how to open and close PDBs, and how certain initialization parameters influence the CDB and PDBs.

To establish a connection to a CDB, you first learned about common users and local users and then how to connect to the CDB and to PDBs using SQL*Plus. We showed you how to set up a service for a PDB and connect using tnsnames.ora. We explained how to change the current container from the CDB$ROOT to a PDB. You also created a common user and a local user.

After teaching you how to connect to the CDB and to PDBs, we showed you how to start up and shut down container databases. You learned that the STARTUP and SHUTDOWN commands for the CDB are basically the same as for a non-CDB. You saw that you can open and close PDBs in addition to using the STARTUP and SHUTDOWN commands on PDBs.

Finally, you learned that several initialization parameters influence the CDB and PDBs. Parameters related to the audit trail, maximum sessions, maximum column sizes, resource plans, enabling pluggable databases, filename conversion for PDB provisioning, and non-CDB compatibility settings were discussed.

Exam Essentials

Know how to establish connections to the different database container types in the Oracle Database 12*c* multitenant architecture. Make sure you understand how to connect to a CDB and a PDB. Know the different methods for each.

Know how to create a connection to a PDB. Know that you must create a valid service and a method to resolve the service name, for example, by using tnsnames.ora.

Know how to alter your session to change the current container. Know how to determine what container your session is currently in.

Demonstrate how to start up a CDB. Understand how to start up a CDB using SQL*Plus. Know the different startup options.

Demonstrate how to shut down a CDB. Know how to shut down a CDB. Know the different shutdown options.

Demonstrate how to open a PDB. Know how to open a PDB. Know how to connect to a PDB and start up a PDB using the different options.

Demonstrate how to close a PDB. Know how to close a PDB. Know how to connect to a PDB and shut down a PDB using the different options.

Know which initialization parameters influence the CDB and PDBs. Know which parameters influence the behavior of the CDB and PDBs.

Review Questions

1. In the Oracle 12*c* multitenant architecture, a common user has access to which PDBs and CDBs?

    A. All PDBs and all CDBs

    B. The current PDB and CDB

    C. All PDBs and the CDB$ROOT container

    D. CDB$ROOT and PDB$SEED

    E. All of the above

2. Which of the following statements is true regarding a local user?

    A. A local user is created at the CDB$ROOT.

    B. A local user has access to the CDB$ROOT and the local PDB.

    C. A local user has access to all PDBs but not the CDB$ROOT.

    D. A local user has access to only the local PDB.

3. Which of these formats represents the correct command to create a common user in SQL*Plus?

    A. CREATE COMMON USER C##cdbuser

        IDENTIFIED BY cdbuser

        CONTAINER = ALL;

    B. CREATE USER c##cdbuser

        IDENTIFIED BY cdbuser

        CONTAINER = CDB$ROOT;

    C. CREATE USER c##cdbuser

        IDENTIFIED BY cdbuser

        CONTAINER = ALL;

    D. None of the above

4. To create a local user in the PDB1 container, which of the following must be true?

    A. The user creating the local user must also be a local user.

    B. The user creating the local user must be a common user and have CREATE USER privileges.

    C. The local username must be unique across all PDBs within the CDB.

    D. The local user must be created by a DBA with access to all PDBs.

    E. None of the above

5. Which SQL*Plus command shows the current container?

    A. SHOW CUR_NAME

    B. SHOW CUR_CONT

    C. SHOW CUR_CDB

    D. SHOW CUR_PDB

    E. SHOW CON_NAME

6. Which Oracle-supplied program will list the current service names that are reachable on the current server?

    A. tnsping

    B. lsnrctl

    C. sqlplus

    D. dbv

    E. None of the above

7. To start up the CDB under normal circumstances, what command should you enter?

    A. From CDB$ROOT, STARTUP FORCE

    B. From CDB$ROOT, STARTUP MOUNT

    C. From any container, STARTUP

    D. From any container, STARTUP OPEN

    E. None of the above

8. Which of the following are valid shutdown scenarios in the CDB? (Choose all that apply.)

    A. SHUTDOWN NORMAL when no other shutdown option will work

    B. SHUTDOWN FORCE when SHUTDOWN IMMEDIATE doesn't succeed

    C. SHUTDOWN TRANSACTIONAL to end all pending transactions and then SHUTDOWN NORMAL

    D. SHUTDOWN IMMEDIATE when SHUTDOWN ABORT doesn't work

    E. None of the above

9. Which of the following is true regarding opening a PDB?

    A. By default, all PDBs are opened when the CDB is opened.

    B. All PDBs are MOUNTED when the CDB is opened.

    C. All PDBs are UNMOUNTED when the CDB is opened.

    D. The status of all PDBs is NEW when the CDB is opened.

    E. None of the above

10. To open a PDB, what conditions must be met?

   A. The ORACLE_SID must be set to the value of the PDB service name.

   B. The PDB must be the current container.

   C. The CDB$ROOT must be the current container.

   D. The user issuing the ALTER PLUGGABLE DATABASE <pdb> OPEN command must be a common user.

   E. None of the above

11. Which of these will open the PDB?

   A. ALTER PLUGGABLE DATABASE pdb1 OPEN FORCE RESTRICTED;

   B. ALTER PLUGGABLE DATABASE pdb1 OPEN;

   C. ALTER CONTAINER DATABASE pdb1 OPEN;

   D. OPEN PLUGGABLE DATABASE pdb1;

   E. None of the above

12. To close a PDB, which of the following conditions must be met?

   A. The PDB must not be currently closed.

   B. The current container must be the PDB.

   C. The current container must not be the PDB.

   D. The current user must be a local user.

13. To close a PDB under normal conditions, which of the following commands should the DBA submit? (Choose all that apply.)

   A. ALTER PLUGGABLE DATABASE <pdb> CLOSE;

   B. SHUTDOWN ABORT

   C. SHUTDOWN

   D. CLOSE PLUGGABLE DATABASE <pdb>;

14. STARTUP FORCE accomplishes which tasks?

   A. It performs a SHUTDOWN ABORT and STARTUP OPEN.

   B. It performs a SHUTDOWN NORMAL and STARTUP OPEN.

   C. It performs a SHUTDOWN IMMEDIATE and STARTUP OPEN.

   D. None of the above

15. During a SHUTDOWN TRANSACTIONAL, what occurs?

    A. Transactions are rolled back and no new sessions are allowed.

    B. Transactions are allowed to complete, new transactions in the same session may start and complete, and no new sessions are allowed.

    C. Transactions are rolled back and all sessions aborted.

    D. Pending transactions are allowed to complete but no new transactions or sessions are allowed.

16. The current container is best described as? (Choose all that apply.)

    A. The CDB$ROOT

    B. Where the current session is running

    C. Either a PDB or the CDB$ROOT

    D. For a common user with multiple sessions, can be multiple containers at the same time

    E. None of the above

17. Which of the following initialization parameters are necessary when creating a CDB? (Choose all that apply.)

    A. PDB_FILE_NAME_CONVERT

    B. ENABLE_CONTAINER_DATABASE

    C. ENABLE_PLUGGABLE_DATABASE

    D. NONCDB_COMPATIBLE

    E. None of the above

18. When creating a PDB from a clone, which initialization parameter maps directory names of source files to target files? (Choose all that apply.)

    A. FILE_NAME_CONVERT

    B. PDB_CONVERT_FILE_NAME

    C. PDB_FILE_NAME_CONVERT

    D. PDB_CLONE_FILE_NAME

    E. None of the above

19. To directly control the number of user connections allowed to a PDB, you use which of the following initialization parameters?

    A. MAX_SESSIONS

    B. CONNECTIONS

    C. MAX_CONNECTIONS

    D. PROCESSES

    E. SESSIONS

20. To increase the MAX_STRING_SIZE for a PDB, what are the appropriate steps? (Choose all that apply.)

   A. Shut down the PDB and restart with the STARTUP UPGRADE command.

   B. Change the MAX_STRING_SIZE parameter to EXTENDED.

   C. Logged on to the PDB as SYSBA, run the $ORACLE_HOME\rdbms\admin\utl32k .sql script.

   D. Restart the PDB.

   E. None of the above

Chapter

13

Oracle Utilities

ORACLE DATABASE 12*c***: ADVANCED ADMINISTRATION EXAM OBJECTIVES COVERED IN THIS CHAPTER:**

✓ **Moving Data, Performing Security Operations and Interacting with Other Oracle Products**

- ※ Use Data Pump

- ※ Use SQL*Loader

- ※ Audit Operations

- ※ Use Other Products with CDB and PDBs—Database Vault, Data Guard, LogMiner

In this chapter we will explore the use of Oracle-supplied database utilities in the Oracle Database 12*c* Multitenant Architecture. We will discuss moving data, performing security operations, and interacting with other Oracle products in the multitenant environment.

The first topic is a more detailed exploration of Data Pump, which was introduced in Chapter 10, "Managing Database Resources." We will use Data Pump to move content in a non-CDB and a PDB. We will demonstrate Data Pump in an exercise.

The second topic introduces SQL*Loader and how it can be used in the multitenant environment.

The third topic further explores the use of audit operations, which were discussed in an earlier chapter.

Finally, we will discuss other products that are used in the multitenant environment: Database Vault, Data Guard, and LogMiner.

Exam objectives are subject to change at any time without prior notice and at Oracle's sole discretion. Please visit Oracle's Training and Certification website (http://www.oracle.com/education/certification/) for the most current exam-objectives listing.

Moving Data, Performing Security Operations, and Interacting with Other Oracle Products

In the new Oracle Database 12*c* multitenant architecture, where the multitenant container database (CDB) can host zero, one, or many DBA-created pluggable databases (PDBs), there are a few key differences between CDBs and non-CDBs when it comes to moving data, auditing, and using Oracle-supplied utility programs and features. In the following sections we'll explore some of the common tools and how they function in the multitenant environment.

As a DBA you will undoubtedly field requests to migrate data from one database to another. You may be asked to clone an entire database, copy only certain schemas, or copy only certain objects from a source database to a target database. Oftentimes the move is not one-for-one, and also it is common for the source and target databases to be of different Oracle versions. Data Pump is one of the tools that the DBA can use to migrate content from point A to point B.

Another useful tool is SQL*Loader, which is a great tool for loading data from external files into tables in an Oracle database. SQL*Loader is source-agnostic, so as long as the data files are in the correct format, the source database system is not of concern. In fact, one of the more important use cases for SQL*Loader is to take data from non-Oracle database sources and load it into Oracle database tables.

Departing from the methods to load data into an Oracle database, we'll turn our attention to auditing activities in the Oracle database. In Chapter 12, we introduced the initialization parameters that have an impact on how audit records are written, and in this chapter we'll demonstrate audit activities.

Next, we'll introduce Database Vault, which is a more secure way to prevent privileged users from gaining access to application data. Then we'll discuss Data Guard, which is Oracle's set of services to implement and manage standby databases. As the final subject, we'll introduce LogMiner, a tool used to analyze the history of database activities by querying the archived and online redo log files.

Using Data Pump

Oracle Data Pump is a set of tools that enable movement of data and metadata from one Oracle database to another. In this section we will introduce the Data Pump components and describe how to use Data Pump in the multitenant environment.

Data Pump Components

Oracle Data Pump is not one program; it is instead made up of a few distinct parts:

- expdp and impdp, the export and import command-line programs
- The Data Pump API PL/SQL package, DBMS_DATAPUMP
- The Metadata API PL/SQL package, DBMS_METADATA

From your operating system command line, execute expdp to start the Data Pump export utility. Execute impdp to start the Data Pump import utility.

The DBMS_DATAPUMP PL/SQL package contains procedures that are executed by the expdp and impdp command-line programs. When you execute expdp and impdp, you pass parameters at the command line, and these parameters are used by the PL/SQL package to enable the exporting and importing of data and metadata for subsets of a database or for a complete database.

Data Pump also uses the DBMS_METADATA PL/SQL package, which provides the tools to extract, manipulate, and recreate dictionary metadata.

DBMS_DATAPUMP and DBMS_METADATA PL/SQL packages are used by Data Pump expdp and impdp, but they can also be utilized by other calling programs.

Using Data Pump with CDBs

You can use Data Pump to migrate tables, schemas, or an entire database. Data Pump can move this content from a non-CDB into a PDB and from a PDB to a non-CDB. Data Pump can also move content between PDBs within the same CDB or between PDBs in different CDBs. Content migration using Data Pump with PDBs is virtually the same as using Data Pump with a non-CDB.

> In Chapter 11, "Introduction to and Creation of Oracle Multitenant Databases," we demonstrate how to create CDBs and PDBs. The exercises in this chapter assume that you have created a CDB and PDBs.

Using Data Pump to Move PDBs within or between CDBs

With the introduction of common users and local users in the multitenant environment, there are some specific differences between how Data Pump export and import operate with PDBs vs. non-CDBs.

If you're using Data Pump to move a PDB within the same CDB, this should not be a problem. However, if you're moving a PDB to another CDB or a non-CDB, either using a privileged schema or full database export, you must consider the impact of the common user or users that you're exporting.

If the target CDB does not have a common user with the same name as the common user or users in the export, then you can create the required common users in the target CDB. Or you could use the REMAP_SCHEMA parameter when you run impdp.

```
REMAP_SCHEMA=C##common name:local user name
```

If the target CDB does not contain the common user or you do not specify the remap on import, impdp will fail because of the common user mismatch on the username, and you'll see the following error message:

```
ORA-65094:invalid local user or role name
```

Using Data Pump to Move a Database into a CDB

One use case for Data Pump is to move a full database into an empty PDB in a CDB. The source database could be a PDB or a non-CDB.

Use Oracle Data Pump expdb to perform a full export of a source database, using the transportable option if you choose. Once you've created a new PDB in a CDB, you can use Data Pump impdp to move the full contents into the PDB.

"Full transportable export/import" is the term used if the transportable option on a full-mode export or import is used.

If you choose the transportable option, Data Pump will also include transportable tablespace data movement. Transportable tablespace data movement, discussed in a previous chapter, can significantly improve the time of the import phase because Data Pump doesn't have to load data and build indexes.

Naming the Import PDB

To tell Data Pump which PDB to use as a source or target, indicate the service name or connect string of the PDB on the command line when using expdp or impdp. Establishing a service name for a PDB was discussed in Chapter 12.

In this example, we'll invoke Data Pump to import data to a PDB named LNE6:

```
impdp hr@LNE6 DIRECTORY=dpump_dir DUMPFILE=ncdb_expdat.dmp SCHEMAS=hr
```

The following are required when using Data Pump to move data into a CDB:

- You must have the CDB_DBA role to administer a multitenant environment.

- You must define a directory object within the PDB that you are exporting or importing because DATA_PUMP_DIR doesn't work with PDBs. Use the CREATE DIRECTORY command in SQL*Plus to complete this task.

- A non-CDB from a full database export of an Oracle Database version 11.2.0.2 and earlier may be imported into a CDB or non-CDB in Oracle Database 12c.

- Oracle recommends that the source database be version 11.2.0.3 or later, because the export file will contain more complete information about registered database options and components. Set the Data Pump Export parameter VERSION=12 when creating a full database export or a full transportable database export to generate a dump file that is ready to import into Oracle Database 12c.

- File-based and network-based full transportable import requires the TRANSPORT_DATAFILES=datafile_name parameter.

- Additionally, network-based full transportable import requires the FULL=YES and TRANSPORTABLE=ALWAYS parameters.

Using Data Pump to Migrate a Non-CDB to a CDB

In Chapter 12 we demonstrated how to use Data Pump to migrate a non-CDB Oracle 11g database to an Oracle Database 12c PDB. Similarly, we can use Data Pump to migrate an Oracle Database 12c non-CDB into a PDB.

In Exercise 13.1, you will create a complete copy of the non-CDB as a full export using Oracle Data Pump, which exports all objects and data. You will not use the Full Transportable option. You will create an empty PDB in a CDB and then use Oracle Data Pump to import the dataset into the PDB.

Data Pump Error

Data Pump does not support any CDB-wide operations in Oracle Database 12*c* Release 1 (12.1). If you are connected to CDB$ROOT or PDB$SEED and attempt to utilize Data Pump, you'll get an error message, as shown here:

```
ORA-39357: WARNING: Oracle Data Pump operations are not typically needed when
connected to the root or seed of a container database.
```

EXERCISE 13.1

Using Data Pump to Migrate a Non-CDB into a PDB

In this exercise, you will use Data Pump to export a non-CDB database that is in an Oracle 12*c* database and use Data Pump import to move the content into a PDB that is in a CDB.

1. Create a new CDB target, or utilize an existing CDB. In this example, we'll use our CONT CDB.

2. Create a new PDB from the PDB$SEED. In this example, we'll call it LNE6. After you've created the PDB, remember to open it in read-write mode before attempting to import into it. Grant appropriate privileges to the Admin user, and create a directory for Data Pump to use with the PDB. Create the target schema and target tablespaces as needed. Also update the tnsnames.ora file to include a new service for the new PDB.

```
SQL> CREATE PLUGGABLE DATABASE lne6
  2  ADMIN USER lne6_admin IDENTIFIED BY system06
  3  /

Pluggable database created.

SQL> ALTER PLUGGABLE DATABASE lne6 OPEN;
Pluggable database altered.
SQL> ALTER SESSION SET CONTAINER=lne6;
Session altered.
SQL> GRANT DBA, IMP_FULL_DATABASE TO lne6_admin;
Grant succeeded.
SQL> CREATE DIRECTORY dpump_dir AS 'c:\temp\';
Directory created.
```

EXERCISE 13.1 *(continued)*

```
SQL> CREATE TABLESPACE example;
Tablespace created.
SQL> CREATE USER hr IDENTIFIED BY hr DEFAULT TABLESPACE example;
User created.
SQL> GRANT UNLIMITED TABLESPACE TO hr;
Grant succeeded.
SQL>

####  $ORACLE_HOME\NETWORK\ADMIN\tnsnames.ora
####  tnsnames.ora entry for the new PDB
####  CONT.lne6
LNE6 =
  (DESCRIPTION =
    (ADDRESS = (PROTOCOL = TCP)(HOST = localhost)(PORT = 1521))
    (CONNECT_DATA =
      (SERVER = DEDICATED)
      (SERVICE_NAME = LNE6)
    )
  )
```

3. Start up the source non-CDB. For this example, we'll use the ORCL database. Alter the non-system tablespaces to read-only mode (if possible) for a consistent export.

```
C:\>Set ORACLE_SID=ORCL
C:\>sqlplus / as sysdba

SQL*Plus: Release 12.1.0.1.0 Production on Sun Feb 2 11:08:21 2014

Copyright (c) 1982, 2013, Oracle.  All rights reserved.

Connected to an idle instance.

SQL> startup
ORACLE instance started.

Total System Global Area 5027536896 bytes
Fixed Size                  2412928 bytes
Variable Size             704646784 bytes
Database Buffers         4311744512 bytes
Redo Buffers                8732672 bytes
Database mounted.
Database opened.
SQL> SELECT tablespace_name FROM dba_tablespaces;
```

EXERCISE 13.1 *(continued)*

```
TABLESPACE_NAME
------------------------------
SYSTEM
SYSAUX
UNDOTBS1
TEMP
USERS
EXAMPLE
USER_TEST

10 rows selected.

SQL> ALTER TABLESPACE users READ ONLY;

Tablespace altered.

SQL> ALTER TABLESPACE example READ ONLY;

Tablespace altered.

SQL> ALTER TABLESPACE user_test READ ONLY;

Tablespace altered.

SQL> CREATE OR REPLACE DIRECTORY DATA_PUMP_DIR AS 'c:\temp';

Directory created.

SQL> EXIT
Disconnected from Oracle Database 12c Enterprise Edition Release 12.1.0.1.0 -
64bit Production
With the Partitioning, OLAP, Advanced Analytics and Real Application Testing
options

C:\>
```

4. Begin the Data Pump export process. We have chosen a full database export here, but you can also selectively export at the schema level.

```
expdp system/system FULL=y DUMPFILE=ncdb_expdat.dmp DIRECTORY=data_pump_dir
LOGFILE=export.log
Export: Release 12.1.0.1.0 - Production on Sun Dec 8 17:32:25 2013

Copyright (c) 1982, 2013, Oracle and/or its affiliates.  All rights reserved.
```

Connected to: Oracle Database 12c Enterprise Edition Release 12.1.0.1.0 –
64bit Production
With the Partitioning, OLAP, Advanced Analytics and Real Application Testing
options

...
. . exported "HR"."EMPLOYEES_HIST"   75.38 MB 1115982 rows
. . exported "HR"."COUNTRIES"   6.437 KB   25 rows
. . exported "HR"."DEPARTMENTS"   7.101 KB   27 rows
. . exported "HR"."EMPLOYEES"   17.07 KB   107 rows
. . exported "HR"."EMPLOYEES_HIST_NEW"   32.18 KB   321 rows
. . exported "HR"."JOBS"   7.085 KB   19 rows
. . exported "HR"."JOB_HISTORY"   7.171 KB   10 rows
. . exported "HR"."LOCATIONS"   8.414 KB   23 rows
. . exported "HR"."REGIONS"   5.523 KB   4 rows

5. Complete the Data Pump import process. In the previous command we exported the
   full database; here we will import part of the database into a PDB. Remember, the
   PDB doesn't know about the DATA_PUMP_DIR so you must have created a database
   directory in the PDB and reference the directory by name on the command line when
   running the import. Also, source database roles may not exist in the target, so review
   any errors and take action if necessary.

```
C:\Temp>impdp LNE6_ADMIN/system06@LNE6 DIRECTORY=dpump_dir DUMPFILE=ncdb_
expdat.dmp SCHEMAS=hr LOGFILE=dpump_dir:import.log

Import: Release 12.1.0.1.0 - Production on Sun Dec 8 20:01:35 2013

Copyright (c) 1982, 2013, Oracle and/or its affiliates.  All rights reserved.

Connected to: Oracle Database 12c Enterprise Edition Release 12.1.0.1.0 -
64bit Production
With the Partitioning, OLAP, Advanced Analytics and Real Application Testing
options

...
Processing object type DATABASE_EXPORT/SCHEMA/TABLE/TABLE_DATA
. . imported "HR"."EMPLOYEES_HIST"                    75.38 MB 1115982 rows
. . imported "HR"."COUNTRIES"                          6.437 KB       25 rows
. . imported "HR"."DEPARTMENTS"                        7.101 KB       27 rows
. . imported "HR"."EMPLOYEES"                          17.07 KB      107 rows
. . imported "HR"."JOBS"                               7.085 KB       19 rows
. . imported "HR"."JOB_HISTORY"                        7.171 KB       10 rows
. . imported "HR"."LOCATIONS"                          8.414 KB       23 rows
```

EXERCISE 13.1 *(continued)*

```
. . imported "HR"."REGIONS"                    5.523 KB      4 rows
...
C:\Temp>
```

> Chapter 14, "Managing Security in a CDB and PDBs," goes into greater detail about users, roles, and privileges in CDBs and PDBs.

Connecting to the PDB and Confirming Data Pump Import Success

As a follow-up to Exercise 13.1, connect to the PDB and verify the contents of the HR schema by selecting the names of the tables in the HR schema. You can compare row counts to the source non-CDB, and you can also compare the export and import log file number of rows exported and imported for each table. Here we'll log on to the PDB as the HR user and verify content. Please note that your table names and row counts may differ from the previous example.

```
SQL> CONNECT hr/hr@LNE6
Connected.
SQL> SELECT table_name FROM user_tables;


TABLE_NAME
----------------------------------------


JOB_HISTORY
EMPLOYEES
JOBS
LOCATIONS
REGIONS
DEPARTMENTS
EMPLOYEES_HIST
COUNTRIES

8 rows selected.

SQL>
SQL> SELECT COUNT(1) FROM COUNTRIES;
```

```
  COUNT(1)
----------
        25
```

SQL>

Note that the count of the rows in the LNE6 PDB HR.COUNTRIES table matches what was in the export and import log files.

Understanding and Using SQL*Loader

SQL*Loader is conceptually straightforward. Data that is to be loaded into the Oracle database is stored in SQL*Loader data files, which are basically text files. The SQL*Loader control file, also a text file, contains the instructions SQL*Loader will use to find the data files and which tables to load into.

There are a variety of options that you indicate in the control file, and we'll go over that in detail in an upcoming section.

There are also different data load paths. The conventional path data load uses SQL INSERT statements to insert rows into database tables. The direct path load writes data blocks directly to the database files, operating on blocks above the high-water mark (HWM) in a table, and doesn't use the DB buffer cache. These enhancements greatly reduce overhead and improve performance.

SQL*Loader will use a control file and one or more data files and insert data into an Oracle database. SQL*Loader will also create a log file, a bad file that indicates rejected records of data, and, if you choose, a discard file that contains records that failed the SQL selection criteria indicated in the control file. The difference between bad records and discarded records is that with a bad record SQL*Loader attempted to load a record but there was something wrong with the record and the load failed, whereas a discarded record had nothing wrong with it but it did not meet the WHERE criteria.

SQL*Loader express mode is activated when you specify the target table on the SQL*Loader command line, for example:

```
C:>\$ORACLE_HOME\bin\sqlldr hr/hr@LNE6 table=countries
```

SQL*Loader express mode uses the database table column definitions and does not use a control file. It will utilize the data file with the same name as the database table and with the extension .dat in the current directory. It will use defaults for the character set, field delimiters, and the names of data, log, and bad files unless you specify them with command-line parameters. We will demonstrate express mode in an upcoming section.

In this section we will introduce the SQL*Loader utility, a tool that you can use to load data from operating system files into tables in an Oracle database. You can use it to load data from multiple data files into multiple database tables.

SQL*Loader is used the same way with PDBs and non-CDBs. Do not attempt to use SQL*Loader to load data from external files into tables in CDB$ROOT. SQL*Loader control files and data files are not the same as database control files and data files.

SQL*Loader Features

Here are some of the activities you can use SQL*Loader to perform:

- Load data from local server file system, disk, tape, or named pipe, from a different server across a network.
- Load data from multiple data files and into multiple database tables during the same load session.
- Use SQL functions (DML) to manipulate the data before loading it.
- Load data based on specifically selected values.

You can use SQL*Loader with or without a control file. In the upcoming sections we will discuss SQL*Loader parameters, the control file, the data files, and the types of data loads.

SQL*Loader Parameters

Start SQL*Loader at the OS command line by entering sqlldr and optional parameters. Unless you're doing only a one-time data load and you get it right the first time, we recommend that you create a parameter file in which to keep the various parameters and values that drive SQL*Loader behavior. After you've modified a long list of parameters on the command line, you'll recognize the time-saving and troubleshooting benefit of using a parameter file instead of entering and editing all the information on the command line:

- Specify the PARFILE parameter on the command line, and for convenience keep the PARFILE in the same directory as your control file and your data files.
- You can also use the SQL*Loader control file OPTIONS clause to set parameter values.

If you specify a parameter on the command line, it will override parameter values that you have specified in a parameter file or in the control file OPTIONS clause. Here's an example of using the PARFILE on the command line:

```
C:\Temp>type sqlldr_parfile.txt
table=countries
userid=hr/hr@lne6
errors=10
silent=errors
C:\Temp>sqlldr parfile=sqlldr_parfile.txt silent=feedback
```

SQL*Loader Control File

The control file is a text file that SQL*Loader uses to locate the data file or files and to determine how data will be formatted, how to handle rejected records, the destination table, field names, whether or not to append rows, and how the data will be manipulated.

There are three main ordered sections to the control file:

- Session-wide information
- Table and field-list information
- An optional input data section

The syntax of the control file is case-insensitive, but quoted text is considered a literal. Statements can extend over multiple lines. Comments begin with two hyphens and go to the end of the line. Comments are not supported in the optional input data section.

In this simplified control file example, a SQL*Loader express mode session generated a copy of a control file and wrote it to the log file; we have copied the control file section and modified it by adding the BADFILE and DISCARDFILE parameters.

```
--Generated control file for possible reuse:
OPTIONS(EXTERNAL_TABLE=EXECUTE, TRIM=LRTRIM)
LOAD DATA
INFILE 'countries.dat'
BADFILE 'countries.bad'
DISCARDFILE 'countries.dsc'
APPEND
INTO TABLE COUNTRIES
WHEN COUNTRY_ID = 'AR'
FIELDS TERMINATED BY ","
(
  COUNTRY_ID,
  COUNTRY_NAME,
  REGION_ID
)
--End of generated control file for possible reuse.
```

This section describes some of the key items in the control file.

LOAD DATA   Indicates the beginning of a new data load.

INFILE   Is the name of a data file to load.

BADFILE   Names the file to write the rejected records to.

DISCARDFILE   Is the target for records not selected in the WHERE clause.

APPEND   Is used to add rows to a non-empty table; use INSERT to add rows to an empty table.

INTO TABLE   Is used to identify tables, fields, and their associated datatypes. Defines the translation between records to be loaded and the database tables.

FIELDS TERMINATED BY   Defines the field termination or field separation character.

WHEN   Specifies one or more field conditions to determine which records to load. Records that do not meet the criteria are discarded.

Finally, we define the fields to be loaded.

SQL*Loader Input Data and Data Files

The INFILE specified in the SQL*Loader control file contains the records to be loaded into the database table or tables. A data file may be fixed record format, variable record format, or stream record format. Specify the record format in the control file by using the INFILE parameter.

Fixed Record Format

In a fixed record format data file, all records in the file are the same byte length. Fixed format is simple to specify, and load performance is better than for variable or stream record loads. Indicate fixed record format and record length *n* as in this example:

```
INFILE 'datafile_name' "fix n"
```

Variable Record Format

When using a variable record format data file, the length of each record is included in a character field at the beginning of each record. Variable is more flexible than fixed record format and performs better than stream record format. Indicate variable record format and the length of the character field at the beginning of each record *n* as in this example:

```
INFILE 'datafile_name' "var n"
```

Stream Record Format

When you don't have the specific size of each record, use the stream record format. SQL*Loader uses the record terminator to determine the end of the line. This is the most flexible format; however, performance may suffer. Indicate stream record format as in this example, where terminator_string is the character string that is used to end a record:

```
INFILE 'datafile_name' ["str terminator_string"]
```

If no terminator_string value is specified, then the default record terminator is the line feed character, \n on Unix, and \n or \r\n (whichever comes first in the record) on Windows. Here's a data file example that would use the stream record format:

```
C:\Temp>type countries.dat
UR,Uruguay,2
TK,Turkey,4
SY,Syria,4
```

```
NP,Nepal,3
MY,Myanmar,3
BG,Bangladesh,3
VT,The Vatican,1
```

SQL*Loader Conventional Path Loads, Direct Path Loads

SQL*Loader can use two different methods to load data: either the conventional path or the direct path. The conventional path load populates tables in the database by executing SQL INSERT statements. The direct path load formats data blocks and writes the data blocks directly to the database files, eliminating database overhead.

SQL*Loader does not create tables in the target database, so the target tables must exist prior to starting the load process. The target table does not have to be empty. To load data using SQL*Loader, the loading user must have INSERT privileges on the table to be loaded. If there is data in the table and the intent is to replace duplicate content using the REPLACE option or empty the table using the TRUNCATE option prior to loading, then the user must have DELETE privileges on the target table.

Conventional Path Loads

The conventional path load, which is the default for SQL*Loader, uses SQL INSERT statements and an in-memory bind array buffer to load data into database target tables. The input records are parsed and each field is copied into the bind array until it is full or there are no more records to process; then the contents of the buffer are inserted into the target table. This is similar to a normal INSERT operation in that DB resources are used for memory, parsing, execution, and searching for available space within data blocks.

Direct Path Loads

The direct path load is significantly faster than the conventional path load. A direct path load parses and converts the input records according to the specifications and builds an array. The array is then converted into data blocks and written directly to the database.

To load data in direct path load mode using SQL*Loader, set the DIRECT parameter to TRUE in the parameter file or on the command line.

```
DIRECT=TRUE
```

Keep in mind that direct path load does not support loading to clustered tables. Also during direct path load, any existing indexes are copied and then merged with the new index keys. For large indexes with few new rows loaded, the time saved by a direct path load may be less than the time required for index maintenance.

Referential and column-check integrity constraints cannot be applied to rows loaded on the direct path, so they are disabled during the load and applied to the table when the load completes. Reenabling the constraints could take longer than the time saved by using direct path.

Comparing Conventional Path and Direct Path Loads

As mentioned previously, the direct path load can be faster than the conventional path load. The conventional path load should be used in the following situations:

- Access to the target table is required concurrently with the data load.
- Inserts or updates will occur to a non-indexed target table concurrently with the data load.
- When loading data into a clustered table.
- When loading a relatively small number of rows into a large table that has referential and column-check integrity constraints or indexes.

Parallel Direct Path

A parallel direct path load allows multiple direct path load sessions to concurrently load into the same data segments, by using the PARALLEL parameter on the command line or in a parameter file.

```
sqlldr USERID=hr CONTROL=hrloader1.ctl DIRECT=TRUE PARALLEL=TRUE
sqlldr USERID=hr CONTROL=hrloader2.ctl DIRECT=TRUE PARALLEL=TRUE
sqlldr USERID=hr CONTROL=hrloader3.ctl DIRECT=TRUE PARALLEL=TRUE
```

SQL*Loader Express Mode

As mentioned earlier, SQL*Loader express mode is a quick way to load by specifying only a table name on the command line. It can be used when the table columns are all number, datetime, or character datatypes and the input data files contain only delimited character data, for example:

```
C:\Temp>type countries.dat
UR,Uruguay,2
TK,Turkey,4
SY,Syria,4
NP,Nepal,3
MY,Myanmar,3
BG,Bangladesh,3
VT,The Vatican,1
```

A control file is not used. SQL*Loader uses the target table column definitions to match up the datatypes and order of the input fields. You can override default values by using parameters and values on the command line.

To run SQL*Loader in express mode, type in **sqlldr** followed by the username parameter and **TABLE=<target table>** at the command prompt.

```
C:\Temp>
C:\Temp>sqlldr hr/hr@LNE6 table=countries
```

```
SQL*Loader: Release 12.1.0.1.0 - Production on Sun Dec 8 22:18:41 2013

Copyright (c) 1982, 2013, Oracle and/or its affiliates.  All rights reserved.

Express Mode Load, Table: COUNTRIES
Path used:      External Table, DEGREE_OF_PARALLELISM=AUTO
SQL*Loader-579: switching to direct path for the load
SQL*Loader-583: ignoring trim setting with direct path, using value of LDRTRIM
SQL*Loader-584: ignoring DEGREE_OF_PARALLELISM setting with direct path, using
value of NONE
Express Mode Load, Table: COUNTRIES
Path used:      Direct

Load completed - logical record count 7.

Table COUNTRIES:
  7 Rows successfully loaded.

Check the log file:
  countries.log
for more information about the load.

C:\Temp>


SQL> connect hr/hr@LNE6
Connected.
SQL> select * from countries;

CO COUNTRY_NAME                            REGION_ID
-- --------------------------------------- ----------
AR Argentina                                      2
AU Australia                                      3
BE Belgium                                        1
BG Bangladesh                                     3
BR Brazil                                         2
CA Canada                                         2
CH Switzerland                                    1
CN China                                          3
DE Germany                                        1
DK Denmark                                        1
```

```
EG Egypt                              4
FR France                             1
IL Israel                             4
IN India                              3
IT Italy                              1
JP Japan                              3
KW Kuwait                             4
ML Malaysia                           3
MX Mexico                             2
MY Myanmar                            3
NG Nigeria                            4
NL Netherlands                        1
NP Nepal                              3
SG Singapore                          3
SY Syria                              4
TK Turkey                             4
UK United Kingdom                     1
UR Uruguay                            2
US United States of America           2
VT The Vatican                        1
ZM Zambia                             4
ZW Zimbabwe                           4

32 rows selected.


SQL>
```

SQL*Loader express mode generates a bad file, and it also generates a SQL*Loader control file and places it in the log file, purely for your convenience.

Default Values Used by SQL*Loader Express Mode

You can override the defaults on the command line, but otherwise SQL*Loader in express mode has these characteristics:

- It uses a file named table-name.dat in the current directory.

- It uses the external table load method. SQL*Loader express mode will switch to direct path load if there are specific errors, such as when the loading user does not have the privilege to create a directory in the PDB:

```
SQL*Loader-816: error creating temporary directory object SYS_SQLLDR_XT_
TMPDIR_0
0000 for file countries.dat
ORA-01031: insufficient privileges
SQL*Loader-579: switching to direct path for the load
```

※ No column names are specified, so the database table column names are used.

※ The order of the columns match from the data file to the database table.

※ The datatypes are aligned.

※ It uses a comma as the field delimiter in the data file.

※ It uses a newline to indicate a new record.

※ It does not use quotes to enclose character fields.

※ The NLS client character set and NLS settings are used for date and timestamp data.

※ Constraints are enforced, and new rows do not overwrite existing data.

※ `DEGREE_OF_PARALLELISM` is `AUTO`, but it will be ignored if SQL*Loader switches to direct path load.

Audit Operations

In Chapter 12, we introduced audit-related initialization parameters that have an impact on PDBs and CDBs. In this section we will focus on the effect of audit operations on the utility programs previously introduced in this chapter: Oracle Data Pump and Oracle SQL*Loader. Both use unified auditing, where all audit records are centralized in one place, viewable in one data dictionary view. But first we'll discuss audit policies in the multitenant environment, focusing on the differences between CDB and PDB, or common and local auditing.

Local and Common Audit Policies

In the multitenant environment, you can set up local or common audit policies. This applies to the `AUDIT` and `NOAUDIT` SQL statements as well as for unified audit policies.

The local audit policy can exist in either a PDB or `CDB$ROOT`. A local audit policy that exists in `CDB$ROOT` can contain object audit options for local and common objects. Local users who have the AUDIT_ADMIN role can enable local policies from their PDBs. Common users with the role can enable local policies from the root or the PDB to which they have privileges. The AUDIT_VIEWER role allows viewing and analyzing audit data.

The common audit policy is available to all PDBs in a CDB, can be enabled only for common users, and can contain only info on common objects. Common audit policies can only be created in `CDB$ROOT`, and only common users who have the AUDIT_ADMIN role can create and maintain common audit policies.

Audit policies are by default local to the current PDB. To create a local or common unified audit policy, follow this example:

```
SQL> CREATE AUDIT POLICY create_table_pol
  2  PRIVILEGES CREATE ANY TABLE, DROP ANY TABLE
  3  roles hr_admin, hr_system_admin;

Audit policy created.
```

SQL Auditing Data Pump Jobs

To monitor and record the use of Data Pump jobs, set up auditing. As mentioned previously Data Pump uses unified auditing.

To set up unified auditing, follow these steps:

1. Create a named unified audit policy, which is a named group of audit settings that you use to monitor database user activity.

2. To create a unified audit policy, use the SQL CREATE AUDIT POLICY statement, and set the COMPONENT clause to DATAPUMP.

   You can audit Data Pump export (expdp), import (impdp), or both.

3. To create a unified audit policy for Oracle Data Pump, consider this syntax:

```
CREATE AUDIT POLICY policy_name
ACTIONS COMPONENT=DATAPUMP { EXPORT | IMPORT | ALL };
```

   This example shows how to audit all Oracle Data Pump import operations.

```
SQL> CREATE AUDIT POLICY audit_datapump_import_pol
  2  ACTIONS COMPONENT=DATAPUMP IMPORT;

Audit policy created.
```

4. Now that you've created the audit policy, use the AUDIT SQL statement to enable it for all users:

```
SQL>
SQL> AUDIT POLICY audit_datapump_import_pol;

Audit succeeded.

SQL>
```

5. Now you can use the NOAUDIT SQL statement to disable it for all users:

```
SQL> NOAUDIT POLICY audit_datapump_import_pol;

Noaudit succeeded.

SQL>
```

   You can audit actions for specific users if you use the BY clause, followed by specific user-names. The same applies to using NOAUDIT to disable an audit policy for specific users. With all unified auditing you must have the AUDIT_ADMIN role. Data Pump is no exception, so you'll need that role before you attempt to audit Oracle Data Pump events.

6. This example shows how to audit both Oracle Database Pump export and import operations.

```
SQL> CREATE AUDIT POLICY audit_datapump_all_pol
  2  ACTIONS COMPONENT=DATAPUMP ALL;

Audit policy created.

SQL> AUDIT POLICY audit_datapump_all_pol BY SYSTEM;

Audit succeeded.
SQL> NOAUDIT POLICY audit_datapump_all_pol BY SYSTEM;

Noaudit succeeded.

SQL>
```

7. Query the DP_ columns of the UNIFIED_AUDIT_TRAIL data dictionary view to access the audit trail for Data Pump operations.

Here's the query you'll need to execute to view the Data Pump operations in the unified audit trail:

```
SELECT DP_TEXT_PARAMETERS1, DP_BOOLEAN_PARAMETERS1
FROM UNIFIED_AUDIT_TRAIL
WHERE AUDIT_TYPE = 'DATAPUMP';
```

Auditing SQL*Loader Operations That Use Direct Path Mode

You can perform auditing on SQL*Loader direct path loads only, to monitor and record user database actions. As mentioned previously, SQL*Loader uses unified auditing.

As mentioned in the previous section on auditing Data Pump activities, you'll need to set up an audit policy specifically for SQL*Loader activities using the CREATE AUDIT command and set the COMPONENT clause to DIRECT LOAD; then enable it using the AUDIT POLICY statement. Here's an example of how to create and audit an Oracle SQL*Loader unified audit policy:

```
SQL> CREATE AUDIT POLICY audit_direct_sqlldr_pol
  2  ACTIONS COMPONENT=DIRECT_LOAD LOAD;

Audit policy created.

SQL> AUDIT POLICY audit_direct_sqlldr_pol BY SYSTEM;
```

```
Audit succeeded.
```

```
SQL>
```

Query the `DIRECT_PATH_NUM_COLUMNS_LOADED` column of the `UNIFIED_AUDIT_TRAIL` to see the audit history of activities that used the SQL*Loader direct path load method, for example:

```
SELECT DBUSERNAME, ACTION_NAME, OBJECT_SCHEMA, OBJECT_NAME, DIRECT_PATH_NUM_
COLUMNS_LOADED
FROM UNIFIED_AUDIT_TRAIL WHERE AUDIT_TYPE = 'DIRECT PATH API';
 DBUSERNAME ACTION_NAME OBJECT_SCHEMA OBJECT_NAME DIRECT_PATH_NUM_COLUMNS_LOADED
----------- ----------- ------------- ------------ ------------------------------
-
HR      INSERT HR REGIONS    6
```

Using Other Products with CDBs and PDBs—Database Vault, Data Guard, LogMiner

There are other products that support the Oracle database and have configuration or behavior differences in a multitenant environment. In this section we will introduce three of these products—Database Vault, Data Guard, and LogMiner—and discuss how they behave with CDBs and PDBs.

Database Vault

Oracle Database Vault is a tool that prevents privileged database users from accessing application data using their system privileges. You can restrict a DBA's access so that they will not be able to see sensitive information like social security numbers, salaries and bonuses, medical records, financial information, or any other information deemed sensitive or confidential.

Oracle Database Vault Overview

The DBA can use Oracle Enterprise Manager Cloud Control 12*c* or SQL*Plus to manage Oracle Database Vault. Oracle Database Vault provides database roles that allow groups of users to perform tasks based on separation of duties. DV_OWNER, DV_ADMIN, and DV_ACCTMGR are the most commonly used roles. With the DV_OWNER and DV_ADMIN roles you can create and manage Database Vault policies. You can manage user accounts with DV_ACCTMGR.

Oracle Database Vault in a Multitenant Environment

In the multitenant environment each PDB has its own Database Vault metadata, including rule sets and command rules. The objects in `DVSYS` and `DVF` common user schemas are available to PDBs. You can create individual policies for each PDB, since the scope of the policies is local.

In the multitenant environment, the `DVSYS` schema is a common user schema that is stored in the `CDB$ROOT`, and all the objects within the `DVSYS` schema are dependent on the common privileges for this schema. As mentioned previously, Oracle-supplied common users do not necessarily follow the naming convention. You first configure Database Vault in the root and then configure it in the PDBs. See Exercise 13.2.

EXERCISE 13.2

Plugging a Database Vault–Enabled PDB into a CDB

In this example, you will start with a source PDB PDB1, a Database Vault–enabled PDB, and plug it into a multitenant container database (CDB) named CONT, using the new PDB name PDB2.

1. Connect to the CDB$ROOT of the target CDB as a user who has been granted the DV_OWNER role, for example:

   ```
   sqlplus c##sec_admin/password@CONT
   ```

2. Grant DV_PATCH_ADMIN to user SYS, which allows SYS to create users but does not allow access to any secured objects, and include the CONTAINER = CURRENT clause.

   ```
   GRANT DV_PATCH_ADMIN TO SYS CONTAINER = CURRENT;
   ```

3. Connect SYS as SYSDBA to the CDB$ROOT.

   ```
   CONNECT / AS SYSDBA
   ```

4. Restart the CDB in read-only mode.

   ```
   SHUTDOWN IMMEDIATE
   STARTUP MOUNT
   ALTER DATABASE OPEN READ ONLY;
   ```

5. Connect to the Database Vault source PDB as a user who has the DV_OWNER role.

   ```
   CONNECT sec_admin@PDB1
   ```

6. Grant DV_PATCH_ADMIN to user SYS in this PDB.

   ```
   GRANT DV_PATCH_ADMIN TO SYS;
   ```

7. Run DBMS_PDB.CHECK_PLUG_COMPATIBILITY to verify if the unplugged PDB is compatible with the target CDB. Set pdb_descr_file to the full path to the XML file that will contain a description of the PDB. Set store_report to TRUE if you want to generate a report if the PDB is not compatible with the CDB. If it is not compatible, a report is generated and stored in SYS.PDB_PLUG_IN_VIOLATIONS temporarily. To determine if a PDB is compatible with the current CDB, run the following PL/SQL block using the XML file output from the unplugged PDB:

   ```
   SET SERVEROUTPUT ON
   DECLARE
   ```

```
    compatible CONSTANT VARCHAR2(3) :=
        CASE DBMS_PDB.CHECK_PLUG_COMPATIBILITY(
            pdb_descr_file => 'c:\temp\oracle\pdb2.xml',
            pdb_name='PDB1')
        WHEN TRUE THEN 'YES'
        ELSE 'NO'
    END;
BEGIN
    DBMS_OUTPUT.PUT_LINE(compatible);
END;
/
```

If the PDB is compatible, then the output will be YES; if it is not compatible, the output will be NO and you can query SYS.PDB_PLUG_IN_VIOLATIONS to learn why it is incompatible.

8. Start up the source PDB in read-only mode, and create an XML file that describes the PDB.

```
BEGIN
  DBMS_PDB.DESCRIBE(
    pdb_descr_file => 'c:\temp\oracle\pdb1.xml');
END;
/
```

9. Create the target PDB with the CREATE PLUGGABLE DATABASE statement specifying the XML file in the USING clause.

```
CREATE PLUGGABLE DATABASE pdb2 AS CLONE USING 'pdb1.xml' NOCOPY;
```

10. Connect to the new PDB as user SYS as SYSDBA.

```
CONNECT SYS@pdb2 AS SYSDBA
```

11. Run noncdb_to_pdb.sql within SQL*Plus.

```
@$ORACLE_HOME\rdbms\admin\noncdb_to_pdb.sql
```

12. Open PDB2 in a read-write restricted mode.

```
ALTER PLUGGABLE DATABASE pdb2 OPEN READ WRITE RESTRICTED;
```

13. Synchronize the PDB:

```
EXECUTE DBMS_PDB.SYNC_PDB;
```

14. Connect to the root as a user who has the DV_OWNER role.

```
sqlplus c##sec_admin/password
```

15. Since you previously granted DV_PATCH_ADMIN to SYS, you will need to revoke DV_PATCH_ADMIN from user SYS with CONTAINER = CURRENT.

```
REVOKE DV_PATCH_ADMIN FROM SYS CONTAINER = CURRENT;
```

16. Connect to the new Database Vault–enabled PDB as user SYS with the SYSDBA system privilege.

```
CONNECT SYS@ pdb2 AS SYSDBA
```

17. Restart this database.

```
SHUTDOWN IMMMEDIATE
STARUP
```

18. Revoke DV_PATCH_ADMIN from user SYS.

```
REVOKE DV_PATCH_ADMIN FROM SYS;
```

Data Guard

Oracle Data Guard provides high availability, data protection, and disaster recovery for Oracle databases. Oracle Data Guard is a set of services that you use to create and manage standby databases as copies of primary databases. When the primary database is unavailable, Oracle Data Guard fails over to a standby database. To provide a very high level of availability, Oracle Data Guard can be used in addition to backup, restore, storage replication, and clustering.

In an Oracle Data Guard environment one primary database can have up to 30 standby destinations, connected by Oracle Net. Geographical location, or more precisely distance from the primary to the standby databases, is not a restriction. You can have multiple remote standby databases that are geographically dispersed, as long as the primary can communicate with the standby.

Physical Standby Database   A *physical standby database* is a physically identical block-wise copy of the primary database. The database schemas are identical between the primary and physical standby. Redo Apply is used to keep the physical standby in sync with the primary.

Logical Standby Database   A *logical standby database* contains the same logical information as the production database but the physical structure and organization of the database can be different. SQL Apply is used to keep the logical standby database in sync with the primary.

Creating a Physical Standby of a CDB

You can create a physical standby of a CDB as you would create a physical standby of a non-CDB primary database. However, there are some differences you need to know about when you create and manage a physical standby CDB:

- The primary or standby role is defined at the CDB, not in PDBs.
- If you switch over to a standby, the entire CDB is switched over.
- Role change DDL is executed in the CDB$ROOT.
- PDBs do not have their own roles.
- The syntax of SQL statements for a physical standby is generally the same for CDBs and non-CDBs, with some exceptions:
  - ALTER DATABASE RECOVER MANAGED STANDBY is not allowed in a PDB.
  - ALTER DATABASE SWITCHOVER TO target_db_name impacts the entire CDB.
  - ALTER DATABASE ACTIVATE PHYSICAL STANDBY impacts the entire CDB.
  - ALTER PLUGGABLE DATABASE [OPEN|CLOSE] is supported on the standby if CDB$ROOT is open.
  - ALTER PLUGGABLE DATABASE RECOVER is not supported on the standby, since standby recovery is at the CDB level.

Creating a PDB in a Primary Database

In this section we'll discuss creating a PDB in a primary database when using a physical standby. A PDB on a primary database is created the same way whether or not you're in an Oracle Data Guard configuration. When you create a PDB as a clone from another PDB within the same CDB, copy the source PDB data files to the standby database. In an Active Data Guard environment this is not necessary since the data files are copied automatically when the PDB is created on the standby database. If you're going to create a PDB from an XML file, remember to copy the XML file and associated data files to the standby database server and directory destination.

If the physical standby database has the Active Data Guard option enabled (open read-only), then copy the set of PDB data files that will be plugged into the primary database to the standby database locations.

Oracle Active Data Guard is a separately licensed Oracle Database option, which provides read-only access to an Oracle Data Guard physical standby database while it remains synchronized with a primary database. This read-only standby can be used for reporting and ad hoc queries while not impacting the primary.

Copy the files to the appropriate location at the standby database where they can be found by the managed standby recovery, before plugging in the PDB at the primary database. If the database files are not ASM, then use the DB_FILE_NAME_CONVERT parameter for the location of the files at the standby. If data files are in ASM, use the ASMCMD utility to copy the files to this location at the standby database

```
<db_create_file_dest>/<db_unique_name>/<GUID>/datafile
```

where the GUID is queried from the V$CONTAINERS view at the source PDB, for example:

```
SELECT guid
FROM V$CONTAINERS
WHERE con_id=3;

GUID
--------------------------------
A491586A99E14806AEFBD366A80D18AD

SQL>
```

The standby database and primary database path name of the data files must be the same, unless you have configured the DB_FILE_NAME_CONVERT initialization parameter on the standby.

Creating a Logical Standby of a CDB

Creating a logical standby of a CDB is the same as creating a logical standby of a non-CDB. However, there are some differences you need to know about when you create and manage a logical standby CDB:

- The primary or standby role is defined at the CDB, not in PDBs.
- If you switch over to a standby, the entire CDB is switched over.
- Role change DDL is executed in the CDB$ROOT.
- PDBs do not have their own roles.
- It is not a requirement to have the same PDBs at the primary and standby, but only tables that exist in the same PDB at both the primary and standby databases are replicated.
- Remember that many DBA views have analogous CDB views whose names begin with CDB_ instead of DBA_, but they have an extra column to indicate the CON_ID, which is associated with the PDB.
- In a logical standby of a CDB some SQL statements do not have the same scope, or they have only a local scope, relative to the same SQL statement in a non-CDB.

A primary or standby role is associated with an entire CDB. So, for example, the following DDL associated with logical standbys affects the entire CDB:

- ALTER DATABASE RECOVER TO LOGICAL STANDBY
- ALTER DATABASE [PREPARE|COMMIT] TO SWITCHOVER
- ALTER DATABASE ACTIVATE LOGICAL STANDBY

- ALTER DATABASE [START|STOP] LOGICAL STANDBY APPLY
- ALTER DATABASE GUARD (Oracle strongly recommends you do *not* use it on a logical standby).

Standby Considerations When Removing or Renaming a PDB at a Primary

If the primary database is a CDB and you're renaming or removing one of its PDBs, the PDB must be closed on the primary and all standby databases to perform UNPLUG and DROP. To RENAME a PDB it must first be put in open restricted mode on the primary and closed on all standby databases. In the following code example, LNE6 is a PDB in the primary CDB.

```
SQL> alter pluggable database open restricted;

Pluggable database altered.

SQL> alter pluggable database lne6 rename global_name to lne7;

Pluggable database altered.

SQL> show con_name

CON_NAME
------------------------------
LNE7
SQL> select name, open_mode from v$pdbs;

NAME                           OPEN_MODE
------------------------------ ----------
LNE7                           READ WRITE
```

Before removing or renaming a PDB at the primary database, you must close the PDB at the standby. Otherwise, the standby will stop recovery for all PDBs, and you will need to close the dropped PDB at the standby and recover the standby database from the CDB$ROOT, as in this example:

```
SQL> ALTER DATABASE RECOVER MANAGED STANDBY DATABASE;
```

Using LogMiner to Analyze Redo Log Files

Oracle LogMiner is a tool you use as a SQL interface to query online and archived redo log files, which contain information about the history of activity on a database. The redo log files record all changes made to data or to the database dictionary. The purpose of the redo log files is to enable database recovery operations. LogMiner can be used as a powerful data-auditing and data-analysis tool, since all changes are recorded in the redo log files. Here are some of the important uses for LogMiner:

- Determine when logical corruption to a database may have occurred.
- Determine how you would perform fine-grained recovery for rows that need to be corrected.
- Determine which tables get the most update and insert activity.
- Track data manipulation language (DML) and data definition language (DDL) statements executed by username and when.

Introduction to LogMiner

The four basic objects in LogMiner are the source database, the mining database, the LogMiner dictionary, and the redo log files. The source database produces all the redo log files that you want to analyze. The mining database is used by LogMiner to perform the analysis. The LogMiner dictionary allows LogMiner to provide table and column names, instead of internal object IDs, when it presents the redo log data that you request. Without a LogMiner dictionary, LogMiner presents objects by internal ID numbers and binary data:

```
INSERT INTO HR.COUNTRIES(COUNTRY_ID, COUNTRY_NAME, REGION_ID)
VALUES('VT','The Vatican', 1);
```

Without the dictionary, LogMiner displays output similar to the following:

```
INSERT INTO "UNKNOWN"."OBJ# 92209"("COL 1","COL 2","COL 3") VALUES (HEXTORAW('56
54'),HEXTORAW('546865205661746963616E'),
HEXTORAW('c102'));
```

Supplemental logging must be enabled before generating log files for LogMiner to analyze. Supplemental logging records additional information in the redo stream so that the information in the redo log files is more useful. (See Exercise 13.3.)

```
SQL> ALTER DATABASE ADD SUPPLEMENTAL LOG DATA;
Database altered.

SQL>
```

The V$DATABASE view tells you if supplemental logging is enabled. Query V$DATABASE like this:

```
SQL> SELECT SUPPLEMENTAL_LOG_DATA_MIN FROM V$DATABASE;

SUPPLEME
--------
YES

SQL>
```

YES or IMPLICIT indicates that supplemental logging is enabled: YES if the SQL ALTER DATABASE ADD SUPPLEMENTAL LOG DATA statement was issued, or IMPLICIT if database-level identification key logging options are enabled.

EXERCISE 13.3

Steps for Using LogMiner

To use LogMiner, you execute procedures in the DBMS_LOGMNR and DBMS_LOGMNR_D PL/SQL supplied packages and query data from the V$LOGMNR_CONTENTS view. The EXECUTE_ CATALOG_ROLE role and the LOGMINING privilege are required to query the V$LOGMNR_ CONTENTS view and to execute the LogMiner PL/SQL packages.

1. Use the DBMS_LOGMNR_D.BUILD procedure or specify the LogMiner dictionary when you start LogMiner.

2. Use the DBMS_LOGMNR.ADD_LOGFILE procedure, or direct LogMiner to create a list of log files for analysis automatically when you start LogMiner.

3. Start LogMiner by executing the DBMS_LOGMNR.START_LOGMNR procedure.

4. Query the V$LOGMNR_CONTENTS view.

5. End LogMiner by executing the DBMS_LOGMNR.END_LOGMNR procedure.

Using LogMiner in a CDB

You can use LogMiner a multitenant CDB. There are some differences when using LogMiner in a CDB compared to a non-CDB, and we'll explain them here:

LogMiner V$ Views and DBA Views in a CDB   The views used to show LogMiner information in a CDB contain the additional column CON_ID, which identifies the container ID associated with the session ID. When you query the same view from a PDB, you'll see only information associated with the current PDB. When you query from the CDB$ROOT you'll see all rows in the CDB. Here's the list of LogMiner V$ views:

- V$LOGMNR_DICTIONARY_LOAD
- V$LOGMNR_LATCH
- V$LOGMNR_PROCESS
- V$LOGMNR_SESSION
- V$LOGMNR_STATS
- V$LOGMNR_TRANSACTION

These views do not contain a session ID column but do contain the CON_ID column:

- V$LOGMNR_CONTENTS
- V$LOGMNR_DICTIONARY

- V$LOGMNR_LOGS
- V$LOGMNR_LOGFILE
- V$LOGMNR_PARAMETERS

The DBA views DBA_LOGMNR_LOG, DBA_LOGMNR_PURGED_LOG, and DBA_LOGMNR_SESSION show the information related to sessions in the current container. Analogous CDB views (CDB_LOGMNR_LOG, for example) include the CON_ID column, and the previous rule regarding scope in PDBs and the CDB$ROOT apply.

The V$LOGMNR_CONTENTS View in a CDB   The V$LOGMNR_CONTENTS view in a CDB and its associated functions are restricted to the CDB$ROOT. The following columns have been added to support CDBs:

- CON_ID—the container ID for the container where the query was executed.
- SRC_CON_NAME—the PDB name.
- SRC_CON_ID—the container ID of the PDB that generated the redo record.
- SRC_CON_DBID—the PDB identifier.
- SRC_CON_GUID—the GUID associated with the PDB.
- SRC_CON_UID—the UID associated with the PDB

Enabling Supplemental Logging in a CDB   The syntax for enabling and disabling database-wide supplemental logging is the same whether you're in a non-CDB or a CDB.

```
SQL> ALTER DATABASE ADD SUPPLEMENTAL LOG DATA;
Database altered.


SQL>
```

Minimal supplemental logging affects the entire CDB. You can connect to a PDB and turn on and off other levels of supplemental logging for that individual PDB.

Using a Flat File Dictionary in a CDB   Connect to a PDB and take a snapshot of that PDB in a flat file, as in this example:

```
EXECUTE DBMS_LOGMNR_D.BUILD('dictionary.ora', -
    '/oracle/database/', -
    DBMS_LOGMNR_D.STORE_IN_FLAT_FILE);
```

You can mine the redo logs only for the PDB whose data dictionary is contained within that flat file. This is not an option for a CDB.

Summary

In this chapter, you learned about the Oracle Database 12*c* Utility programs and how they work in the multitenant architecture. You learned more about how Oracle Data Pump can be used to migrate database content from a non-CDB into a PDB and how to migrate content between PDBs within a CDB or across CDBs. You learned how to use SQL*Loader to load data stored in flat files into a PDB within a CDB, building on the knowledge gained in previous chapters. You learned about the components of SQL*Loader, the record formats, the parameters, the control file and data files, and the advantages of the direct path load over the conventional path load. You also learned how to use SQL*Loader express mode, which is basically running SQL*Loader with a streamlined configuration to load data.

In this chapter, we discussed audit operations that are pertinent to the multitenant environment, discussing local and common audit policies. We discussed how auditing can be applied to the utilities introduced in this chapter, specifically Data Pump and SQL*Loader direct path mode activities.

In the last section of this chapter, we introduced other Oracle products that have unique characteristics in the multitenant environment. We introduced Database Vault as a means to provide a higher level of protection of sensitive or confidential application data that is stored in Oracle Database schemas. We also provided an example of how to plug a vault-enabled database into a CDB environment.

Next, we introduced the Oracle Data Guard option, which provides high availability through the implementation of one or more standby databases that are kept up to date with the primary database. You learned that Oracle Data Guard applies to the entire CDB and all the PDBs that are within the CDB. We introduced physical and logical standby databases, and we discussed how to create a PDB in the primary and synchronize it with the standby databases.

Finally, we introduced Oracle LogMiner, which uses SQL to query online and archived redo log files to determine the history of activity in the database. LogMiner can be used to determine how logical corruption occurred, determine how to perform fine-grained recovery of specific rows of data, determine table activity rates, and track (audit) user activities in the database. You learned about the new CDB-related views for LogMiner.

Exam Essentials

Know the components of Data Pump in the Oracle Database 12*c* multitenant architecture. Make sure you understand the different components of Data Pump, including the programs and types of files.

Understand how to use Data Pump with CDBs.   Know that you use Data Pump to move content into a PDB, a non-CDB into a PDB, or one PDB into another PDB.

Know the components of SQL*Loader.   Understand the different components of SQL*Loader.

Demonstrate how to use SQL*Loader to move records into a PDB.   Demonstrate how to use the various components of SQL*Loader and the different path loads.

Demonstrate how to Audit Data Pump and SQL*Loader jobs.   Understand how to audit these activities in a multitenant environment.

Understand the purpose of Oracle Database Vault.   Understand how Oracle Database Vault can be used to further secure sensitive and confidential data from systems administrators.

Understand how Data Guard behaves in a multitenant environment.   Describe the different configurations of Data Guard and the impact on CDBs and PDBs in the primary and standby roles.

Use LogMiner to analyze redo log files in a multitenant environment.   Understand the purpose of LogMiner and the new and updated data dictionary and CDB views.

Review Questions

1. In the Oracle 12*c* multitenant architecture, what is a common use for Data Pump? (Choose all that apply.)

   A. To migrate a full non-CDB into a CDB

   B. To load the contents of a PDB into another PDB

   C. To load specific tables or schemas from a non-CDB into a PDB

   D. To import a schema from a non-CDB into a PDB

   E. All of the above

2. The DBMS_DATAPUMP PL/SQL package is used for which of the following activities?

   A. Accepting parameters from expdb and importing content into CDB$ROOT

   B. Confirming metadata validity between the CDB$ROOT and the local PDB

   C. Direct path load of content into the CDB$ROOT

   D. Accepting parameters from expdp and exporting content based on the parameters

3. When importing with Data Pump into a CDB and the target CDB does not have the same common username as that of the export, what do you need to do to make sure the import works? (Choose all that apply.)

   A. Create the common user in the target CDB with the same privileges as it had in the source.

   B. Use the SYS schema to complete the import.

   C. Remap the common user schema from the target to a local user in the source.

   D. Remap the common user schema from the source to a local user in the target.

   E. None of the above.

4. To import using Data Pump into the PDB1 container, which of the following must be true?

   A. You must define a directory object within PDB1 and use that as the DUMPFILE directory.

   B. You must define a directory object within CDB$ROOT and use that as the DUMPFILE directory.

   C. You do not define a directory object within PDB1; simply use a DUMPFILE directory on the server.

   D. None of the above.

5. Which of the following are valid scenarios for using Data Pump? (Choose all that apply.)

   A. Connect to CDB$ROOT and import root objects.

   B. Connect to PDB$SEED and import objects.

   C. Connect to a C## common user and import objects.

   D. Connect to a local user and import objects.

   E. None of the above.

6. Which of the following is a SQL*Loader use case?

   A. Loading data from an Oracle table in a source non-CDB directly into a target table in a PDB using a DB LINK connection

   B. Loading data into an Oracle table from a binary database file from a previous Oracle database version

   C. Loading contents from a comma-delimited text file into a CDB$ROOT table

   D. Loading contents from a comma-delimited text file into a table in a PDB

   E. None of the above

7. Which of these comments accurately describes the SQL*Loader components?

   A. The control file contains the source data, the parfile contains the optional parameters, and the data file describes the layout of the data to be imported.

   B. The parfile is required, the data file is a fixed-length list of records to import, and the control file specifies the mandatory BADFILE and DISCARDFILE names.

   C. The optional parfile is used to simplify the management of parameters entered at the command line.

   D. The WHEN clause is required in the control file.

   E. None of the above.

8. When loading data with SQL*Loader, which of the following are true? (Choose all that apply.)

   A. Specify the fixed record format using the INFILE parameter in the control file.

   B. By default, SQL*Loader assumes all records and fields are fixed length unless otherwise specified in the parfile.

   C. Variable record format data load performs better than fixed and stream record format.

   D. The stream record format is the most flexible but performance may suffer.

   E. None of the above.

9. Which of the following describes a SQL*Loader direct path load?

   A. By default all records are written to the database using SQL `INSERT` statements, committed in bulk, and optimized for data loads.

   B. Using the control file parameter `SQLLOAD=DIRECT`, the data file is converted into a binary database file and directly attached to the PDB.

   C. You must truncate the contents of the target table before using the direct load method.

   D. Using the control file parameter `DIRECT=TRUE`, SQL*Loader will utilize the data file as an external table and load it into memory to provide direct access for the user's SQL statements, thus greatly improving performance.

   E. None of the above.

10. When using SQL*Loader in express mode, you need to specify which of the following?

    A. A control file

    B. A parameter file

    C. A variable-length data file

    D. The name of the source data file

    E. None of the above

11. Which of these is true regarding audit operations?

    A. Auditing rules always apply to the entire CDB.

    B. Common auditing policies override local auditing policies.

    C. Common audit policies apply to all objects in all PDBs and the CDB.

    D. Audit policies are by default local to the current PDB.

    E. None of the above.

12. Which of the following is true regarding audit policies and Data Pump jobs?

    A. You must specify `COMPONENT=DATAPUMP` when creating the audit policy.

    B. You must specify `EXPORT` and `IMPORT` separately when creating audit policies.

    C. By default the audit policy applies to both `EXPORT` and `IMPORT`.

    D. The unified audit trail is used only when you specify `COMPONENT=DATAPUMP UNIFIED`.

    E. None of the above.

13. Regarding auditing SQL*Loader, which of the following is true?

    A. By default all SQL*Loader conventional path loads are audited.

    B. By default all SQL*Loader direct path loads are audited.

    C. Only direct path loads can be audited.

    D. None of the above.

14. Which of the following accurately describes Oracle Database Vault?

   A. It is an excellent backup and recovery tool.

   B. It stores user passwords in a secret location, away from system administrators.

   C. It protects the primary database from failure.

   D. It secures application data from superusers.

15. Oracle Database Vault relies on which of the following roles? (Choose all that apply.)

   A. DV_OWNER

   B. DV_ADMIN

   C. DV_ADMINISTRATOR

   D. DV_ACCTMGR

16. When creating a physical standby of a CDB, which of the following must be considered? (Choose all that apply.)

   A. Each PDB functions independently as a primary or standby.

   B. The entire CDB and all its PDBs are in the same role, either primary or standby.

   C. When you fail over the primary to a standby, each PDB must be failed over separately.

   D. When you fail over the primary to a standby, each PDB will fail over automatically.

   E. None of the above.

17. When you create a PDB in a primary CDB, what must you also do in each associated standby CDB?

   A. Do nothing. Data Guard always keeps the physical standby databases synchronized with the primary.

   B. You must clone the primary PDB to the standby CDBs.

   C. You must copy the PDB data files to the standby prior to plugging in the PDB in the primary.

   D. All of the above.

   E. None of the above.

18. When copying files to the standby database and prior to plugging in a PDB at the primary, if the files are not in ASM, which parameter can you use to make sure the filenames are in the correct location?

   A. DB_FILE_NAME_CONVERT

   B. PDB_CONVERT_FILE_NAME

   C. PDB_FILE_NAME_CONVERT

   D. PDB_CLONE_FILE_NAME

   E. None of the above

19. Which of the following are uses for LogMiner? (Choose all that apply.)

   A. Determine when logical corruption occurred.

   B. Determine how you would perform fine-grained recovery.

   C. Determine which tables get the most or fewest updates and inserts.

   D. Track DML and DDL by username and time.

   E. All of the above.

20. Which of the following are requirements for LogMiner? (Choose all that apply.)

   A. Supplemental logging must be enabled.

   B. A LogMiner dictionary.

   C. For a PDB, you can use a flat file dictionary to mine the contents of that PDB.

   D. Redo log files.

   E. All of the above.

Chapter

14

Oracle Security in CDBs and PDBs

ORACLE DATABASE 12*c*: ADVANCED ADMINISTRATION EXAM OBJECTIVES COVERED IN THIS CHAPTER:

- Manage Security in a CDB and PDBs
- Manage common and local users
- Manage common and local privileges
- Manage common and local roles
- Enable common users to access data in specific PDBs

In this chapter we will focus on security considerations in the Oracle Database 12c multitenant architecture. We will discuss managing common and local users, common and local privileges, and common and local roles. We will also enable common users to access data in specific PDBs.

The first topic is about managing common and local users in the multitenant environment. In previous chapters, we defined common and local users, and you learned how to create them. In this chapter, we will expand on what you've learned and demonstrate how to manage the environment.

Next, we will discuss common and local privileges, which we have not discussed at length previously, so in this chapter, we'll present more detail. Then we'll discuss common and local roles, which have been implied in previous chapter examples but will be further explained here.

Finally, we will explain and provide examples of how common users can access data in specific PDBs.

Exam objectives are subject to change at any time without prior notice and at Oracle's sole discretion. Please visit Oracle's Training and Certification website (http://www.oracle.com/education/certification/) for the most current exam-objectives listing.

Managing Security in a CDB and PDBs

In the new Oracle Database 12c multitenant architecture, where the multitenant container database (CDB) can host zero, one, or many DBA-created pluggable databases (PDBs), there are a few key differences between CDBs and non-CDBs regarding the creation and management of users, privileges, and roles. In the following sections, we'll provide narrative for and examples of each of these subjects.

It is important to understand the span of access that a user has in the multitenant environment:

Common Users Common users, as discussed in previous chapters, are defined in the CDB and have access across the PDBs.

Local Users Local users are defined for one PDB within a CDB.

We'll discuss in detail how to create common and local users and provide several examples.

A user *privilege* is the authority or right to run a PL/SQL package, a particular type of SQL statement, or access an object that belongs to another user. Privileges can be granted to common or local users.

A *role* is a named group of privileges and/or other roles that are created by administrators or other users. Roles simplify the administration of privileges for individuals and groups of users. We'll explore roles in detail later in this chapter.

Managing Common and Local Users

In the multitenant environment, a user is either a common user, which has access to all containers in the CDB, or a local user, which has access only to the PDB in which it was created. In the context of a CDB, the word *common* is used to indicate that some entity is common to all containers. In this context, *local* means that an entity is restricted to exactly one container.

Common Users   A common user is a database user who has the same username and password in the root and in every PDB in the CDB.

Local Users   A local user is defined in a PDB and does not have access to the CDB$ROOT or other PDBs, very much like a user in a non-CDB.

In this section, we will explain the difference between common and local user accounts in the multitenant environment. We will describe how to create users and provide examples. We will discuss the current container and scope. We will also provide examples of altering common and local users.

In Chapter 11, "Introduction to and Creation of Oracle Multitenant Databases," we demonstrate how to create CDBs and PDBs. The exercises in this chapter assume that you have created a CDB and PDBs.

The Common Users in a CDB

A common user is a CDB user that has the same identity in CDB$ROOT and in all PDBs and can connect to and perform operations in the root and in any PDB where they have CREATE SESSION privileges. SYS and SYSTEM, as well as the other Oracle-supplied administrative accounts, are examples of common users that are created with each CDB. A common user has the following characteristics:

- Other than Oracle-supplied administrative accounts, the username begins with the characters c## or C##.

- The username contains only ASCII or EBCDIC characters.

- The user resides in the root and uses the same identity to connect to every PDB.

- The schema associated with a common user can be different in each PDB.

It is not essential for a common user to have the same privileges in every PDB. We will demonstrate how to create a common user account later in this chapter.

The ability to create, modify, or delete CDB-wide attributes of a common user or role is restricted to a common user connected to the root. A common user with appropriate privileges can switch between containers and administer PDBs from the root. With the appropriate privileges, the common user can perform operations in PDBs such as granting privileges to local users, which will be discussed later in this chapter.

A common user can plug in and unplug, start up, shut down, and change the read-write state for a PDB. With the right privileges, a common user can specify temporary tablespaces for the CDB. A common user can perform the following operations across PDBs:

▪ Grant privileges to common roles or common users

▪ Recover a CDB using the ALTER DATABASE statement

▪ Execute an ALTER PLUGGABLE DATABASE command while connected to the CDB$ROOT

A common user may switch between PDBs and will use the privileges that are granted to that user in the current PDB. In an Oracle Database Vault environment, the Database Vault restrictions for a PDB apply to the common user when connected to the PDB.

Oracle recommends that you do not change the privileges of the Oracle-supplied common users. You can grant different privileges in each PDB to user-created common users.

Plugging in a PDB and Common Users

One of the nice features of the multitenant architecture is that you can plug in a non-CDB from a previous or current release of the Oracle Database into a CDB as a PDB. This presents an interesting scenario because the non-CDB does not have local or common users, only non-CDB users. If you plug in a non-CDB, the following user translation occurs:

▪ Oracle-supplied administrative accounts such as SYS and SYSTEM are merged with the common user accounts of the CDB.

▪ The passwords of the existing common user accounts are not overwritten.

▪ Modified privileges of a user account apply as locally granted privileges only in the plugged-in PDB and not in any other PDBs.

If a PDB from another source CDB contains a common user and you plug it into a target CDB, then these translations occur:

▪ Common user privileges for these common user accounts in this PDB are not brought over from the source CDB.

▪ If the new PDB has common users who already exist in the target CDB, then the new common user is merged with the target common user, and the target common user password is retained.

▪ If the new PDB has common users who are not defined in the target CDB, then the new common user accounts are locked.

If the new PDB contains common user accounts that are locked because the common user has not been created in the root, you can shut down the new PDB, connect to the root, create common users with the same name as the new PDB common users, and then reopen the new PDB. There's no impact to the privileges and roles that were granted locally to the common users.

The Local Users in a CDB

The local user is not a common user but is local to a specific PDB and can operate in only a single PDB. A user who has the CREATE USER role or greater within a PDB, including common users, can create local users. A local user has the following characteristics:

- The username may not begin with the characters c## or C##.

- The local user is unique in a particular PDB and owns a schema in the same PDB.

- The local user can't be created in the root.

- The local user can't log on to another PDB or to the root.

- If granted privileges, the local user can access objects in a common-user schema in the same PDB.

- If given appropriate privileges, the local user may execute an ALTER PLUGGABLE DATABASE command.

 Chapter 12, "Managing Oracle Multitenant Databases," introduces the concepts of the common and local users, and setting the current container for a session.

The CONTAINER Clause

When you create a new user, the CONTAINER clause differentiates the local user from the common user. If you want to create a common user, make sure your current container is CDB$ROOT and use CONTAINER=ALL when issuing the CREATE USER statement. This is the default if you're logged into CDB$ROOT.

If you want to create a local user in a PDB, set your current container to the PDB and use the CONTAINER=CURRENT clause. This is the default if you're logged into a PDB.

You do not have the option to name a PDB in the CONTAINER clause; it's named either CURRENT or ALL.

When creating a common user, the DEFAULT TABLESPACE, TEMPORARY TABLESPACE, QUOTA, and PROFILE specified must exist in all the containers belonging to the CDB.

The current container is where the current session is running, and each session can have only one current container at any point in time. It can be the root for common users or a PDB for local and common users. Each container has a separate data dictionary, so the current container data dictionary is used for privilege authorization and name resolution.

Granting the Authority to Create User Accounts

Users who have been granted the CREATE USER system privilege can create user accounts. To create common users in the multitenant environment you must have the CREATE USER system privilege. For a common user to create a local user in a PDB, they must have the CREATE USER privilege either granted as a common privilege or granted as a local privilege in the PDB. When you create the user, the current container must be the target PDB.

As the DBA, you can grant CREATE USER to a local or common user and grant CREATE SESSION so that they may log on to the target database. If you grant CREATE USER and CREATE SESSION and include the WITH ADMIN OPTION to a common or local user, that user can then create users and grant them the privilege to log on.

Creating a New User Account

If you have the CREATE USER system privilege, you can create a database user with the CREATE USER statement. This system privilege should be restricted to the database administrator, security administrator, and in some cases, a local PDB application administrator.

Following is an example of how to create a local user account, specifying the password, default tablespace, temporary tablespace, and quota on a tablespace. We also grant this new user the privilege to log on to the PDB.

```
SQL> ALTER SESSION SET CONTAINER=lne6;
SQL> CREATE USER lne_nd
  2   IDENTIFIED BY cgyoomm
  3   DEFAULT TABLESPACE user_data
  4   QUOTA 1G ON example
  5   TEMPORARY TABLESPACE temp
  6   CONTAINER = CURRENT;

User created.
SQL>
```

By default, a newly created user cannot log onto the database. You must grant the CREATE SESSION system privileges or a role that includes the system privilege to the new user, and then they'll be able to log on. Roles and privileges will be discussed more later in this chapter.

```
SQL> GRANT CREATE SESSION TO lne_nd;

Grant succeeded.

SQL>
```

Specifying a Username for a Local User

A local username must be unique within a PDB. A user and a role cannot have the same name within a PDB. Also, a local username cannot start with c## or C##; that prefix identifies a common username. And there is a schema associated with each username. As defined previously, a schema is a collection of objects associated with a username. Within a user's schema, each object must have a unique name.

```
SQL> ALTER SESSION SET CONTAINER=lne6;
SQL> CREATE USER lne_nd
  2   IDENTIFIED BY cgyoomm
  3   DEFAULT TABLESPACE user_data
  4   QUOTA 1G ON example
  5   TEMPORARY TABLESPACE temp
  6   CONTAINER = CURRENT;

User created.

SQL>
```

The new username is stored in the database in uppercase letters, unless you enclose the username in double quotes; then it will be stored in case-sensitive text, as shown in this query of the DBA_USERS data dictionary view. Quoted identifiers are accepted by SQL*Plus but may be invalid with other tools that access database objects.

```
SQL> CREATE USER "local_sample" IDENTIFIED BY password;

User created.

SQL>
SQL> SELECT USERNAME FROM DBA_USERS WHERE COMMON='NO';

USERNAME
-------------------------------------------------------


LNE_ND
HR
local_sample
LNE6_ADMIN

SQL>
```

Assigning a Profile for the User

When you create a user you can assign a profile, which is a set of limits on password access and database resources. The Oracle Database assigns the user a default profile if you do not specify one. In this example, we create a new profile and then create a new user and include the PROFILE clause.

```
SQL> CREATE PROFILE password_reuse
  2  LIMIT PASSWORD_REUSE_MAX 5
  3  PASSWORD_REUSE_TIME 60;

Profile created.

SQL> CREATE USER smith06
  2  IDENTIFIED BY smith06
  2  PROFILE password_reuse;

User created.

SQL>
```

Creating Common Users

To create a common user account, you must have the CREATE USER system privilege, and the current container must be CDB$ROOT. Here are a few guidelines when creating a common user:

- User account names are in the USERNAME column in the ALL_USERS, CDB_USERS, DBA_USERS, and USER_USERS data dictionary views. Common users are indicated by the value YES in the COMMON column.

- Use the CONTAINER=ALL clause to create a common user. If you are logged into CDB$ROOT, the default for the CONTAINER clause is ALL.

- Creating objects in a common user's schemas can cause problems when plugging in or unplugging a PDB.

- When you create a common user and you use the DEFAULT TABLESPACE, TEMPORARY TABLESPACE, PROFILE, and QUOTA clauses, make sure that the tablespaces, tablespace groups, and profiles have been defined in all containers of the CDB. If the objects are not there, you'll get an error message and the user will not be created.

- Schema objects owned by Oracle-created common users (SYS, for example) are shared with the entire CDB. User-created schema objects owned by common users in a PDB cannot be shared with another PDB.

This example shows how to create a common user account by using the CONTAINER=ALL clause. You'll also grant the new user SET CONTAINER and CREATE SESSION privileges. These privileges are required for common users to navigate between containers.

```
SQL> ALTER SESSION SET CONTAINER=cdb$root;

Session altered.

SQL>
SQL> CREATE USER c##my_dba
  2  IDENTIFIED BY secret
  3  DEFAULT TABLESPACE user_data
  4  QUOTA 1G ON user_data
  5  TEMPORARY TABLESPACE temp
  6  CONTAINER = ALL;

User created.

SQL> GRANT SET CONTAINER, CREATE SESSION TO c##my_dba CONTAINER = ALL;

Grant succeeded.

SQL>
```

Creating Local Users

Since we've already created local users in previous examples, we'll just expand on the concepts previously present. As mentioned, to create a local user you must be connected to the PDB and have the CREATE USER privilege. The local username must not start with C## or c##. The CONTAINER=CURRENT clause in the CREATE USER statement is implied when you create a local user.

```
SQL> ALTER SESSION SET CONTAINER=lne6;

Session altered.

SQL> SHOW CON_NAME

CON_NAME
------------------
LNE6
```

```
SQL> CREATE USER another_user IDENTIFIED BY another;

User created.

SQL>
```

It is not permitted to have common users and local users with the same name; this is enforced by the common user naming requirement. You can use the same name for local users in different PDBs. To find the names of existing user accounts, query the ALL_USERS, CDB_USERS, DBA_USERS, and USER_USERS data dictionary views. This example repeats the previous examples of how to create a local user and includes the CONTAINER=CURRENT clause.

```
SQL> ALTER SESSION SET CONTAINER=lne6;

Session altered.

SQL> CREATE USER lne_nd_n
  2  IDENTIFIED BY cgyoomm
  3  DEFAULT TABLESPACE user_data
  4  QUOTA 1G ON example
  5  TEMPORARY TABLESPACE temp
  6  CONTAINER = CURRENT;

User created.

SQL> GRANT CREATE SESSION to lne_nd_n;

Grant succeeded.

SQL>
```

Again, if you have the appropriate privileges as either a common or local user connected to a PDB, you can create local user accounts.

Default Role for a User

A role is a named group of related privileges that you grant to users or other roles. You can assign zero or more default roles to a user. When you create a user, the default role setting for the user is ALL, which means that roles granted to the user will automatically be default roles. When a user creates a session, their default roles are automatically enabled.

Use the ALTER USER statement to change the default roles for the user, for example:

```
SQL> CREATE ROLE lne_boss;
```

```
Role created.

SQL> GRANT lne_boss TO lne_nd, smith06;

Grant succeeded.

SQL> ALTER USER lne_nd DEFAULT ROLE lne_boss;

User altered.

SQL>
```

You must grant a role to a user before you can make that role a default role for that user.

Altering Common or Local User Accounts Using the ALTER USER Statement

Use the ALTER USER statement to alter a common or local user in a multitenant environment. Once a user is created as a local user or common user, you cannot alter it to become the other type.

You can, however, grant common users access to objects in PDBs. In this example, we'll use the ALTER USER statement to alter the common user c##my_dba, created in a previous example, so that this user can access the contents of the V$SESSION view in the PDBs PDB1, PDB2, and LNE6 when logged into CDB$ROOT.

```
SQL> CONNECT sys/system@CONT as SYSDBA
Connected.
SQL> ALTER USER c##my_dba
  3   QUOTA 2G ON user_data
  4   SET CONTAINER_DATA = (cdb$root, pdb1, pdb2, lne6)
  5   FOR V$SESSION CONTAINER = CURRENT;

User altered.

SQL>
```

If you do not include the current container (in this case CDB$ROOT), you will receive an ORA-65057 error message. The ALTER USER statement in this example modifies the settings for the user c##my_dba as follows:

QUOTA 2G   This setting gives the user up to 2 G of space on the user_data tablespace.

SET CONTAINER_DATA   This setting lets user c##my_dba see the active sessions in the PDB1, PDB2, and LNE6 PDBs, as well as the root when they query the V$SESSION view from the root.

```
SQL> CONNECT C##my_dba/secret
Connected.
SQL> SELECT SID, USERNAME, CON_ID
  2   FROM V$SESSION
  3   WHERE USERNAME IS NOT NULL
  4   ORDER BY CON_ID, USERNAME, SID
  5   /

       SID USERNAME                            CON_ID
---------- ------------------------------- ----------
        11 C##MY_DBA                                1
       253 LNE6_ADMIN                               6

SQL>
```

In Exercise 14.1, we will step through the process to create common and local users. We will also attempt to create users that violate the rules for common and local users, resulting in ORA errors.

EXERCISE 14.1

Creating Common and Local Users

In this exercise you will create common users and local users.

1. Launch a command-line window:

   a. From the Windows Start menu, search for "CMD" or press the Windows command button and the R key simultaneously and then enter **CMD**.

   b. At the C:\> prompt, specify an instance identifier (SID), unique to this server and database domain, for the container database you wish to connect to.

   ```
   C:\ set ORACLE_SID=CONT
   ```

2. Set the required environment variables. ORACLE_HOME is required on some operating systems.

   ```
   C:\ set ORACLE_HOME= C:\Oracle\product\12.1.0\dbhome_2
   ```

3. Connect to the root of the CDB specified by the ORACLE_SID, with user SYS as SYSDBA, using OS authentication.

   ```
   C:\>sqlplus / as sysdba
   ```

```
SQL*Plus: Release 12.1.0.1.0 Production on Fri Nov 29 12:36:18 2013

Copyright (c) 1982, 2013, Oracle.  All rights reserved.

Connected to:
Oracle Database 12c Enterprise Edition Release 12.1.0.1.0 - 64bit Production
With the Partitioning, OLAP, Advanced Analytics and Real Application Testing
options

SQL> SHOW USER
USER is "SYS"
SQL> SHOW CON_NAME

CON_NAME
---------
CDB$ROOT
SQL>
```

4. Create a common user in the CDB$ROOT.

```
SQL> CREATE USER c##my_user
  2  IDENTIFIED BY secret
  3  DEFAULT TABLESPACE user_data
  4  QUOTA 1G ON user_data
  5  TEMPORARY TABLESPACE temp
  6  CONTAINER = ALL;

User created.
SQL>
```

5. Attempt to create a local user in the CDB$ROOT. This will fail.

```
SQL> CREATE USER local_user
  2  IDENTIFIED BY cgyoomm
  3  DEFAULT TABLESPACE user_data
  4  QUOTA 1G ON example
  5  TEMPORARY TABLESPACE temp
  6  CONTAINER = CURRENT;
IDENTIFIED BY cgyoomm
              *
ERROR at line 2:
ORA-65049: creation of local user or role is not allowed in CDB$ROOT

SQL>
```

6. Switch to a container PDB and attempt to create a common user. This will fail.

```
SQL> ALTER SESSION SET CONTAINER=lne6;

Session altered.

SQL>
SQL> CREATE USER c##another_user
  2    IDENTIFIED BY cgyoomm
  3    DEFAULT TABLESPACE user_data
  4    QUOTA 1G ON example
  5    TEMPORARY TABLESPACE temp
  6    CONTAINER = CURRENT;
CREATE USER c##another_user
            *
ERROR at line 1:
ORA-65094: invalid local user or role name

SQL>
```

7. Now attempt to create a local user. This will succeed.

```
SQL> CREATE USER local_user
  2    IDENTIFIED BY cgyoomm
  3    DEFAULT TABLESPACE user_data
  4    QUOTA 1G ON example
  5    TEMPORARY TABLESPACE temp
  6    CONTAINER = CURRENT;

User created.

SQL>
```

Managing Common and Local Privileges

A user privilege is the authority or right to run a PL/SQL package, a particular type of SQL statement, or access an object that belongs to another user. Privileges can be granted to common or local users.

Grant privileges to users so that they can accomplish specific tasks within the database. Grant privileges only to users who require the specific privileges necessary to accomplish their tasks. Granting too many privileges can create security issues. Never grant SYSDBA or SYSOPER privilege to users who are not administrators. You should grant privileges to roles and not to specific users since roles allow for an easier and better way to manage privileges.

The following are the general types of privileges in the Oracle database:

System Privileges   These allow the grantee to perform standard administrator tasks in the database. Restrict them to trusted users.

Roles   As previously described, a role groups privileges and roles so that they can more easily be granted to and revoked from users.

Table Privileges   These privileges enable security on DML or DDL.

View Privileges   As with tables, you can apply DML object privileges to views.

Procedure Privileges   You can grant the EXECUTE privilege to procedures in packages and standalone procedures and functions.

Type Privileges   You can grant system privileges to named object types, VARRAYs, and nested tables.

Privileges in the Oracle Multitenant Environment

In the multitenant environment, a user can exercise privileges only in the current container; that is, actions that require privileges have local scope. The exception is for common users who have been granted common privileges to execute operations such as CREATE USER, CREATE ROLE, ALTER USER, and ALTER PLUGGABLE DATABASE.

If a common user has been granted privileges to the CDB views and V$ views and the CONTAINER_DATA attribute has been set for the target PDBs, then the user will be able to see information about PDBs when connected to the CDB$ROOT, as noted in previous examples. Otherwise, the common user cannot query tables or views in a PDB unless using a DB_LINK to which adequate privileges have been granted.

If a common user has the SET CONTAINER privilege, then they can set their current container to a different PDB and exercise privileges in that PDB.

```
SQL> SHOW USER
USER is "C##MY_DBA"
SQL> SHOW CON_NAME

CON_NAME
------------------------------
CDB$ROOT
SQL> SELECT * FROM hr.countries;
SELECT * FROM hr.countries
                  *
ERROR at line 1:
ORA-00942: table or view does not exist

SQL> ALTER SESSION SET CONTAINER=lne6;

Session altered.
```

```
SQL> SELECT * FROM hr.countries;

CO COUNTRY_NAME                              REGION_ID
-- ---------------------------------------- ----------
AR Argentina                                        2
AU Australia                                        3
BE Belgium                                          1
BG Bangladesh                                       3
BR Brazil                                           2
CA Canada                                           2
CH Switzerland                                      1
CN China                                            3
DE Germany                                          1
DK Denmark                                          1
EG Egypt                                            4
FR France                                           1
IL Israel                                           4
IN India                                            3
IT Italy                                            1
JP Japan                                            3
KW Kuwait                                           4
ML Malaysia                                         3
MX Mexico                                           2
MY Myanmar                                          3
NG Nigeria                                          4
NL Netherlands                                      1
NP Nepal                                            3
SG Singapore                                        3
SY Syria                                            4
TK Turkey                                           4
UK United Kingdom                                   1
UR Uruguay                                          2
US United States of America                         2
VT The Vatican                                      1
ZM Zambia                                           4
ZW Zimbabwe                                         4

32 rows selected.

SQL>
```

Commonly Granted Privileges

It's important to remember that in a multitenant environment a privilege is neither common nor local, but a privilege can be granted commonly or locally, and that common users and local users can grant privileges to each other. In the context of the multitenant environment, the term "commonly granted" means that the privilege or role was granted to a common user. Also, the following statements apply:

- A privilege that is granted commonly applies to all existing containers and future PDBs.

- Common users grant privileges commonly to common users or to common roles.

- When granting a common privilege the user is connected to the CDB$ROOT container and uses the CONTAINER=ALL clause in the GRANT statement.

- System and object privileges can be commonly granted.

- A common user's ability to perform activities in the current container is controlled by both locally granted and commonly granted privileges.

- You must not grant privileges to the PUBLIC role commonly, because this will make the role available to all users.

Commonly Granted System Privileges

System privileges granted commonly apply in the root and in all PDBs when the following requirements are met:

- The privilege grantor is a common user and the grantee is a common user or role, or PUBLIC.

- The GRANT statement contains the CONTAINER=ALL clause.

- The common user has been granted the common system privilege with the ADMIN OPTION.

Do not commonly grant system privileges to the PUBLIC role, as mentioned previously.

Here's an example of a common user granting a system privilege to another common user while connected to the root.

```
SQL> CONNECT sys/system@CONT AS SYSDBA
Connected.

SQL> GRANT CREATE ANY TABLE TO c##my_dba CONTAINER=ALL;

Grant succeeded.

SQL>
```

Commonly Granted Object Privileges

An object privilege on a common object applies to that object and metadata links or object links that are associated with it in CDB$ROOT and in PDBs that the grantor has privileges to connect to, if the following requirements are met:

- A common privilege may not be granted or revoked on a local object.
- The grantor must be a common user and the grantee is a common user, a common role, or the PUBLIC role.
- The grantor has been granted the GRANT OPTION for the granted privilege.
- The CONTAINER=ALL clause must be included in the GRANT statement.

This example shows how a common user can grant an object privilege commonly to the common user c##my_dba so that they may select from dba_tables in the current container. Notice that the c##my_dba user has privileges on dba_views in the CDB$ROOT but does not have privileges on dba_views in the PDB.

```
SQL> CONNECT sys/system@CONT AS SYSDBA
Connected.
SQL> SHOW CON_NAME

CON_NAME
------------------------------
CDB$ROOT
SQL> GRANT SELECT ON DBA_TABLES TO C##MY_DBA CONTAINER=ALL;

Grant succeeded.

SQL> GRANT SELECT ON DBA_VIEWS TO C##MY_DBA CONTAINER=ALL;

Grant succeeded.

SQL> connect C##my_dba/secret@CONT
Connected.
SQL> SELECT COUNT(1) FROM dba_tables;

  COUNT(1)
----------
      2317

SQL> SELECT COUNT(1) FROM dba_views;
```

```
   COUNT(1)
----------
      6179

SQL> ALTER SESSION SET CONTAINER=lne6;

Session altered.

SQL> SELECT COUNT(1) FROM dba_views;
SELECT COUNT(1) FROM dba_VIEWS
                       *
ERROR at line 1:
ORA-00942: table or view does not exist


SQL> SELECT COUNT(1) FROM dba_tables;

   COUNT(1)
----------
      2336

SQL>
```

Managing Local Privileges

A local privilege is a privilege that applies only to the PDB in which it is granted. Local privileges in a PDB are synonymous with privileges in a non-CDB. Privileges are applied to a common user or local user and apply to local objects. For a locally granted privilege, the following rules apply:

- It can be used only in the container in which it was granted.
- If granted in the CDB$ROOT, it applies only to the root.
- Common users and local users can grant privileges locally to any other user or role, including the PUBLIC role.
- When granting a local privilege the user is connected to the current container and can use the CONTAINER=CURRENT clause in the GRANT statement.

You can log onto the PDB and grant local privileges to a local user and also to common users, as in this example:

```
SQL> CONNECT lne6_admin/system06@lne6
SQL> GRANT SELECT ON hr.countries TO lne_nd CONTAINER=CURRENT;
```

```
Grant succeeded.

SQL> GRANT SELECT ON hr.countries TO c##my_dba;

Grant succeeded.

SQL>
```

A user can exercise a local system privilege only within the PDB in which it is granted.

Managing Common and Local Roles

A role is a named group of privileges and/or other roles that are created by administrators or other users. Roles simplify the administration of privileges for individuals and groups of users. Managing privileges is much easier when you group them into named groups of related privileges and then grant them to users or other roles. In a non-CDB, a role name may not have the same name as a username or another role; it must be unique. This is also true within a PDB. You may use the same role name in different PDBs, but they're independent of each other. A role is not associated with a specific user schema, so if a user creates a role and then the user is dropped, the role persists independently of the user who created it.

In the following sections, we will introduce the concept of the role and how to create, grant, revoke, and drop roles. Once you have a good grasp on what a role is, we'll introduce common and local roles and creating, granting, altering, and revoking common and local roles.

About Roles

In this section, we will discuss roles in general. Roles are the preferred method for managing user permissions. You can use Oracle-defined roles and create roles of your own that contain the privileges that you need to grant to others. Once you understand roles and privileges and how to manage a user base, you'll truly appreciate the flexibility and usefulness of roles.

You can grant system or object privileges to a role, and you can grant roles to any database user. You can grant roles to other roles, but circular references are not allowed.

```
SQL> create role cross_pdb_role;

Role created.

SQL> create role cross_pdb_role2;

Role created.

SQL> create role cross_pdb_role3;

Role created.
```

```
SQL> grant cross_pdb_role to cross_pdb_role2;

Grant succeeded.

SQL> grant cross_pdb_role2 to cross_pdb_role3;

Grant succeeded.

SQL> grant cross_pdb_role3 to cross_pdb_role;

grant cross_pdb_role3 to cross_pdb_role
*
ERROR at line 1:
ORA-01934: circular role grant detected

SQL>
```

You can indirectly grant a role by granting a role to a role that has already been granted to a user, if the indirectly granted role is not password authenticated or a secure application role.

As mentioned in an earlier section, you can make a directly granted role a default role by using the ALTER USER statement, DEFAULT ROLE clause. You can query the DBA_ROLE_PRIVS data dictionary view to see roles that have been directly granted to a user. The ROLE_ROLE_PRIVS view shows roles that have been granted to roles.

Password-authenticated and secure application roles, discussed shortly, can be default roles or granted indirectly to a user.

Managing Roles

If you have the CREATE ROLE system privilege, you can create a role using the CREATE ROLE statement. Since the CREATE ROLE privilege is very powerful, only security administrators should have this system privilege. When you create a role it has no privileges associated with it, so you'll need to grant privileges or other roles to it afterward.

Role Authentication

Roles can be authorized by the database using a password, by an application using a package, or externally by the operating system, network, or other external source globally by an enterprise directory service.

The CREATE ROLE statement IDENTIFIED BY clause specifies how to authorize the user. If you specify NOT IDENTIFIED or do not specify IDENTIFIED BY, then no authorization is required by the role. Here's an example showing how to create a role that is authorized by a password.

```
SQL> CREATE ROLE bigdata_analyst IDENTIFIED BY hadoop;
```

```
Role created.

SQL>
```

By default, a role is created without a password, as in this example.

```
SQL> CREATE ROLE webviewer;

Role created.

SQL>
```

Granting and Revoking Roles

A user with the GRANT ANY ROLE system privilege (SYS and SYSTEM, for example) can grant or revoke any role except a global role to or from other users or roles of the database.

You can grant system or object privileges or roles that you have the ADMIN OPTION on to a role or other users. The ADMIN OPTION allows administrative powers to be delegated. As mentioned previously, circular references are not allowed. Roles are granted by executing the GRANT statement and revoked by using the REVOKE statement. You also grant privileges to roles and revoke privileges from roles.

Use the SET ROLE statement to enable a secure role for a session. You cannot grant a password-authenticated, aka secured, role that has been created or altered by the IDENTIFIED BY, IDENTIFIED USING, or IDENTIFIED EXTERNALLY clause to a non-secure role.

Dropping Roles

You drop a role by executing the DROP ROLE SQL statement. You must have been granted the role with the ADMIN option or been granted the DROP ANY ROLE system privilege. When you drop a role the associated privileges and indirectly granted roles are immediately removed and reflected in that the user and roles that were granted the role will no longer have those privileges. Dropping a role automatically removes the role from the DBA_ROLES, USER_ROLES, and ROLE_ROLE_PRIVS views.

Dropping a role has no impact on the underlying objects that were granted access to through privileges within the role. The following statement drops the role WEBVIEWER:

```
SQL> DROP ROLE webviewer;

Role dropped.

SQL>
```

Common Roles and Local Roles

In a multitenant environment a common role's identity and password are created in the root, and the common role is known in all containers in the CDB. All Oracle-supplied roles are common roles.

A local role exists in and can be used only within a PDB. A local role does not have commonly granted privileges. Common users can create and grant common roles to other common and local users, either commonly or locally. When a common role is granted to a local user, the privileges of that common role apply only within the local user's PDB, since a local user doesn't have privileges in other containers.

Local users cannot create common roles, but if they have the correct privileges, they can grant common roles to common users as well as local users.

Common Roles

Common roles are visible in the CDB$ROOT and every PDB in a multitenant environment. Commonly granted privileges in a role apply to all PDBs where the grantor has connect privileges and the CDB$ROOT. You must be connected to the CDB$ROOT to create a common role. The grantor must have the commonly granted SET CONTAINER privilege and the ADMIN OPTION for the common role to be granted to others. When a common role contains privileges that are locally granted, these privileges apply only within the PDB in which they were granted.

The PUBLIC Role in the Multitenant Environment

Never grant privileges to PUBLIC commonly. As mentioned previously, this would grant that privilege to all users in the CDB. Oracle grants locally to the PUBLIC role, enabling you to revoke privileges or roles that have been granted to the PUBLIC role in each PDB as needed. Only grant privileges locally to the PUBLIC role.

Create, Modify, or Drop a Common Role

To create, alter, or drop common roles a common user must have the associated privileges CREATE ROLE, ALTER ROLE, or DROP ROLE commonly granted. Common users can create local roles in a PDB.

Creating a Common Role

When you create a common role, you must follow the same naming convention as for common users. Oracle-supplied roles such as AUDIT_VIEWER and DBA do not follow the pattern of other common roles that start with C## or c## and contain only ASCII or EDCDIC characters. When you create a common role, do so in the CDB$ROOT container. You may not create a common role while the current container is a PDB. You do not need to set CONTAINER=ALL when your current container is CDB$ROOT, and you can't specify CONTAINER=ALL when you're in a PDB.

This example creates the c##password_timeout common role, which has password authentication.

```
SQL> CONNECT sys/system@CONT AS SYSDBA
Connected.
SQL> SHOW CON_NAME

CON_NAME
------------------------------
CDB$ROOT
SQL> CREATE ROLE c##password_timeout IDENTIFIED BY secret CONTAINER=ALL;

Role created.

SQL>
```

Altering and Dropping a Common Role

This example alters the password for the c##password_timeout common role. After we alter the role, we'll drop it. We'll then create the role again because we will use it later in this chapter.

```
SQL> CONNECT sys/system@CONT AS SYSDBA
Connected.
SQL> SHOW CON_NAME

CON_NAME
------------------------------
CDB$ROOT
SQL> ALTER ROLE c##password_timeout IDENTIFIED BY pwdtimeout CONTAINER=ALL;

Role altered.

SQL>
SQL> DROP ROLE c##password_timeout;

Role dropped.

SQL> CREATE ROLE c##password_timeout IDENTIFIED BY secret CONTAINER=ALL;

Role created.

SQL>
```

Creating a Local Role

To create a local role you must have the CREATE USER privilege and be connected to the PDB. You may not create a local role in the CDB$ROOT. Local naming conventions apply, so the name of the local role may not start with C## or c##. Optionally, you may include CONTAINER=CURRENT in the CREATE ROLE statement to specify the role as a local role.

```
SQL> ALTER SESSION SET CONTAINER=lne6;

Session altered.

SQL> CREATE ROLE LOCAL_PASSWORD_MAINT CONTAINER=CURRENT;

Role created.
```

Having common roles and local roles with the same name is not permitted and is enforced by the naming conventions. You can reuse a local role name in different PDBs, and the roles are independent of each other. Query the CDB_ROLES and DBA_ROLES data dictionary views, selecting on COMMON = 'NO' to see the local roles.

```
SQL> SELECT * FROM dba_roles WHERE COMMON = 'NO';

ROLE                    PASSWORD AUTHENTICAT COM O
--------------------    -------- ----------- --- -
LNE_BOSS                NO       NONE        NO  N
LOCAL_PASSWORD_MAINT    NO       NONE        NO  N

SQL>
```

Granting and Revoking Common Roles and Local Roles

In the multitenant environment, common users can grant and revoke common roles to and from other common users and local users. Local users can grant common roles to a local or common user in a PDB but the scope of the grant is local, that is, it applies only in the current PDB.

The next example demonstrates granting the common user c##my_dba the c##password_timeout common role for use in all containers.

```
SQL> CONNECT sys/system@CONT AS SYSDBA
Connected.
SQL> GRANT c##password_timeout TO c##my_dba CONTAINER=ALL;

Role granted.

SQL>
```

Similarly, the next example shows how local user lne6_admin can grant the common user c##mydba the AUDIT_VIEWER and c##passord_timeout common roles for use within the lne6 PDB.

```
SQL> CONNECT lne6_admin/system06@lne6
SQL> GRANT AUDIT_VIEWER, c##password_timeout TO c##my_dba CONTAINER=CURRENT;

Grant succeeded.

SQL>
```

The next example shows how a local user lne6_admin can revoke a role from a PDB. Remember that in a PDB CONTAINER=CURRENT is implied.

```
SQL> CONNECT lne6_admin/system06@lne6
SQL> REVOKE lne_boss FROM smith06 CONTAINER=CURRENT;

Revoke succeeded.

SQL>
```

Enabling Common Users to Access Data in Specific PDBs

In the following sections, we will discuss how to set up common users to access data in PDBs. Since common users have by default the same identity across all containers in a multitenant CDB environment, you'll need to grant them the ability to set the current container and grant them access to specific objects within PDB schemas.

We'll first discuss how to grant common users privileges to create objects within PDBs. Next we'll discuss the CONTAINER_DATA concept, and finally we'll show how a common user can access objects related to PDBs in a common view.

Granting or Revoking Privileges to Create PDB Objects

To grant a privilege in a multitenant environment, include the CONTAINER clause in the GRANT or REVOKE statement. Setting CONTAINER to ALL applies the privilege to all existing and future containers; setting it to CURRENT applies the privilege to the local container only. The default value of the CONTAINER is implied to be common if you're a common user and the current container is CDB$ROOT; it is implied to be local if your current container is a PDB. So, when the current container is a PDB, the CONTAINER clause defaults to local, and the privilege applies to the local container. If you issue the GRANT or REVOKE statement from the CDB$ROOT, the privilege is granted or revoked commonly. Here's an example of granting a privilege to a common user that will allow that user to create a table in any PDB.

```
SQL> CONNECT sys/system@CONT AS SYSDBA
Connected.
```

```
SQL> SHOW CON_NAME

CON_NAME
-------------------------------
CDB$ROOT
SQL> GRANT CREATE TABLE TO c##my_dba CONTAINER=ALL;

Grant succeeded.

SQL> CONNECT c##my_dba/secret@CONT
Connected.
SQL> ALTER SESSION SET CONTAINER=lne6;

Session altered.

SQL> CREATE TABLE MY_TAB(X NUMBER, Y VARCHAR2(10));

Table created.

SQL>
```

Viewing Container Data from CDB$ROOT

In a multitenant environment, Oracle restricts access to the X$, V$, GV$, and CDB_ views so that they are not automatically available for all PDBs to a common user querying from the CDB$ROOT. Oracle Database provides access to these tables and views as container data objects. Oracle allows you to grant access on these container data objects to users by specifying the CONTAINER_DATA clause in the ALTER USER statement.

The CONTAINER_DATA column is present in the DBA_VIEWS and DBA_TABLES dictionary views, as well as the ALL_ and USER_ versions of the same. To find information about the CONTAINER_DATA attributes, query the CDB_CONTAINER_DATA data dictionary view, as in the following example:

```
SQL> SHOW con_name

CON_NAME
-------------------------------
CDB$ROOT
SQL> SELECT USERNAME, OWNER, OBJECT_NAME, ALL_CONTAINERS, CONTAINER_NAME
  2  FROM CDB_CONTAINER_DATA
  3  ORDER BY OBJECT_NAME;
```

```
USERNAME              OWNER     OBJECT_NAME          ALL CONTAINER_
--------------------  --------  -------------------- --- ----------
GSMADMIN_INTERNAL     SYS       CDB_SERVICES         Y
GSMADMIN_INTERNAL     SYS       GV_$ACTIVE_SERVICES  Y
C##MY_DBA             SYS       V$SESSION            N   LNE6
C##MY_DBA             SYS       V$SESSION            N   PDB1
C##MY_DBA             SYS       V$SESSION            N   CDB$ROOT
APPQOSSYS             SYS       V_$WLM_PCMETRIC      Y
SYSBACKUP                                            Y
SYS                                                  Y
SYSTEM                                               Y
DBSNMP                                               Y

10 rows selected.

SQL>
```

The results of the query show that the common user c##my_dba can view the contents of v$session for the containers CDB$ROOT, PDB1, and LNE6.

Common User Access to Data in PDBs

Previously we gave an example of granting common users access to objects in PDBs. In the example we used the ALTER USER statement to alter the common user c##my_dba so that this user can access the contents of the CDB_USERS view in the CDB$ROOT and in the PDB1 and LNE6 PDBs when logged into CDB$ROOT.

```
SQL> CONNECT sys/system@CONT as SYSDBA
Connected.
SQL> ALTER USER c##my_dba
  2   SET CONTAINER_DATA = (cdb$root, pdb1, lne6)
  3   FOR cdb_users CONTAINER = CURRENT;

User altered.

SQL>
```

If you do not include the current container (in this case CDB$ROOT), you will receive an ORA-65057 error message. The ALTER USER statement in this example modifies the settings for the user c##my_dba as follows: SET CONTAINER_DATA lets user c##my_dba see the common and local users in the CDB$ROOT and in the PDB1 and LNE6 PDBs when the user queries the CDB_USERS table from the root.

```
SQL> SELECT USERNAME, OWNER, OBJECT_NAME, ALL_CONTAINERS, CONTAINER_NAME
  2   FROM CDB_CONTAINER_DATA
```

```
  3  ORDER BY OBJECT_NAME;
USERNAME               OWNER     OBJECT_NAME            ALL CONTAINER_
--------------------   --------  --------------------   --- ----------
GSMADMIN_INTERNAL      SYS       CDB_SERVICES           Y
C##MY_DBA              SYS       CDB_USERS              N   CDB$ROOT
C##MY_DBA              SYS       CDB_USERS              N   PDB1
C##MY_DBA              SYS       CDB_USERS              N   LNE6
GSMADMIN_INTERNAL      SYS       GV_$ACTIVE_SERVICES    Y
C##MY_DBA              SYS       V$SESSION              N   LNE6
C##MY_DBA              SYS       V$SESSION              N   PDB1
C##MY_DBA              SYS       V$SESSION              N   CDB$ROOT
APPQOSSYS              SYS       V_$WLM_PCMETRIC        Y
SYSBACKUP                                               Y
SYS                                                     Y
SYSTEM                                                  Y
DBSNMP                                                  Y

13 rows selected.

SQL>
```

Now that c##my_dba can see the contents of the cdb_users view, here's an example of the truncated output:

```
SQL> SHOW USER
USER is "C##MY_DBA"
SQL> SHOW CON_NAME

CON_NAME
-------------------
CDB$ROOT
SQL> BREAK ON username
SQL> SELECT username, con_id
  2  FROM cdb_users
  3  ORDER BY username, con_id;

SQL> show user
USER is "SYS"
SQL> ALTER USER c##my_dba
  2  SET CONTAINER_DATA = (cdb$root, pdb1, lne6)
  3  FOR cdb_users CONTAINER = CURRENT;
```

```
User altered.

SQL> SELECT USERNAME, OWNER, OBJECT_NAME, ALL_CONTAINERS, CONTAINER_NAME
  2  FROM CDB_CONTAINER_DATA
  3  ORDER BY OBJECT_NAME;

USERNAME              OWNER    OBJECT_NAME          A CONTAINER_NAME
-------------------- -------- -------------------- - --------------------
GSMADMIN_INTERNAL     SYS      CDB_SERVICES         Y
C##MY_DBA             SYS      CDB_USERS            N PDB1
C##MY_DBA             SYS      CDB_USERS            N CDB$ROOT
C##MY_DBA             SYS      CDB_USERS            N LNE6
GSMADMIN_INTERNAL     SYS      GV_$ACTIVE_SERVICES  Y
C##MY_DBA             SYS      V$SESSION            N LNE6
C##MY_DBA             SYS      V$SESSION            N CDB$ROOT
APPQOSSYS             SYS      V_$WLM_PCMETRIC      Y
SYSTEM                                             Y
DBSNMP                                             Y
SYS                                                Y


USERNAME              OWNER    OBJECT_NAME          A CONTAINER_NAME
-------------------- -------- -------------------- - --------------------
SYSBACKUP                                          Y


12 rows selected.

SQL> connect c##my_dba/secret
Connected.
SQL> SHOW USER
USER is "C##MY_DBA"
SQL> SHOW CON_NAME

CON_NAME
------------------------------
CDB$ROOT
SQL> BREAK ON username
SQL> SELECT username, con_id
  2  FROM cdb_users
  3  ORDER BY username, con_id
  4  /
```

```
FROM cdb_users
     *
ERROR at line 2:
ORA-00942: table or view does not exist]
SQL>
…
USERNAME                 CON_ID
-------------------- ----------
XDB                           1
                              3
                              6
XS$NULL                       1
                              3
                              6
local_sample                  6

122 rows selected.

SQL>
```

Summary

In this chapter, you learned about Oracle Database 12c security and specifically how to manage security in a CDB and PDBs. You learned how to manage common and local users, common and local privileges, and common and local roles and how to enable common users to access data in PDBs.

The first topic was about managing common and local users in the multitenant environment. In this chapter, we expanded on what you learned in previous chapters and demonstrated how to manage users in the multitenant environment. You learned that common users are defined in the CDB$ROOT and have the same identity across all PDBs in the CDB. You learned that all user-created common users must have a username that begins with c## or C## and that when you create the user, you specify CONTAINER=ALL. You cannot create a common user when the current container is a PDB. You learned that local users are specific to a PDB, that they must be unique within a PDB, and that a local username can be repeated across PDBs but that each occurrence of the local username is independent of any other local user with the same name within the same CDB. A local username may not begin with c## or C##.

Next, we discussed common and local privileges. A user privilege is the authority or right to run a PL/SQL package, issue a particular type of SQL statement, or access an object that belongs to another user. Privileges can be granted to common or local users. Privileges determine who has access to what in an Oracle database and determine specific actions that a user may take, so guard privileges well. We introduced system, role, table, view, procedure, and type privileges. You learned that a common user can grant privileges commonly to common users or to common roles. You also learned that local privileges are granted locally and apply only to the current PDB.

Then we discussed common and local roles. You learned that a role is a named group of privileges and/or other roles that are created by administrators or other users. Roles simplify the administration of privileges for individuals and groups of users. Roles are created, granted, revoked, and dropped. Roles can be granted to users or to other roles. Common roles have the same naming conventions as common users, and a common role may not have the same name as a common user. Local roles are assigned locally and have local scope.

Finally, we explained and provided examples of how common users can access data in specific PDBs. We demonstrated granting privileges to common users as one way to directly access PDB objects. We introduced the concept of viewing container data as a common user from the CDB using the CONTAINER_DATA clause.

Exam Essentials

Understand how to create common users in the Oracle Database 12*c* multitenant environment.   Understand the naming conventions for common users. Understand that a common user has the same identity across all containers in a CDB.

Understand how to create local users in the Oracle Database 12*c* multitenant environment.   Know the naming convention for local users (and non-CDBs) and that local users with the same name in different PDBs are independent of each other.

Know how to create common privileges.   Understand the scope of commonly granted privileges.

Demonstrate how to create local privileges.   Understand the scope of locally granted privileges.

Demonstrate how to create common roles.   Understand that a role can be a group of privileges or other roles and that commonly granted roles apply across the CDB.

Understand how to create local roles.   Understand how to create local roles and that they are local to only one PDB.

Understand how common users can access data in specific PDBs.   Describe how to grant privileges to common users so that they can view data related to PDBs, and also so that they may create objects in PDBs.

Review Questions

1. In the Oracle 12*c* multitenant architecture, which of these are characteristics of a common user? (Choose all that apply.)

   A. Appears the same in a non-CDB or a CDB

   B. Appears the same in all PDBs in a CDB

   C. Can access only the CDB$ROOT

   D. Is Oracle-supplied only

   E. All of the above

2. Which of the following are not true about common and local users in a CDB? (Choose all that apply.)

   A. A common user is a database user who has the same username and password in the root and in every PDB in the CDB.

   B. A local user is defined in a PDB and does not have access to the CDB$ROOT or other PDBs, very much like a user in a non-CDB.

   C. A common user is a database user who has the same username in the root and in every PDB in the CDB, but their password may be different in each container.

   D. A local user is defined in every PDB and does not have access to the CDB$ROOT, very much like a user in a non-CDB.

3. Which of the following is true regarding a common user?

   A. A common user may have the same name as a common role, as long as they're not defined in the same container.

   B. Common users can change their passwords to be unique in each PDB.

   C. A common user can create a local user in the CDB$ROOT.

   D. A local user may create a common user in a PDB.

   E. None of the above

4. A local user account must comply with which of the following restrictions?

   A. All local users must be unique in a CDB.

   B. You must define local users from the CDB$ROOT as common users.

   C. A locally created user with the DBA role can shut down a CDB.

   D. None of the above

5. Which of the following is true regarding the CONTAINER clause?

A. CONTAINER=ALL is required when creating a common user.

B. CONTAINER=CURRENT is required when creating a common user.

C. CONTAINER=ALL is implied when creating a common user.

D. CONTAINER=CDB is the default for all common users.

E. None of the above

6. Local users have privileges to:

A. Access all objects in all PDBs.

B. Only local access to the PDB they were created in.

C. Share access with the same local username in another PDB, but only within the same CDB.

D. The CDB$ROOT.

E. None of the above

7. When plugging a non-CDB into a PDB, what happens to the non-CDB users?

A. Oracle-supplied administrative user accounts overwrite the target PDB local user accounts.

B. Oracle-supplied administrative user account passwords overwrite the target common user account passwords.

C. Non-CDB defined user accounts become common user accounts in the target CDB.

D. Non-CDB defined user accounts become local user accounts in the target PDB.

E. None of the above

8. A local user can switch from PDB1 to PDB2 using which of the following SQL*Plus commands?

A. ALTER USER SWITCH TO PDB2;

B. ALTER USER ENABLE PDB SWITCH;

C. ALTER SESSION SET CONTAINER=PDB2;

D. ALTER SESSION SET CONTAINER='PDB2';

E. None of the above

9. From an administrative perspective, which of the following is permitted when creating new users? (Choose all that apply.)

A. Local users can create local users.

B. Common users can create local users.

C. Local users can create common users.

D. Common users can create common users.

E. All of the above

10. Which of the following are permitted by local users with administrative privileges? (Choose all that apply.)

    A. They can create local users.

    B. They can shut down the PDB.

    C. They can alter the pluggable database.

    D. They can alter another pluggable database.

    E. None of the above

11. Which of the following are allowed by user privileges? (Choose all that apply.)

    A. The authority to run a PL/SQL package

    B. The authority to execute a particular type of SQL statement

    C. The authority to access an object that belongs to another user

    D. Granting to common or local users

    E. All of the above

12. Giving good advice to your security administrator is your specialty, so you recommend granting the SYSDBA privilege to all users. Is this a good idea?

    A. This is a good idea because it will make the DBA's job easier.

    B. This is a good idea because it will make the security administrator's life easier.

    C. This is a bad idea because now every user can drop objects and delete the database.

    D. This is a bad idea because every user can now shut down your database.

    E. None of the above

13. Which of the following are characteristics of commonly granted privileges? (Choose all that apply.)

    A. Commonly granted privileges apply to all existing and future PDBs.

    B. System and object privileges can be commonly granted.

    C. It's a good idea to grant common privileges to the PUBLIC role.

    D. None of the above

14. Which of the following accurately describes a local privilege?

    A. It can be used only in the container in which it was created.

    B. Only local users can grant local privileges.

    C. You can grant local privileges only to local users.

    D. None of the above

15. A role is a convenient way to group what? (Choose all that apply.)

    A. Roles

    B. Privileges

    C. Users

    D. Containers

16. A common role must abide by which of the following rules? (Choose all that apply.)

    A. It must use the same naming convention as local users.

    B. It must use the same naming convention as common users.

    C. It can be created in any container in the CDB.

    D. When granted, it applies to all containers in a CDB.

    E. None of the above

17. As the DBA, you pride yourself in making the lives of your developers and end users easier, so you think it's a good idea to grant CREATE ROLE to all users. Is this a good idea? (Choose all that apply.)

    A. This is a great idea, because now the security administrator will not have to worry about who has access to what.

    B. This is a bad idea because anyone can create any role, which could cause your security administrator extra work to manage the roles and associated privileges.

    C. This idea is neutral, because creating roles doesn't cause problems; it's the privileges associated with the roles that can cause security issues.

    D. All of the above.

    E. None of the above

18. One of the nice features of roles is that you can grant a role to another role. Which of the following is invalid? (Choose all that apply.)

    A. Granting a local role to a common role

    B. Granting role1 to role2 and role2 to role3

    C. Granting role1 to role2 and role2 to role1

    D. Granting a common role to a local role

    E. None of the above

19. Is it true that or false that granting privileges to a common user to create objects in any container is not permitted?

- **A.** True, because common users are for administrative purposes only.

- **B.** True, because local users should be allowed to create objects in only a local container.

- **C.** False, because common users can be granted privileges across PDBs with the CONTAINER=ALL clause.

- **D.** None of the above

20. Which of the following SQL statement sequences are invalid? (Choose all that apply.)

- **A.** `CREATE ROLE c##mydba IDENTIFIED BY mydba;`

  `CREATE USER c##mydba IDENTIFIED BY c##mydba;`

- **B.** `CREATE USER c##mydba IDENTIFIED BY mydba;`

  `CREATE ROLE "c##mydba" IDENTIFIED BY mydba;`

- **C.** `CREATE USER "c##mydba" IDENTIFIED BY mydba;`

  `CREATE ROLE c##mydba IDENTIFIED BY mydba;`

- **D.** `CREATE USER "c##mydba" IDENTIFIED BY mydba;`

  `CREATE ROLE "c##mydba" IDENTIFIED BY mydba;`

- **E.** All of the above

Appendix A

Answers to Review Questions

Chapter 1: Performing Oracle User-Managed Backups

1. C, F. The two logging modes that are available in Oracle are NOARCHIVELOG mode—which is the default—and ARCHIVELOG mode. In NOARCHIVELOG mode, the database does not create archived redo logs, and as a result the recovery options are fewer. In ARCHIVELOG mode, the database creates archived redo logs and this results in a much larger number of options.

2. C. You will have to wait until you can shut down the database since it's in NOARCHIVELOG mode. No other option will give you a backup that is recoverable.

3. B. The database should be in ARCHIVELOG mode.

4. B, E. B and E are the correct answers because ARCHIVELOG and NOARCHIVELOG are the two logging modes available in Oracle Database 12*c*.

5. A, C, D. A backup of any database in ARCHIVELOG mode should include the database data files (after they are put in backup mode), the archived redo logs, and the database control file.

6. A. The SCN is a number that represents a point in time in the database relative to transactions within a given database.

7. B, D. The ALTER DATABASE BACKUP CONTROLFILE TO TRACE command will create a trace file with the create controlfile commands inside that are needed to recreate the control file. The ALTER DATABASE BACKUP CONTROLFILE TO 'FILENAME' command will create a backup control file that can be used later to recover the control file should the database control file be lost.

8. A. The ALTER SYSTEM SWITCH LOGFILE command will cause a log file switch, and the log file that was the current log file will then be archived.

9. A, D. Any action that causes the database to shut down abnormally will cause instance recovery to occur when the database is restarted. Thus, a power failure of the database server or use of the SHUTDOWN ABORT command will force instance recovery to occur.

10. E. The FAST_START_MTTR_RECOVERY parameter is used to indicate to the Oracle database how much time to allow for instance recovery. Based on this parameter, the Database Writer process will write to the database data files at a rate that will try to match this target.

11. A, B. The DBWR and LGWR processes are critical to successful database operations and are also critical for backup and recovery purposes. The DBW process is responsible for writing changes that have occurred in the database in memory (the SGA) to the database data files. The LGWR process is responsible for writing from the redo log buffer to the online redo logs after a user issues a commit. The online redo log files then become the truly persistent representation of a committed transaction.

12. C. There is always some divergence between the state of the database persistently (reflected in the database data files) and the actual state of the database with respect to committed transactions (which is reflected in the online redo logs when applied to the database data files during a recovery). Instance recovery time is directly impacted by this divergence. The more recovery that has to be applied during an instance recovery, the longer it will take. The FAST_START_MTTR_RECOVERY parameter is used to indicate to the Oracle database how much time to allow for instance recovery. Based on this parameter, the Database Writer process will write to the database data files at a rate that will try to match this target.

13. A, E. The diagnostic destination directory contains files that are used to diagnose and correct database problems. Thus, the database trace files and the database alert log are contained in this directory structure.

14. C. To back up a database in ARCHIVELOG mode manually, you would want to put the tablespaces in backup mode. This is done most efficiently by using the ALTER DATABASE BEGIN BACKUP command. You would then back up the database data files and then use the ALTER DATABASE END BACKUP command to take all of the database data files out of hot backup mode. Then you would need to perform an online redo log switch and then back up the archived redo logs.

15. B, C. There are two kinds of backups. The first is a physical backup, which we discussed in this chapter a great deal. The second is a logical backup, which we will discuss in other chapters of this book.

16. A, B, D. A valid database backup in NOARCHIVELOG mode requires that you back up all of the database data files, the database online redo logs, and the database control files.

17. E. The V$DATABASE view column LOG_MODE indicates if the database is in NOARCHIVELOG mode or ARCHIVELOG mode.

18. E. The V$ARCHIVED_LOG view provides a list of each online redo log sequence number of that log file and if that log file has been archived. Recall that the online redo logs are used in a circular fashion. Each time an online redo log is used, a sequence number is assigned to the data being stored in that redo log. When the redo log file is switched, the redo log will be archived if the database is in ARCHIVELOG mode. The sequence number of that instance of the log file is what keeps the log file unique. When the online redo log is used again, it will be overwritten and a new sequence will be assigned to it. Thus, once an online redo log is overwritten, the only way to restore data contained in the previous redo log incarnation is to use the archived redo logs.

19. A, C. Previous to Oracle Database 12*c*, the database generally used a multiprocess architecture (with some exceptions). Oracle Database 12*c* provides the ability to use either a multiprocess architecture or a multithreaded architecture.

20. D. There is no ORCL process in the Oracle Database.

Chapter 2: Performing Oracle User-Managed Database Recoveries

1. B. Since the database is in NOARCHIVELOG mode, loss of a data file is going to require the recovery of the entire database. Therefore, you will need to shut down the database and restore it from the last cold backup along with the online redo logs and control files. You can then restart the database.

2. D. When you discover that you have lost an online redo log, and if the database is still up, the first action should be to checkpoint the database. This can serve to reduce the overall risk of data loss. After you checkpoint the database, you can then attempt to clear the online redo log. A backup afterward is highly recommended.

3. D. First, you would restore the missing data files. Notice in the question that there are two data files that were lost. Next, you would mount the database, and then you would recover the SYSTEM tablespace. Since it is the SYSTEM tablespace, you would not be able to open the database first. Then you would open the database with the ALTER DATABASE OPEN command.

4. E. If you lose one or more control files but at least one remains, you should shut down the database. Then use any remaining control file as the source to create new control-file copies for the control files that were lost. Then restart the database. No recovery is required in this situation.

5. A, B, D. You will need to have the database data files, the control files, and the online redo logs in place to be able to restore the database when it's in NOARCHIVELOG mode.

6. C. If the database has not shut down yet, you have an opportunity to preserve your data changes. Issue a checkpoint, which will flush dirty buffers to disk. Then shut down the database normally, if possible (SHUTDOWN, SHUTDOWN IMMEDIATE). You then should mount the database with the STARTUP MOUNT command followed by clearing and rebuilding the log file with the ALTER DATABASE CLEAR LOGFILE command. Finally, attempt to open the database with the ALTER DATABASE OPEN command.

7. A, B, C, D. Change-based recovery allows you to recover the database to a specific SCN. Cancel-based recovery provides the ability to cancel recovery after each archived redo log application. Time-based recovery provides the ability to recover the database up to a specific point in time. Sequence number–based recovery allows you to recover the database up to a specific log sequence number.

8. A, C, D. To perform a full recovery of the database in ARCHIVELOG mode, you would need the database data files, the archived redo logs, and a backup control file.

9. E. NOARCHIVELOG mode does not support any kind of point-in-time recovery of the Oracle Database.

10. C. You should first start the database in mount mode using the STARTUP MOUNT command. You then issue the ALTER DATABASE CLEAR UNARCHIVED LOGFILE command. This will clear the log file if it needs to be archived and recreate the online redo log group. If that command is successful, then you issue the ALTER DATABASE OPEN command. The last step, backing up the database, is very important since your previous backup will not be able to recover the database beyond the point of the cleared redo log sequence number. This is because you have skipped a redo log in the redo log stream.

11. A. You would first take the missing data file offline with the ALTER DATABASE DATAFILE 4 OFFLINE command. You should then restore the data files that have been lost. Then issue the RECOVER TABLESPACE USERS command to recover the USERS tablespace. Use the ALTER DATABASE DATAFILE 4 ONLINE command to bring the USERS tablespace online.

12. D. Since the online redo logs are intact, you will be able to use the NORESETLOGS version of the CREATE CONTROLFILE command.

13. B. Since the database is in NOARCHIVELOG mode, their request cannot be met because point-in-time recovery is supported only in ARCHIVELOG mode.

14. A, C. You can create a backup control file with the ALTER DATABASE BACKUP CONTROLFILE command. You can create a trace file that contains the CREATE CONTROLFILE command.

15. A. First, you would want to restore the three data files that were lost. Then you would want to issue the STARTUP MOUNT command to mount the database to prepare for recovery. You would then recover the database (you could opt to recover just the data files if you wished). Finally, open the database with the ALTER DATABASE OPEN command.

16. E. In this situation, you have gotten yourself in real trouble and you will have data loss. First, you will need to restore the last full database backup and also all archived redo logs that were generated during the backup and since the backup was completed. You will then issue the STARTUP MOUNT command to mount the database, and then issue the RECOVER DATABASE UNTIL CANCEL command. Apply all the archived redo logs that you can. Then cancel the recovery and open the database using the ALTER DATABASE OPEN RESETLOGS command.

17. A. The SCN is a number that represents a point in time in the database relative to transactions within a given database.

18. A. If you have only lost a data file, you should just restore and then recover the data file.

19. A, C. This error will appear if an archived redo log is not available. In this case, you need sequence 11. First you would try to restore archived redo log sequence 11. If log sequence 11 is not available as an archived redo log, you might find that it is available in one of the online redo logs.

20. A, E. The V$LOGFILE view will give you the name of the online redo logs associated with each group. The V$LOG view will provide the current sequence number assigned to each group.

Chapter 3: Configuring and Backing Up Oracle Databases Using RMAN

1. A. Block-change tracking must be enabled with ALTER DATABASE ENABLE BLOCK CHANGE TRACKING. The physical location and name of the block-change tracking file must be supplied.

2. A. The backup set is stored in a proprietary RMAN format, where only used blocks are backed up.

3. D. The following four backup sets would be created:

- One for an archive log backup before the main backup.
- One for the main backup. Since we are using a single channel with no backup-set size restriction, RMAN would create a single backup set.
- One for an archive log backup after the main backup.
- One for the control-file autobackup.

4. A. The BACKUP AS COPY command is used to create an image-copy backup.

5. C. Compressed backups work only with backup sets, not image copies. Thus, compressed backups will work only with the BACKUP command.

6. D. The correct answer is to use the `BACKUP DATABASE PLUS ARCHIVELOG DELETE INPUT` command.

7. D. A full backup is best described as backing up all the used blocks in a data file or any database file. A full backup can be taken on one database file.

8. A. A differential incremental backup backs up only blocks that have been modified since a backup at the same level or lower.

9. B. A level-0 backup is the first backup that is performed when implementing an incremental backup strategy. A level-0 backup copies all the used blocks as a baseline.

10. C. The `TAG` option is used to name a backup with a user-defined character string.

11. E. The correct order of operations is to log into RMAN and then shut down the database with the `SHUTDOWN IMMEDIATE` command. You then mount the database with the `STARTUP MOUNT` command. Once the database is mounted, you back up the database with the `BACKUP DATABASE` command. Finally, after the backup is complete, you open the database.

12. D. Image copies are similar to operating-system copy commands. These equate to bit-by-bit copies of a file.

13. B. The `V$BLOCK_CHANGE_TRACKING` dynamic view shows the filename, status, and size of the block-change tracking file.

14. A. Channel failover is the RMAN feature that provides the ability for other channels to take over the work of a failed channel during backup and recovery operations. Obviously, channel failover requires the allocation of more than one channel.

15. C. The command that sets the persistent setting that directs RMAN to back up to tape is `CONFIGURE DEFAULT DEVICE TYPE TO SBT`.

16. C, E. The `CONTROL_FILE_RECORD_KEEP_TIME` initialization parameter should never be set to 0 if you are using RMAN. If this value is set to 0, there is a potential to lose backup records.

17. A. Backing up in ARCHIVELOG mode is as easy as issuing the `BACKUP DATABASE PLUS ARCHIVELOG DELETE INPUT` command.

18. B, C. The `BACKUP` command can take advantage of multiplexing data files to the same backup set. The `BACKUP` command can also use the block-change tracking capability.

19. C. Use the `CONFIGURE DEVICE TYPE DISK BACKUP TYPE TO COMPRESSED BACKUPSET` command to configure RMAN to always create a compressed backup by default.

20. B. Backup optimization is a feature whereby Oracle will not back up a read-only tablespace as long as that tablespace has been backed up such that it meets the backup retention criteria.

Chapter 4: Using the RMAN Recovery Catalog

1. B, C, E. The recovery catalog provides a means of storing metadata related to a database's RMAN backup and recovery operations. Additionally, it provides the ability to store scripts that can be used by any database connecting to the repository via RMAN. Finally, the recovery catalog provides the means to store backup records for longer than a year.

2. A. The RECOVERY_CATALOG_OWNER privilege is required to create the recovery catalog. The DBA privilege includes RESOURCE and CONNECT and will work, but this role has many additional privileges that are unneeded. SELECT ANY DICTIONARY is not required.

3. B. Use the CREATE CATALOG command to create the recovery catalog schema.

4. A, B. Anytime you execute an RMAN backup operation when connected to the recovery catalog, RMAN will automatically resynchronize the recovery catalog metadata with the database control file. The RESYNC command is used to manually resynchronize the recovery catalog with the database.

5. D. You would use the EXECUTE SCRIPT RMAN command, contained within a RUN block, to execute the backup_database script.

6. C. You would first create the recovery catalog database. Then you create the recovery catalog user, granting that user the recovery_catalog owner role. You then issue the CREATE CATALOG command from RMAN, which will create the recovery catalog schema. Finally, you connect to the target database and register the database with the REGISTER DATABASE command.

7. D. To give the RVPC user rights to specific databases, you must connect to the recovery catalog with RMAN. You then grant those rights to that user from the RMAN prompt using the GRANT command.

8. A, C. The RVPC user can register the database if they are granted the register database privilege. They can also see all recovery catalog database metadata to which they are granted access.

9. D. The script will prompt for the missing substitution variable. The script will return an error if you do not put in a value for the second substitution variable.

10. C, D. Options C and D show the correct format for the RMAN command line. Option C connects to the database locally, while option D connects through Oracle Net. Both methods are completely legal.

Chapter 5: Recovering Databases with RMAN

1. C. Enable control-file autobackups by executing the command `CONFIGURE CONTROLFILE AUTOBACKUP ON`.

2. D. You would shut down the database with the `SHUTDOWN IMMEDIATE` command before the recovery. You would then issue the `RESTORE DATABASE` command followed by the `RECOVER DATABASE` command. After you have recovered the database, you will want to open it with the `STARTUP` command.

3. A, D. The `RESTORE` command is used to restore data files during a database recovery. The `RECOVER` command is used to apply incremental backups and archived redo logs to recover the database to the needed point in time.

4. D. In the event of complete loss of your database, you will need to first restore the database spfile. Once you have restored the database spfile, you will need to restore the database control file. Having restored the database control file, you would restore the database and then recover the database. Finally, since this would be an incomplete recovery (because you lost the entire database, the online redo logs are gone too), you would need to open the database using the `ALTER DATABASE OPEN RESETLOGS` command.

5. B. A loss of the entire database will require an incomplete database recovery. This is because the online redo logs would not be available to perform a complete recovery.

6. C. The `RESTORE DATABASE` command is used to restore database data files. The `UNTIL TIME` parameter is used to indicate the point in time to which you want to restore the database data files.

7. D. Since the retention policy is set to redundancy of 1, the gold_copy backup is not required to meet the retention criteria. Since the backup was not made in a way that will exclude or alter the retention criteria, then the gold_copy backup is no longer needed and may be removed at any time. It is possible that it will still be available for restore purposes, however.

8. C. The online redo logs are never backed up by Oracle no matter what kind of backup you are performing.

9. B. There is no equivalent RMAN command that creates a trace file with the `CREATE CONTROLFILE` statement in it.

10. A. In this case, you would first issue the `RESTORE DATABASE` command using the `UNTIL TIME` option. You would then use the `RECOVER DATABASE` command using the same `UNTIL TIME` option. Finally, since this is an incomplete recovery, you would need to open your database with the `ALTER DATABASE OPEN RESETLOGS` command.

11. B. To perform the restore of data file 4, you would first need to take the data file offline with the ALTER DATABASE command. Once the data file is offline, you would use the RESTORE DATAFILE and RECOVER DATAFILE commands to restore and recover the data file in question. After the restore and recover, you would need to bring the data file back online.

12. C, E. This is not the correct way to address this problem. The command will fail because the database is running. Additionally, this is not the correct way to approach the loss of one of several control files. The better way to approach this loss is to shut down the database and simply copy one of the surviving control files over to where the missing control file existed.

13. A, C, D. The UNTIL TIME clause provides the ability to restore to a specific point in time. The UNTIL SEQUENCE clause provides the ability to restore to a specific redo log sequence number, and UNTIL SCN provides the ability to restore to a specific database SCN number.

14. E. The RECOVER command does not restore data file images. It does restore and apply archived redo logs and incremental backup images during the recovery process.

15. A, B, C, D, E. You will need to restore the data files associated with each tablespace in the database in order to successfully complete the point-in-time database restore operation.

16. C. You would use the SWITCH DATAFILE command (for example, SWITCH DATAFILE 1 TO COPY) to instantly switch to the image copy. Issue the RESTORE command and then start up the database.

17. E. You would run the RMAN command RECOVER CORRUPTION LIST to recover the corrupted blocks using block media recovery.

18. D. The commands will run without error until you attempt to open the database. At that time, the ALTER DATABASE OPEN RESETLOGS command will fail. This will be because data file 4 and the rest of the database will be inconsistent with each other and Oracle does not allow this. If you are going to restore and recover an Oracle database using point-in-time recovery, you must do so with the entire database.

19. E. For this recovery, you would use the RMAN SQL command to issue an ALTER DATABASE DATAFILE OFFLINE command. You would then use the RMAN RESTORE and RECOVER commands to recover the lost data file. Finally, you would use the RMAN SQL command to issue the ALTER DATABASE DATAFILE ONLINE command.

20. C. To restore the database, in this case they needed to connect to the recovery catalog with RMAN. They then started the DSL instance with the STARTUP NOMOUNT command and restored the control file with the RESTORE CONTROLFILE command. After restoring the control file, they mounted the database with the ALTER DATABASE MOUNT command and then restored the database with the RESTORE DATABASE command. After restoring the database, they recovered it with the RECOVER DATABASE command and then opened it with the ALTER DATABASE OPEN RESETLOGS command.

Chapter 6: Tuning and Monitoring RMAN and the Automatic Diagnostic Workflow

1. C. The LIST BACKUP OF DATABASE command provides information on all database backups that are available for restore via RMAN.

2. A. The CROSSCHECK command is used to validate all RMAN-related metadata with associated physical backups on backup media.

3. B. The RESYNC CATALOG command is used to synchronize the recovery catalog with the database control file.

4. D. The DURATION command is used to limit the overall time of a database backup.

5. E. The CATALOG command is used to load backup set pieces that do not already exist into the recovery catalog or the control file.

6. B. Expired backup set pieces are those backup set pieces that do not exist. They are discovered via the CROSSCHECK command and marked as expired. The LIST EXPIRED command reports backup set records that are marked as expired. The DELETE EXPIRED BACKUP command marks the backup metadata in the control file and recovery catalog with a status of DELETED.

7. C, D. The DELETE OBSOLETE command will mark the related metadata records for the backups as DELETED in the control file and the recovery catalog.

8. D. If a backup is expired, it means that a CROSSCHECK command has detected that one or more backup set pieces associated with that backup are missing.

9. B. After you have corrected the reason that the backup set pieces are not available (i.e., replaced a failed disk), you would make the lost backup set available again by running the CROSSCHECK command once the backup set piece becomes available on the backup media.

10. B. The backup will be allowed to run for 2 hours.

11. B, C, E. The backup will fail after the duration period expires, but the data files that were backed up successfully will be able to be used in any restore operation. RMAN will prioritize any data files not backed up in subsequent backups. Also, the backup will not return an error when the duration expires and other commands will be executed.

12. B. This output would be from the V$SESSION view. It contains the current wait event for each session as well as how long the wait has been occurring.

13. E. The V$SESSION_LONGOPS view is used to estimate how long a given running operation has until it is complete.

14. B. The users01.dbf data file has had an unrecoverable operation occur. Because an unrecoverable operation does not generate redo records, the data involved in that operation will be lost in the event of a recovery. The data file should be backed up.

15. B. The #bkps column shows zero, which indicates that the data file has not been backed up. The data file may still be recoverable as long as the archived redo logs are available.

16. C. RMAN will attempt to spread the overall I/O over the total stated duration of the backup listed in the DURATION parameter. This will have the effect of limiting the overall load on the database and reducing the performance impacts of the backup.

17. E. This command lists all database data files that would require that more than three days of archived redo logs be applied in order to be restored.

18. C. ADRCI provides an interface into the ADR repository and provides the ability to review and manage files contained in that directory.

19. A, C, D. The Fault Diagnosability Framework includes a number of components. The ADR component is the persistent file system structure and related metadata that defines the location where files from the Framework should be stored. The alert log and trace files are critical files that are used to diagnose database incidents.

20. A, B. The Fault Diagnosability Framework provides the ability to manage Oracle SRs, including opening the SR and collecting files related to the problem/incident related to the SR and sending those files to Oracle.

Chapter 7: Performing Oracle Advanced Recovery

1. B. RMAN supports duplication of an individual PDB, several PDBs, or the entire CDB to another CDB.

2. B. The RECOVER TABLESPACE command is used to start a TSPITR recovery.

3. B. Active database duplication does not require any backup before the duplication is run.

4. E. The commands in option E are the correct commands to perform an active database duplication given the conditions listed.

5. B. You will use two databases. The first is the target database, and the second is the auxiliary database instance.

6. C. The RESET DATABASE TO INCARNATION command is used to reset the database incarnation.

7. C. The `TS_PITR_CHECK` view is used to determine if a given tablespace (or tablespaces) can be independently transported or if there are other dependencies that will require the transport of additional tablespaces.

8. C. To export from a CDB, you have to log into a specific PDB and export that PDB. Since you log in using the Oracle Net service name, that run of Oracle Data Pump can export only a single PDB.

9. A. The correct answer is `LOG_FILE_NAME_CONVERT`. This setting will direct RMAN to the directory in which it should create the online redo logs.

10. E. The correct command is shown in option E. You would issue the `RECOVER TABLESPACE` command and list the tablespaces to be recovered. You would then use the `UNTIL TIME` parameter to define the point in time to restore the tablespace to. Finally, you would define the location for the auxiliary database instance with the `AUXILIARY DESTINATION` parameter.

11. B. Any database to be duplicated in active mode must be in ARCHIVELOG mode.

12. B. This error message alludes to the fact that there is no backup of the database available to perform TSPITR. A backup before the point in time of the recovery is required to perform TSPITR.

13. A, B. The database must be in ARCHIVELOG mode to perform a TSPITR. Additionally, you must have a backup of the database that occurred at a point in time before the point in time to which you want to perform the TSPITR.

14. C. Use the `TS_PITR_OBJECTS_TO_BE_DROPPED` view to determine which objects will be lost as a result of the pending tablespace point-in-time recovery operation. To preserve the objects, you will want to export them before the TSPITR and import them after the recovery is complete with the Oracle Data Pump or Imp/Exp utility.

15. B. If there is a constraint between two objects in two different tablespaces, you must perform a TSPITR between the two tablespaces. As an alternative, you could disable or drop the constraint. You may not be able to reenable the constraint with validation after the TSPITR, however.

16. D. The `DB_FILE_NAME_CONVERT` parameter is used to define the location in which the data files for the auxiliary-database data files should be created.

17. D. The second `RECOVER TABLESPACE` command will fail because it is trying to perform a recovery to a point in time before the time to which the tablespace was recovered during the first recovery.

18. B. An active database duplication requires that you have access to the target database that is the source of the duplication process. If you have not connected to that database, then the attempt to perform an active database duplication will fail.

19. A, B, C. Oracle Secure Backup (OSB) provides the ability to connect directly to vendor tape devices without needing to use any vendor middleware libraries. When using RMAN you still use the SBT libraries to connect to Oracle Secure Backup. OSB also provides the ability to perform OS backups.

20. A. The LIST INCARNATION OF DATABASE command is used to produce a report of database incarnations.

Chapter 8: Understanding Flashback Technology

1. A, C, E. Flashback Drop utilizes the Recycle Bin, which does not use the undo tablespace; therefore options B and F are incorrect. Flashback Database is a physical recovery method and does not use undo; therefore option D is incorrect.

2. B, D. The Recycle Bin is a logical container of Flashback dropped objects. The objects in the Recycle Bin are stored in the tablespace they were created in.

3. C. Flashback Transaction Query could provide the data requested in a single query. Option A is an invalid choice because the table wasn't dropped. Option B is incorrect because Flashback Query returns data at only a specific point in time, not for a range of times. Option D is incorrect because, although it could produce the data needed for the report, Flashback Version Query would have to be run for each table individually. Option E is incorrect because the user does not want to recover the table at all.

4. A. The user needs to have the SELECT ANY TRANSACTION privilege granted to him. All of the other choices are incorrect.

5. C. AUM will ignore the UNDO_RETENTION parameter if the undo tablespace is not set to autoextend. Option A is incorrect because guaranteeing retention could result in failed transactions, which you specifically want to avoid. Option B is not the best answer because the size of the undo tablespace is not the cause of the issue, but increasing the size of the undo tablespace could increase the amount of undo retained. Option D is wrong because this question is not dealing with the Recycle Bin and because it has no guaranteed retention setting.

6. C, D. Version 10.0 or higher compatibility must be set, so option A is incorrect. Option B is incorrect because there is no such thing as Flashback Logging. Option E is incorrect because ARCHIVELOG mode has no effect on Flashback Transaction Query functionality.

7. A, E. The likely causes are that the RETENTION GUARANTEE option has been set on the undo tablespace and there are no expired transactions to remove to make room for new transactions, or that the user has exceeded the undo quota that has been set by the database resource manager. FLASHBACK GUARANTEE is not a valid option, so option B is incorrect. Flashback queries would not interfere with transactions entering the system, so options C and D are incorrect.

8. D. Flashback Version Query does not change data at all, so option A is incorrect. B could be correct, but only if one of the specified points in time was the current timestamp. Therefore, B is not the best description. Option C is incorrect because Flashback Version Query does not provide the SQL to undo the changes.

9. C. The VERSIONS_XID column contains the unique transaction identifier for the row. None of the other choices are valid pseudocolumn names.

10. A, C. Lists of values are not valid, so both B and E are incorrect. Also, sequence values are not valid, so D is also incorrect.

11. E. A Flashback Drop operation restores dropped objects from the Recycle Bin. It does not use SCN or timestamp ranges, so options A, B, and D are incorrect. Also, Flashback Drop operations don't create objects in the Recycle Bin (they move them out of the Recycle Bin), so C is incorrect. The likely cause is that multiple versions of the table existed in the Recycle Bin and the wrong one was restored.

12. C. The VERSIONS BETWEEN clause of the Flashback Version Query cannot query past table modifications or DDL changes to a table.

13. D. Like the other Flashback options, Flashback Table must be able to find the necessary undo records in order to recover. The use of SCNs is valid in Flashback Table; therefore option A is incorrect. Row movement must be enabled in all cases, not just when a significant number of changes have been made. Therefore option B is incorrect. One of the main features of Flashback Table is that the tablespace can remain online, so option C is incorrect.

14. A. The default action for the FLASHBACK TABLE command is to disable all triggers regardless of their previous state. If the ENABLE TRIGGER clause is added to the FLASHBACK TABLE command, then triggers that were previously enabled will be reenabled after the operation completes.

15. B, C. FLASHBACK_TRANSACTION_QUERY is the correct view to query, and it can be done using either timestamps or SCN ranges. DBA_TRANSACTION_QUERY is not a valid view; therefore options A and D are incorrect.

16. B. Flashback Database relies on flashback logs in the fast recovery area. The Flashback Data Archive and undo tablespace are not required. The RMAN command line is not required to recover to a flashback point; the DBA can execute the FLASHBACK DATABASE command from within SQL Plus.

17. C. The Flashback Database architecture consists of the recovery writer RVWR background process and Flashback Database logs. When the Flashback Database is enabled, the RVWR process is started. The RVWR writes the Flashback Database logs in the fast recovery area. FBDA is the Flashback Data Archive background process; the remaining options are fictitious.

18. A, B, C. The DBA can use Flashback Database to recover to an SCN, a point in time, or a named recovery point that is within the recovery window. Transaction ID and Session ID will not help you recover using the Flashback Database feature.

19. A, C. When creating a Flashback Data Archive, you need to specify the tablespace name and a retention period. The storage quota is optional. You add tables to an archive after the archive is created, not as a prerequisite. You don't need to name a default Flashback Data Archive.

20. C. Do nothing. Once the retention period has passed, rows will be automatically removed from the Flashback Data Archive. Using TRUNCATE on a table that is archived is not allowed. Dropping the archive will definitely clear the old records, but it will also eliminate the ones you wanted to keep.

Chapter 9: Diagnosing the Database and Managing Performance

1. A, C, D. FOREGROUND_DUMP_DEST is not a valid initialization parameter, so option B is incorrect. DIAGNOSTIC_DEST is the new parameter that replaces the parameters in options A, C, and D, so E is incorrect.

2. B. When $ORACLE_BASE is set, it is the default value for DIAGNOSTIC_DEST.

3. C. Option A is incorrect because the correct order is diag/rdbms. Option B is incorrect because the correct order is <dbname>/<instname>.

4. A, E. Options B, C, and D are each fundamental tasks of the Support Workbench problem-resolution process.

5. B. Option A is incorrect because IPS does not delete files not associated with a package that will be sent to Oracle Support. Option C is incorrect because IPS does not open an Oracle service request for each critical error. D is incorrect because IPS does not display critical errors on the database home page.

6. D. All other sequences are incorrect. D is the correct sequence. First, create the new package; then view the package contents. Next, view the manifest; then schedule the job to upload the data for the incident to Oracle Support.

7. B. Option A is incorrect because reduced MTTR is an advantage of BMR. Option C is incorrect because the data files' remaining online is an advantage of BMR. Since A and C are advantages, D is also incorrect.

8. E. Option A is correct because if you attempt to analyze a table or index that has a corrupt block, the ANALYZE command will indicate it. Option B is correct because the dbv command (DB Verify utility) is used to verify the data-structure integrity of an offline data file. DB Verify will let you know if the data file fails the integrity check. Option C is correct unless you have used DBMS_REPAIR.SKIP_CORRUPT_BLOCKS to permit queries to skip corrupt blocks. D is correct because the RMAN BACKUP command will detect corruption by default.

9. A, C. Option B is incorrect because logical corruptions are not repairable by BMR. Option D is incorrect because you must use a level 0 or full backup for the restore. Option E is incorrect because ARCHIVELOG mode is a requirement for BMR.

10. B, C. Option A is incorrect because the syntax is wrong. Option D is incorrect because BLOCK doesn't belong. B is how you recover all corrupt blocks listed in V$DATABASE_BLOCK_CORRUPTION. C is the correct syntax to recover just the one block that you've identified as corrupt.

11. D. Option A is incorrect because there is no direct link on the Software And Support home page to the SQL Advisors. You use either sequence B or C to get to the SQL Advisors and to the Automatic SQL Tuning Advisor page; from there, you can see the results of the most recent Automatic SQL Tuning Advisor task.

12. D. Options A, B, and C are not valid choices when creating a SQL tuning set. During the filter options step, the DBA can choose the SQL attributes, the operator, and the values to use as filter conditions.

13. A. Option B is incorrect because there is no Manual Tuning Task Results option. C is incorrect because there is no Manual SQL Tuning Advisors option.

14. A. Option B is incorrect because the manual SQL Tuning Advisor task does not tune the SQL statements. C is incorrect for the same reason.

15. E. All of the options are correct. The SQL Access Advisor recommends indexing, partitioning, and materialized view changes to improve performance.

16. B. Option A is incorrect because SQL Access Advisor recommendations are not automatically implemented. Option C is incorrect because the DBA can choose which recommendations to schedule and implement from the task result set. D is incorrect because the recommendations are not automatically scheduled for implementation.

17. C. The correct sequence is capture, preprocess, replay, analyze.

18. B, C. Option A is incorrect because the data divergence between the capture and replay databases should be minimized. Option D is incorrect because the database should be started in restricted mode, and then the workload capture process will switch the database to unrestricted. Option E is incorrect because you can define either inclusion or exclusion filters for a workload capture but not both.

19. E. Option A is incorrect because workload capture is for the database, not for individual instances. B is incorrect because the correct procedure is to shut down all instances before you begin workload capture. Option C is incorrect; after the shutdown of all instances, start one instance to begin workload capture, and then start the remaining instances after capture begins. Workload capture and replay are supported in RAC, so D is incorrect.

20. D. Option A is incorrect; DML and SQL results drive data divergence. Option B is incorrect because error divergence, not performance divergence, happens when errors that occur in the capture system don't occur in the replay system. Top SQL statements should behave the same in the capture and replay systems, unless there is a data-divergence issue, so C is incorrect. E is incorrect because the time of day should have no impact on differences between the capture and replay systems. It is possible that other workloads running on the capture and replay systems that have a time-of-day trend might impact performance, but that is an extraneous variable, not a cause.

Chapter 10: Managing Database Resources

1. D. For the instance, set the initialization parameter RESUMABLE_TIMEOUT to a nonzero value, representing the number of seconds for which an operation will suspend until an action is taken to repair the condition or the operation aborts due to the condition.

2. C. In a distributed transaction, the remote RESUMABLE_TIMEOUT initialization parameter applies to the remote part of the transaction, and the remote-session resumable setting applies. Also, local resumable settings do not apply to the remote part of the distributed transactions.

3. D. For the DBA_RESUMABLE view, the NAME column is populated with the username, session ID, and instance number, in that order.

4. A, C. The transportable tablespace set is the self-contained group of tablespaces that encapsulate the objects that you wish to transport along with the exported metadata for the tablespaces.

5. A, C. The SQL query returns the list of target platforms that have the same endian format and do not require RMAN conversion between source and destination databases.

6. B. Execute the `DBMS_TTS.TRANSPORT_SET_CHECK` procedure using the proposed list of tablespaces for the transportable set. Optionally, the last parameter should be `TRUE` to verify referential integrity constraints.

7. B, C, D. Option A is incorrect because the correct view name is `V$DB_TRANSPORTABLE_PLATFORM`. You'll need to verify that there are no restrictions or limitations such as storage or memory, verify that the version levels are the same, and determine where you will perform the conversion.

8. B. The `DBMS_TDB.CHECK_EXTERNAL` function returns the list of external files that will need to be copied to the destination system. The other options are not valid.

9. C. The `DBMS_TDB.CHECK_DB` function must execute with the database open and in read-only mode.

10. A. The segment shrink feature reclaims space above and below the high-water mark without using additional space to perform an operation.

11. A, C, D. The segment shrink feature can be used on tables, indexes, and partitions but not on tables with function-based indexes.

12. D. The segment shrink `SHRINK SPACE` command specifying the table name, and then including the `CASCADE` clause, will reclaim space from the table segment and all dependent index segments, as reported by the `DBMS_SPACE.OBJECT_DEPENDENT_SEGMENT` function.

13. D. A PDB may have its own default temporary tablespace or use the root CDB default temporary tablespace.

14. A. None of the other answers are correct syntax, and therefore they are incorrect.

15. D. Each of these is a true statement about transportable tablespaces; therefore D is the correct answer.

16. A, B. C is incorrect because the tablespace must be in read-only mode. D is incorrect because 8.0-Compatible AQ with multiple recipients are *not* transportable.

17. A. A defragmented block takes up the same amount of space on disk or in cache as a fragmented block. D is incorrect because the segment shrink operation can be performed on indexes as well as tables.

18. C. Use the Transportable Database feature to migrate an entire database from one platform to another, as long as the endian format is the same for both source and target.

19. D. Use the `DBMS_TDB.CHECK_EXTERNAL` supplied function to identify external tables, directories, and BFILES that you'll need to move as part of a transportable database migration.

20. B. A permanent tablespace may be associated with only one container.

Chapter 11: Creating Oracle Multitenant Databases

1. D. A many-to-one relationship exists between PDBs and the CDB.

2. B. The seed PDB plus 252 user-created PDBs are allowed per CDB.

3. B. Options A and C use incorrect terms PDB and SYSTEM.

4. E. The Oracle multitenant architecture is available beginning with Oracle 12c Release 1 (12.1), supports multiple PDBs within a single CDB on a given platform, allows the DBA to shut down tenant PDBs while keeping the host CDB active, and supports multiple PDBs of the same release of Oracle within the same CDB.

5. B, D, E. CDB$SEED and PDB$ROOT do not exist.

6. D. All other options are invalid.

7. A, B, C. Option D is incorrect because the multitenant architecture does not offer platform independence.

8. A, C, E. Option B is incorrect because not all 12c databases are non-CDBs. You can create a CDB that contains only the PDB$SEED database, so D is incorrect.

9. A, B, C, D. Option E is incorrect; you cannot move a CDB into a PDB.

10. D. Option D is the only valid clause that can be used to create a container database.

11. E. Once you create an Oracle 12c database as a non-CDB, you can't alter it to become a CDB.

12. B. The supplied script catcdb.sql adds the necessary dictionary objects to enable container database provisioning.

13. A. Option A is the only correct navigation sequence in the Database Configuration Assistant (DBCA).

14. B. Option A is incorrect because you have not specified a source PDB. Option C is incorrect because when you create a new PDB from PDB$SEED, you must specify an administrator username and password for the new PDB in the CREATE PLUGGABLE DATABASE statement.

15. B. Option A is incorrect because USING is incorrect syntax. Option C is incorrect because you do not explicitly use PDB$SEED as the source for a clone.

16. A, B, D. Option C is the only incorrect answer; it is not a valid package.

17. C. Answers A, B, D, and E are necessary steps to migrate a non-CDB to a PDB.

18. C, D. Option A is incorrect because the requirement is to shut down the non-CDB prior to creating the XML file and copying the datafiles; this is not executed on the target CDB. Option B is not correct, because the PDB needs to be in read/write mode.

19. A, B, C. Option D is incorrect, because the PDB must be closed, not open in read-only mode, before you can unplug it.

20. C. Option C is correct, since none of the other proposed answers are requirements to drop a PDB. The PDB must be closed before you can drop it.

Chapter 12: Managing Oracle Multitenant Databases

1. C. Common users have access to all PDBs and the root container of the CDB. A common user defined in the current CDB does not have access to all CDBs, so option A is not correct.

2. D. The local user by definition has access to only one PDB.

3. C. Option A incorrectly uses the COMMON keyword and Option B incorrectly uses the CDB$ROOT container name.

4. E. Answer A is incorrect because a common user can create local users. Answer B is incorrect because a local user can create a local user, as long as the creating user has sufficient privileges. Answer C is incorrect because each PDB has its own set of local users. Answer D is incorrect because you do not have to be a DBA to create users.

5. E. SHOW CON_NAME is the correct SQL*Plus command.

6. B. At the OS prompt, enter **lsnrctl stat** and the list of currently available services will be displayed.

7. E. Option A is incorrect because FORCE should not be used under normal circumstances. Option B is incorrect because under normal circumstances you would OPEN the CDB. Options C and D are incorrect because the CDB must be started from the root. Under normal circumstances, you would issue STARTUP from CDB$ROOT.

8. E. SHUTDOWN ABORT is used only when no other option will work. SHUTDOWN TRANSACTIONAL will wait for all pending transactions to complete.

9. E. All DBA-created PDBs are in MOUNTED status when the CDB is opened and the PDB$SEED container is in READ ONLY status.

10. E. None of these are required to open a PDB. The Oracle_SID doesn't have to be set to the PDB service name; the PDB doesn't have to be the current container, nor does the CDB$ROOT. A local user with SYSDBA or similar privileges may open the PDB.

11. B. Each of the other commands uses incorrect syntax.

12. A. It is not necessary for the user closing the PDB to be a local user, nor does it matter if the current container is the PDB.

13. A, C. Option B is incorrect because you should not abort a PDB in normal circumstances. Option D is incorrect because CLOSE PLUGGABLE DATABASE is not a valid command.

14. A. Option A is the only correct combination. STARTUP FORCE shuts down the CDB or PDB as would a SHUTDOWN ABORT; then it starts the database and opens it for general access.

15. D. Option A is incorrect because transactions are allowed to complete. Option B is incorrect because no new transactions are allowed. Option C is incorrect because transactions are allowed to complete before the sessions are terminated.

16. B, C, D. Option A is incorrect because CDB$ROOT is not always the current container. Option D is correct because a common user can create multiple sessions in different containers; for each session the current container may be any one of the PDBs or CDB$ROOT where the common user has privileges to connect.

17. C. Answer A is not necessary at CDB creation. It can be used at PDB creation when cloning a PDB from some source other than PDB$SEED. Answer B is not a valid parameter. Answer D is incorrect because it is not necessary when creating a CDB.

18. C. Option C is the only correct initialization parameter name.

19. E. Options A, B, and C are invalid. Answer D, PROCESSES, is used to calculate SESSIONS if SESSIONS is not explicitly set.

20. A, B, C, D. Each option is a valid step in the process to increase the MAX_STRING_SIZE for a PDB.

Chapter 13: Oracle Utilities

1. E. Each of the answers represents a valid and common use for Data Pump in the multitenant environment.

2. D. Answer A is incorrect because expdp is associated with export, not import. Answer B is incorrect because that responsibility lies with DBMS_METADATA. Answer C is incorrect because direct path load is not a function of Data Pump.

3. A, D. Option B is incorrect because using the SYS user to import the contents will not remap or create a new local account. Answer C is incorrect because the mapping would then be the opposite of what you want.

4. A. Answer B is incorrect because the PDB doesn't know about the DUMPFILE directory of the CDB. You must define the DUMPFILE directory at the PDB using the CREATE DIRECTORY statement in SQL*Plus.

5. C, D. Answer A is incorrect because Data Pump does not allow any CDB-wide operations (CDB$ROOT). For the same reason B is incorrect; Oracle Data Pump doesn't allow import operations on PDB$SEED.

6. D. Answer A is incorrect because you do not use SQL*Loader to connect two tables in two distinct Oracle databases. Answer B is incorrect because you do not use a binary source file. Answer C is incorrect because you do not use SQL*Loader to load CDB$ROOT tables.

7. C. Option A is incorrect because the data file contains the source data records and the control file describes the layout of the data to be imported. Option B is incorrect because the parfile is optional. Option D is incorrect because the WHEN clause is not required.

8. A, D. Answer B is incorrect because SQL*Loader assumes the stream record format is to be used if you do not specify variable or fixed-length records. Answer C is incorrect because fixed record format performs the best, all other things being equal.

9. E. Answer A is incorrect because the conventional path load uses SQL INSERT statements. Answer B is incorrect because DIRECT=TRUE directs SQL*Loader to use the direct path load. Answer C is incorrect because truncating is not required prior to a direct path load. Answer D is incorrect because the direct path load copies data from the data file directly into data blocks above the high-water mark in the target database table.

10. E. None of these are required to run SQL*Loader in express mode. The only requirement on the command line is the target table name, which is also the name of the data file.

11. D. Answer A is incorrect because auditing policies can be common or local. Answers B and C are incorrect because common auditing policies apply only to common objects.

12. A. Answer A is true, but you must also indicate EXPORT, IMPORT, or ALL. There is no default value, and UNIFIED is not an option.

13. C. Option A is incorrect because conventional path loads are not audited. Only direct path loads can be audited, but you must create an audit policy and enabling auditing first.

14. D. Option A describes Oracle Secure Backup. Answer B is not correct. Answer C describes Oracle Data Guard.

15. A, B, D. Option C is not a valid role.

16. B, D. Option A is incorrect because the entire CDB and all of its PDBs are in the same role, either primary or standby. Option C is incorrect because each PDB will follow the role of its CDB, so individual fail over or switchover is not necessary.

17. C. Answer A is not correct because Data Guard does not automatically create the PDB in the standby databases. Answer B is incorrect because you do not have to clone the PDB to the standby CDBs.

18. A. Option B and D are not correct initialization parameter names. Answer C is correct when creating a new PDB in a CDB, but not in this scenario.

19. E. Options A, B, C, and D are valid use cases for LogMiner.

20. A, D. Answers B and C are not correct because a LogMiner dictionary is not required, but it makes mining more convenient.

Chapter 14: Oracle Security in CDBs and PDBs

1. B. A common user has the same identity in all containers in a CDB and has the capability to access all containers. Only Oracle-supplied common users in a CDB would appear similar to Oracle-supplied users in a non-CDB; however, non-CDBs do not have common or local users. Common users can create common users, so D is incorrect.

2. C, D. Answers A and B are true; answers C and D are not true. A common user is identified by the same password in all containers. A local user is uniquely defined in each PDB.

3. E. Option A is incorrect because usernames and role names cannot be the same. Answer B is incorrect because common users are identified by the same password in all containers. Answer C is incorrect because you cannot create a local user in CDB$ROOT. Answer D is incorrect because you must create a common user in CDB$ROOT.

4. D. Answer A is incorrect because local users must be unique in a PDB, but they may be independently non-unique across PDBs within the same CDB. Answer B is incorrect because local users are defined locally. Answer C is incorrect because you must be a common user with DBA, SYSOPER, or SYSDBA privileges to shut down a CDB.

5. C. Answer A is incorrect because ALL is not required; it is implied. Answer B is incorrect because CURRENT is implied when creating a local user, not a common user. Answer D is an invalid value option.

6. B. Answer A is incorrect because local users have access only to the PDB they are created in. Answer C is incorrect because local users in one PDB are independent from local users in other PDBs. Answer D is incorrect because local users are not used in the CDB$ROOT.

7. D. Option A is incorrect because the user accounts are merged, not overwritten. Option B is incorrect because the passwords are not overwritten. Answer C is incorrect because the plugged-in user accounts become local user accounts, not common users.

8. E. None of the options A through D are correct because a local user is not permitted to switch from one PDB to another.

9. A, B, D. Answer C is incorrect; local users may not create common users.

10. A, B, C. Answer D is incorrect because a local user does not have privileges on another pluggable database.

11. E. Each answer is a valid capability of a privilege.

12. C, D. Answers A and B are not correct; this is a very bad idea. The SYSDBA privilege allows a user to delete your database.

13. A, B. Option C is incorrect because you should never commonly grant privileges to the PUBLIC role, because that would grant the privileges to all users.

14. A. Option B is incorrect because common and local users can grant local privileges. Option C is incorrect because you can grant local privileges to local and common users.

15. A, B. Option C is incorrect because a role is a group of privileges or other roles, not a group of users. You may of course grant a role to a group of users. Option D is incorrect because a group of containers is a CDB, not a role.

16. B, D. Option A is incorrect because the local user naming convention and the common role naming convention are mutually exclusive. Option C is incorrect because you cannot create common roles in PDBs; you must be in the CDB$ROOT to create a common role.

17. C. Option C is correct because, while creating too many roles can cause a nuisance, it's the associated privileges that can cause damage. Also, you should safeguard the DROP ANY ROLE privilege. Option B is not entirely correct because we added the privileges modifier.

18. C. Options A, B, and D are acceptable options for granting roles, as long as the role grantor has been granted the appropriate roles, locally or commonly. Option C is not allowed because that would create a circular reference.

19. C. Options A and B are not true; common users with assigned privileges or roles may create objects in PDBs.

20. A, D. Options B and C are valid create statements because, while it is not allowed to have a role name and a user name that are the same, independently, "c##mydba" and c##mydba are stored differently in the data dictionary.

Appendix

B

About the Additional Study Tools

IN THIS APPENDIX:

✓ Additional study tools

✓ System requirements

✓ Using the study tools

✓ Troubleshooting

Additional Study Tools

The following sections are arranged by category and summarize the software and other goodies you'll find on the companion website. If you need help installing the items, refer to the installation instructions in the "Using the Study Tools" section of this appendix.

 You can find the additional study tools at www.sybex.com/go/ocp12csg. You'll also find instructions on how to download the files to your hard drive.

Sybex Test Engine

The files contain the Sybex test engine, which includes bonus practice exams, as well as the assessment test and the chapter review questions, which are also included in the book.

Electronic Flashcards

These handy electronic flashcards are just what they sound like. One side contains a question, and the other side shows the answer.

Bonus Lab Exercises

We've included a bonus PDF of additional labs that will allow you to practice what you learned in the book.

Glossary

We have included an electronic version of the glossary in .pdf format. You can view the electronic version of the glossary with Adobe Reader.

Adobe Reader

We've also included a copy of Adobe Reader so you can view PDF files that accompany the book's content. For more information on Adobe Reader or to check for a newer version, visit Adobe's website at www.adobe.com/products/reader/.

System Requirements

Make sure your computer meets the minimum system requirements shown in the following list. If your computer doesn't meet these requirements, you may have problems using the software and files. For the latest and greatest information, please refer to the ReadMe file located in the download.

- A PC running Microsoft Windows XP or newer
- An Internet connection

Using the Study Tools

To install the items, follow these steps:

1. Download the .zip file to your hard drive, and unzip it to your desired location. You can find instructions on where to download this file at www.sybex.com/go/ocp12csg.

2. Click the Start.EXE file to open the study tools file.

3. Read the license agreement, and then click the Accept button if you want to use the study tools.

The main interface appears and allows you to access the content with just a few clicks.

Troubleshooting

Wiley has attempted to provide programs that work on most computers with the minimum system requirements. If a program does not work properly, the two likeliest problems are that you don't have enough memory (RAM) for the programs you want to use or you have other programs running that are affecting the installation or running of a program. If you get an error message such as "Not enough memory" or "Setup cannot continue," try one or more of the following suggestions and then try using the software again:

Turn off any antivirus software running on your computer. Installation programs sometimes mimic virus activity and may make your computer incorrectly believe that it's being infected by a virus.

Close all running programs.   The more programs you have running, the less memory is available to other programs. Installation programs typically update files and programs, so if you keep other programs running, installation may not work properly.

Have your local computer store add more RAM to your computer.   This is, admittedly, a drastic and somewhat expensive step. However, adding more memory can really help the speed of your computer and allow more programs to run at the same time.

Customer Care

If you have trouble with the book's companion study tools, please call the Wiley Product Technical Support phone number at (800) 762-2974, or email them at http://sybex.custhelp.com/.

Index

Note to the Reader: Throughout this index **boldfaced** page numbers indicate primary discussions of a topic. *Italicized* page numbers indicate illustrations.

T